DEVELOPMENTAL PSYCHOLOGY

DEVELOPMENTAL PSYCHOLOGY

AN INTRODUCTION
THIRD EDITION

ROBERT F. BIEHLER

LYNNE M. HUDSON
University of Toledo / Ohio

HOUGHTON MIFFLIN COMPANY
BOSTON
Dallas
Geneva, Illinois
Lawrenceville, New Jersey
Palo Alto

Part-opening photo credits: Part 1, p. 3, David S. Strickler/The Picture Cube; Part 2, p. 99, © Alan Cary/The Image Works; Part 3, p. 203, © Jean-Claude Lejeune; Part 4, p. 319, © Jim Anderson/ Woodfin Camp; Part 5, p. 431, © Eugene Richards/Magnum Photos; Part 6, p. 529, Paul Conklin/Monkmeyer; Part 7, p. 623, E. Roth/The Picture Cube.

Printed in the U.S.A.

Library of Congress Catalog Card Number: 85-60476

ISBN: 0-395-35755-1

BCDEFGHIJ-H-89876

This text was previously published under the title *Child Development: An Introduction.*

Material on pp. 186–187 reprinted from *Developmental Tasks and Education* by Robert J. Havighurst. Originally published in 1952. Third edition copyright © 1972 by Longman, Inc. All rights reserved.

BRIEF CONTENTS

CONTENTS

CHAPTER 4

PRENATAL DEVELOPMENT AND BIRTH 133

CHAPTER 5

THE IMPORTANCE OF ALL STAGES OF DEVELOPMENT 171

PART 4
TWO TO FIVE 319

CHAPTER 10
TWO TO FIVE: PHYSICAL DEVELOPMENT 321

CHAPTER 11
TWO TO FIVE: COGNITIVE DEVELOPMENT 343

PART 5

SIX TO TWELVE   431

CHAPTER 14

SIX TO TWELVE: PHYSICAL DEVELOPMENT   433

CHAPTER 15

SIX TO TWELVE: COGNITIVE DEVELOPMENT   451

CHAPTER 16

SIX TO TWELVE: RELATIONSHIPS WITH OTHERS   485

CHAPTER 23

LATER MATURITY 657

PREFACE

The required text for the very first graduate course taken in 1950 by the senior author of this book was the first edition of the *Manual of Child Psychology* (1946) edited by Leonard Carmichael. At 1,068 double-column pages it was easily the most formidable text the fledgling graduate student had ever encountered but he contented himself with the thought that it probably contained just about all there was to know about developmental psychology. In 1954, the year the senior author taught his first course in developmental psychology, he experienced the ego-building satisfaction of meriting a free examination copy of the second edition of the *Manual* that was published that year. The second edition contained 1,295 double-column pages and served as *the* basic source for lecture outlines. The third edition of the *Manual* (edited by Paul Mussen as the successor to Leonard Carmichael) was published in 1970 and con-

tained 2,391 pages in two volumes. The fourth edition, published in 1983, contains 3,862 pages in four volumes.

This comparison of the various editions of the developmental psychologist's "bible" gives a rough indication of the explosion of scientific knowledge about development that has occurred during the last thirty-five years. But these figures don't tell the whole story. In the 1950s and 1960s, most courses in developmental psychology were concerned with aspects of behavior up to the end of the adolescent years—period. It was assumed that since obvious signs of development stopped at that point, analyses of development should stop at that point. However, starting in the 1970s and continuing to an even greater extent in the 1980s, there has been a trend toward acknowledging that development continues throughout the life span. Research on adulthood and later maturity has expanded to such an extent that scientific information about aspects of behavior during later stages of life now is summarized in handbooks that equal in size and thoroughness the original edition of the *Manual of Child Psychology*. Reflecting this change, courses, and texts for those courses, often include coverage of the transition from adolescence to adulthood and aging.

One inescapable conclusion that can be drawn from these observations is that it is impossible to summarize all, or even most, scientific information about the nature of developmental psychology, particularly in a text that will be covered in one semester or quarter. Authors of texts such as this one must therefore decide how much to include and how much to leave out. The temptation at first is to be as comprehensive as possible. One risk of using an encyclopedic approach, though, is that students may respond to their text in developmental psychology the same way a 10-year-old girl responded to a book on penguins written by an enthusiastic expert. She returned it to the book club with a critique that was a marvel of succinctness. She wrote: "This book gives me more information about penguins than I care to have." In order to avoid giving readers of *Developmental Psychology: An Introduction* more information than they care to have, a selective rather than encyclopedic approach has been adopted. The selection of topics and research reflects the authors' conception of a core of basic knowledge likely to be of interest and value to students. At the same time, it is organized and presented in a manner that facilitates the presentation of supplementary material by instructors in lectures and discussions.

Chapter 1, a capsule history of developmental psychology, outlines a chronology of key ideas introduced by leading theorists and also acquaints the reader with methods to study development. The historical overview serves to familiarize the reader with the names and contributions of scientists whose work is emphasized in later chapters. It also reveals how research interests and conclusions are influenced by the spirit of the times and acquaints students with the concept that replacement of once-accepted ideas by new interpretations reflects a strength, rather than a weakness, of scientific study.

Chapter 2 summarizes the nature of the most influential theories of psychology. An outline of the stage theories of Freud, Erikson, and Piaget calls attention to the progression of age-related aspects of social, interpersonal, and cognitive development discussed in greater detail in later chapters. Descriptions of behavioral theory, social learning theory, and information processing supply background so that subsequent discussions of concepts and conclusions based on those theoretical conceptions can be understood more completely than if they were simply noted in passing.

The beginning of human life is traced in separate chapters on developmental behavioral genetics (Chapter 3) and prenatal development and birth (Chapter 4). Chapter 5 summarizes differences of opinion about the hypothesis that experiences occurring during the first few years are more significant than those that occur at any later stage. Evidence and arguments are presented to support the view that there is change as well as continuity in personality development over the life span, and that all stages of development are important.

Next, chapters covering physical, cognitive, interpersonal, and personality development at four age levels (the first two years, two to five, six to twelve, and adolescence and youth) are presented. For each age level, there is one chapter each on physical, cognitive, interpersonal, and personality development; sixteen in all. These age spans were selected because they represent life stages that are marked off by easily recognizable turning points. Chapters on identical sets of topics for each age span make it possible for instructors to use either an age-span or a topical approach in structuring a course. The chapters might be assigned in order by instructors preferring an age-level progression, or the various chapters on physical development can be assigned, followed by the chapters on cognitive development, and so on.

Two chapters at the end of the book offer an overview of adulthood and later maturity and briefly discuss milestones that occur after adolescence. These final chapters are not meant to supply full life-span coverage and may be omitted in courses covering development through adolescence and youth.

Even though this book is less encyclopedic than many texts on developmental psychology, it still provides the reader with a substantial number of facts, concepts, and theories. Several features of the text help students retain, recall, and apply important information. First, the clear organization of the book makes it possible for the reader to easily grasp how any chapter fits into the whole pattern of the presentation. The history of developmental psychology and the outline of developmental theories presented in the first two chapters provide general background and establish structure for the remainder of the book. The stage theories in particular are referred to frequently in later chapters and serve to make the reader aware how points being discussed at a particular age level fit in the overall scheme of development. Most of the chapters are short and concise, devoted to aspects of a single topic and/or age level, and easy to grasp. Second, lists of Key Points are provided at the beginning of each chapter

and these points are emphasized by marginal notations printed opposite relevant sections of text. The opening page of each chapter lists the Key Points under major headings and provides an overview of the chapter. The margin notes alert students to parts of each chapter that merit special attention and are likely to be stressed (at the instructor's discretion) on exams. Supplementing the Key Points, which often clarify important terms and concepts, a glossary is provided at the end of the book. Finally, concise summaries are provided at the end of each chapter.

Jerome Bruner once observed that "We teach a subject not to produce little living libraries on the subject, but rather to get a student to think as a mathematician [or psychologist] does . . . to take part in the process of knowledge-getting" (1966, p. 72). Although this book is not intended to produce "living libraries," it *is* intended to help the reader become reasonably well-informed about a selection of current scientific knowledge about development. At the same time, an effort is made to persuade readers of this book that they should occasionally think as psychologists, make direct observations (during and after taking course work) of individuals at various stages of development, and relate their conclusions to the conclusions of specialists. At the end of Chapter 1 a description of ways the reader might make personal use of the various methods described in the historical survey is presented, and many of the end-of-chapter Suggestions for Further Study feature do-it-yourself projects.

A Study Guide is offered to enhance learning and understanding. Designed to help students organize information about the Key Points and to learn these points quickly, easily, and thoroughly, the Study Guide can be used in preparing for exams. To facilitate mastery of difficult or hard-to-remember information, suggested study techniques and memorization aids are offered.

Acknowledgments

We would like to acknowledge our indebtedness to the following individuals who read one or more drafts of the manuscript in its various stages of development: Peter Cohen, University of Texas at San Antonio; Gerald Larson, Kent State University; William Hopkins, State University College of New York at Cortland; Mary Main, University of California, Berkeley; Nancy Margand, Washington and Lee University; Irene Miura, San Jose State University; Phyllis Povell, Long Island University, C. W. Post Center; Barry Wadsworth, Mount Holyoke College; Everett Waters, State University of New York at Stony Brook; and Harriet Waters, State University of New York at Stony Brook.

Also, the second author would like to express her appreciation to a number of people who contributed in different ways to the present edition. Dr. Philip Rusche, Dean of the College of Education and Allied Professions at the University of Toledo, provided released time at a critical point in the preparation of the manuscript. Valuable suggestions were received from many colleagues, including William Gray, John Zimmer, Lois Hodgson, and Robert Haaf. Research assistance was provided by several graduate students, including Ken Davis, Mary Lou Rush, Laura Damas, Linda Feigelman-Kalchman, Jerry Stine, and Sara Asmussen. At a more personal level, boundless patience and support were provided by Dr. Richard A. Hudson. And last but least only in size, the coauthor's five-year-old grandson, Benjamin, has been a constant source of inspiration to her. He has enriched her understanding of the process of development and her appreciation for the often remarkable efforts of young children to make meaning in their world.

Robert F. Biehler

Lynne M. Hudson, University of Toledo

DEVELOPMENTAL PSYCHOLOGY

PART 1

THE SCIENTIFIC STUDY OF THE CHILD

KEY POINTS

Baby biography: detailed record of infant behavior

Baby biographies often insightful but unsystematic, irregular, subjective

Coefficient of correlation: index of relationship

Tests: responses to standard questions compared to a key

Questionnaires: children reveal knowledge or opinions by writing answers

Questionnaires provide much data but are subjective, difficult to evaluate

Time sampling: behavior recorded after observing children for a short period

Matched group experiment: similar groups exposed to different conditions

Rating scales: observers judge behavioral traits

Longitudinal approach: same children are studied over a period of time

Longitudinal approach reveals age trends but selection of subjects is crucial

Sociometric technique: children indicate which playmates they like

Clinical interview: child's initial responses determine later questions asked

Clinical interview flexible but subjective

Projective techniques: ambiguous stimuli used to study personality

Standardized interview: responses to standard questions

Interviews provide much information, but it may be inaccurate, distorted, difficult to interpret

Base-line experiment: behavior observed before and after conditions imposed

Cross-sectional approach: characteristics of children of different ages measured

Some age groups in cross-sectional studies may be atypical

CHAPTER 1

HISTORY, SCIENTISTS, METHODS

Some people possess a zest for living—they take advantage of their opportunities, get along with almost everyone they meet, and make positive contributions to society. Others are unhappy—they are unwilling or unable to use their abilities, incapable of forming friendships, and engage in activities that are destructive to themselves and others. From the time human beings first became intrigued by behavior, thoughtful individuals have asked: What are the causes of such differences in human behavior? Can't we use the knowledge we have accumulated to help more people enjoy life and take advantage of their abilities? Since experiences during childhood and adolescence apparently have a significant influence on later behavior, shouldn't it be possible to observe how children develop and how they are influenced by experiences, in order to find ways to help people live happy, fulfilling lives?

Many of the early thinkers who recorded their impressions of human behavior expressed dismay about widespread unhappiness, marital incompatibility, conflict between generations, selfishness, and aggression against others. Today, although we have found ways to conquer most diseases, ease physical suffering, make our lives remarkably comfortable, and even put a man on the moon, we have not substantially reduced the incidence of unfortunate and undesirable forms of human behavior. Part of the explanation, perhaps, is that we have not observed the development of children long enough, or carefully enough, or that we have failed to use the information we possess in the proper manner. This book summarizes past and present information on human development and various interpretations of how this information might be applied to the rearing of children. When you have finished it you should be able to draw your own conclusions about the extent and value of our knowledge of development. Then you will be able to decide how it might best be used by parents, teachers, nurses, social workers, and others who have contact with children.

The information about human development summarized in this book is based on scientific research. While more trustworthy than hunches based on subjective impressions, conclusions based on scientific studies are sometimes difficult to apply. You should, therefore, take into account certain complications and cautions.

Scientific Knowledge and Child Rearing: Some Complications

Recommendations Change as Knowledge Accumulates

As developmental psychologists observe behavior and read reports of studies by their colleagues they benefit from the cumulative nature of science. New ideas constantly replace old ones for a variety of reasons: results published by early theorists permit later researchers to begin at an advanced level of understanding; innovative methods of study are perfected and yield previously undiscovered data; scholars recognize interrelationships that earlier students overlooked; investigators carry out more complete and sophisticated experiments; theorists, through analyzing and synthesizing data, evolve more comprehensive or revolutionary sets of principles. An inevitable by-product of the continual progression of scientific interpretations of development is that current books on child psychology and child rearing often contradict those published just a few years ago. A parent or teacher eager for definitive answers may sometimes find this unsettling and wonder about the wisdom of placing confidence in any book on child psychology. Nevertheless, the demand for expert opinion remains high.

Parents Seek Child-rearing Advice

To a greater extent than in most societies, American parents actively seek information—scientific or otherwise—about child rearing. America is essentially a meritocracy where a person's position in life may often be determined more by merit than family background. There is no denying that some Americans have greater opportunities to achieve success than others, but genuinely capable individuals often work their way to the top through their own efforts regardless of their background. This characteristic of our society appeals especially to recent immigrants and to those from lower socioeconomic situations, but even in families that settled in America generations ago and have achieved wealth and status parents want to do the "right" thing to help their children make the most of their opportunities.

A meritocratic society is based on open competition, however, and parents, in spite of themselves, may measure their success as child rearers by comparing their children's performance with that of others. If a neighbor's child does exceptionally well in some activity or seems to possess every virtue, parents may wonder if that child's parents know something about child rearing that they don't know. Obtaining information about children is not necessarily motivated only by the wish to help a child make the most of opportunities or to keep up with the Joneses, however. If research specialists have engaged in painstaking study of development and subjected their conclusions to scrutiny by others, it makes sense to find out what they have discovered. Even though some parents may be skeptical about changing knowledge and even though motives may differ, most parents are interested in finding out what psychologists have to say about child rearing. This desire for information can be understood more completely by comparing parenthood in the 1880s (before developmental psychology existed as a discipline) with parenthood today.

An American family in the 1880s.
Culver Pictures.

Parenthood Then and Now

Parenthood in the 1880s

If you had been born one hundred years earlier, you would not have been confronted as a young adult with very many decisions regarding parenthood and child rearing. Unless you decided to join the ranks of the tiny minority of old maids and bachelors, it would never have occurred to you that there was any alternative to marriage. Once married, you and your spouse would have probably accepted as matter of course that you would begin almost immediately to have a family.

After the conception of a child, you would have made decisions about pregnancy and birth on the basis of what your parents had done or on the advice of other relatives, friends, or perhaps a family physician. Once your child was born, you would have adopted, without much thought or discussion, infant-care routines that had evolved over time and had been practiced for generations. In the absence of books, magazine and newspaper articles, and television programs on techniques of child rearing, you would have simply done the "natural" thing, or used techniques you remembered or observed. At the appropriate age, your sons and daughters would have learned and accepted traditional sex roles with little or no resistance, largely because of the unquestioning

An American family in the 1980s.
© *Jean-Claude Lejeune.*

way you and your spouse had accepted your sex roles: the father was the breadwinner; the mother took care of the children and house.

All of this made life a lot simpler in the 1880s. But life was also restrictive and precarious in many ways. Relatively few choices could be made, and the limited knowledge of medical practitioners as well as parents about many aspects of conception, prenatal development, birth, child care, and the nature of human development led to frequent miscarriages or stillbirths, high infant and maternal death rates, and much unnecessary unhappiness for both parents and children.

Parenthood in the 1980s

In the last one hundred years, and especially in the last thirty years, more knowledge has accumulated about human behavior and development than in all preceding periods of history. This knowledge has opened up unprecedented possibilities for making life free and full, but it has also made life much more complicated. For along with knowledge has come the need for making a large number of decisions. Consider just a few of the choices available to you that were not available to your great-grandparents.

Today, alternatives to formal marriage are being explored and accepted, and if you join in formal or informal matrimony with a member of the opposite sex, you may devote considerable thought to the question of having children. You may take into account such factors as the population explosion, ecological considerations, careers for both marriage partners, the costs of raising children, and the possibility that parenthood may take precedence over all other roles—particularly for the mother.

So many forms of birth control are available that you have the option of deciding when and how many children you will attempt to have. If you wish, you and your spouse (or prospective spouse) can have an analysis made to ascertain the possibility that incompatibilities in genetic structure might lead to abnormalities in your offspring. If an unwanted pregnancy occurs, or if some disease or condition known to cause abnormalities in fetal development occurs during pregnancy, you may consider a decision (under certain circumstances and depending on your religious convictions) of aborting the pregnancy. If a child is conceived and prenatal development is allowed to proceed, you will be able to choose from several theories and methods of prenatal care. By your selecting a particular obstetrician, the *way* the delivery of the child occurs becomes a matter of choice.

After the child is born, if you become informed about current thinking on child rearing, you will discover that there is a great deal of information available. (Because you are several times more likely than were your great-grandparents to finish high school and study at an institution of higher learning, you are much more likely to be aware of scientific information about development.) If you examine even a small amount of this information, you are likely to find (for reasons just discussed) that interpretations conflict and that ideas about child rearing change in a very short period of time. If you have more than one child, and if you follow up-to-date recommendations, each of your offspring may be reared according to quite different guidelines. Simply being *exposed* to new and different ideas (through books, college courses, magazine and newspaper articles, or television programs) may cause you to frequently alter your opinions about child rearing.

As this brief comparison of parenthood in the 1880s and 1980s indicates, parents of one hundred years ago tended to follow a prescribed pattern, which limited choice but made child rearing straightforward and simple. There were few thoughts about whether what was being done was right or wrong, and most parents did not question the assumption that traditional techniques were the only ones to use. Today few American parents slavishly follow traditional methods of child rearing. We have acquired an enormous amount of information about behavior and development and are in a position to make child rearing more effective than ever. But the extent, variety, and changeable nature of this information leads to speculations and doubts about whether some approaches are better than others. Unthinking but confident acceptance of tradition has been replaced by informed but sometimes insecure choice.

As a consequence of these various factors, you will need to exercise judgment and discretion when you attempt to apply scientific information to behavior. You will also need to take into account how assumptions underlying research influence the way knowledge may be applied.

Conflicts and Changes in Scientific Knowledge

After a hundred years of scientific observation and experimentation, researchers have accumulated a wealth of information about human development. There are differences of opinion, however, about how to interpret this information or apply it to child rearing and education. Some psychologists believe that there are advantages to thinking of a child's personality as being shaped almost entirely by experiences. Their research and recommendations to parents and teachers are based on the assumption that child behavior can be shaped in constructive ways if experiences are arranged in predetermined sequences. Other psychologists are convinced that children come equipped with built-in tendencies that determine behavior. They suggest that parents and teachers allow children considerable freedom to select experiences on their own. Still other psychologists believe that parents and teachers should facilitate development by providing experiences that are matched to the child's current level of functioning. Each of these views has enjoyed favored status at various times during the last thirty years, but at no time has one view been universally accepted.

While conflicting views and shifts in emphasis are particularly confusing to those who wish to encourage the optimum development of children, they are not unique to the field of developmental psychology. After analyzing the history of scientific investigation in various fields of study T. S. Kuhn (1962) concluded that there are frequent **paradigm shifts** in every science. A **paradigm** is a model that serves as a frame of reference, and Kuhn found that all fields of science have been characterized by frequent changes in the popularity of research models. In an analysis of "idealized" and "real" conceptions of science, Arnold Sameroff (1983) comments on the observations of Kuhn on paradigm shifts, as well as related observations by S. G. Brush (1974). He notes:

The standard textbooks in most university introductory courses present the sum of knowledge in a discipline as a continuous discovery of facts, in which each new fact goes a bit beyond the previous one. . . . In reality, science does not proceed in such a continuous mechanistic manner, each new fact being as valuable as the one that came before. . . . Within psychology one can find examples of whole areas of data that seemed important to collect at the time, that now are considered irrelevant. (p. 244)

Three significant characteristics of the nature of science emerge from these observations:

1. At any given point in time there are likely to be conflicting interpretations of scientific information.
2. A point of view that was enthusiastically adopted at one time as *the* best answer to certain types of questions is likely to be replaced by a different view a few years later.
3. Much of the most up-to-date scientific information of today is likely to be superseded by different information some time in the near or distant future.

Before you begin to examine current information about child development, therefore, it will be to your advantage to gain a sense of perspective by becoming familiar with what has occurred in the past. A survey of the history of developmental psychology will not only help you grasp the nature and significance of paradigm shifts, it will also help you evaluate some of the research to be reported in this book. Even though some paradigms are not as popular today as they were a few years ago, the research they generated (and continue to generate) is still valuable. Furthermore, it is beneficial to approach the scientific study of human development with awareness that conclusions that seemed well established just a few years ago have been revised and continue to be revised.

To help you grasp when, how, and why scientific study of development took different forms in different parts of the world during different periods of time, a chronological summary of scientists, methods, and trends will be presented on the remaining pages of this chapter.

An Historical Journal of Developmental Psychology

The historical survey that follows is presented in the form of an imaginary journal that might have been written by individuals who functioned as free-lance investigators. The journal approach has been adopted to encourage you to imagine that you are actually journeying from place to place to find out about current developments. All of the scientists, theories, and studies to be noted in the journal will be dis-

cussed more completely in the following chapters. You are urged, therefore, to read the journal entries not to try to assimilate details but to
grasp how the scientific study of development evolved and how it has
been diverted in different directions at various times in recent history.
When considering any topic as broad and complex as developmental
psychology it is difficult to avoid being overwhelmed by the feeling that
what is described is nothing more than a confusing assortment of unrelated reports. The journal that follows is intended to help establish a
framework. When you later encounter the names and investigations
noted briefly in the journal entries, you should react to them with at
least a degree of familiarity and be able to place them in historical
perspective.

   While you should read the journal to gain an overall impression of the
sequence of events, you are asked to pay particular attention to the
different scientific methods described. Techniques of study will not be
singled out for attention after this opening chapter so they are stressed
on the following pages. To help you concentrate on methodology, brief
notations of different techniques are printed in the margins. Similar **Key
Points** have been chosen for emphasis in all succeeding chapters. The
Key Points are listed on the opening page of each chapter, and, depending on the preference of your instructor, may be stressed heavily or
exclusively on exams. If the Key Points *are* to be featured on exams, you
may wish to examine the Study Guide prepared to accompany this text.
It is designed to help you cement your understanding of text material
identified by the margin notes as you prepare for exams. Various kinds
of memory aids are presented as suggestions for learning difficult sections of the text.

   Philosophers such as Plato, Aristotle, John Locke, and Jean Jacques
Rousseau made observations about human development and child rearing hundreds of years ago. The scientific study of human behavior,
though, might be said to have been given particular impetus by publications of Charles Darwin. Accordingly, the first entry in the imaginary
journal reports impressions gained during a visit with the famous British
scientist.

July 1, 1881   Downe, Kent, England[1]

Visited Charles Darwin at his home today. He is seventy-two and very
frail and weak but still possesses a forceful personality. Wish all of those

---

[1] A few slight liberties have been taken with the sequence of actual events,
and dates and locations have sometimes been deduced from incomplete information. Such minor inaccuracies, however, should not alter the significance
of the information provided.

Charles Darwin with his eldest son, William ("Doddy").
Courtesy of Down House, Downe, Kent.

Baby biography:
detailed record of
infant behavior

critics who refer to him as a "blasphemous heretic" could have eaves-dropped on our conversation. The theory of evolution doesn't force people to choose between the Bible and Darwin; it's simply a matter of two alternative explanations of the same thing. The opening chapters of Genesis with their marvelous description of how God created the world and Adam and Eve are always enjoyable to read. But at the same time it is fascinating to ponder the theory that over a period of millions of years mutations occurred and organisms produced progeny that are different in various ways and that some of these differences contributed to survival more than others did. Darwin's intellectual curiosity has stimulated him to study almost everything he has encountered, including his own children. He showed me what he calls a **baby biography,** a detailed record of the early behavior and development of his first-born child, William Erasmus (nicknamed "Doddy"). He made the original notes thirty years ago but recently revised them for publication in the journal

Mind after he read a similar description made a hundred years ago by a German, Dietrich Tiedemann. I found the biography very interesting, but it may be more useful as a source of ideas to study than as an acceptable scientific record. For one thing, Doddy Darwin is certainly not an average child. And even though his father is an extremely observant man, it was not possible for him to keep a continuous record of all of Doddy's behavior. Consequently, Darwin probably picked out certain types of behavior in his son and ignored others. He was probably influenced by his expectations and also by the fact that the baby was, after all, his child. But a highly detailed diary of the behavior of one child does provide certain kinds of information (such as subtleties and sequences in behavior) that more objective analyses of large numbers of children cannot.

Baby biographies often insightful but unsystematic, irregular, subjective

As we parted, Darwin gave me a letter of introduction to his cousin Sir Francis Galton.

July 10, 1885   London, England

Met Sir Francis Galton today at his Anthropometric Laboratory in the South Kensington Museum. He gave his laboratory that name because he is making an effort to measure as many characteristics of humans as he can. He has accumulated so much information, in fact, that it has become necessary to devise methods for interpreting it. As an example, he showed me some data on the heights of fathers and sons. First he spread out several pages of figures of heights and pointed out that it is almost impossible to make much sense of them. He demonstrated that calculating the *mean* by adding up all the measures and dividing by the number of them provided information about averages, but to discover more revealing relationships he has developed what he calls a **scatter diagram.**

To make one of these scatter diagrams all one has to do is put a tally (mark) in the box indicating the height of father and son. If the tallies are arranged in a diagonal line from the bottom left corner to the top right corner, the relationship is a strong one. But if the tallies scatter so that no discernible pattern is apparent, there is little or no relationship. Sir Francis has developed what he calls the **coefficient of correlation** (or correlation coefficient), a numerical value between $+1.0$ and -1.0 reflecting how strong the relationship is and whether it is positive or negative. A negative value doesn't mean there is a *lack* of relationship; it indicates that a large amount of a characteristic in one individual will be related to a small amount in the other member of the pair being compared. He drew a sample scatter diagram for me and also showed me a formula for calculating the index.

Coefficient of correlation: index of relationship

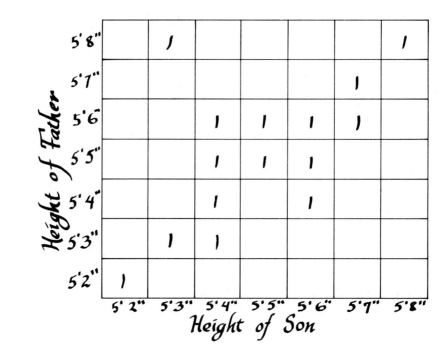

Sir Francis also showed me figures and diagrams that demonstrate what he calls *regression toward mediocrity*. He has found that taller than average fathers tend to have sons slightly shorter than themselves, and that shorter than average fathers have sons slightly taller than themselves. (Since the regression does not always make a person "mediocre" in a literal sense, other scientists have suggested that it would be better to call this *regression toward the average or mean*.) Because regression is found when correlation coefficients are calculated, Sir Francis refers to correlations by the abbreviation *r* (for regression).

Then Sir Francis got started on the subject of measurement. He wants to measure, in the most objective and accurate manner possible, the capacities and abilities of large numbers of people. Since a typical subject will cooperate in providing such measurements for a short period of time only, he has devised various kinds of **tests.** Tests consist of a series of brief questions or situations that the person is asked to answer or perform. Sir Francis pointed out that each individual is exposed to the same situations or asked the same questions in exactly the same way and that responses are measured by various devices or recorded in writing. Answers to written questions can be evaluated by comparing them to a key of correct answers. The number of correct answers can then be totaled, and the result is a numerical index of a particular ability.

Tests: responses to standard questions compared to a key

At the present time Sir Francis is working on a mental test, and he mentioned that he had heard rumors that some psychologists in France are doing the same. As we parted, he suggested that I travel to Paris in the near future and check up on the rumor. Left Sir Francis with one thought dominating all others: there is a tremendous amount of variability in human beings. It's intriguing to try to find some of the factors that make people develop in such different ways.

April 5, 1905 Paris, France

Spent a fascinating day with Alfred Binet and his colleague Theodore Simon. The rumor Sir Francis Galton had heard turned out to be true. Binet has been attempting to measure mental ability for several years and recently completed a very satisfactory test of intelligence. He told me that the previous year he had been approached by the Minister of Public Instruction of Paris and asked if it would be possible to devise a means for determining if some schoolchildren lacked the intelligence to benefit from instruction in regular classrooms. Binet explained that his goal was to devise a measuring scale that could be administered in a short period of time and would yield a numerical index of intelligence. The goal was achieved by making up a series of tests of increasing difficulty and arranging them by age levels. Answers to the tests are evaluated by comparing them to a key, and the final score is reported as the subject's *mental age.*

January 4, 1906 Worcester, Massachusetts

The center of child study in America at the moment seems to be Clark University. Had dinner tonight at the home of G. Stanley Hall, the president of the university. He has established one of the first psychological laboratories in this country, founded the American Psychological Association and several journals in psychology, and carried out hundreds of studies—in addition to running the university. Many of his studies make use of **questionnaires,** which also have been used by Sir Francis Galton and some German researchers.

Questionnaires: children reveal knowledge or opinions by writing answers

Hall explained to me that he first used the questionnaire when he became curious about whether children think of things in the same way as adults. He asked hundreds of elementary schoolchildren to answer a list of questions (one I remember was "What happens when the sun sets?") and discovered that children do not really understand many things adults have assumed they understood. (This discovery has led to quite an upheaval in education.) He gave me a copy of his report "The

Front row, left to right, Sigmund Freud, Stanley Hall and Carl Jung; back row, left to right, A. A. Brill, S. Ferenzi, E. Jones: at Clark University, Worcester, Massachusetts, in September 1909.
Culver Pictures.

Contents of Children's Minds" and of his two-volume work *Adolescence,* which is fascinating.

Hall obtained much of his data on adolescence through questionnaires. This is obviously a quick and easy way to obtain information but it has certain limitations. You can't be sure that all children will interpret the questions the same way or that what they write really reflects what they think. Also, it's difficult to evaluate and analyze their responses with a high degree of accuracy. The Binet-Simon test or its equivalent may be a better way to get some types of information because the questions bring out specific answers that can be evaluated by referring to detailed standards.

Just before I left his home, Hall told me he plans to invite some of Europe's most famous psychoanalysts, notably Sigmund Freud, to a conference to be held three years from now, in 1909. Eagerly accepted his invitation to attend.

Questionnaires provide much data but are subjective, difficult to evaluate

September 10, 1909   Worcester, Massachusetts

Here for the conference at Clark University. Met Sigmund Freud, the "star" of the conference, in the dining car of the train on the way up. He told me he was extremely pleased to receive the invitation to the conference because he does not feel his work has been given the attention it deserves in Europe. In his address, Freud described how he encourages his patients to talk about their childhood experiences. Must say I admire Freud's courage in suggesting that many of these childhood experiences center on sexual impulses. Also am impressed by his suggestion that much of our behavior is influenced by unconscious thoughts and feelings. He promised to send me the manuscript of a book he is going to publish on the unconscious. While I responded favorably to Freud's address, I didn't get the impression that too many of the American psychologists in the audience were terribly receptive. Freud has based his theorizing on personal recollections of himself and his patients. Behavioral scientists in this country prefer to base their conclusions on careful observation and experimentation.

October 5, 1917   Baltimore, Maryland

Had a very unsettling day. Just as I thought I was getting some insight into the conscious and unconscious processes of myself and others, I have been told that such speculations are worthless because they are not scientific. Met John B. Watson in his office at Johns Hopkins University this morning, and he did his best to make me see the error of my ways and to convert me to what he calls **behaviorism.** Watson chose the term *behaviorism* for his point of view because he wanted to emphasize the idea that psychologists should base all their conclusions on observations of overt behavior.

I accept Watson's argument that a behavioristic approach is a valuable method for studying children, but I'm not sure I share his faith in our ability to *shape* behavior. He claims he can produce any kind of person he chooses, and he has written a book for parents urging them to train their children in specific ways. He feels training is essential because he argues that inherited tendencies are insignificant and that a child's personality is almost entirely due to the way the child is treated.

March 7, 1926   New Haven, Connecticut

Interviewed Arnold Gesell today at his Clinic of Child Development at Yale University. He is making motion pictures of the behavior of infants as they respond to standard conditions. Frame-by-frame analyses have provided an extremely detailed description of sequences of behavior in infants. The sequence seems to be amazingly uniform in all children, and Gesell is convinced that early development is almost entirely the result of maturation (that is, growth processes that seem to occur independently of experience). This certainly contrasts with Watson's stress on shaping or training that has influenced thinking about children for the last ten years. Gesell told me of an experiment he and a colleague, Helen Thompson, carried out with a pair of identical twins. One was given training in skills (climbing stairs and building piles of blocks) starting at six months; the other was not given training until about eighteen months; yet both seem to perform equally well at two years. Gesell maintains that development is mediated by a genetic timetable and that all the shaping in the world won't change the rate of growth to any significant extent.

September 29, 1930   Iowa City, Iowa

Spent an interesting day talking with members of the staff of the Iowa Child Welfare Research Station at the State University. About ten years ago child study centers were established in universities in various parts of the country, and I have decided to visit as many of them as I can. Researchers here are interested in discovering ways that different kinds of experiences influence development. Beth Wellman, for example, is seeking to determine if nursery school instruction has an impact on intelligence-test scores. M. Skodak is studying children in institutions. Initial findings suggest that infants who are given a great deal of attention develop faster than those left in their cribs. It looks as if there are exceptions to Gesell's argument that experience has no effect on the rate of maturation.

October 10, 1930   Minneapolis, Minnesota

Am here to visit the Institute of Child Welfare at the University of Minnesota. The institute was established shortly after the Iowa Research Station and is directed by John E. Anderson. He has attracted students interested in carrying out very thorough observational studies. Mary Shirley is using a baby-biography approach not with one infant, but with twenty-five of them. She started out observing and testing her subjects every day, and now she observes them once a week. She intends to continue the study until they are two years old.

   Mildred Parten is studying the social behavior of preschool children. She first observed them in free play and wrote descriptions of the types of behavior they engaged in. She believes that six categories account for almost all types of nursery school social behavior. Parten uses a variation of what is called the **time-sampling technique.** She selects a child and observes him for one minute, then classifies the play observed during that minute into one of the six categories. Next she observes another child for a minute, classifies her behavior, and so on. Over a period of days, she accumulates twenty such samples for each child.

Time sampling: behavior recorded after observing children for a short period

October 20, 1930   Detroit, Michigan

Interviewed specialists in the study of nursery school education at the Merrill-Palmer Institute today. Josephine Hilgard has performed an interesting study of the interrelationships between maturation and learning in young children. Hilgard selected two groups of fifteen nursery school children each and **matched** them according to chronological age, mental age, sex, and their initial ability at three tasks: buttoning, climbing, and cutting with scissors. Then one group received twelve weeks of intensive training in these three skills, while the other group received no training. At the end of twelve weeks, when both groups were tested to determine their skills in the three tasks, the experimental (practice) group was superior in all three skills. At that point, the control group, which previously had been given no training, was exposed to just four days of supervised practice. On the last day of that week, when both groups were tested once again, the two groups had become equal in ability. Up to a point Hilgard agrees with Gesell's emphasis on maturation, but she also notes that general practice in a variety of skills probably contributed to the development of the abilities she measured.

Matched group experiment: similar groups exposed to different conditions

November 1, 1930   Yellow Springs, Ohio

Paid a visit to the Fels Research Institute here in Yellow Springs. Lester W. Sontag, the director, explained the ambitious undertaking he has instituted. Close to one hundred children have been selected, and their behavior—as well as that of their parents—will be studied. Furthermore, the behavior of the offspring of the one hundred children selected will be recorded and analyzed in an effort to identify similarities and differences between generations.

Sontag and his associates have developed **rating scales** to record behavior. Observers are given detailed descriptions of different types of behavior. Then after watching the behavior of parents and children in different situations, the observers mark their ratings on lines representing graduations between opposite types of behavior. As the children mature, an effort will be made to relate the characteristics of children to the child-rearing practices used by their parents. Sontag feels

Rating scales: observers judge behavioral traits

Fels Parent Behavior Rating Scale No. 7.2

Serial sheet no.

Acceptance of child
(devotion-rejection)

Rate the parent's acceptance of the child into his own inner circle of loyalty and devotion. Does the parent act in such a way as to indicate that the child is considered an intimate and inseparable partner? Or does the parent act as though he resents the child's intrusion and rejects the child's bid for a place in his primary area of devotion?

Consider all evidence which in any way may impinge upon the child as acceptance–rejection, however subtle, vague, or indirect. It is not the parent's true feeling, but his *attitude*, as a functioning unit in the child's environment, which we are rating.

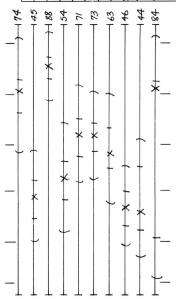

		Number
1 2 3 4 5 6 7 8 9 10		
6/9/40 6/15/40 6/21/40 6/7/40 6/20/40 6/10/40 6/14/40 6/17/40 6/10/40 6/13/40		Period of observation
M M M M M M M M M M		Ratee
122 86 122 25 50 14 32 52 110 86		Age in months at end of period
Jane Bellows Dave Abel Irene Lott Anita Bauer Tommy Westy Susan Darby Paul Stanley Betsy Larson Marilyn Foote Susan Bone		Child

Parent's behavior toward child connotes utter devotion and acceptance into his innermost self, without stint or suggestion of holding back in any phase of his life.

Parent clearly accepts child. Includes child in family councils, trips, affection, even when it is difficult or represents considerable sacrifice.

A "charter member" of the family but "kept in his place." Parent accepts child in general, but excludes him from certain phases of parent's life.

Tacit acceptance. Excludes child so frequently that to the child the rejection attitude may seem to predominate even though parent takes acceptance for granted.

Parent's predominant tendency is to avoid, repulse, and exclude the child, but without open rejection.

Child openly resented and rejected by parent. Never admitted to inner circle. Made to feel unwanted, ostracized.

										Score	Rater: *MJH* Date of rating: 6/26/40
										Tolerance	
										Range	Scored by: *N* Date: 9-17-40 Checked by: *N* Date: 10-17-40
1	2	3	4	5	6	7	8	9	10	Number	Tabulated by: *N* Date: 11-18-40

Rater's remarks: (continue on back of sheet)

One of the Fels Parent Behavior Rating Scales. (Instructions for rater.)
"The Appraisal of Parent Behavior," Alfred L. Baldwin, Joan Kalhorn, and Fay Huffman Breese, Psychological Monographs, *No. 299, 1949, 63, No. 4.*

that this approach will yield insight into the continuity of development and long-term cause-and-effect relationships. He is philosophical about the fact that the most important conclusions of the study may not be drawn until after his death. He gave me a copy of a list of all the scales they intend to use in rating parent behavior and also a detailed set of instructions observers will use in rating one type of behavior.

January 21, 1932   Berkeley, California

Here at the University of California three impressive studies are under way. Each started out as a short-term investigation, but each has now been converted to a continuing research program similar to the study at the Fels Institute.

Jean Walker Macfarlane is directing an investigation referred to as The Guidance Study because its original aim was to determine the impact of guidance supplied to parents. The initial sample consisted of every third child born in Berkeley during an eighteen-month period in 1928 and 1929. Instead of terminating the study as originally planned, Macfarlane has decided to transform it into a long-term investigation of personality development. She intends to obtain cumulative measures of physical and mental growth and personality development up until the time her subjects are eighteen years old and then conduct follow-up studies when they are thirty to forty years of age.

Five years ago Nancy Bayley initiated an intensive investigation of development in the first fifteen months after birth (an approach very similar to that being used by Shirley at Minnesota). At the end of that age span she decided to continue her research indefinitely. The investigation, which is called the Berkeley Growth Study, began with a sample of seventy-four white, full-term, healthy, hospital-born babies of English-speaking mothers. The major emphasis of this study is physical and mental growth, but personality and social factors will be measured as well.

Harold E. Jones and Herbert R. Stolz have just begun an intensive study of the adolescent development of approximately two hundred fifth- and sixth-graders in Oakland. Physiological changes at adolescence are a major emphasis of this investigation, but social relations and teachers' appraisals of classroom behavior will also be analyzed. Even though the original plan was to terminate the study when the students graduate from high school, this investigation, too, will be extended.

The Fels Institute research and the three studies under way here at Berkeley make use of the **longitudinal approach.** The Fels and Berkeley researchers are enthusiastic about this technique because the same subjects will be studied from infancy through childhood, adolescence, and adulthood. This approach avoids the weaknesses of retrospective anal-

Longitudinal approach: same children are studied over a period of time

yses (such as Freud's descriptions of what his patients recalled about childhood experiences), provides maximum information about the overall process of growth, and permits evaluation of the accuracy of predictions of later behavior. On the basis of early observations, the Berkeley researchers plan to record their impressions of what individual children will be like as adults and then check up on their predictions.

While they extol the advantages of the technique, they point out that there are also certain disadvantages. A considerable amount of time, patience, energy, money, and cooperation is needed to embark on a longitudinal study. Staff turnover, lack of cooperation from subjects (particularly those who may move out of the vicinity), and a delayed payoff for their efforts may make it difficult for them to persevere. They also realize that all their results will be based on the behavior of a small group of subjects, and if that group is atypical in significant ways, the results may not apply to other groups or individuals.

Longitudinal approach reveals age trends, but selection of subjects is crucial

February 3, 1932   Stanford, California

Completed my tour of child research centers at American Universities this afternoon by talking with Lewis Terman in his office at Stanford. He and Maud Merrill have supervised a team of test specialists to produce the Stanford-Binet Intelligence Scale, an exceptionally effective test patterned after the Binet-Simon scale. A major improvement Terman has made over the original Binet test is to report scores by dividing mental age by chronological age and multiplying by one hundred. This score, called the **intelligence quotient,** or IQ, is based on a concept first proposed by the German psychologist Wilhelm Stern.

Terman also has instituted a longitudinal study of gifted children. He asked teachers from all over California to help him pick a thousand intellectually gifted children. With the assistance of Melita Oden, he plans to study them for at least thirty years.

November 10, 1934   New York, New York

Sociometric technique: children indicate which playmates they like

Spent an hour this afternoon with Jacob Moreno, an Austrian psychiatrist who recently moved here. He has developed what he calls **sociometric techniques,** which involve asking members of a group to list the names of individuals in the group they like best. Moreno showed me some sociometric diagrams he drew after asking elementary school students to write down the names of their favorite classmates. The diagrams call attention to **stars** (the most popular children) and **isolates** (those who are not chosen at all).

March 1, 1937   Geneva, Switzerland

Have traveled to Switzerland to make the acquaintance of Jean Piaget. He has been engaged in the study of thinking processes of children. His interest in children's thinking was an outgrowth of baby biographies he wrote of his own children. At first Piaget simply described the behavior of his children, just as Charles Darwin kept a diary of the development of his son Doddy. In time, however, he began to record not only spontaneous behavior, but also the reactions of his children to simple "experiments." (One of the first experiments he tried involved a game where he hid a matchbox under a pillow and observed and recorded the reactions of his son.) Eventually, Piaget concluded that he might present more complex problems to older children. He has developed a great many of these problems, and he uses them to understand how children reason at different points in their development. The basic technique, which Piaget calls the **clinical interview,** involves presenting children with a problem, observing them solve the problem, and questioning them about their solutions. Because children do not all respond in the same way, the questions Piaget asks may not be the same from one child to the next. This approach is quite different from the questionnaire approach of G. Stanley Hall or the tests developed by Galton, Binet, and Terman, which consist of a standard series of questions.

Clinical interview: child's initial responses determine later questions asked

On the basis of hundreds of clinical interviews, Piaget has come to the conclusion that intellectual development in children follows a definite pattern, and he is in the process of describing ages and stages.

While I am excited about Piaget's work, I can't help wondering if some of the patterns of cognitive development he is reporting can be attributed more to his orderly mind than to children's thinking. The clinical interview certainly permits Piaget to follow up on points that emerge as he questions his subjects. At the same time, the very flexibility of the technique opens up the possibility that Piaget might interpret answers and ask questions that "lead" to responses fitting his expectations.

Clinical interview flexible but subjective

February 3, 1947   Berkeley, California

Have returned to Berkeley to talk with Erik Erikson, a student of Freud's who emigrated to America. He is studying play constructions made by subjects of the Berkeley Growth Study. (All of the longitudinal studies I learned about on my previous visit are still going strong.) The Berkeley researchers wanted some data on unconscious, as well as conscious, aspects of adolescent behavior, and they have made use of several **projective techniques.** These methods are designed to confront subjects with ambiguous stimulus situations so that they cannot deliberately distort their responses. On a test or questionnaire, particularly one that

Projective techniques: ambiguous stimuli used to study personality

Projective techniques, such as the Rorschach inkblot test are used to induce children to reveal personality tendencies without being aware of it.
Sybil Shelton/Monkmeyer.

taps personality variables, subjects may read some significance into a question and then answer accordingly. Projective techniques make it very difficult for subjects to do this, and so they "project" their thoughts and feelings in an undistorted way when they respond.

The Berkeley Growth Study researchers have already used the Rorschach inkblot test (where subjects are asked to describe what they see in a series of inkblots) and the Thematic Apperception Test (where subjects are shown ambiguous pictures of ordinary and provocative situations and asked to make up a story about them). Erikson is using a doll-play technique to gain further insight into the unconscious thoughts and feelings of adolescent children. He asks each subject to take an assortment of dolls, houses, cars, animals, furniture, blocks, and the like and "make a scene out of an exciting movie." He has found that boys arrange action scenes but that girls are more likely to create domestic tableaus.

Before coming to Berkeley, Erikson did anthropological research with two American Indian tribes, and he told me that he has come to the conclusion that Freud's tendency to stay in Vienna prevented him from becoming aware of the importance of cultural differences when he proposed his description of stages of psychosexual development. Erikson is at work on a modification of Freud's description of stages that will emphasize psycho*social* behavior and trace how it is influenced by the culture in which a child lives.

February 12, 1951   London, England

Interviewed John Bowlby of the Tavistock Clinic and Institute of Human Relations today. Bowlby is just completing a report for the World Health Organization on infants reared in institutions. He has concluded that the overall development of a child deprived of maternal care between six months and three years of age will be retarded and that the effects of early deprivation will be permanent. Even if the child is given extra stimulation and attention later in life, Bowlby feels there is no way to make up for care not supplied earlier.

March 10, 1957   Stanford, California

Am at Stanford University to learn about the work of Robert R. Sears and his colleagues. Sears endorses the view that child behavior is primarily the product of experiences. If this assumption is accepted, then it follows that much child behavior is the product of the parents' child-rearing techniques. Therefore, if relationships can be established between techniques used by parents and different types of child behavior, Sears reasons that informed parents could encourage the development of selected traits in their children. Sears began his career at the Iowa Child Welfare Research Station. From there he moved to the Harvard University Laboratory of Human Development, where he supervised a study of patterns of child rearing. He and his colleagues Eleanor E. Maccoby and Harry Levin trained ten women to conduct intensive **standardized interviews** of almost four hundred mothers of five-year-old children. The mothers were asked to respond to a lengthy series of questions about their own behavior as well as that of their children. The interview records were analyzed by two independent raters with reference to 188 scales that provided information about child-rearing practices used by different women and the impact these had on children. A substantial amount of data from a large number of mothers was obtained, but this method has limitations. For one thing, there is no way of being certain that the mothers gave true descriptions or even that they were able to remember accurately incidents that occurred years or months earlier. And when the responses were classified, further distortions might have occurred. Even so, this study supplies an abundance of information about child-rearing practices and their impact.

From Harvard, Sears came to Stanford, where he has continued his

Standardized interview: responses to standard questions

Interviews provide much information, but it may be inaccurate, distorted, difficult to interpret

1. First of all we'd like to get a picture of the family. How many children do you have?
   1a. How old are they?
   [If more than one child] In this interview we want to talk mostly about X, since he's in the kindergarten group we are working with.

2. Has X been with you all his life, or have you been separated from him at any time?
   2a. [If separated] For how long? How old was he then?

3. And how about his father—has X been separated from his father at any time?
   3a. [If separated] For how long? How old was X then?

4. Now would you think back to when X was a baby. Who took care of him mostly then?
   4a. How much did your husband do in connection with taking care of X when he was a baby?
   4b. Did he ever change the baby's diapers? feed him? give him his bath?

5. All babies cry, of course. Some mothers feel that if you pick up a baby every time it cries, you will spoil it. Others think you should never let a baby cry for very long. How do you feel about this?
   5a. What did you do about this with X?
   5b. How about in the middle of the night?

6. Did you have time to spend with the baby besides the time that was necessary for feeding him, changing him, and just regular care like that?
   6a. [If yes] Tell me about what you did in this time. How much did you cuddle him and sing to him and that sort of thing?

7. Do you think that babies are fun to take care of when they're very little, or do you think they're more interesting when they're older?

8. Now would you tell me something about how the feeding went when he was a baby?
   8a. Was he breast-fed?
   8b. [If not] How did you happen to decide to use a bottle instead of breast feeding?
   8c. [If yes] For how long?
   8d. [If yes] Did you go directly to the cup or did you use a bottle?
   8e. And how about weaning him (from the bottle) (from the breast) to a cup? When did you start this?
   8f. How did you decide it was time to begin this?
   8g. How did you go about this?
   8h. How did he react to being taken off the bottle (breast)?
   8i. Had you been giving him liquid from a cup before?
   8j. How long did it take to get him to give up the bottle (breast) completely?

9. There has been a lot of talk about whether it is better to have a regular feeding schedule for a baby, or to feed him whenever he is hungry. How do you feel about this?
   9a. How did you handle this with X?
   9b. [If schedule] How closely did you stick to that schedule?

10. Have you had any problems about X eating enough, or eating the kinds of food he needs?
    10a. What do you do about it?

Portion of interview schedule devised by Sears, Maccoby, and Levin.
Robert R. Sears, Eleanor Maccoby, and Harry Levin, Patterns of Child Rearing *(Stanford, CA: Stanford University Press, 1957).*

analysis of the impact of different child-rearing practices. Unfortunately, relatively few systematic relationships have been established, but methods developed by Sears and his colleagues are sure to pave the way for valuable research of the same type.

March 15, 1963   Stanford, California

Back at Stanford to observe a fascinating experiment directed by Albert Bandura. A four-year-old girl was shown a film depicting an adult as-

In experiments supervised by Albert Bandura, children were first shown a film depicting an adult assaulting a Bobo doll in a variety of ways (top row of photographs). Then, the children were frustrated (by being interrupted while playing with some highly desirable toys) and taken to a play room containing a Bobo doll. Most of the children responded by imitating the aggressive actions they had seen in the film (middle and bottom rows of photographs).
Courtesy of Albert Bandura.

saulting an inflated doll. Then she was allowed to play with some very attractive toys and, just when she was thoroughly enjoying herself, was abruptly interrupted and taken to a room that contained the inflated doll (as well as many other playthings) she had seen in the film. According to a widely endorsed theory in American psychology, frustration is supposed to lead to aggression, and Bandura predicted that the frustrated child would not only be primed to vent her aggression, but she would do so by imitating the models she had viewed in the film. Sure enough, the little girl used every assault technique she had seen in the movie.

Bandura believes the results of his experiment can be generalized to television. He argues that a child who is frustrated in a real-life situation may express aggression by imitating types of behavior seen on television programs. There may be some truth to this hypothesis, but I see quite a difference beween hitting an inflated doll made expressly for the purpose of being hit and, say, attacking or killing another human being. Even if there are significant differences between behavior in experimental and real-life situations, Bandura has called attention to the influence of models and the potential impact of television. He wants to alert parents to the possibility that their children may learn aggressive forms of behavior from watching too many television programs that feature violence.

Base-line experiment: behavior observed before and after conditions imposed

Some of the experiments carried out by Bandura and other psychologists interested in the impact of different kinds of experiences on child behavior make use of the **base-line experimental technique.** Children are first observed so their "natural" (or base-line) level of behavior of a particular type can be established before they are exposed to conditions arranged by the experimenter; then their behavior is observed again. When studying aggressive reactions, for example, it is important to first find out the level of aggressiveness a child exhibits in ordinary play before measuring the number of aggressive responses exhibited after the subject has been exposed to a frustrating experience.

April 6, 1963   Chicago, Illinois

Am here at the University of Chicago to talk to Lawrence Kohlberg, who has just completed a fascinating pilot study of moral development. When Kohlberg was a graduate student, he read about Jean Piaget's observations on the moral thinking of children. He became so intrigued by the subject that he decided to make it the topic of his doctoral dissertation. In a book published in 1932 and in several subsequent articles, Piaget theorized that the moral reasoning of young children is different from that of older children. Kohlberg decided to carry out a systematic analysis of Piaget's hypothesis by asking ten-, thirteen-, and sixteen-year-old boys to respond to what he calls **moral dilemmas.** (In the moral dilemma Kohlberg showed me this afternoon, I was asked to identify with a man who must decide whether or not to break the law in order to save the life of his wife.) Each boy was asked to describe his reactions to ten moral dilemmas and his tape-recorded responses were later scored for thirty aspects of morality. In addition, the level of moral reasoning was evaluated.

This kind of study is called **cross-sectional** (or **normative**) because age differences are established by studying a sample of children at different ages. An advantage of the cross-sectional approach over the longitudinal approach is that information about age differences can be obtained in a short period of time. Furthermore, a specific aspect of behavior can be studied in detail, and if an important variable is overlooked in an initial study, a supplementary investigation is a simple matter. The biggest problem is selecting subjects at different age levels who are not atypical.

Cross-sectional approach: characteristics of children of different ages measured

In his study, Kohlberg made an effort to select boys who had approximately the same IQ, but he did not attempt to control other potentially significant factors (such as parental attitudes toward morality). Accordingly, there is the possibility that some of the moral reasoning differences reported by Kohlberg may not be solely due to differences in age but to differences in the background of each group. Kohlberg is aware of this weakness, and he told me that he plans to carry out a longitudinal follow-up study by asking the same boys to respond to moral dilemmas every few years.

Some age groups in cross-sectional studies may be atypical

March 3, 1968   Cambridge, Massachusetts

Have come to Harvard to talk to B. F. Skinner, who has just been chosen by psychology department heads in this country as the most influential American psychologist of this century. Skinner's pre-eminent influence on American psychology stems not only from research techniques he pioneered and the principles of learning he established using those techniques, but also from his interest in applying those principles.

Once he had established principles of learning, Skinner began to speculate on how those principles could be applied to human behavior. He wrote a novel, *Walden Two*, in which he described a society where children are placed in the hands of child-rearing specialists who systematically control the children's experiences in order to eliminate undesirable traits (such as jealousy) and encourage desirable ones (such as self-control and perseverance). Skinner has also just completed *The Technology of Teaching*, in which he urges teachers to be systematic in applying learning theory principles in their classrooms. Several of Skinner's followers are currently writing books urging parents to shape the behavior of their children. The basic techniques they recommend center on supplying reinforcement (in the form of praise or a reward of some sort) for desirable behavior and withholding reinforcement when undesirable behavior occurs.

While many American psychologists are highly enthusiastic about Skinner's views on behavior shaping, others have pointed out disadvantages and dangers. The psychotherapist Carl R. Rogers, for instance, feels that Skinner's view of human behavior—which emphasizes that our behavior is controlled by positive and negative experience we have had—is a threat to efforts to improve mental health. Rogers argues that in order for patients in need of psychotherapy to overcome their problems they must develop the conviction that they *can* control their own behavior. Another psychologist who is uneasy about Skinner's theory is Abraham H. Maslow, who fears that too much emphasis on behavior modification causes parents to feel that they must shape their children's behavior. Maslow urges parents to *not* interfere too much but *let* and *help* their children grow.

At present Skinner's influence seems to be at a peak. Many educators and parents are enthusiastically using learning theory principles to attempt to shape behavior. But problems are already becoming apparent, and it would appear that children may become resentful about control by others or lose interest in working for rewards.

March 10, 1971   La Jolla, California

Came here to talk with Carl Rogers because he has always been one of the most outspoken advocates of freedom and self-direction in development. Just a few years after B. F. Skinner's views seemed to be dominating education and child rearing, an abrupt reversal has occurred. Preplanned control of development and learning by parents and teachers has been rejected by many people in favor of permissiveness and self-direction. Such pendulum swings appear to be a fixture of thinking about development, child rearing, and education. In the 1920s John B. Watson urged parents to shape behavior. In the 1930s Arnold Gesell and his associates recommended that parents permit maturation to occur. In the 1950s there seemed to be a shift back toward carefully planned child rearing, as reflected by the research of Robert R. Sears and his colleagues, who sought cause and effect relationships. By the mid-1960s Skinner's arguments in support of behavior shaping and preplanned learning began to attract many supporters. But then America became enmeshed in Vietnam, and reactions against compulsory obedience to authority led to rejection of too much control by either parents or teachers. At present open education, with stress on self-discovery by pupils, is very popular in elementary schools. In high schools and universities students are demanding—and being given—a great deal of freedom to choose courses. Furthermore, tests and grades are being attacked as manifestations of authoritarianism. Many of today's college students seem to regard Rogers as something of a patron saint. When I talked with him today, he pointed out that he has been calling attention to what he considers to be the disadvantages of excessive control by parents and teachers ever since he engaged in a debate with Skinner in 1956. At the moment, many American parents, educators, and students are on the side of Rogers. But it will be interesting to see how long the present trend lasts—and what the results of freedom and self-direction in education will be.

September 11, 1975   Loch Lomond, Scotland

Am on the shores of this beautiful Scottish lake to observe the proceedings of a conference being held at a country house owned by the University of Strathclyde. The theme of the conference is "Mother-Infant Interaction," and psychologists who have specialized in the study of this topic have journeyed here from all over Great Britain as well as from Germany and the United States. As I examine books and articles currently being published on child development, I am struck by the extent to which this appears to be the era of the infant. I get the impression that many more experiments and observations are being carried out on infant subjects today than at any previous time in the history of developmental psychology.

In the United States it seems that the main interest is in *The Competent Infant*, at least that is the title of a virtual encyclopedia of studies of infancy edited by Joseph Stone, Henrietta Smith, and Lois Murphy. British psychologists are fascinated by the "human" qualities of infants. Most of the papers being presented here are concerned with subtle interactions between infants and mothers—with the infant sometimes being the star performer and the mother acting more as a responsive audience.

January 14, 1979   Washington, D.C.

Am in Washington to attend a meeting of the United States National Commission for the International Year of the Child. Growing awareness of the impact of early experiences on later behavior and of the deplorable conditions under which children in many parts of the world mature has prompted leaders from hundreds of countries to join in proclaiming 1979 The International Year of the Child.

I find it interesting to recall that the current desire to use scientific knowledge to foster optimum development in children was the driving force that led to the formation of many American university departments of child development in the 1920s and 1930s. The biggest difference between 1930 and 1980, though, is that today there is much greater awareness of the impact on child development of environmental and cultural differences. The psychologists of the 1930s studied mostly middle-class white American children, usually because such children were readily available as subjects. In the fifty-year period since those first departments of child development were established, we have accumulated an enormous amount of information about all kinds of children. The basic question they faced in the thirties is still the same today, though: How can we use scientific information to help children make the most of their capabilities?

August 25, 1981   Los Angeles, California

Am here to attend the annual convention of the American Psychological Association. As I looked through the program and listened to presentations today, I was struck by the current popularity of **information processing**. Hundreds of experiments have been performed to determine how human beings perceive things, store their perceptions, process them, and retrieve them to solve problems. Results of experiments are often reported in the form of charts and diagrams depicting how information processing procedures occur in sequence. It appears that many developmental psychologists in this country are eager to study thinking by using an alternative approach to that developed by Piaget. So many replications of the Swiss psychologist's studies have been carried out during the last few years that researchers interested in cognitive processes have been eager to find other ways to study this fascinating topic. The information processing approach, with its stress on precise definitions and step-by-step procedures, has provided such an alternative.

April 24, 1983   Detroit, Michigan

Am in Detroit to attend the fiftieth anniversary meeting of The Society for Research in Child Development. In honor of the occasion, the program committee has asked researchers who helped shape the study of development during the Society's history to share their views about how far we have come and to suggest new directions that might further our understanding of development. If there is a single thread that connects these discussions, it is that being human is a very complex activity involving the continual renegotiation of one's role in the physical and social world. We have come a long way in appreciating and understanding these complexities. Parent-child relations are a good case in point. In the formative years of this Society, we looked at how the mother's behavior influenced the child's development. Later we recognized that babies influence mothers as well, that the relationship is bidirectional. As we began to study fathers, we came to appreciate their sometimes unique contributions to children's development. Now, Eleanor Maccoby, the Society's president, is urging us to look more carefully at how parent-child relations develop over time.

Postscript to the Journal

Jean Piaget, who died in 1980 at the age of eighty-five, was fourteen in 1909 and already taking an active interest in science. Therefore, disregarding the accounts of meetings with Darwin and Galton, who were not really developmental psychologists, one individual could have personally interacted with all the leading scientists who have specialized in the study of development.

To help you grasp the nature and significance of the points that have been recorded in this imaginary journal, two summaries are provided on the remaining pages of this chapter: a decade-by-decade outline of research trends, a description of methods *you* might use to study behavior.

A Decade-by-Decade Outline of Research Trends

This first summary consists of a decade-by-decade analysis of significant trends in developmental psychology. Since thousands of studies of children have been carried out each year, it is clearly impossible to summarize all research interests that appeared during any particular period. The points listed, therefore, are not intended to reflect a complete outline of all significant developments, but of trends selected to supply an overview of the kinds of topics developmental psychologists have studied at different times.

1880   Darwin's various books on the theory of evolution arouse great interest in the scientific study of human development.

1890   Galton reports accurate measurements of many human characteristics and introduces the development of statistical techniques for analyzing them.

1900   Influential pioneers publish works that have a profound influence on later psychologists: Binet develops an effective intelligence test; Freud writes and lectures on psychoanalytic theory; Hall establishes several journals of psychology in America and makes extensive use of questionnaires to study child and adolescent behavior.

1910   Watson publishes his articles and books on behaviorism, reflecting and influencing stress on learning by association and on objective observation that become hallmarks of American psychology.

1920   Gesell studies infant behavior and concludes that early behavior is so universal and predictable that it must be controlled by an inner timetable of growth.

1930   Institutes for the study of children's development become well established and highly productive at Iowa, Minnesota, Berkeley, Stanford, and elsewhere. Such departments are often funded because it is reasoned that scientific information should be used to improve the well-being of children.

1940   Piaget publishes in European journals numerous reports of his conclusions about cognitive development. In America, studies of the impact of different child-rearing practices are featured in longitudinal investigations.

1950   Bowlby reports on worldwide studies of institutionalization and stresses the need for early stimulation and effective mothering.

1960   Skinner's books on learning principles lead to discussions of when and how parents and teachers should try to shape child behavior. Translations of Piaget's books on cognitive development arouse considerable interest on the part of American researchers and educators.

1970   Extensive research on infants reveals previously unrecognized competencies. Studies of mother-infant interaction uncover ways mothers and babies influence each other. Interest in using psychological knowledge to help children is as high as it was in the 1930s, but now there is more interest in tracing how environmental conditions influence development and behavior.

1980   Ramifications of parent-child relationships are examined. The information processing paradigm becomes increasingly popular.

This decade-by-decade review of research trends illustrates points made at the beginning of this chapter:

During almost every decade there have been conflicting views about interpretations of data.

There have been frequent paradigm shifts.

The accumulation of scientific knowledge of human development has not followed a consistent, continuous pattern. It has been discontinuous and has taken the form of spurts of interest in different directions.

Some information that seemed important at one time now appears to be irrelevant.

Generalizing from these historical trends, it seems safe to say that there will continue to be conflicts, that new paradigm shifts will occur, and that some information currently viewed as significant will appear irrelevant in the future.

Methods You Might Use to Study Development

This second summary highlights methods of study described in the imaginary journal. Instead of reviewing studies already mentioned, however, examine the methods as if you are using them to gain more systematic and objective information about the behavior of your own child. This approach is used not only to give you a different perspective and reinforce understanding, but also to make you aware that you can use many of the techniques developed by researchers. For purposes of organization, the description that follows outlines techniques you might use to trace aspects of the behavior of a developing child. If you are asked to prepare some sort of term project to satisfy requirements for this course, though, you might use techniques similar to those described to carry out do-it-yourself research during this quarter or semester.

Whenever you want the most accurate answers available to questions about human development, you should consult the information sources described in the Suggestions for Further Study at the end of chapters. Quite often, however, you may be curious about the behavior of particular children in a particular environment at a given point in time. In such situations you might follow procedures such as those described in the following paragraphs.

When your first child is born (which we will assume is a girl), you find yourself so fascinated by her behavior that you decide to write a **baby biography.** Whenever you have the time, you sit down next to her   Baby biography crib or playpen and write down detailed descriptions of what she does, adding interpretive comments about what might have caused the behavior.

When your daughter is a preschooler, you are often entertained by her comments about the people and things she encounters. You find yourself wondering just how much she understands, so you make up a **questionnaire** and ask her to describe her impressions and interpretations of things in her immediate environment.

Some of your daughter's answers strike you as remarkably perceptive, and you find yourself wondering how sharp she is compared to the other boys and girls in the neighborhood. To find out, you make up a simple **test** consisting of questions about your neighborhood (for example, the names of people who live in different houses, which family has the biggest dog, where the nearest fire hydrant is) and ask your daughter and several of her friends to respond. Then you ask an acquaintance who does not know any of the children to evaluate the responses of each child by referring to scoring standards you supply. Finally, you add up the number of points earned by each child and compute a "Neighborhood Knowledge" score.

When you examine these scores, you assume that older children should know more about the neighborhood than younger ones since they have been around longer. To acquire information relating to this point, you prepare a **scatter diagram** showing the relationship between the scores of all children who took your test and their ages in months. (If you are mathematically inclined you might also calculate a **correlation coefficient.**)

The test scores earned by the younger and older children who come to play in your backyard do not seem to be too noticeably influenced by age, since the tallies scatter all over your diagram. You hypothesize that this may be the case because the difference between the youngest and oldest children you tested is only thirty-six months. Accordingly, you ask neighborhood children up to the age of fifteen to take your test. When you compare the scores of children of all ages, you *do* find that there is a definite relationship between neighborhood knowledge and age. You realize, however, that the rough age norms that you have established by using a **cross-sectional** approach may not be very accurate because some of your subjects do not seem to be typical of their age group. (You got the impression that the ten-year-old you tested was preoccupied, and you know that the fifteen-year-old is in a gifted child program at school.) So you decide to do a **longitudinal** investigation and ask each child below the age of five to take your test every two years.

You have a spacious backyard, and many neighborhood children congregate there for play. As you watch them one afternoon, you get the impression that some children are leaders, others followers, and still

Questionnaire

Test

Scatter diagram

Correlation coefficient

Cross-sectional approach

Longitudinal approach

others independent souls. You decide it would be interesting to find out which children assume each of these roles. You realize that it would be impossible to write down everything that every child says or does, so you decide to carry out a **time-sampling** study. You list the names of all the children who are frequent visitors to your backyard on a sheet of paper and draw three columns opposite the names. You head the columns: "Tells others what to do," "Does what others say," "Plays without paying much attention to others." You watch the first child on your list for a minute and put a check mark in the appropriate column if one of the three kinds of behavior is observed. Then you record the behavior of the next child, and so on. You do this for thirty minutes on three different afternoons and total up the tallies in each column. You discover that you now have a quite clear picture of leaders, followers, and independent types.

Time sampling

Your time-sampling study causes you to wonder about the different personality characteristics of your daughter's playmates. So you develop a homemade **rating scale** by listing pairs of traits (such as confident-anxious, daring-cautious, active-sedentary) on either side of a piece of paper and connect them with lines containing equally spaced divisions. Then you ask your spouse and a friend to watch the neighborhood children for several afternoons before putting a mark on the lines indicating how much or how little of a characteristic they think each child displays. Finally, you compare your ratings with the other ratings to see if you and your two fellow observers have reached similar conclusions.

Rating scale

While you are observing children in the backyard preparatory to making your ratings, you speculate about who the most popular children are. To find out you carry out a **sociometric** study by asking each child to tell you the name of the playmate he or she likes best.

Sociometric technique

One day as you watch a television show with your daughter, you wonder if what she sees on TV influences her behavior to the extent that she would go out and immediately imitate some of the actions she has seen. (You recall that after watching Western movies as a child you frequently got out your cap pistol and went in search of playmates to organize a gunfight game.) You happen to notice that a Western titled "Duel of the 'Gunfighters'" is scheduled to be shown on a local TV channel the next day. This prompts you to set up a simple **experiment** featuring experimental and control groups. You make a few telephone calls and find out that three children in the neighborhood always plant themselves in front of a TV in one of their homes and watch that channel at that time. You invite them to come to your backyard for ice cream and play just after they watch the movie. The next day, at the time these three children are watching the Western, you persuade your daughter and two of her friends to watch a rented movie about baby animals. You invite them to join the other children in the backyard for ice cream as

Experimental method

soon as the movie is over. On a table next to the counter from which the ice cream is served you place several cap pistols as well as some stuffed animals. After making sure everyone has a generous helping of ice cream, you move to a remote part of the yard to record the kinds of games the children engage in immediately after they finish their treat.

When your daughter reaches the sixth grade, you become aware that she suddenly seems to be very concerned about right and wrong behavior. You ask her how she feels about different rules and laws and why they should be obeyed. You let her initial answer determine the question you ask as your interview proceeds since you have decided to use **Clinical interview** the **clinical interview** to probe her thinking.

When your daughter is in the ninth grade, you realize that she now keeps to herself thoughts that she expressed openly when she was younger. She also seems very concerned about making a good impression. Both of these tendencies make you wonder if it would be possible to get her to reveal her inner feelings without being aware of it. You realize that your own knowledge of specialized tests is too limited but **Projective** wonder what sorts of tendencies might come to the surface if your **techniques** daughter was asked to respond to a **projective test** given by a trained psychometrist.

When your daughter nears the end of the high school years, she sometimes engages in discussions with you regarding social, moral, and political issues, causing you to wonder if there is a "generation gap" in your family and in other families you know. To find out, you list questions about contemporary topics (such as legalizing marijuana), jot **Standardized** down your own responses, and then **interview** your daughter, several **interview** of her friends, and their parents. You summarize and analyze the different responses to see if any trends emerge.

If you do become intrigued by child development to the point of making systematic observations such as those just described, sooner or later you will probably find yourself trying to relate one conclusion to other conclusions. In other words, you may make an effort to develop a **theory** about certain forms of human behavior so that you can tie together separate conclusions. A theory based on the sorts of observations just described would not be very elegant, but organizing your conclusions would represent an attempt on your part to explain how children develop. In that sense, it would share the goal of psychologists whose work is summarized in the next chapter, which consists of a description of the best-known theories of human development.

Explanation of the Suggestions for Further Study

Scientific knowledge about human development is potentially valuable in a variety of ways. Even though paradigm shifts occur and interpretations of scientific data change, parents, teachers, nurses, social workers, and others who have contact with children can make excellent and varied use of information summarized in this and other books on human development. Therefore, if you presently have contact with children or expect to interact with them in the near future, it will be to your advantage to think about the *personal* significance of what you read on these pages. But even if you are not planning to be a parent in the near future or to engage in a career that involves interacting with children or adolescents, thoughtful reading of this book may give you insights into your own behavior and the behavior of others of all ages. The Suggestions for Further Study that you will find at the end of each chapter are intended to stimulate independent thinking about topics covered. The following types of suggestions are provided:

Specific references to books and articles you might refer to for more complete information about a particular theory, theorist, or topic.

Suggestions for writing a term paper or term project, if either is assigned.

Interviews you might conduct for information about children or child rearing.

Simple observational or experimental studies you might carry out either during the time you are taking a course or after you have completed course work but are actively involved in one or more ways with children.

These latter suggestions are similar to those just noted in the final summary, "Methods You Might Use to Study Development."

Changes in Child-rearing Practices

Suggestions for Further Study

If you would like to read accounts of how approaches to child rearing have changed, look for one or more of these articles or books: "Sixty Years of Child Rearing Practices" by Celia Burns Stendler (*Journal of Pediatrics*, 1950, 36, 122–134); "Trends in Infant Care Ideas" by C. E. Vincent (*Child Development*, 1951, 22, 199–209); "Trends in Infant Care" by Martha Wolfenstein (*American Journal of Orthopsychiatry*, 1953, 33, 120–130); or *Two Centuries of Child Rearing Manuals* (1968) by Samuel Z. Klausner.

History of Developmental Psychology

For a brief history of developmental psychology, look for "Historical Beginnings of Child Psychology" by Wayne Dennis (*Psychological Bulle-*

tin, 1940, *46*, 224–225). An especially interesting account of the history of child study is presented in *The Child* (1965) by William Kessen, who intertwines his own observations with excerpts from works by physicians, philosophers, and psychologists. The earliest account he quotes (by John Locke) was published in 1693. The most recent (by Jean Piaget) appeared in 1947. Wayne Dennis has edited a collection of articles published between 1728 and 1948, titled *Historical Readings in Developmental Psychology* (1972), which includes reports of many of the studies mentioned in this chapter. Robert R. Sears discusses "Your Ancients Revisited: A History of Child Development" on pages 1–74 of *Review of Child Development Research*, 1975, *5*, edited by E. M. Hetherington. Milton J. E. Senn provides "Insights on the Child Development Movement in the United States" in a *Monograph of the Society for Research in Child Development*, 1975, *40*, 3–4, Serial No. 161. Robert Cairns outlines "The Emergence of Developmental Psychology" in Chapter 2 of *History, Theory, and Methods*, edited by William Kessen, Volume I of *Handbook of Child Psychology* (4th ed., 1983), edited by Paul H. Mussen.

Baby Biographies

Charles Darwin's baby biography of his son Doddy appeared in the British journal *Mind* in 1877. This journal is not likely to be available in your library, but the article was reprinted in *Readings in Child Psychology* (1951), edited by Wayne Dennis, pp. 54–64. (At the end of the article [pp. 64–67], Dennis supplies references for sixty-four other baby biographies.) The article is also reprinted in *The Child* (1965) by William Kessen (pp. 118–129). In addition, Kessen provides excerpts from baby biographies written by Wilhelm Preyer (pp. 134–147) and Hippolyte Taine (pp. 181–182). Baby-biography material that is directly related to several later sections of this text can be found in *The Origins of Intelligence in Children* (1952) by Jean Piaget, in which he supplies observations of his children to illustrate the principles and stages of his theory of development. If you read the descriptions of Darwin or Piaget (or of some other baby biographer), you might note the kind of behavior described. Or if you would prefer to function as a baby biographer yourself, keep a record of the actions and reactions of an infant over a period of time, summarize your conclusions, and assess the value of your research.

Binet's Observations on Intelligence Testing

To learn how Alfred Binet developed his test of intelligence and why he devised the techniques he used, read "The Measurement of Intelligence" by Binet and Simon reprinted in *The Child* (1965) by William

Kessen (pp. 188–208). Because this account was written at a time when psychologists were just beginning to refine tests, it is an especially revealing analysis of the problems faced by those who attempt to measure intelligence.

Questionnaires

Ever since G. Stanley Hall inquired into the contents of children's minds, psychologists have asked children to respond to questionnaires. It is a quick, easy way to get information. (The Gallup and Harris polls of public opinion on current affairs use the questionnaire approach.) If you are interested in how adolescents feel about current issues, you might make up a list of questions followed by "Agree" and "Disagree" and ask them to respond. The same questions might be submitted to some of your college classmates and to older adults, particularly parents of teen-agers.

Time Sampling

Observing social behavior can be quite fascinating. If you would like to make a systematic record of some aspect of interactions between children, the time-sampling technique is easy and enjoyable. Select some form of behavior that is of interest (for example, elementary school playground interaction, high school between-class behavior). Then develop a list of observational categories. First, observe children of the age you have selected as they engage in a particular type of behavior and write down what they do. Eventually, you should be able to describe five or so categories that cover most aspects of their behavior. At that point, pick out a child to observe for ten seconds. At the end of that time put a check mark in the appropriate column opposite the child's name. Then select another child, observe him or her for ten seconds, record the behavior, and so on. If you sample behavior on several different occasions, you will have a record of the types of behavior engaged in by different children. Parten's technique is just one of many types of time sampling. A summary of several variations of the basic technique is presented on pages 92–104 of "Observational Child Study" by Herbert F. Wright, Chapter 3 in *Handbook of Research Methods in Child Development* (1960), edited by Paul H. Mussen.

Interviews

If you are interested in feelings and attitudes, you might want to interview some students or parents. (Generally speaking, you are more likely to get responses of greater depth and variety if you interview older children or adults.) To carry out an interview study of adolescents, make up a short list of questions and ask some high school students to respond. (For examples of the kinds of questions you might ask, see the excerpts printed below from *The Adolescent Experience* [1966] by Elizabeth Douvan and Joseph Adelson. One advantage of using some of the questions developed by Douvan and Adelson is that you can compare the responses of your subjects to the summaries in *The Adolescent Experience*.) Another approach would be to ask children of different ages to respond and to compare their answers. If you would like to interview parents, see pages 491–501 of *Patterns of Child Rearing* (1957) by Robert R. Sears, Eleanor Maccoby, and Harry Levin for sample questions. (Part of the interview schedule used by Sears, Maccoby, and Levin is reproduced in Figure 1.3, page 28.)

Items from Interview Schedule for Girls Devised by Douvan and Adelson

1. What are the things you'll have to decide or make up your mind about in the next few years?
2. We find that some girls have a kind of plan or picture of what they get out of school. What ideas do you have about the way you want things to work out for you?
3. Do you want to get married some day?
4. Could you tell me a little about the kind of person you'd like to marry?
5. What kind of work would you like your husband to do?
6. Are there any girls you wouldn't go around with?
7. What do you think makes a girl popular with boys?
8. What do you think about dating?
9. What do you think about the idea of going steady?

. . .

11. Most parents have some ideas about how they want their children to behave. What are the most important things your parents expect of you?
12. Very often girls your age disagree with their parents about something. What disagreements do you have with your parents?
13. Jane sometimes wishes that her parents were different—more like the parents of her friends. What does she have in mind?
14. A girl is told by someone that a close friend of hers has said unkind things about her. What does she do about it?
15. Gladys feels terrible because she did something she thought she would never do. What do you think it would be?
16. What would she do about it?

17. Would she talk it over with anyone?
18. Would you tell me whether or not you agree with the following statements?

    The husband ought to have the final say in family matters.

    It is only natural and right that men should have more freedom than women.

    A man should help his wife with some of the work around the house.[2]

Obtaining an Oral History of Recollections of Child Rearing

You may be familiar with the currently popular technique of oral history in which elderly persons are asked to reminisce about their lives. If you have the opportunity, you might ask a grandparent or older neighbors to give you an oral history of how their parents treated them as children, and also how their impressions of contemporary child rearing compare with the way they were brought up. You might ask questions such as these and tape-record their responses:

How did your mother and father divide up child-rearing responsibilities? Did your mother pretty much handle the job all by herself or did your father help out? How?

Do you think your mother and father agreed about how children should be brought up, or were there differences of opinion? Can you give an example?

When you did anything wrong, how were you punished and who did the punishing?

If you had brothers and sisters, did you feel your parents treated girls and boys in different ways? How?

When you were bringing up *your* children, did you read any books about the subject, or did you do what your parents did, or did you just do what came naturally?

You've probably observed how children are being brought up today. Do you think parents of the 1980s are doing a better job, on the average, than your parents did or than you did? What do you wish parents of the 1980s would do that they don't seem to be doing?

---

[2]Elizabeth Douvan and Joseph Adelson, *The Adolescent Experience* (1966), pp. 441–444. Schedule developed by the University of Michigan Survey Research Center.

Do you think it is easier or harder for parents to bring up children today than it was when you were bringing up your children? Why?

Examining a Journal Containing Reports of Research on Development

You may acquire better understanding of the scientific study of development if you become acquainted with journals in this field of study. Listed below are selected journals containing reports of research on children. Some are devoted exclusively to such research, others publish occasional articles describing studies relating to development. (Not all these publications are journals in the strict sense. Some are annual collections made up of reviews of articles on a topic, or detailed reports of extensive research investigations.)

Adolescence
American Educational Research Journal
American Journal of Orthopsychiatry
Behavioral Science
Child Development
Cognitive Psychology
Developmental Psychology
Developmental Review
Educational and Psychological Measurement
Exceptional Child
Genetic Psychology Monographs
Harvard Educational Review
Human Development
Infant Behavior and Development
Journal of Abnormal Child Psychology
Journal of Applied Behavior Analysis
Journal of Applied Developmental Psychology
Journal of Child Language
Journal of Clinical Child Psychology
Journal of Early Adolescence
Journal of Educational Psychology
Journal of Experimental Child Psychology

Journal of Experimental Education
Journal of Genetic Psychology
Journal of Home Economics
Journal of School Psychology
Journal of Social Psychology
Journal of Youth and Adolescence
Marriage and Family Living
Merrill-Palmer Quarterly of Behavior and Development
Mental Hygiene
Minnesota Symposia on Child Development
Monographs of the Society for Research in Child Development
Personality
Psychoanalytic Study of the Child
Psychological Monographs
Psychological Review
Psychological Reports
Psychology in the Schools
Psychology Today
Science
Scientific American
Young Children

To become familiar with research in developmental psychology, you might examine recent issues of some of these journals. If you ever seek information on a topic by reading research reports, you might write abstracts of pertinent articles by following the outline below:

Author of article

Title of article

Journal in which article appears (including date, volume number, and page numbers)

Purpose (or description of problem)

Subjects

Procedure (or methods)

Treatment of data

Results

Conclusions

Are there any criticisms that you can make of the procedure or of the conclusions? (For example, were there enough subjects? were the subjects "selected" in any way? did the procedure seem to "favor" the predicted results? might you draw different conclusions than those noted in the article?)

Journals of Abstracts and Reviews

Browsing through professional journals is one way to deal directly with facts and theoretical speculations about development. In most cases, however, you are likely to want information relating to a specific question, and it would be too time-consuming to use a "browse" approach. The more efficient procedure is to find a recent article describing research on the point in question and refer to the bibliography of that article for other references. A variety of journals and reference works exists to assist you in doing this. The journals listed below consist of abstracts (brief summaries of results) of articles that appear in the type of journal listed in the preceding section.

Child Development Abstracts and Bibliography
Cognitive Development Abstracts
Exceptional Child Education Abstracts
Psychological Abstracts
PsycSCAN Developmental Psychology
Social Sciences Citation Index (Though it does not include abstracts, it can be used to find articles on a specific topic.)

The journal *Contemporary Psychology* provides reviews of new books in psychology, and the *Annual Review of Psychology* provides information reflected by the title—a specialist in each of several areas of psychology reviews significant studies that have appeared during a given year. The *Review of Educational Research* and the *Review of Child Development Research* feature articles that describe and analyze reports of studies on a particular theme.

To discover the nature of these indices and reference works, you might select a topic of interest, look in the index of one of the journals of abstracts (or scan the appropriate chapter in one of the *Review*s) until you find a reference to a recent article. Look up that article and read it to discover if it provides relevant information. If it does, you can use the bibliography as a source of information about related articles.

Popular Versus Professional Reports

Because of the demand for information on child rearing, newspapers and magazines frequently publish articles on this subject. There are also many TV programs on aspects of development, and books on how to raise children often appear on the best-seller lists. There are often significant differences between such popularized discussions and the reports of experiments found in the journals described in the three preceding Suggestions.

Writers of newspaper or magazine articles, TV scripts, or popular books know they must catch and hold the interest of the reader or viewer. Consequently, many of them highlight the dramatic side of things, oversimplify, and exaggerate. They also are likely to assume that no one will take the trouble to check on what they say and may not be concerned about being completely accurate. In extreme cases, they may make a point by embellishing an incident or part of a report on children.

Psychologists who write reports of experiments in professional journals usually operate under a different set of guidelines. They are expected to describe exactly what they were interested in studying, the characteristics of the children they used as subjects, the procedures they followed, and how they obtained and evaluated their results. This makes it possible for the reader to decide whether their conclusions seem justified. If readers have doubts about the results, they can often replicate the experiment on the basis of the information provided. Scientific articles and books on development may be less dramatic than magazine, TV, and book coverage of this subject, but they are more likely to be accurate—simply because scientists usually tell how they got their evidence. (It sometimes happens that a scientist manipulates data or draws unsupported conclusions. Most of the time, however, such distortions are pointed out, sooner or later, by other scientists.)

To become aware of the often untrustworthy nature of magazine articles, TV programs, or popular books on aspects of development, select a report that arouses your interest, and evaluate it with reference to questions such as these:

Does the author (or narrator) indicate the number and background of the subjects who were studied?

Is there detailed information regarding the procedures used?

Are you told where you could read about the study and draw your own conclusions, or are you just told the name (and perhaps the affiliation) of the investigator?

Are statistical data supplied to back up the conclusions, or are you more or less asked to accept what is reported "on faith"?

Are the conclusions interpreted in a tentative way, or does the author or narrator give the impression that they are clearly established or widely endorsed?

KEY POINTS

Nature, Functions, and Characteristics of Theories

Theories organize facts, guide research

Ideal theory: logical, supplies definitions, makes predictions, falsifiable

Freud: Stages of Psychosexual Development

Libido: basic instinctual energy with strong sexual component

Oral, anal, phallic, latency, and genital stages

Anaclitic identification: boys and girls try to be like mother

Defensive identification: boys try to be like father so as to acquire admired qualities

Id: source of libido

Ego: screens and controls expression of libidinal energy

Superego: one's conscience

Defense mechanisms: control primitive impulses or protect ego

Erikson: Stages of Psychosocial Development

Epigenetic principle: parts have time of special ascendancy

Trust vs. mistrust (first year)

Autonomy vs. doubt (two to three years)

Initiative vs. guilt (four to five years)

Industry vs. inferiority (six to eleven years)

Identity vs. role confusion (twelve to eighteen years)

Intimacy vs. isolation (young adulthood)

Generativity vs. stagnation (middle age)

Integrity vs. despair (old age)

Piaget: Stages of Cognitive Development

Equilibration: seek coherence and stability

Assimilation: incorporate conceptions into store of ideas

Accommodation: modify ideas

Scheme: organized pattern of behavior or thought

Conservation: some properties remain unchanged

Decentration: consider more than one characteristic at same time

Operation: mental manipulation that can be reversed

Sensorimotor stage: acquire first schemes through sense impressions and motor activities

Preoperational stage: form many schemes but not able to mentally reverse actions

Concrete operational stage: capable of mentally reversing actions, but generalize only from concrete experiences

Formal operational stage: able to deal with abstractions, form hypotheses, engage in mental manipulation

Learning Theory

Behaviorism: stress on observable behavior; prediction and control

Pavlovian conditioning: involuntary action aroused by previously neutral stimulus

Operant conditioning: voluntary behavior strengthened by reinforcement

Behavior modification: reinforce desirable, ignore undesirable behavior

Social learning theory: stress on observation and imitation

Bandura: anticipatory control makes it possible to preselect consequences

Information Processing

Information processing: ways input is processed, recovered, and used.

CHAPTER

2

THEORIES

*T*he preceding chapter makes clear how much information about all aspects of development has accumulated since the early 1900s. To impose at least some degree of order on related types of information and to better comprehend what they have learned, scientists propose theories. **Theories of development** represent attempts to organize observations about changes in behavior over time into coherent patterns that help to explain and predict behavior. Patricia Miller observes that "theories have saved developmental psychology from drowning in a sea of data" (1983, p. 2). In an effort to help you avoid drowning in a sea of data as you read this book, theoretical interpretations of development will be summarized in this chapter and will serve as an organizational frame of reference for the chapters that follow. Stages and principles proposed by leading developmental theorists will help you grasp how related sets of information reveal the nature of development.

Nature, Functions, and Characteristics of Theories

Theories organize facts, guide research

Miller notes that **theories** perform two valuable functions: they organize and give meaning to facts, and they guide research. Theories of development often disagree, however, about "which facts are most important for understanding children and what sorts of relationships among facts are most significant for producing this understanding" (Thomas, 1979, p. 3). In a sense, theories act like filters: they screen out some facts and impose a certain pattern on those they let in. In this way, the theoretical perspective of a developmental psychologist influences which questions are considered important to study, which methods are used, and, by implication, which results are found.

The theories discussed in this chapter are Freud's theory of psychoanalysis, Erikson's theory of psychosocial development, Piaget's analysis of stages of cognitive development, learning theory, and information processing. These theories differ in terms of the types of information they try to organize and explain. Some focus primarily on social and emotional development (Freud and Erikson), while others focus on cognitive development (Piaget and information processing). Some focus on internal properties such as thoughts and feelings (Freud and Piaget), while others focus almost exclusively on observable behavior (learning theory).

Ideal theory: logical, supplies definitions, makes predictions, falsifiable

Alfred Baldwin (1980) observes that, **ideally,** a theory should be logical and supply clear definitions. It should make specific predictions about behavior that are verifiable. In addition, a theory should be falsifiable. That is, it should be possible to prove that the theory does not make accurate predictions. Finally, a theory of *development* should call attention to changes in types of behavior that occur as a child develops.

None of the theoretical interpretations to be discussed in this chapter possesses all the characteristics of an ideal theory. Even so, the views to be summarized on the following pages are those discussed most frequently in books on developmental theory (e.g., Baldwin, 1980; Miller, 1983). Each merits consideration because each has made it possible to organize facts and also has stimulated considerable research.

Freud: Stages of Psychosexual Development

Formative Influences

Sigmund Freud was born in 1856 in Freiburg, Austria, to a forty-year-old wool merchant and his twenty-one-year-old second wife. Shortly after giving birth to Sigmund, his mother met an old peasant woman in a pastry shop who informed her that she had brought a great man into the world. The young mother firmly believed this prediction and treated

Sigmund at 16 with mother, Amalie.
Sigmund Freud Copyrights Ltd.

Sigmund as the indisputable favorite of all her children. When Sigmund was four, the family moved to Vienna. Sigmund was an outstanding student as a child, and he graduated early from high school with high distinction. He entered the University of Vienna, specializing in physiology out of admiration for the professor who taught that subject. After earning his M.D. degree, he interned at the General Hospital of Vienna, where he served for several months in the psychiatric clinic. Eventually, he was chosen lecturer in neural pathology and won a grant to study in Paris with the most famous neurologist of that era, Jean Martin Charcot.

Charcot was experimenting with the use of hypnosis to treat mental illness. Freud became intrigued by this technique, and when he returned to Vienna, he entered psychiatric practice with Josef Breuer, who also used hypnosis to treat his patients. One of these was a young woman named Anna O., who had developed paralyses of three limbs, disturbances of sight and speech, and a severe nervous cough as a consequence of nursing her critically ill father. One day she spontaneously described to Breuer how a particular symptom had developed. As she did so, the symptom disappeared. The next day, Breuer hypnotized Anna and urged her to discuss the development of other symptoms, and they also disappeared. In her waking state, Anna was unable to trace the development of most of her paralyses, but once hypnotized, she was able to grasp and explain the connections between experiences and symptoms.

While initially intrigued with the technique, Freud eventually became dissatisfied with hypnosis because not all patients could be hypnotized and because cures induced by hypnosis were often only temporary. He decided to make a more systematic application of the procedure that Anna used spontaneously by asking his patients simply to talk about whatever thoughts popped into their minds. As his patients engaged in such *free association,* Freud observed that dreams and recollections of childhood experiences were frequently of special importance. Unhappy or embarrassing experiences were sometimes so difficult to recall that he frequently had to help the patient overcome *resistance* to talking about them. The therapeutic technique Freud eventually developed that combined free association, dream interpretation, and analysis of resistance he called *psychoanalysis.* (The term *psychoanalysis* also refers to all aspects of Freud's theory, not just his system of therapy.)

Most of Freud's patients were women with symptoms similar to Anna O.'s. Almost all of them reported sexual fantasies, and several imagined that they had been seduced by their fathers. This led Freud to conclude that sexual factors were a normal, not an abnormal, feature of development.

At this stage of his career, Freud experienced considerable anguish and depression because of lack of professional recognition and difficulties in developing his conception of behavior. He therefore decided to psychoanalyze himself. As he examined his own early experiences, he was impressed by recollections of sexual wishes. Eventually, insights from his own analysis and his treatment of others led him to form a comprehensive theory of psychosexual development.

The Nature of Libidinal Energy

To explain behavior Freud proposed that human beings are born with a basic instinctual energy, the **libido.** He was convinced that the basic energy was characterized by a strong sexual component, but he defined "sexual" to include many types of pleasurable sensations, not just those centering on the genital organs. The key to understanding behavior, Freud suggested, is to determine how libidinal energy is being expended. Sometimes libidinal energy may become concentrated on a part of a person's own body; sometimes it is attached to another person or a particular object; sometimes libidinal energy may become blocked and accumulate. When he observed the behavior of children (primarily his own, since he had no child patients), remembered his own childhood, and listened to his patients free-associate, Freud became convinced that libidinal energy was likely to become concentrated on different parts of the body at different age levels. He eventually developed a detailed description of stages of libidinal, or psychosexual, development.

Libido: basic instinctual energy with strong sexual component

Stages of Psychosexual Development

The period from birth to two years Freud called the **oral stage** because the infant concentrates attention on feeding, uses the mouth to examine objects, and gains satisfaction from such activities as sucking a thumb or pacifier. During the **anal stage,** two- to three-year-olds (and their parents) are preoccupied with toilet training. Around the age of four, children typically enter the **phallic stage,** so called because they become curious about anatomical differences between the sexes, the origins of babies, and the sexual activities of their parents. Children may also discover that manipulating the genital organs provides a pleasurable sensation. Freud concluded that between the age of six or so and the time of puberty the libido is not concentrated on any particular part of the body, so he called this the **latency period.** Psychosexual development terminates at adolescence in the **genital stage,** when libidinal satisfaction centers on the genital organs.

Oral stage

Anal stage

Phallic stage

Latency period
Genital stage

Fixation and Attachment of Libidinal Energy

Freud hypothesized that if a child had a traumatic experience, or a series of disagreeable or abnormal experiences, during one of the stages of development, libidinal energy might become fixated. If fixation occurs, the person is predisposed to reduce tension later in life by resorting to the forms of behavior that were of greatest significance during the stage when the trauma occurred. A child who is weaned too early (and fixated at the oral stage), for example, may experience urges to eat and drink to excess as an adult; a child who is exposed to severe toilet training (and fixated at the anal stage) may manifest a compulsive concern about cleanliness in adulthood.

These stages and the concept of fixation account for ways libidinal energy might become centered on the person's own body. Other aspects of development Freud explained by suggesting that libidinal energy would become cathected (attached) to particular individuals, who would literally become *love objects*. He assumed that libidinal energy in an infant would be attached to the mother. Freud noted, however, that many of his female patients revealed in their free associations that they had experienced a strong attraction toward their fathers early in their lives. Furthermore, when Freud analyzed himself, he recalled that he had first gone through a stage when he adored his mother and feared and hated his father but that eventually he came to want to be like his father. To explain these trends in child behavior Freud proposed the *Oedipus complex*,[1] which refers to the tendency for a child (around the age of four) to attach libidinal energy to the parent of the opposite sex and to experience feelings of hostility and rivalry toward the parent of the same sex. If development proceeds normally, the Oedipus complex is resolved when the child of five or so comes to *identify* with the parent of the same sex.

Anaclitic and Defensive Identification

To account for changes in the attachment of libidinal energy, Freud introduced the concept of **identification.** He distinguished between two types, anaclitic (literally translated: "leaning-up-against-type") and de-

---

[1] If you are not familiar with the Greek myth of Oedipus or the play Sophocles based on it, you may wonder why Freud chose the term. Oedipus was separated from his parents at birth. In adulthood, without realizing it, he engaged in battle with his father and killed him. He then, also without realizing it, married his mother. When he discovered what he had done, he blinded himself. Strictly speaking, *Oedipus complex* refers to the love of the boy for his mother and his hostility and fear of his father. The love of a girl for her father (and her feeling of rivalry with the mother) is sometimes called the *Electra complex*, after a woman in another Greek myth who avenged the murder of her father by persuading her brother to kill their mother. In many nontechnical discussions, however, *Oedipus complex* is used to refer to behavior of both male and female children.

Freud proposed that up to the age of four or so, both boys and girls would strive to be like the mother because such anaclitic (leaning-up-against) identification would produce a sense of security. After they reached the age of four, Freud felt, boys would begin to engage in defensive (if you can't lick 'em, join 'em) identification and try to be like their fathers in order to acquire qualities they admired and envied.
© Peter Menzel/Stock, Boston. Leonard Freed/Magnum.

fensive (also called aggressive). **Anaclitic identification** occurs when children pattern their behavior after the primary caretaker, in most cases the mother. The mother provides care when the infant is completely dependent (and must therefore "lean" on her for care and sustenance). Freud thus hypothesized that the child, when capable of a certain amount of independent behavior (around the age of two), gains a measure of security by engaging in some of the activities of the person who had previously provided care. In a sense, the child's own behavior becomes a substitute for some of the satisfactions originally supplied by the parent.

    Defensive identification enters the picture when the child is old enough to recognize sex differences (usually around the age of four or so). Even when she becomes attracted to the father, the girl continues to identify with the mother, and she encounters few difficulties at this stage. But the boy must *transfer* his tendencies toward identification

Anaclitic identification: boys and girls try to be like mother

Defensive identification: boys try to be like father so as to acquire admired qualities

from the mother to the father, even though he resents and fears him. To resolve this Oedipal conflict, the boy employs a defensive maneuver; he makes efforts to be like his father so that he might acquire some of the qualities he envies. (In slang terms, defensive identification means "If you can't lick 'em, join 'em.")

One of the most significant and far-reaching aspects of Freud's theory was his revolutionary suggestion that the attachment or fixation of libidinal energy takes place without conscious awareness on the part of the individual. To explain how this occurs, Freud made a distinction between three levels of consciousness.

Levels of Consciousness and Mental Structures

The three levels of consciousness proposed by Freud are the conscious, the preconscious, and the unconscious. The **conscious** level consists of all mental processes that a person is aware of at a given moment. The **preconscious** (sometimes also called the **foreconscious**) consists of memories stored in the mind that can be readily recalled, particularly by the association of ideas. The third level, which comprises what Freud believed to be the largest part of the mind, is the **unconscious.** This is made up of memories that may influence thinking and behavior but cannot be recalled (except under such special circumstances as dreams, hypnotic states, or free associations).

Freud felt that many types of behavior could be explained in terms of conflicts between levels of consciousness. To clarify the nature of these conflicts, he proposed that personality is made up of three sets of forces or structures: the id, ego, and superego. The **id** is the source of the libido **Id:** source of libido and is entirely unconscious. It is guided by the **pleasure principle** (the seeking of gratification and the avoidance of pain) and is primitive and illogical.

Ego: screens and controls expression of libidinal energy

Experience teaches children that their needs cannot always be met immediately or in a specific way. The primary function of the **ego** is to screen and control the unconscious impulses emanating from the id and to determine how libidinal energy will be expressed in socially acceptable ways. The ego is governed by the **reality principle,** which means that it involves rational analysis of the situations an individual must cope with.

Superego: one's conscience

The third structure to be differentiated is the **superego,** which is essentially one's conscience. The young child's sense of right and wrong is acquired primarily through identification with parents and other adults. Freud hypothesized that children typically would think of actions as right or wrong by imagining how their fathers and mothers would evaluate those actions and respond to them.

Defense Mechanisms

To further explain how conflicts are handled, Freud suggested several **defense mechanisms** that are called into play (by the ego), usually in an unconscious way, when primitive impulses need to be controlled, when accumulating libidinal energy must be released, or when the ego needs to be protected. **Repression** is one of the most common of these mechanisms. Individuals who have had painful experiences will resist remembering them and tend to suppress the memories in the unconscious level of the mind. In some cases, threatening desires may be controlled by **reaction formation,** where individuals assume forms of behavior opposite to those they are struggling to master. (Individuals who are apprehensive about their own strong sexual desires, for example, may lead a crusade against pornography). Or some individuals may resort to **projection** and attribute to others types of behavior they are reluctant to recognize in themselves. Or individuals may engage in **sublimation** by diverting libidinal energy from sex objects to interests and activities that have no direct connection with sex—art or sports, for instance. In situations that individuals feel may be threatening to the ego if they analyze their behavior objectively, they may resort to **rationalizations** by giving "good" reasons for behavior that is weak or unacceptable. If individuals become frustrated and angry because of their inadequacies, they may resort to **displacement** and divert their hostility from themselves to others. Another reaction to frustration takes the form of **regression,** where individuals resort to forms of behavior that provided satisfaction at earlier stages of development.

> **Defense mechanisms:** control primitive impulses or protect ego

   Most contemporary psychologists acknowledge the value of Freud's description of defense mechanisms, even though they may not be willing to accept the idea that libidinal energy is involved or that a primitive id is engaged in a battle with a superego.

Evaluation of Freud's Theory

Freud's impact on the study of human development was diverse. His emphasis on the impact of sex drives on behavior opened up an entirely new era of research. His stage descriptions, particularly of the oral and anal periods of libidinal development, stimulated many observational studies of feeding and toilet training. His theories about the impact of infantile experiences on later behavior led psychologists to study infants and young children intensively and to plan longitudinal investigations in an effort to trace cause and effect relationships. His suggestion that behavior was often controlled by unconscious memories and his description of defense mechanisms contributed to understanding types of

TABLE 2.1
SUMMARY OF FREUDIAN THEORY

Libidinal Development

Basic sexual energy (libido) is concentrated on parts of the body, objects, or individuals. Libidinal development proceeds according to this sequence:

Birth to two years	Oral stage	Mouth is center of satisfaction.
Two to three years	Anal stage	Concern about toilet training.
Three to four years	Phallic stage	Curiosity about sex differences.
Around four to five years	Oedipus complex	Libidinal energy concentrated on parent of opposite sex leads to fear of parent of same sex, who is seen as rival (also explained by switch from anaclitic to defensive identification).
Six to eleven years	Latency period	Resolution of Oedipus complex when child identifies with parent of same sex; libidinal energy not concentrated on any particular part of body, object, or person.
Puberty	Genital stage	Sensual satisfaction through genital organs; libidinal energy concentrated (typically) on member of opposite sex.

Negative experiences (traumatic or repeated) may *fixate* libidinal energy at a particular stage and lead to permanent personality traits.

Levels of Consciousness

Conscious	Everything a person is aware of at a given moment.
Preconscious	Memories a person is not thinking of at the moment but that can be recalled.
Unconscious	Memories that cannot be recalled but that may influence behavior.

TABLE 2.1
SUMMARY OF FREUDIAN THEORY (cont.)

Structure of Personality

Id	Unconscious and primitive source of libido, guided by pleasure principle.
Ego	Screens and controls libidinal energy, guided by reality principle.
Superego	Conscience.

Defense Mechanisms

To control primitive impulses of the id and protect the ego, it may be necessary for the person to resort to *defense mechanisms:*

Repression	Resisting recollection of painful memories.
Reaction formation	Assuming forms of behavior opposite to those that are of concern.
Projection	Attributing to others types of behavior that are difficult to acknowledge in oneself.
Sublimation	Diverting libidinal energy from sex objects to activities not related to sex.
Rationalization	Giving "good" reasons for behavior that is weak or unacceptable.
Identification	Adopting the characteristics of others as if they are one's own.
Displacement	Diverting feelings of hostility from self to others.
Regression	Resorting to immature forms of behavior when frustrated.

child and adult behavior that had previously been difficult to interpret. The technique of psychoanalysis was used by many psychotherapists and led to the development of alternative forms of therapy.

In many respects, however, Freud's impact on American psychology was "indirect" in the sense that investigations were often stimulated by skepticism regarding his theory. Psychologists in this country were bothered by the fact that most of Freud's speculations were based on recollections of child behavior by an extremely small, atypical group of adult subjects. They were also reluctant to accept statements based on abstract theorizing rather than objective observations. Many psychoanalytic concepts, in fact, cannot be tested in an empirical way by an "ordinary" researcher since they often deal with unobservable, unconscious phenomena, which, Freud argued, can be interpreted only by a specialist trained in psychoanalysis.

Today, after sixty years of examination, few psychologists completely endorse all aspects of Freud's theory. But the points regarding the typical child can still assist those seeking to understand development. The way a child is fed and toilet trained, the way parents react to curiosity about sex, the adolescent's experiences with sexual exploration—all may have a significant impact on development. Early experiences retained in the memory but not recalled may influence later behavior in such a way that individuals will not be aware of the reasons they act as they do. Furthermore, several theorists have based *their* interpretations of development on Freudian principles, and an understanding of their views will be facilitated by an awareness of the original theory. For all these reasons, Freud's observations will be referred to frequently in the chapters that follow.

Whereas Freud's theory illuminates some types of development, it does not touch on other aspects of behavior. At this point, therefore, it is appropriate to examine the views of Erik H. Erikson, a psychoanalyst who has used Freud's observations as a starting point for evolving a theory of *psychosocial* development.

Erikson: Stages of Psychosocial Development

Formative Influences

Erik Erikson was born in 1902 near Frankfurt, Germany. His mother divorced his father before Erik was born and later married the boy's pediatrician. The second marriage was a happy one, and Erik's mother frequently invited artists to her home so that the boy not only had the opportunity to hear his stepfather discuss medicine but was also introduced to the arts.

In contrast to Freud, Erikson was not an outstanding student in school, preferring self-directed study to a formal curriculum. He left high school before graduation, wandered around Europe for a year, and then spent the next few years in a series of art schools. Still indecisive about a career in his midtwenties, he was invited to assist a high school friend, Peter Blos, in setting up a school for American and English children living in Vienna. The largest financial backer of the school was a close friend of the Freud family, and through her Erikson became ac-

Erik H. Erikson.
Photograph © 1975 by Jill Krementz.

quainted with the famous psychoanalyst. He made a favorable impression on Freud and was invited to enter psychoanalytic training. Shortly after Erikson completed his psychoanalytic internship, an encounter with an analyst who had returned to Vienna for a visit after establishing a practice in Boston led him to emigrate to America.

In the United States Erikson engaged in private practice and held academic positions at both Harvard and Yale. He became intrigued by anthropology and conducted extensive studies of child-rearing practices in two American Indian tribes, the Sioux of South Dakota and the Yurok of northern California.

The Evolution of Erikson's Theory

As he pondered the behavior of the Sioux and the Yurok Indians, Erikson was struck by the extent to which many of their adjustment problems seemed to result from a lack of continuity between their tribal history and their existence in twentieth-century America. He hypothesized that the Indians found it difficult to develop a consistent identity. Unable to explain this conflict in terms of Freud's concept of libidinal energy, he began to formulate an augmented psychoanalytic theory that incorporated not only biological forces from within but also sociocultural forces from the environment.

This conception of development was supported by therapeutic interviews with war veterans, whom he treated following World War II. He concluded that many of them were experiencing difficulties reconciling their activities and attitudes as soldiers with the activities and attitudes of their prewar civilian life. He used the term **identity confusion** to describe this condition, a problem that the veterans shared with the Indians—lack of a consistent conception of ego or self.

The hypotheses formulated to explain the behavior of Indians and servicemen were corroborated by his research and clinical interviews with children. Gradually, Erikson came to equate the process of growing up with achieving ego identity, which included both an inner aspect (knowing and accepting oneself) and another aspect (knowing and identifying with the group culture). He worked out a complete, consistent conception of **psychosocial** stages of ego development, in which children establish a series of orientations to themselves and their social world (Erikson, 1963, 1968).

The Epigenetic Principle

Epigenetic principle: parts have time of special ascendancy

Erikson based his description of personality development on the **epigenetic principle,** the notion that anything that grows is governed by a genetic ground plan. He linked personality development to fetal development, since "out of the ground plan the parts arise, each part having its time of special ascendancy, until all parts have arisen to form a functioning whole" (1968, p. 92). He proposed that personality forms as the ego progresses through a series of interrelated stages. All of these ego stages exist in the beginning in some form, but each has a critical period of development, a period in which the individual is maximally receptive to the changing expectations of significant persons in the environment. Erikson views personality development as a sequence of these turning points, which he describes in terms of dichotomies of desirable and undesirable qualities. No one avoids the undesirable qualities entirely. Instead, what is sought is a ratio in favor of positive traits.

Stages of Psychosocial Development

The following designations, age ranges, and essential characteristics of the stages of personality development are proposed by Erikson:

Trust vs. Mistrust (Birth to One Year)   Consistency, continuity, and sameness of experience lead to trust. Inadequate, inconsistent, or negative care may arouse mistrust.

Autonomy vs. Doubt (Two to Three Years)   Opportunities to try out skills at own pace in own way lead to autonomy. Overprotection or lack of support may lead to doubt about ability to control self or environment.

Initiative vs. Guilt (Four to Five Years)   Freedom to engage in activities and to use language and express new understandings leads to initiative. Restrictions of activities and parents' failure to respond to comments and questions lead to guilt.

Industry vs. Inferiority (Six to Eleven Years)   Being permitted to make and do things and being praised for accomplishments lead to industry. Limitation on activities and criticism of what is done lead to inferiority.

Identity vs. Role Confusion (Twelve to Eighteen Years)   Recognition of continuity and sameness in one's personality, even when in different situations and when reacted to by different individuals, leads to identity. Inability to establish stability (particularly regarding sex roles and occupational choice) leads to role confusion.

Intimacy vs. Isolation (Young Adulthood)   Fusing of identity with another leads to intimacy. Competitive and combative relations with others may lead to isolation.

Generativity vs. Stagnation (Middle Age)   Establishing and guiding next generation produces sense of generativity. Concern primarily with self leads to a sense of arrested development (or, stagnation).

Integrity vs. Despair (Old Age)   Acceptance of one's life leads to a sense of integrity. Feeling that it is too late to make up for missed opportunities leads to despair.

Sidenotes:

Trust vs. mistrust (first year)

Autonomy vs. doubt (two to three years)

Initiative vs. guilt (four to five years)

Industry vs. inferiority (six to eleven years)

Identity vs. role confusion (twelve to eighteen years)

Intimacy vs. isolation (young adulthood)

Generativity vs. stagnation (middle age)

Integrity vs. despair (old age)

Evaluation of Erikson's Theory

Erikson's description of early stages of psychosocial development calls attention to important relationships between children and their parents. His analyses of behavior during the school years and at adolescence highlight significant facets of the emergence of an individual's self-concept and the establishment of relationships with peers, and his "eight stages of man" represent a first in the now popular life-span approach to development.

However, while he occasionally carried out research investigations, most of Erikson's conclusions are based on personal and subjective in-

Erikson suggests that preschool-age children will first develop autonomy and later acquire a sense of initiative if they are given opportunities to try out skills and engage in independent activities.
Ping Dai.

terpretations that have not been substantiated by controlled investigations of the type that are valued by many American psychologists. As a result, there have been no checks on the tendency to generalize from personal experiences. Erikson, for example, did not decide on a career until he was in his midtwenties. Accordingly he stressed that at adolescence indecision about occupational choice could cause role confusion. But many adolescents make firm occupational choices before they leave high school and may have a much stronger sense of identity than Erikson had at the age of eighteen.

Another factor to consider in Erikson's theory is the eagerness to select types of behavior stressed in the stage descriptions that were congruent with the epigenetic principle. One consequence of this emphasis on the epigenetic principle is that several of the stages, particularly those covering the years three through eleven, seem to stress the same basic qualities. *Autonomy, initiative,* and *industry* all emphasize the desirability of permitting and encouraging children to do things on their own. *Doubt, guilt,* and *inferiority* all focus on the need for parents and teachers to provide sympathetic support. If you keep these reservations in mind, however, you are likely to discover that Erikson's observations will clarify important aspects of development. His various stages of psychosocial development, in fact, serve as an organizational framework for many of the remaining chapters of this book.

Despite their differences, both Erikson and Freud were concerned primarily with social and emotional development. Another important facet of human development centers on intelligence and thinking. At his death in 1980, the Swiss psychologist Jean Piaget had spent fifty years studying cognitive forms of development.

Piaget: Stages of Cognitive Development

Formative Influences

Jean Piaget was born in the small town of Neuchâtel, Switzerland, in 1896. Because his father was a professor of history, Jean was brought up in a scholarly atmosphere. His main boyhood interest was observation of animals in their natural habitats. He pursued this hobby so energetically that he published his first "research" paper at the age of eleven. (He had seen an albino sparrow in a park and reported this in a nature magazine.)

When he entered secondary school, Piaget concentrated on the biological sciences. A series of articles he wrote on shellfish so impressed the director of the natural history museum in Geneva that the fifteen-

Jean Piaget (1970).
Yves De Braine/Black Star.

year-old Jean was offered the post of curator of the mollusk collection. Since he had not yet finished high school, the teen-aged scientist declined the offer. A vacation with his godfather, a scholar specializing in philosophy, resulted in Piaget's fascination with *epistemology*, the branch of philosophy concerned with the study of knowledge.

After graduating from high school, Piaget entered the University of Neuchâtel and earned undergraduate and graduate degrees in natural science, the Ph.D. being awarded when he was only twenty-one. He became intrigued by psychology and studied that subject in Zurich, where he was introduced to Freudian theory and wrote a paper relating psychoanalysis to child psychology. From Zurich he went to Paris, where he obtained a position at the Binet Laboratory and was assigned the task of developing a standardized French version of some reasoning tests developed in England. As he recorded the responses of his subjects, Piaget found that he was much more intrigued by wrong answers than correct ones. The similarities in the wrong answers of children of comparable age convinced him that the thought processes of younger children are basically different from those of older children and adults.

Shortly thereafter, an appointment as director of research at the Jean Jacques Rousseau Institute in Geneva permitted Piaget to concentrate full-time on the study of cognitive development. He did not feel that he could gain the kind of information he wanted by placing subjects in rigidly controlled experimental situations. So as he had done earlier in studying animals, he first observed the spontaneous behavior of his own children (and wrote baby biographies), then observed children in natural play situations. Eventually, he developed a series of questions and tasks to be presented to children in interview fashion, a technique of study he called the **clinical interview.** As he recorded his impressions, Piaget gradually evolved descriptions of the development of many aspects of thought.

Basic Principles of Piaget's Theory

The conception of intellectual development Piaget arrived at after a lifetime of study reflects his basic interests in biology and epistemology. He postulated that human beings are born with two basic tendencies: **organization** (the tendency to systematize and combine processes into coherent systems) and **adaptation** (the tendency to adjust to the environment). Piaget believed that just as the biological process of digestion transforms food into a form which the body can use, so intellectual processes transform experiences into a form the child can use in dealing with new situations. And just as the biological processes must be kept in a state of balance (homeostasis), Piaget believed intellectual processes seek a balance through the process of **equilibration.** Equilibration is a form of self-regulation that children use to bring coherence and stability to their conception of the world and to comprehend inconsistencies in experience.

> **Equilibration:** seek coherence and stability

To grasp these principles of Piaget's theory, imagine an infant who has just reached the crawling stage and is in the process of meeting one entirely new experience after another when put down on the living room floor for the first time. As the infant moves around the floor, dozens of new objects (tables, chairs, lamps) and experiences (a startled yell from father when the baby is about to pull a lamp over) are encountered. Piaget maintains that because of the basic tendencies of organization, adaptation, and equilibration, an infant will be inclined to systematize, combine, and adjust to objects and experiences encountered. Such attempts to establish coherence and stability take place through the operation of two processes: assimilation and accommodation. **Assimilation** refers to the process by which elements in the environment are incorporated in the child's store of ideas about things. The infant exploring the living room floor for the first time will gradually

> **Assimilation:** incorporate conceptions into store of ideas

build up physical and mental conceptions of table, chair, lamp, and so forth by combining tactile and visual impressions of these objects. Initial impressions, however, are bound to be oversimplified. Sooner or later the infant will discover that chairs in the dining room, for example, are not the same chairs as in the living room. Accordingly, it is frequently necessary for children to modify conceptions and alter their responses to things, which is the process Piaget refers to as **accommodation.** As children assimilate (incorporate) and accommodate (modify) their conceptions of objects and experiences, they establish organized patterns of behavior and thought, which Piaget refers to as **schemes.** Schemes can be behavioral (for example, how to grasp objects) or intellectual (for example, realizing that there are different kinds of chairs).

Accommodation: modify ideas

Scheme: organized pattern of behavior or thought

These various tendencies and principles can be illustrated by the example of an infant's experiences with balls of different kinds. From interaction with objects previously encountered, the child of ten months or so will have *organized* the separate skills of looking and grasping into the capability of visually directed reaching. Therefore, when a ball is encountered for the first time, the child benefits from past experience when reaching for it and trying to pick it up. If no previous attempts have been made to pick up an object that rolls, the first efforts may be unsuccessful, so the child will need to *accommodate* to the new object—altering grasping techniques already mastered. As success in doing this is achieved, this new feature will be *assimilated* into a scheme for picking up objects. If the first ball is small and hard, the child will think this typical of all balls until other balls of different sizes and qualities are encountered. When this happens, the need to maintain equilibration will lead the child to reduce inconsistencies between the original and later experiences with balls by assimilating (incorporating) and accommodating (modifying) the earlier scheme for "ball." In time, a cognitive conception of "ball" will be developed that will permit the handling of all types of balls and an understanding of their common qualities.

The Nature of Operational Thought

Organization, adaptation, assimilation, accommodation, and equilibration are basic principles of Piagetian theory. Other principles are used to explain differences between the thinking of younger and older children. These differences became apparent as Piaget used the clinical interview technique with children of different ages. The use of the method can be illustrated by what is probably the best known of all experiments devised by Piaget: the conservation task.

A child is taken to a quiet place by the experimenter, and then water (or juice, or beans, or whatever) is poured into two identical glasses until the child agrees each contains an equal amount. Then water is poured from one of these glasses into a tall, thin glass. At that point the child is asked "Is there more water in this glass (the experimenter points to the tall, thin glass) or this one? Or do they both have the same amount?" Immediately after the child answers, the experimenter asks "Why do you think so?" If the child's response is evasive or vague, the experimenter continues to probe until the underlying thought processes become clear.

In carrying out this and similar experiments with children of different ages, Piaget discovered that children below the age of six or so usually maintain that there is more water in the tall, thin glass than in the short, squat glass. Even though they agree at the beginning of the experiment that the water in the two identical glasses is equal before the pouring takes place, young children stoutly insist that after the water has been poured, the taller glass contains more. When asked "Why do you think so?" many preschool children immediately and confidently reply "Because it's taller." Children over the age of six or so, by contrast, are more likely to reply that the amounts are still equal and explain their judgment by saying, "Well, it *looks* as if there's more water in this one because it's taller, but they're really the same."

The thinking of young children is dominated by their perceptions. Moreover, their perceptual attention tends to be focused on one aspect of an object or situation, a characteristic Piaget called **centration**. In the conservation problem, for example, they are likely to concentrate only on height and equate it with bigness. Finally, they focus exclusively on the final state of the beakers. Piaget believed this is because their thought lacks **reversibility**—they cannot mentally reverse the action or transformation they have observed. For all these reasons, the younger child does not demonstrate an understanding of **conservation**, the idea that certain properties of objects (such as mass or volume) remain invariant despite transformations in their appearance.

Conservation: some properties remain unchanged

By seven or eight years of age, children typically solve the conservation problem described above and give not one but several correct reasons for their judgments, for example, "It's still the same water. It looks like more because this glass is taller, but it's skinnier, too. If you don't believe me, just pour the water back in that glass and see for yourself." This strong conviction occurs in children who have developed and refined a variety of cognitive processes. They can **decenter,** or think of several aspects of a situation simultaneously. They now coordinate present and past experiences (the beakers before and after the transformation). They are capable of reversibility, which allows them to undo mentally the transformation performed physically on the water in the two

Decentration: consider more than one characteristic at same time

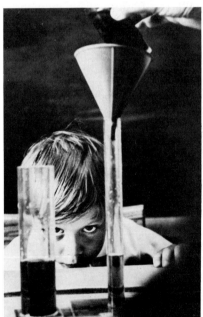

A child reacting to one of the procedures Piaget developed to reveal the nature of preoperational thought. Children below the age of six or so tend to concentrate on one quality at a time and are unable to mentally reverse actions. As a consequence, they are likely to maintain that if liquid is poured from one container into another of a different shape, the quantity of the liquid will be changed.
New York Times Pictures.

beakers. This ability to modify an object of knowledge mentally, to carry out an action in one's head that previously had to be enacted physically, Piaget called an **operation.**

Operation: mental manipulation that can be reversed

Stages of Cognitive Development

In the course of his long career, Piaget and his collaborators, most notably Barbel Inhelder, designed hundreds of problems, which they used to examine the sequence and limits of children's thinking and knowledge at various points in their development. On the basis of clinical interviews with many children, Piaget concluded that there are four clearly distinguishable stages of cognitive development. While he acknowledged that cognitive development is a gradual and continuous process, there were, he believed, periods of relative stability and coherence, which he identified as stages. The four stages are outlined here and will be discussed in detail in later chapters.

Sensorimotor Stage

Infants and young children up to the age of two years acquire understanding primarily through sensory impressions and motor activities, and so Piaget called this the **sensorimotor** stage. During the first months of postnatal existence, infants develop schemes primarily by exploring their own bodies and senses because they are unable to move around much on their own. After they learn to walk and manipulate things, however, toddlers get into everything and build up a sizable repertoire of schemes involving external objects and situations. As a result of these activities, children construct **object permanence,** the understanding that objects continue to exist even when they are not physically present. Piaget considered the development of object permanence to be the primary cognitive task of infancy. Before the age of two, most children are able to use schemes they have mastered to engage in mental, as well as physical, trial and error behavior.

Sensorimotor stage: acquire first schemes through sense impressions and motor activities

Preoperational Stage

The thinking of preschool children centers on mastery of symbols (such as words), which permits them to benefit much more from past experiences. Piaget believed that many symbols are derived from mental imitation and involve both visual images and bodily sensations. Even though their thinking is much more sophisticated than that of one- and two-year-olds, preschool children tend to center attention on only one quality at a time and are incapable of mentally reversing actions. Because they have not yet reached the point of engaging in operational thought,

Preoperational stage: form many schemes but not able to mentally reverse actions

Piaget used the term **preoperational** to refer to the thinking of two- to seven-year-olds.

Concrete Operational Stage

Concrete operational stage: capable of mentally reversing actions, but generalize only from concrete experiences

Children over the age of seven are usually capable of mentally reversing actions, but their operational thinking is limited to objects that are actually present or that they have experienced concretely and directly. For this reason, Piaget described the stage from about seven to eleven years as that of **concrete operations.** At this stage, children's conceptions about the world become increasingly accurate and sophisticated. They think about objects not only in terms of how they interact with them ("My ball is for throwing.") but also in terms of the objects' properties and relations to other objects ("Balls may be hard/soft, large/small, round/not round, etc."). Concrete thinkers master classification, relations, and quantification. Evidence of these emerging skills can be seen in their collections (stamps, dolls, baseball cards) and their competitiveness ("Joan is the best reader, Tom is second best, etc."). They are interested in facts, and especially in records or limits ("What is the tallest building in the world? The longest word in the dictionary? The most home runs hit in a single baseball game?") The thought of children at the concrete stage is rich and varied, but it is confined to reality. In fact, they often confuse reality with possibility, treating their hypotheses as facts. For example, they may assume that the method their teacher used to solve a math problem is the *only* possible solution. Concrete thinkers usually need to manipulate concrete objects physically or recollect specific past experiences to explain things to themselves and others. But ask them to deal with a hypothetical situation, one with which they have had no direct experience, and they are likely to be stymied. They are not able to solve abstract problems by engaging in mental explorations.

Formal Operational Stage

Formal operational stage: able to deal with abstractions, form hypotheses, engage in mental manipulation

When junior high school students reach the point of engaging in mental trial and error by thinking up hypotheses and testing them "in their heads," Piaget said they have reached the stage of **formal operations.** Formal thinkers can reason about propositions even when they have not had direct experience with the content reasoned about or when the content is contrary to fact. Even though they can deal with mental abstractions, early adolescents are likely to be quite unsystematic in their approach to problem solving. It is not until the end of the high school years that some adolescents may consistently exhibit characteristics of formal thought. When they reach that point, they are likely to attack a problem by formulating hypotheses, mentally sorting out possible solutions, and systematically testing the most promising leads.

Evaluation of Piaget's Theory

Norman S. Endler, J. Philippe Rushton, and Henry L. Roediger III (1978) tallied the number of times different psychologists were mentioned in the *Social Sciences Citation Index.* (This index supplies data regarding individuals mentioned in articles appearing in over 180 psychology journals.) Most of the psychologists on the list of the one hundred most frequently noted behavioral scientists had two or three hundred citations. Only two individuals were mentioned over one thousand times: Sigmund Freud and Jean Piaget. The fact that Piaget was mentioned in recent psychology journals many more times than any other contemporary psychologist indicates the impact his work has had.

As you might expect, among the over-a-thousand publications relating to Piaget are many that offer critiques of his work. The earliest criticisms of Piaget focused on methodology, particularly his reliance on the clinical interview. While Piaget felt that flexible interviews revealed subtleties and idiosyncrasies not likely to be discovered through the use of more structured procedures, critics were concerned with the extent to which give and take between interviewer and child or later interpretations of what is said by the child could be influenced by the preconceptions of the examiner. These criticisms have subsided somewhat in recent years, however, in the face of hundreds of studies that have replicated Piaget's basic findings.

Other criticisms remain. Many psychologists argue that Piaget underestimated children's abilities, not only because of stringent criteria he imposed for inferring the presence of particular cognitive abilities, but also because the tasks he used were often complex and far removed from children's real life experiences. The term *preoperational,* for instance, stresses what is absent rather than what is present. Within the last decade, researchers have focused more on what preoperational children *can* do. Their results (summarized by Gelman and Baillargeon, 1983) suggest that preschoolers' cognitive abilities are more advanced in some areas than Piaget's work suggested. Furthermore, there is some evidence (Neimark, 1975) that Piaget may have *over*estimated the formal thinking tendencies of adolescents. It appears that systematic testing of hypotheses is the exception rather than the rule even at the college level. Finally, there is fairly widespread agreement that Piaget's case for four distinct cognitive stages and for the interrelatedness of structures within the stages has been weakened by recent empirical studies (e.g., Brainerd, 1978; Flavell, 1982; Gelman and Baillargeon, 1983).

The fact that many American psychologists have responded with skepticism to Piaget's writings (as well as the writings of Freud and Erikson) helps explain why the two remaining theoretical interpretations to be discussed in this chapter vary in significant ways from the

TABLE 2.2
OUTLINE OF PIAGETIAN STAGES OF COGNITIVE DEVELOPMENT

First two years	Sensorimotor stage	Development of schemes primarily through sense and motor activities
Two to five years	Preoperational stage	Rapid accumulation of schemes, acquisition of abilities to conserve and decenter, but inability to mentally reverse actions
Six to twelve years	Concrete operational stage	Children capable of mentally reversing actions but can solve problems only by generalizing from concrete experiences
Adolescence	Formal operational stage	Many adolescents increasingly capable of dealing with abstractions, forming hypotheses, solving problems systematically, and engaging in mental manipulations

three that already have been summarized. The two views yet to be discussed are learning theory and information processing. As noted in the imaginary diary entries relating to Watson and Skinner in Chapter 1, American psychologists prefer to base their conclusions on observations of overt behavior. They feel uncomfortable when theorists speculate about nonobservable types of behavior, such as unconscious processes, psychosocial behavior, or how children think. Following the lead of Watson and Skinner, many American psychologists have concentrated on studying ways organisms learn. Most of the experiments from which learning theory principles have been derived focused on ways in which associations between stimuli and responses are built up. That is why interpretations of behavior and development based on these principles are referred to as *stimulus-response* (S-R) theories, or as the *learning theory* view of development.

Learning Theory

Learning theory differs from the views already discussed in several ways. Freud, Erikson, and Piaget, acting as individuals, all proposed logically coherent theories that outlined stages of development. Learning theory, by contrast, emerged from the work of several psychologists working more or less independently who proposed various principles that eventually have been combined to form a theory. While it is possible to use these principles to analyze specific aspects of behavior, most learning theorists have shown little interest in stages of development. It is possible and profitable to interpret human development in terms of learning theory principles, but this is done by concentrating on how behavior is changed by experiences. Characteristics of learning theory will become apparent as a brief history of its evolution is examined.

Ivan Pavlov: Early Principles of Learning

Even though learning theory is largely the product of research by Americans, the impetus for its development occurred in the laboratory of the Russian scientist Ivan Pavlov. In his most famous experiment, Pavlov induced a dog to salivate when a bell was rung by building up an association between the bell and food. If the bell was rung several times without food being presented, Pavlov reported, the response that had been conditioned would disappear, or **extinguish.** He also pointed out that once the dog was conditioned to salivate to the sound of the bell, it would tend to salivate to other sounds, such as a whistle. He referred to this as **stimulus generalization.** Such generalized responses could be overcome by supplying reinforcement in the form of food after the bell was rung but never after a whistle was sounded. When this occurred, Pavlov said that **discrimination** had taken place.

   Translations of research reports by Pavlov led to worldwide interest in his work. John B. Watson, an enthusiastic and enterprising American psychologist, was particularly receptive to Pavlov's ideas.

John B. Watson: Champion of Behaviorism

As a graduate student in 1903, Watson wrote a dissertation, *Animal Education: The Psychical Development of the White Rat.* In American psychology at the time, when an experimenter had finished his observations of animal subjects, he was expected to speculate about the state of the animal's consciousness. Watson objected to this, arguing that it was more sensible and scientific to concentrate on overt behavior, which could be observed and described objectively. He spent several years developing his arguments and eventually presented them in a paper entitled *Psychology as the Behaviorist Views It* (1913). He called himself a **behaviorist** to emphasize his belief that psychologists should base their conclusions exclusively on observations of overt behavior. He wrote, "Psychology as the behaviorist views it is a purely objective experimen-

Behaviorism: stress on observable behavior; prediction and control

tal branch of natural science. Its theoretical goal is the prediction and control of behavior" (1913, p. 158).

While Watson was developing his views on behaviorism, he also studied infants. Since the scientific study of behavior was just beginning in the early 1900s, few controlled observations of children had been made. Watson was thus one of the first psychologists to concentrate on the study of newborn babies. Watson simply stimulated infants in various ways and described how they responded. He would expose each baby in the hospital nursery to the same series of experiences—holding their arms at their sides, for example, or making a sudden loud sound, or tickling their feet (Watson and Morgan, 1917)—and then describe their overt physical reactions. As he accumulated data, Watson began to speculate how one experience comes to be associated with another.

When he read about the experiments of Pavlov, Watson became convinced that the conditioned response was a more complete and satisfactory explanation of learning than the views that had been proposed up to that time. In a now classic experiment (Watson and Rayner, 1920) he demonstrated how human behavior could be conditioned. He encouraged an eleven-month-old boy named Albert to play with a white rat. When Albert began to enjoy this activity, Watson suddenly hit a steel bar with a hammer just as the child reached for the rat. In his observations of infants, Watson had discovered that a sudden, loud sound frightened most children. When Albert came to associate the previously attractive rat with the frightening stimulus, he not only responded with fear but generalized this fear to many other white and fuzzy objects.

The success of this experiment and similar experiments with animals carried out by Pavlov and his colleagues in Russia led Watson to believe that by arranging sequences of conditioned responses he could control behavior in almost limitless ways. He was emboldened to make the following claim:

> Give me a dozen healthy infants, well-formed, and my own specified world to bring them up in and I'll guarantee to take any one at random and train him to become any type of specialist I might select—doctor, lawyer, artist, merchant-chief and, yes, even beggerman and thief, regardless of his talents, penchants, tendencies, abilities, vocations, and race of his ancestors. (1925, p. 82; rev. ed., 1930, p. 104)

Watson's impact on the study of child development was substantial but brief. Other psychologists discovered that the kind of learning he had demonstrated so dramatically with Albert applied only to essentially involuntary reflex actions (such as reacting in a fearful way). Furthermore, attempts to build sequences of conditioned responses were rarely successful. And many parents who purchased a book he wrote on child care (1928) were unwilling to follow his advice and play the role of objective child rearer. While Watson's writing on child behavior had only a transitory influence, his views on behaviorism had a lasting impact. Even today many American psychologists think of themselves as behaviorists. They prefer to base conclusions on observations of overt behavior and they seek ways to predict and control behavior.

Starting in the 1920s, hundreds of studies of conditioned responses were carried out, and most of the learning theory principles developed in America stressed the development of associations between stimuli and responses. In the 1930s, however, some developmental psychologists who had carefully observed infants were impressed by the uniformity of the sequence of types of behavior appearing at different age levels. They reasoned that the similarity in the behavior of children from widely different backgrounds could be accounted for only by assuming that development was controlled by innate tendencies. Accordingly, many researchers of the 1930s were interested in aspects of development that appeared to be attributable more to growth processes than to learning. Such forms of behavior are said to be due to *maturation,* and interest in the 1930s and 1940s in the impact of maturation represented—for some psychologists—a paradigm shift away from preoccupation with learning.

The psychologist who was most energetic in promoting the maturational view was Arnold Gesell. Gesell, together with his two chief associates, Frances Ilg and Louise Ames (who became the directors of his research institute after his death), became convinced that Watson's failure to make good on his boast had demolished the belief that behavior could be systematically shaped. They argued for recognition of inner determination of behavior and urged parents to acknowledge the inexorable nature of maturation. Children develop according to a built-in timetable, they maintained, and therefore "control" much of their own behavior. Ilg and Ames began their *Child Behavior* (1955) by observing, "Gone are the days when psychologists likened the child's body to a lump of clay which you the parent could mold in any direction you chose." When making this assertion, they failed to consider the energy and ingenuity of a psychologist named B. F. Skinner.

B. F. Skinner: Operant Conditioning

In a survey of psychology departments conducted in 1967 (Myers, 1970, p. 1045) Skinner was chosen as the most influential American psychologist of this century. Skinner argues that every personality is the product of environmental experiences. It is therefore appropriate to speculate about the experiences that shaped his own behavior. (The background of other theorists mentioned in this book is presented for the same reason: you are encouraged to theorize about causes of behavior, particularly the impact of childhood experiences, so it is reasonable to speculate about the backgrounds of those who have proposed theories of development. In addition, learning something about the personalities of theorists may encourage you to sample their writings.)

Formative Influences

Skinner's father was a draftsman in a railroad shop in Susquehanna, Pennsylvania, when he met and eventually married the daughter of the foreman, a gentleman named Burrhus. He studied law as he worked and in time passed the bar examination. The Skinners settled in Susquehanna, and in 1904 the first of two boys born to the couple was named Burrhus Frederic (which explains the use of the initials B.F.). Young Fred, as he preferred to be called, was always building things; his projects included a merry-go-round, a water pistol, and a steam cannon capable of shooting plugs of potato and carrot over the roofs of houses. Fred attended a small school (his graduating class had eight students) and he came under the influence of a teacher who aroused his interest in literature, the subject he majored in when he entered Hamilton College.

After graduating, Skinner attempted a career as a writer, but became so dissatisfied with everything he wrote that he ended up spending most of his time playing the piano and building ship models. Since he found literature unrewarding, he decided to turn to science and chose to do graduate work in psychology at Harvard. His choice of psychology he attributes to a number of factors: an early interest in animals, a recollection of a troop of performing pigeons he had seen at a country fair, curiosity about episodes of human behavior, and his discovery of books by Pavlov and Watson. The direction his theorizing ultimately took was determined by his early contact with graduate students who were enthusiastic about behaviorism and also involved in research on maze running in rats.

The Skinner Box Leads to Principles of Operant Conditioning

The inventiveness that had produced the steam cannon, his interest in trained animals, and the example set by Pavlov, Watson, and the graduate students he met at Harvard led Skinner to develop a device for investigating the way animals learn through associations. The *Skinner box*, as the apparatus came to be called, is a small enclosure that contains only a bar (or lever) and a tray. Outside the box is a hopper holding a supply of food pellets that are dropped into the tray when the bar is pressed under preselected conditions (for example, when a tone is sounded). Each time the bar is pressed, a record is automatically made

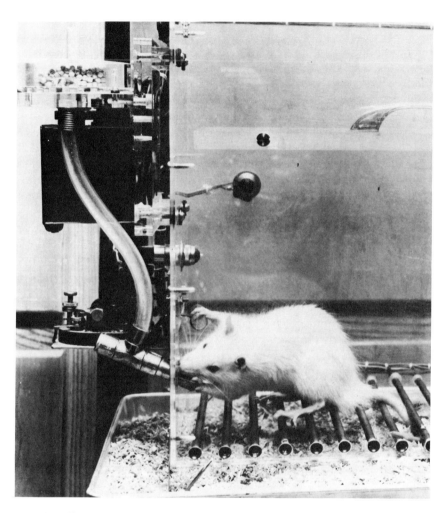

A rat in a Skinner box. The rat's behavior is reinforced with a food pellet when it presses the bar under conditions preselected by the experimenter. The rat does not respond in a reflexive manner, as in the case with Pavlovian conditioning, but engages in self-selected behavior. In the process of exploring the Skinner box, for instance, the rat is almost certain to touch the bar. When that occurs the experimenter supplies a food pellet, and bar-pressing behavior is reinforced. Eventually the rat may be reinforced only when a particular sequence of actions (for example, pressing the bar five times in succession) is performed.
Courtesy of Pfizer, Inc.

on a graph. An experimenter can set the controls of a dozen Skinner boxes, place a hungry rat in each, and engage in other activities while the rats and the machines carry out a series of experiments. Skinner later developed a slightly different apparatus for use with pigeons. In place of the bar, a disk (to be pecked) activates the food-supplying mechanism.

Pavlovian conditioning: involuntary action aroused by previously neutral stimulus

Operant conditioning: voluntary behavior strengthened by reinforcement

On the basis of principles derived from his experiments with rats and pigeons, Skinner developed a theory of **operant conditioning.**[2] He and other behaviorist-associationists had come to recognize that the kind of conditioning practiced by Pavlov and Watson was extremely limited, since an originally neutral stimulus (a bell or a white rat) simply came to arouse an essentially involuntary action (such as salivation or responding with fear). He argued that the kind of learning demonstrated by a rat or pigeon in a Skinner box was much more common and versatile. A voluntary action (pressing the bar or pecking the disk) could be strengthened by reinforcing the behavior under preselected conditions (when a tone was sounded, after a move in a given direction). Skinner proposed that behavior could be shaped in almost any way by supplying reinforcement in a systematic fashion, and he supported his claim by teaching pigeons to—among other things—play table tennis and tap out tunes on a xylophone. These feats were accomplished by first reinforcing the behavior of a hungry pigeon when it voluntarily made a move in the desired direction (for example, pecking a bar on a xylophone) and then refining these movements by supplying food only when a specific sequence of actions occurred (pecking four bars on a xylophone in a particular order).

Science and Human Behavior

Once he had established the principles of operant conditioning, Skinner began to speculate on how these principles could be applied to human behavior. He observed, "The methods of science have been enormously successful wherever they have been tried. Let us then apply them to human affairs" (1953, p. 5). He proposed—in a less flamboyant manner than Watson—that behavior could be shaped in a systematic way. In his novel *Walden Two* (1948) he describes a society based on principles of operant conditioning. The children in this society are placed in the hands of child-rearing specialists who systematically control the children's behavior in order to eliminate undesirable traits (such as jealousy) and encourage desirable ones (such as self-control and perseverance).

---

[2]Skinner chose the term *operant conditioning* to stress that an organism "operates" on the environment when it learns. This type of learning is also referred to as *instrumental conditioning* because what the organism does is instrumental in securing reinforcement. The type of learning first demonstrated by Pavlov is often referred to as *classical conditioning* because it was based on a "classic" experiment (an experiment that was an excellent demonstration of scientific methods and had a significant impact on later studies).

When Skinner had perfected the principles of operant conditioning, he was convinced that the basic weakness of Watson's approach had been overcome. Behavior shapers were no longer restricted to arousing reflex actions by substituting one stimulus for another; they were now capable of controlling any type of behavior. But for behavior control to be effective, Skinner argued, it would be essential to make a fundamental assumption about human nature that conflicted with the view of free will widely accepted since the Renaissance. He concluded that the belief that human beings are capable of shaping their own destinies and that each person's behavior is a result of free choice was incompatible with a scientific analysis of behavior. Skinner acknowledged that his proposal would be difficult for many people to accept because the view of humans as free agents was both well established and appealing. But he argued that the only way to make effective use of scientific knowledge was to endorse totally a view of environmental control. "A scientific conception of human behavior dictates one practice," he explained, "a philosophy of personal freedom another. Confusion in theory means confusion in practice. The present unhappy condition of the world may in large measure be traced to our vacillation" (1953, p. 9).

Choice Between Planned or Accidental Reinforcement

As an organism emitted behavior, Skinner theorized, certain actions would be reinforced and strengthened; others would go unrewarded and be extinguished. Therefore, the behaving organism is controlled by reinforcing experiences, and those who supply reinforcements are in control of behavior. Children will act on their own, but the tendency to repeat certain acts will be determined by which acts are rewarded. If those in contact with a child did not reinforce behavior in a systematic way, Skinner maintained, development would be left to accidental reinforcements. Skinner did not ignore the possibility that inherited factors influence behavior, but he pointed out that these cannot be changed. He suggested that it is more sensible to concentrate exclusively on environmental experiences that *can* be arranged and altered. Skinner recommended that parents and teachers emulate the fictional child-rearing specialists of *Walden Two* by assuming that all behavior is determined by experiences and by doing everything possible to shape the behavior of children systematically.

Behavior Modification

Shaping behavior according to the principles of operant conditioning is referred to as **behavior modification.** The parent or teacher who uses this technique first decides on specific types of behavior to be encouraged and discouraged. Then instances of negative behavior are ignored, and all initial instances of positive behavior are reinforced by praise, candy, money, or tokens that can later be traded in for prizes.

Behavior modification: reinforce desirable, ignore undesirable behavior

The frequency of reinforcement is gradually decreased so that children eventually behave in the desired manner on their own. Suppose, for example, that parents want a three-year-old to stop throwing temper tantrums and to start putting toys away. As much as possible, temper tantrums are ignored, and the parents make sure that the child gains nothing from tantrums. Each time the toys are put away, by contrast, the child is given a hug or kiss, praised, or given a treat. If all goes well, the actions of the parents will modify the behavior of the child so that temper tantrums will disappear and toy-putting-away behavior will increase to the point where it can be maintained by only an occasional reward.

A Debate Regarding Controlled Behavior Versus Free Choice

Many American psychologists agreed with Skinner's view in *Walden Two* and *Science and Human Behavior* that behavior is determined by reinforcement. They were not bothered by the assumption that humans are not free if this would lead to effective control of behavior. Some psychologists, however, urged those who endorsed Skinner's arguments to consider the implications of forcing a choice between controlled behavior and free choice. The psychotherapist Carl R. Rogers, for example, felt that Skinner's view of human behavior was a threat to efforts to improve mental health. In all his therapeutic sessions, Rogers tried to help his clients develop the conviction that they *could* control their own behavior. He pointed out that asking people to assume that they had little or no control over what happened to them was likely to shatter their self-confidence. Rogers engaged in a debate with Skinner (reported in *Science*, 1956, 124, 1057–1066) and wrote *Learning to be Free* (1963), in which he took issue with the argument that our behavior is controlled by reinforcement.

Rogers objected to Skinner's view because of its negative implications for those practicing and receiving psychotherapy. A number of experimental psychologists who endorsed the behaviorist position, however, also became dissatisfied with aspects of Skinner's view of learning and behavior. As an alternative to operant conditioning, they proposed **social learning theory**.

Social Learning Theory

Social learning theory: stress on observation and imitation

Social learning theorists acknowledge the validity of principles of operant conditioning, but they also stress the significance of observation and imitation. In one of the earliest discussions of social learning theory, Neal E. Miller and John Dollard (1941) pointed out that it is not essential for children to have their own spontaneous actions reinforced in order to acquire a new pattern of behavior. Miller and Dollard suggested that children can learn when they are reinforced at a time their behavior *matches* that of another person. A boy might be praised by his mother, for example, when imitating some form of desirable behavior originally displayed by an older brother. A bit later, Albert Bandura joined with Richard H. Walters (1963) in reaffirming the importance of imitation. These theorists also argued that merely observing another person might be sufficient to lead to a learned response. They pointed out that reinforcement is not always necessary.

Sears: Studies of Dependency and Identification

Robert R. Sears, another pioneer in social learning theory, first studied dependency (Sears, Maccoby, and Levin, 1957) and later identification (Sears, Rau, and Alpert, 1965). Sears began with the assumption that child behavior is learned. He then reasoned that parents have control over many factors that influence childhood learning and that they have the primary responsibility for helping children move from dependency to independence. Sears studied dependency because he hoped to discover how associations established when a child was dependent on the parents might influence later behavior. He analyzed identification because he felt (following the lead of Freud, who first emphasized the importance of identification) that this was perhaps the most significant way children acquire more mature forms of behavior. Sears hypothesized that children would first behave like their parents because they wanted to be like their parents and that eventually they would recognize that the behavior was desirable in itself.

In his articles and books, Sears makes clear, more than other learning theorists, why the term **social learning theory** was chosen to refer to that particular set of ideas. He stresses that child behavior is the result of learning but that much of this learning is social in that it occurs when children interact with parents, teachers, and peers. What the child learns is also social in the sense that acquired forms of behavior make it possible for one individual to interact in satisfying ways with other individuals. Sears has been instrumental in contributing many concepts of social learning theory, but the acknowledged leader of this viewpoint is Albert Bandura.

Bandura: The Significance of Anticipatory Control

Bandura is every bit as enthusiastic as Skinner about the potential values of applying principles of operant conditioning to human behavior. (Among other things, he has demonstrated [Bandura, Grusec, and Menlove, 1967] how a child's fear of dogs can be overcome by arranging for the child to watch other children engage in enjoyable interactions with dogs.) But Bandura, like Rogers, was bothered by some of the same

Extreme behaviorist interpretations suggest that preferences (such as these students' choice for competitive sports or for playing in the band) are not due to deliberate choice but are shaped by positive and negative experiences. Albert Bandura, who favors a modified behaviorist position, suggests that individuals can often control their own behavior by anticipating what might happen under given circumstances and then choosing between different kinds of activities.
Hugh Rogers/Monkmeyer and David S. Strickler/Monkmeyer.

potential disadvantages of Skinner's extreme stress on external control. He felt that principles of operant conditioning might be rejected or ignored because the underlying assumptions stressed by Skinner were difficult for many people to accept.

Bandura concluded that behaviorists overemphasized manipulative control because they assumed that reinforcement influences behavior without the conscious involvement of the individual. (He notes: "Humans do not simply respond to stimuli, they interpret them" [1977, p. 59].) He was not convinced that human beings were as helpless as they were made to appear by those who interpreted the behaviorist view in an extreme way. Bandura suggests (1974) that human beings are capable of choosing how they will respond to many situations because many types of human behavior are under **anticipatory control.** That is, children and adults are capable of observing the effects of their actions, and they are also able to anticipate what will happen under certain conditions. As a result, they are able to control their own behavior to a significant extent by imagining what might happen under given circumstances and then choosing between different situations and experiences.

Bandura: **anticipatory control** makes it possible to pre-select consequences

To illustrate what Bandura means by anticipatory control, picture a tenth-grade boy who has developed quite a bit of skill as a musician and enjoys taking clarinet lessons from a much-admired teacher. The boy envies the attention earned by athletes, though, and decides to try out for the school football team. Unfortunately, he lacks ability, makes many mistakes, is ridiculed by teammates, and is ignominiously dropped from the squad after being publicly berated by the not-too-sensitive coach. As a result he develops a negative attitude toward sports. If an extreme behaviorist interpretation is made of these situations, it might be argued that the boy's attitudes toward music and sports are not due to deliberated choices on his part because they have been shaped by positive and negative experiences. If Bandura's conception of anticipatory control is taken into account, however, it might be reasoned that even though the boy's behavior *has* been shaped, he is in a position to control future experiences. If he is later given a choice between taking a physical education class taught by the football coach or performing in the school band, for example, he can control his own destiny by anticipating what is likely to happen in each situation and by selecting a course of action that is almost sure to be fulfilling rather than disagreeable. Bandura's allowance for anticipatory control avoids the implication of Skinner's view that humans are almost always the "victims" of experiences.

Evaluation of Learning Theory

Freud, Erikson, and Piaget provide us with comprehensive, integrated, stage-by-stage analyses of development. American psychologists have

supplied an assortment of related principles, many of which were proposed to highlight aspects of learning. Even though these principles do
not combine to form a theory of development, they have been and
continue to be applied to child rearing, education, and psychotherapy in
a variety of ways. Behavior modification techniques based on these principles can be used by parents to teach toilet training in a day (Azrin and
Foxx, 1976), to make child rearing more systematic and effective (McIntire, 1970; Patterson, 1976; M. Hall et al., 1977), and to enhance intellectual development in preschoolers (Engelmann and Engelmann, 1968).
Programmed instruction, where learning is shaped by presenting
stimuli (questions) designed to elicit correct responses (answers) that are
immediately reinforced, is widely used in American schools. Sometimes
programs are presented by teaching machines or computers; sometimes
they are presented in workbook form. Teachers can use behavior
modification methods to help disadvantaged children prepare for school
(Engelmann, 1969), to become more aware of ways they influence the
behavior of their students (R. V. Hall, 1974; Sherman and Bushell, 1975),
and to establish constructive classroom control without resorting to punishment (Andersen, 1974). Therapists can use behavior modification
techniques to help children overcome abnormal or self-destructive forms
of behavior (Lovaas, 1974; Krumboltz and Thoreson, 1976). Personnel in
correctional institutions can use principles of learning theory to help
delinquents learn acceptable forms of behavior (Cohen and Filipczak,
1971). Adolescents can use behavior modification methods on themselves to control weight (Abramson, 1977) or overcome a "broken heart"
(Wanderer and Cabot, 1978). (These last techniques represent a recent
trend in applications of learning theory principles: having individuals
learn to control their own behavior.)

In addition to serving as the basis for these practical applications,
learning theory has stimulated an enormous amount of research. A basic
reason the learning theory paradigm is so popular with researchers is
that it is much more testable than the rather vague theoretical speculations of Freud, Erikson, and Piaget. Learning theory terms are clearly
defined and hypotheses are stated precisely, making it possible for experimenters to carry out carefully controlled analyses of specific types of
behavior.

Even though principles of operant conditioning have been used in
all the ways described above and even though the learning theory
paradigm has been popular with researchers, there are a number of
shortcomings of this view. Perhaps the most important of these, as far as
this book is concerned, is that most learning theorists (with the possible
exception of Sears) have been more interested in particular types of
behavior than in the process of human development. A second major
weakness (to be explored more fully in later chapters) is that learning

theory principles cannot adequately account for key aspects of language acquisition or cognitive development. A third limitation of this view, emphasized by Rogers and Bandura, is that many learning theorists tend to view children as more or less passive organisms manipulated almost entirely by experiences or the responses of others. (Bandura's version of social learning theory overcomes this limitation.) A final criticism of all forms of learning theory is that too much of the research has taken place in contrived experimental situations. In their eagerness to be precise and to control variables, learning theorists often fail to take into account the complexities of real situations.

Enthusiasm for learning theory, behavior modification, and social learning theory seems to have peaked in the late 1960s and early 1970s. At about the same time, a new research paradigm—*information processing*—began to attract attention and during the last few years interest has accelerated. Even though it is often referred to as information processing *theory*, this approach possesses fewer characteristics of a theory than any of the other theoretical interpretations discussed so far. Even so, the information processing paradigm merits consideration in this chapter because it is the basis for many studies to be summarized later in this book.

Information Processing

Antecedents and Characteristics of Information Processing Research

The information processing approach involves, as the name implies, ways humans process and use information. Robert S. Siegler points out (1983, p. 129) that in the third edition of the encyclopedic *Handbook of Child Psychology*, published in 1970, information processing was mentioned hardly at all and the extremely comprehensive index included only two entries relating to the topic. In the fourth edition of the *Handbook*, published in 1983, by contrast, Siegler presents an eighty-two-page summary of selected research on information processing. The chapter concludes with ten tightly packed, double-column pages of references. Siegler and Patricia H. Miller (1983) offer the following explanations for this explosion of interest in information processing:

Increasing disenchantment on the part of psychologists with the strict behavioristic stress on overt behavior due to awareness of its inadequacies in explaining significant types of behavior (such as language acquisition).

A growing conviction that thought processes are capable of being studied scientifically through use of new methods of investigation, such as measuring the amount of time required for a cognitive process, recording eye movements (such as those used in reading), and error analysis.

The development of computers. Attempts to program computers to perform tasks formerly handled by humans led to interest in how humans themselves process information.

The desire of developmental psychologists to study cognition using an approach not tied to Piagetian theory.

Information processing: ways input is processed, recovered, and used

Researchers who were influenced by one or more of the factors just listed all endorse the guiding principle that humans should be viewed as **information processing** devices. They carry out experiments to analyze in minute detail "The ways in which sensory input is transformed, reduced, elaborated, stored, recovered, and used" (Neisser, 1967, p. 4). The conclusions of studies are often presented in the form of models, diagrams, and charts that depict the steps in types of information processing procedures. Typical results of information processing research can be summarized by outlining one of the most popular models that has been proposed to depict cognitive processes (Atkinson and Shiffrin, 1968).

A Popular Information Processing Model

Our sense receptors are constantly stimulated by visual, auditory, tactile, olfactory, and gustatory stimuli. These experiences are initially recorded in the **sensory register** (SR), so named because the information is thought to be encoded in the same form in which it was perceived. The purpose of the sensory register is to hold information just long enough (one to three seconds) to decide if we want to attend to it further. Two processes that determine whether or not information in the SR will receive additional processing are recognition and attention. As a function of past experience, we are predisposed to recognize certain kinds of information as familiar in some way. And since the environment typically provides us with more information than we can deal with at one time, we attend only to particular stimuli. Once information has been recognized or attended to (or both), it is transferred to the **short-term memory store** (STM). It has been found that the average adult can hold approximately seven unrelated bits of information in the STM for about twenty seconds. (Looking up a telephone number just long enough to dial it illustrates the capacity and nature of the STM.) If information

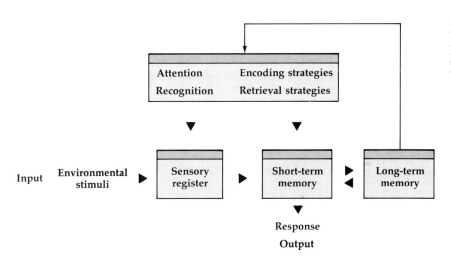

FIGURE 2.1
An information
processing model of
learning

initially transferred to the STM is encoded in an effective way, it will
become part of the **long-term store** (LTM). Factors that facilitate encoding are rehearsal (repetition, with or without attempts to relate new to
old memories), use of imagery, organizing what is to be learned, and
taking advantage of knowledge of how one's memory works (referred to
as **metamemory**). Once something becomes part of the LTM, it is available to be retrieved as an aid to solving problems—provided the person
realizes that relevant information *is* relevant.

Research on subjects of different ages has revealed that younger children are not as effective information processors as older ones. Younger
children are less likely than older ones to attend to the significant aspects of a situation, use rehearsal strategies effectively, or take advantage of metamemory techniques. Furthermore, because they have had
fewer experiences than older children, their LTM is not as well stocked
with potentially valuable bits of information. In general terms, therefore, children increase in capacity and rate of processing and also acquire more effective cognitive skills as they grow older.

Evaluation of Information Processing

In her analysis of information processing, Patricia H. Miller (1983) observes that it currently dominates laboratory research on cognition but
also is spreading to such other areas as intelligence, social development,
and morality. The information processing approach is so popular, Miller
suggests, because it makes it possible to analyze the complexities of

thought. It also appeals to American researchers because of rigorous methodology and the capability of making specific predictions about performance. On the debit side, Miller notes the following weaknesses:

Computer models are similar to, but still significantly different from, human behavior. Many flow charts and diagrams fail to adequately depict the complexities of human thought.

The information processing approach has called attention to differences in the cognition of younger and older children but it does not *explain* development. There is a tendency, Miller notes, for researchers "to proceed on the assumption that change over weeks and months follows the same principles as change over minutes within an experimental session" (p. 295).

Because much information processing research is carried out under rigorous experimental conditions, there tends to be a lack of awareness of differences between the laboratory and the real world.

Despite these weaknesses, it seems likely that the information processing approach will continue to be popular with American psychologists.

Taking Advantage of All Theoretical Interpretations

At the beginning of this chapter, functions and characteristics of theories were described. Theories are proposed to organize and give meaning to facts and to guide research. The *ideal* theory is logical, supplies clear definitions, makes specific predictions about behavior that are publicly verifiable, and is falsifiable. A theory of *development* should call attention to changes in behavior that occur over time. All five of the theoretical interpretations discussed in this chapter have given meaning to facts and guided research, but none of the five really qualifies as an *ideal* theory of *development*. The views of Freud, Erikson, and Piaget call attention to stages in the development of selected aspects of behavior, but all three can be faulted, to a greater or lesser extent, because of lack of clear definitions that make possible predictions that are publicly verifiable. Learning theory and the information processing paradigm both get high marks for providing precise definitions and predictions that can be tested under precisely controlled conditions, but neither contributes very substantially to understanding of continuities and changes in development over time.

Thus, no single theory described in this chapter offers a complete framework for interpreting child development. Taken together, however, they can be of considerable value in helping you to gain insight into development as you consider different stages and types of behavior.

Freud's description of psychosexual stages, for example, will be referred to in later chapters to help you understand how feeding, toilet training, awareness of knowledge of sex differences, and the impact of puberty may influence development. His analysis of levels of consciousness and his outline of defense mechanisms will be used to help you comprehend possible causes of many different types of normal and abnormal behavior.

Erikson's description of psychosocial stages will be used to call your attention to significant aspects of parent-child relationships and to personality characteristics likely to contribute to smooth and favorable development at different age levels. Because Erikson's stages cover the entire life span, they will be used—more than the views of any other theorist—as an organizational frame of reference for the remaining chapters of this book.

Piaget's description of stages will assist you to make quite sophisticated analyses of cognitive development and make you aware of differences between the thought process of younger and older children.

Learning theory will be referred to in explaining how parents might encourage desirable behavior and avoid inadvertently strengthening behavior they would prefer to discourage. Learning theory will also be used to explain how children may generalize responses from one situation to another. *Social* learning theory will be used to clarify your understanding of the ways children move from dependence to independence, how they learn by identifying with and imitating others, and how different approaches to child rearing may influence personality.

Studies of information processing will help you grasp how human beings of different ages sort out perceptions, process them, store them, and retrieve them to solve problems.

The strengths and limitations of each theory are summarized in Table 2.3.

These are just some of the ways the theoretical interpretations you have just read about will help you avoid the feeling that you are drowning in a sea of data as you read further.

A final advantage of the information on theoretical interpretations presented in this chapter is that it will help you understand why widely varying approaches to child rearing are advocated by different authorities. Theorists who endorse psychoanalytic views, for instance, often urge parents to be extremely careful about how they treat infants and young children because they assume that experiences during the early years will be stored in the unconscious and influence behavior later in life. Theorists who are impressed by Erikson's description of psycho-

TABLE 2.3
CONTRIBUTIONS AND LIMITATIONS OF THEORIES OF DEVELOPMENT

Theory	Contributions to Understanding of Children	Limitations
Freud: Psychosexual Stages	Early experiences may influence later behavior, even if they are not remembered. Potential importance of infant feeding and toilet training. Impact of identification with parents. Significance of sexual impulses. Understanding of abnormal behavior and of defense mechanisms. Techniques of psychotherapy.	Based on recollections of a small number of extremely abnormal adults. Speculations not based on objective observations.
Erikson: Psychosocial Stages	Relationships with parents and peers are of great importance. Certain types of feelings about self are of critical importance at different stages of development.	Types of relationships stressed at different age levels are those that seemed particularly significant to Erikson. They may not be significant to all children.
Piaget: Cognitive Stages	The thinking of younger children differs in significant ways from the thinking of older children. Parents and teachers should take into account a child's level of cognitive development.	The clinical method may be too subjective to supply accurate data. Piaget may have made cognitive development seem more orderly than it actually is.
Learning Theories (including Social Learning Theory)	Much child behavior is learned, and parents have control over many factors that influence childhood learning. The way parents guide children from dependence to independence is of significance. Children learn many types of behavior by identifying with and imitating parents, other adults, and peers.	Learning theory principles are difficult to interrelate and do not shed light on continuities of development. It is not possible to explain significant types of behavior (such as some aspects of language acquisition) in terms of learning theory principles.
Information Processing	Makes it possible to study many aspects of cognitive processes in precise ways under controlled conditions.	Does not explain differences between the cognitive processes of younger and older children.

social stages, on the other hand, are more inclined to call attention to important interpersonal relationships at all periods of development. Piagetians, who endorse the principles of equilibration, assimilation, and accommodation, are likely to urge parents to encourage their children to make the most of built-in tendencies to make sense out of what they perceive. Disciples of Skinner, in direct contrast, tend to advocate that parents try to shape behavior as systematically as possible by using techniques of behavior modification. Social learning theorists tend to stress how parents can serve as models or arrange for children to observe desirable types of behavior. Information processing enthusiasts may suggest that parents think of their children as "computers" in order to foster techniques for improving perception, memorization, and problem solving.

   Knowing about each of the theoretical interpretations discussed in this chapter, therefore, will help you understand and evaluate research and also grasp the reasoning behind suggestions offered to parents and teachers for putting research into practice.

Theories of Development

Insightful analyses of the work of many of the theorists discussed in this chapter are presented in *Theories of Child Development* (2nd ed., 1980) by Alfred Baldwin and in *Theories of Developmental Psychology* (1983) by Patricia Miller.

Suggestions for Further Study

Sigmund Freud

To find out more about Freud and the development of his theory, consult *The Life and Work of Sigmund Freud* (1953) by Ernest Jones, who was a close associate of Freud. Volume I, *The Formative Years and the Great Discoveries*, is likely to be of greatest interest to students of developmental psychology. Two inexpensive paperbacks by Freud himself provide quite complete coverage of his life and theories: *An Autobiographical Study* (1935; paperback ed., 1963) and *An Outline of Psycho-Analysis* (1949).

Psychoanalytic Views of Childhood

While Freud had only limited contact with children, a number of his followers specialized in treating children, and a substantial body of psychoanalytic literature on childhood and adolescence has accumulated, much of it by Freud's own daughter Anna. To sample these writings, browse through one or more of the annual volumes of *The Psychoanalytic Study of the Child* or look for these books: *Normality and Pathology in Children: The Writings of Anna Freud* (1965) and *The Magic Years* (1959) by Selma Fraiberg.

Erikson's Description of Development

Erik Erikson's books are of considerable significance in speculating about development and education. In *Childhood and Society* (2nd ed., 1963) he describes how studying American Indians and observing patients in treatment led to the development of his Eight Ages of Man. A capsule description of his stages and a concise biography are found in "Erik Erikson's Eight Ages of Man" by David Elkind, which appeared in the *New York Times Magazine* on April 5, 1970. For a more comprehensive analysis of Erikson and his work, examine *Erik H. Erikson: The Growth of His Work* (1970) by Robert Coles.

Piaget's Theory of Cognitive Development

H. E. Gruber and J. J. Voneche have edited *The Essential Piaget: An Interpretive Reference and Guide* (1979), which Piaget describes in the foreword as "the best and most complete of all anthologies of my work." An inexpensive paperback that summarizes the man and his work is *Piaget's Theory of Intellectual Development: An Introduction* (2nd ed., 1979) by Herbert Ginsburg and Sylvia Opper. Books relating Piaget's ideas to education include *Piaget for Teachers* (1970) by Hans Furth and *Piaget for the Classroom Teacher* (2nd ed., 1980) by Barry Wadsworth. If you are interested in reading Piaget himself, you might consult *The Language and Thought of the Child* (1952), *The Origins of Intelligence in Children* (1952), and *The Psychology of the Child* (1969), which was written with his frequent collaborator Barbel Inhelder.

Watson's Views on Behaviorism and Child Rearing

Watson's provocative observations often outraged his readers. If you would like to sample his style and learn about his views, you might consult *The Ways of Behaviorism* (1928). In the last chapter he explores the question, "Can the Adult Change His Personality?" Watson's claim that he could train any healthy child to become any type of specialist is made in Chapter 5 of *Behaviorism* (1925). Excerpts from *The Psychological Care of Infant and Child* (1928) are reprinted in *The Child* (1965) by William Kessen.

Skinner on Behaviorism

Skinner's *Beyond Freedom and Dignity* (1971) caused almost as much furor as some of Watson's books. A condensation of the book appeared in the August 1971 issue of *Psychology Today*. Another way to learn about Skinner's views is to read his book *About Behaviorism* (1974) or *The Skinner Primer* (1974) by Finley Carpenter. For Skinner's own account of forces shaping his life, see the first volumes of his autobiography, *Particulars of My Life* (1976) and *The Shaping of a Behaviorist* (1979).

Evaluating a Scientific Utopia

To see if you would like to live in a utopia based on Skinner's behavioral principles, read his novel *Walden Two* (1948). After reading the book, consider these questions: What aspects of *Walden Two* strike you as most appealing? What aspects would you find difficult to accept? To compare your hypotheses with the experiences of persons actually living in such a community, read *A Walden Two Experiment: The First Five Years of Twin Oaks Community* (1973) by Kathleen Kinkade or excerpts in the January and February 1973 issues of *Psychology Today*.

Social Learning Theory

Albert Bandura summarized his reasons for proposing an alternative to a strict behaviorist interpretation of learning theory in "Behavior Theory and the Models of Man," which appeared in the December 1974 issue of *American Psychologist*. In *Social Learning Theory* (1977), he offers a comprehensive outline of the nature of this view of behavior and development.

Information Processing

A fairly technical summary of recent research in this area is provided by Robert Siegler in *Handbook of Child Psychology* (4th ed., 1983), edited by Paul H. Mussen.

PART 2

THE BEGINNING OF LIFE

KEY POINTS

Explanation of the Term "Developmental Behavioral Genetics"

Behavioral genetics: genetic factors significant, but influenced by experiences

Contemporary behaviorists more willing to consider genetic influences

How the Genotype Becomes the Phenotype

Genotype: genetic makeup

Phenotype: observable characteristics

Epigenetic model: genetic instructions altered by experiences but self-righting tendency exists

Reaction range model: degree of impact of environment varies depending on characteristic

Research Exploring the Interaction of Heredity and Environment

Mean r between IQ scores of monozygotic twins .74, dizygotic twins .54

With age, IQ scores of monozygotic twins more similar, dizygotic twins more dissimilar

Adopted children resemble biological parents more than adoptive parents in IQ

Adopted children of high-IQ mothers more intelligent than those of low-IQ mothers

Basic Genetic Processes

Chromosomes: particles containing genes

Genes: units of hereditary transmission

Locus: location of hereditary unit

Allele: information in hereditary unit

DNA (double helix model of DNA molecule)

Germ cells: egg and sperm

Meiosis: cell division reducing number of chromosomes in germ cells

Dominant and recessive genes

Multifactorial inheritance due to combinations of genes

X or Y chromosome determines sex

Mortality rates for males higher at all stages of development

Genetic Defects

Phenylketonuria (PKU): metabolic disorder traceable to specific gene

Hemophilia: bleeding tendency due to sex-linked recessive gene

Rh disease: antibodies produced because of dominant-recessive gene incompatibilities

Down's syndrome: mental retardation caused by chromosomal abnormalities

Klinefelter's syndrome: aberrations in male development due to extra X chromosome

Congenital heart defects due to combinations of genes as well as environmental factors

Genetic Counseling

Some genetic defects more likely in particular ethnic groups

Genetic counseling: couple given estimates of likelihood of genetic defects

Planning timing of birth may reduce chances of defects

CHAPTER

3

DEVELOPMENTAL BEHAVIORAL GENETICS

Now that you have some familiarity with the history of developmental psychology, the methods used by behavioral scientists, and developmental theories, we are ready to begin tracing the development of a human being. Since the life of an organism begins at the moment of conception, this chapter is devoted to genetic influences. The next chapter describes prenatal development and birth, and subsequent chapters analyze significant types of behavior at progressive age levels. Before turning to descriptions of genetic processes and abnormalities, however, some background information explaining the title of this chapter is called for.

Explanation of the Term "Developmental Behavioral Genetics"

Behavioral genetics:
genetic factors significant but influenced by experiences

The title of this chapter, "Developmental Behavioral Genetics," is a fairly recent term that was coined to stress the point that environmental experiences exert an influence on inherited tendencies. (In some discussions, the term "behavior genetics" is used.) The use of the word **behavioral** by those who introduced the term can probably be credited to John B. Watson. You may remember from the discussion of Watson in the preceding chapter and in Chapter 1 that he championed behaviorism. He maintained that "Psychology as the behaviorist views it is a purely objective experimental branch of natural science. Its theoretical goal is the prediction and control of behavior" (1913, p. 158). Because he was interested in observable behavior and control of behavior, Watson discounted the impact of inherited factors. In his book on child care, in fact, he asked parents to consider the question, "Isn't it just possible that almost nothing is given in heredity and that practically the whole course of development of the child is due to the way I raise it?" (1926, p. 15).

The same point of view was enunciated almost as emphatically thirty years later by B. F. Skinner, who became the leading spokesman for the behaviorist view starting in the 1950s. Skinner wrote:

> The doctrine of "being born that way" has little to do with demonstrated facts. It is usually an appeal to ignorance. "Heredity," as the layman uses the term, is a fictional explanation of the behavior attributed to it.
>
> Even when it can be shown that some aspect of behavior is due to . . . genetic constitution, the fact is of limited use. It may help us in predicting behavior, but it is of little value in experimental analysis or in practical control because such a condition cannot be manipulated after the individual has been conceived. . . . (1953, p. 6)

Many departments of psychology in American universities have endorsed the behaviorist position as originally defined by Watson and later reaffirmed by Skinner. Researchers trained in such departments were not always as extreme as Watson and Skinner in their dismissal of genetic factors, but they definitely favored the assumption that environmental influences are of paramount importance. Not all psychologists, however, swore allegiance to the behaviorist view. European theorists, in particular, did not hesitate to allow for the influence of built-in tendencies due to genetic constitution. Freud, for example, proposed that the libido is an **instinctual** energy. Erikson stressed the epigenetic principle based on the assumption that anything that grows is governed by a **genetic** ground plan. Piaget suggested that the basic tendencies of organization, adaptation, and equilibration are **inborn.** But quite a few American psychologists also were willing to entertain the notion that inherited tendencies should be considered in tracing development. Arnold Gesell, for example, argued that many types of behavior displayed by infants and young children unfold according to a genetically programmed timetable. Other psychologists disagreed with Skinner's argument that aspects of behavior due to inborn tendencies are of "limited use." Simply because genetic influences are beyond a researcher's control, they maintained, does not mean they should be dismissed out of hand.

As a consequence of these differences of opinion, a sometimes acrimonious debate between "environmentalists" and "hereditarians" was instituted in the 1920s and has continued with various degrees of intensity until the present day. For many years proponents of each position attempted to prove that heredity *or* environment had the most significant impact on a particular type of behavior. Eventually, estimates of the percentage of a given characteristic (such as intelligence) attributable to heredity and the percentage attributable to environment were proposed on the basis of elaborate statistical analyses. In some cases a **heritability** "score" or "index" was reported. The implication of such estimates seemed to be that if one or the other factor was rated at more than 50 percent, it had "won." In the last few years more and more psychologists have begun to acknowledge the futility of waging such "contests" between heredity and environment. Instead, there is a trend toward evaluating ways the two factors interact. Sandra Scarr and Richard A. Weinberg, for instance, published an article in 1980 titled "Calling All Camps! The War Is Over." And Richard Plomin introduced a recent series of articles on behavioral genetics by noting that they "testify to the value of going beyond the question of how much to begin to address issues of how genetic and environmental influence transact in development" (1983, p. 255).

Thus, the rather odd term *developmental behavioral genetics* is intended to emphasize *how* environmental and genetic factors interact. Inclusion of the word *genetics* in the term might be thought of as an indication that contemporary American psychologists are not as extreme in their rejection of inherited factors as Watson and Skinner. They are willing to acknowledge that genetic factors *do* exert a significant impact on individual development. At the same time, by inserting *behavioral* before *genetics*, they stress that inherited tendencies are shaped by environmental experiences.

Contemporary behaviorists more willing to consider genetic influences

How the Genotype Becomes the Phenotype

Genotype: genetic makeup

Phenotype: observable characteristics

In emphasizing how genetic and environmental influences interact, behavioral scientists often refer to the terms **genotype** and **phenotype.** Genotype refers to the genetic makeup of an individual. Phenotype refers to the person's observable characteristics. (*Pheno* is derived from a Greek word that means *to show,* so the phenotype is what shows.) The significance of these concepts is illustrated by the opening statement of a chapter on developmental behavioral genetics in the most recent edition of the encyclopedic *Handbook of Child Psychology.* The authors, Sandra Scarr and Kenneth Kidd, begin the chapter with this statement: "Development is the process by which the genotype becomes the phenotype" (1983, p. 346). To grasp what Scarr and Kidd mean, think of the impression you get when you observe yourself in a mirror, or the impression you give when you interact with acquaintances. You have a unique

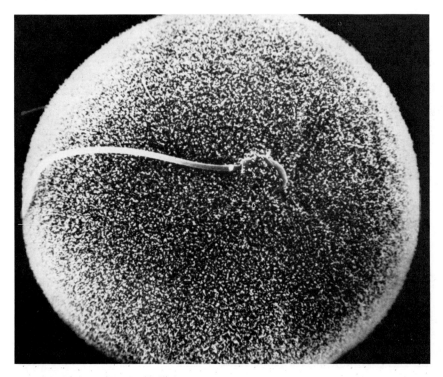

Microscopic view of sperm fertilizing egg.
© *Fawcett/Phillips/Photo Researchers, Inc.*

physical appearance and personality. Those who know you well have learned that you are likely to exhibit certain types of behavior in certain situations. All of the observable characteristics that combine to make you the individual you are represent your phenotype. Your individuality is partly due to the unique arrangement of genes you received when you were conceived, but it also is due to the experiences to which you were exposed as you developed. If you had been exposed to different experiences, your phenotype would be different to a greater or lesser extent.

A number of theorists have proposed models to illustrate ways the genotype becomes the phenotype.

Models of Genotype-Phenotype Interaction

Conrad Waddington (1962) has proposed an **epigenetic model** of development. As noted a few paragraphs earlier, Erikson stressed the epigenetic principle: anything that grows has a ground plan causing the various parts to arise at different stages of development to eventually form a functioning whole. Waddington explains the development of a person's phenotype from the genotype by emphasizing the same principle. The genetic pattern of each individual is determined at the time of conception, and this pattern includes instructions for the timing and eventual limits of many characteristics. But these instructions may be altered in one way or another by environmental conditions or experiences. The rate of growth and the eventual height of a person are genetically programmed at the time of conception, for example, but environmental circumstances may alter the impact of those genetic instructions. Assume that identical male twins, who possess exactly the same genetic pattern, are separated at birth and raised in different homes. One twin grows up under near-starvation conditions and suffers a series of illnesses during the first five years of life. The other twin is provided with an exceptionally nutritious diet and enjoys excellent health. Even though the genetic instructions for growth are the same for both boys, one is likely to be shorter than the other at the time they enter school. If, at the age of six, the first twin is placed in a different environment where he receives an excellent diet and health care, however, he is likely to catch up with his brother and both will be the same height by the time they leave elementary school. This example illustrates the essence of Waddington's theory. The person's genotype lays down the ground plan but genetic instructions will be deflected in different ways by environmental conditions. If negative conditions are removed, however, the organism will right itself by returning to the original "specifications."

Epigenetic model: genetic instructions altered by experiences but self-righting tendency exists

Reaction range
model: degree of
impact of environ-
ment varies depend-
ing on characteristic

Irving Gottesman (1963) explains variability illustrated by the developmental height differences in the pair of twins just mentioned by suggesting there is a *range* of reactions that might emerge from a particular genotype. With physical characteristics the range may be limited, but with complex social and cognitive traits the reaction range may be quite wide. In a classic study of identical twins who were separated at birth and reared in different environments (Newman, Freeman, and Holzinger, 1937), for instance, an IQ difference of twenty-four points at maturity was found for one pair. One twin had been reared in a home that stressed intellectual activities and schooling, whereas the parents of the other girl had not bothered to send her to school for more than a few years. Counting college attendance for the high-IQ twin, the difference in schooling was fourteen years. Gottesman joins with Waddington in emphasizing that there is a constant interaction between genotype and phenotype during development. If the quite extreme difference between the environments of the twins studied by Newman, Freeman, and Holzinger had been reduced during the school years, it is likely that their IQ scores would have become more similar.

Robert McCall (1981) uses the model of a *scoop* to illustrate the interplay between genotype and phenotype. The scoop, which is visualized as narrow at the top but wide at the bottom, represents the course of development. During the first years of a child's life, the amount of variability that might be caused by environmental experiences is somewhat restricted because the range of experiences is restricted. But as environmental experiences accumulate and diversify, the magnitude of the scoop widens and the potentiality for variability increases.

McCall also stresses the often crucial nature of the *timing* of environmental experiences. Two basically similar individuals exposed to the same experience at different points in their development will be influenced differently. Assume that two sisters, one eleven and the other seventeen, are invited to spend a summer vacation at the home of some relatives in the country who own several horses. The eleven-year-old has recently become fascinated by horses and ecstatically rides and cares for the animals from dawn until dusk. The seventeen-year-old *had* been every bit as fascinated by horses when she was eleven, but never had the chance to ride and lost interest. As a high school senior, she is concerned about appearances and fears she might look silly if she took a fall. She declines an invitation to ride the first day of her visit and wanders over to the house next door, where she discovers a handsome young man restoring a battered automobile. The eleven-year-old, who thinks that both cars and boys are yucky, has her interest in horses strengthened to the point that she later becomes a professional riding instructor. Her older sister is never able to understand how any mature woman can be so interested in horses.

Theodore D. Wachs (1983) emphasizes points related to those made by McCall. He suggests that in order to grasp how the genotype becomes the phenotype it is often necessary to ask: "What specific aspects of the environment are relevant for what specific aspects of development, at what specific ages, for what specific individual?" (p. 397). Wachs also notes that the relationship between development and environment is transactional and bidirectional. That is, the developing child is not just a passive set of genetic blueprints upon which environmental influences act; the child often influences the individuals and situations that make up the environment. This point will be further developed when early parent-child relationships are discussed in Chapter 5. Research to be summarized in that chapter has revealed that the personality traits and reactions of infants to early care sometimes shape parental behavior at least as much as parental handling shapes child behavior.

Relating Genotype-Phenotype Models to Theories of Development

The various models of how the genotype becomes the phenotype that have just been summarized call attention to selected aspects of interactions between genetic factors and environmental experiences. These models also stress points emphasized by the more completely developed theories outlined in the preceding chapter. Waddington's epigenetic model, for instance, which proposes that the genotype lays down a ground plan that can be deflected in various directions, is similar to Erikson's theory of psychosocial stages, also based on the epigenetic principle. The significance of the timing of experiences stressed by McCall and Wachs calls attention to the importance of formative influences at particular stages. Freud, Erikson, and Piaget all stress timing in much more comprehensive ways in their stage theories. The basic principle endorsed by behavioral geneticists that experiences shape the ways genetic instructions are carried out is similar to the principle proposed years ago by learning theorists. The behavioral and social learning theories of Skinner, Sears, and Bandura, however, supply more comprehensive analyses of how experiences may influence behavior than models proposed by those who specialize in the study of behavioral genetics. Thus, psychologists who propose models of behavioral genetics join with psychologists who have proposed comprehensive theories of development in seeking to highlight the ways in which genetic and environmental factors interact.

These various conceptions of how the genotype becomes the phenotype serve as background for a brief review of research designed to examine the interplay between heredity and environment.

Research Exploring the Interaction of Heredity and Environment

As noted above, up until recently there was a tendency for researchers to be eager to substantiate that either heredity or environment was more important than the other. A publication that purported to prove that heredity had a more profound influence than environment on intelligence (or whatever) was likely to provoke a salvo of publications presenting or analyzing evidence to prove the opposite. In order to review such studies objectively and comprehensively, it would be necessary to first provide extensive background information on methodological complexities and then summarize and interpret the results of all pertinent studies. Such an analysis would require several hundred pages. Instead of an exhaustive treatment, brief summary comments on typical research will be offered. In keeping with the theme of this chapter emphasis will be on *how* heredity and environment interact, not on how much a particular trait is influenced by one factor or the other.

The following summary of research devoted to exploring relationships between heredity and environment will concentrate on conclusions relating to mental abilities. Intelligence can be measured more accurately than personality traits, interests, emotional disturbances, or conduct disorders (other types of behavior that have been studied by researchers interested in the interaction of heredity and environment). Accordingly, the discussion that follows is restricted to intelligence. For a comprehensive review of research on the other types of behavior, see Scarr and Kidd (1983).

By way of introduction, a summary of a review of several hundred studies by R. C. Nichols (1978) is presented. The research investigations analyzed by Nichols all featured comparisons of measures of the behavior of monozygotic and dizygotic twins. Monozygotic (one-egg twins, also referred to as *identical*) originate from the same fertilized egg and thus have the same genotype. Dizygotic twins (two-egg, also referred to as *fraternal*) originate from two separate eggs, each with a different genotype. They are the equivalent of same-age siblings. These two types of twins serve as ideal subjects for psychologists interested in studying the interaction of heredity and environment since they serve as readily available experimental and control groups. Both types of twins are born at the same time and are exposed to similar environmental conditions, but one pair of children shares an identical genotype, the other pair does not.

Studies of Monozygotic and Dizygotic Twins

Nichols surveyed 211 studies in which up to eleven different measures of the mental abilities of monozygotic and dizygotic twins were obtained

Psychologists interested in studying ways heredity and environment influence behavior and development often compare the behavior of monozygotic twins (who have identical genotypes) and dizygotic twins.
© *Susan Lapides.*

and compared. The mean correlations between mental test scores for monozygotic twins turned out to be .74; for dizygotic twins it was .54.

If you have not had much experience interpreting correlation coefficients, you might, at this point, re-examine the scatter diagram on page 16, as well as the description of the development (by Sir Francis Galton and others) of statistical procedures for interpreting such diagrams. The diagram and the description of the development of the correlation coefficient make clear that both provide an index of the relationships between two variables. A scatter diagram provides graphic

Mean r between IQ scores of monozygotic twins .74, dizygotic twins .54

visualization of the relationship, a correlation coefficient (abbreviated r) provides a numerical index expressed as a value between +1.0 and −1.0. The higher the r, the greater the relationship. There are statistical procedures that can be used to determine if a particular r indicates a significant difference between variables. (A difference is significant if it can be predicted mathematically that it is not due to chance but represents a genuine difference that would almost certainly be found again if the study were repeated.) Knowledge of statistics is not necessary to interpret the information just recorded, however. For purposes of this discussion it is sufficient to say that an r of .74, such as that found by Nichols for mental test scores of monozygotic twins, indicates a quite high degree of relationship. The r of .54 found for mental test scores of dizygotic twins represents a moderate degree of relationship. Even without going to the trouble of calculating a measure of statistical significance, it is usually safe to assume that a difference between rs of twenty hundredths or so, as between the mental test scores of monozygotic and dizygotic twins, is a genuine difference.

A different way of studying twins is to compare measures of the behavior of monozygotic twins who are reared together with similar measures of the behavior of monozygotic twins who were separated at birth and reared in different environments. David Rowe and Robert Plomin (1978) reviewed studies of this type and found that the mean correlation of mental test scores for monozygotic twins reared together was .86, for those reared apart it was .74. For purposes of comparison, they also calculated the mean correlation reported by several investigators between dizygotic twins, which turned out to be .53, almost identical to that reported by Nichols. The mean correlation for IQs of siblings reared together was .54.

A recent study of twins calls attention to developmental changes. Nearly five hundred pairs of twins and their siblings participated in a longitudinal study in Louisville, Kentucky. The subjects were given intelligence tests at intervals from infancy through adolescence. Analyses of the sets of scores revealed that "individual differences in intelligence progressively stabilized by school age, and each child followed a distinctive pattern of spurts and lags in mental development" (Wilson, 1983, p. 298). With age, test scores for pairs of monozygotic twins became more similar, and those for dizygotic twins became more dissimilar. Two-egg twins did not resemble each other in IQ test performance at adolescence any more than ordinary siblings.

While studies of twins are an excellent way to search for relationships between heredity and environment, comparisons of adopted children and those reared by their natural parents also yield informative data. To illustrate the nature of such research, three early "classic" studies and three recent investigations will be described.

With age, IQ scores of monozygotic twins more similar, dizygotic twins more dissimilar

Studies of Adopted Children

When the Iowa Child Research Station was established in the 1920s, several members of the staff instituted an investigation in which IQ scores of adopted children were obtained at intervals from early childhood through adolescence. These scores were compared with measures of the biological mother's IQ and the educational level of the adoptive parents. During the early years of the study, relationships between the IQs of adopted children and the educational level of the adoptive parents were quite high. When the adopted children were tested at adolescence, however, the correlation between the biological mother's IQ and the child's IQ was .44, whereas the correlation between the adoptive mother's educational level and the child's IQ was .02 (Skodak and Skeels, 1949).

Adopted children resemble biological parents more than adoptive parents in IQ

At about the same time the Iowa study was initiated, two other adopted-child studies were carried out. They were done independently (one at Stanford University, the other at the University of Minnesota) and they proceeded in an almost identical manner. The experimental design involved the comparison of a large number of matched families. Considerable effort was made to select pairs of families that differed in only one respect: the presence of an adopted child or a biological child. The correlation between the measures of intelligence of adopted children and adoptive mother reported by the Stanford researchers was .19, and between biological mother and child, .46 (Burks, 1928). The same figures reported by the Minnesota investigators were .24 for adopted child and adoptive mother, and .51 for adopted child and biological mother (Leahy, 1935).

In 1974, two investigations referred to as the Minnesota Adoption Studies were launched. The first, called the Transracial Adoption Study, involved the placement of 176 children in 101 families. Twenty-nine of the children had two black natural parents, 101 had one black natural parent and one natural parent of other or unknown racial background, 25 had white natural parents, and 21 had natural parents of various other racial groups. The adoptive parents all scored in the bright average or superior range on IQ tests. When the adopted children were tested after having lived with the adoptive parents for a number of years, they earned average scores of 110, 20 points higher than average scores earned by children being reared in low-income environments judged to be similar to those of the natural parents (Scarr and Weinberg, 1983). The adopted children, however, scored an average of 6 points below natural children in the same families. When estimates of the educational level of the natural mother and the adoptive parents were compared with child IQ scores, the same trend reported by the earlier investigators at Stanford and Minnesota was found—there was a closer relationship between adopted children and their natural mothers (with whom they had had no contact after the first weeks or months of life) than between the children and their adopted parents (who had reared them since the first year of their lives).

The second Minnesota investigation is called the Adolescent Adoption Study. One hundred and ninety-four adopted children who had spent an average of 18 years in 115 adoptive families were compared to 277 biological children in 120 other families of essentially similar backgrounds. (The families in this study were not matched as carefully as in the earlier Stanford and Minnesota investigations.) The correlations between IQ scores of children and educational level estimates of parents were very similar to those reported in the earlier studies: the correlation for natural parent-child families was .40, and for adoptive parent and child families it was .13 (Scarr and Weinberg, 1983). When the IQ scores of the adopted children tested in late adolescence were compared to educational levels of both biological and adoptive parents, the results corroborated those reported earlier by the Iowa investigators. That is, there was a much higher relationship between educational level of the natural parents and the child's IQ than between similar measures for adoptive parents and child. When these results were compared with those of the Transracial study, the same pattern noted in the Iowa study emerged: the longer adopted children lived with their adoptive parents, the less they resembled them in intellectual performance and the more they resembled their natural parents.

The final study to be mentioned also involved adopted children. A large private adoption agency in the southwestern United States routinely administered IQ tests to unwed mothers living in their residential facility. After close to four hundred children born to these mothers had been placed for adoption in three hundred families, they and their adoptive parents also were given intelligence tests. The correlation between the IQs of biological mother and child was twice as high as that between adoptive parents and child (Horn, 1983). The biological mothers were then divided into high- and low-IQ groups, and the scores of their children compared. Despite the fact that the children of the high- and low-IQ mothers were placed in essentially similar homes with presumably equivalent potential for stimulating mental development, the test scores of the children mirrored the scores of their biological mothers. That is, children of high-IQ mothers scored significantly higher, on the average, than children of low-IQ mothers.

Adopted children of high-IQ mothers more intelligent than those of low-IQ mothers

Relating Research Results to Genotype-Phenotype Models

Even allowing for methodological "impurities," such as the possibility that monozygotic twins are reared in environments that are more uniform than those of dizygotic twins or the myriad ramifications of selective placement of adopted children in carefully screened homes, the combined evidence just summarized reveals that genetic instructions influence such complex characteristics as intelligence. At the same time, it is clear that genetic predispositions are significantly influenced by environmental experiences. Although the interactions of heredity and environment are extremely complex, it is possible to draw a few inferences about how the genotype becomes the phenotype by relating some of the results of studies just mentioned to the models of development described earlier.

Take the finding that adopted children resemble their adoptive parents in measures of intelligence early in life but become less like them as they mature. This result might be interpreted with reference to the epigenetic model of development proposed by Waddington. He suggests that there is a genetic ground plan that determines timing and limits and also causes a return to an original pathway if a deflection occurs. Adopted children (particularly those whose mothers had low IQs) may resemble their superior adoptive parents early in life when they are "deflected" upward by rich home experiences, but become less like them intellectually as they spend more time at school than at home. When the "abnormal" conditions are weakened, there is a return to the genetically programmed course of development.

Or take the finding of the Transracial Adoption Study that children placed in superior homes score an average of twenty points higher than similar children who remain in poor environments. These results might be explained with reference to the reaction range concept of Gottesman. Both groups of children *presumably* had the same genetic potential, but the range of reactions for intellectual functioning varied by twenty points. (It might be predicted on the basis of the results of the Iowa study and the Adolescent Adoption Study, however, that the IQ differences between the groups will decrease as they move through high school.)

Implications of Research on Heredity, Environment, and Intelligence

Before the "truce" in the "war" between environmentalists and hereditarians was declared, interpretations of the research just summarized varied considerably. Psychologists who favored the behaviorist view as expounded by Watson and Skinner tended to discount the reported differences between IQ scores of monozygotic and dizygotic twins or changes over time in the relationships between IQs of adopted children and their adoptive parents. Sometimes results would be questioned because of methodological or statistical inadequacies. In other cases, behaviorists would point out that IQ differences could often be attributed to environmental factors. The IQs of monozygotic twins are more similar than those of dizygotic twins, it was argued, because identical twins are exposed to a more uniform environment.

Psychologists who were more willing to acknowledge the significance of inherited tendencies, on the other hand, interpreted the results just summarized quite differently. They proposed that even allowing for methodological and statistical impurities in individual studies, the accumulated evidence favors the view that intelligence is significantly influenced by heredity. If you would like to sample collections of papers that illustrate such conflicting interpretations, examine *Environment, Heredity and Intelligence* (1970), Reprint Series No. 2 of the *Harvard Educational Review*, or *Intelligence: Genetic and Environmental Influences* (1970), edited by Robert Cancro.

In this decade of interest in behavioral genetics, with emphasis on *how* rather than *how much*, perhaps the best way to sum up the research findings just summarized is to simply note that inherited and environmental factors both exert an influence. Any conclusion that stressed one factor over the other would lead to charges against the authors of bias or favoritism by at least some psychologists.

Now that you are familiar with the nature of current thinking about relationships between inherited and environmental influences on development, genetic processes themselves can be examined.

Basic Genetic Processes

At the moment your life began, you were a single cell about the size of a pinpoint. If that cell could have been compared microscopically to all the other cells of future human beings conceived that day in all parts of the world, it would have been indistinguishable from the rest. At the present time, your body contains approximately sixty trillion cells—all of them produced by that original tiny organism. Depending on the function, they resemble similar cells in other human beings. But (unless you are an identical twin) the basic structure of your cells and the way they are arranged is absolutely unique. You are now easily distinguishable from all the other people in the world conceived the same day you were. Yet your facial features, the color of your hair and eyes—many of the characteristics that make you unique—were determined the moment that original cell was formed. When you think about the great complexity of that original cell, it is almost impossible to comprehend. How did that unique cell become formed in the first place, and how did it become transformed from a single cell into sixty trillion cells—each of which has the same basic structure but each of which also has a special function?

Some at least partial answers to these questions are offered on the following pages.

Units and Processes of Hereditary Transmission

Chromosomes and Genes

The single cell that is the beginning of a human being is created when a sperm fertilizes an egg (or ovum).[1] These two cells are different from all others in the body. In human beings, all cells, with the exception of sperm and egg cell, contain forty-six chromosomes. **Chromosomes** are threadlike particles contained in the cell nucleus, each of which contains up to twenty thousand genes. Genes are the units of hereditary transmission that determine the traits that make each individual unique. As information about genetics has accumulated, the term **gene** has become somewhat ambiguous. Accordingly, geneticists have concluded that a useful distinction can be made between hereditary units as *segments* of a chromosome and the *information* contained in one particular copy of that unit. The location of a hereditary unit in a chromosome is referred to as the **locus. Allele** is the term used to refer to information to be found at a particular locus. M. H. F. Wilkins and F. H. C. Crick of England and James D. Watson, a young American, won the Nobel prize when they developed a model of the molecular structure of the chemical **deoxyribonucleic acid** (called DNA for short). They proposed that a gene is a segment of DNA and that the DNA molecule is in the form of a double helix (coil). Each strand of the helix (see Figure 3.1) consists of four repeating chemical subunits, which may be arranged in a different order. The double helix made it possible to explain how the fertilized egg subdivides and reproduces itself while simultaneously producing different types of cells. The Watson-Crick model suggests that as the fertilized egg divides and subdivides, the two strands in the DNA molecule uncoil, each strand taking with it the exact pattern it needs to reproduce itself.

Chromosomes: particles containing genes

Genes: units of hereditary transmission

Locus: location of hereditary unit

Allele: information in hereditary unit

DNA (double helix model of DNA molecule)

Germ Cells

Sperm and egg cells develop by a process different from that of all other cells because of their potential for combining. Each of these **germ** cells

Germ cells: egg and sperm

---

[1] For the sake of clarity, the terms *germ cell, egg, ovum,* and *sperm* are used in this book. If you have previously studied genetics and reproduction, or if you read other books on this subject, you may find it helpful to keep in mind that germ cells are also called *sex cells, reproductive cells,* or *gametes;* that sperm cells are also called *spermatozoa* (the singular form of which is *spermatozoon*); and that the fertilized egg is also called the *zygote.*

FIGURE 3.1

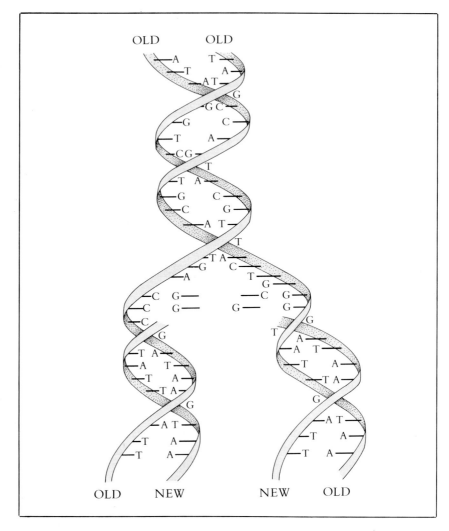

A segment of the DNA molecule as described by Watson and Crick. The letters stand for the pairs of chemicals that make up each rung in the double helix model. A stands for adenine, T stands for thymine, C for cytocine, G for guanine. As the DNA molecule unwinds, the rungs separate, attract duplicate chemical partners, and thus form duplicate genes.

J.D. Watson, The Double Helix *(New York: Atheneum, 1968), p. 211.* © *1968 by J.D. Watson.*

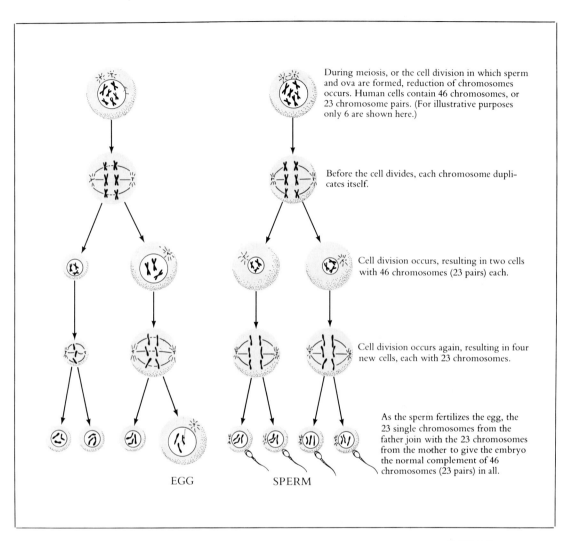

During meiosis, or the cell division in which sperm and ova are formed, reduction of chromosomes occurs. Human cells contain 46 chromosomes, or 23 chromosome pairs. (For illustrative purposes only 6 are shown here.)

Before the cell divides, each chromosome duplicates itself.

Cell division occurs, resulting in two cells with 46 chromosomes (23 pairs) each.

Cell division occurs again, resulting in four new cells, each with 23 chromosomes.

As the sperm fertilizes the egg, the 23 single chromosomes from the father join with the 23 chromosomes from the mother to give the embryo the normal complement of 46 chromosomes (23 pairs) in all.

EGG   SPERM

FIGURE 3.2
The development of germ cells

(given that name because they are the basis for growth—like a germinating flower seed) must contain twenty-three chromosomes, half the usual number. The germ cells develop in the reproductive organs—the testes in males, the ovaries in females. It is estimated that several hundred million sperm are produced by the testes every four or five days. The ovaries, by contrast, contain a permanent supply of an estimated four hundred thousand eggs. During a woman's fertile years, one of these eggs (usually) is released about every twenty-eight days. Depending on the number of fertile years in a woman's life, from three hundred to four hundred eggs will be released from the pool of four hundred thousand. An egg fertilized when a woman is in her thirties will be "riper" than an egg fertilized during earlier years. In some cases (to be discussed later) the ripeness of an egg may be a presumed cause of abnormalities of development. That is, certain types of defects occur much more frequently in children born to women over thirty-five.

Before the germ cells can produce a new human being, they must go through a process of maturation. At the beginning of the maturational process, there are twenty-three pairs of chromosomes in each sperm and egg. As the germ cells develop, a special kind of cell division, called **meiosis** (or *reduction division*, since the number of chromosomes is reduced), takes place. During meiosis, the chromosomes of each germ cell first arrange themselves into pairs, with each pair containing one chromosome from the mother and one from the father. These pairs separate, and then separate again, but the second time they divide lengthwise so that one-half of the original forty-six chromosomes are retained in each new cell. (See Figure 3.2.)

Meiosis: cell division reducing number of chromosomes in germ cells

Aspects of Hereditary Transmission

Mendelian Principles of Hereditary Transmission

Much of our understanding of genetics is based on the laws of hereditary transmission proposed around 1860 by the Austrian monk Gregor Mendel. Mendel experimented with two strains of peas in the monastery garden. Some of these had red flowers; others had white flowers. He discovered that if he mated purebred red and white plants, all the plants produced would be red. When these red plants were mated with each other, however, they produced (on the average) one white plant for every three red ones. After experimenting with several strains of peas for a period of eight years, Mendel proposed the following principles of hereditary transmission:

1. The individual units of heredity (genes) remain essentially constant even when passed from one generation to the next.

2. Genes are found in pairs, one from the mother and one from the father. In some cases both are alike, but sometimes they are different and one will be **dominant** over the other. (Genes from red flowers in pea plants, for example, are dominant over those for white, so the gene for white flowers is called **recessive**.) The red gene is called dominant because whenever the pair of genes that determines flower color in pea plants consists of one red and one white, the flowers will always be red.

3. When germ cells are formed through meiosis, the pairs of genes separate from each other, which explains why the dominant gene may not appear in all sperm or egg cells produced. This separation occurs in a random manner, so it is not possible to predict the kind of gene any particular germ cell will contain.

Dominant and recessive genes

A considerable amount of much more sophisticated research on genetics has been carried out in the hundred and some years since Mendel published his findings. Although his basic principles still stand, scientists have learned that the interaction of dominant and recessive genes may take place in a variety of ways.

Modifications of Mendelian Principles

Chance seems to determine which members of the chromosome pairs will be given to any egg or sperm, which explains why a child may or may not resemble the father, the mother, or neither. One egg, for example, may contain eighteen chromosomes from the woman's mother and five from her father; another egg, the opposite; still another, eleven from the mother and twelve from the father, and so forth. Making accurate prediction more unlikely, some genes may "skip" one or more generations—they remain in the genetic structure but do not always influence development. Furthermore, it has been found that many characteristics depend not just on pairs of genes but also on complex combinations of genes, a situation referred to as **multifactorial inheritance** or **polygenic traits**. At the beginning of meiosis, when the chromosomes become arranged in pairs, genes may *cross over* to opposite chromosomes. As a result, a new combination of genes may be formed in any chromosome. Alleles arranged at loci close together on a chromosome are usually inherited together, but alleles located at opposite ends of a long chromosome are likely to be inherited independently. Finally, it appears that *complete* dominance may be the exception rather than the rule. Even though the allele for a particular trait may be dominant, the recessive allele may not be completely suppressed. As a result, the trait may reflect the impact of a *mixture* of the two sets of genetic information. For all these reasons it is impossible to predict how close parents will come to producing a child with a clear-cut combination of their charac-

Multifactorial inheritance due to combinations of genes

teristics. It may happen, but it probably will not. From time to time (in Hitler's Germany, for example), efforts have been made to mate ideal males and females to produce superbabies. The difficulty of succeeding in attempts to breed children with the best traits of each parent is characterized by a statement attributed to George Bernard Shaw. It is reported that a famous actress wrote to him and proposed that they mate and produce a child. She argued, "With your brains and my beauty, it should be a marvel." Shaw declined the offer, pointing out, "Suppose it has your brains and my beauty?"

Aspects of Sex Determination

Because the germ cells divide twice, four cells are produced from each original cell when meiosis takes place. Within each germ cell there is a pair of chromosomes that will determine the sex of the child if conception takes place. When the original germ cell divides to produce two cells of twenty-three pairs of chromosomes each, and then these daughter cells divide again, this pair of chromosomes (as do all other pairs) splits. In women, all four of these cells contain an X (or female) chromosome. Only one of these—which contains the yolk of the original cell— is a genuine egg cell, capable of being fertilized; the other three (called polar bodies) are absorbed and secreted. In men, however, the pairs of chromosomes that determine sex contain one X and one Y (male). When the first cell division takes place, each new cell contains an X and a Y, but when the second split occurs, the sperm cells which are produced contain *either* an X or a Y chromosome. If a sperm with an X chromosome fertilizes the egg, the child will be a girl. If a sperm with a Y chromosome fertilizes the egg, the child will be a boy.

X or Y chromosome determines sex

Because of the way meiosis takes place (through splitting of chromosomes), there are an equal number of X and Y sperm. However, for some yet to be explained reason, more eggs are fertilized by Y (male) sperm. An estimated 130 to 170 males are conceived for every 100 females (Scheinfeld, 1958), but the ratio of male to female births is 1,053 to 1,000 (according to latest figures released by the National Center for Health Statistics). Thus, the mortality rate of males during the prenatal period is substantially higher than that for females. The same pattern is maintained after birth. Mortality rates for males are higher at every age level. By the age of twenty, females outnumber males. The life expectancy of white males in the United States is 70.2 years; that of females, 77.8.

Mortality rates for males higher at all stages of development

One explanation for sex differences in mortality rates is that females possess a superior resistance to disease. It has been proposed (Purtillo and Sullivan, 1979) that the genes responsible for programming the

The mortality rate for males is higher than for females at all stages of development.
Even though more males are born, by the age of twenty and increasingly thereafter,
females outnumber males.
Patricia Hollander Gross/Stock, Boston.

body's immunological system are located in the X chromosome. Since females have two X chromosomes, they may receive a "double dose" of genes that cause immunities to develop. Another explanation for the lower mortality rate of women is based on the assumption that the female must be strong enough to nourish and carry the fetus through the prenatal period in order to insure the survival of the species. During the course of evolution, it is hypothesized, stronger females survived, while males, whose role in procreation does not require that kind of strength and endurance, were not selected for these qualities.

These comments on mortality rates call attention to the fact that basic genetic processes do not always proceed normally. Given the incredible complexity and delicacy of the formation of egg and sperm, and the way the fertilized egg subdivides over and over again to produce specialized cells, it is not surprising that genetic aberrations occur. While most infants delivered in American hospitals and homes are "normal," about seven out of a hundred begin postnatal life with various kinds of defects that are immediately apparent (Apgar and Beck, 1972). Approximately another seven out of a hundred appear normal at birth but possess genetic instructions that will cause mild or severe abnormalities to appear later in development. Some of the most common defects traceable to genetic aberrations will now be discussed. (Estimates of frequency and kinds of treatment are derived from discussions in Apgar and Beck, 1972; and Reed, 1975.)

Genetic Defects

The defects to be discussed in this section are of three basic types: those traceable to genes (usually recessive), those due to chromosomal abnormalities, and those that are multifactorial. Several of the multifactorial types, which cannot be traced to any particular gene or chromosomal abnormality, may also be traceable, at least in part, to environmental factors to which the mother and fetus were exposed during pregnancy.

Defects Traceable to Specific Genes

Phenylketonuria (PKU)

Phenylketonuria (PKU): metabolic disorder traceable to specific gene

Description: Untreated condition leads to erratic, hyperactive behavior and eventually to severe mental retardation. The enzyme that normally metabolizes phenylalanine (a compound found in protein) does not function properly. As a result, the compound increases in the body tissues and leads to chemical changes that cause injury to brain cells.

Cause: Recessive gene. Through the use of a simple blood test it is possible to detect if any individual is a carrier of the PKU gene, even if it has not appeared in previous generations.

Incidence: 1 in 15,000 births; 1 in 80 whites is a carrier. More common among those of Scandinavian descent and/or those who are blond, fair, and blue-eyed. If two carriers of the PKU gene marry (1 in every 4,900 marriages), there is a 1 in 4 chance that each pregnancy will result in a child with the condition.

Treatment: If the condition is detected at birth (through use of a simple, inexpensive test), the child can be put on a diet containing a minimum amount of phenylalanine. (The special food is produced on a nonprofit basis by a pharmaceutical company.) Strict adherence to the diet prevents brain injury, but some emotional disturbances and learning problems may be residual effects. There are differences of opinion about how long the diet needs to be continued, but a shift to a normal diet is usually not recommended until the child is about five.

Sickle Cell Anemia

Description: Hemoglobin materials in red blood cells crystallize and stick together (because the cells change from a disc to a sickle shape), particularly when the oxygen level is low. Constriction of the blood vessels causes severe pain in muscles and joints, anemia contributing to susceptibility to pneumonia and respiratory infections, and slow-healing sores. If blood vessels leading to the brain are blocked, neurological problems and death may occur.

Cause: Recessive gene. Through use of a routine blood test it is possible to detect if an individual is a carrier of the recessive gene.

Incidence: 1 in 400 blacks; 1 in 10 black Americans is a carrier and in 1 marriage out of 100 between blacks the recessive genes will combine and there will be a 1 in 4 chance that each pregnancy will result in a child with the condition.

Treatment: Analgesics to help relieve pain, drugs to expand size of blood vessels, plasma to increase the volume of the blood. Preventive care includes avoiding fatigue (particularly at high altitudes) and guarding against infection.

Hemophilia

Description: Absence of clotting factor in blood. Internal bleeding in joints causes severe and constant pain. Uncontrolled bleeding, perhaps caused by even a minor scratch, may cause death.

Hemophilia: bleeding tendency due to sex-linked recessive gene

Cause: Recessive gene, sex-linked. The Y chromosome has fewer genes than the X, which opens up the possibility that some X genes may remain unmatched when the egg and sperm unite. In females, the other X chromosome typically has a corresponding gene that blocks the effect of the gene for **hemophilia,** but in males this may not be the case. When there has been a family history of hemophilia, it is possible to predict the odds that a given man and woman will produce a child with the condition. In some cases, however, spontaneous mutations occur.

Incidence: 1 in 1,000 males, only rarely in females.

Treatment: Multiple blood transfusions, injections of concentrates of blood plasma high in clotting power. Preventive care includes exercise to develop resistance (but with care to avoid possible injury), careful planning when surgery or dental work must be done.

Cystic Fibrosis

Description: Error of metabolism that affects the glands controlling production of mucus, saliva, and sweat. Lungs produce a sticky mucus that clogs the air passages and increases susceptibility to respiratory infections. Gummy mucus also blocks the pancreas, interfering with the digestion of food, which often leads to a protruding abdomen. Males tend to be sterile.

Cause: Recessive gene. It is possible to detect the existence of the gene by chemically analyzing perspiration.

Incidence: 1 in 1,000 births; 1 in 20 white American adults is a carrier.

Treatment: Administration of a powdered enzyme at meals to offset lack of pancreatic juices, diet high in salt but low in starches and fats. Administration of antibiotics daily to prevent development of respiratory infections. Preventive care includes having child sleep in a mist tent and positioning the body at several angles to promote discharge of mucus from the lungs.

Rh Disease

Rh disease: antibodies produced because of dominant-recessive gene incompatibilities

Description: Factor in blood (called Rh because it was first discovered in experiments with rhesus monkeys) causes antibodies to attack red corpuscles in a fetus leading to developmental abnormalities or death.

Cause: If the father's genetic pattern contains the gene for Rh-positive (which is dominant) and the mother's gene for Rh-negative, complications may develop because the fetus will have Rh-positive blood but it will be nourished by the mother's Rh-negative blood. The production of antibodies begins only when some of the baby's Rh-positive blood interacts with the blood of the mother (or if the mother had received a transfusion of Rh-positive blood prior to pregnancy). Accordingly, **Rh disease** is usually a problem only with second or later pregnancies.

Incidence: 1 marriage in 9 is between an Rh-positive man and an Rh-negative woman, but only 1 in 10 will have a child with Rh problems after a first child (who usually is not affected).

Treatment: Periodic checks during pregnancy to measure Rh antibodies in the mother's blood. If the antibody count becomes high, the physician may induce labor and give the neonate blood transfusions immediately after birth. In some cases blood transfusions are given to the fetus in utero. Immediately after birth of a child with Rh-positive blood, the Rh-negative mother is given a gamma globulin vaccine that will prevent production of antibodies during the next pregnancy.

Defects Due to Chromosomal Abnormalities

Down's Syndrome (Mongolism)

Description: Most common single form of mental retardation. Individuals with this condition are quite similar in appearance and display the following characteristics: flat face with eyes that superficially resemble those of Mongolians, large head on a chunky body, stubby fingers and toes, flabby muscle tone. Heart and eye defects are common and there are frequent glandular abnormalities. Susceptibility to infections is high.

Down's syndrome: mental retardation caused by chromosomal abnormalities

Causes: Most frequently caused by an extra chromosome in pair twenty-one of the fertilized egg (due to failure of the two chromosomes in that pair to separate when the egg is formed). Sometimes caused by relocation of part of chromosome twenty-one to chromosome fifteen.

Incidence: 1 in 600 births. For women younger than 30, 1 in 1,500 births; for women 30 to 34, 1 in 600 births; for women 35 to 39, 1 in 280 births; for women 40 to 44, 1 in 80 births; for women over 45, 1 in 40 births. The greater tendency for older women to have children with **Down's syndrome** may be due to endocrine changes, slower fertilization of eggs, longer exposure of eggs to toxic agents. In some cases, a malformed sperm may be the cause. There is some evidence that exposure to radiation or an unknown virus may be contributing causes.

Treatment: Thyroid and pituitary preparations to boost growth. Preventive care centers on guarding against infection, careful regulation of diet. When reared with affection and stimulating attention, individuals with Down's syndrome may eventually become at least partially self-supporting through employment in sheltered workshops.

Turner's Syndrome

Description: Females suffer from stunted growth, poorly developed sex organs, low hairline, low-set and prominent ears.

Cause: Chromosomal abnormality of XO type (only one X chromosome instead of two).

Incidence: 1 in 2,500 female births.

Treatment: Administration of estrogens at puberty brings about development of feminine form. Although menstruation occurs in some treated women, they remain sterile.

Klinefelter's Syndrome

Description: Males with small and nonfunctioning testes, deficiencies

Klinefelter's syndrome: aberrations in male development due to extra X chromosome

in male hormone production, enlarged breasts. In some cases mental retardation and behavior problems are exhibited.

Cause: Chromosomal abnormality of XXY type (an extra X chromosome).

Incidence: 1 in 400 male births.

Treatment: Surgery (if necessary) to reduce breast size, administration of androgens to promote secondary male characteristics. Despite treatment, males with this condition remain sterile.

XYY Syndrome

Description: Males who are unusually tall, impulsive, exhibit tendencies toward antisocial behavior and violence. Low intelligence is common but not universal.

Cause: Chromosomal abnormality of XYY type (an extra Y chromosome).

Incidence: 1 in 1,000 male births.

Treatment: None. Preventive care is difficult because awareness of abnormal chromosomal pattern might lead parents to *expect* antisocial and violent behavior, thereby inadvertently encouraging it. Not all males with the XYY pattern exhibit the syndrome.

Defects Due to Multifactorial Causes

Cleft Lip and Cleft Palate

Description: Child is born with mild or severe clefts in the upper lip or palate.

Cause: Multifactorial. Errors in DNA coding, perhaps caused by a virus or drugs or excessive vitamins taken by the mother at about the eighth month of pregnancy.

Incidence: 1 in 700 births; 1 in 1,000 whites, 1 in 500 Japanese-Americans, 1 in 2,000 blacks have the condition.

Treatment: Special arrangements and techniques for feeding infants. Corrective surgery during the first months and years. Orthodontic treatment when the teeth are formed.

Club Foot

Description: Twisted or deformed foot.

Cause: Multifactorial. Group of genes interacting with some yet to be identified factor cause a temporary halt in the development of the foot during the eighth and ninth week of pregnancy.

Incidence: 1 in 300 births, twice as many boys as girls.

Treatment: Nonsurgical manipulation, sometimes using a cast or corrective shoes attached to a metal bar. Various kinds of surgery.

Congenital Heart Defects

Description: Defects of various kinds in the heart itself or the blood vessels that lead to and from the heart.

Cause: Multifactorial. Viruses, drugs, or radiation to which the mother has been exposed during the first eight weeks of pregnancy.

Incidence: 1 in 100 births.

Treatment: Various kinds of surgery, diet, therapy.

> Congenital heart defects due to combinations of genes as well as environmental factors

Diabetes

Description: Chronic metabolic disorder resulting in elevated blood glucose levels, which prevent the body from metabolizing carbohydrates properly. The condition is most likely to appear between the ages of 8 to 12, 40 to 50, and in the late 70s.

Cause: Multifactorial. No test is available to determine if a person is a carrier, but the likelihood of the condition can be estimated by examining family health histories.

Incidence: 1 child in 2,500. About 12 million Americans have diabetes in one form or another, about 1 in 4 is a carrier.

Treatment: Injections of insulin or glucagon. Frequent tests (at least once a day) of urine are needed to determine the amount of insulin required. Preventive care stresses control of weight and strict adherence to a diet with little or no sweets, fried foods, or alcohol.

Genetic Defects: Summary

The following points emphasize common threads found in the types of genetic defects just described:

1. Certain defects appear much more frequently in particular ethnic groups. PKU, for example, is most likely to be found in blond, blue-eyed Scandinavians. Sickle cell anemia occurs in blacks. (It is believed

> Some genetic defects more likely in particular ethnic groups

that the gene that causes sickle cell anemia is common in those of African descent because it provided protection against malaria. Africans who inherited one abnormal gene and one normal gene had a quality in their blood that prevented malarial parasites from multiplying. Accordingly, blacks who inherited the gene were more likely to survive than those who did not.)

2. Some defects are found exclusively or more frequently in males or females. Abnormal combinations of X and Y chromosomes leading to Turner's, Klinefelter's, or XYY syndromes are found only in one sex or the other. Boys are more likely than girls to have hemophilia or to be born with club feet.

3. It is possible to determine if individuals contemplating marriage possess recessive genes or chromosomal abnormalities that might lead to certain defects.

4. By analyzing family health histories, it is possible to estimate the likelihood that children conceived by any particular couple might be born with several other kinds of defects.

5. There are a number of things prospective parents might do to try to prevent birth defects by planning when they will have children.

These various points call attention to the potential values of genetic counseling.

Genetic Counseling

Genetic counseling: couple given estimates of likelihood of genetic defects

Genetic counseling is quite a new field, and as information about hereditary causes of abnormalities in development accumulates, it is likely to become used by more and more couples contemplating parenthood. At present it is possible for any man and woman to visit a **genetic counseling** center (usually affiliated with a large hospital or university) and request a genetic analysis. (A list of genetic counseling centers can be obtained from the National Foundation/March of Dimes, Box 2000, White Plains, N.Y. 10602.) On the basis of laboratory tests and preparation of a family history, the couple can learn about the chances that they will have a child with one or more of the defects just summarized. If it is discovered, for example, that they both possess the defective gene that causes PKU, sickle cell anemia, cystic fibrosis, or hemophilia, they will know in advance that they have a one-in-four chance of having a child with a particular condition. They may also discover the existence of an abnormal arrangement of chromosomes. By accumulating information about family health histories, they may become aware of the potentiality of having a child with such multifactorial defects as diabetes, cleft palate, club foot, or congenital heart defects.

The genetic counselor might also point out to the prospective parents

Genetic counselors can give couples planning to have a child estimates of the probability that certain types of genetic defects might occur.
© *Robert V. Eckert, Jr./EKM-Nepenthe.*

that they can reduce the possibility of having a child with certain types of birth defects (such as Down's syndrome) by planning to have children when the wife is between twenty and thirty-five and the husband younger than forty-five. They should also plan an interval of at least two years between children. If they have wondered about having a large family, they might take into account that beginning with a third child genetic defects become increasingly likely.

Planning timing of birth may reduce chances of defects

These discussions of types of genetic disorders and of genetic counseling may be somewhat misleading in the sense that about two-thirds of the conditions described have been traced to single genes or particular chromosomal patterns. Disorders traceable to specific genetic factors *should* be stressed when prevention is of prime importance. Concentrating on specific genes and chromosomal patterns may help prospective parents avoid having a child with an incurable condition or a permanent handicap. Many disorders, and most "normal" aspects of development, however, cannot be attributed to any known gene or combination of genes. Furthermore, as illustrated by some of the kinds of treatment described for certain disorders, the impact of some genetic instructions can be altered by environmental conditions.

These comments on genetic counseling have called attention to a number of things prospective parents might do to take into account genetic factors before conception takes place. The next chapter on pre-natal development and birth describes what occurs after conception.

Summary

1. **Developmental behavioral genetics** is a term that refers to the study of ways environmental experiences and conditions influence inher-ited tendencies. Instead of trying to prove, as earlier theorists were prone to do, that heredity is more important than environment or vice versa, contemporary researchers typically investigate ways the two factors interact.

2. In analyzing the interaction between genetic and environmental fac-tors on behavior and development, psychologists often speculate about how the **genotype** (a person's genetic make-up) becomes the **phenotype** (the observable characteristics of a person). A number of genotype-phenotype models have been proposed. One stresses a self-righting tendency; others emphasize that the impact of environ-mental experiences varies depending on timing and the characteris-tics affected.

3. The interaction of heredity and environment in establishing a per-son's level of intelligence has been studied intensively. Many re-searchers have reported that monozygotic twins resemble each other in intelligence more than dizygotic twins. Other researchers have discovered that adopted children resemble their biological parents more in intelligence than they resemble their adoptive parents.

4. The cells that combine to form a human being typically contain forty-six chromosomes, each of which contains several thousand genes. Genes are the units of hereditary transmission, and their impact on the development of an individual varies depending on the informa-tion **(allele)** found at a particular location **(locus)** in a chromosome. Each gene is a segment of the deoxyribonucleic acid **(DNA)** molecule, which has a structure resembling a double helix.

5. **Germ cells** (sperm and egg) are produced by the process of **meiosis,** which reduces the number of chromosomes from forty-six to twenty-three. When a sperm fertilizes an egg, the chromosomes in each combine to produce the forty-six chromosomes found in the cells of most humans. (If a sperm with a Y chromosome fertilizes the egg, the child will be a boy. If a sperm with an X chromosome fertilizes the egg, the child will be a girl.) Genes that determine traits are arranged in pairs, one from the mother, one from the father. Sometimes one gene in a pair will be **dominant** over the other and determine a

particular trait, but many characteristics are due to combinations of genes (multifactorial inheritance).

6. Because of the complexity of the process of cell division, as well as exposure to toxic conditions, genetic defects sometimes occur. Females are less likely than males to develop defects, perhaps because the X chromosome contains genes that lead to the development of immunities. Some defects (such as phenylketonuria, hemophilia, or Rh disease) are traceable to specific genes. Other defects (such as Down's syndrome and Klinefelter's syndrome) may be due to chromosomal abnormalities. Still other defects (such as congenital heart defects) are due to multifactorial causes.

7. Couples planning a family may obtain estimates of the likelihood of having children with certain types of defects by taking advantage of genetic counseling. Even without knowledge about their genetic structure, they may be able to reduce the likelihood of defects by planning to have children when the mother is between twenty and thirty-five and the father younger than forty-five.

Genetics

Suggestions for Further Study

If you would like to find out more about heredity and genetics, two books by Amran Scheinfeld are highly regarded: *Your Heredity and Environment* (1965) and *Heredity in Humans* (1972). You might also look for *The Genetic Code* (1962) by Isaac Asimov.

Developmental Behavioral Genetics

A comprehensive but technical discussion of developmental behavioral genetics by Sandra Scarr and Kenneth Kidd can be found in Chapter 6 of *Infancy and Developmental Psychobiology*, edited by M. M. Haith and J. J. Campos, Volume II of *Handbook of Child Psychology* (4th edition, 1983), edited by Paul H. Mussen. Volume 54 (1983) of the journal *Child Development* contains fifteen articles on behavioral genetics by many of the leading researchers in this field.

Genetic Defects

For comprehensive but clearly written descriptions of genetic defects and how they might be prevented, examine *Is My Baby All Right? A Guide to Birth Defects* (1972) by Virginia Apgar and Joan Beck.

KEY POINTS

Prenatal Development

Amnion: fluid-filled sac

Placenta: membranous organ that envelops embryo

Embryo: prenatal organism from time nourishment by placenta begins

Ribonucleic acid (RNA): carries instructions, assembles chemicals

Fetus: prenatal organism from third month after conception to birth

Teratogens: harmful agents that may cause abnormalities in development

Impact of teratogens is greatest during period of embryo (three to eight weeks)

Impact of teratogens depends on timing, constitution, dosage

Poor maternal nutrition influences physical and intellectual development of child

Infectious diseases contracted by mother may cause fetal abnormalities

Embryo and fetus unable to break down drugs taken by mother

If mother uses hard drugs, infant may be born addicted

Smoking during pregnancy has significant adverse effect on fetus and baby

Excessive drinking by mother may cause permanent damage to child

Infant defects more likely if mother is over thirty-five or under eighteen

Extreme extended anxiety during pregnancy may cause complications

First rule of prevention: detect pregnancy early

Amniocentesis: analysis of amniotic fluid to detect abnormalities

Birth

Average labor for first-borns: ten to fourteen hours

Natural childbirth intended to reduce tension in mother

Natural childbirth may reduce, but not eliminate, pain

APGAR score: Appearance, Pulse, Grimace, Activity, Respiration

Reproductive risk high in disadvantaged homes, when parents are anxious

Low-birth-weight infants from disadvantaged backgrounds most likely to experience problems

Views on the Significance of Life Just After Birth

Gentle birth may benefit parents more than infant

No evidence from controlled studies that early contact has a lasting impact

CHAPTER

4

PRENATAL DEVELOPMENT AND BIRTH

*I*t is not possible to treat developmental behavioral genetics and prenatal development in separate chapters without some overlap. The two topics are different but also inextricably intertwined, since extremely significant genetic processes occur during the prenatal period. In the preceding chapter, genetic aspects of the remarkable transformation of a single fertilized egg into a human being made up of approximately 60 trillion cells were the focus of attention. In this chapter, the nature and sequence of stages in development occurring between fertilization and the time of birth is described. Genetic as well as environmental factors are analyzed.

Prenatal Development

Approximately once every twenty-eight days (usually about midway in the menstrual cycle) an ovum is released in one of a woman's two ovaries. The egg produced in the ovary moves down a Fallopian tube (also called the oviduct) toward the uterus. If sperm are ejaculated into the vagina during the three to seven days the ovum is in the Fallopian tube and if some of them move through the cervix and uterus up into the tube, they are attracted to the egg by a hormonal force that draws them toward it. If one of the sperm enters the egg during the twenty-four-hour period it is ready for fertilization, the surface is changed so that no other sperm can enter. At the moment of penetration the nuclei of the two cells merge, and a new cell is formed containing twenty-three pairs of chromosomes, one half from the mother, the other half from the father. At that moment the sex and heredity of the new organism are determined.

Various Forms of Fertilization

Even if sperm are ejaculated into the vagina during the time the ripe ovum is moving down the Fallopian tube, fertilization may not take place. Many sperm are trapped in the mucous secretions of the vagina and cervix. Other sperm enter the "wrong" Fallopian tube. The fluids in the "right" Fallopian tube move the ovum in a direction opposite to that of the sperm and the "upstream" journey of most of the sperm that have penetrated that far terminates in one of the many folds of the tube. If the male's semen does not contain an estimated 60 million to 200 million sperm per ejaculation, none of the sperm may reach the ovum. (A normal, healthy male deposits between 300 to 500 million sperm into the vagina at a single ejaculation.)

Fertilization may also fail to occur if the woman is unable to release ova or if the Fallopian tubes are blocked. If a couple has repeatedly attempted to conceive without success, even after taking special care to monitor the woman's temperature so that intercourse can be timed to occur when the sperm and ovum are both fresh, they may consider several alternatives. Drugs to stimulate ovulation may be given to the woman, although one possible disadvantage of this technique is that several ova may be released at once and multiple births may occur. Blocked Fallopian tubes may be opened surgically. If the husband's sperm count is low, his sperm may be collected, frozen, and concentrated until a sufficient number have accumulated to be used in artificial insemination procedures. If the husband is sterile, sperm from a donor with similar characteristics may be obtained. Sperm from either the husband or a donor, or a combination of sperm from both, may be introduced into the uterus of a fertile woman with a syringe. If the Fallopian tubes cannot be opened, ripe ova may be surgically removed from the mother, allowed to mature in an incubator for about three hours, and then placed in a container with sperm from either the husband or a donor. If fertilization occurs, after about two to four days, when the fertilized egg reaches the eight-cell stage, it may be implanted in the woman's uterus with a catheter. The first successful use of this technique took place in England in 1978. A different technique, first used successfully in California in 1983, involves artificially inseminating a fertile woman with sperm from the husband of an infertile woman. After five days the embryo is washed out of the donor's uterus and implanted in that of the infertile woman. Yet another alternative, first used in 1978, involves **surrogate mothering,** in which sperm from the husband of an infertile woman are used to artificially inseminate a woman who agrees to carry the baby to term and then give it to the couple.

Development of the Embryo and Fetus

Whether fertilization occurs by natural or contrived means, by the time the fertilized egg reaches the uterus, it has divided several times and formed a spherical cluster of several dozen cells. This cluster floats in the uterus while it continues to divide. After seven to ten days it burrows into the lining of the womb and attaches itself. As cell division continues, fingerlike extensions, called *villi*, develop. The **amnion,** a fluid-filled sac in which the developing organism will float, also begins to form at this time. The amnion serves to protect and cushion the organism throughout prenatal development.

Amnion: fluid-filled sac

During the third week after conception, the villi multiply and interlock with the tissues of the uterus to form the **placenta** and the umbilical cord. The placenta is a membranous organ that lines the uterine wall and partially envelops the embryo. The umbilical cord emanates from the placenta and connects with the embryo at the navel. It contains two arteries and one vein that nourish the developing organism and remove its wastes. Up until this time, the fertilized egg has been sustained by its

Placenta: membranous organ that envelops embryo

Embryo: prenatal
organism from time
nourishment by
placenta begins

own yolk. Now it is nourished by the mother, and when this occurs, the
organism is referred to as the **embryo.** The mother's blood flows into the
placenta and the umbilical cord from arteries in the wall of the uterus
and provides food and oxygen to the developing organism. Consequently, alterations in the mother's blood stream may affect the development of the embryo. If the mother contracts a virus or takes a drug,
for example, her blood chemistry may be altered in such a way that the
process of cell division is distorted. The incredible sensitivity and complexity of the chemical balance involved in DNA molecules, which are to
produce trillions of cells, explain why an estimated one-third of all
pregnancies may miscarry. If there are abnormal genes in the fertilized
egg or if something triggers an incorrect sequence of chemical reactions,
the embryo of the villi or amnion may not develop properly, and growth
will cease. J. M. Tanner (1970, p. 89) estimates that 30 percent of all
embryos are spontaneously aborted, usually without the mother's
knowledge, because of such abnormalities of development. He reports
that chromosomal abnormalities are found in between 3 and 4 percent of
fertilized ova but in only .25 percent of newborn infants. These figures
indicate that 90 percent of all fertilized eggs containing chromosomal
abnormalities are aborted spontaneously.

If development proceeds normally, once the embryo is implanted in
the uterine wall cell division occurs at a rapid pace. It is during this
period that development seems most remarkable. Single cells of specific
types become recognizable as cell division continues. This occurs because the DNA in the genes leads to the formation of amino acids, which
in turn form proteins that cause the development of different types of
cells.

In the nucleus of each cell is a double strand of DNA. The genes are
specific segments in the strands of DNA. It may be helpful for you to
picture them as beads on a twisted double-stranded necklace. Before
each cell divides, the two strands of DNA unwind. Each strand then
directs the chemical synthesis of a new complementary strand, creating
two double-helical DNAs where one had previously existed. After this
process occurs, the cell is ready to divide into two new cells, each containing one of the two identical double-helical DNAs.

The information coded in the nucleus of the new cells must then be
communicated to the other parts of the cell. This function is performed
by **ribonucleic acid,** or RNA. There are three basic types of RNA. **Messenger** RNAs carry instructions from the genes in the cell nucleus to the
rest of the cell. The specific functions of any given cell are determined by
the proteins that messenger RNAs direct the cell to synthesize. **Transfer**
and **ribosomal** RNAs then assemble the amino acids necessary to produce these proteins. As cell division takes place, many specific types of

Ribonucleic acid:
(RNA) carries in-
structions, assem-
bles chemicals

cells develop and each type is characterized by a unique protein composition. What causes cells with identical genetic material to synthesize some proteins and not others—and hence to become one type of cell and not another—is a mystery that many researchers are currently trying to solve.

As the process of cell division takes place, the embryo begins to differentiate into three distinct layers:

The **endoderm** (inner layer), from which will develop the lungs, liver, and intestines

The **mesoderm** (middle layer), from which will develop the muscles, bones, circulatory, and excretory systems

The **ectoderm** (outer layer), from which will develop the skin, hair, teeth, and the nervous system

Three weeks after conception, the heart of the embryo begins to beat. It is not until about eight weeks after conception, however, that the embryo (which is now about an inch long) begins to assume a more or less human form. Most of the organs of the body appear during this period, and the development of the nervous system is especially rapid. From the start of the third month after conception until birth, the developing organism is called the **fetus**. During this period the organs and nervous system mature to the point where the fetus becomes capable first of activity and eventually of independent existence. The mother may sense fetal movements at the end of about sixteen weeks of development, even though the fetus is only about six inches long at this time. The organism is not likely to survive, even with elaborate hospital care, if born much before twenty-six weeks after conception.

Fetus: prenatal organism from third month after conception to birth

The Impact of Teratogens at Various Stages of Prenatal Development

The sequence of development just described takes on special significance when the impact of **teratogens,** or harmful agents (such as diseases and drugs), is considered. The Greek word *tera* means monster, and the term teratology originally was used to refer to the interest of early medical theorists in classifying physical deformities. Today, the science of teratology is concerned with understanding causes of abnormalities in development. Before knowledge about causes of abnormalities in prenatal development is summarized, the *timing* of the impact of teratogens on the embryo and fetus at different stages will be

Teratogens: harmful agents that may cause abnormalities in development

Weeks

3

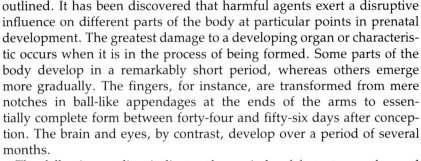

$\frac{3}{16}$ "

4

$\frac{5}{16}$ "

5

$\frac{1}{2}$ "

6

$\frac{5}{8}$ "

7

$\frac{3}{4}$ "

8

1"

(to scale)

outlined. It has been discovered that harmful agents exert a disruptive influence on different parts of the body at particular points in prenatal development. The greatest damage to a developing organ or characteristic occurs when it is in the process of being formed. Some parts of the body develop in a remarkably short period, whereas others emerge more gradually. The fingers, for instance, are transformed from mere notches in ball-like appendages at the ends of the arms to essentially complete form between forty-four and fifty-six days after conception. The brain and eyes, by contrast, develop over a period of several months.

The following outline indicates the periods of fastest growth—and greatest susceptibility to the harmful impact of teratogens—for different parts of the body. The drawings in the margins illustrate the appearance of the embryo and fetus at different stages of development. For the period of the embryo (third to the eighth week) the drawings represent the actual size of the developing organism. The figures under the drawings for twelve, sixteen, twenty, and thirty-eight weeks indicate length in inches. (Information and illustrations are derived from Moore, 1982.)

Period of the Ovum (Weeks 1 and 2)

Egg is fertilized and implanted; mitosis occurs at a rapid rate.

Teratogens do not appear to exert a specific negative influence during this period.

Period of the Embryo (Weeks 3 through 8)

Third week: Heart and central nervous system begin to form.

Fourth week: Heart begins to beat, even though it is "outside" the embryo's body; central nervous system develops rapidly; eyes, arms, and legs begin to form.

Fifth week: Heart, central nervous system, eyes, arms and legs continue to develop. Ears start to form; vertebrae of the back begin to appear.

Sixth week: Development of heart and central nervous system tapers off; eyes, arms, and legs continue to develop; ears and teeth begin to form. All vertebrae are laid down and a skeleton (of cartilage rather than bone) takes shape.

Seventh week: Heart becomes encased in chest cavity. Development of arms and legs tapers off; eyes, ears, and teeth continue to develop; palate and external genitalia begin to form. Buds that will become fingers and toes appear on extremities of arms and legs.

Eighth week: Development of eyes and teeth tapers off; ears, palate, and external genitalia continue to develop. Fingers and toes take shape rapidly. Face takes on human shape.

Weeks

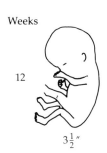

12

$3\frac{1}{2}''$

Because the various parts of the body are in the process of being formed between the third and eighth weeks, the impact of teratogens is greatest during this period. Organs undergoing their period of most rapid development at the time they are exposed to teratogens are most severely damaged.

Period of the Fetus (Weeks 9 through 38)

By the ninth week the fetus is about one inch long. Development of the ears, palate, and external genitalia taper off early in the fetal period. Brain development continues. Organs of the body, which are now more or less formed, increase in size. The fetus begins to use muscles at about the twentieth week. The eyes open and the ears become functional at about the twenty-fourth week.

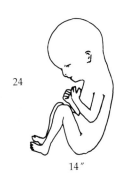

24

14''

Teratogens that exert an influence during the last twenty-five weeks cause minor structural abnormalities or restrict growth.

The same information can be summarized in a different way by noting critical periods of development for basic organs:

Central nervous system—third to fifth week
Heart—third to sixth week
Arms and legs—fourth to seventh week
Eyes—fourth to eighth week
Teeth and palate—sixth to eighteenth
External genitalia—seventh to twelfth week
Brain—third to thirty-eighth

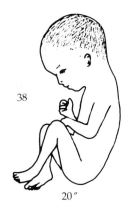

38

20''

In a survey of over fifty thousand pregnancies (Heinonen, Slone, and Shapiro, 1976), it was found that 6 percent of the babies were born with structural malformations. The researchers estimated that two-thirds of these were probably caused during the first twelve weeks of prenatal development either by genes or teratogens or both. The remaining one-third—37 different kinds of abnormalities found in 911 of the babies—were called *anytime* malfunctions because they could have originated at any time during pregnancy.

Teratogens may have a disruptive influence on the developing embryo and fetus by damaging chromosomes, causing mutations, interfering with cell division, or triggering biochemical changes. Whether exposure to a toxic agent actually leads to an abnormality depends not only

Impact of teratogens is greatest during period of embryo (three to eight weeks)

Impact of teratogens
depends on timing,
constitution, dosage

on timing, but also on the constitution of the embryo or fetus (due to genetic factors as well as the health of the mother), and the concentration or dosage of the agent. An expectant mother who is a heavy drug user, for example, is more likely to bear a child with abnormalities than one who uses drugs only occasionally during pregnancy. If two pregnant women consume identical amounts of a nonprescription drug, though, one may have a normal child, the other a child with some sort of birth defect. The constitution of one mother and/or her embryo may include an immunity that will counteract the agent, whereas the other mother and embryo may have constitutional susceptibilities to the same agent.

Factors That May Have a Negative Impact on Prenatal Development

Nutrition

After the placenta and umbilical cord form, the development of the embryo is sustained by the mother's blood stream. Therefore, factors affecting the mother's health also affect the health—or more importantly the development—of the embryo and fetus. One of the most significant factors in health is nutrition, and what the mother eats is of considerable importance. The significance of the expectant mother's diet first attracted widespread attention during World War II, when pregnant women in Europe were forced to live under conditions of near starvation. Analyses of reports from various countries (Keys et al., 1950) led to the conclusion that poor maternal diet slowed the growth of the fetus, particularly during the last four months of pregnancy. Evidence was also reported (Ebbs et al., 1942) that expectant mothers with poor diets were more likely than those with adequate nutrition to miscarry, have premature infants, or experience prolonged labor. Subsequent investigations carried out in the 1950s did not always corroborate the findings of the wartime studies. In an analysis of all research carried out through the 1960s, the Committee on Maternal Nutrition of the National Research Council (1970) concluded that it was difficult to separate diet from other factors, particularly when studying women from lower socioeconomic levels. Researchers (Cravioto, DeLicardie, and Birch, 1966) in Mexico, however, *were* able to control nonnutritional factors quite effectively. They found evidence leading to the conclusion that when both mother and child had poor diets, children were likely to be below average in height and weight and also earn lower scores on an intelligence test. Furthermore, an analysis of children who developed under prenatal and postnatal conditions of extreme malnourishment led Myron Winick (1976, pp. 16–17) to conclude that brain-cell division might be substantially slowed—to the point that the later intellectual capability of the child would be affected.

Despite the difficulties in interpreting inconsistent data, the Committee on Maternal Nutrition of the National Research Council concluded that there is sufficient evidence regarding the impact of nutrition to support the following recommendations (1970, pp. 132–133):

Women who expect to bear children should strive to maintain an adequate diet *throughout* the child-bearing years, not just during pregnancy.

As soon as a woman knows she is pregnant, she should seek advice from a physician or public health agency regarding proper diet while she is carrying the fetus.

An average weight gain of twenty to twenty-five pounds is considered reasonable and desirable during the course of pregnancy. Attempts to limit weight gain to less than twenty pounds may lead to malnutrition that could adversely affect both the mother and the fetus.

Routine use of vitamins during pregnancy is of doubtful value, and excessive use of a few vitamins (for example, vitamin D) might lead to fetal abnormalities. Some supplements (especially iron and folic acid), as well as vitamins recommended by a physician for special nutritional deficiencies, may be beneficial.

Diseases

It is now clearly established that if an expectant mother contracts certain infectious diseases during the first months of pregnancy, abnormalities in fetal development may occur. The best-known of these diseases is rubella (German measles). In some states laws have been passed to assure that all girls will be immunized against this disease. In other states a woman will not be issued a marriage license until she provides proof of immunization.

Other diseases that may lead to birth defects if they are contracted by a woman during the first three months of pregnancy are mumps, chicken pox, hepatitis, polio, diphtheria, and some types of influenza. If a pregnant woman has syphilis, her child may be born with congenital syphilis and suffer from brain damage as well as bone and liver abnormalities—if it lives. An expectant mother with syphilis can be given antibiotics that may prevent the spread of the disease to the embryo or fetus, *provided* she contacts a physician early in pregnancy. If a pregnant woman has active genital herpes at the time of delivery, the infant may

Poor maternal nutrition influences physical and intellectual development of child

Infectious diseases contracted by mother may cause fetal abnormalities

142

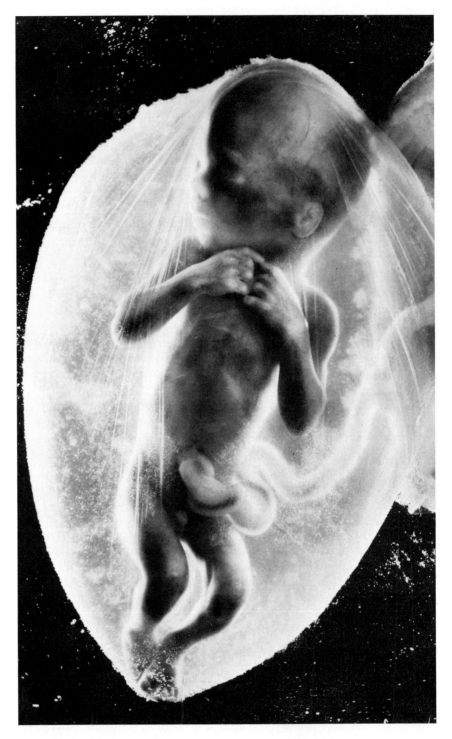

Four-month-old fetus.
Photograph by Lennart Nilsson, A Child Is Born *[New York, Seymour Lawrence (an imprint of Dell Publishing Co.), 1967. Used by permission of Delacorte Press/Seymour Lawrence.].*

contract the disease. More than half of all infants who are infected with herpes at the time of birth die or suffer severe damage. As with syphilis, medical attention during pregnancy and especially at the time of birth often makes it possible to protect the baby.

Even mild and seemingly innocuous diseases may lead to abnormalities in fetal development. Toxoplasmosis, for instance, a disease caused by a parasite often present in uncooked meat and in cat feces, may cause brain damage, hydrocephalus, epilepsy, or abnormalities in the eyes and ears of an embryo if the expectant mother contracts it during the first three months of pregnancy. About one out of every three or four women have had a mild case of toxoplasmosis earlier in life and are immune to later infections. A blood test can determine if such an immunity does exist. If it does not, the expectant mother should eat only thoroughly cooked meat. If she has a cat, she should have a veterinarian test it for toxoplasmosis, isolate it from other cats, feed it dry cat food, and have someone else empty the litter box. Whether she has a cat or not, she should avoid contact with cats.

Prescription and Nonprescription Drugs

In 1960 a West German drug firm placed on the market a nonprescription sleeping pill and nausea preventive called thalidomide. It was used by many pregnant women to alleviate morning sickness. A tremendous increase in the number of children born with deformities of the limbs, heart, and digestive tract led to an investigation, which revealed that the abnormalities appeared in babies born to women who had used thalidomide between the fourth and sixth weeks after conception. (Frances Kelsy, an alert member of the Food and Drug Administration, prevented the drug from being sold in this country. Some obstetricians, however, gave their patients free samples distributed by a company applying for the rights to sell thalidomide in the United States, and some Americans purchased it abroad.)

Despite the extensive publicity of the thalidomide tragedy and repeated warnings by public health officials in the 1960s of the potential dangers of other drugs, an investigation of over 150 expectant mothers completed in the 1970s (Hill, 1973) revealed that they were taking an average of ten different drugs during the course of their pregnancy, *not* including vitamins, iron, caffeine, nicotine, or alcohol. Although some of these drugs (such as aspirin and antihistamines) have not been *proven* to cause damage to the embryo, others (such as certain tranquilizers and antibiotics) *do* appear to lead to defects. The likelihood of damage to the embryo and fetus is increased if several drugs are taken at about the same time (Wilson and Fraser, 1977). The expectant mother who takes drugs may be able to reduce certain bothersome symptoms without suffering side effects. The embryo and fetus, however, do not yet pos-

Embryo and fetus
unable to break
down drugs taken
by mother

sess enzymes found in the liver of mature humans that break down drugs. Furthermore, because of the substantial difference in the size of the mother and the unborn child, the dosage of a drug is magnified many times for the embryo or fetus.

Other Drugs

Research on the possible adverse effects of marijuana use on fetal development is difficult to assess. For every study that seems to supply evidence that marijuana causes birth defects or chromosomal anomalies that might cause abnormalities in children not yet conceived, there is likely to be a study that leads to the opposite conclusion. (For a review of such contradictory studies, see Brecher, 1973, pp. 451–463.) A major difficulty in evaluating such research is that many individuals who use marijuana also use other drugs. Among possible negative effects of marijuana (Tinklenberg, 1975) that might influence heredity or prenatal development are damage to chromosomes, delayed genetic damage, fetal brain damage, and abnormalities in sex differentiation in male fetuses. Marijuana might also adversely affect the capability of the parents to care for newborn infants, if account is taken of the antimotivational syndrome produced in some marijuana users (who must make an effort to carry out even routine tasks) and the possibility that marijuana may intensify neurotic or psychotic tendencies. Many studies (for example, McGlothlin et al., 1970) of the impact of LSD and heroin on fetal development have proven inconclusive, largely because so many of the mothers who used these drugs also were heavy smokers, had extremely poor diets, and/or suffered from infectious diseases of various kinds. If a pregnant woman is addicted to either heroin or methadone, however, her child is likely to be born addicted. If the baby, often born prematurely, is not given the drug shortly after delivery, it may die of severe withdrawal symptoms (Harbison, 1975). Even if treated for withdrawal symptoms, infants born to heroin or methadone addicts are likely to be malformed in various ways. Because of severe respiratory problems, they are twice as likely to die within days after birth as babies born to nonaddicted mothers from similar backgrounds (Ostrea and Chavez, 1979).

If mother uses hard
drugs, infant may
be born addicted

Tobacco

Smoking and Health: A Report of the Surgeon General (1979) reviews over two hundred studies of relationships between smoking, pregnancy, birth, and the behavior of infants and children. The general conclusions are summarized in the introduction to the entire *Report*:

> The weight of the evidence demonstrates that smoking during pregnancy has a significant adverse effect upon the well-being of the fetus and the health of the newborn baby.

There is abundant evidence that maternal smoking directly retards the rate of fetal growth and increases the risk of spontaneous abortion, of fetal death, and of neonatal death in otherwise normal infants. More important, there is growing evidence that children of smoking mothers may have measurable deficiencies in physical growth, intellectual development, and emotional development that are independent of other known risk factors. Children of mothers who smoke during pregnancy do not catch up with children of nonsmoking mothers in various stages of development. (p. ix)

Smoking during pregnancy has significant adverse effect on fetus and baby

By 1984 evidence of the harmful impact of smoking on the developing fetus had become so conclusive that Congress passed a law mandating that a warning to pregnant women be printed on all packages of cigarettes.

Alcohol

It has been found (Hanson, Jones, and Smith, 1976; Rosett and Sander, 1979) that women who are chronic alcoholics have a much greater tendency than average to bear children with a variety of physical and mental defects. (This is often referred to as the Fetal Alcohol Syndrome, abbreviated FAS.) Furthermore, even when children of alcoholic mothers are placed in excellent foster homes, they do not seem to show noticeable improvement, suggesting that prenatal damage caused by alcohol is permanent. The possibility of fetal damage traceable to alcohol is not restricted to chronic drinkers. James W. Hanson (1977) reported that 12 percent of the babies born to women who consumed an average of two ounces of 100-proof alcohol a day before and during pregnancy were born with defects. Only 2 percent of a control group of women who drank lightly or not at all had similar defects. Two explanations have sometimes been proposed to account for such findings:

Excessive drinking by mother may cause permanent damage to child

1. Alcohol consumption decreases appetite, which may lead to a poor maternal diet before and during pregnancy.
2. Women who drink heavily may do so because they are tense, if not neurotic, and tension may directly or indirectly cause prenatal complications.

Even allowing for these qualifications, the negative impact of alcohol on fetal development is well established. A woman who has an adequate diet but also drinks excessively runs the risk of having a child who will lag in physical and mental development and perhaps be handicapped by heart, eye, and limb defects.

Radiation

The dropping of the atom bomb on Hiroshima revealed the potentially harmful nature of radiation. Several pregnant Japanese women who had been within a mile and a half of the explosion gave birth to babies with damaged brains and skulls. Alerted by this discovery, as well as by other evidence that was accumulating, medical scientists found that pregnant women who had received heavy doses of X rays, either for treatment of some kind or to determine the placement of the fetus in the uterus, gave birth to babies with malformed eyes and brains. Expectant mothers are now urged to avoid exposure to X rays. If an obstetrician desires information about fetal position, ultrasound, a technique that sends sound waves through the expectant mother's body, can be used to produce a picture that is equivalent to an X-ray plate.

Age of Mother and Number of Pregnancies

As noted in the discussion of genetic causes of abnormalities in the preceding chapter, there is an increasing tendency with age for a woman to bear a child with Down's syndrome. Beyond the age of thirty-five, the tendency increases sharply. Possible explanations for this tendency include overripe ova and hormonal changes, conditions which also may lead to abnormalities other than Down's syndrome. The proportion of babies born with abnormalities is also higher for mothers under the age of eighteen. Many teen-age mothers are unmarried and avoid seeking medical advice until pregnancy is well advanced. They may also have poor diets and be uninformed about the possible dangers of drugs, alcohol, and tobacco. Even if a young woman in her teens does make an effort to prepare herself for pregnancy and is given excellent medical care, she is likely to give birth prematurely and/or experience difficult labor. The reproductive apparatus may not be fully mature and some of the hormones needed for reproduction may not have reached optimum levels.

Infant defects more likely if mother is over thirty-five or under eighteen

First-born children may have a tendency to have defects for a variety of reasons. The parents may not be aware of possible genetic abnormalities, circulation between the uterus and placenta tends to be slower during initial pregnancies, the first-time expectant mother may be tense and anxious about the unknown aspects of pregnancy, and labor is longer. If a subsequent pregnancy occurs at least two years after the first, the likelihood of defects is reduced, but with every subsequent pregnancy after the third, there is an increasing possibility of stillbirth, prematurity, or congenital malformation (Apgar and Beck, 1972, p. 430). Second and third children born to a couple, therefore, should be least likely to have defects, provided the parents make an effort to take advantage of the knowledge and experience they acquired during the first pregnancy and birth.

Emotional Factors

If a woman experiences extreme or continued anxiety or unhappiness during pregnancy, there is a possibility that hormonal changes associ-

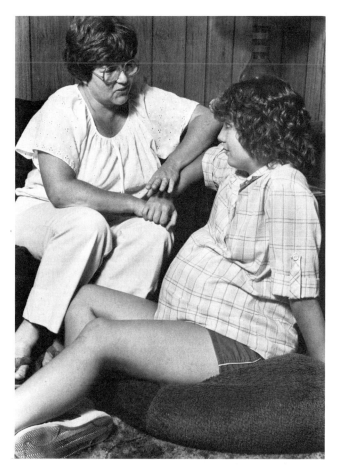

The proportion of babies born with abnormalities is higher for mothers under the age of 18 (and over the age of 35).
© *Tom Ballard/EKM-Nepenthe.*

ated with emotion may alter her blood chemistry (Sontag, 1941). If this occurs, the development of the fetus may be affected, particularly if emotional reactions are extreme within the first few weeks after conception (Stott, 1971). L. T. Strean and A. Peer (1956), for example, found evidence that a child may be born with a cleft palate if the expectant mother experienced emotional stress between seven and ten weeks after conception. (This condition might also be due to heredity or to the influence of a drug or virus at the critical stage of fetal development.)

R. C. McDonald (1968) concluded that emotional factors were most likely to be associated with abnormalities in fetal development when these characteristics were found in the expectant mother: extreme anxiety, high levels of dependency, sexual immaturity, and ambivalent feeling about pregnancy. McDonald noted, however, that many anxious women *do* have normal pregnancies and deliveries. He hypothesized that endocrine changes likely to cause complications in pregnancy and birth may occur only when a woman experiences a very high degree of anxiety over an extended period of time. Generalizing from animal studies, R. L. Webster (1967) has suggested that anxious mothers may eat less and that some complications of prenatal development may therefore be due to poor nutrition.

Extreme extended anxiety during pregnancy may cause complications

A factor to consider in evaluating the impact of prenatal stress is that a woman who is emotionally upset during pregnancy may be quite likely to feel the same way after her baby is born. Therefore, some abnormalities in infant behavior might be attributed to postnatal care, not to prenatal stress. This point is underscored by studies of colic in infants (Stewart et al., 1954; Lakin, 1957), in which it was found that insecure women who were unaccepting of their role as mothers were much more likely to have babies characterized by excessive crying and digestive upset. Maternal tenseness and anxiety during pregnancy is one explanation for the colicky behavior of the infants. Another possible explanation is that the colic was caused by the tense and anxious way the mother cared for the infant after birth.

Preventing Problems in Prenatal Development

This outline of factors that may have a negative impact on prenatal development can be used to call attention to preventive measures that can be taken. Perhaps the single most important guideline is for a woman to determine as early as possible whether fertilization has taken place by making use of inexpensive pregnancy tests available in drugstores, student health centers, and family planning clinics. Teratogens have the greatest impact on the embryo between the third and eighth weeks after conception, when the various parts of the body are being formed. In the absence of a test, a woman may not be aware that she is pregnant until well into the embryonic period.

First rule of prevention: detect pregnancy early

As soon as she is aware that she is pregnant, the expectant mother can take steps to promote optimum health and avoid exposure to potentially harmful conditions or agents. The following guidelines can be derived from the outline of negative factors just discussed. (Some medical authorities stress that, ideally, a woman should systematically maintain excellent health and avoid potentially harmful conditions *throughout* the child-bearing years. Some teratogens appear to exert a negative influence not just on an embryo or fetus, but on the genetic structure of the woman or her reproductive organs.)

To reduce the possibility of prenatal damage or complications the expectant mother should

1. take advantage of knowledge of good nutrition and of the potential dangers of certain types of foods and food additives.
2. protect herself against diseases such as rubella, polio, or toxoplasmosis through immunization or avoidance of infection.
3. avoid use of all drugs except those prescribed by a physician.
4. try to avoid, or at least severely limit, smoking and drinking.
5. avoid X rays.
6. plan to have children when she is between twenty-two and twenty-eight years old.
7. space children at least two years apart and consider limiting family size to three children.

Determining Fetal Abnormalities in Utero

Despite all efforts to avoid teratogens, a woman who knows she is pregnant may be exposed to conditions or agents known to cause damage to the embryo or fetus. If that is the case, or if there is reason to suspect abnormalities due to any of the genetic causes described in the preceding chapter, the prospective parents may request that a physician use a technique called **amniocentesis.**

The procedure usually is done between the thirteenth and sixteenth week of pregnancy. A physician performs **amniocentesis** by inserting a long, hollow needle in the expectant mother's abdomen to draw off some of the amniotic fluid, which contains cells shed by the fetus. (Sound waves are used to inform the physician how to insert the needle so that it enters the amnion as far away as possible from the vital organs of the fetus.) The cells drawn off from the amnion are grown in a culture and analyzed to determine the genotype of the fetus. By use of various tests, it is also possible to detect indications of various diseases, as well as the likelihood of respiratory distress that may occur at the time of birth. Amniocentesis is most useful, however, as a means for determining chromosomal abnormalities leading to such conditions as Down's syndrome.

If the analysis of the cells of the fetus indicates a chromosomal abnormality or if an expectant mother knows she has been exposed to a teratogen during the early weeks of pregnancy, the prospective parents may have the option (depending on their religious convictions) of considering an abortion.

Amniocentesis: analysis of amniotic fluid to detect abnormalities

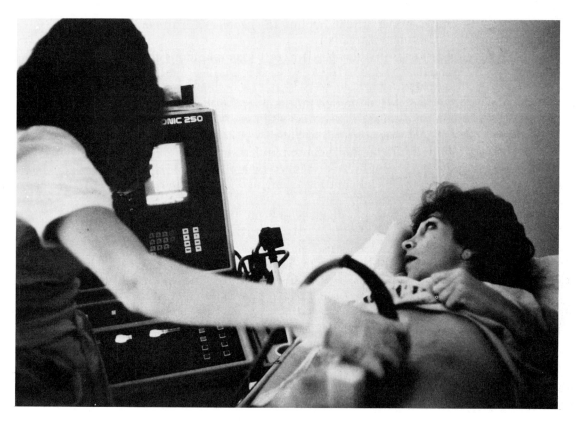

Because exposure to X-rays may lead to abnormalities in the development of a fetus, sonograms produced by sound waves are now used to provide information about the position of a fetus as the time of birth approaches.
© *Erich Hartmann/Magnum.*

Birth

The Birth Process

Position of the Fetus

Approximately nine months after conception, the fetus has increased in size and complexity from a single, barely visible cell to a recognizably human creature weighing about seven and one-half pounds. In order to accommodate itself to the uterus, this sizable organism assumes a position of maximum compactness, with the legs tucked up and crossed. Sometime before birth, most fetuses assume a head-down position, with the chin close to the chest, which favors passage through the pelvis and vagina. Some fetuses, however, assume a head-up position (called breech presentation) or even an oblique position (transverse lie). When the head (or rump) of the fetus settles into the pelvis, it is referred to as the *lightening* because the change in position reduces pressure on the upper abdomen of the mother and she experiences it as a lightening effect. This may take place gradually over a period of days or shift quite abruptly and noticeably. In a woman carrying her first child, it usually occurs two to four weeks before delivery. In a woman who has previously given birth, it may not occur until labor begins.

Labor and Delivery

The exact causes of the onset of labor are unknown, but it is apparently triggered by hormonal changes as well as reactions of the uterus when it has been stretched to a maximum point (Reynolds and Danforth, 1966, pp. 458–465). The mother becomes aware of these changes when contractions of the uterus produce labor pains. At first spaced about ten to fifteen minutes apart and of mild intensity, these contractions become more frequent and intense as labor continues. The beginning of labor is also indicated by the appearance of a clot of mucus that had formed a plug in the cervix and was released as the cervix dilated; frequently, the amniotic sac bursts at the beginning of labor. The duration of labor may vary from three to twenty-four hours and still be considered normal (Bryant and Danforth, 1966, p. 519), but the average time for first-born babies is ten to fourteen hours.

> Average labor for first-borns: ten to fourteen hours

   The placement of the body and head of the fetus is an important factor in determining ease of delivery. The opening in the mother's pelvis is usually an inch smaller than the circumference of the head of the fetus, but the skull bones of the fetus overlap in such a way that the head can be molded without damage to the brain. The size of the head is smallest when the fetus is in the head-down, chin-to-chest position, and the compression of the skull takes place most expeditiously in this type of delivery. Once the head slips through the pelvis, it must pass through the vagina. The tissues of the vagina have become softened during pregnancy and can be stretched to a considerable extent, but if the attending physician thinks they may be torn as the fetus emerges, a small incision (which can be easily stitched after delivery) may be made to enlarge the opening. (The medical term for this procedure is *episiotomy*.)

Natural and Surgical Adjustments to Facilitate Birth

The uterus seems to come equipped with a slowing-down mechanism that controls the size of the fetus and adjusts it to the size of the mother. If a small mother is carrying a child genetically programmed to become a

152

Stages of birth. During the first stage of labor the cervix dilates to permit passage of the baby's head from the uterus. Top left: *The baby's head is beginning to pass through the pelvic opening and is being slightly molded by the pressure. During the second stage of labor the baby begins passage through the vagina. Note how the head is beginning to turn toward the mother's back.* Top right: *The amniotic sac has not yet ruptured and bulges in front of the baby's head. The mother can speed the second stage of labor by tightening her abdominal muscles in concert with the contractions of the uterus.* Middle left: *The amniotic sac has ruptured and the crown of the baby's head appears at the outlet of the vagina.* Middle right: *Toward the end of the second stage, the baby's head emerges. Notice how the baby's body has turned.* Bottom: *As the baby's head emerges the contractions continue, the rest of the body slides out, and the baby is born. The third stage of labor, the delivery of the afterbirth (the placenta, the amniotic and chorionic membranes, and the rest of the umbilical cord) takes about 20 minutes.*

Reproduced with permission from the Birth Atlas, *published by Maternity Center Association, New York.*

6-foot 6-inch, 280-pound adult, for example, the rate of fetal growth is slowed during the last months of pregnancy. This built-in feature of prenatal growth was demonstrated by the mating of male-female pair and a female-male pair each consisting of a large horse and a small pony. The pair in which the mother was a horse had a large newborn foal; the pair in which the mother was a pony, a small foal. In a few months, however, both foals were the same size, and at maturity both were about halfway between their parents in size (Tanner, 1970, p. 91).

Many obstetricians use a specially designed instrument called the *forceps* to grip the unborn baby's head and help pull the child through the pelvis. Some doctors, fearing that use of instruments may cause brain damage, use the forceps only if the fetus appears to be in distress due to oxygen deprivation or pressure of the head or if there is prolonged labor. Other physicians make routine use of forceps during the final stages of delivery, particularly in first births. Proponents of routine use of forceps (for example, Guttmacher, 1973, pp. 217–218) argue that use of the instrument spares the fetal head from prolonged pressure and relieves the mother of much of the strain of the last stage of labor.

If the mother's pelvis is small or oddly shaped, or if the head of the fetus is large, or if uterine contractions are weak or absent, or if the fetus does not assume a head-down and chin-to-chest position (to mention only some of the reasons), the obstetrician may resort to Caesarean section (used in approximately 16 percent of all deliveries [Hausknecht and Heilman, 1978]). This operation consists of incising the lower abdomen of the mother, cutting into the uterus, and removing the fetus.

Use of Anesthesia

Depending on the mother's anatomy and attitude, the position of the fetus, and other factors, labor may involve considerable pain. Up until 1853, when Queen Victoria inhaled chloroform during the birth of her son Leopold (her seventh child), there was widespread opposition to any kind of pain relief during delivery. This opposition was due to the belief (promulgated by male theologians) that pain suffered by a woman during birth was punishment for original sin. (No doubt many women of earlier times wondered if God had been completely fair and had provided males with a sufficiently demanding way to atone for *their* original sin. Eve ate the apple first, but Adam also disobeyed, and his punishment consisted of working for his bread and putting up with a few thistles and thorns.)

During the 1590s a female resident of Edinburgh who had obtained a medicine to relieve pain during childbirth was burned at the stake by order of King James VI (Speert, 1966, p. 19) because she had violated the biblical injunction "In sorrow thou shalt bring forth children" (Genesis 3:16). If King James had given birth to nine children, as Victoria did, he might have felt differently about the matter. (He might have also listened to biblical scholars who pointed out that the word that had been translated "sorrow" might also have been translated "labor," leading to the implication that a woman was expected to *work* at giving birth but not necessarily to suffer pain.)

The first use of anesthesia for childbirth took place in Britain in 1847. James Young Simpson, the physician who used it, was widely and bitterly attacked but proved to be as adept at finding divine sanction for his view as his critics were in discovering biblical passages to uphold theirs. He pointed out that verses 21 and 22 of the second chapter of Genesis describe how the Lord prepared Adam for the ordeal of the creation of Eve from one of his ribs by causing him to slumber. Thus the only time in biblical history a man gave birth, he was completely anesthetized. Queen Victoria's use of chloroform effectively silenced much of the opposition in Britain and America (particularly since she knighted Simpson, who served as her anesthetist). As a variety of different anesthetics were perfected, some form of pain relief came to be used in most hospital deliveries, often to excess.

Natural Childbirth

Early Development of the Natural Childbirth Movement

In 1914 Grantly Dick-Read, a London physician, was called to assist a poor woman who was having a baby. He prepared to give her an anesthetic, but she declined it. After the baby had been born, he asked why she had not taken advantage of the anesthetic, and she replied, "It didn't hurt, it wasn't meant to, was it, doctor?" (1959, p. 7). The woman's innocent question stimulated Read to observe how different women responded to delivering a child. Some were obviously in need of an anesthetic, but others seemed to be remarkably calm and apparently without pain. He became convinced that for many women the pain of labor was due primarily to tension and fear aroused by stories of agonizing childbirth told by relatives and friends.

Natural childbirth intended to reduce tension in mother

Read gradually evolved an approach he called **natural childbirth.** In order to reduce tension in the expectant mother, detailed information about anatomy and physiology was provided so that she would be completely aware of the entire process of prenatal development and birth and of the emotional and physical rewards of relaxed and conscious childbirth. Training in relaxation, breathing, and general physical fitness was also designed to reduce tension and ease delivery. Read encouraged the expectant mother to think about managing the birth of her child on her own. He also recommended that the father play an active role in both prenatal preparation and delivery.

There was considerable initial resistance to Read's suggestion that pain during childbirth was not inevitable, but by the time the first edition of his *Childbirth Without Fear* was published in the United States in 1944, his previous books had attracted many followers. Women who had used the technique and successfully achieved natural childbirth were particularly enthusiastic and were eager to spread the word. It should be noted, though, that apparently only half of Read's patients achieved completely natural birth. Richard D. Bryant and David N. Danforth note (1966, p. 527) that Read is reported to have given an anesthetic to 242 of 481 of his patients.

Emergence of the Psychoprophylactic Method

At about the same time natural childbirth was becoming popular in America, a different way to reduce pain at birth was being developed in Russia. The Soviet doctors who developed the method began with the same assumption as Read—that pain was not an inevitable part of labor—but they used Pavlovian principles to explain how many women had been conditioned to be tense during labor. They hypothesized that stories of agonizing childbirth led women to build up an association between pain and labor. The Russian doctors reasoned that if pain *was* a conditioned response, replacing it with a different, positive response should be possible. In time, they developed what has come to be called the **psychoprophylactic method** (abbreviated PPM) to accomplish this purpose. One technique encourages the expectant mother to substitute a new response (breathing) for fear or pain when a uterine contraction occurs. By concentrating on breathing, the woman also inhibits awareness of pain, just as a skier competing in a slalom race might not be aware she has injured herself because of her intense concentration on completing the course as rapidly as possible. The PPM approach was adopted by the Russian government as the official method of childbirth in 1951, and it was introduced in France shortly after by Fernand Lamaze (1958), who learned of it on a visit to Russia. It was publicized in this country by Marjorie Karmel (1959), a young American woman who was introduced to PPM by Dr. Lamaze when she sought an obstetrician because her baby was due while she was in Paris.

Natural Childbirth Methods Do Not Always Eliminate Pain

In the years since the Read and PPM methods were introduced in this country, it has become apparent that some women *are* able to have painless childbirth. But as the statistics regarding Read's own practice of the method reveal, this is not true for all women, no matter how faithfully they follow instructions or how fervently they believe in the

Expectant parents learning techniques of natural childbirth in a Lamaze class. Husbands learn how to monitor stages of the birth process and provide coaching and support for their wives during labor.
© *Mariette Pathy Allen/Peter Arnold Inc.*

Natural childbirth may reduce, but not eliminate, pain

method. Consequently, some proponents of the technique (for example, Chabon, 1966) now stress that a woman *may* experience no pain but that in choosing natural childbirth she should concentrate primarily on taking an active part in the birth of her child and do her best to minimize the use of drugs and surgical intervention. Many obstetricians stress that a woman in labor should feel free to request or authorize assistance if she feels she needs it. Her own anatomical physiological characteristics, and those of the fetus she is carrying, may make it necessary to have the attending physician provide an anesthetic and play an active role in the delivery.

Preparing for Natural Childbirth

The term **natural childbirth** no longer refers only to the Read method but refers to any approach that stresses the preparation of the mother and father for childbirth and their participation in the process. For this reason many advocates of the method prefer the term **prepared birth** to *natural birth*. In practice, such approaches often combine techniques recommended by Read with aspects of PPM. Couples who elect to try prepared childbirth attend classes for eight to twelve weeks before the delivery date. They learn how the mother can control specific groups of muscles she will use during labor and how she can use different breathing patterns at different stages of the birth process. They visit the hospital and become familiar with the delivery room and the procedure that will be followed. The husband assists and coaches during the training period and also at the time of delivery. (The husband may assist in the delivery by helping his wife pace breathing patterns, spotting tense muscle groups, and timing labor contractions.)

Drugs Taken During Labor May Influence Infant

One of the major arguments offered by enthusiasts for prepared childbirth is that drugs taken by the mother during labor will have an undesirable influence on the newborn baby (Tanzer and Block, 1972, pp. 42–58). In a review of research on this question, Watson A. Bowes and several associates (1970) found that medication given to the mother during labor had a significant retardant effect on sensorimotor functioning of the infant for as long as four weeks after birth. The researchers concluded, however, that this was "transient narcosis" and that there were "probably few long-term untoward effects" (1970, p. 23). The baby may take up to four weeks to overcome the effects of drugs given to the mother because a dosage sufficient to anesthetize an adult has a much greater impact on a seven-pound infant, whose blood stream must be detoxified by the immature liver and kidneys (Brazelton, 1970, p. 2).

In a later review of studies on the impact of drug use, Yvonne Brackbill concludes that "the effects of obstetrical medication are *not* transient" (1979, p. 109, italics added). Brackbill later notes, however, that the most reliable studies she cites did not extend beyond the first twelve months. Her statement that the effects of drugs are "not transient," therefore, might be qualified by the phrase "up until the end of the first year." It appears, then, that her conclusion is not really in conflict with that of Bowes and his associates. Since there is the possibility that drugs taken at the time of delivery may have at least a temporary impact on child behavior, Brackbill feels that the mother, rather than the obstetrician, should make the decision about use of medication during labor. (She notes [pp. 115–116] that there is evidence that particular doctors and hospitals follow a "standing order" policy, where every woman who enters a delivery room is given a standard series of drugs at prescribed intervals.)

Final Stages of the Birth Process

Once the baby's head emerges, the physician checks to make sure the umbilical cord has not wound itself around the neck and, if this problem does not need to be dealt with, supports the head and assists the passage of the shoulders through the vagina. After the shoulders are through, the rest of the body emerges rapidly, and the moment the entire body is outside the mother's body is the official time of birth. Some physicians cut the cord immediately because they feel it is easier to care for the newborn baby in a crib. Others, who believe that it is desirable to make sure the baby receives all the blood in the cord, wait until the cord stops pulsating. (If the mother has received large amounts of drugs during labor, the cord may be cut as soon as possible to minimize the amount of blood interchange between mother and baby.) Once the baby is born, the placenta is expelled, often with the physician's assistance, and the birth process is complete.

Conditions during the final stage of labor and delivery may cause a shortage of oxygen (anoxia) in the fetus that may lead to damage of the cells in the brain stem (Teuber and Rudel, 1962), and some form of cerebral palsy may result. Brain damage may also be caused by delayed breathing, and if the infant does not begin to breathe spontaneously, a slap on the buttocks may be given or various types of resuscitation apparatus may be used. The functioning of the infant is usually evaluated with reference to the Apgar Scoring Method (Apgar et al., 1958) which involves rating color, heartbeat, reflex irritability, muscle tone, and respiratory effort. A healthy baby appears completely pink, has a heart rate over one hundred, grimaces and cries when the sole of the foot is slapped, is active, and breathes without extreme effort. (Thus, the **APGAR score** evaluates *Appearance*, *Pulse*, *Grimace*, *Activity*, and *Respiration*.) If the infant fails to meet one or more of the Apgar score criteria, the physician may supply various treatments depending on the diagnosis of the problem.

APGAR score:
Appearance
Pulse
Grimace
Activity
Respiration

Another highly regarded technique for evaluating the condition of a newborn infant makes uses of the Brazelton Neonatal Behavioral Assessment Scale (BNBAS), developed by T. Berry Brazelton (1973). A trained observer rates a neonate on factors such as neurological intactness, interactive capacities, social attractiveness, and need for stimulation. The Brazelton Scale has proven to be effective in identifying children who are rated high in terms of what is often referred to as a *continuum of reproductive casualty* or *reproductive risk*. These terms call attention to the tendency for certain types of complications occurring during the prenatal period and at birth to cause problems later in development. The Brazelton Scale was devised to identify children who seem likely to experience difficulties because of abnormalities that take place during the reproductive process.

In an analysis of reproductive risk, Arnold Sameroff and Michael Chandler (1975) conclude that four factors are frequently mentioned as likely to lead to later disorders in development: anoxia (oxygen deficiency), prematurity, newborn status, and socioeconomic influences. They reviewed studies of the later behavior and adjustment of children who were judged to be high in reproductive risk due to the influence of the first three factors and concluded that the effects of anoxia, prematurity, and low ratings on neonatal assessment scales often were overcome—provided the children were reared in middle- or upper-income homes by parents who did not manifest high levels of anxiety. Children who were reared in disadvantaged environments or by parents of any economic level who were rated high in anxiety were much less likely to overcome early handicaps. (Sameroff and Chandler note that there is evidence that many children of high-anxiety parents contributed to the insecurity of the parents because they were difficult to care for.)

Reproductive risk high in disadvantaged homes, when parents are anxious

Sameroff and Chandler support the hypothesis originally proposed by Conrad Waddington (1966) that humans come equipped with self-righting tendencies. They conclude, however, that these self-righting tendencies are most likely to produce a positive effect when the child is reared in a favorable physical and psychological environment. If the environment is poor and/or if the parents are unable to provide confident care, the child may be unable to overcome early handicaps.

Preterm Birth

Between 7 and 8 percent of all births in the United States occur before full term. The term *premature baby* is commonly used to refer to such infants, but many scientists and medical practitioners prefer the term *low-birth-weight infant* or *short-gestation-period infant*. Furthermore, it has been suggested (Kopp and Parmelee, 1979) that it may be helpful to distinguish between *small-for-dates infants*, who have low birth weights regardless of the time of delivery, and *preterm infants*, who are born before the expected date but whose weights *are* appropriate for their gestational age. The reason for this distinction is that low birth weight appears to be more predictive of difficulties in development than early birth per se.

Among the possible causes of preterm birth are maternal health and nutritional status prior to and during pregnancy; maternal age, height, and weight; weight gain; smoking; use of drugs during pregnancy; uterine problems; and lack of prenatal care (Bergner and Susser, 1970). Many of these factors are related directly or indirectly to poor economic and social conditions, and the percentage of preterm births is higher for disadvantaged mothers than for those from more favored backgrounds.

(For reasons to be discussed more completely in later chapters, it appears that low-birth-weight infants who are reared in good environments often overcome early signs of retardation in development [Sameroff and Chandler, 1975], but this may not be the case for infants who are reared in poor environments. Thus, it is important to consider home background in assessing the long-term, as well as the immediate, effects of preterm birth.)

Until the 1970s, investigation of the early and later development of preterm infants led to the conclusions (Crowell, 1967) that many of them were likely to be retarded in physical and mental growth, suffer speech difficulties, and have poor visual acuity. Starting in the late 1960s, however, detailed investigations of preterm infants revealed that such conclusions needed to be analyzed and qualified. It was discovered, for instance, that routine hospital procedures used with preterm infants often caused preventable problems. In the 1940s and 1950s, for example, many preterm infants were kept in incubators with high oxygen levels and low temperatures, fed on diluted formulas (because of imperfect methods of tube feeding) and handled as little as possible (to reduce the possibility of infection). In time it was discovered that excessive amounts of oxygen caused a type of blindness, that nutrients from the diluted formulas were diverted from growth to maintenance of body temperature (leading to near starvation), and lack of handling retarded physical, cognitive, and emotional growth. In the 1970s, excellent hospital care of preterm infants eliminated these conditions. Temperature and oxygen levels in specially designed incubators are carefully monitored, care is taken to supply an adequate diet, and the infant is physically handled (without having to be removed from the specially designed incubator) and stimulated at frequent intervals. As a result of such practices, the number of preterm infants who develop physical, cognitive, speech, or visual anomalies has been substantially reduced.

In summarizing research on preterm infants, Claire B. Kopp and Arthur H. Parmelee (1979, pp. 47–59) report that infants who are below average in weight for their gestational age and whose mothers come from disadvantaged backgrounds are most likely to exhibit developmental anomalies of various kinds. They also report that when satisfactory care is provided, preterm infants later appear to earn average scores on intelligence tests, but that boys, in particular, may experience problems in school. Finally, they note that there is often unevenness in some of the ways preterm infants mature.

It is not possible on the basis of available data to pinpoint the source of these various characteristics. In some cases behavioral anomalies may be due to the prenatal conditions or birth complications noted earlier in the summary of possible causes. In other cases, the way parents treat preterm infants may perpetuate, retard, or shape particular traits. Mary Shirley (1939), for instance, speculated that some of the characteristics of

Low-birth-weight infants from disadvantaged backgrounds most likely to experience problems

children who had been born preterm might have been intensified by the tendency for parents to be overprotective and anxious when handling such infants. And in some cases it appeared that the same parents later seemed to feel obliged to urge the child to make up for a slow start. (If such types of parental behavior do occur, they might account for some of the unevenness of development noted by Kopp and Parmelee.)

Views on the Significance of Life Just After Birth

A number of theorists have suggested that the moments immediately following birth are especially significant not only for the baby but for the parents as well.

The Alleged Values of Gentle Birth

In the mid-1970s Frederick Leboyer, a French obstetrician, attracted a substantial amount of publicity by emphasizing the significance of experiences at the time of birth. In *Birth Without Violence* (1975) Leboyer maintains that the bright lights and rough treatment that are features of many hospital births cause a birth trauma. (He backs up his argument by noting personal recollections of how he reacted to his own birth.) When Leboyer delivers a baby, he insists on dim lights and a quiet atmosphere. The emerging infant is handled with great tenderness and placed on the mother's bare stomach as soon as birth is complete. The newborn infant is then stroked and massaged until the umbilical cord stops pulsating and breathing is established, after which a leisurely warm bath is given. Many obstetricians have pointed to some possible disadvantages of the Leboyer approach, such as the difficulty of examining a baby placed on the mother's abdomen in a dimly lighted room. They note that potential complications might go undetected under such circumstances. Furthermore, researchers have presented evidence (to be summarized in the next chapter) that newborn infants do not appear to be neurologically mature enough to experience an emotional reaction such as the extreme trauma described by Leboyer.

It is difficult to assess Leboyer's hypothesis regarding the long-term impact of gentle birth. It seems likely that a selective factor operates when a woman requests that form of delivery. If an expectant mother has heard about the technique, either by reading Leboyer's book or by being told about it by an obstetrician who is enthusiastic about the method, she is likely to approach birth—and child rearing after birth—with a set of expectations. Therefore, if a baby delivered Leboyer-style later seems less disposed to develop emotional or behavior problems than a child delivered in the usual way, it is not possible to attribute such behavior just to the birth process. The same or similar interest in gentle handling, or a particularly thoughtful child rearing, may be manifested by the mother throughout the early years of the child's life.

Objective evaluations of the impact of the Leboyer technique indicate that infants delivered in his gentle style appear to be more relaxed the first few moments after birth than infants delivered in the usual way (Oliver and Oliver, 1978). The relaxed attitude of Leboyer infants might be attributed, however, to the soporific effect of the warm bath they are given just after delivery. In a carefully controlled study (Sorrells-Jones, 1982) twenty mothers were randomly assigned to Leboyer and conventional delivery groups. The mothers assigned to the Leboyer group were all ignorant of the alleged long-term advantages of gentle birth and later reported that they had assumed they were being treated like all other women giving birth in that particular hospital. As in the study just cited, Leboyer babies were calmer during the first few minutes after birth, but tests of reflexes, social responsiveness, and cognitive and motor abilities at three days, six weeks, and three months, revealed no differences between the two groups of babies.

Even if the *baby* may not be neurologically mature enough to be influenced by gentle treatment at the time of birth, it is possible that a more serene delivery room atmosphere might be beneficial to the mother (and perhaps the father, if he is assisting). Many women who gave birth in the 1950s and early 1960s (before natural childbirth techniques became popular) resented the sterile, impersonal, "baby-factory" atmosphere of some hospital delivery rooms. If they had looked forward to the birth of a child as a moment to be treasured, they were understandably bitter when doctors and nurses treated the arrival of their child as a routine matter to be handled in much the same fashion as the assembly of a stereo amplifier. It seems possible, therefore, that some (perhaps much) of the enthusiasm for Leboyer's book might be attributed to expectant parents' desires to make the birth of their child something memorable. Instead of assuming that a newborn baby is mature and sophisticated enough to be aware of subtleties in the way it is handled, however, it may be preferable to concentrate on the feelings of the parents regarding the atmosphere of the delivery room. That many parents of the 1980s *are* interested in the way their child is delivered is indicated by the number of books on the subject, as well as by new interest in home delivery, midwifery, and birthing rooms in maternity hospitals.

Gentle birth may benefit parents more than infant

The Alleged Values of Early Contact

John H. Kennell and Marshall H. Klaus (1976) agree with Leboyer that skin-to-skin contact between a newborn baby and both parents may

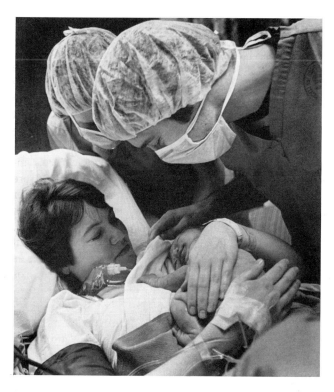

Kennell and Klaus hypothesize that if both parents have contact with a baby immediately after birth, the child will benefit in long-lasting ways. Evidence from carefully controlled studies does not support their early-bonding hypothesis.
© Milton Feinberg/The Picture Cube.

have quite remarkable long-term effects. They propose that if the mother has skin-to-skin contact with her baby within the first twelve hours after birth, and a total of sixteen hours of contact during the first three days, a mother-infant bond will be formed that will influence interactions between the two throughout the early childhood years. A similar, although less intense, bond may be formed if the father and the baby have skin-to-skin contact during the same period of time. Together with Diana K. Voos (Kennell, Voos, and Klaus, 1979) they offer what they feel is evidence that mothers who have early skin-to-skin contact during the first three days behave differently toward their babies than mothers who are prevented by hospital routine from having more than occasional contact (for example, only at feeding time). Early-contact mothers are reported to display the following types of behavior more frequently than limited-contact mothers: closer proximity to infants being examined by doctors, greater tendency to soothe crying, more eye-to-eye contact and more fondling at feeding time, greater tendency to breastfeed longer, and greater tendency to talk to their children throughout the childhood years. Kennell and Klaus hypothesize that because of the early contact, or of a clear parent-child bond established by early contact, or a combination of the two, the later behavior of children who enjoyed skin-to-skin contact the first three days is different from that of noncontact children. Extended-contact children were reported by the researchers to earn high scores on intelligence and language tests given when they were about four years of age.

Unfortunately, the research on which Kennell and Klaus base most of their conclusions is open to question. The subjects of the study that provides the most direct support for their hypothesis were a small number of largely unmarried, lower socioeconomic level black mothers and their babies. P. H. Leiderman, who collaborated with Klaus on early studies, points out that the mothers in this study received "specific and nonspecific social and psychological support from the institution and clinical researchers over the five-year period during involvement in the study" (Leiderman, 1978, p. 48). Thus, the behavior of the extended-contact children later in life cannot be attributed only to skin-to-skin contact during the first three days after birth. It might have been due to the extensive interest and support of the researchers and the continued impact this had on the behavior of the mothers as they interacted with their children over the entire preschool span of years.

Leiderman (1978) and several other investigators tested the Kennell and Klaus hypothesis with a degree of control. In a review of several studies of this type Michael Rutter and Norman Garmezy (1983) summed up the results in terse fashion: "Empirical findings have shown that (the Kennell and Klaus) bonding model is invalid and should be abandoned" (p. 779).

Even though the early-contact hypothesis of Kennell and Klaus may not be supported by evidence, parents who are eager to develop a close relationship with a new baby might try to arrange for both mother *and* father to handle their child shortly after it is born. The reason both parents might wish to be present at the birth of their child is that there is evidence (Parke, 1979) that fathers who participate in the delivery (as in the Lamaze method) and who handle newborn infants are often at least as nurturant as mothers. Parke reports, for example, that fathers who had early contact with a baby were just as responsive as mothers to the infant's signals and were equally adept at bottle-feeding. (It appears, though, that fathers seem to identify more with sons than daughters, particularly first-born sons. Parke summarizes research evidence indicating that during the first three months of infant-parent interactions

No evidence from controlled studies that early contact has a lasting impact

fathers vocalize more with boy babies and stimulate them more than girl babies.)

Prospective parents might make arrangements to try to have immediate contact with their newborn child by following natural childbirth procedures and by selecting an obstetrician who will cooperate. If circumstances and complications prevent immediate contact, however, parents who had hoped to handle their newborn baby might keep in mind this point: in most American hospitals in the 1950s and 1960s very few mothers had contact with their newborn children because the mothers were under sedation and/or were prevented by hospital routine from handling their infants except at prescribed feeding times. Yet many of these mothers must have formed a strong attachment to their children because there is no evidence that there was a marked decrease in maternal responsiveness on a large scale during those decades. It would appear, then, that early contact may encourage the formation of attachment between parent and child, but it is not essential.

Theorists such as Leboyer, Kennell, and Klaus may have stressed the importance of birth because it is such a dramatic event. Experiences that follow birth are less exciting, but they may be of greater significance because of two factors: the increasing maturity and sensitivity of the developing child and the accumulation of experiences. The nature and interaction of these two sets of factors during the months after birth will be discussed in the next two chapters, which are devoted to development during the first two years.

Summary

1. As soon as a sperm fertilizes an egg, cell division begins. About a week after fertilization, the spherical cluster of cells that has been formed as the cells divide and divide again attaches itself to the mother's womb. A fluid-filled sac (the **amnion**) develops as well as a membranous organ (the **placenta**) that envelops the embryo. The process of cell division continues as strands of the deoxyribonucleic (DNA) molecule unwind and form new cells. **Ribonucleic acid** (RNA) carries instructions and assembles chemicals that determine the function of each new cell formed.
2. The impact of harmful agents **(teratogens)** that may lead to abnormalities in development is greatest between three and eight weeks after conception (the period of the **embryo**), when the organs of the body are being formed. The impact of teratogens depends on which organs of the body are being formed at the time exposure occurs, the constitution of the embryo, and the concentration or dosage of the harmful agent.

3. Factors that may have a harmful influence on the development of the embryo and the **fetus** (as the fetal organism is called from the third month after conception) include poor maternal nutrition, infectious diseases contracted by the mother, and prescription, nonprescription, and hard drugs taken by the mother. Smoking or excessive drinking during pregnancy may cause a variety of problems. Extreme, extended anxiety may also lead to certain types of complications.

4. In order to minimize the negative impact of teratogens and potentially harmful practices, it is desirable for women to detect pregnancy as early as possible. A woman who suspects or knows that she is pregnant should maintain a proper diet and avoid drugs of all kinds. It is possible to determine the presence of certain defects in a fetus by analyzing the amniotic fluid **(amniocentesis)** between the thirteenth and sixteenth weeks of pregnancy.

5. As the time of birth approaches, the fetus typically assumes a head-down position, settling into the pelvis of the mother. The average time of labor for first-born infants is ten to fourteen hours. Many women favor natural childbirth methods, which often reduce (but do not necessarily eliminate) tension and pain.

6. As soon as the baby is delivered, it is evaluated with reference to the **APGAR** scoring method (*Appearance, Pulse, Grimace, Activity, Respiration*). Infants who have low APGAR scores, particularly those who are also low birth-weight infants, are likely to be rated high in reproductive risk. Such infants are least likely to overcome early handicaps if they are reared in disadvantaged homes.

7. In recent years it has been argued that infants will receive permanent benefits if they are treated gently immediately after birth and have skin-to-skin contact with both parents. Neither of these hypotheses is supported by scientific evidence.

Suggestions for Further Study

Conception and Contraception

If you have questions about the nature of conception and how it might be controlled, an extremely detailed analysis is presented in *Human Reproduction: Conception and Contraception* (1980), edited by E. S. E. Hafez and T. N. Evans. Less technical accounts of many of the same topics are provided in *Birth Control and Love* (1969) by Alan F. Guttmacher; *Birth Control* (1970) by Garrett J. Hardin; and *Woman's Choice: A Guide to Contraception, Fertility, Abortion, and Menopause* (1970) by Robert H. Glass and Nathan G. Kase.

Birth

If you would like more information about the process of birth, consult *Textbook of Obstetrics and Gynecology* (4th ed., 1982), edited by D. N. Danforth. A number of books have been written expressly for expectant parents. One of the best of these is *A Child Is Born* (1966), with a series of remarkable photographs by Lennart Nilsson and an informative text by Axel Ingelman-Sundberg and Claes Wirsen. Another excellent book of the same type is *A Baby Is Born* (1964), a simplified and popularized version of the *Birth Atlas* (6th ed., 1978), published by the Maternity Center Association. A list of exercises and a general set of guidelines for the expectant mother can also be obtained from the Association (Maternity Center Association, 48 E. 92nd Street, New York, New York, 10028). *Methods of Childbirth* (1983) by Constance A. Bean provides descriptions of several methods of childbirth, a list of childbirth education associations (by states, pp. 195–201) and an extensive bibliography. A comprehensive book written by one of America's most respected obstetricians is *Pregnancy, Birth, and Family Planning: A Guide for Expectant Parents in the 1970s* (1973) by Alan F. Guttmacher. A popular, inexpensive paperback is *Pregnancy and Childbirth* (1979) by Tracy Hotchner.

Prenatal Development and Care

Not so many years ago a common belief was that an expectant mother could influence the later development of her unborn child if she exposed herself to certain experiences and environments. (If a mother hoped her child would become a musician, for example, she would attend concerts and recitals during her pregnancy.) There is no proof that such a prenatal regime ever had the intended effect, but recent scientific discoveries have called attention to a number of factors and conditions that *do* seem to influence the development of a fetus. The most important of these have been outlined in this chapter, but for more complete information you can examine *The Child Before Birth* (1978) by Linda Ferrill Annis. *The Complete Guide to Pregnancy* (1983) by David N. Danforth and Michael J. Hughey gives complete and technical coverage of prenatal development.

  For practical suggestions regarding such matters as diet, exercise, and the like, see *Guide for Expectant Parents* (1969) by the Maternity Center Association; *Preparing for Childbirth: A Manual for Expectant Parents* (1969) by Frederick W. Goodrich, Jr.; or contact your local county health department for pamphlets published by such agencies as the Children's Bureau, Office of Child Development, U.S. Department of Health, Education and Welfare (Washington, D.C. 20201); the Public Affairs Committee (381 Park Avenue South, New York, N.Y. 10016); or The National Foundation—March of Dimes (Box 2000, White Plains, N.Y. 10602). (Addresses are provided in case you are unable to obtain publications of these organizations from a local source.)

Natural Childbirth

If you would like more information about natural childbirth, these books are recommended: *Childbirth Without Fear: The Principles and Practice of Natural Childbirth* (2nd ed., 1959) by Grantly Dick-Read; *Painless Childbirth: Prophylactic Method* (1958) by Fernand Lamaze; *Thank You, Dr. Lamaze: A Mother's Experiences in Painless Childbirth* (1959) by Marjorie Karmel; *Natural Childbirth and the Christian Family* (1963) by Helen Wessel; *Six Practical Lessons for an Easier Childbirth* (1967) by Elizabeth Bing; *Awake and Aware: Participating in Childbirth Through Prophylaxis* (1969) by Irwin Chabon; or *Why Natural Childbirth?* (1972) by Deborah Tanzer and Jean Libman Block.

Information and educational materials are available from these organizations:

American Society for Psychoprophylaxis in Obstetrics (APO)
7 West 96th Street
New York, N.Y. 10025

International Childbirth Education Association (ICEA)
P.O. Box 5852
Milwaukee, Wisconsin 53220

Maternity Center Association
48 East 92nd Street
New York, N.Y. 10028

You might keep in mind while reading books by some of the more enthusiastic proponents of natural childbirth that their commitment to the technique may lead them to select reports emphasizing the advantages of natural childbirth (when it is successful) and call attention to the undesirable aspects of delivery involving drugs and assistance by the attending physician. On the other hand, some obstetricians who are highly critical of natural childbirth give the impression that they may distrust the technique partly because the physician takes a subordinate role to the mother. Objective reviews of all available evidence on topics such as use of anesthesia during labor (for example, Bowes et al., 1970) provide a more balanced view than articles or books written by adherents of a given point of view.

Interviewing Parents About Childbearing

You might find it interesting to ask parents of different ages to describe their recollections about the birth of their children. For maximum value, try to get brief reports from mothers (and fathers) of different ages about obstetrical procedures used, as well as their feelings and attitudes toward the birth of a child. If possible, you might start with your grandparents or others of about the same age and work down to new parents in their early twenties. You might also find it interesting to get responses from recent parents who preferred an obstetrician who used "traditional" delivery procedures, as well as parents who chose natural childbirth. If you compare your interview responses with those of classmates, you could get firsthand information about trends in delivery techniques and also discover the range of differences in attitudes toward birth. You might ask questions such as these:

What are your recollections of the birth of your first child?

Did you select a particular doctor for a particular reason?

Do you remember your thoughts and feelings the last few days before the baby was due?

What was the actual procedure that was followed after labor began?

Did you feel that the doctor and nurses were sympathetic and supportive, or just businesslike?

What were your feelings immediately after the child was delivered?

What were your feelings the first time you held the child after the birth process had been completed? What were your feelings a few days later?

KEY POINTS

Are the First Stages of Development the Most Important?

Marasmus attributed to lack of mothering

Imprinting thought to occur during a critical period

Effects of early deprivation initially thought to be irreversible

Infancy thought to be a critical period because of rapid acquisition of abilities

Cognitive critical period hypothesis led to stress on preschool education

The Significance of Later Stages of Development

Years from six to ten seen as crystallization period

Erikson: necessary to "refight battles" during adolescence

Modifications of Thinking About Infancy as a Critical Period

Sensitive, rather than critical, periods

Well-cared-for children able to overcome severe early deprivation

Rejection of belief in a "magic period" in cognitive development

How Critical Is Early Experience?

Successful achievement of developmental tasks leads to happiness and approval

Academic achievement of elementary school children compared to that of others

Elementary school children often need to solve their own problems

Goodness of fit: fortunate meshing of child and parent characteristics at a point in development

Predictions of adult adjustment based on child behavior often inaccurate

Some Concluding Observations on Continuity and Change

Humans have an impressive adaptive capacity

CHAPTER

5

THE IMPORTANCE OF ALL STAGES OF DEVELOPMENT

*N*ow that you have some familiarity with genetic, prenatal, and birth influences on development, it is time to analyze changes in significant types of behavior as a human being matures, interacts with others, and is exposed to experiences.

There are two basic ways to organize a discussion of development from infancy through old age. The first is to discuss various types of behavior at succeeding stages of development: the first two years, two to five years, six to twelve years, and so on. The second is to concentrate on particular types of behavior (e.g., physical, cognitive), and compare manifestations of each type of behavior at different age levels. The age-by-age approach has the advantage of calling attention to continuities in the overall process of development and is easy to comprehend because it follows the actual pattern exhibited by a growing child. The topic-by-topic approach, on the other hand, calls attention to continuities and discontinuities in specific types of behavior. The reader can concentrate on one topic at a time and does not have to juggle several different types of behavior at once.

In an effort to take advantage of the strengths of each approach, the following chapters are organized to permit either (or both) an age-level or a subject-matter analysis. Chapters are arranged in sets of four for the following age spans: the first two years, two to five years, six to twelve years, adolescence and youth. Adulthood and later maturity are each discussed in a single chapter. These age divisions have been selected because they represent easily identifiable periods of development that coincide with turning points in a person's life (e.g., entering elementary school, entering secondary school). The topics discussed in each quartet of chapters (and in the final two chapters) are physical development, cognitive development, relationships with others, and personality development. This organizational scheme makes it possible to analyze changes in types of behavior and at the same time call attention to continuities. You (and/or your instructor) can examine the nature of development as it actually unfolds (by reading the chapters in order) or concentrate on age changes in particular types of behavior (by reading every fifth chapter).

For purposes of analysis it is essential to concentrate on one topic at a time, but in actuality all of the characteristics of a person are interrelated. The achievement of sexual maturity, to note just one example, has a pervasive influence on physical, *and* social, *and* personality development and also stimulates cognitive evaluation of what is happening and what it means. Thus the decision to discuss a particular topic under a particular heading must often be somewhat arbitrary. Simply because an aspect of development is analyzed in a chapter titled "Physical Development" does not mean that it is exclusively a physical phenomenon.

Are the First Stages of Development the Most Important?

Before embarking on an analysis of various types of behavior at succeeding age levels, however, it will be of interest and value to discuss—in advance—whether certain stages of development are considered to be more important than others. Before you read the next paragraph, mentally answer this question: Do experiences during the first five years of life have a more significant impact on behavior and personality than experiences at any other stage of development? If your answer to that question was "Yes," you are in distinguished company.

Varying Opinions About the Significance of Early Experiences

The belief that experiences during the first few years of life have a more profound influence on human development than experiences that come later has been expressed or implied by individuals from all kinds of backgrounds during all eras of history. Three hundred years before the birth of Christ, for example, Plato wrote:

And the first step, as you know, is always what matters most, particularly when we are dealing with those who are young and tender. That is the time when they are taking shape and when any impression we choose to make leaves a permanent mark.

Verses from the King James version of the Bible express the same view: "Train up the child in the way he should go: and when he is old he will not depart from it" (Proverbs 22:6). Poets such as Alexander Pope and William Wordsworth wrote "Just as the twig is bent the tree's inclined," and "The child is father of the man." Writing a century later, Sigmund Freud agreed with Wordsworth when he observed (1949):

It seems that neuroses are only acquired during childhood (up to the age of six), even though their symptoms may not make their appearance until much later . . . analytic experience has convinced us of the complete truth of the common assertion that the child is psychologically father of the man and that the events of his first years are of paramount importance for his whole subsequent life.

American psychologists also emphasized the importance of early experience, although for much different reasons than Freud. As noted in Chapter 2, most American psychologists have favored the learning theory view of behavior. The impact of inherited predispositions is minimized, and it is assumed that a newborn child is similar to a lump of clay ready to be molded. If that assumption is accepted, it follows that early experiences are particularly important since they determine the initial "shape" of a child's behavioral characteristics and personality. In his novel *Walden Two*, B. F. Skinner describes how newborn children are placed in the hands of child-rearing experts who shape desirable traits in a systematic fashion. The clear implication is that once shaped, such traits will remain essentially permanent.

Postwar Peak of Emphasis on Early Experience

Support for the hypothesis that experiences during the first years of life are more significant than those that occur at any later stage might be said to have reached a peak during the years following World War II. Several investigators with backgrounds in medicine, biology, and psychology independently called attention to the extreme importance of the very first relationship between infant and caretaker. Three of the most influential of these theorists were René Spitz, Konrad Lorenz, and John Bowlby.

Spitz: The Impact of Institutionalization

During the course of his duties as a doctor on the staff of a European hospital during World War II, Spitz noted a condition called **marasmus** (Greek for "wasting away"). Certain infants in pediatric wards were listless, apathetic, and unresponsive. In some cases their unresponsive behavior was so extreme that they refused nourishment and several died. When Spitz looked for causes of the condition, he discovered that all the infants suffering from marasmus had been deprived of contact with their mothers. In some cases the mothers had been killed in air raids; in other cases they had returned to war-related jobs immediately after giving birth. Spitz concluded that contact with the mother was apparently necessary for normal development in infancy and he decided to test that hypothesis. He found two groups of babies being reared in institution nurseries: infants in a prison nursery, who were cared for by their inmate mothers, or by full-time substitutes, and provided with an abundant supply of toys; and infants in a foundling home who were isolated in cribs and were handled only at feeding time. The foundling home babies displayed many symptoms of marasmus whereas the prison nursery infants, who received maternal care, did not. Spitz concluded (1945) that these results supported the hypothesis that early contact with the mother is essential for normal development.

Marasmus attributed to lack of mothering

Lorenz: Imprinting and Critical Periods

At about the same time as Spitz was describing marasmus, the Austrian ethologist Konrad Lorenz began to publish reports of his observations of bird behavior. Ethologists study animals in their natural habitats, and in the course of observations of newly hatched goslings Lorenz noticed a curious phenomenon. He discovered that the baby birds would adopt as their mother any moving object they happened to follow during the first few hours after they were hatched. Ordinarily, this moving object was the mother, but on a number of occasions Lorenz happened to walk past newly hatched birds and *he* was adopted as the mother. Even as mature birds, they would cluster around him and follow him wherever he went. This tendency for a specific type of behavior to be locked in at a particu-

Konrad Lorenz being followed by goslings who adopted him as their "mother" since he was the first moving object they saw during a critical period shortly after they were hatched.
Thomas McAvoy, Time-Life Picture Agency.

lar point in development is called **imprinting.** The fact that it occurs only during a very short period of time early in life led to use of the term **critical period** to describe when it occurs.

    Psychologists who read reports of the research of Lorenz and other ethologists began to speculate about the possibility of critical periods in human development. Some wondered if the findings of Spitz might not be related to the observations of Lorenz.

Imprinting thought to occur during a critical period

Bowlby: Impact of Institutionalization Seen As Irreversible

Spitz had taken motion pictures of the children he had studied in foundling homes, and when he showed these in a series of public lectures, a wave of interest in reform was set in motion. The British psychologist John Bowlby was asked by the World Health Organization to survey all available information on the impact of institutionalization. His findings (1952) supported the earlier conclusions of Spitz: children deprived of maternal care early in life exhibited symptoms of marasmus and were retarded in almost all aspects of development. Bowlby also concluded, on the basis of his initial interpretation of available evidence, that the effects of early deprivation were irreversible. Thus, it appeared that there might be a critical period in human development similar to the one that Lorenz had observed in birds. It was hypothesized that if children were not given maternal care during the first three years of their lives, they would never be able to recover. Bowlby's hypothesis called attention to the extreme importance of **attachment behavior,** often defined as the establishment of an emotional bond between infant and caretaker.

Effects of early deprivation initially thought to be irreversible

Arguments Stressing the Significance of Infant Capabilities

At about the same time that the infant-caretaker bond was being treated as critical, many researchers became fascinated with newly discovered capabilities of infants. They concluded that the first two years were a critical period not only because of early relationships, but also because of the rapid acquisition of abilities. An encyclopedic book titled *The Competent Infant* (1973), for example, contained over two hundred articles stressing the accomplishments of infants. In the introduction, the editors, L. Joseph Stone, Henrietta T. Smith, and Lois B. Murphy, offered these comments on the significance of the first few years of life:

Infancy thought to be a critical period because of rapid acquisition of abilities

[The] enormous thrust of the new comprehension of infancy appears on the verge of becoming—as we are convinced it should—a new and dominant focus for all of psychology. We are on the threshold of new concepts of what is universal in human development and of discovering ways in which human nature may be creatively and constructively shaped. We may discover in infancy some of the sources of vulnerability that make for later emotional disturbance or destructive defenses; we may be approaching the identification of specific events and experiences and relationships that make for later competence, confidence, and generosity. Without becoming Watsonian ("Give me a child for his first seven years . . .") or Skinnerian (Walden II [sic] manipulators, we may yet provide powerful information to guide wise parental choices and social decisions. (p. 10)

Several other books similar to *The Competent Infant* appeared at about the same time, and the editors or authors expressed much the same view as Stone, Smith, and Murphy. Michael Lewis, for example, observed that "The infant, although limited in its response repertoire, is a highly complex and sophisticated organism. And while growth characterizes all living things, the rapid rate of growth most characterizes these early years. At no time in its history will the human being again experience more dramatic, intense and dynamic change" (1967, p. 17). And T. G. R. Bower began a book on infancy with these words: "Few would dissent from the proposition that infancy is the most critical period of development, the period in which the basic frameworks of later development are established" (1977b, p. vii).

Speculations About a Critical Period in Cognitive Development

The provocative observations of Spitz, Lorenz, and Bowlby, as well as books such as *The Competent Infant*, led some theorists to speculate that the first years of life might be of crucial significance not only in the formation of attachment behavior, but also in the development of cognitive abilities. Benjamin Bloom (1964), for example, analyzed data regarding age changes in cognitive functioning and hypothesized that children achieve 50 percent of their adult intelligence by the age of four, 80 percent by the age of eight. Bloom also argued that if children lived in an impoverished environment for the first four years of their lives, they might lose as many as 2.5 IQ points a year and that this loss would be irreversible. Shortly before Bloom published his book, Martin Deutsch (1964) had reported that disadvantaged children showed gains in cognitive functioning after being exposed to intensive preschool experiences. The reports by Bloom and Deutsch appeared at a time when the Great Society program of the administration of President Lyndon Johnson was being planned. One of the goals of the Great Society program was to attempt to equalize educational opportunities. The hypothesis that deprivation early in life led to permanent decreases in cognitive development motivated the establishment of Head Start schools for disadvantaged children. Psychologists who endorsed the cognitive critical period hypothesis predicted that enriched preschool experiences, such as those to be provided in Head Start programs, would lead to permanent gains in intellectual functioning.

Cognitive critical period hypothesis led to stress on preschool education

The assumption that the preschool years might be a critical period in cognitive development led not only to Head Start and related programs for disadvantaged children but eventually to programs for early instruction for *all* children. A book titled *How to Teach Your Baby to Read* (1964) by Glenn Doman was widely purchased by upper- and middle-class parents, as was *Give Your Child a Superior Mind* (1968) by Siegfried and Theresa Engelmann. Engelmann and Engelmann described techniques parents were to use in efforts to speed up and expand the cognitive abilities (such as concepts described by Piaget) of their preschool children. In addition, the number of middle- and upper-class children who were enrolled in nursery schools increased with the publication of popular reports of Bloom's hypothesis about the critical nature of the first four years. Many parents seem to have believed that children who did not attend nursery school would be unable to compete during the elementary school years with those who did. Parental concern about preschool experiences was influenced by toy manufacturers who stressed (often in distorted fashion) Bloom's hypothesis about the crucial importance of the first four years. One advertisement for "creative" playthings, for example, proclaimed that "New research shows will to learn is established before the first day of school or it's never established at all" (*New Yorker*, October 3, 1964, p. 185).

Another outgrowth of the conviction that the first years of life functioned as a critical period in cognitive development was an investigation called the Harvard Preschool Project. This project, directed by Burton L. White, was funded by the Head Start Division of the Office of Economic Opportunity. It was designed to discover if certain experiences during the first six years of life could be structured so that children would be better prepared for schooling. White and his associates began their task by first describing the characteristics of six-year-olds who possessed overall *competence* and those who did not. After specific abilities leading to competence were defined, the Harvard researchers attempted to discover the kinds of experiences that led to these abilities by making detailed observations of thirty-four families: half selected because they seemed likely to produce competent children; the other half selected because they seemed likely to have children below average in competence. The way parents handled their children in the home was observed at length, and the abilities of the children were measured in a variety of ways.

After completion of the first part of the study, White and his colleagues concluded that the age span from ten to eighteen months is a critical period in development. The Harvard researchers believed that aspects of the child's own development and interactions with the mother during the critical ten- to eighteen-month period set the stage for all subsequent development. They hypothesized that "Much of the basic quality of the entire life of an individual is determined by the mother's actions [the first] two years" (White and Watts, 1973, p. 242). They noted three factors they believed make the ten- to eighteen-month age span so critical:

1. During these months, children develop their capacity for receptive language, which means they are able to engage in effective communication with others for the first time.

*During the late 1960s and early 1970s, many psychologists believed that infancy was
a critical period in personal-social and cognitive development and urged parents to
stimulate their children in particular ways. Later research, however, led to doubts
about the significance of critical periods. Accordingly, contemporary parents might
simply interact with their young children for the joy of it.*
Mark Antman/The Image Works.

2. Shortly after their first birthday, children learn to walk. Their ability
   to get around, coupled with insatiable curiosity, constantly lead them
   to get into things. The way the mother handles these dynamic ex-
   plorers will determine the nature of many subsequent parent-child
   relationships.
3. When children have explored their environment and interacted with
   others for twelve months or so, they begin to develop a clear sense of
   separate identity.

Thus White and his colleagues believed that competent children got
that way because of their treatment by their mothers during the first two
years.

After completing the first phase of the Harvard Preschool Project,
White wrote *The First Three Years of Life* (1975) to explain to parents how
they might foster competence in their children. (The book is composed
of descriptions of typical behavior, recommended child-rearing practices, and appropriate "educational" materials for age levels up to three
years.) In the concluding chapter, White observed that people fre-

quently asked him questions such as "Is it really all over by three? Isn't there anything else I can do? Can't I compensate for mistakes?" He then noted, "Answering these questions is rather difficult for me because to *some* extent I really believe it *is* too late after age three" (1975, p. 257). He qualified this statement by adding that the flexibility of human beings declines with age.

It should be abundantly clear by now that in the 1960s and 1970s there was considerable support for the hypothesis that the first few years of life were *the* most critical period of development. Not all psychologists were convinced that infancy was more important than any other stage, however.

The Significance of Later Stages of Development

The Elementary School Years as a Crystallization Period

Jerome Kagan and Howard Moss carried out an analysis of Fels Institute longitudinal data. They discovered that for many traits, elementary school behavior was a better predictor of adult behavior than preschool behavior. This led them to suggest that the first four years of school (the years from six to ten) are a critical period in development in that they

Years from six to ten seen as crystallization period

"crystallize behavioral tendencies that are maintained throughout young adulthood" (1962, p. 272). Thus, Kagan and Moss suggested that in some respects, at least, the elementary school years might be more significant than the first few years after birth.

Refighting Battles During the Adolescent Years

Two influential theorists with backgrounds in psychoanalysis have suggested that adolescence is perhaps the most important stage of development. If the number of pages devoted to different psychosocial stages in the works of Erik Erikson is used as a criterion, at any rate, it can be argued that he perceives adolescence as more important than any other period of development. He summarizes the significance of adolescence in this way:

In puberty and adolescence all samenesses and continuities relied on earlier are more or less questioned again, because of a rapidity of body growth which equals that of early childhood and because of the new addition of genital maturity. . . . In their search for a new sense of continuity and sameness, adolescents have to refight many of the battles of earlier years. (1963, p. 261)

The refighting of battles is so extensive, in Erikson's view, that the growing person does not establish a really significant sense of identity until the adolescent years—or after.

Peter Blos was the friend of Erikson who invited him to join in forming the private school in Vienna that was mentioned in the brief biography of Erikson in Chapter 2. Both Erikson and Blos eventually studied with Freud and emigrated to America. While Erikson was engaging in the various activities summarized in Chapter 2, Blos was practicing psychoanalysis with adolescents. At about the same time that Erikson published his first book describing psychosocial stages, Blos wrote a book on adolescence. In that work (and in subsequent publications), Blos suggests that much adolescent behavior can be understood by thinking of it as a "struggle to regain or retain a psychic equilibrium which has been jolted by the crisis of puberty" (1962, p. 11). He amplifies this statement by noting that "Late adolescence is a decisive turning point, and consequently a time of crisis" (p. 130).

Therefore, even when many psychologists were arguing that infancy was the most critical period of development in the 1960s and 1970s, at least some theorists were arguing that it definitely was not "all over by three." Since that time, a number of follow-up studies of research that led to initial support for the hypothesis that infancy is a critical period have led to modified interpretations. The nature and significance of these various studies and hypotheses will now be summarized.

> Erikson: necessary to "refight battles" during adolescence

Modifications in Thinking About Infancy as a Critical Period

The surge of support for hypotheses stressing that infancy is a critical period in development peaked in the 1960s. Evidence and analyses from a variety of sources soon led to modifications of many of these hypotheses, however. Ethologists concluded that observations of imprinting and critical periods were not as clear-cut as they had first seemed (Lorenz, 1970, pp. 124–132). After reviewing many studies of imprinting, Robert Hinde (1963, 1983) suggested that it might be preferable to substitute the term **sensitive period** for *critical period*. Hinde joined other students of animal behavior in stressing the point that experiences occurring early in life involve **probabilities** that certain forms of learning may take place. There is a *tendency* for some species of birds to imprint an attachment to another bird, person, or moving object they follow around a few hours after they hatch, but such learning does not always occur.

(While most ethologists and psychologists have become cautious about generalizing from the results of imprinting studies, some theorists

> Sensitive, rather than critical, periods

still believe that imprinting during critical periods may occur in human development. The hypothesis of Klaus and Kennell that skin-to-skin contact during the first few hours after birth will produce a long-lasting attachment bond is a case in point. As noted at the end of the preceding chapter, however, evidence that leads to doubts about the validity of the Klaus and Kennell hypothesis is stronger than evidence in support of it.)

A number of investigators, including Bowlby, who had originally concluded that the impact of institutionalization was irreversible, made additional observations and reported that in some cases infants deprived of maternal care displayed essentially normal development when placed in supportive home environments. (Reviews of such research are provided by Thompson and Grusec, 1970, and Rutter, 1972, 1979.) Some of these researchers suggested that retarded development in institutionalized children was not due exclusively to lack of mothering (and attachment) but to lack of stimulation. That is, the children were not given many opportunities to explore their environment, nor did they receive very many responses from caretakers. When they were placed in stimulating environments and given supportive and responsive care, they overcame deficiencies in development (Clarke and Clarke, 1976).

Initial enthusiasm for discoveries of unexpected capabilities of infants that had contributed (along with research on critical periods) to the belief in infancy as *the* most important stage of development was moderated. Jerome Kagan, for instance, who had joined with Howard Moss in the early 1960s in pointing out that behavior during the elementary school years was a much better predictor of adult behavior than traits exhibited in infancy, reaffirmed that judgment (1971). Several other psychologists (e.g., Sameroff, 1974, Kessen, 1979) reviewed available longitudinal research and agreed with Kagan that there is little evidence that experiences in infancy have an unchangeable influence on later behavior.

The hypothesis that there is a critical period in cognitive development was also revised as evaluations of the impact of early educational experiences were reported. In a summary of follow-up studies of Head Start programs presented in the Report of the U.S. Commission on Civil Rights, for instance, this conclusion was noted: "None of the compensatory education programs appears to have raised significantly the achievement of participating pupils within the period evaluated by the Commission" (1967, p. 138). Thus, the hypothesis that enriched experiences during a hypothetical cognitive critical period would lead to substantial increases in intelligence was not supported. Furthermore, Benjamin Bloom (1968) revised his original view regarding irreversibility of IQ losses and observed that while experiences during the preschool years are important, change may take place later. Although Burton White still

Well-cared-for children able to overcome severe early deprivation

During the 1960s many parents sent their children to nursery schools because of the belief that the preschool years were a critical period in cognitive development. Subsequent research led to the conclusion that there is no "magic period" of intellectual development.
© *Elizabeth Crews.*

maintained in 1975 that it may be "all over by the age of three," other specialists in childhood education who published reports around the same time no longer supported the critical period hypothesis. For example, E. Zigler, who was director of Head Start for a number of years, noted:

I, for one, am tired of the past decade's scramble to discover some magic period during which interventions will have particularly great pay-offs. . . . My own predilection is that we cease this pointless search for magic periods and adopt

Rejection of belief in a "magic period" in cognitive development

instead the view that the developmental process is a continuous one, in which every segment of the life cycle from conception through maturity is of crucial importance and requires certain environmental nutrients. (1975)

Furthermore, twelve psychologists who made up the Consortium on Developmental Continuity, Education Commission of the States, and who directed different types of programs for disadvantaged children, prepared a report titled *The Persistence of Preschool Effects.* Toward the end of the report they express the opinion that "there is as of now no indication of a 'magic age' at which early intervention is most effective." (1977, p. 108)

In a follow-up report published seven years later (Murray et al., 1984), members of the Consortium noted that children who had attended preschool programs did seem to have received long-term benefits from the experience. The authors of the report reaffirmed the Civil Rights Commission conclusion that no permanent increases in IQ scores resulted from preschool attendance, but they noted other evidence of positive influence. Children who had attended preschool programs were less likely than control children to fail a grade or be placed in special classes. Since preschool experience did not seem to have produced permanent improvement in intellectual functioning, the superior academic performance of the children must have been due to factors other than intelligence. At the end of their report, the Consortium members supply an explanation. They note that "Program mothers' aspirations for their children were higher than the children's aspirations for themselves, while this pattern was not evident for the controls. Program children were 'proud of' achievement-related actions more often than control children" (p. 488). It seems reasonable to conclude, therefore, that the superior academic performance of children who had attended preschool compared to those who had not was due to a desire to achieve experienced by the children because they were selected for preschool instruction and reinforced by their mothers. Thus, the improvement was apparently *not* due to early experiences that enhanced cognitive functioning during a critical period, but to attitudes toward schooling that were established as a result of preschool attendance. A similar explanation can be applied to other reports of the long-term positive impact of preschool experience (e.g., Weikart and Schweinhart, 1984).

How Critical Is Early Experience?

Before proceeding, it will be instructive to summarize points emphasized so far in this chapter.

1. Since before the time of Christ, the assumption that early experiences substantially shape later behavior has been almost universally accepted.
2. Belief in the importance of experiences during the first months and years of life reached a peak in the 1960s, partly as an outgrowth of reports of the impact of institutionalization and speculations about critical periods, partly because of discovery of unexpected infant capabilities.
3. As initial conclusions about infancy as a critical period were evaluated, doubts about the long-term impact of early experience began to be expressed. A tempering of enthusiasm about infant competencies also occurred. Types of behavior observed in infancy rarely were found to be predictive of behavior in childhood and adulthood. Some theorists suggested that the elementary school or adolescent years might be more important stages of development than the first few years. Evidence accumulated revealing that children often were able to overcome the effects of extreme deprivation suffered early in life.

As you read the last few points just listed it is possible that you might have found yourself thinking, "Are you trying to tell me that the way children are treated the first years of their lives isn't of vital importance?" If so, your reaction was similar to that of psychologists who had devoted their professional lives to the study of infant behavior.

Differing Views on the Significance of Early Experience

When they became aware that a number of psychologists were suggesting that experiences that occur later in life may "cancel" those that occur during the first few years, researchers who had specialized in studying infant behavior felt compelled to disagree. L. Alan Sroufe, for instance, noted that "What children experience, early and later, makes a difference. We cannot assume that early experience will somehow be cancelled out by later experience" (1979, p. 840). Michael Lewis and Mark Starr summed up a review of longitudinal research with this statement, "Our answer (to the question "Does childhood show the man?") is both that in principle childhood does show the man and that this principle is not open to denial by fact. Rather the continuous nature of development should be taken as a premise" (1979, p. 668). It seems fair to rephrase the observations of Sroufe, Lewis, and Starr in this way: we should assume that early experiences are important even though we cannot prove it on the basis of current research evidence.

By stressing the importance of later stages of development, though, psychologists such as Kagan and Moss and Erikson and Blos ask, in effect, "Why *can't* we assume that early experience will somehow be cancelled out—at least in part—by later experience?" To draw your own conclusions about the possibility that later experiences may have at least as significant an impact on certain types of behavior as experiences during the first few years, consider the developmental tasks individuals are expected to achieve at different ages in our society.

The Nature of Developmental Tasks

Successful achieve-
ment of develop-
mental tasks leads
to happiness and
approval

Robert J. Havighurst was impressed by Erikson's analysis of stages of psychosocial development, but he concluded that the same basic rationale could be applied in a different way to shed light on other facets of development. Erikson describes stages in terms of positive and negative qualities; Havighurst lists what he calls developmental tasks for different age levels. Havighurst defines developmental tasks as tasks that arise "at or about a certain period in the life of an individual, successful achievement of which leads to his happiness and to success with later tasks, while failure leads to unhappiness in the individual, disapproval by the society, and difficulty with later tasks" (1952, p. 2).

Havighurst's developmental tasks for different stages of development are listed below.

Infancy
1. Learning to walk
2. Learning to take solid foods
3. Learning to talk
4. Learning to control the elimination of body wastes

Early Childhood
1. Learning sex differences and sexual modesty
2. Achieving physiological stability
3. Forming simple concepts of social and physical reality
4. Learning to relate oneself emotionally to parents, siblings, and other people
5. Learning to distinguish right and wrong and developing a conscience

Middle Childhood
1. Learning physical skills necessary for ordinary games
2. Building wholesome attitudes toward oneself as a growing organism
3. Learning to get along with age-mates
4. Learning an appropriate masculine or feminine social role

5. Developing fundamental skills in reading, writing, and calculating
6. Developing concepts necessary for everyday living
7. Developing conscience, morality, and a scale of values
8. Achieving personal independence
9. Developing attitudes toward social groups and institutions

Adolescence
1. Achieving new and more mature relations with age-mates of both sexes
2. Achieving a masculine or feminine social role
3. Accepting one's physique and using the body effectively
4. Achieving emotional independence of parents and other adults
5. Achieving assurance of economic independence
6. Selecting and preparing for an occupation
7. Preparing for marriage and family life
8. Developing intellectual skills and concepts necessary for civic competence
9. Desiring and achieving socially responsible behavior
10. Acquiring a set of values and an ethical system as a guide to behavior

Early Adulthood
1. Selecting a mate
2. Learning to live with a marriage partner
3. Starting a family
4. Rearing children
5. Managing a home
6. Getting started in an occupation
7. Taking on civic responsibility
8. Finding a congenial social group

Middle Age
1. Achieving adult civic and social responsibility
2. Establishing and maintaining an economic standard of living
3. Assisting teen-age children to become responsible and happy adults
4. Developing adult leisure-time activities
5. Relating oneself to one's spouse as a person
6. Accepting and adjusting to the physiological changes of middle age
7. Adjusting to aging parents

Later Maturity
1. Adjusting to decreasing physical strength and health
2. Adjusting to retirement and reduced income
3. Adjusting to death of spouse
4. Establishing an explicit affiliation with one's age group
5. Meeting social and civic obligations
6. Establishing satisfactory physical living arrangements

Havighurst published his list of developmental tasks in 1952, which accounts for the possibility that some of them may have impressed you as a bit outdated. It is not as easy to define "appropriate" sex roles today, for example, as it was in 1952. In the 1980s, approximately half of all high school graduates go on to college, so "achieving economic independence" is no longer a task of adolescence for many young Americans. And changing attitudes toward marriage and the family have altered the meaning of some of the tasks for early adulthood, e.g., "selecting a mate." Even so, the developmental tasks as described provide an excellent overview of important aspects of development and make it possible to draw some inferences about the possibility that later experiences may have at least as significant an impact on certain types of behavior as experiences during the first few years. If you will compare the tasks for infancy with those of adolescence and adulthood, for instance, you may detect possible explanations why the behavior of infants is not predictive of later behavior. The kinds of attributes needed for walking, talking, and learning toilet control are obviously much different from those needed for learning social roles or developing a conscience. To grasp why Kagan and Moss referred to the elementary school years as a "crystallization period," examine the following comparison of the developmental tasks for early and middle childhood. (The analysis is organized with reference to tasks listed by Havighurst for the elementary school years.)

Differences Between Tasks for Early and Middle Childhood

Building a Wholesome Attitude Toward Oneself

The self-concept of the preschool child centers on the formation of feelings of autonomy and initiative (to focus on the qualities stressed by Erikson). The independence of the preschooler develops, however, in the protective atmosphere of the home, immediate neighborhood, and perhaps a nursery school. A child's self-concept is influenced by the reactions of parents (and perhaps nursery school teachers) who are typically sympathetic and supportive and eager to foster positive traits. Furthermore, because developmental changes during the preschool years are often rapid and dramatic, parents may focus on recent attainments and overlook inadequacies, attributing them to immaturity and assuming that they will disappear with age. The preschool child's self-concept is also somewhat "insulated" because of egocentric thinking. Children below the age of five are not acutely aware of the feelings or responses of others and may therefore fail to comprehend (except in

There are significant differences between the developmental tasks of preschool and elementary school children. Preschoolers, for instance, spend considerable time engaging in relaxing free play. Elementary school pupils, in contrast, are expected to concentrate on mastering academic assignments.
Michael Weisbrot and Family. © Elizabeth Crews.

extreme instances) when their behavior is reacted to negatively by others.

By contrast, the self-concept of the elementary school child centers on the establishment of a sense of industry. Failure to experience a sense of industry leads to inferiority, which is likely to be a more pervasive cause of feelings of inadequacy than doubt or guilt experienced by a preschool child. Unlike autonomy and initiative, which are largely shaped by the reactions of parents, a child's conception of his or her ability to work by and with others is also influenced to a significant extent by the reactions of peers and teachers. Teachers, who must divide their attention among twenty to thirty pupils and who must maintain control of the class and also demonstrate their ability to foster learning, are not as likely as parents to be tolerant and sympathetic when confronted by unsatisfactory behavior. The self-concept of the elementary school child is not only increasingly influenced by the reactions of peers but also by classmates' academic and social abilities. Elementary school children, along with their parents and teachers, become concerned about how well they perform compared to others. As children move through the elementary grades they become progressively capable of socialized thinking. Greater awareness of the feelings of others may lead to previously unrecognized feelings of rejection and embarrassment and perhaps erode the self-confidence that had been established during the preschool years.

Mastery of Basic Academic Subjects

The preschool child is rarely expected to complete formal assignments involving academic skills. Even more rarely is the performance of a preschool child on almost any kind of task publicly compared to the performance of others: If a preschool child "fails" some undertaking, parents and nursery school teachers are likely to respond with sympathy, support, and encouragement.

The elementary school child is expected to master certain prescribed academic tasks. Depending on the school, the teacher, and the grade level, the child might be expected to work more or less independently. Success is likely to be determined as often by comparison to the achievements of others as by evaluation of improvement over each child's previous performance. Failure to do as well as others may be reacted to by teachers or parents with disappointment (or even punishment), and encouragement to improve may involve pressures of various kinds (for example, the promise of money or a gift for higher grades).

Academic achievement of elementary school children compared to that of others

Getting Along with Age-mates

The preschool child almost always plays with age-mates under the surveillance, if not supervision, of parents or nursery school teachers. When children experience problems in getting along with others, they are likely to arouse a supportive rather than a critical response from adults. Interactions with other children are not very complex and involve the assignment of temporary rather than stable roles. And as was the case with the formation of a self-concept, the egocentric thinking of preschoolers at least partially insulates them from subtle negative responses from others.

The elementary school child engages for the first time in frequent unsupervised play with age-mates. The protected play atmosphere of backyard or nursery school is replaced by more of a "law of the jungle" atmosphere when children are on their own. The games and pastimes that elementary school children participate in with peers are complex and often lead to the assignment of quite stable roles that highlight differences between individuals (for example, the child who is chosen captain of a team versus the child who is the last one picked when choosing sides). The acquisition of socialized thinking causes elementary school children to become aware of how others react to them, and they may become very much concerned about how popular they are with others.

Learning an Appropriate Sex Role

The preschool child is just beginning to become aware of sex roles and is not concerned or self-conscious about behaving in sex-inappropriate ways or of participating in activities with members of the opposite sex. If the family has been disrupted by divorce or if the mother works, children of this age are not likely to suffer in their relations with peers.

Elementary school children become increasingly aware of sex-appropriate behavior. (They may or may not favor revised conceptions of the liberated female, depending on the attitudes of the parents and the family situation.) Because of greater awareness of the thoughts of others (due to socialized thinking), they may be concerned about how peers respond to sex-inappropriate behavior (for example, a boy may be upset if he is called a sissy). Lack of a male model in father-absent homes may have a significant impact on the behavior, maturity, and academic performance of boys during this age span. If the mother works, the independence and academic achievement of both boys and girls may be influenced.

Learning Skills Necessary for Games

Preschool children typically engage in loosely organized games and quite often children of different ages participate. As a consequence, differences in skill are difficult to evaluate and may not be of any significance. There may be more stress on fantasy, imagination, and getting along with others than on actual physical skills.

Elementary school children frequently engage in competitive games, and by the middle grades they may be involved in Little League or similar adult-directed sports activities. Athletic skill, for boys in particular, may be the single most important factor in determining acceptance by peers. Differences in the athletic prowess of children become clear and are magnified by the reactions of parents to the performance of children in organized competitive sports.

Development of Conscience and Morality

Preschool children develop only rudimentary understanding of moral codes. If they break rules or behave in immoral ways, their behavior may be excused by adults and attributed to immaturity. Since children at this age are egocentric thinkers, they are not likely to grasp how much they may hurt someone else's feelings by thoughtless behavior.

Elementary school children are expected to learn and abide by the laws and regulations of society, community, and school and to honor rules when they play with age-mates. If they break a law, or ignore a school regulation, or fail to comply with the rules of a game, they may be punished or ostracized. Growing sensitivity to the feelings of others may lead to guilt about behavior that causes distress to others.

Achieving Personal Independence

Many parents do their best to promote competence and independence in preschool children. The competence of the young child is evaluated, however, largely in terms of individual performance in protected and supervised home and nursery school settings. Because preschoolers function in quite circumscribed environments, parents and teachers can often manipulate circumstances to suit the child. (If a four-year-old boy dislikes his nursery school teacher, for instance, or if he is bullied by an older pupil in the school, the parents can easily arrange for him to attend a different school.)

The elementary school child is expected to achieve most of the developmental tasks that have just been discussed outside of the home, either in school classrooms or in interactions with peers. Accordingly, it may be difficult or impossible for parents to manipulate circumstances in efforts to improve a problem. (A fourth-grade boy who doesn't like his teacher, for example, will probably just have to put up with him or her for nine months. And if a bully asserts himself in out-of-school situations, a victim may despair about finding ways to avoid intimidation.) Elementary school children must learn to become independent in the strict sense of that word—they have to learn to make many of their own adjustments and solve many of their own problems.

Elementary school children often need to solve their own problems

This analysis of differences between the developmental tasks faced by individuals at two early stages of development calls attention to the different kinds of demands made at different age levels. Since demands differ, it seems reasonable to expect that a characteristic that was important at one stage of development may not be significant a few years later. And conversely, a characteristic that was not apparent at one level of development might take on significance just a few years later. The course of a child's life may be diverted by changing conditions, and traits that were appropriate at one age level may not serve a child as well a few years later. Furthermore, the reactions of parents and others to certain traits may change over the years. These points were illustrated by a longitudinal study of temperament.

Changes in Significant Traits and "Goodness of Fit"

Alexander Thomas and several colleagues (1963) instituted a longitudinal study of temperament in the 1960s. They found that they were able to classify most of their infant subjects into three temperament types:

easy, difficult, and slow to warm up. (These temperament types will be described in detail in a later chapter. For purposes of this discussion the labels are sufficient to indicate basic differences.) In a follow-up report published fourteen years after the study was initiated, Thomas and his associates concluded: "Our long-term study has now established that the original characteristics of temperament tend to persist in most children over the years" (1970, p. 104). They qualify that statement by noting: "Of course a child's temperament is not immutable. In the course of his development the environmental circumstances may heighten, diminish or otherwise modify his reactions and behavior" (p. 104). They also point out that "not all children in our study have shown a basic constancy of temperament" (p. 105) and suggest that *inconsistency* of temperament may be a basic characteristic of some children. In yet a later report, they offer this explanation for consistency or lack of consistency:

One temperamental characteristic may be enormously influential in the child-environment interactional process at one age period and in certain life situations but not particularly important at a later period. A temperamental trait may assume an importance at the older age period which it did not have earlier. Or the same characteristic may play an important role in development at sequential age stages. (1977, pp. 28–29)

A slow-to-warm-up child with relaxed and understanding parents, for example, may experience few difficulties while at home during the preschool years but become upset if exposed to an impatient and demanding teacher during the elementary school years. This example illustrates what Thomas and Chess refer to as the **goodness of fit** concept, which sheds light on other aspects of personality consistency and inconsistency. Some children, even difficult ones, may be fortunate enough to have parents with characteristics and attitudes that are in harmony with (or at least not in conflict with) their temperaments. A father who prides himself on his drive and dogged competitiveness, for instance, may respond positively to a difficult child because he can boast that his offspring "really has a mind of his own." But goodness of fit may change as the child matures. The father who admired self-willed behavior in his seventeen-month-old son may feel differently by the time the same child matures into a seventeen-year-old adolescent and takes the family car in defiance of a parental directive that it not be used on a particular night.

Other evidence of ways initial personality tendencies might be diverted by experiences, changing demands, and "goodness of fit," was provided by one of the many analyses of the Berkeley longitudinal data.

Goodness of fit: fortunate meshing of child and parent characteristics at a point in development

In some cases, goodness of fit occurs between parent and child characteristics. In other cases, parents may find it difficult to understand or interact with their children.
Melissa Shook/The Picture Cube.

Adaptability, Resiliency, and Unpredictability

After analyzing data on behavior disorders as well as all the other information accumulated on the subjects of the Guidance Study, various members of the research staff at the University of California made predictions of how successful and well adjusted each child would be as an adult. After the subjects had reached the age of thirty, comparisons were made between child and adult behavior. Surprisingly, 50 percent of the children in the sample who were later studied as adults became

more stable and effective individuals than had been predicted; 20 percent turned out to be less effective than had been predicted. In commenting on these findings, Jean Walker Macfarlane observed:

Predictions of adult
adjustment based
on child behavior
often inaccurate

We have found from a review of life histories that certain deficits of constitution
and/or environment, and certain unsolvable interpersonal conflicts have long-
term effects upon the individual, up to age thirty. We have also found that much
of personality theory based on pathological samples is not useful for prediction
for the larger number of persons. Many of our most mature and competent
adults had severely troubled and confusing childhoods and adolescences. Many
of our highly successful children and adolescents have failed to achieve their
predicted potential. (1964, p. 125)

As a partial explanation for this conclusion, Macfarlane notes:

We had not appreciated the maturing utility of many painful, strain-producing,
and confusing experiences which in time, if lived through, brought sharpened
awareness, more complex integrations, better skills in problem solving, clarified
goals, and increasing stability. Nor had we been aware that early success might
delay or possibly forestall continuing growth, richness, and competence. (1964,
p. 124)

Macfarlane and her coworkers were impressed by the resiliency of the
human organism. Some children, however, seem to lack sufficient
adaptability to situations that others take in stride; some children are
faced with conflicts and problems of such magnitude that even the most
adaptable succumb. The inaccuracies of the predictions of the Guidance
Study researchers reveal the difficulties and complexities of tracing the
causes of mental health and mental illness. Children who have "ideal"
parents and who are exceptionally well adjusted in school, Macfarlane
hypothesizes (1964, p. 125), may develop unrealistic expectations about
how well they will do when they embark on a career or may spend too
much time and energy attempting to maintain an image. Children who
come from homes where apparently undesirable techniques of child
rearing are used or who experience much misery and unhappiness in
school may thereby become equipped to cope with and overcome extreme demands in later life.

Other evidence of the desirability of a certain amount of "tempering"
is provided by Thomas and his colleagues (1970) in their first follow-up
study of temperament and personality. They found that some easy-to-
rear children developed unexpected problems when they left the home
environment. They offered this explanation:

In general easy children respond favorably to various child-rearing styles. Under
certain conditions, however, their ready adaptability to parental handling may

itself lead to the development of a behavioral problem. Having adapted readily to the parents' standards and expectations early in life, the child, on moving into the world of his peers and school, may find that the demands of these environments conflict sharply with the behavior patterns he has learned at home. If the conflict between the two sets of demands is severe, the child may be unable to make an adaptation that reconciles the double standard. (1970, pp. 105–106)

Thomas and his colleagues illustrate their point with a case history of a girl who had been "reared by parents who placed great value on individuality, imagination, and self-expression" (p. 105). When this child entered school, she found it extremely difficult to adjust to classroom routine, did poor work, and found it difficult to make friends. The parents were asked to encourage their daughter to accept the fact that it was necessary to follow the teacher's instructions and that she should occasionally abide by the play preferences of classmates. Within six months the child was enjoying school and making friends. In many respects this case history illustrates one of the same points made by the Guidance Study researchers: a child who seems to have been blessed by favorable determinants of personality may still encounter problems of adjustment.

The results of these studies might be summarized this way. A well-adjusted four-year-old with loving, supporting parents will not automatically become a happy, successful, popular student by the time he or she leaves elementary school. A happy, successful, popular sixth-grader will not automatically become a happy, successful, popular high school senior. And when the time comes for you to attend a high school reunion twenty or thirty years after you graduated, you will discover firsthand that happy, successful, popular high school seniors do not automatically become successful, satisfied adults. This may be true in some cases, but it may also turn out that some adolescents who gave the appearance of being miserable, confused nonentities throughout the high school years surprisingly end up as adults who "have it made."

One explanation for lack of stability or predictability in personality and adjustment centers on differences between the developmental tasks that must be mastered at different age levels. Other explanations can be imagined by taking into account the "goodness of fit" concept. Still other explanations will become apparent as we trace development through infancy, childhood, adolescence and youth, adulthood, and old age. Perhaps the basic message to remember from this chapter, then, is that all stages of development are important. While it seems irrefutable that early experiences will have some influence on later behavior, each individual will continually change and develop as new experiences are encountered.

Some Concluding Observations on Continuity and Change

At first glance it might seem that some of the speculations noted in this chapter lead to the question: If early experiences are *not* predictive of adult behavior and if new battles have to be fought at every period of development, why should parents (or anyone else) worry about what happens to infants? Instead of feeling *disappointed* that infancy does not seem to be of crucial importance, however, parents and others who interact with children might feel *comforted*. During the years when the critical period concept was widely endorsed, parents were under a tremendous amount of pressure. Arguments that it was "all over by three" (or even earlier) as far as personality and intelligence were concerned caused many conscientious parents of the 1960s and early 1970s to worry excessively about doing the "wrong thing." The conclusions summarized in this chapter lead to a much more relaxed philosophy of child rearing. Instead of assuming that the infant is so delicate and sensitive that even the slightest misstep will cause permanent harm, parents might assume that the first few years of life are not *that* critical. What occurs later in development may have a greater impact on adolescent and adult behavior than what occurs in infancy. Accordingly, there will be plenty of time to make up for early "mistakes." Parents, teachers, and others who interact with children might also take into account the conclusions of two venerable developmental psychologists: Marjorie Honzik and John E. Anderson.

Honzik was a member of the team of researchers who carried out the longitudinal studies at Berkeley. In writing a report on the behavior problems exhibited over the years by the subjects of one of the studies, she concluded it as follows:

May we pay our respects to the adaptive capacity of the human organism, born in a very unfinished and singularly dependent state into a highly complex and not too sensible world. Unless handicapped by inadequate structure and health and impossible and capricious learning situations, he threads his way to some measure of stable and characteristic patterning. We see, even in the raw frequency figures presented in this report, the variety of coping devices he uses for his complex set of tasks. He starts out with overt expression of his needs and feelings and attempts immediate and direct solutions to his problems. Many of his overt and direct problem-solving attempts are not tolerated, so he learns when necessary to side step, to evade, to withdraw, to get hurt feelings and, also, to submit overtly even while his releases and problem-solving continues internally until controls are established. If he is under fairly stable and not too discontinuous pressures and secures enough approval and support to continue his learning and enough freedom to work out his own compromise overt-covert

Humans have an impressive adaptive capacity

solutions, he becomes, to use the vernacular, "socialized," and even without this optimum combination, he frequently arrives at a stable maturity. When we look at the hazards of the course, we are not sure that we have begun to understand how or why. (1954, pp. 220–221)

Anderson was founder and long-time director of the Institute of Child Welfare at the University of Minnesota. At a time when the psycho-analytic concept of fixation of libidinal energy during infancy was being stressed by several theorists (e.g., Ribble, 1943), Anderson summarized the implications of such interpretations. He observed:

Many discussions of child personality . . . seem to be projections backward upon the child of concepts that seem necessary for the author's conception of adult behavior. . . .
Various generalizations on the personality of the infant and young child which follow from these impressions and interpretations can be made: (a) Infants and young children are essentially passive recipients of stimulation who display little energy or activity on their own; (b) are very delicate and tender, and have little capacity to resist or survive and are especially sensitive to lack of affection to which they cannot adapt for even short periods; (c) are unusually susceptible to, and carry the effects of, traumatic episodes indefinitely; (d) carry forward all their memories and experiences, which later come out to plague them; (e) in their behavior and the products resulting, are subject to all the implications and values that inhere in adult reactions in similar situations. (1948, pp. 410–411)

Anderson then cited research evidence to support the following conclusions: the child is not passive but active, has a substantial capacity to withstand all manner of stresses and strains, recovers quickly from injury, and is impressively resilient and able to bounce back after negative experiences.

The observations of Honzik and Anderson should not only help you relax a bit if you will be interacting with young children; they should also make you feel less fatalistic about your own future development—and more interested in the later chapters of this book. Freud argued that neuroses are acquired by the age of six; Skinner suggested that early shaping will be permanent; White maintained that "it is all over by three." If you accept these arguments uncritically you would have to assume that there isn't too much you can do—on your own—about your present or future behavior. You were fixated and/or shaped by experiences and treatment over which you had little or no control at a time of life you can only dimly remember. In order to change your ways of responding to life's events, you would either have to submit to psychoanalysis by a psychiatrist or to reshaping by a behavior modification therapist. You might find yourself thinking, "What's the point in reading about human development from a personal point of view? I've had it. I am what I am and that's it."

There are alternatives to the views of Freud, Skinner, and White, however. Carl Rogers, for instance, argues that those who experience adjustment difficulties can learn to control their own behavior. Erikson's interpretation of psychosocial stages calls attention to the point that each phase of development requires new adjustments. Albert Bandura's version of social learning theory supports the view that as you mature and gain experience you become better able to anticipate what will happen in new situations and thereby improve control of your own behavior. Furthermore, the lists of developmental tasks for different age levels and the discussion of differences between the preschool and elementary school years reveal that different kinds of demands are made at different age levels. If you will turn back a few pages to the lists of developmental tasks for early adulthood and middle age, you will see that many of the tasks that you currently face, or will face in the future, are substantially different from those you have achieved so far. Therefore, even if you have not always surmounted all previous developmental tasks with ease, it is entirely possible that you possess the adaptive capacity to make successful adjustments at this stage of your life. (Hang in there. The best is yet to come.)

With these observations as background, it is time to turn to an analysis of significant types of behavior during the first two years of life. After comparing the behavior of children as neonates and preschoolers, R. Q. Bell, G. M. Weller, and M. F. Waldrop (1971) made this observation: "Newborn behavior is more like a preface to a book than a table of its contents yet to be unfolded. Further, the preface is itself a rough draft undergoing rapid revision" (1971, p. 132). Taking into account the significant changes in physical, social, cognitive, and personality development reflected by the developmental tasks for later age levels, it seems reasonable to say that the rough draft of each child's personality continues to undergo rapid revision during the elementary school years and in adolescence. The plot thickens (to continue to use the book metaphor suggested by Bell and his associates) as the child matures, but even in adulthood it may not be possible to figure out exactly how it is going to come out. It is important, therefore, to pay careful attention to all stages of development.

Summary

1. The belief that experiences during the first few years of life have a more profound influence on human development than experiences that come later has been expressed during all eras of history.

Scientific support for the early experience hypothesis reached a peak after World War II. It was reported that infants deprived of contact with their mothers exhibited **marasmus** (wasting away), ethologists described how **imprinting** occurred during **critical periods** just after birth, and evidence of the negative impact of early institutionalization accumulated. Some psychologists argued that infancy was of supreme importance because of the rapid acquisition of abilities; others argued that the preschool years were a critical period in cognitive development.

2. Not all psychologists of the postwar era agreed that "it was all over by three," however. Some argued that the years from six to ten were a **crystallization period** because certain tendencies that persisted into adulthood emerged at that time. Others maintained that adolescence was a stage of life during which it was necessary to "refight battles" in the sense that new ways of adapting to new demands had to be found.

3. As scientists of the 1970s rigorously tested hypotheses stressing the importance of infancy, they found that it was more accurate to speak of **sensitive,** rather than critical, periods. It was also discovered that at least some institutionalized children successfully overcame severe early deprivation. Follow-up studies of children exposed to intensive preschool instruction revealed that initial gains in intelligence and achievement quickly faded, leading to the conclusion that there is no "magic period" in cognitive development.

4. One explanation why experiences during infancy may not have a permanent impact on later behavior is provided by an analysis of **developmental tasks** at different ages. In contrast to preschool children, for instance, elementary school children are publicly compared with age-mates in academic achievement. Elementary school children are also expected to solve many of their own problems for the first time. Many of the developmental tasks that need to be achieved during the elementary school years, therefore, demand skills different from those that were of significance during the preschool years.

5. A related explanation for lack of continuity between behavior in infancy and at later stages is that personality tendencies that develop early in life may be diverted by experiences as the child matures. Furthermore, child and parent characteristics may lead either to **goodness of fit** or to conflicts at various stages of development. A trait that was admired by the parents early in a child's life may be perceived as negative or irritating later on.

6. Evidence of ways initial personality tendencies might be diverted by experiences, changing demands, and goodness of fit has been provided by longitudinal studies. Researchers at Berkeley found that predictions of adult adjustment based on child behavior were often

inaccurate. Some children who had been expected to do well had problems as adults whereas many children who had been expected to have problems turned out to be mature and competent adults. It was concluded that humans have an impressive adaptive capacity. Another conclusion that can be drawn from all the points just summarized is that all stages of development are important.

The Significance of Early Experiences

Suggestions for Further Study

If you would like to read detailed and technical evaluations of various hypotheses about the significance of experiences during the first few years, consult these two sources: *Constancy and Change in Human Development* (1980), edited by Orville G. Brim and Jerome Kagan; and "Socioemotional Development" by J. J. Campos, K. C. Barrett, M. E. Lamb, H. H. Goldsmith, and C. Stenberg, Chapter 10 of *Infancy and Developmental Psychobiology*, Volume II of *Handbook of Child Psychology* (4th ed., 1983) edited by Paul H. Mussen.

PART 3

THE FIRST TWO YEARS

KEY POINTS

Factors That Influence Growth

Target-seeking tendency: deprived child later catches up

Principles of Developmental Direction

Cephalocaudal growth: head to tail
Proximodistal growth: inside to outside

The Development of Motor Skills

Sequence of motor development: head, arms, hands, legs

Reflex Activity During the First Months of Life

Rooting reflex: head turns when cheek is touched
Grasp reflex: palm closes around object
Subcortical reflexes controlled by lower brain

Various Hypotheses About Crib Death

Crib death: sudden infant death syndrome (SIDS)

Crib death infants have low Apgar scores, respiratory difficulties, are lethargic

Development of the Brain and Nervous System

Speech control localized in left hemisphere, spatial relationships in right

Perceptual Development During the First Two Years

Neonates look for edges
Two- to five-month-olds respond to patterns with many elements
Habituation: tendency to lose interest in a continual stimulus

Initial Forms of Learning

Pavlovian conditioned response weak in infants
Earliest operant conditioned responses involve sucking

CHAPTER 6

THE FIRST TWO YEARS

PHYSICAL DEVELOPMENT

*I*f a sperm fertilizes an egg and the process of cell division takes place without being interrupted or distorted, approximately nine months later a child will be born. After the newborn baby emerges from its mother's body and the umbilical cord is cut, the baby begins to function as an independent human being. The official time of birth is the moment the baby is completely clear of the mother's body. Independent existence might be said to begin when the baby takes its first breath, sometimes on its own, sometimes in response to a slap on the buttocks by the attending physician. Once breathing begins, the onset of the process causes the valves in the heart to alter the pattern of the circulation of the blood. In the uterus the blood was circulated to the placenta for aeration. When the baby is separated from the placenta, the blood is pumped to the lungs to be aerated.

From birth to the age of one month the baby is called a *neonate* (from the Latin *neo*, "new," and *natus*, "born"). The average newborn baby weighs a few ounces over seven pounds and is twenty inches long (boys, on the average, are slightly larger than girls), but because the legs are drawn up, the baby looks smaller. By adult standards, the body looks out of proportion, since the head accounts for a quarter of total length (compared to a tenth in a mature individual). Once the birth process is over, the baby sleeps much of the time—as much as twenty hours a day. When awake and active, its behavior often appears aimless, diffuse, and uncoordinated. Yet this seven-pound, out-of-proportion, sleepy, and apparently disorganized organism possesses the basic equipment needed to survive. The newborn baby also comes equipped with a genetic ground plan that controls growth. During the first two years, the physical changes that take place are quite remarkable.

Factors That Influence Growth

The average infant, who weighed a bit more than seven pounds and was twenty inches long at birth, weighs about twenty pounds and is approximately thirty inches tall at the age of one year. After the first year, average weights and heights do not supply very helpful information about growth because of several factors. At most age levels, boys, on the average, are heavier and taller than girls; but girls, on the average, develop at a more rapid rate. (It has been estimated [Garai and Scheinfeld, 1968] that in terms of maturity the newborn girl is equivalent to a four- to six-week-old boy.) Because of genetic and prenatal influences, some children will be taller and heavier than others, some will be shorter and lighter, and some will be slow or rapid maturers. Genetic factors also have much to do with body build, but extremely good or poor nutrition (and other environmental factors) may have an impact on weight and sometimes height. (The impact of environmental conditions on genetic instructions for height and weight is an excellent illustration of why the study of behavioral genetics has emerged.) Improved nutrition, along with better health practices and living conditions, probably accounts for the progressive increase in size of American and some European children during the last one hundred years (Malina, 1979). This is known as the *secular trend,*[1] and although it is still continuing in many countries, it appears to be leveling off in developed societies, such as the United States, England, and Japan (Roche, 1979). The rate of maturation varies from one country and geographic area to another. M. Geber and R. F. A. Dean (1957) and F. Falkner and several associates (1958) found that African black infants are advanced in skeletal maturation, and a number of investigations (reviewed by Crowell, 1967, p. 166) have yielded data indicating that black children in Africa and the United States are also advanced in motor development for about the first two years. While the *average* European child lags behind African infants, some nationality groups are more precocious than others. C. B. Hindley and four other European researchers (1966) compared the age of walking of children from five cities. Children from Brussels and Stockholm started to walk a month earlier, on the average, than those from Paris, London, and Zurich. Such differences in rate of motor development might be attributed to differences in opportunities for exercise or amount of encouragement, to nutrition, or to genetic factors.

Thus there are wide variations in growth rates between children, but a quite consistent pattern of growth characterizes each individual child. The child who is a fast maturer of a particular body build, for example, will be consistent in rate and structure. In a study carried out in Britain, A. Merminod (1962) found that the height of two-year-olds (who are almost exactly half their adult height on the average) correlates approximately 70 percent with ultimate height. The extent of genetic control over growth is emphasized by what J. M. Tanner refers to as a **target-seeking tendency:**

Children, no less than rockets, have their trajectories, governed by the control systems of their genetical constitution and powered by energy absorbed from the natural environment. Deflect the child from its growth trajectory by acute malnutrition or illness, and a restoring force develops so that as soon as the missing food is supplied or the illness terminated the child catches up toward its original curve. When it gets there, it slows down again to adjust its path onto the old trajectory once more (Tanner, 1970, p. 125).[2]

Target-seeking tendency: deprived child later catches up

The tendency to return to an original growth curve after a short period of deflection appears to be stronger in females than males (Tanner, 1962,

---

[1]Here *secular* refers to a trend that lasts from century to century or extends over a period of time.
[2]Perhaps you recognized that what Tanner calls the target-seeking tendency is similar to Waddington's epigenetic model of genotype-phenotype interaction described in Chapter 3.

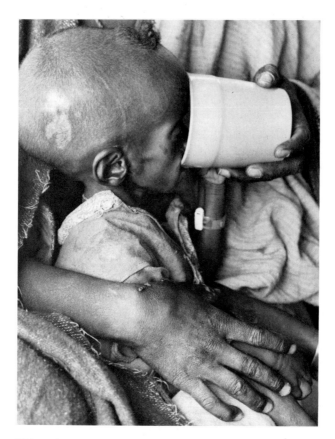

*This undernourished child has almost certainly suffered a slowing of growth. If given
an adequate diet for the next several years, however, the child may "catch up" to the
genetically determined growth pattern because of the target seeking tendency.*
Chris Steele Perkins/Magnum Photos.

p. 127). That is, a girl who is subjected to poor nutrition or emotional
stress is less likely to show a slowing of growth than a boy in the same
situation. It is also clear that it is difficult for a child to make up for
extended deprivation, particularly when it occurs early in life.

The pattern of growth for the body as a whole tends to be consistent,
then, but it is also cyclical. For some reason yet to be understood, the
rate of gain in height between March and August during a child's
growth years is as much as two and one-half times as great as in the fall
and winter months. On the other hand, two-thirds of the annual gain in
weight takes place between September and February (Tanner and Taylor, 1969, p. 137). Not all parts of the body follow the same rate of

growth, however. The brain completes 95 percent of its growth by the age of ten, for example, while the heart may not reach its ultimate size until after the age of twenty. At birth the head accounts for one-quarter of total length and the legs for one-fifth, but by the age of two the head accounts for less than a fifth and the legs for one-third of total height.

Principles of Developmental Direction

Even allowing for all of these variations, the overall growth of the body and nervous system follows a lawful pattern. Development proceeds from the head region to the extremities, which is referred to as **cephalocaudal growth** (from the Latin *cephalus,* meaning "head," and *cauda,* meaning "tail"). It also proceeds, simultaneously, from the interior of the body to the exterior, which is referred to as **proximodistal growth** (from the Latin *proximus,* meaning "nearest," and *distantia,* meaning "remote").

Cephalocaudal growth: head to tail

Proximodistal growth: inside to outside

One early manifestation of these principles of growth is the development of **prehension,** which refers to the ability to pick up a small object (such as a small block) by using the thumb and fingers. In a trend-setting study, H. M. Halverson (1931) made motion pictures of how young children sitting in a high chair responded when a block was placed in front of them. Not until the age of seven months could children actually grab the block in the palm with any degree of consistency or precision, and the ability to use fingers and thumb to pick up the block was not achieved until the ninth month. This sequence occurs because—in keeping with cephalocaudal and proximodistal development—the nerves and muscles nearest the head and spinal cord mature before those of the extremities of the body. Another way of expressing this principle is to say that large-muscle control precedes fine-muscle control. In picking up a block, a child learns to control the muscles involved in palming an object before achieving finger control.

The Development of Motor Skills

The most obvious and dramatic illustration of the nature of physical development is provided by the mastery of locomotor behavior. On the basis of an intensive study of children during their first two years, Mary Shirley (1933) described the sequence illustrated in Figure 6.1. As you can see, in keeping with the principles of developmental direction, the typical child first acquires the ability to hold up the head, then refines the use of arms and hands, and finally gains control of legs and feet.

Sequence of motor development: head, arms, hands, legs

When you examine the ages at which Shirley observed the locomotor

FIGURE 6.1
Sequence of mastery
of locomotor
behavior

Mary M. Shirley, The First Two Years, *Institute of Child Welfare Monograph No. 7,
Minneapolis, University of Minnesota Press, Copyright 1933, renewed 1961 by the
University of Minnesota.*

activities depicted in Figure 6.1, you should take account of the fact that
she was an objective observer watching each of her subjects for only a
short period of time. Parents, who have almost constant contact with
their young children and are "rooting" for them to stand and walk as
early as possible, are likely to encourage and arouse more effort than a
dispassionate visitor. They also are likely to give credit for a good try
and to be lenient in determining exactly when a particular skill is mastered. Consequently, if parents compare the motor performance of their
child, the age levels described by Shirley, they may conclude that they
have a remarkably precocious baby. It is preferable to concentrate on the
sequence of skills depicted in Figure 6.1 rather than use the noted age

TABLE 6.1
AGE PLACEMENT IN MONTHS FOR ITEMS FROM THE BAYLEY INFANT
SCALE OF MOTOR DEVELOPMENT (WITH COMPARISON TO AGES
REPORTED BY SHIRLEY)

Skill	Age in Months	Age Reported by Shirley
Lifts head at shoulder	0.1	0.1
Dorsal suspension—lifts head	1.7	2.0
Sits with support	2.7	4.0
Sits alone momentarily	5.4	6.0
Walks with help	9.9	11.0
Stands alone	11.3	14.0
Walks alone	11.8	15.0
Walks upstairs with help	18.7	
Walks upstairs alone, marks time	22.7	
Walks downstairs alone, marks time	22.9	
Ascending short steps, alternate feet, unsupported	31.0	
Descending short steps, alternate feet, unsupported	49.0	

Sources: Ages reported by Nancy Bayley: "Comparisons of Mental and Motor Test Scores for Ages 1–15 Months by Sex, Birth Order, Race, Geographical Location and Education of Parents," *Child Development*, 1965, *36*, 379–411. Ages reported by Mary M. Shirley: *The First Two Years*, Institute of Child Welfare Monograph No. 7, Minneapolis, University of Minnesota Press, © Copyright 1933, renewed 1961 by the University of Minnesota.

levels for estimating rate of development. For that purpose, a test of infant development would be more appropriate.

On the basis of her initial observations of the sixty-one subjects of the Berkeley Growth Study, Nancy Bayley (1936) reported age placements for over one hundred motor skills on what was originally called the California Infant Scale of Motor Development. She later used this information to standardize the Bayley Infant Scale of Motor Development (1965, 1969) by testing nearly fifteen hundred infants. Table 6.1 depicts some items and age levels from this scale. (To facilitate comparison, the age levels for skills reported by Shirley are also supplied.) As you can see, the age levels described by Bayley are consistently earlier than those noted by Shirley, perhaps because Shirley recorded behavior only when it occurred during one of her observations, whereas Bayley arranged for the babies she studied to attempt all the skills on her scale.

The sequence of motor development described by Shirley and Bayley can be explained by taking into account the principles of cephalocaudal and proximodistal growth. These principles also help explain the nature of some of the reflexes displayed by infants.

Reflex Activity During the First Months of Life

Newborn infants come equipped with reflex actions that permit them to do much to maintain their own survival and comfort. Breathing—with or without assistance—ordinarily begins just after birth, and most babies will obtain nourishment the first time they are exposed to a breast or bottle. This occurs because of two reflexes. If the cheek of a newborn baby is touched, the baby's head will turn to that side. This reaction is called the **rooting reflex,** and its importance can be easily understood—in order to eat, the child must find the source of food. Once the rooting reflex causes the mouth to come into contact with the nipple of the breast or bottle, the **sucking reflex** is activated. Some babies start to suck immediately; others may need to be "primed" by having the nipple moved around in the mouth.

The neonate also possesses some reflexes that serve a protective function. The newborn infant may exhibit a **withdrawal reflex,** involving sudden jerking away of the legs when the sole of the foot is stimulated. Neonates blink their eyes shut if an object is moved close to the face and also "defend" themselves against an approaching object by pulling the head back and moving their hands in front of their bodies (Bower, Broughton, and Moore, 1970).

Still other reflexes illustrate the nature of the development of the brain and nervous system. If a pencil or similar object is placed in the palm of the neonate's hand, the **grasp reflex** will cause the fingers to tighten around it. If the sole of the foot is stroked, the toes may fan upward and outward in the **Babinski** (or plantar) **response,** named after J. Babinski, the French doctor who first described it in 1896. (Karl C. Pratt [1954, p. 260] points out that there is considerable variability in the Babinski response and that lack of a "classic" pattern does not necessarily indicate any abnormality in development.) If there is a sudden sound or movement (someone knocking over a can of powder, for example, or bumping the table when changing a diaper), a baby lying on his or her back will respond with the **Moro reflex** (named after E. Moro, the German doctor who first described it in 1918) by first stretching out the arms and legs and then bringing them together.

To account for the fact that the grasp and Moro reflexes were present in the behavior of neonates but had pretty much disappeared by the age of five or six months, Myrtle McGraw (1943) suggested that the original reflexes were activated by lower and older parts of the brain. Since the older parts of the brain are below the cortex, reflexes controlled by the

Rooting reflex: head turns when cheek is touched

Grasp reflex: palm closes around object

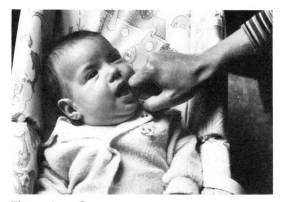

The rooting reflex

The sucking reflex

The grasp reflex

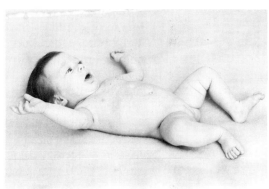

The Moro reflex

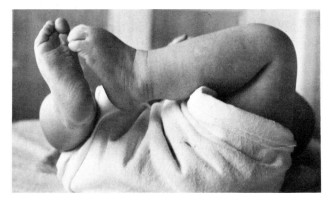

The withdrawal reflex

Some of the significant reflexes of the newborn infant.
Photographs, top to bottom, by David Nudell; David Nudell; Roy Pinney/Monkmeyer; Lew Merrim/Monkmeyer; Nolan Petterson/Black Star.

Subcortical reflexes
controlled by lower
brain

lower brain are called **subcortical.** McGraw hypothesized that when the cortex developed and began to function more actively, the subcortical control of the nervous system was inhibited. This explanation is now widely accepted, and if the grasp and Moro reflexes do not diminish or disappear by the time an infant is six months old, it may be taken as an indication that the brain and nervous system are not developing normally.

Various Hypotheses About Crib Death

Crib death: sudden
infant death syn-
drome (SIDS)

The tendency for subcortical reflexes eventually to be replaced by voluntary actions of the same type may be a contributing cause of **crib death,** also referred to as the **sudden infant death syndrome** (SIDS). Crib death is the unexplained death of an infant that typically takes place between the second and fourth month after birth. An ostensibly healthy baby simply stops breathing, usually in the night, without apparent cause and without giving any signs of having struggled or suffered. Approximately two out of every thousand children born in America are victims of crib death. Even though the condition has been analyzed extensively, no widely accepted or proven explanation has yet been proposed, which means that no satisfactory prescription has yet been offered.

Crib death infants
have low Apgar
scores, respiratory
difficulties, are
lethargic

In a review of research on crib death, S. Broman (1984) noted that the following factors frequently have been reported by those who have studied this condition: unmarried low-income mother under the age of twenty who is a smoker and anemic; male infant born prematurely with a low Apgar score and respiratory difficulties. After studying the characteristics of SIDS infants, Naeye, Messmer, Specht, and Merritt (1976) concluded that crib death victims tend to be temperamentally lethargic. They were found to be below normal in physical tone and alertness, which may make them more vulnerable when respiratory problems (including colds) develop. As for the timing of crib death, Lewis P. Lipsitt (1979) speculates that the tendency for crib death to occur between two and four months of age suggests that this is a period when subcortical reflexes are beginning to be supplanted by voluntary or learned reactions. Thus, the infant is at an in-between stage of development. If respiratory problems occur (for example, mucus blocking the nasal passages), an infant may not struggle to gasp for breath because built-in defensive reactions are disappearing and learned protective reactions are not yet well established.

A different explanation for crib death is that it is caused by undetected abnormalities in the central nervous system. A related hypothesis is that lesions in the respiratory center of the brain stem cause disorders in breathing. Many normal babies may briefly cease to breathe while asleep (a condition called *apnea*), but infants with respiratory center abnormalities may suffer extended periods of interrupted breathing that lead to cardiac arrest and death (Steinschneider, 1975).

Even though specific causes of crib death have yet to be pinned down, manufacturers of hospital equipment have perfected tiny monitors (about the size of a quarter) that can be attached to the chests of infants suspected of being prone to crib death. The rate of breathing as well as the heartbeat is monitored while the infant is asleep, and any indication of an interruption of the normal pattern activates light and sound warning systems to alert nurses or parents that an attack of apnea may be about to occur. Picking up the child and providing stimulation is likely to cause respiration to continue.

Development of the Brain and Nervous System

Mention of subcortical reflexes and speculation about the causes of crib death call attention to the nature and significance of brain development.

FIGURE 6.2

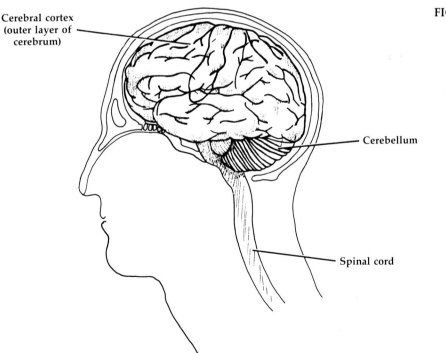

FIGURE 6.3

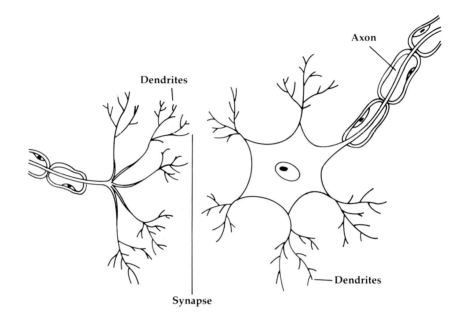

In keeping with the laws of developmental direction, the brain develops, for the most part, from the bottom to the top and from the inside to the outside. That is, the brain stem develops before the cortex, and the inside of the cortex develops before the outside. The cerebellum, however, which is responsible for regulation and coordination of complex voluntary muscular movements, is an exception to the general trends of neurological development. The cerebellum is the last of the brain to develop, even though it is just in back of the spinal cord and below the cortex. The development of the brain is thought to occur as neurons multiply, migrate (to use a term favored by developmental neurologists), and interact. Individual neurons that make up the human nervous system communicate with each other through dendrites and axons. Dendrites are branched projections of the nucleus of nerve cells that function to *receive* signals from other cells. The axon is a long fibrous projection that *transmits* information to other cells. The area of communication between neurons is called a **synapse.**

As neurons develop and pathways between them are established, the brain becomes capable of controlling a greater variety of physical and cognitive activities. It appears that the brain is genetically programmed to develop according to a timetable that prepares the maturing organism to process appropriate stimulation at particular stages of development (Parmalee and Sigman, 1983). If stimulation occurs before the nervous system is ready for it, neurons seem to protect themselves by rejecting the sensory input. Premature infants, for example, are exposed to many more stimuli than infants who develop in utero for the full nine-month gestation period. Despite receiving an abnormal amount of stimulation compared to full-term infants, preterm babies do not exhibit accelerated neurological or physiological growth. Once the nervous system *is* ready to respond, however, it appears that "appropriate" stimulation facilitates normal development.

Hypotheses About the Hemispheres of the Brain

As the cortex develops, the different hemispheres of the brain begin to exert control over different types of emerging behavior. In a comprehensive analysis of research on brain development, Marcel Kinsbourne and Merrill Hiscock (1983), two leading authorities on brain functioning, conclude that there is little empirical evidence to support hypotheses that there are fundamental differences—such as abstract versus concrete thinking or logical versus intuitive reasoning—between hemispheres of the brain. There *is* substantial evidence, however, that speech control is localized in the left hemisphere for more than 95 percent of right-handed individuals and as many as 70 percent of left-handers. (While language processing is concentrated in the left hemisphere, it appears that the right hemisphere has substantial capacity for linguistic comprehension and limited capacity for control of expressive speech. This conclusion is based on the finding that some individuals who experience incapacitating damage to the left hemisphere are still able to comprehend speech and may be able to use speech to a limited degree.) Grasp of spatial relationships and aspects of visual memory are localized in the right hemisphere.

Speech control localized in left hemisphere, spatial relationships in right

Developmental neurologists have debated how and when localization of speech and visual functions take place. Three hypotheses have been proposed: localization of function of the two hemispheres of the brain—referred to as **functional lateralization**—increases with age, decreases with age, or remains essentially the same throughout the life span. On the basis of their review of research, Kinsbourne and Hiscock conclude that the evidence favors the view that lateralization is present at birth and continues through the life span. One interesting bit of evidence they cite to support this conclusion takes the form of observation of asymmetries in the posture of infants. The tonic neck reflex, which features inclination of the head and all four limbs, involves movement to the right in most infants. Additional evidence of a right-sided motor bias—presumably due to localization of function—is provided by the much greater tendency for infants to reach for and hold objects in the right hand.

FIGURE 6.4

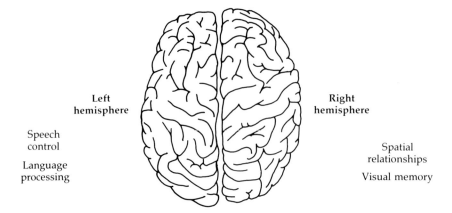

Left
hemisphere

Right
hemisphere

Speech
control

Spatial
relationships

Language
processing

Visual memory

In summarizing their conclusions on lateralization of the brain, Kinsbourne and Hiscock note that in the 1970s the following hypotheses about brain function were proposed:

Functional lateralization increases with age and is a major factor in mental development.

Lack of dominance of one hemisphere of the brain is associated with failures in mental development.

The more completely lateralized the brain becomes, the more refined behavior becomes.

They suggest that evidence accumulated during the last ten years has led to the conclusion that none of these hypotheses can be clearly substantiated. It appears, therefore, that at present there are few clearly established principles describing localization of function of the brain other than the fact that the left hemisphere controls speech and the right controls spatial and visual perception.

Scientists who have been interested in the development of the brain and nervous system often study how infants and young children respond to stimulation. Other researchers who have analyzed responses to stimulation have been interested in early perceptual development.

Perceptual Development During the First Two Years

Responses to Visual Patterns

Robert L. Fantz developed an ingenious technique for studying how infants respond to visual patterns. (His methods prompted dozens of

The infant "looking chamber" used in Fantz's study of perception in young infants. The experimenter peers through a small hole in the screen and observes the reflected image on the infant's eyeball. This technique makes it possible to record the amount of time infants look at different patterns.
Photograph by Dr. Robert Fantz.

studies and led to new appreciation of the responsiveness of infants.) Fantz constructed a comfortable crib with a depression designed to hold an infant's head in a steady position. This crib was placed within an enclosure topped by a screen upon which cards could be placed. Fantz would settle an infant down in the crib and attach to the screen cards on which different patterns had been drawn. Immediately after attaching the patterns, Fantz peered through a small hole in the screen and observed the reflected image on the surface of the infant's eyeball. This made it possible to determine the amount of time the infant concentrated on each pattern.

In an early study, Fantz (1958) observed preferences between two patterns. In a subsequent study (1961), he measured duration of gaze for patterns presented in succession. His early findings led him to conclude that during the early months of life infants can concentrate on one-eighth-inch stripes at a ten-inch distance, that they prefer patterns to plain colors, that they can differentiate among patterns of similar complexity, and that they show interest in a pattern similar to a human face. In a later study, Fantz (1963) found that neonates from ten hours to five days old attended more to a schematic face and a concentric circle pattern than to unpatterned colored squares.

The pioneering studies by Fantz stimulated dozens of other researchers to devise similar experiments. Marshall Haith analyzed the results of hundreds of reports and presented his conclusions in a book titled *Rules That Babies Look By* (1980). Here are some of the basic looking rules neonates seem to follow:

Neonates look for edges

1. If awake and in either not-too-bright light *or* darkness, they maintain a detailed, controlled visual search.
2. When a visible pattern is encountered, they search for edges.
3. If an edge is found, they stay in that general vicinity. They try to cross the edge, but if such eye movements are not possible, they scan for other edges.

These rules apply to neonates, but Haith concluded that starting only a month later, infants begin to direct their gaze back and forth across specific features. It is not until sometime later, however, that infants engage in *extensive* visual exploration of complex patterns.

After reviewing their own research, as well as dozens of other studies carried out by others, Fantz, Fagan, and Miranda (1975) concluded that the difficulty neonates experience in concentrating on details of patterns is due to immaturities of the eye and nervous system. By the time they are two months old, though, maturation of the eyes and brain, as well as practice in using the eyes, equips babies to differentiate between distinctive features of a pattern. The acquisition of ability to distinguish between details seems to predispose two- to five-month-old infants to respond to patterns that are made up of many elements, angles, and contours. At about the age of five months, a third phase in the development of visual perception takes place, when infants show a preference for three-dimensional objects over two-dimensional pictures or photographs. Fantz hypothesized that this preference is due to experience with reaching, grasping, and manipulation of objects. It appears that once babies have handled something, they prefer to look at the real thing instead of a picture of it.

The kinds of differences Fantz found between the visual perception of one- and two-month-old infants were highlighted by research carried out and analyzed by Philip Salapatek (1975). Salapatek found that one- to four-week-old babies concentrate on a single feature of a pattern, usually at the edges of the design. Salapatek concluded that the visual

FIGURE 6.5
Schematic plots of
visual scanning of a
real head by 1- and
2-month infants

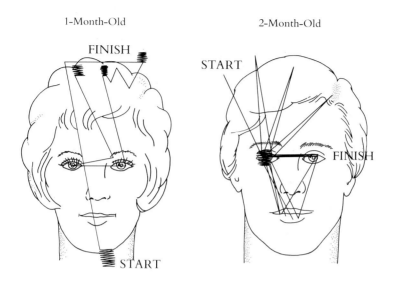

1-Month-Old   2-Month-Old

The lines drawn over these representations of a human face record the eye movements
made by 1- and 2-month-old infants as they watched an adult who leaned over them.
As you can see, the 1-month-old baby concentrated on the top and bottom edges of the
head; the 2-month-old baby focused on internal features, particularly the eyes.
Philip Salapatek, "Pattern Perception in Early Infancy," from L. B. Cohen and Philip Salapatek,
eds., Infant Perception: From Sensation to Cognition, Vol. I, Basic Visual Processes (New
York: Academic Press, 1975), p. 201.

scanning of neonates might be thought of as reflexive sensory discharge
activated by peripheral parts of the stimulus pattern that stand out. By
the end of the second month, however, and increasingly thereafter,
infants reveal that they become intrigued by internal features of a pattern. These differences between the scanning behavior of one- and two-
month-old babies will become clear if you examine Figure 6.5 above.

> Two- to five-month-
> olds respond to pat-
> terns with many
> elements

In a recent review of research on early visual perception, Martin S.
Banks and Salapatek (1983) conclude that the results of such studies
reveal that infants exhibit differential preferences among stimuli in various patterns and that these preferences change with age. It is not yet
possible, however, to describe the exact nature of such age changes.
Banks and Salapatek report the same inability to delineate specific age
trends in form discrimination, color vision, and depth perception, although information on these types of visual perception is accumulating
at a rapid pace.

Habituation Implies Memory and Learning

Habituation: tendency to lose interest in a continual stimulus

When infants respond to different segments of a visual pattern, they are exhibiting shifts in attention. Psychologists who first studied visual as well as auditory perceptual phenomena by using techniques similar to those introduced by Fantz soon realized that shifts in attention often imply memory and learning. When a visual pattern or sound is first presented, an infant is likely to attend to it. However, if the stimulus is presented a number of times in succession or if it is presented for an extended period, most infants lose interest. Their attentiveness is likely to perk up, though, if a different pattern or sound is introduced. This

The blissful look on this baby's face may indicate that habituation—the tendency to be lulled into a relaxed state by a continual stimulus—has been induced by the father's harmonica playing. (Habituation also refers to the tendency of a child to lose interest in a steady stimulus.)
David S. Strickler/The Picture Cube.

tendency to lose interest in a stimulus is called **habituation** and it has been studied intensively.

Visual Recognition Memory as an Indicator of Intelligence

As an outgrowth of the work of Fantz, psychologists interested in information processing have carried out studies of what is called **visual recognition memory.** Such studies (reviewed by Fagan, 1982) are based on the habituation tendency for an infant to become bored with an old stimulus and to devote more attention to a new stimulus. The fact that a child switches attention from an old to a new pattern is taken as evidence that the old pattern has been encoded in some way. If the old pattern is reintroduced among new patterns the next day, it frequently happens that the child indicates, through eye movements and increased heart rate, that recognition has occurred. It has been discovered that infants as young as five months are able to later recognize a pattern even if it has been previously exposed for only a few seconds. Furthermore, they may retain the encoded information for anywhere from two to fourteen days, depending on the nature and variety of the patterns presented.

Perhaps the most intriguing aspect of research on visual recognition memory in infants, though, is that there is some evidence that pattern recognition during the first months of life may predict later levels of intelligence. It is too early to be sure about this hypothesis, but it appears that infants who do well on visual recognition tasks later earn high scores on measures of intelligence. Thus, being able to discriminate between patterns and recognize them when presented later may be one of the earliest signs of brightness. As Fagan puts it, "tests of visual recognition tell us about the infant's developing ability to perceive, to abstract, to categorize, and to transfer information" (1982, p. 89).

The Infant as an Information Processor

A variety of other techniques for studying habituation and related phenomena have been developed in the last decade or so, and hundreds of articles describing experimental studies have been published. After reviewing many of these, Gary M. Olson and Tracy Sherman (1983) concluded that the "infant of 3 to 6 months has become an extremely active information processor" (p. 1039). They point out that before the end of the first year infants are quite capable of encoding (or forming mental representations) of environmental information. Olson and Sherman suggest that during the second year sensory and perceptual skills become much more refined and that there is extensive growth in the child's basic fund of knowledge. Also during the second year these three major developments occur: the emergence of symbolic representation, the development of recall abilities, and the development of imitation capabilities. The way these three factors contribute to cognitive development will be discussed in the next chapter.

Although perceptual development during the first months of life depends on physical maturation (which explains why it is included in this chapter), it also reveals aspects of cognitive development (such as memory and information processing). The same is true of initial forms of learning. The first learned responses that have been observed under controlled conditions are primarily reflexive, but the cognitive aspects of learning soon become apparent. Accordingly, even though learning is usually thought of as a cognitive activity, it is appropriate to discuss initial forms of learning in a chapter on physical development during the first two years.

Initial Forms of Learning

Pavlovian Conditioning

A number of investigators have attempted to establish Pavlovian conditioned responses in neonates. In Pavlovian conditioning, an essentially involuntary reflex action comes to be actuated by a previously neutral stimulus. In order to establish Pavlovian conditioned responses in neonates, the experimenter must use stimuli that a newborn baby can respond to and also must arouse reflex actions that are part of the infant's repertoire. In a review of studies of Pavlovian conditioning, H. E. Fitzgerald and Yvonne Brackbill (1976) note that neonates have been induced to respond to a variety of sounds, mild electric shock, and lights. Types of reflex actions that have been aroused by such stimuli are heart-rate changes, blinking, sucking, and foot withdrawal. It should be noted, however, that not all psychologists are convinced that genuine conditioned responses have been clearly established in neonates. Arnold Sameroff and Patrick Cavanagh (1979), for example, argue that what some researchers call *learned* responses might more properly be classified as types of behavior that occur when an infant is in a **state of preparedness to react.** And Gary M. Olson and Tracy Sherman characterize the results of classical conditioning studies as "weak or negative" (1983, p. 1029).

The apparatus pictured here illustrates one technique experimenters have used to try to establish a Pavlovian conditioned response in young children. Infants respond to puffs of air directed at the eyes by reflexively blinking the lids closed. After a puff of air directed at the eyes is

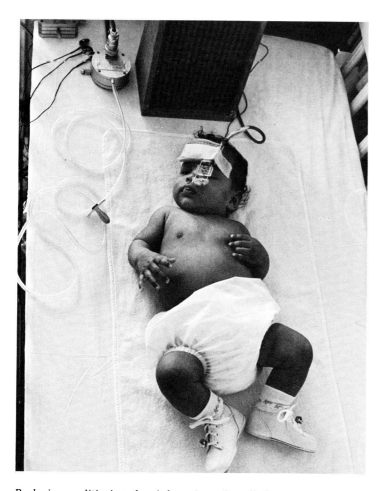

Pavlovian conditioning of an infant. A gentle puff of air (which causes the eye to blink) is produced by the mechanism attached to the baby's forehead. A tone is paired with the air puff. After a number of such presentations, the tone itself elicits the eye blink. Photograph by Jason Lauré. Courtesy of Lewis P. Lipsitt.

associated several times with a tone sounded through a loudspeaker close to the baby's head, the baby may blink when the tone is sounded, even though the puff of air is omitted.

Pavlovian conditioning involves an essentially involuntary response. The organism responds, but without exerting any deliberate control over the actions. A much more significant kind of learning occurs when an organism makes precise movements in response to a specific stimulus and does this when it wants to.

Pavlovian conditioned response weak in infants

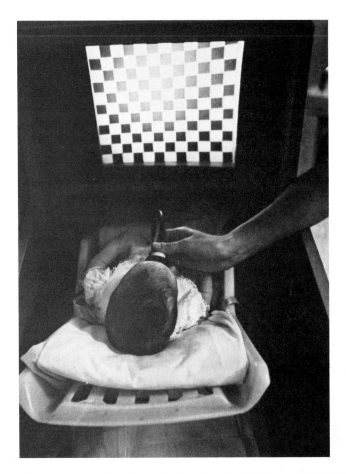

Operant conditioning of infants. Experiments like this one indicate that the behavior of very young infants can be shaped by reinforcement. The nipple on which this four-month-old is sucking controls the brightness of the pattern projected on the screen. When the infant sucks at a rapid rate, the picture becomes brighter and reinforces the higher frequency of sucking behavior.
E. R. Siqueland and C. A. DeLucia, "Visual Reinforcement of Nonnutritive Sucking in Human Infants," Science 1969, 145, 1144–1146. Photos taken in laboratory of Einar R. Siqueland at Brown University by Jason Lauré.

Operant Conditioning

Learning that involves strengthening actions *initiated* by an organism occurs when operant conditioned responses are established spontaneously. In order to establish operant conditioned responses, therefore, it is necessary to reinforce types of behavior that can be initiated and controlled by the organism. The newborn human infant is not capable of making very many responses of this type, but nonnutritive sucking and head turning fit this description.

In one of the earliest studies of operant conditioning, Hanus Papoušek (1961) conditioned head-rotation movements in neonates. A bit later Reuben E. Kron (1966) used an apparatus for controlling and recording sucking behavior in newborn infants. Kron found that as early as the first day of life infants would alter their sucking pattern when the flow of milk was turned on or off. He concluded that the day-old infant is capable of developing an operant conditioned response. Lewis P. Lipsitt has supervised or stimulated a series of infant-conditioning studies. Einar R. Siqueland and C. A. DeLucia (1969), for example, were able to establish nonnutritive-sucking responses in babies as young as one month by using an apparatus (pictured here) that allowed the infants to alter visual patterns when they sucked on a nipple wired to a slide projector. These studies and many others of the same type (reviewed by Sameroff and Cavanagh, 1979, pp. 355–362) indicate that infants are capable of acquiring learned responses as soon as they can control their own behavior. Both Pavlovian and operant conditioned responses become easier to establish toward the end of the first year and increasingly so thereafter.

Earliest operant conditioned responses involve sucking

(Changes in physical development during the years from two to five are discussed in Chapter 10, beginning on page 321.)

Summary

1. During the first two years of life, physical development is rapid and dramatic. Growth is controlled by a genetic timetable but environmental factors may have a positive or negative influence. A child who suffers from malnutrition or illness, however, is later likely to catch up because of a **target-seeking tendency** that leads to a return to the genetically programmed plan.
2. The overall growth of the body and nervous system follows a lawful pattern. Development proceeds from the head region to the extremities, which is referred to as **cephalocaudal** growth. It also proceeds, simultaneously, from the interior of the body to the exterior, which is referred to as **proximodistal** growth. These laws of developmental direction are illustrated by the sequence of motor development: the child first gains control of the head, then the arms and hands, and then the legs and feet.
3. The earliest physical reactions of infants take the form of reflexes that contribute to survival or comfort. If the baby's cheek is touched, the **rooting reflex** causes the head to turn in that direction (which facilitates finding the nipple when feeding). The **grasp reflex** occurs when the baby's hand closes around an object placed in the palm. Several of the reflexes that are displayed during the first months of life are

called **subcortical** because they are controlled by the lower brain. As the cortex develops, these reflexes diminish or disappear.

4. One explanation for **crib death,** or the **sudden infant death syndrome** (SIDS), is that it occurs at a time (two to four months of age) when subcortical reflexes are being supplanted by voluntary or learned responses. Other explanations stress that crib death victims have low Apgar scores, suffer from respiratory difficulties, and are lethargic.

5. Many hypotheses about neurological development have been proposed during the last few years. Some of these stress that certain types of thinking and creative activities result from differences in function between the two hemispheres of the brain. At present the only conclusions about brain function that are clearly established by research are that speech control is localized in the left hemisphere (in right-handed persons) and spatial relationships in the right.

6. As a result of the perfection of ingenious experimental techniques, many studies of early perceptual development have been carried out recently. When neonates are confronted by visual stimuli, they tend to look for edges. Two- to five-month-olds respond to patterns with many details. A particularly interesting aspect of early perceptual development centers on **habituation:** the tendency to lose interest in a continual stimulus. The related observation that a child switches attention from an old to a new pattern is taken as evidence that the old pattern has been encoded in some way.

7. **Pavlovian** conditioned responses, where an essentially involuntary reflex action (such as blinking or sucking) comes to be activated by a previously neutral stimulus (such as a tone), have been established in neonates. Some psychologists, however, point out that such responses are weak and might be more accurately described as a state of preparedness to react. **Operant** conditioned responses, where a self-controlled form of behavior (such as head turning or nonnutritive sucking) is strengthened by reinforcement (in the form of food or a visual stimulus), have been established in neonates by several investigators.

Suggestions for Further Study	## Physical Growth During the First Two Years A concise but complete analysis of physical growth in childhood is presented by J. M. Tanner in Chapter 3 of *Carmichael's Manual of Child Psychology* (3rd ed., 1970), edited by Paul H. Mussen. ## Physiological and Neurological Development The best single source for detailed technical information about early physiological and neurological development is *Infancy and Developmental*

Psychobiology, edited by Marshall M. Haith and Joseph J. Campos, Volume III of *Handbook of Child Psychology* (4th ed., 1983), edited by Paul H. Mussen. Chapter 3, by Arthur H. Parmelee and Marian D. Sigman, is on "Perinatal Brain Development and Behavior"; Chapter 4, by Marcel Kinsbourne and Merrill Hiscock, is about "The Normal and Deviant Development of Functional Lateralization of the Brain"; and Chapter 7, by Martin S. Banks and Philip Salapatek, is on "Infant Visual Perception."

Observing the Behavior of Young Children

You might gain greater understanding of several of the points noted in this chapter (and also enjoy yourself) if you look for opportunities to observe one or more children under the age of two. If you know someone with a child less than six months old, you might find it of interest to check out the various reflexes described in this chapter. Perhaps the most interesting of these is the grasp reflex which can be activated by putting your finger or a pencil in the palm of the baby's hand. Many children grab so tenaciously you can almost lift them up. (Quite a few babies *are* able to support their own weight when the grasp reflex is activated, but please do *not* test for this capability. Just make a simple check of grasping ability.) If you know someone with a child between the ages of six months and a year, you might check to see if the subcortical reflexes have disappeared. You might also observe the child in action and compare his or her physical performance with the information provided by Shirley and Bayley in Figures 6.1 and 6.2. Note whether you detect signs of cephalocaudal and proximodistal growth. With a child of the same age, you might check on habituation. First, hold a picture with a well-defined pattern over the baby's head as it lies on its back. After a minute or so, hold a different picture next to the first one and observe the movement of the infant's eyes. If the baby switches its glance from the first picture to the second and then keeps it there, you might conclude that the baby had become habituated (or bored) with the first stimulus and responded with interest to a new stimulus.

NOTE: Suggestions for observing the cognitive, social, and personality development of children under the age of two are offered at the end of each of the next three chapters. Therefore, if you arrange to observe a young child, you might examine the Suggestions for Further Study in all these chapters on the First Two Years before you make a home visit. It should be possible for you to study all four types of behavior at the same time.

KEY POINTS

Piaget: Stages of the Sensorimotor Period

First sensorimotor stage: formation of primitive schemes

Primary circular reaction: satisfying bodily activity repeated

Functional assimilation: tendency to use a capability

Object concept: object exists even when not perceived

Secondary circular reaction: duplication of activity involving an object

Coordinated schemes: separate skills combined to achieve goal

Tertiary circular reaction: exploration, interest in novelty

Final sensorimotor stage: thought replaces activity, delayed imitation

Various Views of Relationships Between Language and Thought

Piaget: language depends on thought

Chomsky: language independent of thought

Vygotsky: language and thought separate until two, then interrelated

Language Development

Neonates able to discriminate between sounds

Cooing first reflexive, then responsive

Babbling peaks between nine and twelve months

Vocal contagion: child vocalizes with parent

Mutual imitation: parent and child repeat sounds initially made by child

First word: child emits sound, is reinforced, builds association

Holophrastic speech: one-word communications

Telegraphic speech: nonessential words omitted

Some children referential, others expressive speakers

Motherese higher in pitch, slower, abbreviated

CHAPTER

7

THE FIRST TWO YEARS

COGNITIVE DEVELOPMENT

*F*or reasons noted in the discussion of theories in Chapter 2, the most complete and widely respected description of cognitive development during the first two years has been proposed by Jean Piaget. To help you grasp the overall structure of Piaget's description of stages in early cognitive development, here is a brief review of the basic concepts of his theory that were described in Chapter 2.

Piaget: Stages of the Sensorimotor Period

Piaget believes human beings inherit two basic tendencies: organization (the tendency to combine processes into coherent systems) and adaptation (the tendency to adjust to the environment). Adaptation occurs through two complementary processes: assimilation (the tendency to incorporate experiences into one's view of the world) and accommodation (the tendency to modify one's conceptions in response to new or inconsistent experiences). These various tendencies lead to the development of schemes (organized patterns of behavior). Piaget refers to the first two years as the **sensorimotor** period because the child develops schemes primarily through sensorimotor activities. There are six stages in this period.

Stage 1: Variations of Reflex Activity (Birth to One Month)

Stage 1: The sucking behavior of the neonate illustrates how the infant begins to develop schemes. Piaget started observing his children immediately after they were born by sitting next to the cradle and making detailed descriptions of their behavior. He recorded how the rooting and sucking reflexes were aroused the first time the babies had an opportunity to feed; he then noticed that as early as the second day variations of these basic responses began to appear. The first variation was that the babies made sucking movements between feedings; the next was that they would suck almost anything that touched their lips (for example, their thumbs or a blanket). Before the end of the first month, they engaged in sucking for the sake of exercise (thumb sucking) in addition to sucking for the sake of food. From these changes in behavior Piaget concluded that as early as the first days of life the baby assimilates and accommodates to form schemes regarding sucking activities.

First sensorimotor stage: formation of primitive schemes

Stage 2: Primary Circular Reactions (One to Four Months)

After the first month, the complexity of the behavior of the child develops at an accelerated pace, basically through what Piaget refers to as the **primary circular reaction.** A primary circular reaction occurs when the infant engages in an activity (by chance or the intervention of his parents) that leads to a satisfying state of affairs. The infant seeks to repeat such satisfying activities, and when it succeeds in doing so, the act becomes part of its repertoire of behavior.

Primary circular reaction: satisfying bodily activity repeated

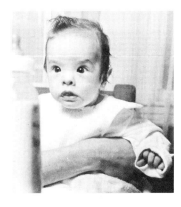

The development of schemes. The infant in these photos has associated the sucking scheme with the nursing bottle.
Excerpted from Infants and Mothers: Differences in Development, *T. Berry Brazelton, M.D., Copyright © 1969 by T. Berry Brazelton, M.D. Reprinted by permission of Delacourt Press/Seymour Lawrence.*

The primary circular reaction is illustrated by the way Piaget's children came to engage in thumb sucking. The hand of the young child is frequently held close to the mouth, probably because the arms and hands are usually tucked up close to the face in the fetal position, which young infants continue to assume after birth. Piaget noticed that when the thumb or fingers of one of his children first came into contact with the lips, the sucking reflex was activated. Once this occurred, the infant tried to move his hand to his mouth, and by the end of the first month, he was mature enough to be able to do this. (On one occasion, when his son Laurent was one month old, Piaget moved the infant's hand from his mouth to his side thirteen times in succession. Each time, Laurent moved it back to his mouth.) At first, Piaget's children sucked any part of the hand, but they quickly developed a preference for the thumb, perhaps because it is the most nipplelike appendage available. Another aspect of his children's sucking behavior that attracted Piaget's attention was their tendency to anticipate sucking before feeding actually started. At first, almost any contact with the mother aroused this response. In time, it began only when the child was held in the customary feeding position.

Piaget believes the self-starting aspect of human behavior is due to curiosity and the inborn tendency of the child to seek stimulation. When children become capable of an activity, an inherited tendency makes them do it. This is what Piaget terms **functional assimilation.** Observing how his children looked at objects, Piaget noticed that at the age of one

Functional assimilation: tendency to use a capability

month Laurent would spend as long as an hour looking at the fringe on his cradle. When he was two weeks older, Laurent engaged in systematic visual exploration of his bassinet. By the third month he was more likely to look at things, such as a toy hanging from the top of the bassinet, that were moderately novel. This progression from fixed attention to visual exploration to interest in novel objects led Piaget to conclude that children come equipped with a tendency to use their eyes, that they seek stimulation, and that they quite early in life develop schemes based on visual perception. This last conclusion is based on the reasoning that Laurent must have developed a quite consistent conception of what his bassinet was like to be capable of recognizing the addition of something new when the toy was attached. (The same line of reasoning was noted in discussing experimental studies of habituation in the preceding chapter.)

What Piaget refers to as functional assimilation has been observed and described in different terms by many other psychologists. Robert W. White (1959), for instance, analyzed various views of motivation that had been proposed in American psychology up to the mid-1950s and concluded that too many of them led to the assumption that children had to be stimulated to learn or even respond. White rejected this conception and proposed instead that human beings are born with built-in curiosity and manifest a desire to interact with their environment. He referred to this tendency as a drive toward **competence** or **effectance.** Observations of normal human infants (or of puppies or kittens) tend to support White's argument that young organisms have an urge to explore and try out their abilities. The same tendency has also been demonstrated many times under controlled conditions. Anneliese F. Korner and Evelyn B. Thoman (1970), for example, observed what happened when infants who were crying in their cribs were picked up and placed on the shoulders of their mothers. In most cases the babies stopped crying quite abruptly when they were provided with the opportunity to just look around. The chance to satisfy the drive of curiosity by engaging in visual exploration was strong enough to take their minds off whatever had been bothering them in their cribs. Taking into account the likelihood that the only thing the infants were able to see when in their cribs was either the ceiling or the side of the crib, it is possible that many of them were crying out of sheer boredom.

Harriet Rheingold, who has made a career of studying infants and young children in many different kinds of situations, endorses the hypothesis that boredom bothers babies. She notes (1973, p. 183) that placing a child in a nonstimulating environment (such as an empty crib) often leads to fussing and crying. When she observed infants in institutions, Rheingold reports that she was impressed by the apparently irrepressible (at first) urge of infants to occupy themselves, even when they had practically no playthings to handle or objects or people to look at. Children who have access to many interesting objects seem to possess an innate urge to explore with zest and enthusiasm whenever the opportunity arises. In an experiment with twelve- and eighteen-month-old children, Rheingold (1973) arranged for the mothers to carry their children into a room, put them down on the floor, and then simply sit and watch as the infants amused themselves in two adjacent playrooms containing toys. All the children left their mothers within seconds and explored the rooms with considerable energy. Rheingold believes that the children deserved to be called *enterprising* because they took the initiative to discover and interact with the playthings on their own. Furthermore, they obviously got a great deal of pleasure out of it.

Stage 3: Secondary Circular Reactions (Four to Eight Months)

From the fourth to the tenth month, the major change in the intellectual development of the child consists of adding to reactions centering on the body (initial, or **primary,** reactions) and to those involving the external environment (later, or **secondary,** reactions). Awareness of the external environment is illustrated most clearly by what Piaget calls the **object concept:** understanding that an object continues to exist even when it is no longer perceived. (Such understanding is also referred to as **object constancy** or **object permanence.**) Piaget formulated this concept when he observed Laurent's reactions as his mother came to the bassinet and then left it. At first, Laurent would stare at her when she was present but almost immediately look away when she left. It seemed apparent that his reaction was "Out of sight, out of mind." After he was four months old, however, Laurent would continue to stare at the spot she had vacated, and when he was a bit older, he would look in the direction of his mother's voice (when he was not able to see her). By his behavior he revealed that he had developed a scheme of "mother," which involved both visual and auditory stimuli. However, not until Laurent actively searched for his absent mother by looking around and listening intently, did Piaget feel that a true object concept had developed. By these actions, Laurent was revealing that his scheme of "mother" had sufficiently developed that he understood that she continued to exist even when he could not see or hear her.

Object concept: object exists even when not perceived

   The key aspect of **secondary circular reactions** is the ability of the child to reproduce activities involving objects (not just bodily movements) initially discovered by chance. When Laurent accidentally discovered that he could make a sound by hitting a rattle, for example, he repeated the act. Another feature of this stage is the ability of the child to inter-

Secondary circular reaction: duplication of activity involving an object

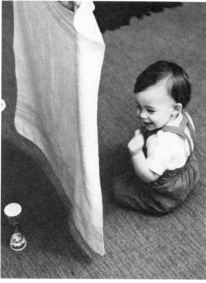

Development of object concept. In the first photo the concealed toy does not exist for the infant. The child in the last two photos, however, has formed an object concept. The toy continues to exist even though he cannot perceive it, which enables him to search for and find it.
George Zimbel/Monkmeyer.

rupt an act and then return to it. Lucienne, for example, was playing with a small box one day when Piaget came up to her crib. She turned her attention to him for a few minutes, but then confidently reached for the box and resumed play with it. Still another feature that appears toward the end of this stage is the ability to recognize an object that is partially hidden. When nine-month-old Laurent's rattle was completely hidden by a cloth, he acted as if it no longer existed. But when one end of it protruded from the cloth, he reached for it.

During the stage of secondary circular reactions, then, the child shifts from concentrating on her or his own body to interest in the external environment; object concepts develop that lead the child to understand that something continues to exist even though it is not being perceived; chance actions leading to satisfaction are repeated; an activity that is interrupted will not be forgotten; and sensing only part of an object may be sufficient to permit the child to react to it as a whole.

Stage 4: Coordination of Secondary Schemes (Eight to Twelve Months)

As noted in discussing cephalocaudal and proximodistal development at the beginning of Chapter 6, the average child develops the ability to pick up an object between thumb and fingers (prehension) at around nine months. By the time children have matured to the point where they can manipulate objects with considerable precision and control, they have also reached the point where their interactions with the environment have produced a sizable repertoire of schemes, paving the way for new combinations of schemes.

Piaget became convinced that schemes became coordinated as he watched his children cope with problems such as searching for a matchbox hidden in a hand or under a pillow. In dealing with such novel situations, Laurent and Lucienne would try techniques they had previously developed through spontaneous activities. In the course of manipulating objects, for example, they would pick up pillows. When the box was placed under the pillow, they would apply the previously learned skill (picking up an object just for its own sake) to the new situation (picking up a pillow to search for an object). This switch from playful to purposeful manipulation is the major feature of Stage 4, and it explains why the stage is referred to as a **coordination of secondary schemes:** separate skills learned in interacting with the environment are put together, or coordinated, to achieve a specific goal. Other changes during this stage are the development of the ability to imitate actions (provided the child has already mastered them through spontaneous activity) and more sophisticated understanding of the object concept.

Coordinated schemes: separate skills combined to achieve goal

Coordination of secondary schemes occurs when a child combines separate skills to achieve a particular goal. This child coordinates skills of picking up and rotating objects to solve the problem of getting a long object through the bars of the crib. George Zimbel/Monkmeyer.

Stage 5: Tertiary Circular Reactions (Twelve to Eighteen Months)

Shortly after their first birthdays, children begin to perfect their locomotor abilities, and when they are able to walk, their investigation of the environment takes on greater self-direction. They no longer must limit themselves to objects made available by others (or within crawling distance); they can roam around and explore things on their own. The degree to which children at this age actively seek new and interesting things is the key feature of the **tertiary circular reaction stage.** The first type of circular reaction centers on the infant's own body; the second on external objects or events; the third is characterized by exploration and interest in novelty.

Piaget explains the fifteen-month-old's fascination with novelty for its own sake by suggesting that the large number of schemes built up during the first year makes the child familiar with many things. Schemes become so clearly established that children are capable of recognizing

Tertiary circular reaction: exploration, interest in novelty

Tertiary circular reaction. The active seeking out and manipulating of new objects is characteristic of this stage.
James R. Holland/Stock, Boston.

objects and events that do not fit into their growing conception of the world. The tendencies to seek equilibration, and to assimilate and accommodate, stimulate the child to examine new objects carefully and either incorporate them into an existing scheme or form a new one. The child's acquisition of the ability to move around and seek out new objects and situations coincides with the development of tertiary circular reactions.

This potential for both physical and mental exploration leads children to engage in constant manipulation of their world and explains why children of this age explore with unrelenting vigor wastebaskets, objects on coffee tables, knobs on television sets, pots and pans in lower cupboards, and the like. As they investigate things, children expand their understanding of relationships between themselves and the objects they handle, thereby learning to institute and imitate all kinds of actions, not just those that happen to be similar to actions done on their own immediately preceding the acts they imitate.

Stage 6: New Means Through Mental Combinations (Eighteen to Twenty-Four Months)

Final sensorimotor stage: thought replaces activity, delayed imitation

Children in Stage 5 have built up a repertoire of schemes that make it possible for them to deal with new situations by trying out a variety of techniques mastered in the course of exploring their environment. Before they are two years old, children usually will show the first signs of substituting thinking for action. A fifteen-month-old child confronted with a problem is likely to run through a series of physical actions in an effort to find a solution. Two-year-olds, on the other hand, may hesitate and by eye movements indicate that they are engaging in mental trial and error. Another kind of behavior providing evidence that a cognitive image has been formed is imitation of an action hours or days after the model was observed. Lucienne, for example, observed a little boy engage in a temper tantrum. She was quite fascinated since she had never before seen such behavior. When she wanted to get out of her playpen the next day, she did an excellent imitation of the screaming and foot stamping she had observed. The final characteristic of this stage is that object concepts now function as effective mental images. If an object is removed from sight, children will clearly show they comprehend that it still exists.

Summary of Sensorimotor Stages

The basic changes that take place as a child progresses through these stages can be summarized as follows:

Stage 1—Variations of Reflex Activity
Birth to One Month. Development of variations of reflex activity (of sucking, for example) indicates formation of primitive schemes.

Stage 2—Primary Circular Reactions
One to Four Months. Visual exploration progresses from staring to scanning to looking at moderately novel objects. Such activities indicate formation of primary circular reactions: schemes based on exploration by children of their own bodies and senses.

Stage 3—Secondary Circular Reactions
Four to Eight Months. Object concept (permanence) begins to develop as children come to realize that things continue to exist even though they are not present to sense. The switch in emphasis from exploration of their own bodies and senses to exploration of the physical environment leads children to secondary circular reactions: spontaneous reactions involving external objects or events are deliberately repeated.

Stage 4—Coordination of Secondary Schemes
Eight to Twelve Months. Development of many schemes through secondary circular reactions paves the way for combining them. Children have developed enough awareness of their bodies and environment to engage in purposeful manipulation.

Stage 5—Tertiary Circular Reactions
Twelve to Eighteen Months. Development of ability to walk, increased skill at manipulating things, understanding of many schemes, and recognition of novelty all lead to active exploration of the environment (tertiary circular reaction).

Stage 6—New Means Through Mental Combinations
Eighteen to Twenty-Four Months. Experiences with exploration and manipulation equip the child with enough clearly established schemes to be able to engage in mental manipulation; that is, actions can be thought out.

Evaluations of and Alternatives to Piaget's Theory

While Piaget's description of sensorimotor stages has been acknowledged for thirty years as the most important single explanation of early cognitive development, other theorists have offered alternative hypotheses. In an analysis of infant cognition, P. L. Harris (1983) summarizes the views of three psychologists who have proposed theoretical interpretations that differ from those of Piaget. J. J. Gibson (1979) is not convinced that there are six stages in the sensorimotor period. He suggests that the only difference between a neonate and a two-year-old is increasing skill at picking up information from the environment. Gibson also suggests that it may not be necessary for young children to interpret what they perceive; they may merely need to *extract* pertinent information from available sources. Jerome Kagan (1979) has carried out numerous studies of infant attention. He differs from Piaget in stressing that young children form schemes not so much to draw conclusions about objects and events as to direct their attention toward particular aspects of their world. Kagan also suggests that visual inspection in the absence of manipulation is often a sufficient basis for the foundation of early schemes. Jerome Bruner (1973) emphasizes the importance of intentional skills that are gradually placed in the correct order to achieve a particular goal. Bruner also has placed greater stress than other theorists on the importance of language.

In his analysis of early cognitive development, Harris notes a number of aspects of Piaget's theory that can be questioned; e.g., the suggestion that young infants are substantially less sophisticated about interpreting observations than older ones and the claim that the capacity to represent an invisible state of affairs does not develop until the end of the sensorimotor period. For the most part, however, Harris concludes that most aspects of Piaget's description of early cognitive development have stood up very well under intensive experimental evaluation.

A final aspect of Piagetian theory that merits mention serves as a bridge between this section on initial stages of cognitive development and the next section on language development.

Various Views of Relationships Between Language and Thought

Piaget: Language Depends on Thought

Piaget (1967) maintained that language acquisition cannot take place until cognitive development has paved the way. Piaget also proposed that language development by itself is not sufficient to foster cognitive development. The Piagetian view, therefore, is that language depends on thought but that thought is not dependent on (or significantly influenced by) language. A number of researchers (e.g., Cromer, 1974; Langer, 1975) have supplied evidence to support both of Piaget's propositions. They have demonstrated that nonlinguistic concepts (or schemes) emerge before linguistic concepts. For instance, a child first develops a scheme for an object and then learns the word that stands for that object. In addition, the ability of a child to use language does not seem to foster related aspects of cognitive development. A child can be

Piaget: language depends on thought

taught the meaning of *more* and *less,* for instance, but that does not equip him or her to solve problems requiring understanding of those concepts.

Chomsky: Language Is Independent of Thought

The American linguist Noam Chomsky (1968), on the other hand, suggests that language is basically **independent** of thought. He has proposed what he calls the **language acquisition device** to account for language development. (Inclusion of the word *device* in this designation is a bit unfortunate since it conjures up a vision of a miniature computer in the brain. What Chomsky means by the term is that tendencies to use language are inborn.) If a child is exposed to language, the inborn tendencies will be activated. Chomsky bolsters his argument by pointing out that language develops the same way in virtually all children despite the fact that they differ in cognitive skills. Thus, Chomsky maintains that language and thought are separate.

*Chomsky: language **independent** of thought*

Vygotsky: Language and Thought Separate at First, Then Interrelated

Yet another hypothesis regarding the relationship between language and thought has been proposed by the Russian psychologist Lev Vygotsky (1962). Vygotsky suggests that thought and language are separate until about the age of two. One- and two-year-olds go through the stages of sensorimotor development described by Piaget and begin to acquire rudimentary language skills. But these are separate accomplishments. After the age of two, however, language and thought become interrelated. The child begins to develop an understanding of language and also uses language as an aid in reasoning. One form of evidence in support of Vygotsky's view has been reported by A. Karmiloff-Smith (1979), who observed that children sometimes invent their own linguistic forms to help themselves grasp concepts.

Vygotsky: language and thought separate until two, then interrelated

Arguments in support of the views of Piaget, Chomsky, and Vygotsky have been proposed not only by the theorists themselves but by other researchers who have tested their hypotheses. At the same time, each view has been criticized. The available evidence is not sufficient to substantiate that any particular theory is clearly superior to the others. Accordingly, perhaps the safest conclusion to draw is that there is an element of truth in all three.

Language Development

Speech Perception Sets the Stage for Language Development

In an article titled "Auditory Development and Speech Perception in Infancy," Richard N. Aslin, David B. Pisoni, and Peter W. Juzczyk (1983) comment on the tremendous surge of interest in these topics that has occurred since 1970. In the last few years hundreds of studies have been carried out to investigate auditory sensitivity in infants through the use of newly developed measuring instruments as well as ingenious techniques of experimentation. The results of many of these studies reveal that even during the first days of postnatal existence infants are capable of making quite subtle distinctions between the sounds to which they are exposed. Some of the most interesting experiments concentrate on the abilities of infants to discriminate between speech sounds. Since being able to detect differences in speech sounds plays such an important role in the acquisition of speech, the results of studies of auditory development are discussed as an introduction to this section on language development even though audition is a form of perceptual development.

Experiments by Peter D. Eimas, one of the most active researchers in this area of study, illustrate the nature of many experiments designed to analyze speech perception. In collaboration with several associates (Eimas et al., 1971) he exposed one- and four-month-old babies to recorded speech sounds. The infant subjects were able to keep the recordings turned on by sucking on a nipple that contained a switch. At the beginning of an experimental session, a baby could hear a *pa-pa* sound coming from a loudspeaker. Most subjects responded with interest and sucked vigorously on the nipple to keep the recording playing. They became bored or habituated with the sound (and/or tired of sucking) very quickly, however, and at that point the recording was switched from *pa-pa* to *ga-ga*. As soon as the infants heard the new sound they perked up and their rate of sucking increased significantly. Eimas reasoned that in order for this change of interest to occur, the babies had to be able to distinguish between *pa* and *ga*.

Neonates able to discriminate between sounds

Subsequent studies by Eimas and others (reviewed by Aslin, Pisoni, and Juzczyk) have led to the conclusion that infants perceive sounds in a manner approximating that of adults and that the mechanisms underlying this ability appear to be innate. Support for the second conclusion is supplied not only by the fact that neonates can discriminate between sounds, but also by studies in which infants from different countries have been exposed to recordings of speech in their own, as well as foreign, languages. These studies reveal that children from diverse backgrounds respond to speech sounds in much the same way. It seems reasonable to assume, therefore, that innate tendencies found universally rather than exposure to speech by others are the key factors in early speech perception. Just a few days after birth, though, infants respond differentially to the voices of familiar and unfamiliar individuals. A number of investigators (e.g., DeCasper and Fifer, 1980) have found that even three-day-old infants demonstrate a preference for their mother's voice over that of a stranger. There is some evidence (Spence and De-Casper, 1982) that this preference may exist because the mother's voice was perceived by the fetus while in utero during the last months of pregnancy.

The significance of recent research on speech perception, then, is that infants start postnatal existence equipped with abilities that contribute to their acquisition of language. They also seem to come equipped with a vocalization self-starter since they spontaneously begin to experiment with voice production very early in their lives.

Cooing and Babbling

Cooing usually begins sometime between the first and second month of life. The onset of cooing is believed to be controlled by biological maturation and occurs at about the same time that the subcortical reflexes begin to disappear and the cerebral cortex begins to function more actively. The first phase of cooing is called **reflexive,** since the age of onset is approximately the same for both deaf and hearing infants, and the initial rate of cooing is unaffected by environmental responses. Within a few days or weeks, however, cooing becomes **responsive.** In this phase the rate of infant cooing is influenced by the way parents respond to vocalizations, at least for hearing children. Infants whose parents coo back vocalize significantly more than infants whose parents do not respond.

Cooing first reflexive, then responsive

Somewhere between four and six months babbling begins. Infants begin to combine consonants and vowels into speechlike syllables which are repeated, for example, *ma-ma* and *da-da*. The frequency of babbling increases gradually, typically peaking somewhere between nine and twelve months and declining thereafter as meaningful speech begins to develop (deVilliers and deVilliers, 1978).

Babbling peaks between nine and twelve months

Use of a "Private" Language

Before the end of the first year, some children begin to use sounds as forms of communication. In a sense, they develop their own language

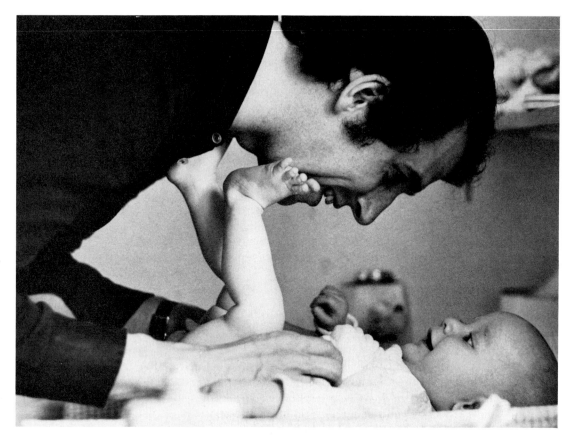

Cooing becomes responsive when parents respond to spontaneous vocalizations made by young children.
© *Thomas Hopker/Woodfin Camp.*

before they begin to use their native language. M. A. K. Halliday (1975), for instance, recorded the language repertoire of a ten-month-old boy. Even though the child did not use a single word listed in an English dictionary, he used "words" of his own. To request someone to hand him a toy bird, for example, the child said "Bih." This sound was used consistently to refer to the toy bird, and his parents readily understood what the child was trying to convey, particularly when he underlined his meaning with gestures and facial expressions.

It appears that normal babies develop prespeech languages of their own, provided they have opportunities to interact with at least one interested adult who is willing to try to interpret their utterances. The uniqueness of each child's private language was emphasized when T. G. R. Bower (1977b, p. 143) observed that even identical twins used different sounds to secure the same purpose.

The ability of a young child to communicate effectively by using his or her own private language may, paradoxically, retard the use of the first word and subsequent vocabulary acquisition. A child with responsive parents may be able to communicate quite satisfactorily by making exclusive use of her or his own language. Only when the parents make an effort to substitute real words for the child's private words, is it likely that the child will begin to use utterances that are recognizable to nonfamily members. The momentous occasion when a child first uses a bona fide English word *as* a word usually takes place around the first birthday.

The First Word

A very plausible explanation for the way children reach this important plateau in language development has been proposed by Jean Piaget (1952a) on the basis of observations of his own children. Like all normal babies, Piaget's daughter Lucienne spontaneously began to emit sounds early in life. When she was slightly less than two months old, Lucienne would sometimes increase her vocal activity in response to sounds made by her father. She was unable to reproduce the exact sounds he made, but the fact that she was stimulated to "talk" led Piaget to refer to her reaction as **vocal contagion.** She did not really talk *back* but talked along *with* her father, as if his vocalizing activity was contagious. By the time she was three months old, Lucienne was able to imitate sounds made by her father, provided she had just made them herself. Piaget called this **mutual imitation,** emphasizing that it could only take place if Lucienne had instituted the interchange and if both father and daughter made mutual (or similar) sounds. Continuing this pattern, Lucienne eventually used a recognizable sound in the presence of her father to refer to a specific object.

This sequence may become clearer if you imagine that a mother and baby have engaged in mutual imitation involving the sound *ma-ma*. That is, the mother hears the baby spontaneously emitting the *ma-ma* sound as the child plays at babbling. The mother picks up a cue and says "ma-ma" just after the baby does. That prompts the baby to repeat "ma-ma" several times, which arouses an equal number of *ma-ma* responses from

Vocal contagion: child vocalizes with parent

Mutual imitation: parent and child repeat sounds initially made by child

the mother. After this "duet" has been refined over a period of time, the mother points to herself and says "ma-ma." The child responds with the same sound, and if the mother responds to this behavior with smiles or expressions of delight, the child may associate the sound with her. When the child consistently associates the sound *ma-ma* with the mother, a word has been learned.

The learning theorist explains the acquisition of the first word in much the same way as Piaget, differing primarily in terms used. Instead of referring to *vocal contagion* and *mutual imitation,* a learning theorist would point out that the sequence just described is an excellent illustration of *operant conditioning.* First the child emits a sound of its own volition. Then particular sounds (for example, *ma-ma*) are reinforced when the parent makes similar sounds, smiles, plays with the child, and so forth.

First word: child emits sound, is reinforced, builds association

Reinforcement strengthens the tendency of the child to use the *ma-ma* sound, and when this response is well established, the parents build up an association between the sound and an appropriate object (the mother) by enthusiastically reinforcing the child when the sound is used to refer to the object. In *Verbal Behavior* (1957), B. F. Skinner offers an analysis of the development of language based on sequences of emitted sounds and reinforcements.

While the acquisition of the first word can be explained quite adequately in terms of imitation and reinforcement, such is not the case with many aspects of early language development. Even two-year-olds, for example, speak and understand sentences they have never heard their parents say. They also put together words in ways that have never been reinforced. Detailed criticisms of learning theory explanations of language development, as well as alternate theories of language acquisition, will be discussed in Chapter 11, "Two to Five: Cognitive Development."

From Single Words to Word Combinations

Once a child learns to use one or more words, a single word may be used to communicate a variety of messages. Such use of language is called **holophrastic speech.** (*Holo* is Greek for *whole,* so holophrastic speech refers to the use of a single word as a whole "phrase.") A matter-of-fact "Milk," uttered by a fourteen-month-old just after a glass of milk is placed on the table, may be translated by a perceptive parent as "That's a glass of milk." An urgent "Milk," uttered as a child entreatingly pats the refrigerator door, will be taken as "I want a glass of milk." A tentative "Milk," uttered just after an accidental push of a glass of

Holophrastic speech: one-word communications

milk off a table, might be interpreted as "Oops. The glass of milk fell on the floor. Now how do you suppose that happened?" (It seems that such an interpretation might be justified if the child first gazes sadly at the mess on the floor and then slowly transfers that sorrowful gaze to the parent.)

These various possible interpretations of a child's use of holophrastic speech reveal the extent to which initial attempts to convey meaning through speech depend on the listener's awareness of the situation. If a parent is not able to see the situation or gestures accompanying the word, the meaning may not be clear. In order to use speech to communicate without resorting to other cues, it is almost always necessary to combine words into at least rudimentary sentences, for example, "That's milk," "Sally want milk," "Milk fall."

Many of the two-word utterances used by children are sometimes called **telegraphic** because they resemble telegrams in which nonessential words have been left out. "Milk fall," for example, gets the point across even though the child leaves out words that would be included by an adult using correct grammar. After analyzing the speech of young children, Martin D. S. Braine (1963) concluded that many telegraphic utterances may be formed from a quite limited pool of words. This occurs because an all-purpose word (called a *pivot* by Braine) may be used in essentially the same way with a variety of other words (called *open-class* words). One child studied by Braine, for example, said "All-gone vitamins," "Allgone eggs," "Allgone watch," "Allgone sticky" (after washing his hands), and "Allgone outside" (after the front door was closed). In this case *allgone* is the pivot word, and *vitamins, eggs,* and so on are open-class words.

Telegraphic speech: nonessential words omitted

Changing Opinions About the Use of Rules

Almost all psycholinguists of the 1960s and early 1970s seem to have been influenced by the idea that children follow consistent rules when they begin to speak. Telegraphic speech and pivot words, for example, were originally thought to be formed according to discernible patterns. More recent studies of the speech of young children cast doubt on the validity of hypotheses regarding use of rules. Martin D. S. Braine, for example, who thought he had detected consistently applied rules in children's use of pivot and open class words in 1963, came to a different conclusion in 1976. He reviewed all studies he could find of records of the spontaneous speech of young children from several countries and decided there is little evidence that two-year-olds follow rules as consis-

tently as he and other students of language had first thought. Braine
suggested that children exhibit certain patterns when they begin to
put words together but they do not seem to consistently use rules.
He coined the term *groping patterns* to call attention to the tentative
way young children experiment with word combinations to express
ideas.

Vocabulary Development and Styles of Acquisition

Katherine Nelson (1973) found that during the period between twelve
and eighteen months, children gradually acquire a vocabulary of approximately fifty words. Nelson found considerable overlap in the

As they develop language skills, some young children tend to be referential *speakers,
using words primarily to refer to objects or situations. Others tend to be* expressive
speakers, using words primarily to express feelings or desires.
© *Elizabeth Crews.*

words learned by different children, probably due to the overlap in their cognitive and social experiences. Among the most common categories were names for people, animals, parts of the body, food, clothing, and toys. In a later study of vocabulary development, Nelson (1981) looked for differences, as well as similarities, in the ways children acquire and use speech. Many children are **referential** speakers. They tend to use words to refer to objects or people. Vocabulary development in referential children is likely to center on naming an object ("dog"), or stressing one of its qualities ("big") or making an observation about it ("run"). Other children, however, tend to be expressive speakers. They use words to express feelings or desires. The initial vocabulary of such children is likely to include words such as "Hi," "want," or "like."

Some children referential, others expressive speakers

Nelson conceptualizes referential and expressive styles not as mutually exclusive types but as ends of a continuum. Individual children may have a preference, then, for one style over the other, but they are not exclusively referential or expressive speakers. At present very little is known about the factors that contribute to these preferences. In Nelson's (1981) sample, expressive speakers tended more often to be secondborn and from less educated families. What remains to be specified is the way these factors shape language use in the family.

Children build vocabulary, then, by modifying what were originally babbling sounds so that they function as words understandable by others. An interesting aspect of language acquisition is that *parents* also modify their speech as their children begin to talk.

Motherese

Most of the research on early verbal communication has involved mother-child pairs, and the modified speech used by mothers with their young children is called **motherese.** (The terms *baby talk* and *simplified speech* are sometimes used as synonyms.) Motherese differs both quantitatively and qualitatively from the speech used with older children and adults. It is typically higher in pitch (Garnica, 1977), which may function to attract and hold the young child's attention. It is also slower. In one recent study the mean rate of adult-adult speech was sixty-one words per minute, while the comparable rate with one- and two-year-olds was thirty-four words per minute (Ringler, 1978). Several researchers have documented that adults speak in shorter sentences when talking to children and increase the length of their utterances gradually as the children's language proficiency improves. In the same study cited above, Ringler found that one in three responses of mothers to one-year-olds

Motherese higher in pitch, slower, abbreviated

For Better or For Worse®

were abbreviated utterances (e.g., "Yes" in response to a question), while the ratio was one in five with two-year-olds. In that same period, repetitions declined, as did the relative frequency of declarative statements. Questions to children, however, increased, as did the use of function words (e.g., prepositions, conjunctions, and articles). A final example of the mothers' sensitivity to their children's limited cognitive and linguistic skills is reflected by the fact that over 80 percent of the nouns they used with children referred to concrete objects that were physically present.

Gradually increasing the length and complexity of conversational statements made to young children appears to facilitate language acquisition. It has been found (Cross, 1978) that mothers of children who display accelerated language skills are more likely to comment on and correctly state messages conveyed in telegraphic fashion by young children. If a child says "My book," for instance, parents are more likely to foster language development if they respond by saying "Yes. The book is yours," than if they simply murmur "Uh-huh." A richer, more advanced rephrasing of the child's simple utterance is thought to help the beginning linguist encode more advanced ways of speaking. As we shall see a bit later, though, rephrasing a grammatically incorrect statement the correct way will not necessarily cause a two- to five-year-old to make a change. In some ways, children at the next stage of development are more logical about grammatical constructions than those who devised the English language. If the past tense of *scold* is *scolded*, if *fold* becomes *folded*, and *mold* becomes *molded*, why shouldn't *hold* become *holded*?

Ways children learn to deal with inconsistencies of the English language will be discussed in Chapter 11—which deals with cognitive development during the years from two to five—starting on page 343.

Summary

1. Jean Piaget's description of cognitive development during the first two years outlines the stages of the **sensorimotor** period. From birth to one month **primitive schemes** are formed through variations of reflex activity. From one to four months **primary circular reactions** develop, involving repetition of satisfying bodily activities. Such activities illustrate **functional assimilation:** the tendency to use a capability. Between four to ten months **secondary circular reactions,** or the duplication of activities involving an object, appear. Awareness of the external environment is illustrated by emergence of the **object concept:** the realization that an object exists even when it is not perceived. **Coordination of secondary schemes,** where separate skills are combined to achieve a goal, occurs between eight and twelve months. **Tertiary circular reactions,** characterized by exploration and interest in novelty, are exhibited between twelve and eighteen months. During the final stage (eighteen to twenty-four months) thought replaces activity, and the child engages in imitation.
2. Various views of relationships between language and thought have been proposed. Piaget argued that language depends on thought. The American linguist Noam Chomsky suggested that language is independent of thought. The Russian scientist Lev Vygotsky proposed that language and thought are separate until the age of two, then interrelated.
3. During the first month of their lives, human infants demonstrate the ability to discriminate between sounds. A bit later they demonstrate that they can produce different sounds, first by cooing in reflexive ways and then in responsive ways. Babbling, in which speech-like syllables are repeated, peaks between nine and twelve months.
4. A plausible explanation for the way children come to speak a first word was proposed by Piaget. He suggested that the first step in the process is **vocal contagion,** in which a child vocalizes with a parent. Next, **mutual imitation** occurs, with both parent and child repeating sounds initially made by the child. Finally, the child uses a recognizable sound to refer to a specific object. Learning theorists have offered a similar explanation that outlines this sequence: the child emits a sound with reference to an object, is reinforced, and builds an association between the sound and an object.
5. Once a child learns to use one or more words, a single word may be

used to communicate a variety of messages, which is referred to as **holophrastic** speech. A bit later the child typically combines two words into rudimentary sentences that function as **telegraphic** speech.

6. As they build vocabularies, some children seem to be **referential** speakers, using words to refer to objects and qualities. Others tend to be **expressive** speakers, using words to express feelings or desires.

7. Many parents modify their speech as their children begin to talk. **Motherese,** as such speech is often called, is higher in pitch and slower than ordinary speech and involves abbreviated (or telegraphic) modes of communication.

Suggestions for Further Study

The Sensorimotor Period

If you would like more complete information about Piaget's description of the sensorimotor period of intellectual development, read pages 26–71 of *Piaget's Theory of Intellectual Development: An Introduction* (2nd ed., 1979) by Herbert Ginsburg and Sylvia Opper. Other books you might consult are *Understanding Piaget* (1971) by Mary Pulaski; and *Piaget's Theory of Cognitive Development: An Introduction for Students of Psychology and Education* (2nd ed, 1981) by Barry Wadsworth. If you would like to read Piaget's own account of cognitive development, including excerpts from his baby biographies of his own children, see *The Origins of Intelligence in Children* (1952).

Early Language Development

Two books to consult for more information about early language development are *A First Language: The Early Stages* (1973) by Roger Brown and *Language Acquisition* (1978) by P. A. and J. G. deVilliers.

Studying Early Language Development on Your Own

If you know someone with a child in the eighteen- to twenty-four-month age span, you might ask the parents about the child's vocabulary and use of words. You might inquire about the first word (what it was and when it was uttered), and ask them to list the words in the child's vocabulary. If possible, also spend at least thirty minutes with the child in a provocative and relaxed social situation and record all words (and nonwords) uttered. (If the situation is too sterile, and/or if the child is a bit apprehensive about the presence of a stranger, you might not get much of anything to record. Accordingly, it may help if you do your recording unobtrusively or from a hidden vantage point.) Analyze the list of words supplied by the parents and/or uttered by the child to determine if you have chosen a referential or expressive talker. You might also ask the parents whether the child has developed personal sounds that function as words, and whether they use "motherese" when conversing with the child. If they do, you might mention the conclusions of Cross (1978) that parents who respond to a child's utterances by elaborating on them seem to encourage language acquisition.

KEY POINTS

Research on Attachment Behavior

Stranger anxiety and separation anxiety typically appear before end of first year

Securely attached infants perceive mother as accessible, responsive

Mothers of resistant babies perceived as inept

Mothers of avoidant babies reserved, dislike contact

Mother typically at top of hierarchy of attachment figures

Infant Care Techniques Likely to Encourage Optimum Development

Effective mothers have good sense of timing

Infants and mothers need to take turns

Important for infants to learn they can produce consequences

Moderate rather than rich stimulation may be best for infants

Supportive programs help parents improve infant-handling skills

Mothers of competent children talk, respond, enrich, encourage, explain

Implications of Ineffective Mothering

Sex-typed and androgynous parents likely to respond to infants in different ways

Implications of Increasing Numbers of Employed Mothers

In 1970s disapproval of day care for young children

In 1980s research indicates day care children less dependent on mother

Child Abuse

Child abusers express aggressive impulses freely, were abused themselves

Child abusers must cope with frustrations, often live in social isolation

CHAPTER

8

THE FIRST TWO YEARS

RELATIONSHIPS WITH OTHERS

*A*fter discussing the birth process in Chapter 4, mention was made of hypotheses regarding the significance of initial child-parent relationships. John Kennell and Marshall Klaus (1976) argue that skin-to-skin contact between parent and child shortly after birth will have a lasting positive impact on mutual feelings of love. This hypothesis is similar to the concept of imprinting proposed by ethologists such as Konrad Lorenz. As noted in the evaluation of the research of Kennell and

Klaus on bonding just after birth and in the summary of revisions of thinking about critical periods presented in Chapter 5, there is little empirical support for the argument that the very first interactions between infants and caretakers are highly significant. Even so, many psychologists (as noted in Chapter 5) maintain that infancy is *the* most important stage of development, despite arguments by other theorists that early experiences may be less important than those that occur later. There is still a great deal of interest in attachment behavior. The infant's relationship with the primary caretaker may not be as important as some theorists have maintained, but it is still of considerable interest and it has been studied extensively.

Research on Attachment Behavior

Theorists who speculated about the possibility of critical periods in human development continued to study attachment behavior. For instance, René Spitz, who called attention to marasmus in motherless infants, specialized in the study of mother-child relationships after he had published his reports on the impact of institutional care. He reported (1965) that around the age of eight months, after an infant-mother attachment had been formed, infants began to show a marked fear of strangers. John Bowlby, who had been asked to make a survey of the impact of institutionalization after the observations about marasmus by Spitz had been publicized, carried out research and theorized extensively about the nature of attachment in *Attachment and Loss* (1969). He agreed with Spitz that **stranger anxiety,** as the reaction eventually came to be called, typically did appear around the age of eight months. Bowlby was also one of the first psychologists to notice that toward the end of the first year children begin to exhibit **separation anxiety.** If separated from the mother even for brief periods, many one-year-olds cry, scream, and manifest unmistakable signs of anxiety. If children of that age are separated from the mother for an extended period of time, or permanently because of the death of the mother, Bowlby noted that anxiety reactions were severe and prolonged. Mary Ainsworth, an American psychologist who carried out a carefully designed study of attachment behavior in Uganda (1967), came to similar conclusions about stranger and separation anxiety. She eventually developed ingenious experimental techniques for studying these two types of behavior. Because Ainsworth has developed a research paradigm that has been, and continues to be, used extensively, the next section outlines the nature of her research.

Stranger anxiety and separation anxiety typically appear before end of first year

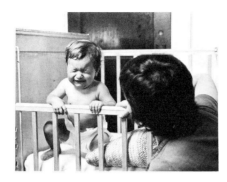 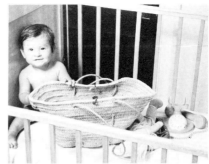

Stranger anxiety often appears at around eight months. This child is frightened by the appearance of a strange person and does not begin to relax until the stranger—who represents a drastic departure from the scheme for mother—withdraws.
Philip Jon Bailey.

Ainsworth's Studies of Stranger and Separation Anxiety

Four of the most carefully planned investigations of stranger and separation anxiety were carried out by Ainsworth, Blehar, Waters, and Wall (*Patterns of Attachment*, 1978). Over one hundred infants approximately one year old were observed in laboratory, as well as home, situations. (A summary of the sequence of situations the infants were exposed to in the controlled environment of the laboratory is presented in Table 8.1.) Observers tape-recorded a play-by-play account of what each baby and mother did, and in some cases, still or motion pictures were made of the baby's activities. The various records of infant and mother behavior were then coded, tabulated, and analyzed.

Ainsworth and her associates designed their investigation to shed light on several incompletely answered questions about stranger and separation anxiety. As soon as these two types of behavior were first described, some psychologists (for example, Schaffer and Emerson, 1964) reasoned that they indicated that an infant had formed an attachment to the mother. This hypothesis seemed valid since both types of behavior reveal that an eight-month-old infant is noticeably upset when the mother disappears or is replaced by a stranger. It soon became apparent, however, that not all infants reacted in the same way or to the same degree. The response of the child seems to depend on the situation. M. Lewis and J. Brooks (1975), for example, exposed seven- to nineteen-month-old children to strange adults and children at close

TABLE 8.1
DESCRIPTION OF PROCEDURES USED BY AINSWORTH IN STUDYING STRANGER AND
SEPARATION ANXIETY

Number of Episode	Persons Present	Duration	Brief Description of Action
1	Mother, baby, & observer	30 secs.	Observer introduces mother and baby to experimental room, then leaves. [Room contains many appealing toys scattered about]
2	Mother & baby	3 min.	Mother is nonparticipant while baby explores; if necessary, play is stimulated after 2 minutes.
3	Stranger, mother, & baby	3 min.	Stranger enters. First minute: Stranger silent. Second minute: Stranger converses with mother. Third minute: Stranger approaches baby. After 3 minutes mother leaves unobtrusively.
4	Stranger & baby	3 min. or less[a]	First separation episode. Stranger's behavior is geared to that of baby.
5	Mother & baby	3 min. or more[b]	First reunion episode. Mother greets and/or comforts baby, then tries to settle him again in play. Mother then leaves, saying "bye-bye."
6	Baby alone	3 min. or less[a]	Second separation episode.
7	Stranger & baby	3 min. or less[a]	Continuation of second separation. Stranger enters and gears her behavior to that of baby.
8	Mother & baby	3 min.	Second reunion episode. Mother enters, greets baby, then picks him up. Meanwhile stranger leaves unobtrusively.

[a] Episode is curtailed if the baby is unduly distressed.
[b] Episode is prolonged if more time is required for the baby to become re-involved in play.
Source: Ainsworth et al., *Patterns of Attachment* (Hillsdale, N.J.: Lawrence Erlbaum Associates, 1978), p. 37.

range and at a distance. They found that strange adults who came close to the children were quite likely to arouse a fear response, but if adult strangers remained at a distance, no signs of fear appeared. They also discovered that strange *children* of about the same age, whether near or far, aroused a *positive* reaction.

Ainsworth and her associates arranged the sequence of situations listed in Table 8.1 to seek causes of individual differences in both stranger and separation anxiety. After analyzing the tabulated results, they concluded that consistent patterns of infant-mother interaction were found in both laboratory and home situations and that these influenced how the child reacted in the experimental situations.

In their first investigations, Ainsworth and her associates identified three patterns of infant-mother interaction, which they designated Groups A, B, and C. In later studies, when the types of child and maternal behavior became more clearly established, terms that described the behavior of the infants in each group were added to supplement the original alphabetical designations. In Table 8.2 you will find a summary of infant behavior, maternal characteristics, and the infant's hypothesized perception of the mother for each of the three groups.

As you can see, Group B (securely attached) infants responded to the sequence of situations described in Table 8.1 by initially exploring freely when the mother was present (Episode 2). They tended to be cooperative and outgoing when a stranger joined the mother (Episode 3) but were visibly upset when separated from the mother (Episodes 4 and 6). When the mother returned (Episodes 5 and 8) Group B babies responded with obvious relief and made strenuous efforts to establish physical contact with her. The mothers of these securely attached babies were judged to enjoy bodily contact with their infants, to be responsive to the baby's signals, and to have a good sense of timing (for example, they knew when to pick the baby up and when to put the baby down). On the basis of the responses of Group B babies in the experimental episodes, Ainsworth and her associates concluded that they appeared to perceive the mother as an accessible and responsive person and as a secure base from which to explore. They seemed to be confident that the mother would be available to provide support if needed and that she would do this effectively.

Securely attached infants perceive mother as accessible, responsive

The mothers of anxiously attached and resistant (Group C) babies seemed to have good intentions and to be eager to provide physical contact, but they lacked the sensitivity and timing of Group B mothers. Ainsworth and her associates hypothesized that Group C babies have learned that their mothers are inept, which causes such children to be both anxious and resistant. They do not feel that they can count on the mother for satisfactory support and are angry and resentful about it.

Mothers of resistant babies perceived as inept

The mothers of anxious and avoidant Group A babies were noticeably

TABLE 8.2
DIFFERENCES IN MOTHER-INFANT INTERACTION REPORTED BY AINSWORTH

Type of Infant Behavior	Infant Behavior before, during, and after Separation from Mother	Behavior and Characteristics of Mother	Infant's Hypothesized Perception of Mother
Group B securely attached (about 70% of sample)	Active exploration when alone with mother. Visibly upset by separation. Respond strongly to mother's return, eagerly seek physical contact, quickly soothed. Cooperative and outgoing with strangers (when mother present)	Enjoy bodily contact with baby. Responsive to baby's signals. Good sense of timing.	Mother perceived as accessible and responsive. Mother serves as secure base from which to explore.
Group C anxiously attached and resistant (about 10 percent of sample)	Anxious even when alone with mother, disinclined to explore. Upset by separation. Make strong efforts to gain contact with mother but simultaneously display anger or resentment. Likely to be distressed when strangers approach (even when mother is present)	Seem to enjoy bodily contact with baby but not skilled in interacting with baby. Not sensitive to baby's signals. Poor sense of timing.	Infant lacks confidence in mother as an accessible and responsive person. Infant expects to be frustrated rather than comforted when upset. Mother does not function as a secure base from which to explore, which leads to anxiety and limits exploration.
Group A anxious and avoidant (about 20 percent of sample)	Disinterested and perfunctory exploration when alone with mother. Show little distress when separated. Avoid contact with mother when reunited. Not excessively wary of strangers, but avert gaze from mother (as if ignoring her) when strangers approach.	Do not enjoy bodily contact with infant. Rigid and compulsive. Little emotional expression. Impatient, resentful, or angry when baby interferes with own plans and activities.	Infant expects that efforts to gain comfort will be rebuffed. When subjected to stress, infant defends self by avoiding contact. Mother not recognized or acknowledged as a supportive person.

Source: Ainsworth, Blehar, Waters, and Wall, 1978; Ainsworth, 1979a, Ainsworth, 1979b.

different from the other mothers. They seemed to have an aversion to physical contact and sometimes revealed that they had negative feelings about their children. They were rigid, reserved, impatient, and self-centered. Ainsworth and her colleagues concluded that the basic response of infants to such mothers was to try to avoid contact. Group A babies did not exhibit anger or resentment about the mother's ineffectiveness but acted disinterested, uninvolved, and withdrawn. (In Eriksonian terms, anxiously attached and resistant Group C babies and anxious and avoidant Group A babies both exhibit signs of mistrust.)

Ainsworth's method of study and her classification scheme have become basic tools used by many other researchers interested in studying stranger and separation anxiety. Inevitably, when a large number of researchers replicate and analyze an original study, exceptions and omissions are noted. Some psychologists (for example, Thompson and Lamb, 1983) have called attention to a number of methodological complications and have suggested that the results of Ainsworth-type studies be interpreted tentatively. Others (for example, Waters, Vaughn, and Egeland, 1980) have concluded that Ainsworth puts too much stress on the mother and not enough on the child. Anxiously attached and resistant Group C babies, for example, tend to be evaluated less favorably as neonates on the Apgar and Brazelton scales. Their behavior in the strange situation might be due at least in part to inherited predispositions, which also shaped the behavior of the mothers. Still other researchers (for example, Lamb et al., 1983) have questioned that all babies can be classified into the three types described by Ainsworth. Even though Ainsworth's conclusions about the reactions of infants to stranger and separation situations need to be interpreted as general trends rather than clearly established facts, they have shed much light on an intriguing aspect of child behavior.

Mothers of avoidant babies reserved, dislike contact

How Crucial Is the Attachment Relationship?

One of the most intriguing points about research on attachment centers is the question of how much interactions between infant and caretaker influence later personality development. As a result of his studies of institutionalized children and attachment, John Bowlby (1973) hypothesized that through interactions with caretakers during the first year of life, children form **working models** of their world and themselves that exert a lasting influence on later behavior. For example, an anxiously attached and resistant infant (as classified by Ainsworth), whose mother seemed unable to respond to her baby's signals effectively, might develop a working model of the world as unresponsive and of self as unloved. These initial working models, Bowlby suggests,

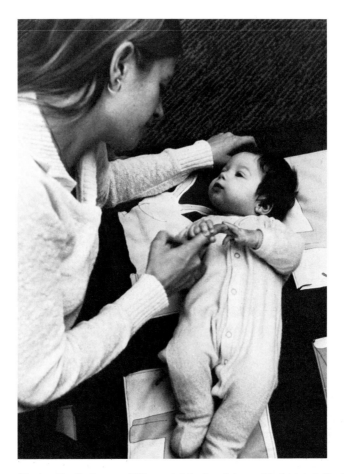

During the first year of life most infants relate positively to adults (such as father and grandfathers) with whom they have frequent contact. It appears, though, that in most cases the mother remains at the top of a hierarchy of attachment figures.
© *Suzanne Arms/Jeroboam.*

will establish patterns that will persist and continue to influence personality development throughout childhood, adolescence, and adulthood. Bowlby also hypothesized that it is essential for an infant to develop a relationship with *one* primary caretaker. Institutionalized infants who were cared for in routine fashion by several attendants were often found to have significantly more personal and emotional problems later in life than those who were given substantial care by one person.

When Ainsworth's findings are interpreted with reference to Bowlby's hypotheses, some perplexing questions are raised. Will mothers of anxiously attached or anxious and avoidant babies cause their children to develop potentially harmful working models? If no single individual takes primary responsibility for an infant, will adjustment problems be likely to appear later? Taken together, these two questions might appear to lead to a double-bind or no-win situation for a conscientious and thoughtful mother who seems to lack infant-care skills. She might find herself brooding, "I don't seem to be able to get my baby to respond but I know it's essential for me to take the primary responsibility for child care. It looks as if we're stuck with each other and I'm probably going to make a mess out of my child's life." Fortunately, the situation does not appear to be that hopeless.

As noted in Chapter 5, there is evidence (Rutter, 1979, Clarke and Clarke, 1976) that institutionalized children who received only perfunctory care as infants later were able to overcome an abominable start in life. Furthermore, revisions of the critical period hypothesis, together with evaluations of the significance of aspects of development that occur after infancy, lend support to the view (which served as the theme of Chapter 5) that all stages of development are important. Erikson's description of psychosocial stages and Havighurst's lists of developmental tasks call attention to the fact that different personal and social qualities take on significance at different age levels. Finally, you are reminded of the observations of Honzik and Anderson praising the adaptability of the human organism. It does not seem likely, therefore, that mothers who don't seem to quite get the hang of interacting successfully with their babies are going to do irreparable harm. If they so desire, they can improve their infant-care skills by reading about effective techniques (to be summarized later in this chapter), or by enrolling in a program of instruction in infant care. Finally, mothers might take comfort in learning that they need not take the entire responsibility for child care.

A Hierarchy of Attachment Figures

Rudolph Schaffer and Peggy Emerson (1964) found that many infants seem capable of forming a number of attachments at the same time. Furthermore, satisfying attachments are formed with adults of varying ages and of either sex. Michael E. Lamb (1979), for instance, reports that seven- to thirteen-month-old infants show no preference between their mothers and fathers, although the mother may be sought more frequently when the child is frightened. The fact that the mother appears to be preferred in stress situations has led some theorists (for example, Bowlby, 1969; Ainsworth, 1979a) to suggest that there is a **hierarchy** of attachment figures. Under normal circumstances, infants may respond

Mother typically at top of hierarchy of attachment figures

equally well to several familiar caretakers. If infants are distressed or ill, however, they seem to seek the person they have identified as the primary caretaker (usually the mother).

Two reasons young children may seek the mother rather than the father when distressed are familiarity and availability. In most homes, even those where the father may share infant-care responsibilities, the mother has more frequent and sustained contact with the child. Consequently, the mother is more likely to be present to supply comfort and sympathy when they are needed in everyday "emergencies" and the child thus learns to turn to her more or less habitually when distressed. In a review of studies on father-infant interaction, Campos and others (1983, p. 879) concluded that fathers *can* be as responsive as mothers to an infant's needs, but it is not clear that they *are* as responsive. One reason may be that just mentioned: they have not had as many opportunities as mothers to be responsive. Other reasons may stem from findings that fathers tend to respond to infants in different ways than mothers. Campos and his colleagues note the following ways that fathers and mothers differ in interacting with infants: fathers provide bursts of stimulation, mothers are more rhythmic; fathers respond to motor cues, mothers to social cues; fathers engage in more stimulating and unpredictable play; fathers respond more to boys, mothers to girls.

Regardless of who interacts with a young child, there seem to be certain infant care techniques that are likely to encourage optimum development.

Infant Care Techniques Likely to Encourage Optimum Development

Stern: Repetition, Timing, Optimal Stimulation

Daniel Stern (1977) has spent years poring over videotapes of the facial and bodily activities involved in early mother-child interactions. Such analyses have led him to conclude that an **episode of engagement** (pp. 79–80) between mother and infant typically involves the intention on the mother's part to maintain the baby's attention or enter into some sort of game (for example, peekaboo) to arouse pleasure. Usually the mother will repeat a brief routine of speech and physical movements (for example, saying "You're a sweetie-pie" while nuzzling the baby's face) several times in succession. Stern concluded that in order to interact

Effective mothers have good sense of timing

successfully with a baby, mothers must have an excellent sense of timing, engaging in a particular type of activity at the precise moment the baby seems ready for it. Even the most sensitive mother, however, is sure to encounter periods of time when the baby is either not in the mood for play or the mother misinterprets the infant's signals. An important point about a successful episode of engagement appears to be gauging the amount of stimulation the baby can handle at a given point in time. Sometimes a mother may confront the infant with too many verbal and physical stimuli. In other cases, she may not stimulate the baby appropriately to arouse a positive response. Just as the mood of the baby governs the success or failure of a particular interaction, so the mood of the mother plays a part. If the mother is tired or tense, she may be less sensitive than usual. Or if she fails to get a response from her baby after several minutes of effort and experimentation, she may experience the feeling that she is being rejected by her child and lose her enthusiasm for play.

Schaffer: The Need to Take Turns

H. Rudolph Schaffer (1977a) is another psychologist who has made detailed analyses of mothering. He agrees with Stern that effective mothers are exceptionally adept at picking up subtle cues to gauge the mood of a baby and that they have an excellent sense of timing. In addition, Schaffer stresses the need for mother and infant to take turns—after the baby started an interchange. Most successful mother-baby interactions apparently begin with the mother's response to some spontaneous activity of the infant. If the mother's response stimulates the child to build up to a smile and perhaps reach out or engage in some other form of activity, it seems important for the mother not to interrupt the baby's behavior as it builds toward a crescendo. Instead, she should act as an interested, receptive audience until the baby has "performed" and at that point respond enthusiastically.

Infants and mothers need to take turns

Finally, Schaffer emphasizes that it is extremely important for babies, quite early in life, to acquire the feeling that they can produce consequences. The suggestion that infants should learn that they can produce consequences serves as an antidote to descriptions of behavior modification techniques by some learning theorists. Some behaviorists who were impressed by the potentiality of behavior modification when it was first described unwittingly reinforced the view that parents should always be the shapers and the child should always be the shapee. (More recent analyses of behavior modification have placed greater stress on ways individuals can shape their own behavior.) They also failed to recognize all of the implications of withholding reinforcement to extinguish types of child behavior that were bothersome to adults. B. C. Etzel and J. L. Gewirtz (1967), for instance, wanted to demonstrate how caretakers could reduce crying in infants. They no-

Important for infants to learn they can produce consequences

ticed that nurses in pediatric wards promptly picked up infants who started to cry. They explained to the nurses that this reaction strengthened tendencies to cry and suggested that crying could be reduced if responses were withheld. The experimenters reported that when nurses permitted two infants to "cry themselves out" a few times, the overall rate of crying diminished.

C. A. Aldrich and several associates (1945a, 1945b) on the other hand, observed crying behavior in hospital nurseries and concluded that the main cause was hunger. They also discovered that prolonged crying spells were almost three times as frequent in the hospital as at home. (Home babies had about four prolonged crying spells a day, and their total crying time per day was rarely more than an hour.) These findings led Aldrich to hypothesize that the home babies cried less because they received more attention. With the cooperation of several associates (1946), he increased the amount of time nursery babies were cared for from 0.7 hours a day to 1.9. The mean amount of crying dropped from 113 to 55 minutes per day. Mary D. Ainsworth (1972) corroborated these findings. She studied infant-mother interactions in twenty-six families and concluded that babies whose mothers responded promptly to crying from the outset tended to cry little and had developed a variety of other modes of communication by the end of the first year. Not responding to cries in the hope of not spoiling the child tended to have exactly the opposite effect.

Taken together, these studies might be interpreted as indicating that responding to an infant's cries most of the time will reduce the amount of crying and perhaps lead to greater peace of mind and body for infant *and* parents. If parents resolutely refuse to respond to crying for an *extended* period of time in an effort to extinguish such behavior, the baby might go hungry (and express displeasure ever more vocally as the hunger pangs increase in intensity), or perhaps lack of reinforcement will cause the infant to develop a sense of mistrust (which Erikson believes should be avoided as much as possible). This illustrates a problem sometimes encountered when operant-conditioning principles are applied to child behavior. An experimenter who shapes the behavior of a rat or pigeon in a Skinner box can usually control the situation so that only one variable is reinforced or not. The human infant is much more complex than a rat or pigeon, however, and withholding reinforcement with the intention of extinguishing one response may inadvertently shape other types of behavior in unintentional or unexpected ways.

Schaffer argues (1977a, p. 56) that withholding all reinforcement when babies cry would be likely to cause children to develop a sense of helplessness. The infant uses cries and other forms of behavior to communicate needs and desires. If no one responds, the baby is likely to take on characteristics of children reared in deprived environments. In Schaffer's opinion, therefore, it is perhaps more important for children to learn before the end of the first year that *they* can successfully use behavior-modification techniques on their parents than for the opposite to occur.

Ainsworth: Control, Contact, and Delight

Mary Ainsworth analyzed her own work on mother-infant interaction and reviewed the work of others (Ainsworth and Wittig, 1972) and concluded that the following factors seemed to favor development:

1. The provision of an environment that helps the child develop the feeling of having some control over what happens. (This same point is stressed by Schaffer.)
2. Seeing things from the infant's point of view and responding promptly and appropriately to the baby's signals.
3. Frequent and sustained physical contact, especially during the first year of life, including the ability to soothe the baby's discomfort through physical handling.
4. The establishment of feelings of mutual delight between mother and child.

Bower: The Disadvantages of Overstimulation

T. G. R. Bower is still another specialist in the study of the responses of infants to others. Bower believes, as do Stern and Schaffer, that it is a mistake to bombard infants with stimuli. Overstimulation might take the form of too much interaction, trying to induce babies to respond to something they are not ready to respond to, and prolonging or overemphasizing a particular interaction. Bower believes that babies overburdened with people, things, and experiences, may be faced with interpretive problems beyond their capabilities. The concept that an infant needs time to sort out experiences helps explain why mothers who are willing to take turns seem to have successful interactions with their children.

Support for Bower's hypothesis is supplied by research studies by Burton L. White of the impact of stimulation on infant development. In an early investigation (White and Castle, 1964), week-old institutionalized infants were given twenty minutes of extra handling a day. At the end of thirty days, developmental-test ratings of the handled infants were compared to ratings of nonstimulated babies. The only difference was a greater amount of visual attention shown by the stimulated infants. This prompted White (1967) to provide another group of institutionalized infants with extra stimulation by enabling them to look out of their cribs, or at intriguing objects suspended over their cribs, or at patterned crib bumpers. Compared to control infants, who were placed in plain cribs with high sides, the rich-environment babies showed greater visual attentiveness as well as accelerated reaching behavior.

In an effort to determine the effectiveness of different kinds of enrichment, White and Held (1966) placed one group of infants in the rich-environment cribs, another group in cribs that were equipped on each side with large disks from which pacifiers projected, and still another group in plain cribs with high sides. The infants in the two-disk cribs developed reaching behavior faster than those who had been placed in the rich-environment cribs, who, in turn, were ahead of the control-group babies. Apparently the rich-environment infants had so many things to look at that they neglected to reach for objects. The babies in the two-disk cribs, on the other hand, concentrated all their attention on the single, within-reach object attached to either side of their cribs. (This finding is similar to the hypothesis noted in discussing physical development in Chapter 6 that premature infants do not appear ready to respond to ahead-of-schedule stimulation.)

Moderate rather than rich stimulation may be best for infants

Variations of Mother-Infant Interactions

Stern, Schaffer, Ainsworth, and Bower agree that some mothers seem to have an aptitude for interpreting infant behavior, timing their responses, and allowing for instantaneous changes in interest and mood. But it may also be that some mothers are simply luckier than others. As noted in Chapter 5 Alexander Thomas and his associates (1963) felt that babies could be classified into three general types: easy, difficult, and slow to warm up. Mothers who are fortunate enough to have an easy baby will probably be more successful at satisfying interactions than mothers of difficult infants. It is entirely possible, of course, that some mothers might at least partly "produce" difficult babies in just a few days of mistimed, ineffective handling and that some babies are slow to warm up because the mother doesn't know how to establish successful episodes of engagement.

It would be a mistake to assume, however, that babies and mothers are entirely consistent in their interactions. Not only do mother and child have good and bad days and minute-by-minute changes in mood; there are likely to be changes in relationships over time. Schaffer (1977a, p. 53) points out that the way mothers treat and handle their children changes as the infant matures. Furthermore, there is evidence (Moss, 1967, and Lewis, 1972) that mothers tend to treat girls differently from boys, particularly as the children grow older. Before the age of three months, mothers cuddle boys and girls about the same extent. After three months, girls are cuddled to a significantly greater extent. (Moss hypothesizes that mothers may be positively reinforced by the responsiveness of female infants and negatively influenced by the irritability of many male infants.)

A mother may respond to her baby, therefore, not only in terms of the infant's personality traits but also because of its sex and changes in behavior that occur as development takes place. The impact of rapid physical and cognitive development also causes *children* to alter their patterns of response to their mothers (and other adults) during the first two years. The child who exhibited anxiety when separated from the mother at the age of twelve months, for instance, may be eager to move away from her and explore independently at the age of twenty-four months.

While it may be desirable to encourage an infant to develop a feeling of control over others and his or her environment, there will inevitably come a time—usually before the age of two—when the child will have to begin to learn that he or she must also defer to the wishes of others. The necessity for learning that sometimes it is necessary to take into account the desires of others leads to an interesting question about effective child care: Will parents who are sensitive to a baby's needs and capable of responding effectively to the baby's behavior be equally adept at handling a three-year-old who balks at restrictions, or a ten-year-old who has difficulty getting along with others, or a fifteen-year-old who resents authority?

It seems likely that an ability to see things from the child's point of view will serve a caretaker well in all of these situations, but there are certainly significant differences between the types of behavior just noted and the behavioral repertoire of a six-month-old infant. Parents who find that they just don't seem to see things the way an infant sees them, accordingly, might console themselves with the thought that they may be more successful dealing with an older child. Some educators choose to teach preschool children; others prefer to teach the primary, elementary, or high school grades. It seems likely that most teachers choose a particular grade level because they feel an affinity for children of that age. Perhaps many parents also have an affinity for a particular age level. However, unlike teachers, who are presented with a new batch of students of the same age each September, parents have no choice in the matter and must interact with children throughout the span of development. The need to deal with a child at all ages may cause problems. Perhaps only rarely will a caretaker be equally effective in dealing with children of all ages (which might be thought of as another reason for endorsing the view that no particular stage of development is crucial).

Parents who interact with their children in a variety of ways, show interest in what they do, show that achievements are admired and appreciated, and communicate love in a warm and sincere way are likely to encourage competence in their offspring.
Anna Kaufman Moon/Stock, Boston.

If it is true that some parents have aptitudes for interacting with infants while others have a knack for handling older children, the question arises: Can those who are not "natural" caretakers with children of a particular age level learn how to become more skillful? It seems likely that at least some of the qualities necessary for successfully interacting with infants (to take the age level being analyzed in this chapter) can be acquired by referring to the conclusions of Stern, Schaffer, and Ainsworth. Any parent who is willing to try can let the child instigate activities, can respond promptly, and can use repetition when responding. It may be, however, that not all parents will be able to properly interpret a baby's signals or correctly assess rapid changes in mood. (Group C mothers in the Ainsworth studies, for instance, had good intentions but were ineffective.) If this is the case, caretakers may simply have to do the best they can when they are a bit baffled by the behavior of an infant and console themselves with the hope that they may have greater empathy with the child when she or he is older.

Supportive and Early Intervention Programs

It may be possible, though, for parents who sense that they are not skilled in handling an infant, particularly one that Thomas and Chess would classify as difficult, to improve their child-rearing skills. A number of *supportive programs* for infants and parents have been developed in the last few years. Dorothy S. Huntington notes (1979, p. 849) that such programs are often designed to accomplish the following goals: release guilt about a child's behavior, enhance the self-esteem and self-image of parents, encourage the development of inner controls in place of physical reactions (particularly with parents who have physically abused their children), supply understanding and awareness of individual differences between children and the nature of their needs, and provide new ways of interacting with a child.

Several psychologists have developed **early intervention programs,** primarily for use with lower-class, educationally deprived mothers. (Several such programs are described by Beller, 1979.) One of the best known of these is the Florida Parent Education Program, developed by Ira J. Gordon (1969). The basic goals of the Florida program are to enhance the cognitive and personality development of the child and to promote the mother's self-esteem and her conviction that she can affect what happens to her and her child. Women from the community were trained by Gordon and his associates to visit socially and economically disadvantaged mothers in their homes and teach them games and exercises that were developed by taking into account Piaget's observations on cognitive development (which were discussed in Chapter 7).

Supportive programs help parents improve infant-handling skills

When the later cognitive and social behavior of children who had been through the Florida program was compared with that of control children who had not, it was reported (Gordon and Guinagh, 1974) that the early training had produced lasting gains in intellectual functioning but not in personality traits. It was also reported that mothers were most likely to report enhanced feelings of self-esteem and control if they had been trained to teach other mothers the techniques.

Effective Child-Care Techniques (Ten to Twenty-four Months)

All the techniques just summarized are appropriate for use with infants who have not yet learned to walk and talk. As they approach their first birthdays and develop locomotor and language skills, children function as quite different organisms than they did when they were babes in arms.

At the time the cognitive critical period hypothesis was widely endorsed, Burton L. White was asked to direct a project (the Harvard Preschool Project, funded by the Head Start Division of the Office of Economic Opportunity) to discover if certain experiences during the first six years of life could be structured so that children would be better prepared for schooling. White and his associates began their task by first describing the characteristics of six-year-olds who possessed overall *competence* and those who did not. After specific abilities leading to competence were defined, the Harvard researchers attempted to discover the kinds of experiences that led to these abilities by making detailed observations of thirty-four families: half selected because they seemed likely to produce competent children; the other half selected because they seemed likely to have children below average in competence. The way parents handled their children in the home was observed at length, and the abilities of the children were measured in a variety of ways. Mothers of children who were rated as highly competent used the following types of child-care techniques (White and Watts, 1973, pp. 242–243):

Talked to the child often and in understandable terms

Made the child feel that what she or he was doing was interesting

Provided many objects for the child to play with and arranged for the child to have access to a variety of situations

Mothers of competent children talk, respond, enrich, encourage, explain

Led the child to expect that help and encouragement would be supplied most, but not all, of the time

Demonstrated and explained to the child primarily when the child asked for instruction and assistance

Some parents seem to be more skilled than others in responding to their children in sensitive, security-building ways.
© *Erika Stone.*

An analysis of these various techniques leads to the conclusion that during the first two years of child-adult interactions, effective caretakers are very adept at responding to activities initiated by the child. This responsiveness appears to be especially important during the first year of life, as revealed by the list of effect techniques reported by Stern, Schaffer, and Ainsworth, but it appears to be significant later as well. Examination of the techniques used by the successful mothers described by White and his associates leads to the conclusion that throughout the first two years effective caretakers encourage the child to explore and interact. Explanations seem to be more effective when the child asks for them.

Implications of Ineffective Mothering

These conclusions lead to two intriguing questions: *Why* are some mothers more sensitive and effective than others? Is it always a good idea for the *mother* to take primary responsibility for child rearing? In regard to the first question, there are many possible answers, and few of them can be evaluated with any degree of precision or certainty. A psychoanalyst might propose that mothers of anxious and avoidant Group A babies (as classified by Ainsworth) might have suffered fixation during the oral and anal stages and thereby acquired neurotic tendencies that were communicated to the child. In addition, a psychoanalyst might suggest that a woman who seemed to find it difficult to develop a warm relationship with her child might have failed, during her own infancy, to view *her* mother as a love object. A follower of Erikson might trace part of the behavior of ineffective mothers to failure to achieve a sense of trust or autonomy during the first two years (and to develop other positive traits during later stages of psychosocial development). Klaus and Kennell, taking into account the possibility of imprinting during a critical period, might attribute the behavior of mothers who do not enjoy bodily contact with their children to lack of skin-to-skin contact the first few hours after birth. Other theorists might suggest that mothers of Group A babies were born with characteristics of temperament that predisposed them to resist cuddling. Such behavioral characteristics might have caused their parents to be confused or unresponsive not only during infancy but throughout the formative years.

In addition to factors that already have been discussed, another possible explanation for differences in attitudes toward mothering centers on perceptions of sex roles.

Due to interactions between inherited predispositions (such as hormonal balances), cultural sex stereotypes, and experiences, some women (and men) may be more attracted to and comfortable with infant-care responsibilities than others. Sandra Bem (1975, 1976, 1981) has

Sex-typed and androgynous parents likely to respond to infants in different ways

studied the extent to which individuals can be classified as **sex-typed** (the tendency to exhibit forms of stereotyped masculine or feminine behavior) or high in psychological androgyny[1] (the integration of both masculine and feminine traits in the same individual). Sex-typed females, for example, respond favorably when asked to care for an infant but may refuse to try to nail two boards together (because it is a "masculine" rather than "feminine" form of behavior). Sex-typed males may be extremely reluctant to handle a baby or even wind a package of yarn into a ball (apparently because they will be made to appear "effemi-

---

[1] Androg*y*nous, spelled with a *y*, is defined in dictionaries and usually used to indicate possessing both male and female characteristics. As used in some books and articles by psychologists, however, androgyny refers to the tendency for persons to think of themselves as human beings rather than as males or females. Androg*e*nous spelled with an *e*, refers to the impact of the male sex hormone, androgen.

nate"). Adults of both sexes who are rated high in psychological an-drogyny appear able to move between masculine and feminine roles without difficulty or self-consciousness.

Furthermore, some individuals appear to be undifferentiated (that is, low in both masculinity and femininity); others Bem classifies as femi-nine males (low in independence), masculine males (low in nurturance), feminine women (low in independence), or masculine women (low in nurturance). It would seem logical to assume that the response of any father or mother to skin-to-skin contact with a newborn baby (as well as later interactions) would depend on the tendencies that have been de-scribed by Bem. A sex-typed female would presumably be more likely to form an attachment than an undifferentiated woman or one classified as a masculine woman. A sex-typed male might not be influenced by early contacts or might even refuse to handle the child. A male classified high in psychological androgyny, by contrast, might respond positively to early contact and enjoy sharing infant-care responsibilities with the mother.

Other factors that might influence a woman's reaction to early contact with a newborn baby include her attitude toward pregnancy, the amount of discomfort she suffered during pregnancy, and the ease or difficulty of labor and birth. Furthermore, a new mother might discover after the first few days that she resents, rather than enjoys, the respon-sibilities of infant care. (This might be particularly true if she has been employed.)

Characteristics of the child may also shape the mother's attitudes toward child care. If the baby is attractive, easy to care for, and respon-sive, a woman classified by Bem as masculine might be won over. If the baby is unattractive, difficult to care for, and given to uncontrollable crying and unpredictable demands, a sex-typed woman who had looked forward to motherhood might become disenchanted.

Until recently, the answer to the second question—Is it always a good idea for the mother to take care of child rearing during the first two years?—probably would have been an unhesitating "Yes." Today, be-cause of changes in American culture, as well as research by behavioral scientists, the answer may sometimes be "Perhaps not." To understand part of the reasoning behind that statement, some relevant cultural fac-tors should be taken into account.

Implications of Increasing Numbers of Employed Mothers

One of the most significant developments in American society in the 1980s has been the increasing number of women employed outside the

About half of all mothers of preschool children are employed at least part-time, which has led to an increase in use of day care. Many day care arrangements involve supervision by grandparents.
© Susan Lapides.

home. New conceptions of sex roles, the "women's movement," stress on self-fulfillment, the need to augment family income during a period of inflation, and other factors have contributed to the tendency of women to seek some form of employment. In 1965 only 20 percent of all mothers of preschool children were employed; by 1982 the proportion had risen to 48 percent and the trend is expected to continue. Because of the high divorce rate, as well as an increasing tendency for women to keep children born out of wedlock instead of placing them for adoption, it has been estimated that approximately 40 percent of children born in America at present will spend at least some time in a single-parent home. Fifty-six percent of all single mothers work, compared with 37 percent of married mothers. At present (according to estimates by governmental agencies) 55 percent of preschool children whose mothers work outside the home are cared for during the day by relatives (father, grandmother, siblings), 32 percent are cared for by a nonrelated woman in her home, and 13 percent attend a day care center.

The classification "preschool children" includes all children up to the age of five, of course, and many substitute-care arrangements probably involve two- to five-year-olds. There are no accurate statistics available, but it seems likely that most mothers care for their own children during at least the first year. An attachment bond is thought to be formed during the first year of a child's life, typically with the primary caretaker, and once that bond is formed, stranger and separation anxiety are likely to be manifested by the child. After initial anxiety about separation, however, children over the age of eighteen months or so increasingly begin to relate to others and are not upset about separation from the mother. Two-year-olds taken to a nursery school for the first time, for example, often cry and exhibit anxiety the first few minutes after the mother leaves, but typically get over initial fear in short order and begin to enjoy themselves.

Aspects of Substitute Care Arrangements

The most significant point about a substitute care arrangement probably centers on how soon it begins after the birth of a child. If a child is placed under the care of another person after an attachment bond has been formed and after separation anxiety has been overcome, development might be expected to proceed satisfactorily. But even if a six-month-old (or even younger) child is placed under the care of another person, development might be expected to proceed satisfactorily *provided* the substitute mother established a supportive relationship. A supportive relationship would include factors such as those described by Erikson in his analysis of the stage of trust versus mistrust, as well as techniques just enumerated in the description of sensitive and effective mothers. A satisfactory substitute might be the child's grandmother, or father, or a child-care professional. In some cases, it might be argued, an infant would be better off under the care of such an individual than under the care of the mother.

Suppose that within a few weeks after a woman gives birth it becomes clear that she clearly fits in the category of anxious and avoidant Group A mothers described by Ainsworth. As noted in Table 8.2, these characteristics include: "Do not enjoy bodily contact with infant. Rigid and compulsive. Little emotional expression. Impatient, resentful, or angry when baby interferes with own plans and activities." In such cases, the child would seem to be better off under the care of someone else who possessed the characteristics of securely attached, Group B mothers (who enjoy bodily contact, are responsive, and have a good sense of timing). Perhaps some women who elect to place very young children under the care of others have enough self-insight to realize that they are doing more harm than good when they care for the child themselves. In other cases, a woman may quickly develop the feeling that she is "just not cut out to be a mother" but be apprehensive about looking for a substitute out of fear she will harm her child. The same kind of apprehension might be felt by a woman who *must* get back to work. Guilt about placing a young child in the care of others might be particularly likely to occur if the mother reads books on child care published in the 1960s and 1970s. These were the decades when the early writings of Lorenz, Spitz, and Bowlby had called attention to the hypothesis that the first years were a critical period in development. Because of the well-publicized critical period hypothesis, many of the first evaluations of day care stressed negative factors. Claire Etaugh (1980) surveyed the most popular child-care books published in the 1970s and concluded that only seven out of twenty-four approved of mothers of young children working. Some developmental psychologists (e.g., Hogan, 1974) who were concerned about the devastating impact of institutionalization reported in early studies suggested that children under the age of three be *forbidden* to attend day care centers. Others (e.g., Blehar, 1974) studied children in mediocre day care centers and reported a variety of problems in development.

In 1970s, disapproval of day care for young children

Current Evaluations of Day Care

During the 1980s, concern about day care is not as extreme as it was ten years ago. One reason for a somewhat more favorable attitude is a result of doubts about the existence of a critical period in the establishment of attachment. As noted earlier, studies by Lorenz and others led to the conclusion that there are *sensitive*, rather than critical, periods in development. In addition, Bowlby, Rutter, Clarke and Clarke, and other researchers found evidence that children deprived of contact with the mother or other single caretaker during the first year of life later often establish satisfactory relationships with others. Furthermore, observational and experimental studies of the impact of day care on young children supported the following conclusions (reported in a review by Clarke-Stewart and Fein, 1983):

1. Most children maintain attachment to the mother even when other individuals provide care several hours a day. (The mother typically stays at the top of the attachment hierarchy.)
2. Compared with home-reared children, the quality of a day care child's attachment may differ in the direction of greater distance, avoidance, and independence from the mother.
3. For most day care children, patterns of greater avoidance and distance probably reflect a sensible adaptive reaction to separation from the mother rather than a pathological disturbance.
4. Reactions to separation are most likely to be extreme if day care begins during the first year, before a stable attachment between mother and child has been formed. (Additional research findings on the impact of day care on two- to five-year-olds will be summarized in Chapter 12.)

In 1980s, research indicates day care children less dependent on mother

While the research results just noted might help parents reduce feelings of guilt about arranging for someone else to care for their young child, these conclusions should not be interpreted as a blanket endorsement of day care. Many of the day care centers studied by researchers were affiliated with institutions of higher learning where personnel were well aware of research on critical periods and the need for responsive care. Not all day care centers or alternative arrangements are equally good. Some are mediocre, some are probably not too different from the kind of care provided in institutions, and some highly publicized day care arrangements are clearly harmful. Before making a decision about day care, therefore, parents should consider various possibilities and evaluate the kind of care that will be provided.

Picture a husband and wife who are both engaged in careers. They both like their jobs and together they have established a very satisfactory standard of living they wish to maintain. They want to have a child but both agree that the wife should take only a short maternity leave and then return to her job. The baby is born and the mother cares for it during the first ten months. At that point the mother decides she must return to her job. She and her husband begin to explore day care alternatives even before the baby is born. They discover that they have three basic options: a day care center, an arrangement where a woman provides day care for children in *her* home, and a full-time baby sitter who would care for the child in *their* home. They visit a number of day care centers and day care homes and interview a dozen potential baby sitters. They also talk to all their acquaintances (and friends of their acquaintances) who have recently arranged for day care. They discover that day care centers vary enormously in terms of the qualifications of the personnel, the kind of care provided, and the "atmosphere." They find just as much variability in women providing home care and in those who offer to baby-sit full time. Some have impressive graduate degrees, some give the impression that they love caring for children, and some make it clear (unintentionally) that they care for children only because they need the money. Eventually, the parents choose a home-care arrangement operated by a sensitive woman who seems to have a gift for establishing rapport with young children. They select this option because of recommendations from others, but also because they feel there are advantages to an arrangement where their child will become accustomed very early in life to interacting with peers.

The increase in the number of employed mothers leading to greater use of day care is one cultural phenomenon of the 1980s. Another (unrelated) trend is the prevalence of child abuse.

Child Abuse

According to the National Center on Child Abuse in Washington, D.C., one out of every forty-three American children under the age of fourteen was abused in some way or another in 1982. This rate of mistreatment represents a sharp increase from figures compiled twenty or even ten years ago. Part of the increase in the rate of child abuse is attributable to greater awareness of the problem and more accurate statistics. New laws, for instance, require doctors and hospital personnel to report injuries to children not traceable to accidents. Even allowing for such factors, however, it is clear that child abuse is alarmingly prevalent in contemporary American society.

In a review of books and articles on child abuse, R. D. Parke and C. W. Colmer (1975) note that hypotheses regarding causes can be summarized under three headings: psychiatric, sociological and social-situational. Parke and Collmer report that the authors of the first articles on child abuse (published in the 1950s and 1960s) often suggested that basic causes were traceable to characteristics of child abusers that became apparent when psychiatric analyses were made. Among traits frequently found in parents who abused their children were low self-esteem, self-centeredness, rigidity, impulsiveness, immaturity, and hypersensitivity. Parke and Collmer note that while child abusers often display one or more of these traits, no consistent pattern that characterizes such parents as a group has emerged. The most common factor appears to be a tendency to express aggressive impulses too freely (Spinetta and Rigler, 1972). There *is* consistent evidence, however, that child abusers were themselves abused as children and that their parents were often demanding and aggressive individuals who disregarded their children's needs.

Child abusers express aggressive impulses freely, were abused themselves

One of the sociological explanations for child abuse focuses on the American attitude toward violence. Murders occur ten times more frequently in this country than in England (Geis and Monahan, 1975). The assault and battery rate in America is about five times the rate in Canada (Steinmetz, 1974). In a survey of middle-class American families, 93 percent of the parents reported that they used physical punishment (Stark and McEvoy, 1970). Violence is featured on American television to a much greater extent than it is in any other country. Ross Parke and Ronald Slaby (1983), for instance, reported that for all types of television programs, an average of 7.5 violent acts are depicted every hour. It is not possible to determine precisely how the various trends indicated by these statistics are related to child abuse, but some theorists (for example, R. J. Gelles, 1973) hypothesize that the extent to which violence permeates our society might predispose parents to resort to physical aggression when angered by the behavior of a child.

A widely accepted theory in psychology is that frustration leads to aggression (Dollard, Doob, Miller, Mowrer, and Sears, 1939). Those who provide sociological explanations of child abuse suggest that individuals who are likely to experience frequent feelings of frustration because of such factors as unemployment, poverty, and crowded living conditions may be particularly inclined to react with violence when the behavior of a child adds yet another frustration or irritation. In addition, it appears that child abusers often live in self-imposed social isolation, that is, with little or no contact with neighbors or relatives. As a result, the child is more likely to be in lengthy contact with parents, which increases the possibility of annoyance. Furthermore, the absence of other people may cause parents to feel less inclined to control their anger since they will assume that they will be unobserved if they beat a child.

Child abusers must cope with frustrations, often live in social isolation

Social-situational interpretations of child abuse emphasize that the experiences of parents who were abused by their parents predispose them to be punitive themselves. If physical punishment used by such parents causes the child to stop annoying behavior, the tendency toward punitiveness is reinforced. Furthermore, if the child builds up an immunity to habitual forms of punishment, the parents may feel obliged to resort to more extreme physical abuse. Other social-situational explanations of child abuse focus on characteristics of the victims. Infants born prematurely (who are difficult to care for and may have a variety of abnormalities), children who are sick, and babies who cry excessively are frequent victims of parental violence. One of the reasons premature babies are frequent victims of parental abuse may be that such infants are often placed in an incubator during the first weeks of postnatal existence (A. Leifer et al., 1972). The mother is thus prevented from having contact with her child during what may be a maternal sensitive period. This may account, in part at least, for her failure to later develop strong feelings of attachment.

A variety of techniques for attempting to prevent and control child abuse have been developed. These include parent group discussions, home support programs, hotline services (where a frustrated parent can talk to a sympathetic and supportive listener), crisis nurseries and drop-off centers (where a child can be left until a frustrated parent on the brink of resorting to physical abuse is able to gain control), and educational programs designed to provide information about techniques that might be used to control violent tendencies and replace them with non-punitive reactions.

(Changes in relationships with others during the years from two to five are discussed in Chapter 12, starting on page 375.)

Summary

1. The development of **attachment** behavior, or the relationship between an infant and the primary caretaker, has been studied extensively. After an attachment has been formed, many infants exhibit stranger anxiety and then separation anxiety toward the end of the first year. Mary Ainsworth developed an experimental technique for studying both types of behavior and found three infant-mother interaction patterns. **Securely attached** infants perceived their mothers as accessible and responsive. **Resistant** babies, by contrast, seemed to perceive their mothers as inept. The mothers of **avoidant** babies impressed observers as reserved women who disliked having contact with their children.

2. When the critical period hypothesis was strongly endorsed in the 1950s and 1960s, John Bowlby and other theorists speculated that it was essential for an infant to develop a strong attachment to a primary caretaker. Subsequent research has led to the conclusion that infants often establish satisfactory relationships with several caretakers, although the mother typically remains at the top of a hierarchy of attachment figures.

3. Regardless of who does the caretaking, certain infant-care techniques seem to encourage optimum development. Effective mothers seem to have a good sense of timing, know how to take turns, and make it possible for infants to learn that they can produce consequences. They also provide moderate rather than overly rich stimulation. Starting at around the age of ten months, infants seem to be encouraged to develop competence if their parents talk, respond, enrich, encourage, and explain. Caretakers who have difficulty inducing infants to

respond positively may learn how to acquire effective child-care techniques through supportive programs.

4. Some women may be more effective caretakers than others because they are **sex-typed** (tending to exhibit forms of stereotyped feminine behavior), and feel comfortable with the mother's role. A sex-typed male, on the other hand, may find it more difficult to care for a young child than an **androgynous** male, who has a more flexible conception of sex roles and is not upset about functioning as a "mother."

5. At present about half of all mothers of preschool children are employed, which has led to an increase in day care. In the 1960s and early 1970s, when the critical period hypothesis was widely endorsed, many theorists argued that placing a young child under the care of someone other than the mother would be harmful to the child. More recent research suggests that when placed in a carefully selected day care arrangement, young children do not seem to suffer negative consequences. Quite often the major change in their behavior as a result of being placed under the care of others is that they become more independent of the mother.

6. During the last twenty years a noticeable increase in child abuse has occurred. Parents abuse their children for a variety of reasons, but quite often they have tendencies toward expressing aggressive impulses freely. In addition, they were likely to have been abused themselves as children. It has been found, too, that many of them must cope with frustrations and that they also live in social isolation.

Attachment, Stranger and Separation Anxiety

Suggestions for Further Study

If you would like to peruse the accounts that led to the surge of interest in attachment behavior and stranger and separation anxiety, sample these books: *Attachment* (1969) and *Separation: Anxiety and Anger* (1973), Volumes I and II of *Attachment and Loss* by John Bowlby, or *Patterns of Attachment: A Psychological Study of the Strange Situation* (1978) by Mary D. Ainsworth, Mary C. Blehar, Everett Waters, and Sally Wall.

Infant-Mother Interaction

Two brief, readable books on the nature of successful interactions between infants and their mothers are *Mothering* (1977) by Rudolph Schaffer and *The First Relationship* (1977) by Daniel Stern. T. G. R. Bower offers his views on early relationships in Chapters 1, 4, and 9 (in particular) of

A Primer of Infant Development (1977b). Mary Ainsworth summarizes her conclusions on the subject in "The Development of Infant-Mother Attachment" in *Review of Child Development Research*, Volume III, edited by B. M. Caldwell and H. N. Ricciutti (1974). A collection of short papers by many of the individuals just noted, plus other students of early relationships, can be found in *Studies in Mother-Infant Interaction* (1977b), edited by Rudolph Schaffer.

Father-Infant Interaction

Recent trends in our society have led to greater tendencies for fathers to interact with infants and young children. Ross D. Parke offers a comprehensive review of research on this subject in Chapter 15 (pp. 549–590) of the *Handbook of Infant Development* (1979), edited by Joy D. Osofsky. Among other things, he notes that fathers may be as influenced as mothers by contact with a newborn baby (p. 561), that fathers treat male babies differently from female babies (p. 566), and that father-infant attachment can be just as strong as mother-infant attachment (p. 570).

Other comprehensive sources of information about father-child interaction are *The Father: His Role in Child Development* (1974) by D. Lynn, and *The Role of the Father in Child Development* (1976), edited by Michael E. Lamb.

Supportive and Early Intervention Programs

For descriptions and analyses of programs designed to help parents of young children become more confident and effective, see "Supportive Programs for Infants and Parents" by Dorothy S. Huntington, Chapter 26 (pp. 837–851) of the *Handbook of Infant Development* (1979), edited by Joy D. Osofsky. For descriptions and analyses of programs designed to supply help and instruction to parents of disadvantaged children, see "Early Intervention Programs" by E. Kuno Beller, Chapter 27 (pp. 852–894) of the same volume.

Day Care

For a comprehensive review of research on the ramifications of day care, refer to "Early Childhood Programs" by K. Alison Clarke-Stewart and Greta G. Fein, Chapter 11 of *Infancy and Developmental Psychobiology*, edited by Marshall M. Haith and Joseph J. Campos, Volume II of *Hand-*

book of Child Psychology (4th ed., 1983) edited by Paul H. Mussen. For a less technical account written for parents, read *Daycare* (1982) by Clarke-Stewart.

Making Firsthand Observations of Child-Parent Interactions

If you have the opportunity to observe interactions between a child in the six- to eighteen-month range and one of his or her parents, you might analyze those interactions with reference to information presented in this chapter. Does the caretaker have a good sense of timing, for instance, know how to take turns, or permit the child to learn it can produce consequences? You might also look for signs of stranger or separation anxiety by carrying out simple procedures similar to those used by Ainsworth (described in Table 8.1). Ask the mother to put the child on the floor together with some toys before moving to a chair some distance away. Next, have a strange person enter the room and approach the baby. Depending on the infant's reaction, then ask the mother to leave the room. Finally, have the mother return and see what happens when they are reunited. Describe the child's reactions to these various actions.

KEY POINTS

Varying Views on the Consistency of Personality

Personality: unique combination of psychophysical characteristics that determine behavior

Early unanimity of opinion about personality consistency now questioned

How Consistent Is Personality?

Determinants of personality: constitutional, group membership, role, situational

Cohort effect: impact of a particular set of cultural factors on individuals born at same time

Stable traits: passivity, aggressiveness in males, dependency in females

Comprehensive analyses of longitudinal data reveal consistency

Desire to achieve and sex roles stable; attitudes unstable

Implications of Various Hypotheses About Personality

Behavioral geneticists expect personality to change

Learning theorists and psychoanalysts view child as shaped by experiences

Stress on shaping or fixation causes parents to blame selves for abnormal child behavior

Ways Infants Influence Their Parents

Infants respond to soothing in consistent ways

Behavior of baby may influence mother's reactions

Realizing that some infant behavior is innate could lessen parental guilt

Temperament as the Root of Personality

Temperament: heritable, early appearing, or stable aspect of personality

Stable traits of temperament: irritability, activity level, smiling, laughing, wariness

Views Stressing Reciprocal Child-Parent Relationships

Some distrust, shame, and doubt desirable

The Significance of Emotional Expression

Neonatal emotions: interest, disgust, distress, startle reaction

Emotions appear when they serve an adaptive function

Infants interpret emotional expression as early as three months

CHAPTER

9

THE FIRST TWO YEARS

PERSONALITY DEVELOPMENT

Analyses of physical development led J. M. Tanner (1970) to conclude (as noted in Chapter 6) that there is a target-seeking tendency in human growth. If children do not receive adequate nourishment or are seriously ill for a period of time early in life, they seem to catch up to their genetically programmed growth pattern after an adequate diet is supplied or an illness overcome. For a time in the 1960s there was considerable support for the belief (as noted in Chapter 5) that early childhood was a critical period in cognitive development. Subsequent evaluations of that hypothesis, however, led to the conclusion that there is no "magic period" in cognitive development, although there is some evidence that attending a preschool may have a positive impact on the later academic achievement of disadvantaged children. (It seems likely, however, that this impact is due more to the subsequent attitude of children and parents toward schooling than to the intellectual stimulation of the preschool experience.)

For a time in the 1960s and early 1970s there was also support (as noted in Chapters 5 and 8) for the view that the first months of life functioned as a critical period in the establishment of attachment behavior. It was hypothesized that if a child did not develop a close relationship with a primary caretaker, later social and personality development would be adversely affected. Subsequent evaluations of that hypothesis, however, led to doubts that interactions with a primary caretaker are as crucial as they once seemed.

Thus, in terms of physical, cognitive, and social development, there are reasons to doubt that experiences during the first two years will establish patterns of behavior that will be highly resistant to change. When it comes to personality development, however, the common expectation has been that there *will* be continuity. Most theorists have assumed that personality traits that become apparent during the first two years are likely to persist throughout a person's life. Many theorists have argued that a basic reason for consistency is that early experiences shape personality in lasting ways, although there are strong differences of opinion about *how* that shaping occurs. These points will become clear as varying views on the consistency of personality are summarized.

Varying Views on the Consistency of Personality

Gordon W. Allport (1937) surveyed accounts of personality in books on philosophy, theology, law, sociology, and psychology and concluded that there were about fifty different meanings of the term. Dozens of psychologists have offered definitions, some of which you may have encountered in other courses. Before embarking on an evaluation of personality, therefore, we should agree on a working definition. In this

Personality: unique combination of psychophysical characteristics that determine behavior

and the following chapters, **personality** will be defined as an individual's unique combination of psychophysical characteristics that determine behavior (Murray and Kluckhohn, 1948). The basic combination of psychophysical characteristics will remain essentially the same throughout life, it is typically assumed, but the behavioral manifestations of those characteristics will change over time. A tendency toward aggres-

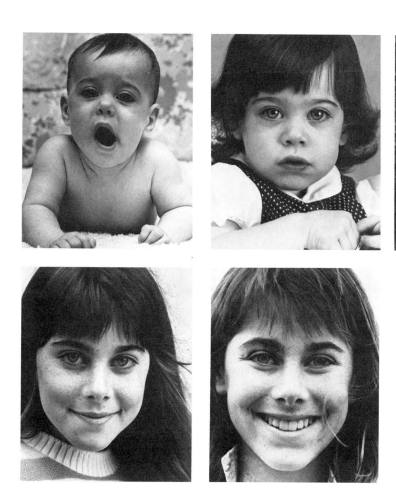

Up until recently there was virtual unanimity of opinion that even though the physical appearance of this girl changed as she matured, her personality would remain essentially the same. Recently, a number of theorists have suggested that changes in personality might be expected to occur as individuals are exposed to varying experiences.
© *Erika Stone.*

siveness, for example, may appear early and persist throughout a person's life but be expressed differently in infancy, adolescence, and adulthood.

Belief in the consistency of personality has been so strong that in his presidential address to the convention of the American Psychological Association in 1955 E. Lowell Kelly expressed the view that it was perhaps the only issue about which there was unanimity of opinion among psychologists. He noted, "Whether one is an extreme hereditarian, an environmentalist . . . or an orthodox psychoanalyst, he is not likely to anticipate major changes in personality after the first few years of life" (1955, p. 659).

As noted in the discussion of behavioral genetics in Chapter 3, hereditarians believe that many types of behavior are substantially influenced by inherited predispositions. Since a person's genetic structure does not change, it follows that the same influences will persist throughout life. It is logical to expect, therefore, that personality traits traceable to genetic factors will remain quite consistent. Environmentalists, such as B. F. Skinner, discount the impact of genetic factors and argue instead that a newborn infant is like a bit of clay ready to be molded by experiences. Because the initial molding determines basic features, early formative influences are assumed to have a particularly potent and lasting influence. In his novel *Walden Two,* Skinner describes how infants are taken away from their parents immediately after birth and placed in the hands of child-rearing experts, who shape desirable traits in a systematic fashion. The clear implication of such treatment is that once shaped the traits will remain essentially permanent. Psychoanalysts who adhere to the gospel of Freud in orthodox (or faithful) ways, assume that the fixation of libidinal energy during the oral or anal stages will establish personality traits that will persist and influence behavior throughout later childhood and adulthood. All three types of theorists mentioned by Kelly agree that there are not likely to be major changes in personality, but they disagree emphatically about the causes of such consistency. Within the last few years, however, the unanimity of opinion about the unchanging nature of personality that Kelly perceived in the 1950s has dissipated.

Early unanimity of opinion about personality consistency now questioned

A number of psychologists have recently suggested that personality traits *do* change over the years. Some theorists (e.g., Mischel, 1968) maintain that behavior is specific to the situation and that if situations change markedly, reactions (and personality traits) will change. Other researchers (e.g., Nesselroade and Baltes, 1974) have criticized the methods used by psychologists who have presented evidence to support the view of consistency in personality. Still others (e.g., Kagan, 1980) have concluded that early forms of behavior only occasionally are predictive of adult behavior and that whatever stability in personality does exist can be attributed to stability in environmental experiences. However, each of these arguments has been countered by other psychologists, who marshal evidence to support the view expressed by Kelly. There may no longer be unanimity of opinion about the stability of personality, but there is still considerable support for that assumption.

How Consistent Is Personality?

To evaluate the question of how much consistency there is in personality over the life span it is first necessary to come to some agreement about what personality is. Then some of the problems faced by those who study personality over a period of years need to be considered. Finally, an analysis of the results of longitudinal studies should be made. These various points will now be discussed.

The Nature of Personality

A bit earlier personality was defined as the unique combination of psychophysical characteristics that determine behavior. A particularly insightful description of psychophysical characteristics that determine behavior has been offered by Henry A. Murray and Clyde Kluckhohn (1948), the psychologists who proposed the definition just given. They describe four types of personality determinants: constitutional, group membership, role, and situational. **Constitutional** determinants are inherited characteristics and predispositions (sex, height, facial features, body chemistry, and so on). **Group membership** determinants include the general culture (for example, American, French, Japanese) in which a child is reared and all the cultural subgroups that influence personality development (such as class, family, peer group, friends). **Role** determinants include not only the general, more or less permanent self-concept of a person but also the specific and variable roles assumed in different situations (reflected, for instance, in the behavior of a boy who feels self-conscious when he writes a poem in English class as contrasted with his behavior as captain of the football team). **Situational** determinants are all the experiences of the individual that contribute to the development of personality—not only frequently repeated experiences that have a cumulative impact but also traumatic or especially significant single experiences that alter the entire course of a person's life.

Opinions about the nature and impact of many of these determinants already have been noted in earlier chapters. Differing views about constitutional determinants were treated at some length in the analysis of developmental behavioral genetics in Chapter 3. Even though the heredity-environment controversy was discussed with reference to intelligence, the same basic arguments apply (in less easily traceable ways) to personality. Role determinants were noted in the review of Erikson's theory, particularly the section on identity formation. The potential significance of traumatic experiences was noted in the discussion of Freudian theory. If you will take a moment to think about factors that

Determinants of personality: constitutional, group membership, role, situational

may have influenced your own personality, you will probably have little difficulty recognizing that all four types of determinants are important. The fact that personality development is influenced by many determinants, some of which cannot be isolated or analyzed objectively, means that there are many problems faced by those who attempt to study personality over a period of time.

Problems Faced by Those Who Study Personality

In the imaginary historical journal presented in Chapter 1, mention was made of longitudinal studies carried out at the Fels Institute, the University of California at Berkeley, and Stanford University. In most cases the researchers were interested not only in tracing the development of personality, but also in attempting to identify some of the causes of behavioral traits. Accordingly, each team of psychologists selected a sample of subjects and began to accumulate information not only about the children, but also about their parents and others (e.g., siblings, teachers) who exerted an influence on their behavior. Many of the methods and techniques described in Chapter 1 were used. During infancy and early childhood, the behavior of the children and their parents was evaluated on rating scales. (Turn back to Figure 1.2, page 22, for an example of a Fels Parent Behavior Rating Scale.) Observational records, sometimes made through the use of time-sampling techniques, were compiled. The parents were interviewed. (Refer to Figure 1.3, page 28, for an example of an interview schedule used by Robert R. Sears and his colleagues.) When the subjects reached school age, ratings were obtained from teachers. As they matured, increasing use was made of questionnaires, self-reports, and tests. After they left school, the subjects, at intervals, received questionnaires requesting information about various aspects of their lives. In some cases, the adult subjects were persuaded to take tests of different kinds or fill out personality or interest inventories. After the more comprehensive longitudinal studies had been under way for twenty years or so, records on each subject filled an entire filing cabinet.

To grasp the magnitude of the problem faced by a researcher who wants an answer to the question of consistency in personality, put yourself in his or her place. Suppose you want to determine if a trait such as aggressiveness is manifested consistently over a span of years. What sorts of descriptions would you look for in the data for different age levels? How would you expect a three-year-old who engaged in a great deal of shoving in nursery school to manifest aggressiveness at age thirty? Even if you felt you could identify types of behavior to look for, you might conclude, on perusing the data very carefully, that aggressiveness at age three was due to marital discord between the parents

One of the problems faced by those who carry out longitudinal personality studies centers on changes in ways a particular trait may be expressed at different age levels. During the preschool years, for example, aggressiveness may be expressed physically; in adulthood, it is more likely to be expressed visually or verbally.
Michael Weisbrot and Family; © Nancy Bates/The Picture Cube.

while aggressiveness at age thirty was caused by a drive for achievement. Thus, you would not only need to look for manifestations of the same basic personality trait at different ages; you would also need to speculate about whether the same type of behavior was caused by different determinants. You would probably also discover that the same terms (such as aggressiveness) were used in different ways in different sets of data. The definition of aggressiveness on a rating scale used to evaluate the behavior of elementary school pupils, for instance, might be quite different from the definition of aggressiveness noted on the profile of a personality inventory given to the subjects when they were eighteen. In addition, you might conclude that it is not always possible to make direct comparisons between data based on the observations of others, data supplied by the subjects when asked to record impressions of their own behavior, and test data. Finally, you might conclude that the behavior of the subjects of your particular study had been influenced in unique ways by the fact that they had reached young adulthood during

Cohort effect: impact of a particular set of cultural factors on individuals born at same time

a particular historical period (e.g., World War II). This is often referred to as the **cohort effect,** and it acknowledges that in the rapidly changing world of today each generation (or subgeneration) of individuals will be influenced by quite different sets of cultural, social, and political factors. Accordingly, at least some of the personality traits of any group of subjects will have been influenced by determinants that will differ in idiosyncratic ways from the determinants that influenced other groups of subjects, or that are influencing contemporary children, adolescents, or adults.

This brief analysis mentions only a few of the problems faced by those who engage in research on personality development, but it is sufficient to make the point that it is virtually impossible to come up with clear-cut conclusions. With that point in mind, it is time to examine some of the conclusions that *have* been drawn by those who have analyzed longitudinal data.

Conclusions Reached by Those Who Have Studied Personality

Stable traits: passivity, aggressiveness in males, dependency in females

Jerome Kagan and Howard A. Moss (1962) analyzed the voluminous data accumulated by researchers at the Fels Institute, paying particular attention to stability of behavior. They found that children rated as passive as early as the age of two retained this characteristic to such an extent that they concluded it was apparently due to biological factors. Other traits that appeared to be stable were aggressiveness in males and dependency in females. Kagan and Moss suggested that these traits might be traced to constitutional variables that are later reinforced by "behavioral rules promoted by the child's culture" (p. 119). Males are expected to be independent whereas, for example, girls may be criticized or even punished if they are too aggressive. Achievement, defined as "behavior aimed at satisfaction of an internal standard of excellence" (p. 120), was found to be quite stable throughout the childhood years.

Comprehensive analyses of longitudinal data reveal consistency

Several researchers have made separate analyses of the huge amount of data accumulated on and from the subjects of the various longitudinal studies carried out at the University of California at Berkeley. The most comprehensive of these was the work of Jack Block (1971), who set out specifically to evaluate consistency of personality. His general conclusion is summed up by this statement: "The unity or consistency of personality is compellingly apparent in these data and is manifest in so many and so diverse ways as perhaps to establish the [concept of consistency] once and for all" (p. 268).

In a review of longitudinal studies of personality development, Howard A. Moss and Elizabeth J. Susman (1980) evaluated the Fels and Berkeley studies, as well as many others. They concluded that the most consistent personality traits appear to be those that are influenced by well-established cultural expectations. Strength of desire to achieve and sex roles are both socially valued traits and both are quite stable. Attitudes, by contrast, which are susceptible to changing cultural values, are among the least stable personality characteristics. Types of behavior reflecting a personality "style," such as introversion or activity level, were found to be stable starting during the preschool years, while motivational characteristics (such as a desire to achieve) first emerged in middle childhood.

Desire to achieve and sex roles stable; attitudes unstable

Given the kinds of complications mentioned earlier, it should come as no surprise that some psychologists have been skeptical about the conclusions just summarized. Walter Mischel (1968), for instance, has maintained that the view that personality is stable is incorrect. (Jack Block [1977], however, argues that Mischel based his conclusions on selected data that do not give a complete picture of all relevant research.) Robert Nisbet (1969) has pointed out that there is a tendency for the Western mind to *look* for continuities, connections, and stability. Greek philosophers sought relationships and tended to minimize discontinuities, Nisbet suggests, while Oriental philosophers were more inclined to perceive and accept change and impermanence. Thus, in our society, the expectation of continuity has become a tradition. Jerome Kagan, who collaborated with Howard Moss in the early evaluation of Fels Institute data, has concluded (1980), after twenty years of additional analysis of research on personality, that very few early personality traits are predictive of later behavior and that whatever stability does exist in personality is due to continuing social influences.

Before proceeding, it will be helpful to summarize points discussed so far:

1. Hereditarians, environmentalists, and psychoanalysts all have endorsed the assumption that there is continuity in personality. Hereditarians attribute continuity to genetic predispositions, environmentalists to the shaping of behavior by early experiences, psychoanalysts to the impact of fixation.
2. Recently, a number of psychologists have argued that personality changes through the years and that any continuity that does exist is traceable to continuity in experience.
3. It is virtually impossible to conclusively prove on the basis of available research data that either of the views just noted is correct. There is some evidence of consistency in a few traits and in general impressions of personality, but the evidence is difficult to interpret.

Since there are differences of opinion, and since no particular view can be proven, you should feel free to draw your own conclusions about the consistency of personality and how much it is influenced by experiences during the first two years. Before you form even tentative conclusions, however, you might find it helpful to evaluate some of the implications of arguments proposed by hereditarians, environmentalists, and psychoanalysts.

Implications of Various Hypotheses About Personality

Genetic, Behavioral, and Psychoanalytic Hypotheses

Before the emergence of developmental behavioral genetics, there was often an either-or approach to evaluations of the impact of genetic factors on personality development. As noted in Chapter 3, however, the tendency at present is to consider how the two factors interact. The discussion of developmental behavioral genetics in Chapter 3 included mention of several models of genotype-phenotype interaction. The epigenetic model of Conrad Waddington (1962) stresses that the genetic pattern of each individual is determined at the time of conception and that the pattern includes instructions for the timing and eventual limits of many characteristics. These instructions are altered in various ways by environmental conditions or experiences, but Waddington suggested that a self-righting tendency often occurs. Irving Gottesman (1963) proposed that the degree to which experiences modify inherited predispositions depends on the characteristic. Robert McCall (1981) and Theodore Wachs (1983) both stress the impact of particular experiences at particular points in development. Thus, many behavioral geneticists favor the view that personality changes through the years and that later experiences may sometimes offset or cancel out earlier experiences.

Behavioral geneticists expect personality to change

The strongest proponents of the environmental view in American psychology have been the behaviorists who studied learning. You may recall from Chapter 3 that John B. Watson asked parents of the 1920s to consider the question: "Isn't it just possible that almost nothing is given in heredity and that practically the whole course of development of the child is due to the way I raise it?" (1926, p. 15). B. F. Skinner did not go quite as far as Watson in suggesting that inherited factors have practically *no* impact on behavior, but he pointed out that genetic influences cannot be changed. He argued that behavior is shaped by experiences and that if parents did not try to control child behavior in a systematic fashion they would do it in unplanned and haphazard ways.

Fixation is a basic principle of psychoanalytic theory, and Freud concluded (as noted in Chapter 5) that "analytic experience has convinced us of the complete truth of the common assertion that the child is psychologically father of the man and that the events of his first years are of paramount importance for his whole subsequent life" (1949). Many psychoanalysts still subscribe to that view.

Implications of Views of Personality Development

Of the three views just summarized, that favored by behavioral geneticists is the most flexible in stressing the possibility of personality changes after the first few years. Skinner and Freud both support the assumption that infants are essentially passive recipients of stimuli, with little or no control over their own behavior. Skinner maintains that young children are shaped by their parents; Freud argues that any person's future behavior is determined by the kinds of fixations experienced during the first six years. Learning theorists and psychoanalysts have not always recognized the devastating impact their hypotheses might have on parents. If it is assumed that children have little or no control over their own behavior, it follows that any personal, emotional, or social problems that they display have been caused by the way they have been treated.

> Learning theorists and psychoanalysts view child as shaped by experiences

One of the first theorists to call attention to the disturbing implications of the Skinnerian and Freudian views was Leo Kanner, author of a classic text on child psychiatry (1935, 1972). In his counseling sessions with parents of disturbed children, Kanner noticed a frequent pattern. He reported that many of the parents who came to him for counseling entered his office for the first time, sat down, hung their heads in shame, and said "We know it's all *our* fault." To try to convince such parents that it was not necessarily all their fault, Kanner wrote a book titled *In Defense of Mothers* (1941), in which he humorously but effectively punctured theories stressing the view that children are molded (or fixated) almost entirely by others.

> Stress on shaping or fixation causes parents to blame selves for abnormal child behavior

In the course of therapeutic sessions with disturbed children, Kanner encountered a number of cases of what he eventually described (1943) as **infantile autism.** Children displaying this condition (which was later observed in a variety of forms by other psychotherapists) were extremely unresponsive and seemed almost unreachable by their parents. The term *autism* is derived from the Greek word for "self" and it was chosen to describe the autistic child's resemblance to an individual totally involved with self. The condition, which occurs in about five children out of every ten thousand births, becomes apparent very early in life. Because Skinnerian and Freudian interpretations of personality de-

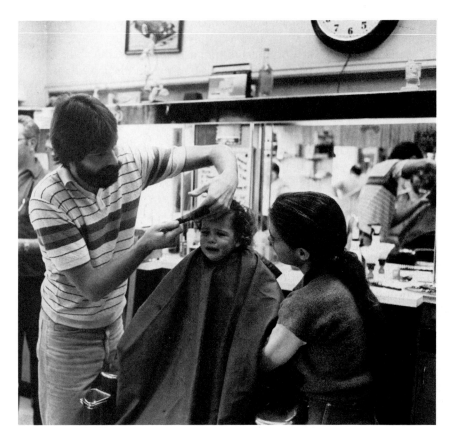

Behavioral theorists and psychoanalysts stress that behavior is shaped by experience over which a person has no control. Thus, traumatic experiences during a first haircut might be expected to fixate personality tendencies. Other psychologists are not as convinced that experiences during the first years are crucial, and have greater faith in the ability of individuals to overcome early negative experiences through their own efforts. Robert Eckert/The Picture Cube.

velopment dominated psychological thinking at the time autism was first identified, many parents of autistic children assumed that they had caused the condition by using inept techniques of child rearing. Since that time, there has been a shift away from Skinnerian and Freudian interpretations of early behavior and much greater willingness to accept the hypothesis that autism is due primarily to characteristics of the child, not the way the child is treated by parents. (Many theorists trace autistic behavior to a genetic defect, but some suggest that the condition may be caused by an unknown drug or virus, or an allergic response to some unidentified substance in the environment.)[1] The parents of autistic children have been described as "strained or apprehensive or overserious" by theorists (Tinbergen, 1974) who argue that the parents' behavior shapes the child's behavior. An alternative explanation (favored by Kanner) is that the parents of an autistic child recognize very early that the infant is disturbingly unresponsive, and this causes them to become strained, apprehensive, and overserious.

Analyses of and speculations about autism illustrate a trend in thinking about early child-parent relationships that has gathered momentum during the last few years. Until recently, it was almost universally assumed that young children were molded almost entirely by the way they were handled by their parents. Today there is considerable interest in ways infants, even as early as the first few hours after birth, influence their parents.

Ways Infants Influence Their Parents

The hypothesis that certain types of child behavior influence parents is supported by hundreds of studies, which are reviewed in *The Effect of the Infant on Its Caregiver* (1974), edited by Michael Lewis and Leonard Rosenblum, and *Child Effects on Adults* (1977) by Richard Q. Bell and Lawrence V. Harper. To illustrate the nature of this research, two frequently cited investigations by Beverly Birns will be described.

Differences in Soothability and Cuddling

In her first investigation, Birns (1965) exposed 30 two- to five-day-old babies to a soft tone, a loud tone, a cold disk, and a sweetened pacifier. She found consistent differences in response intensity to these stimuli and also observed that reactions to different stimuli tended to lead to essentially the same state of arousal. That is, one infant would respond in an intense way regardless of whether it was exposed to a tone, cold disk, or sweetened pacifier; another would respond in a consistently mild way. The results of the study led Birns to carry out a follow-up investigation with Marian Blank and Wagner H. Bridger (1966). In this study 30 two- and three-day-old babies were taken out of the nursery an hour before feeding time on the assumption that they would be in an

---

[1]Research on various types of autism and speculations about causes are succinctly summarized by Rutter and Garmezy, 1983, pp. 785–794.

irritable mood. Their irritability was further aroused by flicking the soles of their feet. At that point efforts were made to soothe them by offering a sweetened pacifier, sounding loud and soft continuous tones, gently rocking their bassinets, and immersing their feet in warm water. The behavior of the babies was also observed when no attempts at soothing were made. Some infants were easily aroused to a high level of irritability and did not respond markedly to any of the attempts at soothing; others became only moderately irritated and were easily soothed. Furthermore, one soothing stimulus turned out to be as effective as any other.

Infants respond to soothing in consistent ways

The differences in sensitivity to stimulation and in soothability described by Birns appeared so soon after birth that the way the babies were handled is not likely to have caused these differences. Moreover, if infants were as sensitive to techniques of handling as some theorists have suggested, they would presumably alter their behavior in response to different stimuli. One would certainly expect that a pacifier (providing direct oral satisfaction) would arouse more of a reaction than placing an infant's foot in warm water. Yet the babies observed by Birns responded to a variety of stimuli in a consistent way. The results of these studies therefore lend support to the conclusion that some babies have an innate tendency to accept or resist mothering.

In summing up the conclusions of her second study, Birns states:

> One need only observe a few infants to become aware of the different feelings evoked by a "baby who cries no matter how hard you try to calm him" and one who quiets within moments of soothing. The baby's behavior thus may affect the mother's feelings toward him. In addition, the mother-child relationship may be influenced by how effectively the mother responds to her child's individual predispositions. (1966, p. 321)

Behavior of baby may influence mother's reactions

Rudolph Schaffer and Peggy Emerson (1964) carried out another frequently mentioned study supporting the view that inborn differences in infants may influence maternal behavior as much as mothering techniques may influence the child. They studied two groups of one- to two-year-old children. One group responded favorably to being cuddled by their mothers; the other group reacted negatively. The researchers were unable to detect any consistent differences in the way the cuddlers and noncuddlers had been handled by their mothers. They did discover, however, a distinctive cluster of traits for each type. Cuddlers were quiet and inactive, slept more, and liked soft playthings. Noncuddlers were restless and wakeful, stood and walked earlier, and disliked being confined in any way. The extent to which each type had these traits, together with lack of evidence that they had been produced by any identifiable child-rearing practices, suggests that the tendency to respond positively or negatively to cuddling may be due to innate factors.

Individuality in Early Childhood

Alexander Thomas and several associates decided to carry out a longitudinal study (mentioned in Chapter 5) to discover the extent to which personality differences appear at birth and how stable such differences are during the span of development. Thomas and his colleagues selected 130 infants and asked their parents to describe how the babies behaved in specific situations. These descriptions were then analyzed with regard to such qualities as rhythmicity, adaptability, intensity, persistence, and distractability. *Behavioral Individuality in Early Childhood* (1963) describes the results of the investigation up to the time the children were two years old. At that stage, the researchers concluded, "Each child has an individual pattern of primary reactivity, identifiable in early infancy and persistent throughout later periods of life" (p. 84). Thomas and his associates stressed the same point made by Birns: their observations convinced them that a baby's primary reaction pattern is likely to influence the attitudes and reactions of his parents, especially when the baby asserts individuality right from the moment of birth. Thomas, who was a psychiatrist (and presumably had encountered the same sort of parental guilt Kanner had observed in counseling sessions) concluded his report with this statement:

> The knowledge that certain characteristics of their child's development are not primarily due to parental malfunctioning has proven helpful to many parents. Mothers of children often develop guilt feelings because they assume that they are solely responsible for their children's emotional difficulties. This feeling of guilt may be accompanied by anxiety, defensiveness, increased pressures on the children, and even hostility toward them for "exposing" the mother's inadequacy by their disturbed behavior. When parents learn that their role in the shaping of their child is not an omnipotent one, guilt feelings may lessen, hostility and pressures may tend to disappear, and positive restructuring of the parent-child interaction can become possible. (P. 94)

Realizing that some infant behavior is innate could lessen parental guilt

Birns and Thomas and his colleagues thus emphasize that an infant may influence the parents as much as they influence the infant. If attempts at soothing an irritable neonate are not successful or if a child reacts negatively to cuddling, originally confident parents may begin to feel anxious and apprehensive about their skill at handling the baby. If they resort to a variety of methods recommended by different authorities, none of which brings about an improvement, they may despair and panic. Thomas and his colleagues suggest that parents consider the possibility that the behavior of the child is due to inborn temperament and adjust their infant-care techniques to the personality of the child.

While some of their subjects were unpredictable and some did not fit

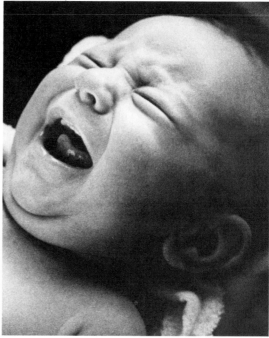

Newborn infants display wide differences in behavior. It is possible that distinctive patterns of neonatal behavior are produced by experiences during the prenatal period and at the time of birth. Another explanation is that each infant's behavior pattern arises primarily from inherited predispositions.
Michael Weisbrot and Family; © Michael Hayman/Photo Researchers.

patterns shared with others, Thomas and his associates concluded that most children they observed manifested one of three clusters of traits. Each of these types seemed to respond favorably to certain child-rearing techniques. A summary of the types of temperament and general child-rearing techniques appropriate to each is presented in Table 9.1.

Temperament as the Root of Personality

Thomas and his associates classified their subjects in terms of temperament, but the article in which they reported their findings was titled "The Origin of Personality." Thus, they emphasized a point endorsed by many other psychologists that temperament is considered to be the origin (or the root) of adult personality. Joseph J. Campos and several colleagues (1983) note that "Many theorists view temperament as an

TABLE 9.1
TYPES OF CHILD TEMPERAMENT AND EFFECTIVE CHILD-REARING TECHNIQUES

Type of Temperament	Characteristics of Children	Effective Child-rearing Techniques
Easy (found in 40 percent of sample)	Positive mood, regularity in bodily functions, moderate reaction tendencies, adaptable, positive approach to new situations.	Many different approaches will bring about a favorable response. Main danger is to avoid having children become used to only one approach. Prepare children for variety of reactions from others (for example, teachers).
Difficult (found in 10 percent of sample)	Negative mood, irregularity in bodily functions, intense reaction tendencies, slow to adapt, withdrawal from new situations.	Treat children objectively, patiently, nonpunitively, consistently. Essential requirement for parents is to recognize need for unusually painstaking handling.
Slow to warm up (found in 15 percent of sample)	Somewhat negative in mood, low intensity of reaction, slow to adapt, likely to withdraw from new situations.	Allow children to adapt to environment at own pace, but when children show interest in new activity, encourage them to try it.

Source: Based on research carried out by Alexander Thomas, Stella Chess, and Herbert G. Birch reported in "The Origin of Personality," *Scientific American*, 1970, 223, 102–109.

important subdomain in the broader field of personality psychology. That is, according to one's theoretical predilections, temperament may be considered as the heritable, the early appearing, or the stable aspect of personality" (p. 827). A widely accepted definition of **temperament** was offered by Gordon W. Allport (1937):

> **Temperament:** heritable, early appearing, or stable aspect of personality

Temperament refers to the characteristic phenomena of an individual's emotional nature, including his susceptibility to emotional stimulation, his customary strength and speed of response, the quality of his prevailing mood, and all peculiarities of fluctuation and intensity of mood; these phenomena being regarded as dependent on constitutional make-up, and therefore largely hereditary in origin. (P. 54)

In terms of the determinants of personality described by Murray and Kluckhohn, therefore, temperament would fit in the constitutional category. It seems possible that at least some of the conflicts of opinion about the consistency of personality noted earlier are due to failure on the part of different theorists to make a distinction between temperament and personality. Some psychologists may have conceived of personality as essentially the same as temperament; others may have used a

One of the most stable traits of temperament is irritability. It is possible that this adult—who gives the appearance of being easily irritated—was also easily irritated as an infant and adolescent.
Jebb Dunn/The Picture Cube.

broader conception that included all the determinants (or the equivalent) described by Murray and Kluckhohn. Because temperament is generally thought to be largely constitutional in origin, it might be expected that this aspect of personality would remain quite stable throughout the life span. There is quite consistent evidence (reviewed by Campos et al., 1983), in fact, that particular aspects of temperament *are* stable. Among traits that appear to remain most constant throughout the life span are irritability, activity level, smiling, laughing, and vigilance or wariness. Thus, a neonate who displayed irritability during the first few days of life might be expected to impress others as an irritable adolescent or senior citizen later in life (assuming that irritability during the first weeks was due to temperamental factors and not to temporary circumstances such as illness).

Stable traits of temperament: irritability, activity level, smiling, laughing, wariness

There seems to be reason to believe, therefore, that the three temperament types described by Thomas and his associates reflect built-in tendencies that are not shaped by parental treatment but *are* likely to influence parental behavior. Some theorists (e.g., Lewis and Rosenblum, 1974) have pointed out that even though an infant's behavior may influence parents, the parents still control the situation. In some cases, however, the parents might not be able to control their own behavior or that of the child as completely as they would like. Parents of a difficult child, for instance, might not be able to control feelings of irritation or disappointment or be successful in inducing the baby to respond as positively as desired to signs of affection.

Evidence that infants display differences in temperament and that these differences influence the reactions of their parents leads to a different conception of child personality than that proposed by psychoanalysts and behaviorists. Freud and Skinner pictured infants as passive recipients of stimuli who are at the mercy of experiences over which they have no control. The research of Birns, Schaffer and Emerson, and Thomas supports the view that, even as infants, children "control" at least some of their own behavior and influence the behavior of others as well.

Of the various theorists discussed in Chapter 2, Freud and Skinner place greatest emphasis on the one-way nature of early experiences. They view the child as the recipient of stimulation provided by parents. The speculations of Erikson and of social learning theorists, on the other hand, give greater recognition to reciprocal interactions between parents and child. This point will become clear as observations of Erikson and Sears on personality development during the first two years are summarized.

Views Stressing Reciprocal Child-Parent Relationships

Erikson: The Significance of Trust and Autonomy

Erikson suggests that the basic psychological attitude to be learned by infants is that they can trust their world. Trust, as he defines it, includes feelings that parents can be trusted to provide care and support, as well as an infant's sense of personal trustworthiness. A sense of personal trustworthiness emerges as children become increasingly capable of controlling their own behavior and also become aware that others respond to them positively.

Toward the end of the second year the basic consideration of the parents is to help the child to develop a sense of autonomy and avoid a sense of shame or doubt. In contrast to Freud, Erikson points out that children at the age of two or so are mastering their entire musculature, not just the muscles that control elimination. But he agrees with Freud that toilet control is likely to be of special significance. If parents are impatient with children and try to shame them into mastering the process of elimination, children may feel not only inadequate but guilty as well. But autonomy involves not just mastery of muscles; it is found in all signs of independence. Toward the end of the second year, children begin to want to do many things for themselves. While it is important for children to develop confidence in their own abilities, the development of at least a degree of shame and doubt is desirable. You are reminded that in describing his stages as dichotomies, Erikson does not mean to imply an all-or-nothing choice. He believes that both qualities at each stage are necessary but that the positive factor should be more highly developed than the negative. One-year-olds should not develop an uncritical trust in everything; they should learn that some aspects of the world are untrustworthy. Two-year-olds should develop a sense of autonomy, but they should also begin to learn that in some situations they should be ashamed of their actions. They should also learn to have doubts about their abilities to master tasks that are beyond them.

While Erikson's observations on trust and autonomy seem eminently sensible and supply excellent general guidelines for some aspects of child rearing, it is not possible to substantiate these qualities as the most crucial features of early personality development. Furthermore, trust and autonomy are extremely elusive and complex qualities. It does seem logical to assume, however, that a child who first develops a sense of confidence in self and parents and then acquires feelings of independence will be off to a good start in adapting to experiences that will be encountered later.

Some distrust, shame, and doubt desirable

Sears: The Significance of Reinforcement, Identification, and Imitation

Sears proposed that during the first months of their lives infants seek to reduce biological drives. In the process, they learn that certain types of behavior bring about certain responses from others. If a hungry infant cries, for instance, and one of the parents immediately appears to sup-

ply milk, crying-to-announce-hunger behavior is reinforced. As repeated reinforcements occur, the baby learns to associate crying with a
response from the parents.

Sears also proposed that during the first two years children make their
first moves from dependence to independence (or autonomy, as Erikson
describes it). He agreed with Freud that identification plays an important role in this transition but Sears also stressed imitation. These various processes are often interconnected, since a child who wants to be
like someone else will engage in the kinds of behavior displayed by that
individual. A two-year-old who insists on "helping" mother or father
sweep the driveway by pushing a broom around imitates actions that
contribute to feelings of identification as well as independence.

Views stressing interaction between child and parents lead to the
intriguing question of how infants who are incapable of speech communicate with their parents. That question, in turn, leads to consideration of emotional expression.

The Significance of Emotional Expression

Trends in the Study of Emotion

In a chapter on socioemotional development in the latest edition of the
Handbook of Child Psychology (1983), Joseph J. Campos and several of his
colleagues note that "One of the most striking developments in contemporary psychological theory is the resurgence of interest in the field of
human emotions. Until very recently, emotions suffered from a not-
very-benign neglect" (p. 785). They point out that the study of emotions
was shunned by psychologists from the 1950s to the 1970s for a variety
of reasons: it did not seem possible to measure emotions scientifically,
emotions seemed superfluous in learning theory explanations of behavior, and emotions were too closely associated with romanticized and
unscientific language. (Even in these enlightened times, many psychologists still prefer to use the term *affect* as a substitute for *emotion*.) Starting
in the 1970s, however, a number of techniques were developed for
measuring emotional expression with precision. Thus, even those who
were faithful adherents to the behaviorist stricture that all conclusions
should be based on overt behavior were able to study emotions in a
respectable way. As a consequence, psychologists once again began to
analyze emotion and speculate about how it contributes to understanding of behavior and development. Recent studies and speculations have
made it clear that emotions influence social, perceptual, and cognitive processes.

The major methodological breakthrough in the study of emotion has centered on analyses of facial expression as indicators of emotion. Several systems have been developed, such as the Facial Action Coding System (FACS) (Ekman and Friesen, 1978). The FACS system makes it possible to record all visible changes of a person's facial musculature as recorded on videotape. (There are several different ways to record movement of just the eyebrows, for instance.) After specific facial movements have been identified, formulas are used to identify different emotions. Through use of such techniques, researchers have been able to chart the course of early emotional development.

Emotional Development in Infancy

Carroll E. Izard (1977), who has proposed a widely accepted description of emotional development, suggests that three basic factors are involved:

1. Newborn infants come equipped with four discrete emotions.
2. Later emotions emerge at times when they serve an adaptive function.
3. Emotions emerge simultaneously with, but not as a result of, perceptual, motor, and cognitive abilities.

Neonatal emotions: interest, disgust, distress, startle reaction

The four emotions displayed by newborn infants are **interest, disgust, distress,** and a **startle reaction** that anticipates surprise. These emotions are considered to contribute to a newborn infant's adaptation to independent existence. Interest promotes cognitive development, disgust may protect a baby from ingesting noxious substances, distress serves to communicate needs to caretakers, and the startle reaction serves as a primitive form of defense. During the next four months, according to Izard, **anger, surprise,** and **joy** appear. Joy emerges between one and three months of age, a time when infants typically begin to discriminate between social and nonsocial objects. A child who registers joy when a caretaker approaches, for example, will reinforce approach responses on

Emotions appear when they serve an adaptive function

the part of the caretaker. Anger emerges at a time when the infant is becoming capable of voluntary behavior. Expressing anger when unable to achieve a goal may secure assistance. **Fear** and **shyness** emerge during the second half year, and play a significant role in the expression of fear of strangers. Fear also may function as a protective factor as the child develops locomotor abilities. There is evidence, for example, that as soon as they become capable of crawling, infants reveal a fear of height (Gibson and Walk, 1961; Campos et al., 1978). They will decline to crawl off the edge of a raised platform.

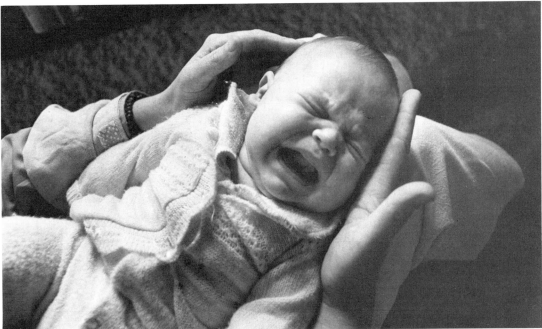

Two emotions that appear during the first months of life are interest and distress.
J. Berndt/The Picture Cube; © Jerry Howard/Positive Images.

Evolutionary Explanation for Attachment

Izard's analysis of the adaptive aspects of emotional development is similar to an explanation for attachment behavior proposed by Bowlby (1973) that is based on Darwin's theory of evolution. Bowlby proposes that in the course of evolution particular members of our species survived because mother and infant both possessed innate tendencies to be close to each other. These tendencies included such infant behavior as crying, smiling, and clinging, which elicited caretaking responses in the mother. Bowlby hypothesizes that during the long period of history when human beings lived in small nomadic groups infants born with tendencies that aroused a caretaker response were most likely to survive. Babies who did not evoke caretaker responses were more likely to die because of lack of adequate care or protection from predators.

Bowlby acknowledges the findings of Birns, Schaffer and Emerson, and Thomas and his associates regarding differences in the degree to which infants engage in types of behavior likely to arouse a maternal response. He also suggests that the infant's attachment behavior will become progressively weaker if the caretaker does not adequately respond. One explanation for the wide differences in infant attachment behavior (and temperament) is that some babies inherit weaker tendencies to smile, vocalize, and seek attention and cuddling than others. During the nomadic period of human history, some infants who inherited few attachment tendencies survived apparently because their mothers happened to possess compensatingly strong maternal tendencies.

Emotional Expression as a Form of Communication

Izard's account of emotional development and Bowlby's explanation for attachment behavior both stress the extent to which emotional expression serves as a medium of communication between infant and caretaker. Caretakers respond, or alter their responses, by interpreting facial expressions, vocalizations (such as cries), and bodily activity. Since adults have had ample opportunities to learn to associate certain types of emotional expression with various feelings, moods, and physical sensations, their ability to interpret emotions does not seem surprising. What is surprising, though, is evidence that infants demonstrate abilities to interpret signs of adult emotional expression very early in their lives. Mothers of three-month-old infants, for example, were instructed to maintain a deadpan facial expression as they held their babies (Tronick et al., 1978). When the infants smiled at their mothers but failed to get a response, they stopped smiling and acted upset. The

Infants interpret emotional expression as early as three months

same researchers asked mothers to make believe they were in a depressed state by registering depression, moving slowly, talking in a monotone, and not touching their children. In response to this type of maternal behavior, the infants averted their gaze and sometimes began to cry, suggesting that they too were upset.

Evidence of the way older infants interpret emotional expression has been provided by variations of the Ainsworth strange situation experimental arrangement. Mothers were instructed (Boccia and Campos, 1983) to either emit a curt hello while frowning or a cheerful hello while smiling when strange persons entered a room in which their children were playing. Eight-month-old infants took their cues from their mothers and displayed marked cardiac acceleration and overt signs of distress (such as clinging to the mother) to the frowned-at strangers, but not to the smiled-at strangers. One-year-olds have demonstrated the ability to interpret the emotional expression not only of their mothers but also of unfamiliar adults. A motorized toy was sent moving across the floor of a room containing a child, the mother, and a newly familiar adult (Klinnert et al., 1983). When the "stranger" registered joy, the children approached the toy; when the "stranger" registered fear, they avoided it.

It is clear, then, that very early in their lives children use emotions to communicate with others and are capable of interpreting the emotional expressions of others in quite subtle ways.

How Critical Are the First Two Years?

In the discussion of continuity and change in development in Chapter 5, the question How critical are the first two years? was introduced. Now that you have some familiarity with research findings about development during the first two years, that question should be considered again. In Chapter 5, differences of opinion about the significance of the first two years were noted. In the introduction to a book on infancy, for example, Michael Lewis wrote, "At no time in its history will the human being again experience more dramatic, intense and dynamic change" (1967, p. 17). T. G. R. Bower began a book on infancy with these words: "Few would dissent from the proposition that infancy is the most critical period of development, the period in which the basic frameworks of later development are established" (1977b, p. vii). On the other hand, a number of psychologists (e.g., Mischel, 1968; Kagan, 1980) have suggested that infancy may not be as important as many theorists have assumed. Among arguments proposed by those who play down the significance of infancy are the following: we *expect* to find continuity in development, infant behavior is rarely predictive of adult behavior, the mother-infant bond has been overemphasized, and later experiences are likely to exert a greater impact on adult personality than infantile experiences.

You will not be able to draw your own conclusions about how much experiences during the first two years influence later behavior until you have read about changes in behavior that occur at later stages. Comparing the behavior of a neonate with that of a two-year-old certainly supports the view of Lewis that infancy is a time of "dramatic, intense and dynamic change." During the first two years of life, a child chalks up some remarkable achievements. At the same time, achievements that are yet to come are often more remarkable, and perhaps more significant in terms of their impact on adult forms of behavior. Perhaps the best way to sum up these chapters on the first two years, therefore, is to repeat the observation of Bell, Weller, and Waldrop quoted at the end of Chapter 5: "Newborn behavior is more like a preface to a book than a table of its contents yet to be unfolded. Further, the preface is itself a rough draft undergoing rapid revision" (1971, p. 132).

(Changes in personality development during the years from two to five are discussed in Chapter 13, starting on page 399.)

Summary

1. A good working definition of personality is that it is a unique combination of psychophysical characteristics that determine behavior. For many years there was unanimity of opinion that personality would not change after the first few years of life. Recently, however, several theorists have suggested that personality *does* change as a person matures and is exposed to different experiences. In order to evaluate the question of consistency of personality, it is helpful to take into account that there are **constitutional, group membership, role,** and **situational** determinants of personality.
2. In evaluating personality consistency, the **cohort effect,** or the impact of a particular set of cultural factors on individuals born at the same time, needs to be considered. Personality traits that appear to be stable, even between cohorts, are passivity, aggressiveness in males, dependency in females, the desire to achieve, and sex roles. Attitudes are often unstable, changing as a person responds to changes in the social and political climate of the times. Comprehensive analyses of voluminous data from longitudinal studies suggest that there is recognizable consistency in personality over the life span, but this consistency may be difficult to prove in empirical terms.
3. Different theorists have expressed opinions about significant influences on personality development. Behavioral geneticists, who are

interested in ways experiences alter inherited predispositions, expect change. Learning theorists and psychoanalysts argue that personality is molded by experiences, but for different reasons. Skinner and his colleagues stress **shaping,** Freud and his followers emphasize **fixation.** If accepted uncritically, both of these explanations may cause parents to assume that they are entirely to blame for any abnormal behavior exhibited by their children.

4. To counteract the tendency for parents to assume that they are solely responsible for all of a child's behavior, several researchers have studied ways the behavior of newborn infants may influence their parents. It has been found, for instance, that starting a few hours after they are born, infants respond—or fail to respond—in quite consistent ways to attempts at soothing. An implication of this finding is that an infant's inborn tendencies may influence the way the parents react to a child. Acceptance of the hypothesis that some types of infant behavior are innate, and not the result of how the child has been treated, should lessen parental guilt.

5. In speculating about inborn, or constitutional, aspects of personality, it is helpful to consider the concept of **temperament,** defined as the heritable, early appearing, or stable aspect of personality. Researchers have found that stable traits of temperament include irritability, activity level, smiling, laughing, and wariness. Thus a person may exhibit a tendency toward irritability as an infant, child, adolescent, and adult.

6. Erik Erikson's description of psychosocial stages of development stresses the point that there is a reciprocal relationship between child and parent behavior. A sense of trust on the part of the child, for instance, is strengthened by the way parents handle the infant, but parental confidence and responsiveness are strengthened by signs that the child trusts them. While children should first develop trust and then autonomy, they should also learn that some aspects of their world should be distrusted and that shame and doubt are appropriate in some situations.

7. Since young children are not able to express their feelings in spoken language, ways they express and interpret emotions have been of interest to researchers. It has been found that newborn infants display four recognizable emotions: interest, disgust, distress, and a startle reaction. Later emotions, such as anger, surprise, and joy, appear at a time when they serve an adaptive function. A four-month-old child who registers joy, for example, will reinforce approach responses on the part of caretakers at a time when such responses are important. Infants not only communicate feelings to others through emotions; they also correctly interpret the emotional expressions of others as early as at three months of age.

Suggestions for Further Study

Consistency of Personality

If you would like to read a concise analysis of the results of longitudinal studies of personality, peruse "Longitudinal Study of Personality Development" by H. A. Moss and E. J. Susman, Chapter 11 of *Constancy and Change in Human Development* (1980), edited by O. G. Brim and J. Kagan. To get the flavor of comprehensive analyses of voluminous data on personality development over the life span, sample *Lives Through Time* (1971) by Jack Block.

The Effects of Infants on Their Parents

Two collections of articles tracing ways that infants shape their parents are *The Effect of the Infant on Its Caregiver* (1974), edited by Michael Lewis and Leonard A. Rosenblum, and *Child Effects on Adults* (1977) by Richard Q. Bell and Lawrence V. Harper.

The Significance of Emotions

For more information about the development of emotions and the ways emotional expression influences interactions with others, consult one of the following: *Human Emotions* (1977) by C. E. Izard, "Socioemotional Development" by J. J. Campos, K. C. Barrett, M. E. Lamb, H. H. Goldsmith, and C. Stenberg; Chapter 10 in *Infancy and Developmental Psychobiology*, edited by M. M. Haith and J. J. Campos; Volume II of *Handbook of Child Psychology* (4th ed., 1983), edited by Paul H. Mussen; and *Emotions, Cognition, and Behavior* (1984), edited by C. E. Izard, J. Kagan and R. B. Zajonc.

Observing Emotional Expression in a Young Child

If you have the opportunity to observe a child in the six-month to two-year age range, you might make fairly systematic observations of emotional expression. First, observe the child in a variety of situations and see if you can determine if the emotions described by Izard have appeared on schedule. (Six-month-olds should register interest, disgust, distress, surprise, anger, and joy in appropriate situations. After the age of one year, fear and shyness should be added to those just listed. In the absence of a facial expression rating scale, you will simply need to make inferences about the emotions being experienced on the basis of general impressions.) If the mother will cooperate, you might also replicate some of the experiments described in the latter part of this chapter. Ask her to assume a deadpan expression, for instance, or act depressed, and observe the reaction of the child. You might also see what happens if you present the child with a new toy placed in the middle of the floor but ask the mother to mimic fear as the toy is unwrapped. Record the behavior of the child and then analyze it to see if there is evidence that the child has been influenced by the emotional expressions of the mother.

PART
4

TWO TO FIVE

KEY POINTS

Aspects of Health and Growth

Skull bones protecting brain are soft in young children

Health problems likely first year in school

Controlling weight of preschooler simplifies weight control later

Physical Development

Preschoolers at peak of efficiency as energy users

The Interaction of Maturation and Learning

Gesell: early development assumed to be controlled by maturation

Young children can learn skills early (if maturation has taken place)

More mature children learn more rapidly

Current emphasis more on encouragement than training

Play

Groos: play must serve an adaptive function

Freud: play is an effective means for wish fulfillment

Piaget: from **practice** to **symbolic** to **pretense** play

Play features: self-motivated, involves pretense, no rules, active

Play permits children to explore and experiment without risk

Play permits children to practice roles

Play fosters imaginative and creative abilities

Play permits release of emotional tension

Older preschoolers play roles in more comprehensive ways

Older preschoolers interact with playmates in cooperative ways

Variety of playthings likely to foster many types of play

CHAPTER 10

TWO TO FIVE

PHYSICAL DEVELOPMENT

*B*etween the ages of two and five, the typical American child adds about three inches of height and a bit more than four pounds of weight per year. The average five-year-old is about three and one-half feet tall and weighs forty pounds. The way those inches and pounds are distributed as they are acquired, though, changes the appearance of children during the preschool years. The chubby appearance of the typical two-year-old, with a round face and limbs, gives way to a leaner look. The arms and head become longer and the head smaller in proportion to the rest of the body.

Aspects of Health and Growth

The Physical Resiliency of Young Children

As noted in earlier chapters, a child's growth plan is genetically programmed at the time of conception but nutritional and/or health factors may alter it to some extent. If children fail to receive adequate nutrition or if they suffer from a lengthy illness that limits appetite and opportunities for exercise, they may not achieve their programmed height and weight. If proper nutrition is later supplied, however, the child is likely to make up for early deprivation because of the self-righting impact of the target-seeking tendency (Tanner, 1970).

The physical resiliency of young children is illustrated by the target-seeking tendency, but it is revealed in a very direct way by their healing rate. If a three-year-old boy and his grandfather both cut their fingers at the same time, the boy's finger will heal six times faster than that of the grandfather (deNouy, 1937). In addition to being physically resilient, young children are also physically flexible. Preschoolers are able to arrange their limbs in ways that you cannot duplicate (unless you have had prolonged gymnastics or ballet training). If excessive pressure is placed on the limbs of a young child, a green-stick fracture rather than a clean bone break may occur. As the skeletal system matures, ossification (hardening) occurs. While less hard bones are an advantage in some parts of the body (such as the arms and legs), they are a disadvantage in the skull. The softness of the skull bones means that the brain is not as well protected in young children as it is in adults. Parents and teachers should warn preschoolers that they must never hit another child on the head and also protect themselves from being hit on the head. Laws requiring parents of young children to use child-restraint systems when they ride in automobiles are intended to reduce the number of children who are killed or who suffer severe brain injury as a result of being catapulted into the windshield in an accident, or even as a result of a panic stop.

Skull bones protecting brain are soft in young children

Health Factors During the Preschool Years

While young children are resilient and have a fast healing rate, they are also susceptible to infectious diseases as soon as they begin to interact with other children and adults. In one survey carried out by the U.S. Department of Health (1977), for instance, 124 episodes of upper respiratory problems per 100 children per year under age six were reported. To put it a different way, the average preschooler is likely to have one and one-quarter colds (or the equivalent) per year. Ear infections are extremely common and rank as one of the most frequent medical problems treated by pediatricians (Starfield and Pless, 1980, p. 280). And if some type of flu suddenly becomes epidemic, two- to five-year-olds are likely to be victimized as much as older children and adults. Thus, the first year a child attends a nursery school is likely to involve health risks. But keeping a child out of nursery school for health reasons may simply postpone the inevitable until kindergarten begins. Regardless of when it occurs, the first year in some sort of school is likely to be attended by a certain number of health problems.

Health problems likely first year in school

Obesity

A chubby infant may often be thought cute, but a fat five-year-old may be teased by peers. Changes in the proportions of the body with growth, as well as more strenuous exercise, cause most preschoolers to lose the potbelly they possessed as toddlers. Some children, however, not only retain the potbelly but become more noticeably obese as they mature. There is now quite a bit of evidence (summarized by Starfield and Pless, 1980, p. 282) that fat preschoolers tend to become fat adolescents and adults. The more overweight the child, the more likely it is that he or she will be obese later in life. It has been hypothesized that the number and size of the fat cells in the body is a major factor in obesity. Consequently, parents may be able to simplify the weight control of their offspring as adolescents and adults by providing a nonfattening diet during the preschool years. (Another factor contributing to obesity centers on the timing of puberty. It will be discussed in Chapter 14.)

Controlling weight of preschooler simplifies weight control later

The "Sickly" Child

As just noted in discussing infectious diseases, the year following a child's enrollment in a nursery school or kindergarten is likely to be marked by fairly frequent illnesses. Thus, children may seem "sickly" to their parents when they are first exposed to a variety of infectious agents. By the time they enter the primary grades, though, resistance to diseases increases and most children are thought of as healthy. Some children, however, seem to establish a pattern of frequent illnesses that may persist the rest of their lives. After evaluating longitudinal surveys of health records, Starfield and Pless concluded, "The popular concept of the sickly child may have some scientific basis" (1980, p. 302). In some cases a child may be prone to develop infectious diseases because of deficits in the immunologic system. But certain diseases, such as anemia, cystic fibrosis, and various types of nutritional deficiencies, may also cause a child to have chronic health problems.

Physical Development

The most direct way to get a clear picture of changes in physical development during the years from two to five is to visit a nursery school and watch the children at play. Differences between two- and five-year-olds are apparent not only in physical size, but also in coordination of both small and large muscle activities. Most two-year-olds have a well-coordinated walk, but they run with difficulty. If they get on a tricycle, they may use only one pedal at a time. Great effort and concentration may be required to get food on a spoon, and spills at the dining table are common. When getting dressed, they may help by pushing their arms and legs into shirt sleeves and pants, but they cannot get into these garments by themselves. They negotiate stairs one step at a time, putting down first one foot and then the other before moving to the next step. Most five-year-olds, by contrast, can run easily and use play equipment with considerable skill. They can handle tricycles with proficiency and may also be able to ride a bicycle (with or without training wheels). They can handle spoons and forks well (although knives may still be a problem), and spills while eating are more likely to be due to carelessness than to lack of coordination. They can dress themselves easily, although tying shoe laces may still be a problem. They can go up and down stairs by alternating feet and climb with agility.

Preschoolers at peak of efficiency as energy users

During the preschool years, human beings (because of low body weight and mass) are at a peak of efficiency as energy users (Brody, 1959). They also are inclined to be active and eager to use their newly perfected physical skills and abilities. To prove these two points to yourself, pick out an energetic child at play during a kindergarten recess. Write down everything he or she does (e.g., run from door of school room to fence, run back, run to jungle gym, climb on jungle gym for three minutes, run to fence and back, run to horizontal bar and hang upside down, run to fence, etc.). Then, if you really want to appreciate how efficiently energetic five-year-olds are, carry out the same actions yourself. (You might want to have a friend around to explain what you are doing in case someone happens to observe you dashing back and forth with no apparent purpose.) If you are too lazy and/or inhibited to actually carry out the actions you have observed and recorded, *imagine*

During the preschool years human beings are at their peak of efficiency as energy users.
© *Jane Scherr/Jeroboam, Inc.*

that you are doing the same things as the child in the same amount of time. Either way you will probably become aware that young children have lots of pep.

The energy of young children, together with their tendency to expend that energy on what impresses workaholic adults as aimless activities, has led theorists at different times to speculate about the interaction of maturation and learning. This question has been a topic of debate at intervals since the 1930s: Should children be allowed to engage in self-selected activities during the preschool years, or should they be exposed to instruction intended to speed up development?

The Interaction of Maturation and Learning

In the 1920s and 1930s, when institutes of child study were being established in American universities, many researchers were interested in tracing development during the first few years of life. As noted in Chapter 6, Mary Shirley carried out an intensive study of twenty-five children during the first two years of their lives and charted changes in locomotor skills. Arnold Gesell also was interested in tracing physical development and made motion pictures of children behaving in a variety of situations.

When he compared films of different children, Gesell was struck by the similarity of behavior at different age levels. Because the same types of behavior appeared at about the same time and in the same sequence, Gesell reasoned that early development must be guided by a built-in master plan. When a form of behavior seems to appear in the absence of training or experience, it is said to be due to maturation, and Gesell became the champion of the maturational view in American psychology. He wrote about the importance of maturation so extensively and so enthusiastically that other psychologists decided to test some of his hypotheses. One of the most energetic and inventive of these researchers was Myrtle McGraw.

Gesell: early development assumed to be controlled by maturation

The Impact of Early and Later Training

McGraw: The Study of Johnny and Jimmy

When Gesell published an article (Gesell and Thompson, 1929) in which he described how one of a pair of identical twins failed to learn locomotor skills any faster than his brother even when exposed to early training, McGraw accepted it as a challenge. She received permission from the parents of twin boys to use them as subjects in an elaborate experiment. The experiment began when the boys were less than a year old. At that time, doctors believed they were identical twins. A few months after the experiment was under way, however, it became apparent that they were *not* identical. Consequently, the results of the study were not as simple to interpret as they would have been if the boys had possessed identical genetic make-ups.

The basic approach McGraw followed was to give one twin (Johnny) intensive practice in a number of skills early in life. When the other twin (Jimmy) was several months older, he was given similar training, but he was more mature by then. The skills of the two boys were then compared immediately after training was completed and again after an interval of three or four years.

Starting at the age of two months, Johnny and Jimmy spent the hours from nine until five, five days a week, at a medical center. Johnny was given training by McGraw; Jimmy stayed in a crib or a playroom. It is apparent that McGraw wanted to test Gesell's hypotheses with a vengeance, because she taught Johnny how to roller skate and swim before he was a year old. As a matter of fact, by the age of sixteen months, Johnny was so expert on wheels he would skate through a tunnel from the building of the medical center where McGraw's experimental room was set up to another building, which housed the swimming pool. Johnny was also given training in riding a tricycle, climbing, and jumping off pedestals (among other things).

While it took only a few weeks for McGraw to train Johnny to skate, swim, climb, and jump, it took almost ten months of training before he became proficient on a tricycle. At this point, he was twenty-two months old, which was the age Jimmy started training sessions. Jimmy learned how to manipulate a tricycle as well as Johnny after just a few weeks but did not become as proficient in skating, swimming, climbing, or jumping, even after months of training. In analyzing the causes of these differences, McGraw (1939) had to take into account that since the boys were not identical twins there was a possibility genetic factors played a part. She also discovered that the parents of the boys seemed to feel obligated to make a bigger fuss over Jimmy to compensate for all the attention Johnny was receiving from McGraw. This seemed to lead to differences in the attitude of the boys toward the experiment and some of the activities.

Despite these complications, it seems clear that McGraw demonstrated that very young children could be taught skills no one had previously thought possible. Johnny's exploits did not necessarily disprove Gesell's hypothesis, however, since it could still be argued that learning took place only after maturation had set the stage. Johnny's accomplishments might seem less startling if it is assumed that no one had ever thought of teaching an eleven-month-old child to roller skate and swim before McGraw came along. It might be argued that roller skating is basically the same as walking and that swimming occurred because movements originally due to subcortical reflex were maintained through exercise and repetition. When Johnny was put on a tricycle and asked to develop a skill that involved a pattern of movements not related to locomotor or reflex activities, he experienced difficulties—until the maturation of his nerves and muscles made learning possible. (The skill Gesell and Thompson taught their twins was ladder-climbing, which also involves a pattern of movements and which also could not be learned until maturation set the stage.) Finally, some of Johnny's superiority in skating and swimming seemed to have been a function of such factors as being used to falling (since he had just learned to walk), a lower center of gravity (since he was shorter than Jimmy at the time training began), and a lack of awareness of potential danger (Jimmy was older and wiser when he began training).

Young children can learn skills early (if maturation has taken place)

Hilgard: Older Children Learn More Rapidly

The same basic experimental design utilized by McGraw was followed by Josephine Hilgard, who carried out an experimental study (1932) of interrelationships between maturation and learning. Hilgard arranged for one group of two- and three-year-old children to be given training for twelve weeks in buttoning, ladder-climbing, and the use of scissors. A matched control group was given no specific training. At the end of the twelve-week period, the trained group did better at the skills. The control group, then three months older than the experimental group had been at the onset of its training, was given just one week of instruction. At the end of this week the control group was as proficient as the experimental group, which had received three months of training at an earlier age level. Hilgard concluded that general physiological maturation, plus experiences other than the specific training, had contributed to the faster development of the skills by the control group.

More mature children learn more rapidly

From Readiness to Acceleration to Responsiveness

During the 1930s books by Gesell stressing the significance of maturation, Shirley's descriptions of the unvarying sequence of stages in locomotor development, and the Hilgard study all contributed to the concept of **readiness.** Many psychologists and educators became convinced that children would learn only after physical and neurological development, plus the normal experiences of childhood, had prepared them to learn. Tests were devised to determine if children were ready to enter first grade, and when children were rated as immature, their parents were advised to have them spend another year in kindergarten. In the 1950s and 1960s this view came to be widely rejected, the critical period hypothesis became popular, and faith in the importance of instruction was renewed. Some psychologists urged parents to do everything possible to accelerate physical, as well as intellectual, development. Books and articles outlined techniques parents might use to teach one- and two-year-olds to walk, talk, and even read (Doman, 1964) much earlier than they would on their own.

Current emphasis more on encouragement than training

Within the last few years studies revealing previously unrecognized capabilities of infants and young children seem to have led to a compromise in which parents are urged to provide encouragement and guidance but not instruction intended to try to speed up development. In the 1930s and 1940s Gesell more or less told parents that child behavior would unfold in a particular way at a particular point in development no matter what they did. In effect, parents were told to play the role of interested spectators. In the 1960s some psychologists told parents they should shape behavior as systematically and as rapidly as possible. It was argued (Engelmann and Engelmann, 1968) that if children were stimulated to master sequences of physical and mental skills early in life, they would be more capable and competent later in life. In this period the parent was seen as the molder and accelerator of development. In the 1970s many of the psychologists whose work is being summarized in these chapters on development during the first few years have put the child back in the central position. But, unlike Gesell, they have been intrigued by the subtle ways parental reactions are likely to foster maturing forms of behavior initiated by the child.

Because of the conflicting opinions just summarized, many parents wonder how much instruction at home or in a preschool is necessary or desirable. Statements by toy manufacturers or magazine articles arguing that "the will to learn must be established before the age of five" (or the equivalent) are not nearly as common today as they were in the mid-1960s, but they are occasionally encountered. And books claiming to describe techniques parents can use to "raise" a child's IQ are still to be found in libraries and bookstores. If they read such books, though, parents will discover that the approaches described usually require formal lessons and that these lessons involve a considerable amount of drill and rote memorization. The schoolroom atmosphere (even including a chalkboard) recommended in many books of this type conflicts with several of the characteristics of effective child care noted earlier (for example, permitting and encouraging the child to do many things independently). Parents of the 1980s may not wish to try to speed up development by providing instruction, but they may still wonder: How much should we allow our child to "just play"? An analysis of play will reveal that it involves a great deal more than aimless fooling around that has no substantial impact on the acquisition of skills. Play fosters (and reflects) aspects of cognitive, social, and emotional development, but it is very much a physical activity and also a product of interactions between maturation and learning. Accordingly, a discussion of play logically fits in this chapter and serves as an introduction to the remaining chapters on development during the preschool years.

Play

Theories of Play

Theorists in various fields have speculated about the nature and significance of play for hundreds of years. Some of the most influential of these theories will now be summarized.

Groos: The Adaptive Value of Play

K. Groos, an early theorist who delineated aspects of play that either anticipated or influenced many contemporary psychologists, stressed its **adaptive** aspects. Groos was impressed by Darwin's theory of evolution and, on the basis of observations of animals (1898) and humans (1901), he concluded that play must serve an adaptive function since it has been

Groos: play must serve an **adaptive** function

reported for as long as individuals have depicted or written about be-havior. Young animals and children are shown at play in pictures created thousands of years ago, and this led Groos to reason that the period of immaturity following birth occurs to make it *possible* for organ-isms to play. Human beings are more complex than any other species, and our period of immaturity (and play) is longer than that of any species. Groos suggested that play permitted children to practice adult activities and to engage in activities for their own sake, not to achieve some specific end. He also concluded that children initially concentrate on **experimental** play that leads to development of sensory and motor skills, and that they later engage in play that serves to foster interper-sonal relationships. The speculations of Groos served as the basis for many subsequent analyses of play.

Freud: Play as a Means for Wish Fulfillment

Freud: play is an ef-fective means for wish fulfillment

In his writings, Freud suggested that play provides children with an effective means for wish fulfillment. When an adult experiences a con-flict between the id (guided by the pleasure principle) and the ego (guided by the reality principle), frustration may result as the person seeks ways (consciously or unconsciously) to resolve the conflict. A child faced with a similar conflict may be able to resolve it by fulfilling wishes in play activity. A neighborhood nemesis who makes life dis-agreeable for a child, for example, may be assigned the role of an enemy in a game with toy space soldiers and blasted into oblivion with a guided missile. (Adults can *imagine* the same sort of thing, but it doesn't give the same sense of satisfaction.) Thus, a child can deal with a negative or fearful situation in play and make it more acceptable. In addition, a child who plays the role of loved individuals (such as the parents) may be able to fulfill the wish to be like them.

Erikson: Play as Therapy

After Erikson had become established in America, he served for a time as a faculty member at the University of California at Berkeley. While there, he asked subjects of one of the longitudinal studies to make play constructions out of an assortment of dolls, toys, and props. He found that boys tended to create constructions that involved active themes whereas girls were inclined to arrange static constructions. Although Erikson's interpretations of the significance of these constructions (which centered on differences in both sex organs and sex roles) have been sharply criticized (e.g., Janeway, 1971), his research contributed significantly to the development of play therapy. Most (but not all) forms of psychotherapy with adults are based on verbalizations. Young children often lack the vocabulary to express their thoughts in speech, but they *are* able to express themselves in play. In the process, they give therapists clues as to their problems, compensate for traumatic experiences by mastering them, and gain release of tension.

Piaget: Play as Assimilation and Consolidation

Piaget's view of play is an outgrowth of basic principles of his theory and of his stages of cognitive development. Adaptation (to review points outlined in the discussion of his theory in Chapter 2) results from the interplay of assimilation and accommodation. In assimilation, children incorporate experiences into existing schemes, but the way they do

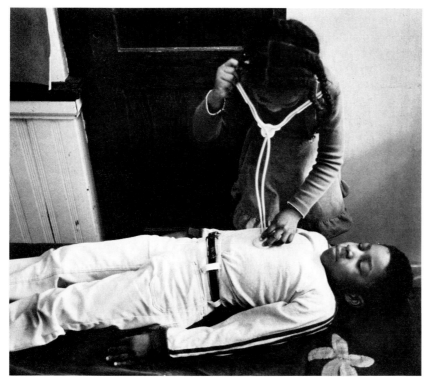

Pretense play, in which children pretend they are engaging in activities they have observed, reaches a peak at about the age of five.
© *Jean-Claude Lejeune.*

this depends on their stage of cognitive development. During the first stages of the sensorimotor period, for example, infants engage in **practice** play by repeating a satisfying bodily activity. At the secondary circular reaction stage, they will intentionally duplicate (or practice) an activity involving an object. At the preoperational level (to be described in detail in the next chapter), preschoolers switch from practice play to **symbolic** play when they are able to grasp that something can stand for something else. Thus a broom can be used not just as a broom, but as a gun or a horse. In both practice and symbolic play, consolidations occur. When we consolidate a position, we strengthen or reaffirm it in some way, and that is what happens when children play. As they practice and embroider on experiences in play, children strengthen and expand their understanding of schemes.

Piaget: from **practice** to **symbolic** to **pretense** play

Piaget suggested that symbolic play is exclusively solitary during the first two years of life. Starting in the third year, though, children begin to engage in social, or interactive, **pretense** play. Pretense play increases to about the age of five, and then decreases (Rubin, 1977). Interestingly, solitary pretense play tends to increase for a brief period around the age of six, just as interactive pretense play decreases. It has been hypothesized (Rubin, Fein, and Vandenberg, 1983, p. 721) that this brief return to solitary pretense play occurs because when children enter school they become involved in games with rules. Engaging in solitary pretense play gives them a chance to practice and consolidate game skills without pressure. As they engage in pretense play, preschoolers become increasingly capable of substituting inappropriate objects for the real thing. A three-year-old may need to hold something resembling a cup to pretend she is drinking tea; a five-year-old can make do with any small object or even nothing at all.

Features of Play

Several other theories of play have been proposed by contemporary psychologists. Their contributions (as well as those of Freud, Erikson, and Piaget) can be summarized in the form of a set of six features of play noted by Kenneth Rubin, Greta Fein, and Brian Vandenberg (1983):

1. Play is intrinsically motivated. It is not stimulated by physiological drives or social demands.
2. Play is characterized by attention to means rather than ends. It is engaged in for its own sake.

3. Play is guided by the question: What can I do with this object? Play is therefore different from exploration, which is guided by the question: What is this object and what can it do?
4. Play involves pretense. It stresses the make-believe use of objects.
5. Play is characterized by freedom from externally imposed rules. Play is not the same as games, which *do* depend on rules.
6. Play involves activity.

Play features: self-motivated, involves pretense, no rules, active

A different way to look at play is to summarize its various functions.

Functions of Play

When children are allowed to engage in self-selected play activities, they have opportunities to discover many things at their own pace and in their own way. In contrast to formal instruction (at home or in school), self-initiated play makes it possible for a child to explore and experiment without risk. If a child cannot answer a question or carry out a task presented by a parent or teacher, tension may develop. The child may feel inferior or inadequate and become reluctant to try new tasks for fear of failure. But in a play situation there is usually no pressure to produce a particular result and no concern about failure if an intended outcome does not occur. A "wrong" response, in fact, may trigger a new and unexpected way of doing things.

Play permits children to explore and experiment without risk

In the process of "playing around," children can experiment with types of behavior in nonthreatening situations. Instead of actually fighting with another child, for instance, three-year-olds can make believe they are fighting. In the process, they get feedback about what *might* happen if they engaged in a genuine altercation with another child. S. Miller (1973) refers to such make-believe fooling around as *galumphing*. Galumphing may seem a pointless waste of time to a workaholic adult, but it permits young children to learn about the nature and consequences of certain types of potentially risky interactions with others.

A related function of play is that it permits children to experiment with roles of various kinds. When they assume the role of father or mother, or police officer or store clerk, children are able to identify with those individuals. In the process, they have the chance to try out adult forms of behavior and also experience the feeling that they have something in common with persons they admire.

Play permits children to practice roles

Another function of play is that it permits practice without pressure to accomplish some specific task. A young child who is given an expensive set of blocks, for example, may disappoint parents if initial manipulation of the pieces seems more or less aimless. An impatient father might even go to the trouble of constructing an elaborate castle or skyscraper to demonstrate what he thinks should be done with the materials. In such cases, the child may "know" better than the father that it is necessary to gain familiarity with the blocks before attempting an ambitious project. In the process of play involving such objects as tricycles and jungle gyms, children strengthen muscles and develop coordination.

Play fosters imaginative and creative abilities

Yet another function of play is that it fosters imaginative and creative abilities and tendencies. When left to their own devices, children often find remarkably inventive uses for mundane objects. A five-year-old boy found an old garbage can cover on the way to a neighbor's house, for instance, and he and three playmates used it in a dozen different ways in the space of thirty minutes. First it was a flying saucer, then a shield, then a hat, then a "sled," and so on. The dramatic situations invented by young children can also be much more entertaining than the plots of many of the most popular TV series.

Play permits release of emotional tension

A final function of play, stressed by Freud and Erikson, is that it serves to release tension. Most types of psychotherapy with children utilize play not only to provide clues to the therapist as to the causes of problem behavior, but also to help the child get rid of pent-up emotion. Children often spontaneously use play to get emotional catharsis.

Age Trends in Sociodramatic Play

Differences in the types of play engaged in by younger and older preschoolers have been charted by Sara Smilansky (1968), who has studied sociodramatic play, a form of pretense play in which children use props and assume roles. Types of behavior exhibited by younger and older preschoolers for aspects of sociodramatic play are summarized below.

Role Play

Indicated by the roles chosen and how the child plays a role. Roles chosen at the beginning level reflect the child's attempts to understand and sort out who he or she is (e.g., mommy, daddy, baby, animals). Roles chosen at advanced levels reflect the child's attempts to understand and sort out the world around him or her (e.g., police officer, doctor). Ways the child plays the role at the beginning level center on imitation of one or two aspects of the role (e.g., the child announces,

Two-year-olds seem to prefer realistic toys, perhaps because such familiar objects are easier to relate to existing schemes. Older children often get a great deal of enjoyment out of "abstract" toys, perhaps because they enjoy expanding and embellishing conceptions they have already formed.
Guy Gillette/Photo Researchers.

"I'm the mommy" and rocks the baby). Ways the child plays roles at the advanced level center on elaboration of the basic character being imitated (e.g., child announces, "I'm the mommy," feeds the baby, goes to a meeting, prepares dinner).

Older preschoolers play roles in more comprehensive ways

Using Props

Indicated by the type of prop used and how the child uses the prop. Props used at the beginning level reflect how the child uses a real object (e.g., a real phone), or a replica of the object (e.g., a toy phone). Props used at the advanced level reveal that the child can use any object as a prop (e.g., a block for a phone), or a pretend prop (e.g., holding a hand to the ear and pretending it is a telephone). How the child uses the prop at the beginning level involves simple physical manipulation (e.g., dialing the phone). Use of props at the advanced level is characterized by their use in a play episode (e.g., calling the doctor on the phone because the baby is sick).

Make-Believe

Indicated at the beginning level by the way the child imitates actions performed by others (e.g., holding the phone to the ear). At the advanced level, the child's actions are part of an episode of make-believe (e.g., the child says, "I'm going to call the baby-sitter").

Time

The amount of time a child devotes to a play episode. At the beginning level there may be only fleeting involvement (e.g., the child picks up a toy phone, dials a number, goes on to another toy). At the advanced level the child may stick with a type of play for ten minutes or more (e.g., carry out several imaginary telephone conversations).

Interaction

Relationships with others. At the beginning level the child typically acts out a role without apparent awareness of others (e.g., The child "calls" someone on the phone but then engages in a monologue). Next, the child interacts with others at various times when the need arises to share props or have a partner in play. Eventually, cooperative effort around a theme occurs. The child acts out a role cooperatively with others, recognizing the benefits of working together (e.g., the child plays the role of a secretary and hands the phone to her employer after answering a call and saying "May I say who is calling?").

Older preschoolers interact with playmates in cooperative ways

Verbal Communication

Verbalization or conversation. At the beginning level, verbalization centers on use of toys (e.g., "I had the phone first"). At the advanced level, there may be a dialogue about the selected play theme or constant chatter reflecting selected roles (e.g., "What do you want to eat?" "I'd like a hamburger, french fries, and a milk shake").

These changes in sociodramatic play outlined by Smilansky can be explained by the observations of Piaget on cognitive development. Children who exhibit types of play at the beginning levels have a limited repertoire of schemes and they engage in short, literal play episodes. Children at the advanced levels have had more opportunities to assimilate and accommodate. They expand, revise, and embellish play episodes.

Training Versus Arranging the Play Environment

Because play serves all the functions just listed and is the primary "occupation" of preschool children, several developmental psychologists have speculated about the potential value of teaching children *how* to play. Since play contributes to the development of relationships with others and fosters imaginative and creative abilities (among other things), theorists have wondered whether children should simply be left to their own devices. (This interest in guiding play might be thought of as a current focus of interest in the maturation learning debate.) A number of attempts have been made, for instance, to train children to solve problems as they play and to engage in fantasy. The rationale for such training is that children who solve problems and use their imaginations in play will continue to engage in those forms of behavior on their own and in school.

While some short-term positive results have been reported (reviewed by Rubin, Fein, and Vandenberg, 1983), the results are somewhat inconsistent. For reasons noted in analyses of the critical period hypothesis in earlier chapters, it does not seem likely that long-term gains from such training will be found. If a fade reaction occurred after children attended Head Start programs that involved intensive instruction for several months, it does not seem logical to expect that brief instruction in play techniques will have a lasting impact. Differences between the demands made on and activities engaged in by preschool and elementary school children were summarized in Chapter 5. Such differences are so substantial that there would appear to be little carryover from an informal play experience to a formal school experience. Furthermore, changes in cognitive abilities that occur between the preschool and elementary school years mean that children respond to situations in different ways at the age of three and the age of seven.

Instead of attempting to provide play training, therefore, parents might concentrate on trying to arrange an environment that will encourage different types of play. When buying toys and play equipment, parents might seek to provide variety. Construction materials such as playdough and crayons, for example, tend to foster solitary play and are appropriate for times when no playmates are available. Transportation toys and housekeeping toys, on the other hand, tend to encourage interactive play. Parents might also keep in mind that toys contribute to the formation of sex roles. If girls are given only dolls, baby carriages, and miniature kitchens, they will almost be forced into playing the role of housewife-mother. It has been found that when girls have access to "boys" toys, they frequently enjoy playing with them. Accordingly, preschool girls might be given blocks and construction sets and transportation toys along with more traditional "female" playthings. In addition to realistic toys, children might also be provided with "unstructured" materials that can serve a variety of play purposes. Asking a neighbor for the large cardboard carton that was left by a local appliance

Variety of playthings likely to foster many types of play

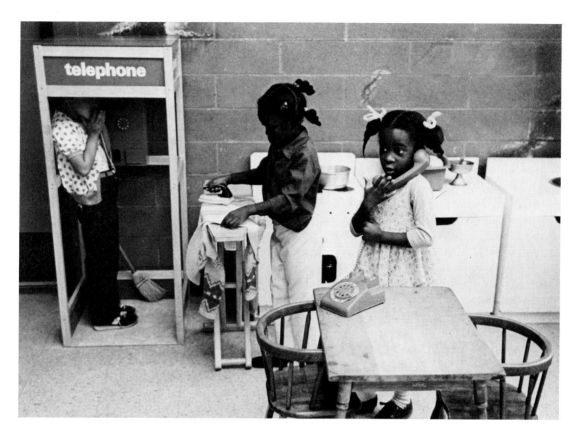

Many toys given to preschool-age girls may tend to strengthen sex-role stereotypes if they encourage identification only with the mother-housewife role. To reduce such tendencies, parents might give girls opportunities to play with materials (such as construction sets) that widen their play horizons.
© *Elizabeth Crews.*

firm that delivered a refrigerator, for example, might trigger several days of imaginative play. To encourage experience in assuming roles and interacting with age-mates, parents might make it a practice to invite children of the same age as their preschool son or daughter to their homes. When no other children are available, parents might be willing to go along with fantasy play instituted by their children. Finally, they might restrict television viewing to programs such as "Sesame Street," "Mr. Rogers' Neighborhood," non-violent cartoon shows, Walt Disney movies, and the like.

(Physical development during the six- to twelve-year span is discussed in Chapter 14, starting on page 433.)

Summary

1. Young children are resilient, not only in terms of overcoming illness and injuries quickly, but also in terms of physical elasticity. One reason for the physical flexibility of young children is that their bones have not completely ossified (hardened). While this is an advantage in many ways, the fact that the skull bones are soft means that parents should do everything possible to prevent blows to a young child's head since the brain is not as well protected as it will be later.

2. As soon as children begin to interact with peers, they are exposed for the first time to many kinds of infectious diseases. As a result there are likely to be health problems the first year a child attends any kind of school. Nutrition plays an important part in the maintenance of good health, but parents should try to prevent overeating because children who are overweight as preschoolers tend to have weight problems later in life. Preschoolers are at a peak of efficiency as energy users, and they should be encouraged to be active not only to strengthen muscles and the cardiovascular system, but also to reduce tendencies toward obesity.

3. Many psychologists have been interested in the interaction between maturation and learning early in life. Some theorists, such as Arnold Gesell, argued that early development was controlled by built-in tendencies and that children should be allowed to develop skills on their own. Myrtle McGraw, on the other hand, demonstrated that young children can be trained to acquire certain skills at very early ages (provided maturation had prepared the way). In the 1930s, Josephine Hilgard showed that more mature children learn more rapidly, but in the 1950s and 1960s, when the critical period hypothesis was widely endorsed, there was considerable stress on training children to ac-

quire skills as early as possible. Re-evaluation of the critical period hypothesis has led to current emphasis on encouragement rather than training.

4. The primary activity of preschool children is play, and it has been studied extensively. An early theorist proposed that play must serve an adaptive function; since it is so universal, it might be concluded that it has contributed to the survival of most species. Freud pointed out that play is an effective means of **wish fulfillment,** Piaget described how children move from **practice** to **symbolic** to **pretense** play. Features of play that emerge when all theories are considered include the following: it is self-motivated, involves pretense, does not stress rules, and is active.

5. Play serves many functions: it permits children to explore and experiment without risk, it lets children practice roles, it fosters imaginative and creative abilities, and it allows the release of emotional tension.

6. As preschoolers mature, they engage in different kinds of play. Older children are more likely than younger ones to play roles in comprehensive ways and to interact with playmates in cooperative ways. Since children engage in play spontaneously, it is generally felt that they should be provided with a variety of playthings likely to foster many types of play rather than be exposed to a great deal of instruction or training.

Suggestions for Further Study

Growth and Health

Physical growth is discussed by J. M. Tanner in *Carmichael's Manual of Child Psychology* (3rd ed., 1970), edited by Paul H. Mussen. Physical health is analyzed by Barbara Starfield and I. B. Pless in *Constancy and Change in Human Development* (1980), edited by Orville G. Brim and Jerome Kagan.

Play

For a concise review of research on play, consult "Play" by Kenneth H. Rubin, Greta G. Fein, and Brian Vandenberg in *Socialization, Personality, and Social Development,* edited by E. M. Hetherington, Volume IV of the *Handbook of Child Psychology* (4th ed., 1983), edited by Paul H. Mussen. More complete discussions of play can be found in *Child's Play* (1971), edited by R. E. Herron and B. Sutton-Smith, and *Children's Play* (1980), edited by K. H. Rubin.

Observing Preschool Children

Spending an hour or so at a nursery school would give you an opportunity to observe aspects of physical development as well as the nature of preschool play. If you do have the chance to observe two- to five-year-olds in free play situations in a nursery school (or backyard), you might first concentrate on physical differences. Pick out the youngest- and oldest-appearing children in the group and note differences in appearance and in coordination. Then take notes on the kinds of play children engage in. You might note age and sex differences and also check to see if the features and functions of play described in this chapter become apparent. Finally, keep a record of the toys and equipment used and decide if you would want to provide different types of play materials if you were in charge of arranging the play environment.

KEY POINTS

The Nature of Preoperational Thought

Preoperational thinking: tendency to focus on one quality, inability to reverse

One-track thinking may cancel aspects of understanding

Objects classified in one category at a time

Cognitive development may lead to improved memories

The Nature of Egocentric Speech and Thought

Egocentric thinking: difficulty in taking another's point of view

Questions About Preoperational and Egocentric Thought

Socialized thinking may occur early under simplified conditions

Piaget: attempts to speed up cognitive development lead to superficial learning

The Cumulative Depressant Effect of an Impoverished Environment

Impoverished environment has cumulative depressant effect

Attitude toward school best predictor of adult achievement

Child-rearing Techniques That Foster Cognitive Development

Parents of preschoolers should talk, respond, enrich, encourage, explain

Factors Parents Might Consider Regarding Nursery School

Nursery school attendance does not necessarily lead to better school performance for middle-class children

Full-time mothering may lead to overinvestment

Vocabulary Acquisition Does Not Seem to Depend on Instruction

By age six many children know 14,000 words

Most words seem to be encoded in absence of instruction

Language Development

Overextensions illustrate assimilation and accommodation

"Inconsistent" grammar may be due to consistent schemes

Confusion of opposites may be due to inability to decenter

CHAPTER

11

TWO TO FIVE

COGNITIVE DEVELOPMENT

*I*n Chapter 7 you were acquainted with the six stages in the sensorimotor period of development described by Jean Piaget. During that period children acquire the object concept and learn to coordinate schemes so that they can engage in mental manipulations and think out simple problems. During the next three years children begin to carry out mental manipulations in more complex ways. But their thinking still differs in significant ways from that of older children and adults. Piaget's concept of an **operation** can help explain the distinction between the thinking of three-year-olds and that of ten- or fifteen-year-olds.

The Nature of Preoperational Thought

Operations, Conservation, Decentration

You are reminded that an operation is a mental action that can be reversed. Two- to five-year-olds are not able to engage in operational thinking, which explains why Piaget refers to this as the **preoperational** period. Preoperational thinking (to reinforce points mentioned earlier) can be clarified by examining the Piagetian concepts of conservation and decentration. Conservation refers to the idea that certain properties of objects (for example, volume, mass, or substance) do not change when the shape or appearance of an object changes. Decentration refers to the ability of a child to keep from centering attention on only one quality at a time (or, to put it another way, the ability to concentrate on more than one quality of an object or situation). Operational thinking, conservation, and decentration are all illustrated by Piaget's experiment in which children are asked to tell what they think happens when water is poured from one container into a differently shaped container. When children up to the age of five respond in such situations, they reveal that they concentrate on only one quality at a time (for example, height) and are unable to mentally reverse what they have seen. The inability of two- to five-year-olds to handle operations (that is, to mentally reverse actions) is perhaps the most distinctive feature of their thinking. But other aspects of cognitive development are revealed by the ways preschoolers assimilate, accommodate, and form schemes representing their ever-widening experiences.

Schemes, Assimilation, Accommodation

In his analysis of cognitive development Piaget stresses the formation of schemes. As children perceive people and events and interact with objects and other individuals, they assimilate new experiences to already existing schemes or accommodate their thinking by modifying such schemes. To strengthen your grasp of these various processes, put yourself in the place of a three-year-old who goes off to nursery school for the first time, after having been more or less confined to home and neighborhood. The family has a cocker spaniel, and the child has learned that

Preoperational thinking: tendency to focus on one quality, inability to reverse

it is called Fluffy and that it is referred to as a dog. On the way to school the first day the child sees a Great Dane and a Chihuahua, which represent totally new animals, since Fluffy has been the only dog encountered up to that time. Upon asking what these strange animals are called, the child is told, "They are dogs, like Fluffy." In sorting out the meaning of these first encounters with other dogs and the bit of information that they *are* dogs, the child fits some features into an already existing scheme but also alters that scheme. Fluffy has four legs and barks, and so do the other dogs. So those features are assimilated. But Great Danes are much bigger than Fluffy, while Chihuahuas are much smaller (among other things), so the child must revise (accommodate) the original scheme for *dog*.

One-track Thinking

When preoperational children are confronted with something that does not fit any already developed scheme (or when they form new schemes), they tend to center their attention on one feature at a time. In Piaget's water experiment, children below the age of five may be misled into saying that a taller glass holds more water than a shorter one (when actually they hold the same amount) because they concentrate on height. The same tendency to center attention on a single attribute characterizes the spontaneous formation of schemes. The process illustrated by the example of dogs occurs each time a child is exposed to a new experience or a variation of a previous experience. If the number of new experiences, objects, and persons that a child encounters in the first few days in a nursery school (or on excursions away from home) is considered, it is apparent that young children engage in an enormous amount of cognitive activity. Tendencies that influence ways a preschooler sorts out these various impressions are illustrated by some of the clinical interview procedures devised by Piaget.

If you were to take eight blocks and arrange them about an inch apart in a row, most preschoolers could probably count them. If you then asked a four-year-old child to form a row of the same number of blocks (by selecting from a supply you provided), your subject would probably carry out your request by putting a block just below each of the blocks already in line. But if you then took the first row of blocks and spaced them about three inches apart, you might be surprised at the confusion this simple change would produce. If you asked the child (who had just demonstrated an ability to form a line containing the same number of blocks), "Do I have more blocks (pointing to the long row), or do you have more blocks (pointing to the short row), or do we have the same?" the likely response would be, "*You* have more blocks." The tendency for

One-track thinking may cancel aspects of understanding

the child to concentrate on the single feature of length tends to cancel out the just-demonstrated point that each row contains the same number of blocks.

Now, picture yourself carrying out other Piaget experiments. You ask the four-year-old to watch as you put pieces of cardboard on a table. Some of the pieces are square, some are round, and some are triangles. There are large and small pieces of each shape. After you place several of each shape and size in a random order on the table, you say to the child, "Put together things that are alike—that are the same." The child will probably respond to this request by moving the pieces around in a somewhat disorganized way, putting some similar objects together but not following a consistent procedure (for example, putting all large pieces together, or all pieces of the same shape together).

Next, you ask a five-year-old to observe as you place plastic flowers of different types (say tulips, zinnias, and petunias) on the table. The assortment includes three yellow, two red, and two orange flowers of each type. If you say, "Put together flowers that are alike—that are the same," the child will probably sort flowers either by color or type. Then you ask, "Suppose a girl (or boy, depending on the sex of your subject) takes all the yellow tulips and makes a bunch of them, or else makes a bunch of all the flowers. Which way does she have a bigger bunch?" Your subject will probably reply, "She would have more tulips." Chil-

Objects classified in one category at a time

dren at the preoperational level find it difficult to think of an object as belonging to more than one classification category at a time. It is not until children reach the elementary school years that they comprehend that the same object or person can be classified in several ways at the same time.

You try still another Piagetian experiment independently with both the four- and five-year-old children. This time you take several sticks. The smallest is three inches long, the next is three and one-half inches long, and so on by half-inch increments. You put these down in scrambled order in front of each child and say, "Put these sticks in a row from the shortest to the longest." The four-year-old will probably put the sticks in something approximating a row, but it is not likely that they will be arranged in order from shortest to longest. The five-year-old is likely to come closer to carrying out your request, but may experience some difficulty in placing all the sticks in exact order. After the four- and five-year-olds have arranged the sticks, you put the sticks in the proper order, very neatly arranged. Next, you ask each child first to arrange another set of sticks just like yours and then make a drawing of the arrangement. Now you wait six months and then ask the two children to draw a picture of the sticks that they arranged and drew the last time you saw them. You might be amazed to discover that the four-year-old, who had trouble copying the arrangement of sticks and making a drawing of the arrangement just after it had been done in your initial inter-

FIGURE 11.1

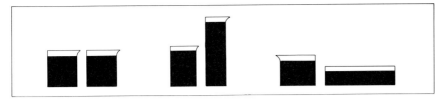

Preschoolers maintain that the amount of liquid in one of two equal-sized containers changes when it is poured into a container of a different shape. (Illustrates the tendency for preoperational thinkers to concentrate on one quality at a time as well as their inability to reverse.)

Preschoolers maintain that a spaced-out row of eight blocks contains a greater number of blocks than a tightly spaced row of eight blocks. (Illustrates how preoperational thinkers tend to be influenced by how things look rather than how they must logically be.)

Preschoolers are likely to group objects in a somewhat unsystematic and inconsistent manner. (Illustrates the tendency for preoperational thinkers to classify objects in loose and disorganized ways.)

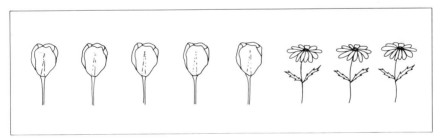

When asked if there are more tulips or more flowers, preschoolers are likely to maintain that there are more tulips than flowers. (Illustrates the difficulty preoperational thinkers have when they are asked to think of an object as belonging to more than one classification at a time and to deal with relations between a part and the whole to which it belongs.)

Preschool children may not be able to arrange a series of sticks in order from smallest to largest. (Illustrates the difficulty preoperational thinkers have dealing with ordinal relationships.)

Cognitive develop-
ment may lead to
improved memories

view, draws a more accurate picture of the sticks arranged in order half a
year later. Piaget and Inhelder (1973) discovered that preschoolers actually improve their recollections of some arrangements of objects. Apparently, children retain an image of the arrangements they have
previously seen. But they later interpret these images more accurately
because of the rapid changes in cognitive development that take place
during the preschool years.

The block experiment illustrates how the thinking of preoperational
children is dominated by their perceptions. When the just-counted
blocks are rearranged, the child's thinking is dominated by how things
look, not by how they must logically be. The experiment in sorting
geometric shapes reveals the tendency of preoperational children to
group things in loose and confused ways. The flower experiment shows
how difficult it is for a preoperational child to deal with relations between a part and the whole to which it belongs. The experiment in
arranging sticks reveals the difficulty the preoperational child experiences with ordinal relationships (placing things in order). All the experiments demonstrate a common characteristic: the inability to think
simultaneously about several aspects of a situation. As the memory experiment reveals, however, in just a few months the thinking processes
used by children may change quite dramatically.

Even though Piaget's designation of this stage as preoperational calls
attention to the inability of preschoolers to handle operations, young
children still formulate and modify schemes at an impressive rate. Considering the number of new experiences to which young children are
exposed, it is not surprising that they tend to focus on one attribute at a
time. Piaget's observations on the one-track thinking of young children,
particularly their tendency to engage in what he called **egocentric
speech and thought,** has led to a certain amount of controversy during
recent years.

The Nature of Egocentric Speech and Thought

Egocentric thinking:
difficulty in taking
another's point of
view

Egocentric, as used by Piaget, does not mean selfish or conceited. It
signifies that young children find it difficult to take another person's
point of view.[1] In their conversations with others and in experimental
situations in which they are asked to describe how something would
look if viewed by someone else (Piaget and Inhelder, 1956), preschool
children reveal that they have difficulty seeing things from another person's perspective. Quite often, nursery school children will engage in

---

[1] Piaget defined egocentrism in various, often broad, ways (Ford, 1979). The
essence of the concept is summed up, however, by the statement that it is the
inability to take another's perspective.

what Piaget called a **collective monologue.** A pair of children may give the appearance of having a conversation, pausing after having said something to listen to the partner, but their statements and responses will bear little relationship to each other. Each child's utterances will follow a particular line of thought. But there is little reciprocal interchange, where something said by one individual elicits an appropriate response from the other. In certain situations, when one child asks another a specific question or when a mutually interesting point comes up, preschool children *do* engage in genuine conversations (Garvey and Hogan, 1973). Piaget suggested, however, that such **socialized speech** does not usually appear with any consistency until after children reach the age of seven years or so.

Piaget's conclusions regarding egocentric and socialized speech were originally based on records of vocal interchanges between children in natural settings. He later devised some simple experiments to determine the extent to which a child is able (or unable) to take another's point of view. One of these experiments features a model of three easily distinguishable mountains. (Each mountain is a different color, one has snow on it, another a house, and the third a red cross.) A child is asked to sit on one side of a table on which the model is placed. Then the examiner produces a doll and puts it at some other position on the table. The child is then asked to indicate what the doll sees by selecting from a set of ten pictures the one that represents the mountains seen by the doll. Piaget and Inhelder (1956) found that children up to the age of seven or eight years tend to pick out a picture that represents their point of view rather than that of the doll. He concluded that despite the fact that children who are approaching eight years of age know that the appearance of something changes when they walk around it, they are prevented from selecting the correct picture by their egocentrism—their inability to visualize something from another's point of view. Egocentric thinking, in turn, can be understood by considering the principle of decentration. Preoperational children typically concentrate on one thing at a time. This tendency causes them to focus on their own point of view even when asked to imagine a different point of view.

Questions About Preoperational and Egocentric Thought

Are Children Less Egocentric than Piaget Says They Are?

A number of psychologists have questioned Piaget's conclusions regarding egocentricity and the explanation that egocentricity manifests a child's inability to decenter. Margaret Donaldson, for instance, suggests

Piaget observed that because of tendencies toward egocentric thinking, preschool-age children often talk to each other without paying too much attention to what the other child is saying.
Bob Kalman/The Image Works.

that children below the age of seven or eight "fail" the mountain experiment mainly because they do not understand what they are to do. In *Children's Minds* (1978), she describes experiments that are specifically designed to "make sense" to children. In one experiment, for example, a child is asked to hide a boy doll behind a wall so that a policeman doll cannot see it. In another experiment a simplified version of Piaget's mountain task is presented in a very slow and deliberate manner. Donaldson reports that when children below the age of eight are asked to deal with realistic and familiar problems, they are *not* egocentric. She also suggests that young children have difficulty classifying objects primarily because of problems of communication. She reports that they can solve conservation problems if instructions are presented in language they can understand. Donaldson concludes that parents and teachers might foster cognitive development by talking *about* words (p. 93) to help children acquire language skills. This may in turn lead to deeper and earlier understanding.

Another psychologist who has criticized Piaget's conclusions about preoperational thought is Rochel Gelman. She reports (1979) that when conditions are communicated to young children at their own level, pre-schoolers are capable of solving simplified versions of many of the Piagetian experiments. Gelman argues, for example, that when children are asked to distinguish between "winners" and "losers" instead of specifying "more" or "less," they are able to correctly answer questions about aspects of conservation. She believes that Piagetian concepts should be tested by specifically devising tasks and experimental settings to suit the preschool child.

Socialized thinking may occur early under simplified conditions

The results of the experiments described by Donaldson and Gelman suggest that Piaget may have overemphasized the orderliness of the sequence and timing of aspects of cognitive development. On the other hand, simply because researchers have developed ingenious experimental techniques that enable *their* subjects to solve certain types of problems earlier than Piaget's subjects does not mean his observations should be rejected or ignored. If parents and preschool teachers make a concerted effort to see things from the child's point of view, arrange conditions to suit the child, and use terms that are familiar to the child, a child may demonstrate certain types of understanding somewhat earlier than Piaget predicts she or he will. But if parents, teachers, siblings, or peers do *not* make any special efforts to think and talk as a preschool child does, the trends described by Piaget would probably appear "on schedule."

While it may make sense for those who interact with preschool children to follow Donaldson's suggestion and talk *about* words, it might not be advisable for adults (outside of experimental situations) to try to frequently adjust their thought and speech to suit the child. If parents and teachers spend too much time deliberately thinking and talking in preoperational terms, it would seem possible that they might slow down the rate at which a child would move to concrete operational thinking. These observations lead to the question: Should parents and preschool teachers make systematic efforts to encourage children to conserve, decenter, and overcome egocentric thinking at a faster than normal rate?

Should Efforts Be Made to Speed Up Cognitive Development?

Aware that preschool children are typically preoperational and unable to conserve, some psychologists in the 1960s (for example, Engelmann and Engelmann, 1968) speculated about the possibility of speeding up cognitive development. They reasoned that preschool children who learned how to solve conservation problems, for example, might function as concrete operational thinkers at an earlier than average age. Precocious concrete operational thinkers might then begin to function as formal thinkers ahead of schedule, making them capable of solving many kinds of problems at a younger age than if they had not received early instruction.

Piaget: attempts to speed up cognitive development lead to superficial learning

When he learned that American psychologists such as Engelmann were referring to his descriptions of cognitive development in their efforts to speed up mastery of concepts, Jean Piaget expressed the opinion that such attempts would lead to superficial rather than genuine learning (1966). To test his accelerated intelligence view (as well as Piaget's contention that it would produce only superficial learning), Engelmann set out to teach six-year-old children the concept of specific gravity. He then invited Constance Kamii and L. Dermon, advocates of the Piagetian view, to test the children to determine whether or not they had gained genuine understanding. Kamii and Dermon (1972) concluded that the children had gained only partial understanding of the concept, that they still functioned at the preoperational level, and that they applied the rule they had learned in rote fashion. Engelmann argued that this seemed to be the case only because the children lacked information that would have been necessary for them to use the rule with understanding. He claimed that they could be taught this information and then would be able to apply the concept. Kamii and Dermon evaluated this argument and discovered that the children had to be told what information they would need. (They were not able to ask for it on their own.)

More comprehensive evidence regarding attempts to speed up cognitive development by presenting instruction during the preschool years was provided by follow-up studies of Head Start programs. As noted in Chapter 5, the Report of the U.S. Commission on Civil Rights (1967) indicated that none of the Head Start programs studied had significantly raised achievement levels of pupils in the primary grades. In commenting on this report, Susan W. Gray and Rupert E. Klaus (1970) observed that not even the best possible program could be expected to "inoculate" children and make them "immune" to the impact of continued existence in a poor environment. This point can be grasped more completely by considering the depressant effect of the cumulative impact of conditions associated with poverty in America.

The Cumulative Depressant Effect of an Impoverished Environment

The low-income woman who is expecting a child often receives little or no benefits from health knowledge and services. A low-income woman who seeks medical advice during pregnancy is likely to receive it from a series of different medical practitioners on the staff of a clinic. If she receives medical aid at the time of delivery, the doctor may be a stranger to her. If she is uneducated, she may not know of the availability of programs and information that might contribute to a healthy pregnancy and a safe and uneventful delivery. A low-income mother may not be aware of the importance of a good diet during pregnancy (or even be able to maintain such a diet). She may not protect herself from exposure to infectious diseases. She may take a variety of drugs without realizing that even aspirin or the equivalent may cause abnormalities in fetal development. For all these reasons, a child of a low-income mother may be born with physical defects, some of which may go undetected for several years because regular health care is not available.

The low-income mother may not know about the physical and psychological care of infants and may not even benefit from "tradition" if she has no contact with older female relatives. Because of poverty, the parents may not be able to provide much in the way of clothing or playthings for the child. Also because of poverty, and possibly because both parents must work, the child may only rarely venture beyond the immediate neighborhood. The child from a low-income home may never ride in a car or a bus or be taken to a large department store and may be ignorant of objects and experiences that are completely familiar to more favored children. Many inner-city children, for example, have no conception of a farm or a garden.

When the time comes to enter school, the child may be apprehensive at worst or unenthusiastic at best because of the attitudes of parents and older siblings and playmates. If parents, siblings, or older peers were school dropouts, they may harbor negative feelings about teachers and education. And these may be communicated directly or indirectly to the child. If older children have negative experiences in school, they may describe these in exaggerated fashion and make the uninitiated younger child feel anxious about what lies ahead. Even if the parents do not feel negatively toward education, they may take little interest in what goes on in school, fail to show up for parent conferences, and be indifferent to report cards. Because of lack of familiarity with many objects and situations depicted in instructional materials, together with an absence of encouragement from parents, a child from a low-income home may get off to a poor start in the primary grades. Inability to read or write will then lead to ever-increasing problems and cause the child to fall further and further behind. By the time the student reaches the secondary grades, she or he may have given up on school and may resolve to just put in time until it is legally permissible to drop out. Awareness that many older children in the neighborhood are unable to find employment contributes to attitudes of fatalistic resignation, anger, or resentment. The possibility of higher education seems so remote that it may never be considered at all. Even if an adolescent does respond to the

A child who lives in a slum may fail to overcome early handicaps (such as inadequate prenatal care or birth complications) and suffer in many ways from the cumulative depressant effect of a poor environment.
George Malave/Stock, Boston.

urging of a teacher and resolve to work for high grades, the attempt may be cut short because there is no place at home to study, no desk or reference works to use, and no encouragement from parents.

The child from a low-income home may never see a doctor or dentist and may go to school hungry and dressed in hand-me-down clothes. If a language other than English is spoken in the home or neighborhood, the child may find it difficult to understand the teacher, converse with class-mates, or read instructional materials. When asked to complete assign-ments or take tests, the child may have difficulty following instructions, interpreting questions, or supplying answers. If the child becomes aware that parents and neighbors are treated in demeaning ways or are accorded little respect from others, feelings of self-doubt and low esteem may be intensified.

There are exceptions to the portrait just presented, of course, but this description includes most of the elements found in a detailed study of disadvantaged children by Frank Riessman (1962). One of the most significant points about the description just provided relates to ways factors (such as inadequate prenatal care or birth complications) appear to lead to a lasting impact on a child growing up in a poor environment. E. E. Werner, J. M. Bierman, and F. E. French (1971) revealed how potent a poor environment can be when they carried out a longitudinal study of all 670 children born on the island of Kauai in 1955. Each newborn infant was rated on a scale of severity of prenatal and birth complications. Later, periodic assessments were made of physical health, intelligence, social maturity, and environmental variables. This comprehensive study found, significantly, that most children from middle- and upper-income homes who were judged to have had a poor start because of prenatal or birth complications seemed to have overcome their early handicaps by the time they entered school. On intelligence tests, for instance, they scored only slightly below children from similar backgrounds who were judged to have had uneventful prenatal and birth experiences. Children from lower economic backgrounds who had experienced difficulties at the beginning of their lives, however, seemed to remain at a disadvantage. They scored from nineteen to thirty-seven points lower on IQ tests than children from similar backgrounds who were judged to have had normal prenatal and birth experiences. On the basis of this finding, as well as other analyses of their data, Werner and her associates concluded that the single most important variable leading to retardation or aberrations in development in disadvantaged children is the poor environment in which they mature. This conclusion is supported by other research summarized by Arnold Sameroff and Michael J. Chandler (1975, pp. 205–210).

Impoverished environment has cumulative depressant effect

If the pervasive devitalizing nature of a disadvantaged environment is considered, it is not surprising that brief exposure to an enriched environment (such as that provided by Head Start programs) is insufficient to "inoculate" or "immunize" a child for life. However, results of follow-up studies by the Consortium for Longitudinal Studies (Murray et al., 1984), which were noted in discussing the cognitive critical period hypothesis in Chapter 5, support the conclusion that preschool experience for disadvantaged children may lead to improved academic achievement. Children who attended Head Start schools were less likely to be held back or be placed in special classes than control group children. Since gains in IQ faded in a few years, the most logical explanation for the superior school performance of preschool graduates centers (as noted in Chapter 5) on attitudes of the children and their parents regarding school achievement. Support for this hypothesis is supplied by the results of an intensive longitudinal study (Kraus, 1984) of children who entered two New York City kindergartens in 1953. The final statement in the report is "Given children of equal ability, the most significant predictor of adult achievement was parental attitudes toward school and toward education. This was particularly true among black families" (p. 363).

Attitude toward school best predictor of adult achievement

The importance of attitudes toward education as a key factor in the education of disadvantaged children is underlined by the results of what was probably the most successful of all attempts at compensatory education, the Ypsilanti Perry Preschool Project (Weikart and Schweinhart, 1984). This project was designed to be an ideal model for others to follow. A carefully planned educational program was presented to disadvantaged children by a trained team of instructors, with a staff-child ratio of one adult to every five children. Each week, a staff member visited the child's home and spent ninety minutes giving the mother instructions, advice, and support. In follow-up studies, it was found that graduates of this program did substantially better in all the grades through high school than control children. The attitude of the participants and their parents toward schooling was singled out as a particularly important factor. In summing up the results of the latest report, the directors of the project observe:

Not so long ago preschool education was seen by many as the single solution. Then it was not a solution at all. It would indeed be rash to use the evidence of the Perry Preschool Study and other such studies as a basis for reinstating preschool education as a single solution. Preschool education is not nearly enough. Poverty still grinds down those who seek to overcome it. But, at least, preschool education may be able to help. (P. 499)

Child-rearing Techniques That Foster Cognitive Development

In the discussion of infant-parent relationships in Chapter 8, differences between effective and ineffective mothers were noted. Just as some mothers seem better able than others to encourage responses from infants, some parents seem better able than others to foster cognitive development during the preschool years. Burton H. White and his colleagues (1973) called attention to this point when they carried out the Harvard Preschool Project and studied children (and their mothers) rated high and low in competence. Techniques used by mothers whose children were judged to be above average in competence included the following:

Letting the child initiate activities and then responding in ways that extend and expand those activities

Taking turns, giving the child ample opportunities for self-expression

Arranging conditions and providing responses so that children develop the feeling that they can produce consequences

Seeing things from the child's point of view

Establishing feelings of mutual delight

Talking, responding, enriching, encouraging, explaining

*Disadvantaged children who attended Head Start schools often exhibited superior aca-
demic achievement in grade school compared to children who had not been exposed to
such experiences. Such academic gains probably were due to attitudes, however, not
cognitive stimulation.*
Alan Carey/The Image Works.

Jean Carew, who had collaborated with White on the Harvard Preschool Project, decided to make a similar study of children from a variety
of social class and cultural backgrounds (Carew, Chan, and Halfer,
1976). The children, who were either one or two years old at the start of
the study, were observed several times in their homes and neighborhoods until they were between thirty and thirty-three months old. The
children's intellectual development was assessed using both standardized tests and home observations. On the basis of the assessment, the
researchers assigned each child to a **well-developing** or **less well-
developing** group and observed how the parents of subjects in each
group interacted with their children. The researchers discovered that
parents of well-developing children provided them with more educational toys, took them on more educational outings, read to them more
often, and allowed them to "help" with household chores. In addition,
well-developing children spent less time watching television and more
time interacting with their fathers. Mothers of well-developing children
were more likely than mothers of less well-developing children to im-

part new information, ask challenging questions, and show how to do something. They tended to acknowledge when their children were right and correct them when they were wrong. They were more likely to label objects and events, comment on activities, explain, make comparisons, go back over experiences, and talk about imaginary things and situations. These various techniques can be summed up by the last entry just noted in the list of techniques likely to promote competence: talking, responding, enriching, encouraging, explaining.

Carew, Chan, and Halfer reported that the parents of well-developing children exhibited many of the same caretaker characteristics, regardless of their social class. The only significant difference they observed between mothers from lower- and middle-class backgrounds was their use of restriction and punishment. Lower-class mothers restricted and punished their children more frequently than middle-class mothers, who were more likely to rely on distraction. When middle-class mothers did restrict their children, they tended more often to justify their restrictions, that is, to explain to children why they could not do something. Other researchers who studied a larger number of subjects, however, have concluded that certain caretaker characteristics may be more likely to appear in low-income homes than in middle- or upper-income homes. Robert D. Hess and Virginia Shipman (1965), for instance, found that a significant number of children who were born into low-income families were cared for by mothers who were inattentive and unresponsive, used impoverished language, lacked self-confidence, ran the home in a disorganized way, and often functioned at the preoperational level of cognitive development. Taken together, the results of these two studies suggest that mothers who use effective techniques for encouraging cognitive development are to be found at all economic levels, but that a larger proportion of low-income mothers probably will be rated as ineffective.

Factors Parents Might Consider Regarding Nursery School

If parents have time to interact extensively with preschool children, if they use techniques such as those just described, and if they *enjoy* interacting with their children, it would seem that they could supply an excellent environment for cognitive development in the home. Unless a child has restricted opportunities to interact with other children in the neighborhood, there may be little reason for parents to feel that attendance at a nursery school is essential. Joan W. Swift (1964) found that middle-class children who attended nursery school did not seem to perform better in school or on intelligence tests over the long run than

Parents of pre-
schoolers should
talk, respond, en-
rich, encourage,
explain

Nursery school at-
tendance does not
necessarily lead to
better school perfor-
mance for middle-
class children

Many parents enroll their children in nursery schools to give them experience in interacting with others and/or to give mother and child time to be apart from each other. Two- to five-year-olds who stay at home (and have occasional interactions with peers in home settings, though) are not likely to be at a disadvantage compared to nursery school graduates during the elementary school years and beyond.
© *Chuck Kidd Photography.*

children who did not attend. (Swift noted, however, that children from disadvantaged backgrounds *did* benefit, a conclusion later corroborated by the Consortium for Longitudinal Studies.) Accordingly, the primary factor for middle-class parents to consider (assuming they have the time, inclination, and ability to use techniques such as those listed above) when deciding for or against nursery school might center on the question: Will it be better for parents and child if they each engage in separate activities for part of the day?

Full-time mother-
ing may lead to
overinvestment

In relation to this point, it should be noted that full-time mothering may not always be desirable. There is some evidence (Birnbaum, 1971) that educated women who devote themselves to full-time mothering may **overinvest** in their preschool children. That is, they may provide more attention than a child can handle (a point related to arguments against overstimulating infants that were noted in Chapter 8). Furthermore, one study comparing the behavior of children of working and nonworking mothers (Moore, 1975) reported that while boys who received full-time mothering during their preschool years were advanced in cognitive abilities, they were rated as more conforming, fearful, and inhibited as adolescents. It would be a mistake to assume that these findings mean that a woman should *avoid* functioning as a full-time mother, even if she enjoys it and finds it fulfilling. But mothers of preschool children who are indecisive about seeking or accepting a job might take into account that maternal employment during the preschool years does not seem to have negative effects on the development of the young child (L. W. Hoffman, 1979). In fact, there may be advantages since working mothers report that they are more satisfied with their lives than nonworking mothers (Dubnoff, Veroff, and Kulka, 1978). There is evidence that the mother's satisfaction with her role increases her effectiveness as a parent (Gold and Andres, 1978).

If parents do decide (perhaps after consulting with the child) to arrange for nursery school experiences, they may be faced with a choice between schools. Some nursery schools offer a classic Montessori form of instruction, others are based on Piagetian concepts and stress a great deal of self-instruction and interaction between age-mates, and still others feature behavior-modification techniques. In small towns, perhaps only one school will be available, but in populated areas there may be several to choose from. Because of the number and complexity of the variables involved, it is all but impossible to carry out a trustworthy comparison of the impact on later child behavior of different kinds of nursery school experience. This probably explains why no comprehensive effort to carry out such a study has been attempted. (It would be essential, for example, to obtain *detailed* information about a child's abilities and attitudes before entering school as well as information about the variety and subtleties of the child-rearing techniques used by the parents in the home. Such information is extremely difficult to obtain.) Furthermore, there are undoubtedly differences between schools practicing the same basic approach that are a function of the personalities of the director and the teachers. Accordingly, parents might select a nursery school by considering questions such as these:

What do parents of children who attended a particular nursery school have to say about it?

What do children who attended a particular nursery school have to say about it?

What impressions do parents form after having visited the school, observed teachers interacting with children, and talked to the teachers?

How does the child feel about the school that is being considered after a few trial sessions?

Vocabulary Acquisition Does Not Seem to Depend on Instruction

Whether or not children attend nursery school, between the years of two and five most of them master a quite remarkable intellectual achievement—typically without formal instruction. After a child utters

Children seem to have a built-in tendency to use language. Many children understand the meaning of 14,000 words by the age of six and they get plenty of practice using words as they talk to others.
© *Rose Skytta/Jeroboam, Inc.*

his or her first word, it might be expected that additional words would be learned at a rapid rate. Such is not the case, however, because as they approach their second birthday the average child has a vocabulary of about fifty words. Assuming that the child uttered the first word at the age of twelve months, that works out to about one new word a *week* during the second year. One reason for this unimpressive rate of vocabulary acquisition is probably traceable to limitations imposed by cognitive functioning. Perhaps a more basic reason is that between their first and second birthdays children have a lot to keep them occupied. Learning to walk and get around and explore things amounts to a full-time job, with little free time left to devote to learning new words. Once they move into the preoperational stage of cognitive development, though, and have mastered locomotor skills, children make up for lost time with a vengeance. By the time they are six, it has been estimated (Carey, 1977) that many children know as many as fourteen thousand words.[2] That works out to about one new word every waking *hour*. Perhaps the most amazing aspect of this amazing achievement is that it occurs, for the most part, without formal instruction. Some words are taught by parents or nursery school teachers, and some are learned as a result of a request for instruction on the part of the child. Most words, though, seem to be picked up simply because young children are primed to function as information processors. A child may encounter a new word just once in a book, conversation, or television commercial and encode it well enough to recognize it the next time it is encountered. It is difficult to comprehend completely how this remarkable achievement occurs, but insights are provided by analyzing aspects of language acquisition with reference to cognitive development.

By age six, many children know 14,000 words

Most words seem to be encoded in absence of instruction

Language Development

To grasp how language development reflects cognitive development, keep in mind points that have just been summarized regarding preoperational thinking. Two- to five-year-olds form schemes through physical or mental manipulation, and these schemes are constantly revised through the processes of assimilation and accommodation. Preschoolers are unable to decenter, which means that they concentrate on one quality at a time. They are also preoperational, which means that they are unable to mentally reverse actions. Aspects of language acquisition that

---

[2]Six-year-olds do not *use* fourteen thousand different words when they talk, but they are able to recognize or interpret the meaning of that many words. In terms of their everyday vocabularies, they actually use a few thousand words.

illustrate each of these characteristics of early cognitive development will now be considered.

First Words: Schemes, Assimilation, Accommodation

Most of the words that children learn first (Nelson, 1973) refer to parts of the body, to actions, or to familiar objects or individuals. These types of words reflect initial stages of cognitive development described by Piaget. In the early stages of sensorimotor thinking (described in Chapter 7), children explore their own bodies. Next, they build up schemes through their own actions and by interacting with familiar objects and individuals. While these observations on word acquisition reflect general trends, many children seem to specialize in particular types of first words.

M. F. Bowerman (1976) found that some children seem to concentrate almost exclusively on objects, others specialize in names of people, and still others favor social phrases (for example, Hi, want). Bowerman hypothesizes that such differences are based on cognitive styles that are present before language is acquired. Cognitive styles, in turn, might be based on innate tendencies influenced by circumstances that lead to the development of particular types of schemes. A girl with many siblings and relatives in the house, for example, might be inclined to develop social phrases; a boy who has contact only with his mother—and dozens of playthings—might concentrate on learning names of objects.

As soon as a child forms a scheme and learns the name of an object, there is a tendency to apply that term to all similar objects. A learning theorist would call this generalization. But some psychologists who study language development prefer the term **overextension** (Clark, 1973). Once a child learns the word *dog,* for example, all four-legged animals may be called dogs. When a parent corrects the child by saying "No, honey, that's not a dog, that's a cat," the child will learn to correct the overextension (or to *discriminate,* in learning-theory parlance). This process is an illustration of the Piagetian principles of assimilation and accommodation. First the child notices similarities between dogs and cats and assimilates these identical elements in forming a revised scheme for *dog.* Then, when the child learns that cats differ from dogs in significant ways, accommodation takes place. The revised *dog* scheme is modified, and a *cat* scheme is formed.

Overextensions illustrate assimilation and accommodation

Early Two-Word Utterances: Inability to Decenter

In their initial use of language, children usually concentrate on expressing one idea at a time, a point that is revealed by the earliest two-word utterances formed by children. Before the age of two, most children progress from using holophrastic speech to the point when they begin to use telegraphic speech. Just as one-word expressions serve a variety of purposes, two-word utterances can be used in a variety of ways. Roger Brown, who has written one of the most complete accounts of early language acquisition (1973), describes at least eleven ways that two-word utterances are used. The child may *name* something ("Allgone milk") or indicate the *location* of an object ("Milk table"). Between the ages of two and three, children form more elaborate utterances. Most of these, however, are still telegraphic in that nonessential (to the child, if not to a grammarian) words are omitted.

Brown bases many of his conclusions about early language on records of the spontaneous speech of three children who are quite famous among contemporary students of language acquisition. Their names are Adam, Eve, and Sarah, and their speech was recorded (sometimes in writing, sometimes by microphones sewed in their clothing) when they were between eighteen and twenty-seven months old. When the children began to use sentences, they almost exclusively used nouns and verbs (with an occasional adjective thrown in). They omitted prepositions (*in, on*), conjunctions (*and, or*), articles (*a, the*), and auxiliary verbs (*have, did*). A rather verbose adult might say "I am eating delicious cake that has been tastefully served on a beautiful plate." A two-year-old might convey the same message by saying "Eat cake." The child maintains the proper word order, eliminating all but the essentials, and is likely to remain faithful to this telegraphic mode of speech even when asked to repeat a sentence. For example, if the verbose adult attempted to encourage a two-year-old to acquire a larger vocabulary by enunciating the elegant sentence about delicious cake served on a beautiful plate and then asked the child to repeat the whole thing, the child might listen attentively and still say, "Eat cake."

Consistent (Mis) Usage: Application of Schemes

Brown traces the sequence of early language acquisition by concentrating on **morphemes,** the smallest units of meaning. Morphemes include words (for example, *milk*) as well as parts of words that have meaning (for example, *ing*). Brown has plotted the appearance of fourteen grammatical morphemes and their order of acquisition. Children learn to add *ing,* for example, before they learn *in* and *on.* They learn to add an *s* to make a word plural before they learn to add an *s* to express possession. Adding an *s* to a verb form (*walks*) comes still later. Even though Adam, Eve, and Sarah acquired types of morphemes in the same sequence, they used different morphemes. Such individuality in the acquisition of language is not surprising. Every child will form a different assortment of schemes because of exposure to different objects, individuals, and experiences.

Other characteristics of early language development are illustrated by the acquisition and use of **wh-questions** (who, what, when, where, why). At first (around two years of age), children use inflections rather than *wh*-words to ask questions. Next, they use telegraphic-type questions: "What man doing?" At around three years of age, question sentences become longer, but children tend to follow the order of subject and verb that they have learned in declarative sentences. Instead of saying "Why can't the dog come?" for example, the three-year-old will say "Why the dog can't come?" inserting "Why" in front of "The dog can't come."

In their use (and misuse) of language, children reveal consistencies that make a great deal of sense. A child who forms a question by simply putting "Why" in front of a previously learned phrase, for example, is applying schemes in a logical way. So is a child who assumes, after learning to form a plural by adding *s*, that all plurals can be formed the same way. Jean Berko demonstrated this tendency when she asked four-year-olds to form the plural of names of imaginary and real animals (see Figure 11.2). If a single imaginary animal in a picture was a *Wug*, four-year-olds reasoned that two of them shown in another picture were *Wugs*. If a single longnecked water bird was a *goose*, two of them were *gooses*.

"Inconsistent" grammar may be due to consistent schemes

Other evidence of the extent to which children use language according to their own rules (some of which are more consistent than the rules of English grammar) is provided by ways children respond to premature attempts at instruction in proper usage. A mother and a four-year-old just home from nursery school engaged in this conversation (reported by Cazden, 1968):

Child: My teacher holded the baby rabbits and we patted them.
Mother: Did you say your teacher held the baby rabbits?
Child: Yes.
Mother: What did you say she did?
Child: She holded the baby rabbits and we patted them.
Mother: Did you say she held them tightly?
Child: No, she holded them loosely.

(As noted earlier, if the past tense of *scold* is *scolded*, and the past tense of *fold* is *folded*, and the past tense of *mold* is *molded*, why isn't the past tense

FIGURE 11.2

This is a wug.

Now there is another one.
There are two of them.
There are two _____.

Jean Berko Gleason, "The Child's Learning of English Morphology," *Word*, 1958, 14, 150–177.

of *hold, holded*?) An example of how a child may find it necessary to adapt to apparent inconsistencies in the speech of parents is illustrated by this interchange. A three-year-old girl was looking at a picture in the book *Three Billy Goats Gruff*. She carefully pointed to each goat and said "Look! Three billy goats eated." Her mother, busily working near her, simply said "Ate." The girl once again counted the figures in the picture and said "Three billy goats eated." Her mother responded again by mechanically saying "Ate." At that point the little girl shrugged her shoulders and said "OK! *Eight* billy goats eated." (Reported by Dennis A. Warner, 1978.)

Confusing Opposites: Inability to Reverse

Still other aspects of early language acquisition can be explained (in part, at least) by focusing on the distinguishing feature of Piaget's concept of an operation. M. Donaldson and R. Wales (1970) became interested in finding out how children acquire understanding of opposites. They showed preschool children two cardboard trees equipped with hooks from which paper apples could be hung. Different numbers of apples were hung from each tree out of the child's view and then displayed. The children were then asked "Does this tree have more (or less) apples than the other?" Donaldson and Wales had expected that the difference between *more* and *less* would be clearly understood by three- and four-year-olds. They were surprised to discover that most preschoolers did not know the difference well enough to use the words correctly with any degree of consistency. The children in their study correctly replied that a tree had more apples sixty-three out of sixty-nine times. The same children were able to correctly explain when a tree had *less* apples only fifteen out of fifty-five times.

Subsequent studies by Eve Clark (1973) have revealed a similar tendency for young children to confuse the opposites *little* and *big, same* and *different, before* and *after.* Clark hypothesizes that the confusion is caused by the tendency of a child to focus on only one end of the continuum implied by opposites, particularly the end that emphasizes the greatest amount or extent. Terms such as *more* and *less* are usually applied to the same objects and situations, and they appear in the same position in a sentence. A three- or four-year-old who is involved in sorting out schemes relating to all sorts of objects and experiences seems to concentrate on the *most* or the *biggest.*

It seems possible that the inability of preschoolers to differentiate between more and less may be related to their inability to explain what happens when water is poured from one container into a container of a different shape. Three- and four-year-olds maintain that a tall container contains more because they center their attention on the single quality (height) that stands out. Perhaps children of the same age who confuse "more" and "less" are misled by the same tendency to focus on a single noteworthy quality. Furthermore, the inability of preschoolers to think operationally may limit understanding of opposites. In a sense, a child has to "reverse" *more* in order to understand *less.* A young child cannot reason out the water problem by mentally pouring water back into the original container. The same inability to mentally reverse may make it difficult for a child to deal with opposites. (Changes in cognitive development during the years from six to twelve are discussed in Chapter 15, starting on page 457.)

Confusion of opposites may be due to inability to decenter

Summary

1. Two- to five-year-olds are preoperational thinkers. They tend to focus on one quality at a time and are unable to mentally reverse what they have observed. These tendencies cause preschoolers to cancel out understanding illustrated by demonstrations. When asked to classify objects they concentrate on one category at a time. In an ingenious experiment, though, Piaget demonstrated that older preschoolers improve in their understanding of the arrangement of objects viewed months earlier. The image is retained, the understanding of what the image means improves.

2. On the basis of observations and clinical interviews Piaget proposed that preschoolers engage primarily in *egocentric* thinking—they find it difficult to take another's point of view. A number of American investigators have found, however, that under simplified conditions *socialized* thinking (the ability to see things the way others see them) occurs earlier than Piaget predicted. Several American psychologists have also attempted to teach young children to become concrete operational thinkers ahead of schedule. Piaget felt that such attempts were misguided since he argued that they produced superficial rather than genuine understanding.

3. Starting in the 1960s, psychologists became aware of the cumulative depressant effect on cognitive development of an impoverished environment. Since this was a time when the critical period hypothesis was accepted, it was reasoned that providing disadvantaged children with intensive training during the preschool years would lead to permanent gains in intelligence and school achievement. Some children who attended such programs *did* show gains in later achievement, apparently because of acquired attitudes, however, and not because of intellectual enhancement.

4. Even though it may not be desirable or possible to convert preoperational into concrete operational thinkers ahead of schedule, parents might encourage full use of a child's cognitive abilities by talking, responding, enriching, encouraging, and explaining.

5. When considering nursery school attendance for a two- to five-year-old, parents might note that such attendance will not necessarily lead to better school performance in the elementary grades. On the other hand, mothers who decide to keep their children at home should guard against overinvesting in their development. They should give their children plenty of opportunities to explore and discover on their own.

6. Between the years of two and six, children may increase their vocabularies from around fifty words to over fourteen thousand words. This amazing feat is typically accomplished without much formal instruction.

7. As they learn to apply words to things, young children often resort to *overextensions*, generalizing logically but incompletely from previous experiences. Such "mistakes" occur because the child first assimilates similarities (between dogs and cats, for example) before realizing there are differences (which leads to accommodation). A similar tendency to reason logically sometimes leads to grammatical errors, when a child assumes that the English language is more consistent than it is. Confusion of opposites, though, seems to be due largely to the inability of preoperational thinkers to decenter.

Piagetian Experiments: Preoperational to Concrete Operational Thought

An excellent way to gain greater understanding of Piaget's description of cognitive development is to carry out some of his clinical interviews. To grasp differences between preoperational and concrete operational thought, ask a child in the four- to seven-year age range to play the following "games" with you. (It would be even better if you compare the performance of a four-year-old and a seven-year-old.) The simple experiments described below can be carried out with easily obtained "equipment" and should take no more than a few minutes. Begin by asking the age of your subject. (It would be prudent to verify this with a parent or teacher.) Next, explain that you would like her or him to play a few games with you. Then follow instructions provided below. (Note: if your subject is completely baffled by the first problem, you might avoid confusion and frustration by not presenting the more difficult problems, and you might then select a slightly older subject.)

Conservation of Number

Purpose: To discover if the child grasps that the number of objects in a row remains the same even if the distance between them is changed. Children of four or so will be unable to decenter and are likely to say that a longer row has more blocks—even though they can count the blocks in both rows. Older children will be able to understand that the number is constant, even when the appearance of the blocks is changed.

Equipment: Twenty blocks, poker chips, or the equivalent.

Procedure: Place the blocks (or whatever) in front of the child and space out eight of the blocks about an inch apart in a row. Place the remaining blocks in a pile close to the child. Then say: "Can you count the blocks? How many are there?" (Point to the blocks you have arranged in a row. If the child cannot count them accurately, give assistance.) Then say: "Now take as many of these blocks as you need to make the same number." (Give assistance if necessary.) Describe how the child proceeds.

Next, take the blocks in the row nearest you and space them about three inches apart. Take those in the other row and space them about one inch apart. Point to the longer row and say: "Let's say these are my blocks" (point to the long row) "and these are your blocks" (point to the short row). "Do I have more blocks, or do you have more blocks, or do we have the same?" Record the child's response.

Then ask: "Why do you think so?" Record the child's response.

Finally, take the blocks which were spaced three inches apart and move them so that they are one inch apart, just below the other row. Then say: "Now, do you have more blocks, or do I have more blocks, or do we have the same?" Note the child's response and reaction. (Does the child seem surprised, bothered, unimpressed?)

Conservation of Area

Purpose: To discover how the child handles a different situation involving conservation. A child who is able to handle the problem presented in the preceding experiment may encounter difficulty when confronted with the same basic problem presented in a different form. In solving the conservation of number problem the child must grasp the fact that the number of blocks stays the same even though the space between them is changed. In this experiment the child must understand that four blocks placed on pieces of paper of equal size take up the same amount of space, even though they are arranged differently.

Equipment: Eight small blocks, poker chips, or the equivalent; two pieces of paper or cardboard at least 8½ by 11 inches.

Procedure: Place the two pieces of paper in front of the child, and arrange the blocks in a pile to one side. Say: "Let's pretend these are fields owned by two farmers. They are exactly the same size, and each farmer has the same amount of space for cows to graze in. One farmer decides to build a barn" (you might say "silo" if you use poker chips), "and we will make believe this is the barn." (Take one of the blocks and place it near one corner of one piece of paper.) "The other farmer builds a barn, too." (Put a block on the other piece of paper in the same position as that on the first.) "Do they still have the same amount of space for their cows to graze in?" Record the child's response.

Then say: "Now let's suppose that both farmers make a lot of money and build three more barns. One farmer's barns are built this way" (place three blocks right next to the block already on one sheet of paper), "the other's barns are built this way" (place three blocks several inches apart at different places on the other piece of paper). "Do they still have the same amount of space for their cows to graze in, or does one farmer have more space than the other?" Record the child's response.

Then ask: "Why do you think so?" Record the child's response.

Finally, take the blocks which were scattered and place them together so that both sets of blocks are arranged in exactly the same way on each piece of paper. Then ask: "Now, does each farmer have the same amount of space for cows to graze in, or does one have more space than the other?" Note the child's response and his or her reaction.

Conservation of Continuous Quantity

Purpose: To discover if a child who can understand conservation of number can also grasp conservation of quantity. Children at the level of concrete operations may be unable to generalize from the block experiment and will solve the following problem only if they have had sufficient experience with liquids in glasses of different size.

Equipment: Two plastic or glass tumblers of the same size, one plastic or glass bowl or vase (or a tall, thin tumbler).

Procedure: Pour water into one of the equal-sized tumblers until it is about two-thirds full, into the other until about one-third full. Put these down in front of the child and say: "Is there more water in this glass (point to one), "or this one" (point to the other), "or are they the same?" Record the child's response.

Then, pour water from the fuller glass into the emptier one until they are equal and ask: "What about now? Is there more water in this glass" (point to one), "or this glass" (point to the other), "or are they the same?" Record the child's response.

(A child who says one has more water can be encouraged to pour liquid back and forth from one glass into the other until satisfied that they are the same.)

Next, empty the water from one glass into the bowl (or vase) and ask: "Is there more water in this one" (point to the full glass), "or this one" (point to the bowl or vase), "or do they contain the same amount of water?" Record the child's response.

Then ask: "Why do you think so?"

Finally, pour the water from the bowl or vase back into the glass and ask: "Now, is there more water in this glass" (point to one), "or this glass" (point to the other), "or are they the same?" Note the child's response and reaction.

Conservation of Substance

Purpose: To discover if a child understands that the amount of a substance remains the same even though its shape is changed. The child who is unable to decenter will concentrate on only one quality and, therefore, will be unable to grasp that the amount stays constant. The older child will be able to allow for both qualities at once and will be able mentally to *reverse* the action which changed the shape of the substance, showing the capability of dealing with *operations*. However, difficulty may be experienced in dealing with an abstract (not actually present) situation of a similar type, indicating that the child is at the level of *concrete operations*.

Equipment: A small amount of plasticene or clay.

Procedure: Take a piece of plasticene or clay and divide it as equally as possible. Roll the pieces into two balls and ask the child if the two are the same size. If the answer is that one is bigger than the other, ask the child to remove as much as necessary from the larger ball until satisfied that they are identical. Then take one ball, roll it into a sausage shape and ask: "Is there more clay here" (point to ball), "or here" (point to sausage), "or do they both have the same amount of clay?" Record the child's response.

Then ask: "Why do you think so?"

Then, roll the sausage shape back into a ball and ask: "Is there more clay here" (point to one ball), "or here" (point to the other ball), "or are they the same?" Note the child's response and reaction.

Then say: "Suppose I put these two pieces on two scales. Would this piece be heavier, or this piece, or would they be just as heavy?" Record the child's response.

Then, roll one ball into a sausage shape and ask: "What would happen if I weighed these now? Would this one" (point to ball) "or this one" (point to sausage) "be heavier, or would one be as heavy as the other?" Record the child's response.

Then ask: "Why do you think so?"

Early Language Development

If you would like to learn more about language development, one of the best sources of information is *A First Language: The Early Stages* (1973) by Roger Brown. More recent books on language development include *Language and Maturation* (1977) by Paula Menyuk; *Psychology and Language* (1977) by H. H. and E. V. Clark; *Language Development and Language Disorders* (1978) by Lois Bloom and M. Lahey; *Readings in Language Development* (1978), edited by Lois Bloom; and *Early Language* (1979) by P. and J. de Villiers.

A Piagetian interpretation of early language development is offered by E. L. Moerk in "Piaget's Research as Applied to the Explanation of Language Development" in *Merrill-Palmer Quarterly*, 1975, *21*, 151–169. Techniques parents might use to encourage language development are described by Moerk in "Processes of Language Training in the Interaction of Mother-Child Dyads" in *Child Development*, 1976, *47*, 1064–1078.

Recording the Speech of Young Children

A different way to gain insight into language development is to keep a record of the utterances of a young child. Subjects two to three years of age are probably the best to choose, since this is a period when children are beginning to use language extensively but without complete awareness of adult sentence structure. Record (on a tape recorder or in writing) everything children of different ages say on several different occasions and analyze their utterances in terms of such factors as consistency in grammar, parts of speech used, vocabulary, and other characteristics that attract your attention. You might also compare the speech you have recorded with the utterances of two- and three-year-olds recorded by Brown and Bellugi in an article in *Harvard Educational Review*, 1964, *34*, 133–151, or to descriptions of early language provided by Brown on pages 63–111 of his *A First Language* (1973).

KEY POINTS

Parent-Child Relationships

Authoritative parents: self-reliant, competent children

Authoritarian parents: insecure, hostile children

Permissive parents: dependent, immature children

Authoritative techniques: encouragement, limits (with explanations), appreciation, affection

Authoritative parents serve as models, help children set standards

Increasing awareness of interdependency of family members

Early use of coercion leads to increased coercion later

Use of external pressure discourages internalization of control

Explanations, plus anxiety, likely to inhibit misbehavior

The Impact of Day Care and Preschool Experience

Day care children competent and mature but aggressive and noncompliant

Excellent day care may lead to advanced development, but gains not likely to be permanent

Relationships with Peers

Adult-child interactions often involve support (scaffolding)

Sociable conversation and aggression in same-age groups

Peers serve as models and as reinforcing agents

From two to five, children move from parallel to associative and cooperative play

Sex cleavage: tendency for children to prefer same-sex playmates

CHAPTER 12

TWO TO FIVE

RELATIONSHIPS WITH OTHERS

*H*uman infants begin life as dependent beings. They engage in many types of behavior that help them respond in ways that contribute to their survival, but if others do not care for them, they will die. (They influence the behavior of their caretakers in many ways, but they are still dependent on them.) Infants also begin life as egocentric creatures. They are concerned primarily about satisfaction of their own needs, and the quickness and devotion with which these needs are satisfied (in most cases) during the first months of life reinforce this self-centeredness. In the short time between birth and the second birthday, children move from dependency on others to the capability of an impressive amount of self-directed behavior. Two-year-olds have excellent vision and highly developed senses; they can walk, manipulate things, feed themselves, control their processes of elimination (most of the time), and use words to express wants and desires. They have overcome most of the anxiety experienced as one-year-olds when separated from their mothers and are eager to explore new experiences on their own. They begin to seek and enjoy the companionship of their age-mates and start to interact with individuals outside their immediate family. All these skills, abilities, and tendencies infuse two-year-olds with a sense of power and independence.

This sense of autonomy is a mixed blessing, however. Parents who have been delighted by almost all their offspring's accomplishments during the first year begin to realize that some of the tendencies and abilities appearing after that time may lead to complications and even trouble. Most parents are proud and excited when a one-year-old daughter or son begins to walk or says a first word. When a two-year-old refuses to follow a request to cease some activity, however, parental delight may turn to anger or dismay. An eleven-month-old who grabs a floorlamp and brings it down with a crash after having taken a few wildly uncoordinated but incontestably independent steps is not likely to be looked upon as a troublemaker. In fact, the parents may brag about the incident. But a two-year-old who deliberately knocks over a lamp in retaliation for being forcibly restrained from banging on the piano (after having spat out "No" to a request to stop) is almost sure to arouse a much different response.

When children become capable of moving around, getting into things, and expressing themselves verbally, they are confronted for the first time with the realization that they must sometimes subordinate their wishes to the wishes of others. They discover that their parents no longer cater to all their desires. And as they begin to play with siblings or peers, they realize that a certain amount of give-and-take is expected and that they cannot always have their own way. Starting around the age of two, then, children learn that they are expected to move from self-centered dependence to independent coexistence. They also learn that only certain types of behavior are considered appropriate in certain situations. The way these types of behavior develop and are influenced by parents is called the process of **socialization.**

Psychologists have sought information about the various ways a child acquires social forms of behavior. They have studied how children identify with and imitate parents and peers and how they learn to adapt to group interaction. Some of the ways socialization takes place will be discussed on the next few pages.

Parent-Child Relationships

Because the child from two to five years old is capable of independent behavior and mature enough to attend nursery school, the preschool years provide an exceptional opportunity for studying parent-child relationships. Researchers can observe children interacting during free-play periods in a nursery school (an ideal situation for obtaining evidence regarding personality differences) or in home situations and then compare descriptions of child behavior with information obtained from parents about their child-rearing practices. Furthermore, actual interactions between parents and their children in home and experimental situations can be recorded. Dozens of studies of this type have been carried out. Many early investigations were reviewed and analyzed by E. S. Schaefer (1959); studies carried out during the subsequent decade were reviewed by Wesley C. Becker (1964). Investigations by Diana Baumrind not only substantiate findings of many early studies, but also stand out because of the clarity of the implications that can be drawn from her conclusions. Baumrind's research, therefore, will be stressed in this analysis of parent-child relationships during the preschool years.

Three Types of Child Rearing

In an early study, Baumrind (1967) asked teachers and independent observers to rate the behavior of three- and four-year-olds who had been selected because of particular types of behavior patterns. Their parents were interviewed, and observers visited homes and recorded all parent-child interactions where one person tried to influence another during the period from dinner to bedtime. All of these impressions were analyzed and compared, leading eventually to descriptions of techniques used by mothers classified into three basic types. The techniques of control used by each type of mother and the types of child behavior associated with each included the following patterns:

Authoritative mothers established firm control but gave reasons for restrictions. They respected the child's wishes but also expected the child to take into account the needs of others. They were warm, supportive, and loving. Their children were likely to be socialized and independent, self-reliant, explorative, assertive, and competent.

Authoritative parents: self-reliant, competent children

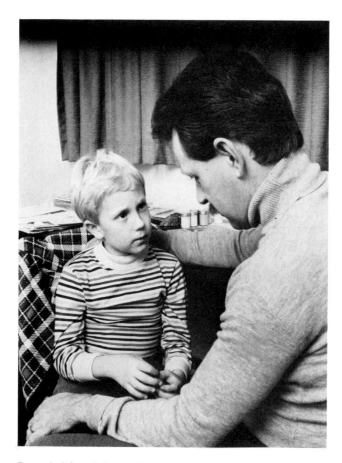

Baumrind found that authoritative parents set firm and consistent limits but were willing to explain and negotiate those limits in warm and sincere ways.
© *Michael Heron/Woodfin Camp.*

Authoritarian parents: insecure, hostile children

Authoritarian mothers set absolute standards and used punitive techniques to enforce them. They did not permit their children to challenge restrictions but presented them as inviolable rules. They were not very affectionate. Their children were likely to be somewhat discontented, insecure, and hostile under stress.

Permissive parents: dependent, immature children

Permissive mothers were nonpunitive, acceptant, and made few attempts to shape behavior. They tended to be disorganized and ineffective in running the household. A maximum amount of self-regulation was encouraged. Their children were likely to be dependent, immature, and to lack self-reliance or self-control.

Authoritative Techniques of Child Rearing

From her original sample, Baumrind (1971) selected children who clearly exhibited the three patterns of behavior she had noted in her earlier studies and made detailed analyses of the control techniques used by parents of each type. Children who were rated as competent, mature, independent, self-reliant, self-controlled, explorative, affiliative, and self-assertive were found to come from homes where parents used an authoritative approach made up of techniques that can be converted into the following guidelines:

1. Permit and encourage the child to do many things independently.
2. Urge the child to try to achieve mature and skilled types of behavior.
3. Establish firm and consistent limits regarding unacceptable forms of behavior; explain the reasons for these as soon as the child is able to understand; listen to complaints if the child feels the restrictions are too confining; give additional reasons if the limits are still to be maintained as originally stated.
4. Show that the child's achievements are admired and appreciated.
5. Communicate love in a warm and sincere (but not excessive) way.

Authoritative techniques: encouragement, limits (with explanations), appreciation, affection

Explanations for the Advantages of Authoritative Approaches

Some of the reasons authoritative child-rearing techniques seem to lead to competence in children are revealed by Baumrind's analysis of the three approaches she discovered and described. Parents of competent children were *authoritative* because they had confidence in their abilities as parents. Consequently, they provided a model of competence for their children to imitate. When they established limits and explained reasons for restrictions, they encouraged their children to set standards for themselves and to think about *why* certain procedures should be followed. And because the parents were warm and affectionate, their positive responses were valued by their children as rewards for mature behavior. *Authoritarian* parents, by contrast, made demands and wielded power, but their failure to take into account the child's point of view, coupled with their lack of warmth, led to resentment and insecurity on the part of the child. Children of authoritarian parents did as they were told, but they were likely to do so out of compliance or fear, not out of a desire to earn love or approval. Permissive parents were likely to appear disorganized, inconsistent, and unsure of themselves, and their children were likely to imitate such behavior. Furthermore, such parents did not demand much of their children; nor did they discourage immature behavior.

Authoritative parents serve as models, help children set standards

Autonomy, Initiative, and Child-rearing Techniques

Baumrind's conclusions regarding the impact of authoritative, authoritarian, and permissive child-rearing approaches can be related to the stages of psychosocial development proposed by Erikson. The child of two and three years of age is at the autonomy vs. doubt stage; the four- and five-year-old is at the initiative vs. guilt stage. Erikson suggests that autonomy is most likely to develop if children are encouraged to do what they are capable of doing at their own pace and in their own way—but with judicious supervision by parents. He suggests that initiative is most likely to develop if children are given freedom to explore and experiment and if parents take time to answer questions. Erikson's suggestions for parental behavior are very similar to techniques used by the authoritative parents observed by Baumrind. Such parents encouraged their children to set standards for themselves, were warm and affectionate, and responded positively to the child's accomplishments.

It would seem likely that two- and three-year-olds might experience doubts about their capabilities if their parents were either authoritarian (causing the child to feel insecure) or permissive (serving as disorganized models). In addition, it seems likely that authoritarian parents might cause their children to experience shame if they made excessive demands (regarding toilet training, for instance). Four- and five-year-olds might be expected to experience guilt if authoritarian parents made too many demands and failed to take into account the child's point of view. Permissive parents might inadvertently foster guilt because of inconsistencies in child-rearing practices and because their behavior seems to encourage dependency and immaturity in children.

The Reciprocal Nature of Parent-Child Relationships

The tendency for Freudians and behaviorists to view children as essentially passive recipients of stimuli has been noted frequently in earlier chapters. The well-established conception that children are shaped by parental behavior has caused many researchers to concentrate almost exclusively on the controlling role of parents when observing and hypothesizing about child-parent interactions. A criticism of Ainsworth's research on attachment behavior (noted in Chapter 8), for example, is that it implies that the three types of reactions to stranger and separation anxiety situations she described are due primarily to differences in the behavior of the mothers. The same criticism can be made of Baumrind's analysis of types of child rearing. There is a strong implication that children exposed to each of the three types of child rearing develop particular characteristics only because of the kind of control used by the parents. In the last few years many developmental psychologists have begun to question the view that child-parent interactions are a one-way street. The studies of infant temperament by Birns, and by Thomas and his associates, were at the forefront of a trend that has gained momentum in recent years: recognition of ways children influence parents and of the reciprocal nature of parent-child relationships.

Two related trends are greater awareness of the interdependency of family members (parents, children, and siblings) and recognition that parents, as well as children, change in response to changing conditions and perceptions. The interdependency of family members has been demonstrated in a variety of recent studies of both well-functioning families and families with problems. It has been shown, for example, that mothers are more effective in controlling young children when the father is present (Lytton, 1979). The parents and siblings of highly aggressive children use coercion more frequently than parents and siblings of less aggressive children (Patterson, 1982). And when parents are having problems in their own relationship, they perceive their children's behavior problems as more serious than they are and react more negatively to them (Christensen, Phillips, Glasgow, and Johnson, 1983). The trend toward greater acceptance of the view that there is change as well as continuity in personality was discussed at length in Chapters 5 and 9. Analyses of longitudinal studies reveal that there are often significant changes in personality and attitudes toward child rearing over the years as a result of changing conditions and perceptions. A woman who started out enjoying the responsibilities of being a mother may undergo a reversal of feelings if, for example, her husband walks out on her and she must find a job to support her children. Because of changes in "goodness of fit," a father who responded positively to his son as a five-year-old may respond negatively to him as a fifteen-year-old. Thus, changes in child behavior may contribute to changes in parent behavior, and changes in parent personality may lead to differences in relationships with children.

Increasing awareness of interdependency of family members

Adaptation Level Theory and Parent-Child Relationships

While there is reciprocal interaction between parents and their children and while changes may occur in personality and relationships, there is still likely to be quite a bit of consistency in the way parents deal with their children. Certain habitual patterns of interaction and mutual expectation may be established early and tend to persist. Eleanor Maccoby and John Martin (1983) have taken the concept of **adaptation level,** which originated in studies of perception, and applied it to family dynamics. Adaptation level refers to an expectancy that develops as a result of prior experiences with a stimulus. When a particular kind of stimulus falls within an expected range (the adaptation level), we may not respond to it. But if it goes beyond the expected range, we do respond. When you drive your car, for instance, you are used to the sound of the engine when it is functioning normally. Ordinarily, you don't pay any attention to that sound. But if the engine of your car suddenly starts to make abnormally loud or irregular sounds, you do respond. Maccoby and Martin suggest that the same sort of pattern occurs in parent-child relationships.

If an ordinarily easy-going and compliant child uncharacteristically acts self-willed and disobedient in a home situation, the parents may respond quickly and decisively. If a child in another family was self-willed from the very beginning, though, the parents might treat resistance as normal behavior. Only when the disobedience becomes extreme will they be likely to respond more decisively than usual. (In terms of the engine analogy just noted, the first child might be compared to a smooth-running, easy-to-drive, responsive luxury car; the second child might be compared to a poorly tuned, hard-to-handle, cantankerous pickup truck.)

The habitual behavior of the child is one aspect of adaptation level theory; the habitual behavior pattern of the parents is another. Parents who use authoritative child-rearing techniques, for example, encourage the likelihood that a child will comply with their requests because compliance has become the expected response. Parents who have tendencies to use authoritarian techniques, by contrast, may resort to coercion when they first deal with signs of independence. Because coercion is likely to work in the short run, it will be reinforcing for parents and be likely to develop into a preferred strategy. Two unfortunate things are likely to happen as a result. First, the parents develop an expectation that external pressure is necessary to ensure compliance, and the child delays compliance until the expected external pressure is applied. Second, as the child comes to expect a given level of coercion from the parent, increasingly higher levels of coercion become necessary to get the child's attention and ensure subsequent compliance. Under such circumstances, noncompliance becomes the expected response in the minds of both parent and child. The harmful consequences of setting this coercive cycle in motion become apparent when the nature of socialization is considered. One goal of socialization is to have children learn to inhibit tendencies to engage in disapproved forms of behavior in the absence of external pressure or surveillance. Early reliance on coercion tends to lead to the necessity for ever-increasing amounts of coercion and decreases the likelihood of self-control, often referred to as **internalization.**

Early use of coercion leads to increased coercion later

Authoritarian parents who use coercion early in life may find that it is necessary to increase the degree of coercion used to secure obedience as their children grow older.
Edwin Lettau/Photo Researchers.

Encouraging Self-Control (Internalization)

The process of internalization of culturally approved behavior appears to be inhibited, rather than encouraged, by coercive control techniques. Children are likely to attribute their compliance in the presence of coercion to the power of the adult enforcer. Since compliance is associated with the presence of the powerful adult, children feel no obligation to comply in the adult's absence. (If they come to dislike the dictatorial adult, they may sometimes be motivated to *not* comply.) When children control impulses without strong external pressure, on the other hand, they are likely to attribute compliance to their own behavior and feelings. Because compliance is associated with attributes of their own, rather than the socialization pressures of the parents, children are likely to comply in the future even when parents are not present. Parents who want to encourage internalization, then, should heed what M. R. Lepper (1981) calls the **minimum-sufficiency principle:** use no more external pressure than is necessary to ensure compliance.

Use of external pressure discourages internalization of control

While coercion tends to be an ineffective way to encourage self-control, punishment is sometimes necessary when children misbehave. Punishment is not restricted to physical forms of discipline but includes such reactions as disapproval or rejection (although rejection in the form of withholding love is to be avoided). There is evidence (Parke, 1977) that children are more likely to internalize control when punishment of their transgressions is accompanied by verbal explanation. (This is a variation of the authoritative parenting approach described by Baumrind that involves explaining why restrictions are necessary.) J. Aronfreed (1968), who has studied internalization intensively, suggests that, with young children, anxiety may be a more important factor in establishing self-control than explanation. Picture a three-year-old boy who misbehaves, is chastised for his behavior, and is then given an explanation why the behavior was unacceptable and must not be repeated. On the basis of his observations and speculations, Aronfreed suggests that the boy will refrain from repeating the transgression in the future not so much because of the explanation but because of fear that the parent will breathe fire, emit sparks, and resort to more stringent forms of punishment than were applied the first time. When reasons for not misbehaving are given to young children, they appear to be more effective when they stress physical consequences rather than the rights or feelings of others (Parke, 1977). Stressing the rights of others does not seem to become effective until children are seven or eight, apparently because a certain degree of cognitive sophistication must be achieved before such explanations can be grasped.

Therefore, parents of preschoolers who want to encourage their children to internalize controls should follow the procedures used by authoritative parents: establish firm and consistent limits regarding unacceptable forms of behavior, explain why the limits are necessary, listen to complaints about restrictions, and renegotiate limits, if appropriate. When a transgression of stated or unstated limits occurs, exhibit dissatisfaction in emphatic (but preferably nonphysical) ways and stress physical consequences. Authoritative parenting techniques other than those centering on limits are also likely to enhance internalization. When parents show that they admire and appreciate what their children do and communicate love in a warm and sincere way, they enhance a child's self-esteem. Children who think highly of themselves are likely to behave well to please others (and themselves).

Explanations, plus anxiety, likely to inhibit misbehavior

The Impact of Day Care and Preschool Experience

The analysis of relationships with others presented so far in this chapter has concentrated on child-parent relationships. This emphasis is appro-

One of the reasons children of authoritative parents are likely to develop a positive self-concept is that the parents communicate love and appreciation in warm and sincere ways.
© *Hazel Hankin/Stock, Boston.*

priate because most children interact with their parents more than with any other persons during the preschool years. More and more children, however, are being placed in day care arrangements and in some cases may see more of a nursery school teacher or a substitute caretaker than of their parents. Accordingly, research implications to supplement those presented in the discussion of day care in Chapter 8 will now be summarized.

The earlier discussion of day care for children up to the age of two focused on the topics of attachment and critical periods. During the 1960s and early 1970s, when the critical period hypothesis was widely endorsed, some psychologists expressed fears that placing young children under the care of others would interfere with the development of attachment. Studies of the impact of day care on two-year-olds reviewed in Chapter 8, however, suggest that day care children are less dependent on the mother but that she still stays at the top of the attachment hierarchy. Studies of the impact of day care or nursery school experience on two- to five-year-olds (reviewed by Clarke-Stewart and Fein, 1983) support the conclusion that such children continue to be more independent than home-reared children but reveal other differences as well.

Clarke-Stewart and Fein report that day care children tend to be more socially competent and mature than home care children. They are more self-confident, assertive, outgoing, and knowledgeable about the social world. They are also less compliant and more belligerent, irritable, aggressive, and hostile. In interpreting these findings you should keep in mind that many studies of the impact of day care feature children who attend organized day care centers that are essentially the same as nursery schools. As noted in Chapter 8, though, day care center arrangements are not nearly as common as child care provided by a relative or a single woman in her home. If a child is cared for by a grandmother or a woman who takes care of only one or two "clients," the results of much research on day care will not be directly relevant.

In speculating about reasons for the characteristics reported by those who have studied the impact of day care (primarily in centers), Clarke-Stewart and Fein note the following potentially significant factors: opportunities for interaction with peers and nonparental adults, possible exposure to instruction by day care personnel, and possible tendency for day care personnel to encourage independence. If one three-year-old spends several hours a day interacting with adults and peers in a group situation and another stays at home in the care of the mother, it is logical to expect the day care child to be more independent and socially sophisticated than the other. If day care personnel provide instruction in the sorts of skills and abilities that are measured on intelligence tests, it is also logical to expect that day care children will perform at a higher level than home care children. This, in fact, is what has been reported. In

Day care children competent and mature but aggressive and noncompliant

When children play with others of about the same age they tend to engage in sociable conversation. Opportunities for conflicts also increase, however, and they tend to engage in more aggressive behavior as well.
© *Elizabeth Crews.*

various studies day care children have been found to perform better than home care children in tests of vocabulary, verbal expression and comprehension, creativity in use of materials, and eye-hand coordination. But there is no consistent evidence that early superiority of day care children in either social or intellectual skills is permanent. As noted in the preceding chapter, virtually all the preschool educational programs established during the Head Start years were found to produce temporary gains in IQ. Even in the best programs, though, these gains faded within a few years (although academic achievement was influenced in positive ways, apparently because of attitudinal factors).

Parents who are undecided about day care and/or preschool experience might take into account this conclusion of Clarke-Stewart and Fein:

If children are placed in a decent program after 2 years of age, effects, if any, are likely to be positive. Children's development of social and intellectual skills is

Excellent day care may lead to advanced development, but gains not likely to be permanent

likely to be advanced, and there are no apparent detrimental effects on their emotions. Developmental acceleration is especially likely in programs that offer systematic educational activities and opportunities for social interaction and exploration of materials. (1983, p. 980)

The following point might be added: it is likely that advancement in social and intellectual skills that occurs during the preschool years as a result of day care and/or nursery school experience will disappear by the time the children reach the second grade or so. Accordingly, parents who consider day care might base a decision more on convenience for family members than on the belief that day care will foster development in long-lasting ways. The same line of reasoning might be applied to nursery school attendance for older preschoolers. Parents might base a decision about nursery school attendance more on factors such as the desirability of having mother and child be free of each other's company for a few hours a day rather than on a conviction that it is necessary for social or cognitive development. There is no clear-cut evidence that children who attend nursery schools are superior in either social or academic skills later in life to children from similar backgrounds who stayed home with a responsive adult during the preschool years.

Relationships with Peers

During the first two years of their lives, children interact most frequently with their parents or parent-substitutes. If they have older siblings or attend a day care center, they may engage in limited interactions with other children, but relationships with others the same age do not ordinarily begin before the age of three or so.

Differences Between Adult-Child and Child-Child Interactions

While adult-child interactions are related to child-child interactions, there are important differences between the two types of relations. In adult-child interactions, the adult usually assumes primary responsibility for directing and maintaining the interaction. In child-child encounters, these responsibilities rest with the children. Child-child interactions, then, are more difficult for children to sustain. To illustrate the differences between the two types of interactions, imagine a simple game of ball. When a parent and child play, the child is typically allowed to control which type of game will be played with the ball. When the child has difficulty catching the ball, the parent suggests that the child put both arms together and move closer. When the child's interest wanes, the parent varies the game or suggests a different activity. In short, the activity is likely to go smoothly because it is guided by a knowledgeable, competent adult who takes the child's abilities into account when structuring the activity. Many researchers refer to this type of parental support as **scaffolding** (Hodapp, Goldfield, & Boyatzis, 1984). In contrast, a game of ball between two young children is likely to be less successful. Because of the egocentricity of young children, even agreeing on what game to play may be a problem. Because turn-taking skills are not well established, one child may try to maintain possession of the ball. Because neither child is skillful enough to throw accurately or to advise the other how to catch, the game is likely to last only as long as both children are content to chase the ball.

Adult-child interactions often involve support (scaffolding)

Differences Between Same-Age and Mixed-Age Interactions

Clearly, there are many things that are best learned through interacting with an experienced adult. But there are other things that children learn primarily through interacting with other children. And even in child-child interactions, the socialization opportunities are different in same- and mixed-age groups. Mixed-age groups resemble adult-child interactions in the sense that children's roles are defined to a significant extent by relative age and experience. In same-age groups, however, children are on an equal footing and their roles are more often defined through social interaction and negotiation. The ways in which the composition of social groups influences behavior is illustrated in a study of children in six cultures conducted by Whiting and Whiting (1975). In each culture sociable conversation and aggression were more frequent among peers, that is, among children of roughly comparable age and experience. In mixed-age groups, the Whitings found that assistance seeking and other dependent behaviors were most frequently directed to older children by younger children. Nurturing behaviors, on the other hand, were more commonly directed to younger children by older children. The Whitings also found evidence that the effects of mixed-age interaction varied from culture to culture. Cultures that provide more opportunities for children to interact and assume responsibility for younger children (for example, Mexico) produce more nurturant children.

Sociable conversation and aggression in same-age groups

There is some recent evidence that the effects of mixed-age interaction also depend to some extent on the relationship among the interactors. Stoneman, Brody, and MacKinnon (1984) observed four- to seven-year-olds interacting with their eight- to ten-year-old siblings alone and in the presence of the older sibling's friend. They found that interactions involving the younger child were more positive when the older sibling's friend was present. In these triadic interactions the younger siblings were likely to behave more like the older children's peers. They complied less frequently with their older siblings' management attempts and more frequently attempted the manager's role themselves. (As most readers with an older sibling might have predicted, their management attempts were less successful with older siblings than they were with the older siblings' friends.) Stoneman, Brody, and MacKinnon also examined sex differences in children's patterns of interaction. They found that boys were less likely than girls to comply with their friends' management attempts. Like many other researchers, they also found that boys were more likely than girls to play alone, to play outdoors, and to engage in competitive physical activity.

Differences in Compliance and Conformity

Compliance has been the focus of many studies of emerging social interaction skills. V. J. Crandall and several associates (1958) studied the ways nursery school children complied with or conformed to the demands of their peers and of adults. They discovered that peer-compliant children were readily influenced by the opinions of others and were likely to seek praise and attention from others. But they were also rated as energetic, spontaneous, friendly, and relaxed. Children who were more adult-compliant were rated as nonaggressive and withdrawn. The child who seeks approval from peers appears to engage in easygoing, relatively nonaggressive give-and-take, while the child who seeks adult approval appears to be more anxious and submissive. Part of the reason some children from this study sought adult approval might have been that they were unable to secure peer approval. Perhaps the need for belonging was satisfied in the peer-compliant group but not in the children who sought adult approval. If so, peer approval was reinforcing, and so it was desired.

There seems to be a tendency for nursery school children who are eager to gain peer approval to imitate the behavior of classmates. W. W. Hartup and B. Coates (1967), for example, arranged for preschoolers to observe a child (a confederate of the experimenters) who was very generous in sharing things. The sharing behavior of many of the children increased, particularly in those the model had previously responded to in a favorable way. The results of this study reveal that peers serve both as models and as important reinforcing agents. Consequently, many of the hypotheses accounting for the way parents influence socialization also apply to the way children influence each other; children recognize that peers are engaging in forms of behavior that are

Peers serve as models and as reinforcing agents

worth emulating, and they imitate models who are rewarded or who reward them.

Age Trends in Social Interaction with Peers

Two- to five-year-olds seem to build the skills necessary for interacting with others gradually. At first they keep to themselves, observing play-mates from a distance. Next, they play more or less independently *beside* others. Eventually, they engage in cooperative types of play in which specific roles are assigned. This sequence was first described by Mildred Parten (1932), who observed the free play of children in a nursery school and noted the types of social behavior they engaged in. Eventually, she was able to write quite precise descriptions of these six types of behavior.

Unoccupied Behavior: Children do not really play at all. They either stand around and glance for a time at others or engage in aimless activities.

Solitary Play: Children play alone with toys that are different from those used by children within speaking distance. They make no attempt to interact with others.

Onlooker Behavior: Children spend most of their time watching others. They may make comments on the play of others but do not attempt to join in.

Parallel Play: Children play *beside*, but not really with, other children. They use the same toys in close proximity to others, yet in an indepen-dent way.

Associative Play: Children engage in rather disorganized play with other children. But, there is no assignment of activities or roles; individ-ual children play in their own ways.

Cooperative Play: Children engage in an organized form of play, where leadership and other roles are assigned. The members of the group may cooperate in creating some project, dramatize some situa-tion, or engage in some sort of coordinated enterprise.

Having developed these descriptions, Parten then used the **time-sampling** technique. She observed a one-minute sample of the behavior of the child selected. At the end of that time, she classified the child's play into one of the six categories. She then repeated this procedure with another child, and so on. Over a period of days she accumulated a record of twenty such samples for each child. An analysis of these rec-

Parallel play. Children play beside but not really with others.
© Elizabeth Crews.

Associative play. Children engage in disorganized play with others. No roles are assigned because the play remains unstructured.
David S. Strickler/Monkmeyer.

Cooperative play. Roles are assigned as children engage in structured play activities.
© B. Griffith/The Picture Cube.

ords showed that two-year-olds were most likely to engage in **parallel** play (they played *beside,* but not really with, others). Older children were more likely to enjoy **associative** or **cooperative** play (they interacted with others first in somewhat disorganized ways and eventually by engaging in coordinated activities and by assigning specific roles).[1]

Because Parten's categories are age-related, it might be concluded that the earlier-appearing forms, including solitary play, are less desirable and should be discouraged. Parten herself never drew such a conclusion. What Parten did conclude was that with increasing age children were able to sustain longer and more complex social interactions. She did not mean to imply that there was something inherently wrong with solitary play. (Parents, in fact, often view children's inability to entertain themselves as a problem.) Nor did Parten suggest that solitary play is necessarily immature. In fact, even the oldest children in Parten's study engaged in a lot of solitary play. Solitary play can vary considerably in complexity, from the child who puts together a puzzle to the child who constructs a troupe of puppets and puts on an original puppet show single-handed. Thus, high levels of solitary play should not be a cause for concern unless children are also failing to develop their abilities to interact positively with others.

K. E. Barnes (1971) replicated Parten's study and compared the social behavior of preschool children of this generation with the descriptions of the behavior of children observed forty years earlier. The time samplings obtained by Barnes indicated that young children reared in the 1970s were much less socially oriented than those reared in the 1930s. Barnes hypothesized that the time contemporary children spend watching television, plus the decrease in family size, might account for the change toward more self-centered behavior.

The Nature and Apparent Causes of Sex Cleavage

An interesting trend in peer relations that begins in early childhood is **sex cleavage,** the tendency for children to prefer interacting with same-sex peers. Hartup (1983) suggests that parents may foster these preferences by providing sex-typed toys for their sons and daughters and by seeking same-sex playmates. Maccoby (1980), however, hypothesizes

From two to five, children move from parallel to associative and cooperative play

Sex cleavage: tendency for children to prefer same-sex playmates

---

[1]You may have recognized that the age trends reported by Parten are very similar to the stages of sociodramatic play described by Smilansky, which were summarized in Chapter 10 in the discussion of play.

that sex cleavage may represent the child's own strategy for adapting to the different styles of interaction developed by boys and girls. Girls may opt to play with other girls, for example, because they find the physically active, competitive, rough-and-tumble style of boys' play incompatible with their own. Boys, on the other hand, may find girls' activities too tame, may find girls' tendency to structure situations according to specific rules too confining, and may be disappointed or frustrated by the tendency of girls to withdraw or seek adult intervention at the first sign of a struggle (Jacklin and Maccoby, 1978). Whatever the reasons, young children usually prefer to interact with same-sex peers. However, parents may want to encourage some cross-sex play. The very differences that make interaction with same-sex peers more comfortable may make cross-sex play potentially enriching. Girls who need to be more assertive are likely to find more assertive models in cross-sex interactions. Likewise, boys who need to develop the caring, nurturing side of their personalities will find that cross-sex play provides more opportunities for these socialization experiences.

The Nature of Early Friendships and Popularity

Two- to five-year-olds who attend nursery school are convenient subjects for study, and dozens of analyses of social interaction have been made. Some researchers make use of observational methods of different kinds (particularly time sampling); others prefer sociometric techniques (in which members of a group indicate which individuals they like best); some combine the two. Studies of the consistency of playmate choices (described in a review by Hartup, 1983) indicate that friendships become more stable with age. Two- and three-year-olds tend to flit from one playmate to another and select a different classmate on successive sociometric interviews, but five-year-olds may be faithful to one or two companions for an extended period of time. The personality traits of preschool children chosen frequently by their peers include friendliness, sociability, social visibility, and outgoingness (Hartup, 1983, p. 133). Children who seek assistance from peers and are eager for their approval tend to be more popular than those who seem interested primarily in attracting attention. Preschoolers seem to like having a playmate seek their help or approval but are bothered by someone who pesters them. There is some evidence that brighter children are more popular than those below average in intelligence. Children are not likely to be popular if they are aggressive, violate rules, or behave in strange ways. (Changes in relationships with others during the six- to twelve-year span are discussed in Chapter 16, starting on page 485.)

Summary

1. Diana Baumrind analyzed the impact of three types of child rearing. She found that children of **authoritative** parents tended to be self-reliant and competent. Children of **authoritarian** parents, by contrast, tended to be insecure and hostile. Children of **permissive** parents tended to be dependent and immature. Authoritative parents encouraged independence, established firm and consistent limits (giving explanations for such limits), and communicated love in a warm and sincere way. Authoritative child rearing may be effective because the parents serve as models of competence for their children to imitate and also help their children set standards.

2. A recent trend in the study of early parent-child relationships revolves around greater awareness of the **interdependency** of family members. Parents influence children, children influence parents, and parents and siblings influence each other.

3. In interacting with young children, some parents begin by resorting to coercion. Unfortunately, use of coercion early often makes it necessary to use increased coercion later. Furthermore, use of external pressure tends to discourage the internalization of control. When young children, who may not be able to completely comprehend explanations, are **emphatically** told why they have misbehaved, it appears that they are likely to avoid repeating the disapproved action because of anxiety about the seriousness of reprisals rather than complete understanding of the explanation.

4. Because of the trend toward employment of mothers, many contemporary American children may see more of a day care professional or a nursery school teacher on weekdays than their parents. It appears that children who spend considerable time at day care centers may display greater overall competence and maturity than home-reared children of the same age. They also appear to be more aggressive and noncompliant. While excellent day care may lead to advanced social development during the preschool years, such gains are likely to fade during the elementary school years.

5. When preschool children interact with their parents in play situations, they are often given support **(scaffolding).** When they interact with peers of the same age, they are not given such "concessions." In same-age groups, they are likely to engage in sociable conversation and also forms of aggression. Preschoolers acquire many skills in same-age groups by imitating the behavior of peers and by being reinforced by peers for acceptable actions.

6. Studies of play groups formed by nursery school children reveal that between two and five years children move from **parallel** to **associa-**

tive and **cooperative** play. At first they play beside others; then they engage in types of play that involve progressively more integrated interactions. Many spontaneously formed groups of young children comprise members of the same sex (**sex cleavage**). This tendency may be due partly to sex stereotypes and partly to boys' and girls' preferences for different styles of play.

Suggestions for Further Study

Child Rearing

Because of the complexity and subtlety of the processes involved, studies of the impact of child-rearing practices are difficult to summarize. The brief comments in this chapter reflect general conclusions, and you may wish to examine one or more of the actual studies mentioned for further information. The details of the methods and conclusions of such investigations can be found in *Patterns of Child Rearing* (1957) by Robert R. Sears, Eleanor E. Maccoby, and Harry Levin; *Identification and Child Rearing* (1965) by Robert R. Sears, Lucy Rau, and Richard Alpert; *Birth to Maturity: A Study in Psychological Development* (1962) by Jerome Kagan and Howard A. Moss; "Child Care Practices Anteceding Three Patterns of Preschool Behavior" by Diana Baumrind, *Genetic Psychology Monographs*, 1967, *75*, 43–88; or "Current Patterns of Parental Authority," *Developmental Psychology Monographs*, 1971, (1), 1–103, also by Baumrind. In *Child Rearing* (1968), Marian Radke-Yarrow, John D. Campbell, and Roger V. Burton describe a replication of the Sears study (described in *Patterns of Child Rearing*) and also present a summary and critique of other research on child rearing. Recent research and analyses are reviewed in "Socialization in the Context of the Family" by Eleanor Maccoby and John Martin in *Socialization, Personality, and Social Development*, edited by E. Mavis Hetherington, Volume IV of *Handbook of Child Psychology* (4th ed., 1983), edited by Paul H. Mussen.

Day Care

Research on day care and other preschool experience is reviewed in "Early Childhood Programs" by K. Alison Clarke-Stewart and Greta Fein in *Infancy and Developmental Psychobiology*, edited by Marshall M. Haith and Joseph J. Campos, Volume II of *Handbook of Child Psychology* (4th ed., 1983), edited by Paul H. Mussen.

Peer Relationships

For more information about interactions between children consult "Peer Relations" by Willard W. Hartup in *Socialization, Personality, and Social Development*, edited by E. Mavis Hetherington, Volume IV of *Handbook of Child Psychology* (4th ed., 1983), edited by Paul H. Mussen.

Observing Preschool Social Behavior

An excellent and interesting way to become aware of interactions between peers during the preschool years would be to visit a nursery school and carry out a simple replication of the Parten study. First, across the top of a sheet of paper write a description of the six types of social behavior described on page 391. Then, write brief descriptions of the children you are going to observe (unless you know their names) on lines along the left-hand margin. Observe the first child on your list for twenty seconds and make a check mark under the appropriate play description. Observe the next child, and so on. Wait five minutes, and start over again. Continue to make observations and records until you have several check marks for each child. Finally, ask the nursery school teacher for the ages of the children, summarize your results, and draw conclusions.

If the nursery school teacher is willing to cooperate, you might ask her for information about friendships and popularity and perhaps even request that she carry out a simple sociometric study by asking the children to name their favorite playmate. You might relate such information to your findings about types of play.

KEY POINTS

The Significance of Sex-typed Behavior

Preschoolers develop "cognitive map" of sex roles

Children imitate behavior of multiple models

Awareness and observation of sex-stereotyped behavior leads to imitation

Androgenized girls develop masculine traits despite being treated as girls

Boys and girls treated differently starting in infancy

Males depicted as authority figures on TV, females as helpers

The Development of Aggression

Some male aggressiveness traceable to biological factors

Boys encouraged to be aggressive, observe many aggressive male models

Frustrated children tend to imitate aggressive acts

Hypothesis: viewing violence on TV leads to aggressive behavior

Violent acts frequent on TV, consequences minimized, "good guys" resort to violence

Recent research: TV violence increases aggression, decreases sensitivity

Aggressive behavior strengthened by reinforcement, observation

Prosocial Behavior

Children who express distress more likely to help others in distress

Preschoolers recognize suffering, experience guilt, don't always know how to help

Sympathetic models likely to be imitated: warm, express pleasure

Prosocial behavior encouraged by discussion, models, pleasure

Emotional Factors in Personality Development

Between two and five, "physical" fears decrease; "imaginary" fears increase

Fears may be overcome by explanations, example, positive reconditioning, confidence

Preventing fears by allowing freedom to explore

Anxiety may be minimized by providing support, satisfying needs, encouraging independence

CHAPTER

13

TWO
TO
FIVE

PERSONALITY
DEVELOPMENT

*I*n discussing personality development during the first two years in Chapter 9, we summarized arguments for and against the hypothesis that infancy is a critical period. Although they stress the importance of the first two years for different reasons, Freudians and behaviorists propose that early experiences are of supreme importance in shaping behavioral traits that will persist. The fact that infants *must* be cared for has led many theorists to assume that they are shaped by what caretakers do to them and that they have little control over their own behavior. Some psychologists, however, have supplied evidence that even during infancy children exhibit personality traits of their own and that they influence how others respond to them. Both of these tendencies become more apparent with each succeeding month of development between the years of two and five. When children are able to walk and talk with ease, develop a strong sense of their independence, interact with individuals other than their parents (and siblings), and are exposed to experiences outside the home, their individuality becomes increasingly apparent. And the more they develop personalities of their own, the greater the variety of responses they arouse from others.

Psychologists who strongly endorse the critical period hypothesis suggest that personality development during the preschool years is essentially a continuation of trends established in infancy. But between the ages of two and five, children encounter many experiences (e.g., playing with age-mates in comparatively unsupervised situations) that are unlike anything encountered earlier. Furthermore, they become clearly aware for the first time that certain characteristics and types of behavior are displayed by and expected from boys and girls. Awareness of such sex-typed behavior often has a profound influence on personality development. It seems reasonable to assume, therefore, that significant formative influences on personality are likely to occur during these years. The nature of some of these influences is revealed by the theorizing of Freud, Sears, and Erikson about personality development during the years from two to five.

The Significance of Sex-typed Behavior

Freud: The Importance of Identification

In recognition of the fact that children first become clearly aware of differences between males and females between two and five, Freud designated this the **phallic** stage of psychosexual development. To account for shifts in the feelings of boys and girls for their mothers and fathers, he proposed the Oedipus and Electra complexes. To explain the dynamics behind these two complexes, he emphasized the importance of identification. Freud distinguished between two types, **anaclitic** (leaning-up-against-type) and **defensive** (or aggressive). Freud proposed that anaclitic identification occurs when the child of two or so, who has been completely dependent on his or her mother the first few months of life, imitates some of her activities. He reasoned that two-year-olds may become apprehensive about certain aspects of their new-found independence and seek security by engaging in some of the activities performed by the person who has previously cared for them. This explanation may account for the identification behavior of two-year-olds, but at the age of three or four, when children typically become aware of sex differences, boys begin to identify with their fathers. Defensive identification was proposed to explain this switch. As noted in Chapter 2, Freud hypothesized that the four-year-old boy (who is experiencing the Oedipus complex) fears and resents his father as a rival. The boy realizes that the father is more powerful, and so he identifies with the "aggressor" and tries to become more like him. By doing this, the boy defends himself against anxiety.

Sears: Identification and Child Rearing

Robert R. Sears, Lucy Rau, and Richard Alpert carried out an ambitious study (reported in *Identification and Child Rearing*, 1965) in an effort to evaluate Freud's theory of identification. They considered this an important area for research because they felt it might yield a unitary process that would account for several types of behavior that become established early in a child's life—particularly sex typing and formation of adult roles. Sears was one of the originators of social-learning theory, and he was interested in analyzing the development of identification in terms of stimulus-response principles. He hypothesized that since the young child must be cared for by others, the development of sex-appropriate and adultlike behavior would be strongly influenced by early *dependency* in the child. He also theorized that if there were a unitary process that accounted for sex typing, the formation of adult roles, and other types of behavior, there would be considerable consistency in child behavior, traceable to child-rearing practices.

To test these hypotheses Sears and his colleagues obtained information on forty four-year-olds attending a summer nursery school. The children were observed in free play and in experimental and doll-play situations and were then interviewed, as were both fathers and mothers. The mothers were observed interacting with their children in standard situations. In one phase of the study, for example, the mother was asked to fill out a questionnaire in a room where her child had nothing to do—which caused most children to pester their mothers. In another phase the child was asked to solve a jigsaw puzzle with or without the mother's help. (Both of these situations made it possible to evaluate the degree of dependency shown by a child.)

When all the data were processed and analyzed, Sears and his colleagues found more consistency in the behavior of girls than boys. They concluded that this could be interpreted as support for Freud's concept of anaclitic identification. The children being studied were four years old, which meant the boys theoretically were experiencing the Oedipus complex and were in a process of shifting from anaclitic to defensive identification. The researchers failed, however, to find evidence that dependency was a unitary process. They observed, "By age four, *overt dependency behavior* does not reflect a unitary drive or habit structure that can be interpreted as the unique source of reinforcement for all the other behaviors we have studied" (1965, p. 249).

Regarding the development of sex-typed behavior, a comparison of child behavior and parental practices led Sears and his colleagues to conclude: "Children of both sexes initially adopt feminine-maternal ways of behaving" (p. 261) due to a monitoring process based on the mother's responsiveness and also to direct instruction (not always intentional or verbalizable). "The boy develops a cognitive map of the male role at some point in his first three or four years and begins to shape his own behavior toward that role" (p. 261). The boy is able to do this more effectively if male models (particularly the father) are available. In contrast to the influence of the mother on the development of feminine behavior, the *responsiveness* of the male model is not an important factor. "Masculinity and femininity both appear to be more influenced by parental attitudes toward the control of sex and aggression than by any aspect of the availability of the behavior of models" (p. 261). If the parents encouraged freedom of expression and were nonpunitive, both boys *and* girls were likely to develop masculine traits.

> Preschoolers develop "cognitive map" of sex roles

Even though Sears concluded that dependency did not appear to be a unitary trait, his results might be interpreted as support for the Freudian concepts of anaclitic and defensive identification. At first, both boys and girls adopt forms of behavior exhibited by the mother, particularly if she responds positively to them. It seems quite reasonable to explain this as identification that involves dependency on (or anaclitic identification with) the primary caretaker. Around the age of three or four, the boy begins to imitate the father's actions, but masculine behavior will be practiced even though the male model does not respond to the child. It seems plausible to explain this by suggesting that the boy identifies with the father not because he feels dependent, but because he hopes to acquire some of the father's envied power. The same explanation might account, in part at least, for the tendency of a girl who is not "protected" by the mother to imitate masculine types of behavior.

Bandura: Impact of Imitation

At the same time Sears was evaluating the impact of identification on social learning, Albert Bandura began a series of investigations of the

Preschool children begin to acquire sex-typed behavior by imitating older members of the same sex.
Frank Siteman/Stock, Boston; Erika Stone.

influence of observational learning. Bandura has observed (Bandura and Walters, 1963) that what personality theorists (such as Freud and Sears) called *identification* is labeled *imitation* by experimental psychologists. Bandura believes that both terms might be referred to as observational learning. Bandura suggests thinking of the three terms as synonyms, instead of drawing fine distinctions between them. Bandura also believes that attempts to explain all types of behavior in terms of traditional stimulus-response principles, with emphasis on reinforcement of specific acts, are not completely satisfactory. He feels that more allowance should be made for changes in behavior due to observation and imitation, with or without reinforcement.

Bandura and his colleagues carried out experiments (Bandura, Ross, and Ross, 1963a, 1963c) to discover the kinds of models most likely to be imitated. They concluded that individuals who supplied rewards or who were perceived as possessing power were often—but not always—imitated. They also discovered that some types of behavior may be imitated in the absence of any apparent reinforcement. Regarding the learning of sex-typed behavior, Bandura and his colleagues observed:

Theories of identificatory learning have generally assumed that within the family setting the child's initial identification is confined to his mother, and that during early childhood boys must turn from the mother as the primary model to the father as the main source of imitative behavior. However, throughout the course of development children are provided with ample opportunities to observe the behavior of both parents. When children are exposed to multiple models they may select one or more of them as the primary source of behavior, but rarely reproduce all the elements of a single model's repertoire or confine their imitation to that model. (1963a, p. 534)

Children imitate behavior of multiple models

Other studies of the same type (reviewed by Walter Mischel, 1970, pp. 29–39) have supported Bandura's conclusion that sex-typed behavior is often learned through imitation of a variety of models and in the absence of any form of tangible reward.

Kohlberg: Cognitive Awareness of Sex Differences

Lawrence Kohlberg (1966) points out that by the age of five children have definite awareness of sex differences. (Freud based his explanation of the Oedipus complex on the same observation.) Kohlberg suggests that children of that age also have come to acquire knowledge of stereotypes about masculinity and femininity. (This hypothesis is similar to the conclusion of Sears that "The boy develops a cognitive map of the

male role at some point in his first three or four years and begins to
shape his own behavior toward that role" (1965, p. 261). Many aspects
of the development of sex-role behavior, therefore, might be attributed
simply to observation and the desire of a boy or girl to behave the way a
man or woman does. Aware that he is a male, a boy who sees an older
brother shave, watches college and professional athletes on television,
or observes his father mow the lawn will think of these as masculine
activities and tend to imitate them. Aware that she is a female, a girl who
sees an older sister put on lipstick, observes the behavior of females
depicted on television programs, and observes her mother cook dinner
will think of these as feminine activities and tend to imitate them. As
Bandura's conclusion suggests, children are exposed to so many models
that the emerging self-concept of any particular child is likely to be a
synthesis of many impressions. Sears, Bandura, and Kohlberg offer explanations for the way sex-role behavior may be learned. There is some
evidence, however, that certain aspects of the behavior of males and
females in our society may be due to innate biological differences between the sexes.

*Awareness and ob-
servation of sex-
stereotyped be-
havior leads to
imitation*

Biological Influences on Sex-typed Behavior

The basic problem in speculating about the causes of what have come to
be called male and female traits is that under ordinary circumstances it is
impossible to separate completely biological from environmental causes.
The infant *must* be cared for, and the child cannot be reared in a vacuum.
It is thus inevitable that he or she will have occasion to see how other
males or females behave. The development and use of pregnancy hormones in the 1950s, however, inadvertently led to a situation where
biological and environmental factors relating to sex differences could be
examined separately. Before use of these hormones was discontinued, it
was discovered that some women treated with them (to prevent unwanted abortion) gave birth to masculinized daughters, that is, females
in whom the influence of the androgens (hormones that develop and
maintain masculine traits) caused the development of male sex organs.
In several cases, this condition was diagnosed at birth, and the masculine sexual organs were surgically modified. While the surgery corrected the external physical aspects of masculinization, it did not cancel
out the continued impact of the androgens. Masculinization could be
controlled with injections of cortisone so that the girls grew up with a
female physique, and most were eventually capable of bearing children.
These girls, therefore, as they matured, saw themselves and were seen
as girls, yet they continued to be influenced by the androgens. This

situation provided an excellent opportunity for studying the origin of sex differences.

John Money and Anke Ehrhardt (1972) found twenty-five androgenized girls (ranging in age from four to sixteen years) and matched each of these with a normal girl of the same age, socioeconomic background, IQ, and race. All fifty girls and their mothers were asked a standard series of questions and were given tests of sex-role preferences. The purpose of the study was to see if "prenatal androgens may have left a presumptive effect on the brain, and hence subsequent behavior" (1972, p. 98). It was discovered that the fetally androgenized girls manifested **tomboyism** to a much greater extent than the control group. The androgenized girls were much more likely to engage in activities involving energy expenditure and competitiveness; they preferred clothes that were utilitarian and functional (and avoided fashionable dresses); they were indifferent to dolls and later to human infants; but they were attracted to toy cars, trucks, and guns. Many of the control girls, by contrast, loved to play with dolls and took every opportunity to get close to human infants.

Androgenized girls develop masculine traits despite being treated as girls

Furthermore, all twenty-five of the controls said (in reply to a question) that they wanted to have babies of their own when they grew up. One-third of the androgenized girls, on the other hand, said they would prefer not to have children, and although the remainder did not reject the idea, they were not enthusiastic about it either. When asked whether they would prefer a career to marriage (and being a housewife) when they grew up, the majority of the androgenized girls chose a career first. The majority of the control girls answered that they felt marriage was the most important goal of the future, and the older girls in the sample showed a high interest in romance and boy friends. The androgenized girls, by contrast, took little interest in dating.

Money and Ehrhardt concluded, "The most likely hypothesis to explain the various features of tomboyism in fetally masculinized genetic females is that their tomboyism is a sequel to a masculinizing effect on the fetal brain" (p. 103). They theorized that this effect strengthened pathways in the brain that led to competitive energy expenditure (not necessarily aggression) and weakened those that led to maternal behavior. Money and Ehrhardt also analyzed several other types of cases where bisexual abnormalities had occurred. In summing up the significance of their research on hermaphroditism, they stressed the degree to which behavior seems to be controlled by genetic factors—if the fetal brain is androgenized, masculine traits will appear regardless of what the parents and others do. (The conclusions of Money and Ehrhardt have been criticized for various technical reasons by a number of researchers—summarized by Huston, 1983, p. 417—but it seems likely that biological factors do have some influence on sex-typed behavior.)

Environmental Influences on Sex-typed Behavior

Money and Ehrhardt stress biological influences on sex-typed behavior, but environmental factors influence the emergence of such forms of behavior in myriad ways. To appreciate the extent of environmental influences, consider findings of investigations revealing ways sex-typed behavior is shaped starting at birth. Some of the points noted below have been mentioned in earlier chapters, but they are repeated here to make clear the cumulative impact of factors that shape sex roles. (No specific references to individual studies are noted in the following summary because of the magnitude of research on this topic. For information about specific studies, consult Huston, 1983.)

Parents of newborn infants rate daughters as smaller, softer, and having finer features than sons, despite the fact that such differences are not identifiable when the sex of the child is not known.

Starting as early as the first few weeks after birth, mothers tend to cuddle girls more often than they cuddle boys.

In interacting with infants and toddlers, adults engage in more activity with boys. Boys are stimulated in more robust ways and encouraged to be more active than girls.

Boys and girls treated differently starting in infancy

When given an assortment of playthings to present to infants and young children, both male and female adults more often give dolls to girls, objects like rubber hammers to boys.

By the age of three, children have acquired knowledge of sex stereotypes for toys, clothing, household objects, games, and work. In their play, they choose "appropriate" toys, props, and roles. They reinforce peers who use playthings in sex-appropriate ways and criticize those who depart from sex-stereotyped forms of behavior.

By the age of five, children know most of the sex stereotypes presented in questionnaires designed to test such knowledge.

Starting as early as the preschool years, boys' rooms contain more "educational" toys (e.g., construction sets) and more "instructional" decorations (e.g., informative posters). Girls' rooms typically contain a large number of dolls; decorations feature flowers and ruffles.

The television programs children watch feature males in almost three-fourths of all leading roles. Male and female characters engage in sex-stereotyped activities. Males are depicted as authority figures (even to the extent of speaking the message for products used by females and touted in commercials). Females are depicted engaging in jobs such as nursing or clerical work or devoting themselves to domestic and parenting roles. (Black males shown on TV have higher occupational status than white females.)

Males depicted as authority figures on TV, females as helpers

Male characters in children's books engage in active achievement of goals; females are typically depicted as passive onlookers.

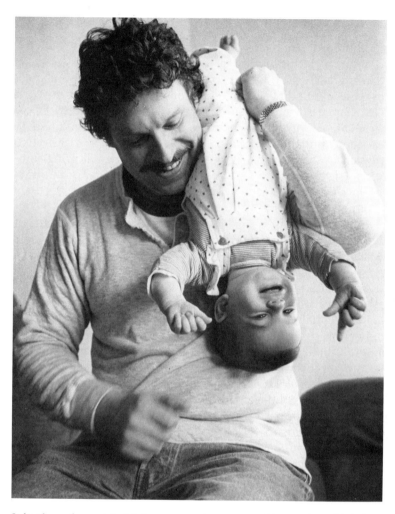

It has been observed that fathers engage in more roughhouse play with infant sons than with infant daughters, which may function as an early (and often unintentional) way of establishing sex-role stereotypes.
© *Elizabeth Crews.*

Starting during the preschool years, sex cleavage causes children to play in same-sex groups and to engage in stereotyped male and female activities. Such interactions serve to reinforce the tendencies that led to sex cleavage in the first place.

Starting during the preschool years, teachers give more positive attention to girls, more negative attention to boys, even though the behavior of boys and girls is similar. (Teachers seem to *expect* boys to cause more trouble than girls.) Inexperienced teachers, in particular, tend to reward pupils for engaging in sex-stereotyped behavior (e.g., praising girls for handwriting, boys for construction projects).

Attempting to Counteract Sex-typing Indoctrination

Taking into account the cumulative impact of such indoctrination, it is not surprising that sex typing occurs, even if biological factors are discounted. Because sex typing is influenced in such diverse ways, combating children's tendency to accept traditional male and female roles as inevitable is not a simple task. Attempts to break down sex stereotypes seem to be most effective when a systematic program of "education" takes place over a period of time. To repeat a suggestion made earlier, starting when children are infants, parents might try to remain aware of ways they unwittingly reinforce traditional sex roles (by the kinds of toys they provide, for instance, or ways they respond to behavior). In addition, they might select books that depict female characters engaging in a variety of activities. When female characters on television programs are shown as achievers rather than as subordinates (such as nurses and secretaries) who carry out the orders of males, parents might call attention to the potential women have to become successful in a variety of occupations. Finally, parents might try to serve as models for the development of androgynous tendencies by engaging in activities that demonstrate that both males and females can engage in activities that are not restricted to one sex or the other.

The Development of Aggression

Various Explanations for the Greater Aggressiveness of Boys

Aggression is a form of behavior that is influenced by many of the factors just discussed. There is substantial evidence (reviewed by Feshbach, 1970, and Parke and Slaby, 1983) that boys tend to be more aggressive than girls. At least part of the tendency for males to be aggressive appears to be due directly or indirectly to biological factors. There is some evidence of a link between the male sex hormone testosterone and aggressive responses to provocation. Furthermore, at least partly because of biological factors, males are more active and have greater strength (at most ages) than females, characteristics that predispose males to engage in physical interactions with others. It also appears that certain aspects of temperament (which is usually defined as a constitutional determinant of personality) may predispose children to both arouse and express aggression. A boy who is active, irritable, and would be rated by Thomas as a "difficult" child might arouse more physical forms of control from parents (and later from other adults and bigger peers) than a "difficult" female child or an "easy" child. If treated physically, the child might be provoked into responding physically. Finally, in almost all cultures in all parts of the world males are found to be more aggressive than females. Such differences might be attributed in part to direct biological influences (such as hormones) and in part to influences derived from biological differences (such as roles assigned to males as providers and females as child bearers and rearers).

The summary you just read of factors that shape sex-typed behavior calls attention to the extent to which males in our society are encouraged by environmental influences to be more aggressive than females. Boys are treated in rougher fashion than girls by parents and given toys that encourage aggressive play. In real life situations (e.g., play of older boys, sports events) and in news, sports, and dramatic television programs, boys repeatedly observe male models acting in aggressive ways. It is not surprising, therefore, that males are not only rated as more aggressive than females very early in life but that aggressiveness is found to be the most stable trait in boys (Kagan and Moss, 1961).

Some male aggressiveness traceable to biological factors

Boys encouraged to be aggressive, observe many aggressive male models

Developmental Trends in Aggression

While aggressiveness in general is a stable trait, there are changes with age in ways aggression is aroused and expressed. Seymour Feshbach (1970) reviewed many studies of aggressiveness in children and concluded that it was instructive to make a distinction between two basic types of aggression. **Hostile** (or person-oriented) **aggression** is directed at other children and is provoked by behavior that threatens self-esteem (for example, a boy tells another boy, "You're stupid") or is interpreted as intentional (for example, a girl is convinced that another girl deliberately hit her). **Instrumental aggression** is aimed at attaining or retrieving some object or privilege and is usually provoked when some goal-directed activity is blocked (for example, a boy pushes a playmate away

Dozens of studies support the conclusion that boys engage in more aggressive behavior than girls.
Elizabeth Hamlin/Stock, Boston.

from a pile of blocks he needs to complete a miniature castle). Willard Hartup (1974) observed aggressive interactions between preschool children and first-graders. He found that the younger children engaged in aggressive interactions more frequently but that most of these were of the instrumental type. Hartup speculates that younger children may not respond to comments that would provoke a response from an older child because they have not yet developed a clear self-concept and are not aware of the intention of malice. As they grow older, children engage in fewer aggressive acts, but they are more likely to be provoked by threats to their self-esteem. They not only have formed a concept of themselves; they are also better able to interpret what is on the other person's mind. When preschool children are on the receiving end of derogatory remarks, they use physical means of responding as frequently as they use verbal reactions (for example, counterthreats or derogatory remarks). Primary grade school children, on the other hand, use physical retaliation only about 20 percent of the time. Hartup also found that boys engaged in more aggressive acts than girls but that this difference was due almost entirely to differences in the amount of hostile aggression: boys were more likely to attack persons when angered.

Television and Aggressive Behavior

Bandura's Studies of the Impact of Imitation

In one of their series of experiments designed to test the impact of imitation of models on child behavior, Albert Bandura, D. Ross, and S. A. Ross (1963b) arranged for five-year-old children to observe models engage in aggressive acts. The children first saw a live female adult attack an inflated plastic figure (often called a Bobo doll) with her fist, her foot, a hammer, and a cap pistol, throw it up in the air, and sit on it while pummeling its face. The same sequence of acts was then depicted in a film of an adult and in a cartoon, both of which simulated television programs. Each child who had observed the model and seen the films, as well as each child in a control group who had not, was then frustrated (by being interrupted just when enjoying play with some very attractive toys) and taken to a room that contained an identical inflated figure and many other toys.

When social learning theory was being formulated, several psychologists (Dollard, Doob, Miller, Mowrer, and Sears, 1939) proposed that frustration leads to aggression. Bandura and his colleagues took this hypothesis into account and reasoned that the children who had been interrupted were likely to react with aggression. On the basis of their previous research on the impact of imitation, they predicted that the aggressive reactions to frustration would be patterned on those of the models the children had observed. The reactions of the children in the experimental and control groups supported the frustration-aggression hypothesis, as well as the prediction that aggressive acts would be imitated. Children in both groups engaged in aggressive acts. However, those who had observed the model attacked the inflated figure not only more frequently but often in exactly the same way and in the same sequence as the model. The experimenters suggested that these results might also apply to television viewing and argued that a child who is frustrated and reacts in an aggressive way will tend to engage in violent acts similar to those seen on television programs. A five-year-old who watches a cartoon where one character hits another over the head with a board, for example, may carry out the same action if frustrated by a playmate shortly after seeing the cartoon. A teen-ager frustrated to the breaking point may grab a gun and start shooting, imitating the behavior seen thousands of times in Western, war, and crime television programs.

The Bandura study (and several others like it, reviewed by Feshbach [1970, pp. 211–214]) was accepted by some theorists as proof of a link between television and violence. Critics pointed out, however, that the inflated figure used in many of these studies was expressly designed to be hit and kicked and that children were well aware of this. Simply

Frustrated children tend to imitate aggressive acts

Hypothesis: viewing violence on TV leads to aggressive behavior

because children imitated the way a model hits a toy designed for the purpose of being hit did not prove, they argued, that they will hit other children. Children who hit the inflated figure in the same way as the models might have been simply trying out some new assault techniques for use with Bobo dolls, techniques they had not tried before that looked like fun.

The Surgeon General's Report on Television and Violence

When Robert Kennedy was assassinated, though, even congressional leaders who had been skeptics became convinced of the need for a careful review of all research on causes of violence in our society. They appointed The Surgeon General's Advisory Committee on Television and Social Behavior and asked its members to review all available information on the link between television and violence. Their conclusions are reported in a five-volume set of documents issued under the general heading *Television and Social Behavior* (1972). A summary report is titled *Television and Growing Up: The Impact of Televised Violence* (1972). The general conclusion of the committee was that some studies supported the hypothesis that television viewing leads to violence and others did not. Some critics of the report argued, however, that the members of the committee were not selected in a way that guaranteed a balanced combination of views and backgrounds. Others (for example, Liebert and Neale, 1972) questioned the interpretation of some studies and the general conclusion of the committee.

Subsequent Research on the Impact of Televised Violence

The vague conclusions of the Surgeon General's Report led to renewed interest on the part of researchers in the question of how violence shown on television contributes to aggression. In a review of more than twenty-five hundred studies published since the report, Ross Parke and Ronald Slaby (1983) first note that American children between the ages of two and eighteen watch an average of well over three hours of TV programming every day. When weekends and vacations are taken into account, it turns out that children in our society spend more time watching television than they spend engaging in any other single waking activity, including school. Parke and Slaby then note that for all types of programs an average of 7.5 violent acts are depicted every hour. In weekend daytime programs presumably intended for children, violent acts are depicted at the rate of 17.6 per hour. Because television program codes prohibit showing negative effects of violence (e.g., blood, agony), the painful consequences of violent acts are rarely communicated to the viewer. Victims simply lie where they have fallen; they do not suffer nor are they likely to be shown being treated in a hospital, where the extent of their injuries would become apparent. In addition, the "good guys"

Violent acts frequent on TV, consequences minimized, "good guys" resort to violence

perform as many violent acts as the "bad guys" and frequently break the law while they are doing it. There is also evidence that younger children respond to violent acts as isolated events and do not take into account either motives or consequences.

In contrast to those who wrote the summary of the Surgeon General's Report, Parke and Slaby muster impressive evidence to support the hypothesis that a steady diet of televised violence *does* cause children to engage in subsequent aggression. They note that "Exposure to televised violence has been shown not only to increase the viewer's own level of aggression, but also to decrease the viewer's behavioral and physiological responsiveness to aggression by others" (1983, p. 603). (This latter point is often referred to as the **emotional desensitization hypothesis.**)

Recent research: TV violence increases aggression, decreases sensitivity

It would appear, therefore, that parents who would like to reduce the tendency for their children to react to frustration with violence—and also try to maintain emotional sensitivity to the suffering of others—should carefully monitor television viewing by their children. They should not assume that cartoon and dramatic programs prepared for viewing by children will be less likely to encourage aggression than adult programs. If anything, the opposite may be the case. Since over 70 percent of all television programs have been found to include at least some violence, it will probably be impossible for parents to completely prevent their children from occasionally seeing one character attack another. In such cases, though, parents might comment on the dramatization by expressing disapproval of the action, perhaps noting that it was unnecessary and that other ways of resolving the conflict would have been much more effective and lasting. They might also ask their children to imagine how seriously the victim would be injured if such an attack occurred in real life. Finally, parents might arrange for their children to watch programs such as "Sesame Street" and "Mr. Rogers' Neighborhood." For reasons to be discussed a bit later in this chapter, by watching such programs *with* children and commenting on the lessons dramatized and illustrated, parents can encourage positive forms of social behavior.

While television viewing may be a significant cause of aggression, ways children interact with parents and peers also contribute to the development of aggressive behavior.

The Reinforcement of Aggressive Behavior

G. R. Patterson, R. A. Littman, and W. Bricker (1967) emphasize the extent to which aggressive behavior on the part of preschool children is reinforced by the reactions of peers. Visualize a boy who is spending his first day in a nursery school. He sees a beautiful tricycle on the playground and runs toward it, arriving simultaneously with a little girl. The girl tentatively grabs the handle bars, the boy gives her a hearty shove, causing her to stumble backwards and fall. The girl, frightened and upset, huddles on the ground and starts to whimper. The boy triumphantly mounts the tricycle and rides away. A few minutes later, another boy who had been an interested spectator of the scuffle—and who had never previously thought of using physical force against playmates—shoves the same little girl away from an easel when he wants to paint a picture. He is both surprised and pleased when he easily gets the easel all to himself. Patterson and his colleagues suggest that such interactions cause tendencies toward aggressiveness to be strengthened either through direct reinforcement or observation.

Aggressive behavior strengthened by reinforcement, observation

Patterson also found (1976a) that aggressive behavior is frequently reinforced in the home. He compared children referred to clinics because of excessive aggressive tendencies with children of the same age, sex, and background who had low levels of aggression. Both sets of children were observed in home and school situations interacting with parents, siblings, and peers. Patterson discovered that excessively aggressive children grow up in home situations that involve a great deal of aggression on the part of all family members. Parents and siblings of the aggressive children frequently expressed disapproval, either verbally or physically. They were also likely to tease the child or make demands. Furthermore, when the child responded with anger, the reactions of other family members often tended to reinforce the behavior. They might laugh, give the aggressive child their undivided attention, comply with the child's demands, or react aggressively themselves. When children in the aggressive group aroused an angry response from other family members, a reciprocal reinforcement pattern often developed leading to several quick "rounds" of aggressive and counteraggressive acts.

Patterson stresses reinforcement in his analysis of highly aggressive children and their families, but other explanations might also be considered. It is possible that all family members in aggressive homes share similar inherited predispositions that cause them to react with abnormal degrees of anger when they are frustrated. In addition, the possibility that either or both parents serve as aggressive models who are imitated by their children should be taken into account.

Aggressive behavior stands out because of its very nature. But young children also spontaneously engage in helpful, cooperative, and generous forms of behavior. Such types of behavior are called **prosocial** by psychologists. (When someone is *pro* something, they are in support of it; most forms of prosocial behavior are supportive.) Because prosocial behavior leads to positive relationships between individuals, psychologists have been interested in how it develops and how it might be encouraged.

Children who exhibit strong tendencies to help others in distress often tend to express distress themselves when they are hurt, troubled, or frightened.
© *Suzanne Szasz/Photo Researchers.*

Prosocial Behavior

Factors That Arouse Helping Behavior

A pioneering investigation of the prosocial behavior of preschool children was carried out by Lois Barclay Murphy (1937). She arranged for teachers in several nursery schools to keep records of sympathetic, cooperative, imitative, and aggressive forms of behavior exhibited by three-year-olds. She discovered that certain children, particularly popular children who cried loudly and dramatically, seemed to attract sympathetic responses more than others. An interesting finding was that children who displayed considerable sympathetic behavior also displayed high levels of aggressive behavior. It appeared that the same sort of tendencies that prompted a child to make an overt sympathetic response (for example, trying to comfort a sufferer with a hug) also prompted physical assertiveness in different situations. Murphy also observed the reactions of three-year-olds to a situation where a two-year-old was placed in a playpen with no toys. She found that some children remained aloof to the predicament of the two-year-old while others made a variety of attempts to help, and if these failed, made remarks intended to console the child. A final technique devised by Murphy involved asking children to respond to pictures showing children crying or in uncomfortable, dangerous, or painful situations. Most of the children revealed that they identified with the plight of the subjects of the pictures, but their interpretations were made primarily in terms of actual experiences they had had in similar situations.

In the half century since Murphy wrote her report, dozens of similar studies of prosocial behavior have been carried out. Many of these were reviewed by James H. Bryan (1975), who found that the relationship between helping behavior and aggressiveness first noted by Murphy has been corroborated repeatedly. Bryan also reported that children who expressed distress in everyday activities were more likely to help someone else in distress, suggesting that children who have strong feelings about their own plight have feelings almost as strong about the plight of others. Another factor that contributed to the inclination to help others was the amount of pleasure experienced in helping situations. Apparently, if the victim who is helped responds with gratitude, and/or if the child enjoys playing the role of "savior," helping behavior is reinforced. Bryan found that in some studies girls were reported to be more generous than boys. He speculated that this might be due to a tendency for girls to have had more experience being helped by parents and teachers. Bryan also reported that older children are more likely to help peers.

Children who express distress more likely to help others in distress

In a later review of research, with emphasis on technical and detailed analysis of results, Marian Radke-Yarrow, Carolyn Zahn-Waxler, and Michael Chapman (1983) were not as convinced as Bryan that a strong relationship between helping behavior and aggressiveness always exists. They concluded that the relationship is often complex and difficult to establish with certainty. They also concluded (on the basis of studies of overt responses) that there are no sex differences in sharing cooperation, or empathy. At the conclusion of their analysis of sex differences in all aspects of prosocial behavior, though, they note: "We would hazard the hypothesis that there are differences between boys and girls in how and when and why they perform prosocial acts and that such qualitative differences are more revealing of the nature and nurture of sex differences in prosocial behavior than are quantitative differences in frequency" (1983, p. 523). They do not supply any details of the nature of such qualitative differences, however.

Martin L. Hoffman (1978) has described stages in the development of the ability of preschoolers to identify with the distress of others. This

helps explain why older children are more likely than younger ones to
help peers. At the first stage (up to about the end of the first year),
children are unable to differentiate self from others. If ten-month-old
children observe someone else in distress, they may respond as if they
had suffered the painful experience themselves. If another child is observed to fall and cry, for example, an eleven-month-old observer may
also cry and seek comfort from a parent. At the second stage (around the
end of the first year), after children have achieved person permanence
and are aware of others as separate entities, they assume that a sufferer's feelings are identical to their own. Hoffman describes an incident
(p. 241), for instance, where a thirteen-month-old child observed an
adult looking sad and offered the person his favorite doll.

At around the age of three or so, children are able to engage in
rudimentary role taking, that is, they are sometimes able to put themselves in another person's place. Before the end of the preschool years,
most children are able to clearly recognize signs of happiness and
sadness. They realize as well that the feelings of others may differ from
their own. Children also become capable of experiencing guilt. Two-
year-olds may feel guilty when they become aware that something they
have done has caused another to suffer. After the age of three or so
children may also feel guilty when they realize that they did not act in a
sympathetic way when they should have. Sometimes, however, the
preschooler may feel sympathetic toward someone else but not know
exactly *how* to help. Hoffman suggests that the basic reason preschoolers
are unable to completely comprehend the feelings of others is due to
preoperational and egocentric thinking.

> Preschoolers recog-
> nize suffering, expe-
> rience guilt, don't
> always know how
> to help

Television and Prosocial Behavior

Several investigators have been intrigued by the question: Do children
learn *positive* forms of behavior when they watch television shows?

In his review, Bryan summarizes a number of studies in which the
impact of models on prosocial behavior has been measured. He reports
that models engaging in helping behavior who are most likely to be
imitated are perceived as warm individuals who express happiness
about their altruistic behavior (for example, "I really felt good when I
helped that little old lady pick up her groceries"). Furthermore, models
(such as parents) are more likely to encourage helping behavior if they
are consistent about practicing what they preach and if they are in a
position to dispense rewards.

> Sympathetic models
> likely to be imitated:
> warm, express
> pleasure

Aletha H. Stein and Lynette K. Friedrich (1975) were interested in the
extent to which actual television shows influence child behavior. They
arranged for three- to five-year-olds to watch violent programs ("Bat-

man" and "Superman"), neutral programs (nature and circus features), and several episodes of "Mr. Rogers' Neighborhood" (which uses a low-key approach calling attention to a variety of positive types of behavior). Simply viewing the "Mr. Rogers" episodes led to increases (in some children) in cooperative behavior, task persistence, rule acceptance, tolerance of delay, and verbalization of feelings. The children were less attentive to the "Mr. Rogers" programs than to the violent or neutral programs, which helps explain why Stein and Friedrich found that asking them to comment on what they were viewing or to act out similar situations seemed to increase the impact of the prosocial messages.

Implications of Research on Prosocial Behavior

If the various studies of prosocial behavior are examined for the purpose of developing guidelines for parents and teachers eager to encourage helpfulness and related traits in preschool children, the following suggestions emerge:

1. Invite children to talk about situations in which they have suffered in some way (to make them aware of their feelings and to encourage them to recognize similar feelings in others).
2. Express pleasure when helping someone else and encourage children to become aware of and to express the pleasure they feel when they help others.
3. Do not berate a young child for not showing sympathy in situations where you think it is justified. Unless the child has had personal experiences of a similar type, he or she may not possess the cognitive maturity to be able to comprehend how the sufferer feels.
4. Try to serve as a positive model to be imitated by exuding warmth and pleasure when helping others, being consistent, and rewarding acts of kindness.
5. Watch TV programs such as "Mr. Rogers' Neighborhood" *with* children, and encourage them to talk about the desirable actions that are depicted and perhaps also act out similar situations.

Prosocial behavior encouraged by discussion, models, pleasure

Aggressive behavior and prosocial behavior both increase during the years from two to five because children increasingly interact with others in unsupervised situations. When children get around more, do more things with more people, and acquire deeper cognitive awareness, they widen their horizons. They also become more exposed and vulnerable. As a consequence, children of this age are likely to experience fear and anxiety in new and different ways.

Emotional Factors in Personality Development

Fear

Age Trends in Fears

Arthur Jersild and F. B. Holmes (1935a) carried out a series of classic studies of fear in young children. Subsequent investigations have not been as comprehensive nor have they produced any contradictory data. Even though these studies were carried out forty years ago, therefore, they are still valuable as sources of information about the fears of young children. Jersild and Holmes collected some data by exposing subjects to fear-provoking stimuli under experimental conditions. The investigators found that from the age of two to five, children showed a decrease in fear of noise, strange objects and persons, pain, falling, sudden loss of support, and sudden movement. During the same age span, there was an increase in fear of imaginary creatures, the dark, animals, ridicule, and threat of harm (for example, from traffic, deep water, fire, or other potentially dangerous situations). These latter fears develop as children gain greater awareness of things and become capable of anticipating potential danger.

Between two and five, "physical" fears decrease; "imaginary" fears increase

Overcoming Fears

In addition to studying age trends in fear, Jersild and Holmes (1935b) examined the effectiveness of different ways of dealing with fear. They concluded that ignoring the child, ridiculing or punishing, or forcing the child into the feared situation did more harm than good. Methods that were effective in helping the child overcome fear included the following:

Fears may be overcome by explanations, example, positive reconditioning, confidence

1. **Explaining the Situation** The child who is afraid of thunder, for example, might be less frightened if told that it is caused by hot and cold clouds bumping together.
2. **Setting an Example** This is most likely to be effective if the child sees other children of the same age who are not afraid in a particular situation. If older children or adults show no fear, the two- to five-year-old may not be inclined to imitate their behavior. Three-year-olds who are afraid of large dogs, for example, may be unimpressed if their father fearlessly pats a Great Dane because they are likely to think, "If I were that big, I wouldn't be afraid either." But if a child the same age pats the dog, a three-year-old might be emboldened to try it. Albert Bandura and F. L. Menlove (1968) showed films to preschoolers who were afraid of dogs. One of the films depicted a five-year-old playing happily with a dog; another showed models of various ages interacting with dogs. Both films were effective in reduc-

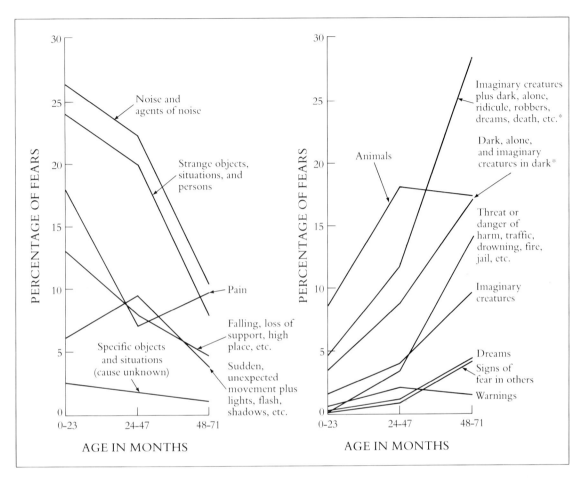

Age trends in fears based on 146 observations of children for periods of 21 days and occasional records of 117 additional children. Starred items represent a cumulative tally of two or more categories that also are depicted separately.
Reprinted by permission of the publisher from Arthur T. Jersild and Frances G. Holmes,
Children's Fears *(New York: Teachers College Press, 1935).*

FIGURE 13.1

ing fear reactions, although the multiple-model version appeared to have a greater impact, which may have been due more to seeing the fearless behavior repeated than to the different ages of the models. Perhaps most effective of all would be a film or a "live" situation in which several children of the same age as the fearful child show fearless behavior with dogs.

3. **Positive Reconditioning**   This is a technique Mary Cover Jones (1924) used to help a child overcome a fear similar to that Watson

An effective technique for preventing or minimizing some types of fears is to give ad-vance information about situations and experiences likely to make a child feel ap-prehensive or afraid.
Dani Carpenter/The Picture Cube.

produced in Albert. Albert developed the fear in the first place because he associated the rat with a frightening stimulus (a loud, unexpected sound). To help a child overcome a fear, this process can be reversed so that positive associations are substituted for negative ones. For a fear such as Albert's, for example, a feared animal might be put in a cage some distance from the child at a time ice cream and candy are served. There is the potential danger in this technique, however, that the association might develop in a way opposite to that intended. Instead of overcoming fear of the animal, the child might generalize the fear of animals to ice cream, food in general, or eating. Accordingly, it may be preferable simply to let the child adapt to the feared object. For example, a caged animal might be put in a far corner of the room where a child is playing. Over a period of time the child might be allowed to approach the cage and examine the animal.

4. **Helping the Child Gain Confidence in Dealing with the Feared Object or Situation**   Perhaps the most effective way to help a child overcome a fear is to teach him or her to become competent in dealing with it. A child who is afraid of the dark, for example, might be supplied with a night light wired to a bedside switch. When the switch is pushed, the child, in effect, controls the dark. Or a child who is fearful of dogs might be given a puppy and helped to train it.

Preventing Fears

As part of their studies of fear, Jersild and Holmes also analyzed how fears might be prevented from developing in the first place. They found that a common factor in many of the fears of young children was the sudden or unexpected nature of a stimulus. Suppose, for example, a mother or father decides to clean the living room floor in the presence of a young child who has not been exposed to a vacuum cleaner. If, without warning, the vacuum is turned on a few feet away from the child, the unexpected loud noise might easily lead to a fear reaction. A more prudent course of action would be to turn on the vacuum in another room and gradually move it closer to the child. Or suppose a relative gives a two-year-old a jack-in-the-box for Christmas. If the child is permitted to unlatch the top the first time, the doll figure that suddenly pops up may cause fear of the toy. A better course of action would be to hold the toy for the child and release the top slowly at first. Once the child understands how it works, the doll can be popped up more quickly. Under these circumstances, the child is more likely to delight in playing with the toy.

The most difficult variation of giving a warning occurs when an element of pain may be involved. A common example is a visit to the doctor or dentist. If the parents say "It won't hurt a bit" and it does hurt, children may lose faith in the parents and the doctor and generalize their fear to all situations involving medical treatment. On the other hand, if the parents go too far in describing how much it is going to hurt, children may become so tense the pain will be magnified.

If a child must undergo surgery, it is now standard practice in many hospitals to take children on a dry run of the entire procedure the day before, explaining what will be done, where they will go, how they will feel when it is over, and what can be done to control pain. This policy was established when it was discovered thirty or so years ago that some children who went into surgery unprepared and had to spend several days in a hospital (at a time when visiting hours were severely restricted) were haunted by the experience the rest of their lives.

Another aspect of fear prevention was neatly illustrated by an experiment carried out by D. G. J. Schramm (1935). Young children were placed in a chair so that their movements were restricted. Then, one at a time, a frog, a rabbit, a rat, and a parakeet were placed on a tray that was moved toward the children. Almost all of the children acted afraid, and some were terrified. A different group of children the same age were then allowed to roam around a room where the same animals were placed in the middle of a table. The children could approach or ignore them as they wished. None of these children showed any fear. These results suggest that if parents allow children to approach a potentially frightening situation in their own way and at their own pace, problems might be minimized.

Preventing fears by allowing freedom to explore

But if children feel they are trapped and have no way of avoiding the situation thrust upon them, even a relatively innocuous object or experience may induce a panic reaction. A well-meaning father, for example, was pushing his three-year-old daughter (who was apprehensive about dogs) in the miniature fire engine she had inherited from an older brother. A large, amiable neighborhood dog ambled onto the scene, and the father decided this was a golden opportunity to help his daughter learn to like dogs. He energetically pushed the fire engine toward the dog. The little girl started to scream and tried to climb out, but her father shoved her back, telling her all the while about the "nice doggie." By the time they were close to the dog the little girl was screaming uncontrollably, and the puzzled father had to carry her into the house, where it took the mother twenty minutes to calm her down. If he had been aware of the Schramm study, he might have realized that his daughter felt helpless, while she saw the dog as powerful. If the father had held the dog on a leash and permitted the daughter to approach the controlled animal on her own, she might have felt that *she*, and not the dog, was in control of the situation.

Anxiety

The Nature of Anxiety

Jersild and Holmes concluded that perhaps the best fear preventative was the development of a sense of security. One way to define security is as an absence of anxiety. Jersild (1968, pp. 348–365) has pointed out some key differences between fear and anxiety. He notes that fear is usually a reasonably rational (legitimate) response to a tangible threat or danger. Anxiety, on the other hand, involves inner conflict that may appear irrational to others. Furthermore, fears are likely to disappear if children learn how to handle them. But anxiety may persist even after children gain knowledge and experience; they must gain insight into the "inner" danger and develop confidence in their ability to handle it.

Explanations of Anxiety

In Freud's view, the early dependency of the child on the mother accounted much for anxiety. He attributed stranger and separation anxiety to the child's fear of losing the love and protection of the mother. Freud also proposed that anxiety may be produced by conflicts between the id, ego, and superego. A child may experience anxiety when confronted by a conflict between a need for gratification and conditions in the environment that limit its satisfaction. A child in a store, for example, whose parents have said they will not buy a much desired toy may suffer anxiety in the struggle between the desire to steal the toy and awareness that it is wrong to take things without paying for them.

Still another explanation for causes of anxiety is provided by Erikson's description of the stages of autonomy versus doubt and initiative versus guilt. Two-year-olds are in the process of establishing themselves as autonomous individuals. They need to develop feelings of independence as they assume responsibility for their own behavior. But there are bound to be experiences that cause these budding individualists to doubt their ability to handle everything on their own. Despite occasional setbacks and moments of doubt, however, most three-year-olds remain undaunted and are eager to initiate activities and explore new experiences. If preschoolers are allowed to try out their powers and if their parents are patient in answering questions, Erikson suggests, the children will develop a sense of initiative and self-confidence. If children are made to feel their questions and activities are a nuisance, they may feel guilty about trying to do things on their own and experience anxiety.

Minimizing Anxiety

If the observations of Freud and Erikson are taken into account, the following factors can be listed as possible causes of anxiety in two- to five-year-olds: fear of losing love and protection of the mother; conflict between desires and social codes and restrictions; concern about physical and psychological safety; lack of acceptance by others; threats to self-esteem; experiencing too much shame or doubt; and being made to feel guilty about trying to do things on one's own. The following guidelines might be offered as ways to minimize the development of anxiety in children:

Anxiety may be minimized by providing support, satisfying needs, encouraging independence

Avoid withholding love as a means of punishment for misbehavior.

Continue to provide support and protection even as the child makes efforts to assert independence.

Help children cope with conflicts between desires and restrictions. (If a child takes something from a store without paying for it, for example, explain gently but firmly why the object must be returned or paid for, instead of berating or punishing the child.)

Do everything possible to make the child feel secure, not only by arranging for physical safety but also by establishing the feeling that parents are always available to provide love and support. Give extra support and reassurance when a child has unfortunate or belittling experiences with peers.

Guard against making a child feel excessively ashamed of misdeeds.

Be patient when a child is eager to try doing things alone and do not provide assistance unless it is asked for or absolutely essential.

Respond positively to expressions of initiative even if these cause extra effort and bother for older members of a household.

Set realistic goals for a child and avoid being hypercritical of incomplete achievement.

(Changes in personality development during the years from six to twelve are discussed in Chapter 17, starting on page 505.)

Summary

1. One of the most noticeable aspects of personality development between two and five is the appearance of **sex-typed** behavior. As a result of his intensive studies of preschool children, Robert Sears concluded that boys, in particular, develop a **cognitive map** of sex roles starting around the age of three. Albert Bandura, another prominent social learning theorist, noted that children imitate the behavior of multiple models as they acquire sex-typed behavior. Lawrence Kohlberg stressed that cognitive awareness and observation of sex-typed behavior lead to imitation.

2. Evidence favoring biological influences on sex-typed behavior was presented by John Money and Anke Ehrhardt, who reported that girls who had received doses of hormones that led to production of the male sex hormone androgen developed masculine traits despite being treated as girls. There are numerous environmental factors, however, that shape sex-stereotyped behavior. Starting in infancy, for instance, boys and girls are treated differently. Throughout their lives, children repeatedly observe male characters on television programs functioning as authority figures while females are depicted as helpers.

3. There is quite consistent evidence that boys are more aggressive than girls. At least some of the greater aggressiveness of males can be traced to biological factors. At the same time, boys are encouraged to be aggressive, and they observe many aggressive male models, whom they may imitate.

4. Bandura's studies of the tendency for frustrated children to imitate aggressive acts led to the hypothesis that viewing violence on television leads to aggressive behavior. Analyses of television programs reveal that violent acts are extremely frequent, that painful or lethal consequences are minimized, and that "good guys" resort to violence as much as "bad guys." There is now considerable research support for the conclusion that watching violent acts on television increases tendencies toward aggression and diminishes sensitivity to the consequences of aggression. Children also acquire tendencies toward aggressive behavior when they observe actual incidents, imitate them, and are reinforced by gaining desired ends through aggressive behavior.

5. During the preschool years children spontaneously exhibit tendencies toward **prosocial** behavior, offering help and sympathy to others. Children who express distress themselves appear to be more likely to help others in distress. Preschool children recognize suffering, experience guilt if they have hurt others, and may sometimes want to help without knowing exactly how to do it. Parents who want to encourage prosocial behavior should discuss situations involving pain and pleasure with their children, serve as sympathetic models, and express pleasure when helping others.

6. Between the years of two and five, "physical" fears (e.g., noise, falling) decrease, but "imaginary" fears (e.g., imaginary creatures, threats of harm) increase. Parents may help children overcome fears by supplying explanations, setting a fearless example, associating the feared object with something pleasant (*positive reconditioning*), and building the child's confidence in being able to handle feared situations. It also seems preferable to permit children to explore new situations at their own pace and in their own way.

7. Anxiety, which involves inner conflicts and is less rational than fear, may be minimized if children are given support, if their basic needs are satisfied, and if they are encouraged to be independent.

Suggestions
for
Further
Study

Sex-typed Behavior

For information about research on ways sex stereotypes are encouraged in our society, consult "Sex-typing" by Aletha Huston in *Socialization, Personality, and Social Development,* edited by E. Mavis Hetherington, Volume IV of the *Handbook of Child Psychology* (4th ed., 1983), edited by Paul H. Mussen.

Aggression

For information about research on aggression, peruse "The Development of Aggression" by Ross D. Parke and Ronald G. Slaby in the same volume of the *Handbook of Child Psychology* noted above. A concise summary of research on television as a socializer of aggression begins on page 593 of the Parke and Slaby chapter.

Checking on the Impact of Television

To get some firsthand impressions of ways television viewing influences sex-typed and aggressive behavior, you might ask some young children to name their favorite television programs. Then make it a point to watch those programs. As you watch, record the following impressions and types of information:

What sorts of roles do male and female characters play?

How are males and females depicted in commercials?

In both programs and commercials, are males presented as authority figures who get things done and females as helpers who admire masculine accomplishments?

How many violent acts carried out by "good guys" and "bad guys" are depicted?

What happens to the victims of violent acts? Do they act as if they are suffering or have been severely injured (if not presumably dead), or do they just appear to be rendered unconscious?

Were the violent acts justified, or were nonviolent ways of taking care of the situation ignored by the persons who used violence?

Did you feel any sympathy for the victims of the violent acts as you watched what happened to them?

Prosocial Behavior

Even though written in 1937, *Social Behavior and Child Personality* by Lois Barclay Murphy still provides insights into the early development of sympathy for others. For a review of recent research on prosocial behavior, see "Children's Cooperative and Helping Behaviors" by J. H. Bryan in *Review of Child Development Research*, 1975, *5*, edited by E. M. Hetherington; "The Development of Social Cognition" by Carolyn U. Shantz in the same volume; or "Empathy, Role-Taking, Guilt, and Development of Altruistic Motives" by Martin L. Hoffman in *Moral Development and Behavior* (1976), edited by Thomas Lickona. A quite technical summary of research is presented in "Children's Prosocial Dispositions and Behavior" by Marian Radke-Yarrow, Carolyn Zahn-Waxler, and Michael Chapman in *Socialization, Personality, and Social Development*, edited by E. Mavis Hetherington, Volume IV of the *Handbook of Child Psychology* (4th ed., 1983), edited by Paul H. Mussen.

Fear, Anxiety, and Emotional Development

If you would like more information about fear and anxiety in children, consult the review of studies on pages 863–883 in "Emotional Development" by Arthur Jersild, Chapter 14 in the *Manual of Child Psychology* (2nd ed., 1954). More recent research is reviewed and discussed in *The Development of Affect* (1978), edited by Michael Lewis and Leonard A. Rosenblum.

Use of operant conditioning techniques to help children overcome fears is described in "Behavioral Treatment of Children's Fears: A Review" by A. M. Graziano and others in *Psychological Bulletin*, 1979, *86*, 804–830.

PART 5

SIX TO TWELVE

KEY POINTS

Growth and Physiological Development

Girls mature at more rapid rate, some adolescents complete growth before others start

Growth spurt in girls two years earlier than in boys

Average age of puberty: girls, 12.5; boys, 14

Early-maturing girls tall early, shorter and heavier later

Exercise during elementary school years contributes to cardiovascular health

Boys who are active, extroverted, daring, and athletic likely to be accident prone

Relationships Between Puberty and Sex Typing

Contemporary elementary school girls aspire to a variety of careers

Varying Conclusions Regarding Sex-typed Behavior

Well-established sex differences: girls more verbal; boys better in math, more aggressive

Some evidence that boys more dominant, curious; girls more fearful, compliant

Parents may not be aware they are shaping sex-stereotyped behavior

Boys should be encouraged to become sensitive, girls to desire to achieve

CHAPTER 14

SIX TO TWELVE

PHYSICAL DEVELOPMENT

*D*uring the elementary school years physical maturation and growth lead to significant changes in appearance and behavior. Children grow rapidly and the proportions of the various parts of the body alter to make twelve-year-olds appear much more mature than six-year-olds. Differences in the physiques of males and females become more noticeable, and girls who reach puberty before they leave the sixth grade become directly aware of biological differences between the sexes. Physical changes, in turn, influence social relationships between boys and girls and also have an impact on emerging concepts of self. Because physiological changes at the time of puberty exert an increasing influence on male-female relationships and the formation of identity, certain topics discussed earlier under headings of social and personality development will be analyzed in this chapter (and later chapters) on physical development.

Growth and Physiological Development

A Growth Spurt Precedes Puberty

J. M. Tanner (1970, 1972), a leading authority on physiological development, has observed that there are two significant facts that stand out about human biological development. The first is that girls mature at a more rapid rate, on the average, than boys. The second is that some individuals complete their adolescent development before others start theirs. The first of these points can be illustrated by a hypothetical demonstration. If you were to ask teachers of all of the grades in an elementary school to have their pupils line up in order from shortest to tallest along the fence of the playground, you would become aware of several things. First of all, you would probably notice increasing differences between extremes in height and variations in body build. Next, you might notice that many girls would be at the tall end of the fifth- and sixth-grade lines. Many boys, however, would be at the tall end of the other lines. Finally, you might realize that some of the girls in the upper-grade lines looked substantially more mature than any other children on the playground. The tendency for girls to be taller (and to look more mature) starting around the fifth grade is due to a growth spurt just before the advent of puberty. Because girls mature at a more rapid rate than boys, they experience their growth spurt about two years earlier (Tanner, 1970). While the most obvious manifestations of the growth spurt are an increase in height and greater maturity of appearance, the physiological changes that follow the spurt are of greater significance. The average age at which American girls reach menarche (begin menstruation) is between twelve and thirteen, with a range from nine to sixteen. For boys the average age of puberty is fourteen, with a range from eleven to eighteen. Many American girls, therefore, reach puberty before they finish the sixth grade.

Girls mature at more rapid rate, some adolescents complete growth before others start

Growth spurt in girls two years earlier than in boys

Average age of puberty: girls, 12.5; boys, 14

The growth spurt in girls occurs about two years earlier than it does in boys. Around the sixth or seventh grade, therefore, boys may feel (and be) dwarfed by dance partners.
© *Elizabeth Crews.*

Differences in Rate of Maturation

Differences in rate of maturation may have a significant impact on several aspects of behavior because many of the physiological changes that accompany maturity are obvious, while others trigger a variety of changes and reactions. The first menstrual period may be a difficult and traumatic experience for a girl, particularly if she has not been provided with information about sexual maturity. The appearance of secondary sexual characteristics influences the reactions of peers, parents, and teachers. (**Secondary** sex characteristics include breast development, rounded hips, and the appearance of a waistline in girls; broadening of the shoulders and replacement of fat with muscle tissue in boys. In both sexes, pubic, axillary [armpit], facial and body hair appear; the texture of the skin changes, and the voice deepens. Changes in the sex organs are referred to as **primary** sexual characteristics.) The reactions of others, in turn, influence the budding adolescent's self-concept.

The growth spurt and the appearance of the primary and secondary sexual characteristics follow such a standard pattern and individual children tend to be so faithful to a fast, average, or slow rate of maturation, that the timing of maturation is generally considered to be due to genetic factors. However, it may also be influenced by nutrition. Evidence demonstrating the importance of nutrition is provided by a secular trend in sexual maturity: the average age of menarche in this country has occurred about two months earlier each decade over the last fifty years. It appears, however, that the average age of menarche is not likely to get much lower than it is at present (Tanner, 1970).

Stanley M. Garn (1980) summarizes evidence indicating that a "fast" growth pattern is likely to lead to different results than a "slow" growth pattern. Early-maturing girls, for instance, tend to be taller earlier in life but shorter as adults, apparently because under a rapid rate pattern, growth stops earlier than average. Slow-maturing girls get off to a "delayed" start, but continue to grow over a longer period of time and thus end up taller than average. Early-maturing girls not only are tall early and short later; they also tend to be fatter and heavier as adolescents and adults. By contrast, women who are slender when mature often report that they reached puberty later than average. These differences are also reflected by the ultimate height and weight of children eventually born to early- and late-maturing females. Early-maturing women tend to have daughters and sons who are early maturers and who are taller from infancy through adolescence, but shorter as adults. Late-maturing women tend to have children with an opposite pattern. (An interesting aspect of this tendency is that sons seem to resemble early- and late-maturing mothers in ultimate height and weight more than daughters.)

Early-maturing girls tall early, shorter and heavier later

It appears, therefore, that one cause of obesity is the timing of puberty for both mothers and their children. Thus an elementary school girl who is the tallest pupil in her sixth-grade class may have had an early-maturing mother with tendencies toward obesity. If so, she is likely to repeat that same pattern.

Aspects of Growth

While overall growth during middle childhood is quite steady, different parts of the body do not always grow in synchrony. Uneven growth of the long bones and the muscles supporting them may cause "growing pains," and it is not unusual for children to awaken in the night complaining of leg cramps. Children may also think of themselves as ugly ducklings if one part of their anatomy is, for a time, disproportionate (Schuster, 1980). Uneven growth also characterizes the development of individual organs. Asymmetrical growth of the eyeball may cause a child to be nearsighted at one point and farsighted at another. Recent neurological research suggests that brain growth, too, is uneven. Two major spurts in brain growth are believed to occur during middle childhood, one between six and eight years and another between ten and twelve years (Epstein, 1979). The timing of these growth spurts corresponds to the onset of concrete and formal operational thought, and Epstein believes these spurts are the biological basis for the stages of cognitive development described by Piaget. Increases in the complexity of neural networks that occur during these two periods are due principally to **myelination,** the process of coating nerve fibers with a fatty substance called myelin. Myelin insulates nerve impulses from interference from unrelated signals and speeds up neural transmission.

Motor Skills and Activities

Myelination, coupled with the increased size and capacity of the heart, contributes to the improved motor abilities of six- to twelve-year-olds. Initially, the large muscle (gross motor) abilities are far superior to the small muscle (fine motor) skills. Most children can run and ride a tricycle before they can tie their shoes and write legibly. Both gross and fine motor abilities improve gradually during middle childhood, and the rate of skill development is approximately the same for both sexes. Girls do not perform quite as well as boys on tests of common physical skills (throwing, catching, jumping, running), but these differences are not statistically significant and probably reflect differing opportunities for

During the elementary school years children should be encouraged to be active in order to develop physical skills and strengthen their cardiovascular systems.
© *Elizabeth Crews.*

practice rather than differing potentials. In addition to becoming better organized, children's physical activities become more purposeful. They run not just for the sake of running, but to reach a base or increase their speed in the fifty-yard dash. Because they are less egocentric and are able to understand and follow rules, they are able to sustain team games, which require cooperation. The benefits of improved physical coordination are not confined to the playground. In the classroom, children's handwriting becomes more uniform and their letters smaller in size. Reading skills improve as their eyes become more proficient at holding a line as they scan left to right. Some preschool children have sufficient finger coordination to begin playing a musical instrument. Learning to read music, however, will depend more on cognitive than psychomotor skills.

The Importance of Exercise

Activity levels during middle childhood vary considerably. Some children are continually moving—walking, running, riding bikes, playing sports—while others are more sedentary, preferring fine motor activities such as playing a musical instrument or building models. In recent years physicians and physiologists have demonstrated that the spontaneous physical activity of many young children, especially girls, is not of sufficient intensity and duration to facilitate cardiovascular health (e.g., Gilliam, Freedson, Geenen, and Shahraray, 1981), and risk factors associated with coronary heart disease have been found in substantial numbers of elementary school children. All children, regardless of their interests or abilities, need regular physical exercise. It increases coordination, strength, and endurance, and it promotes better sleeping and eating patterns.

Exercise during elementary school years contributes to cardiovascular health

Accident Proneness

A final point about physical development during the elementary school years centers on accident proneness. By the time they enter school, both boys and girls have developed considerable physical proficiency, to the point that they enjoy challenging physical activities. (Just watch what happens on an elementary school playground when the midmorning recess bell rings and the pupils stampede out of their rooms.) At the same time, children at these grade levels are not always able to anticipate consequences (because they are not yet formal thinkers). As a result of these two sets of factors, elementary grade children are particularly likely to have accidents of various kinds. Some children, however, appear to be much more accident prone than others.

One of the most comprehensive studies of accident proneness (Manheimer and Mellinger, 1967) produced the following portrait of a child most likely to end up in a hospital emergency room: a boy with a high activity level, an extroverted personality, and tendencies toward independence, exploration, daring, roughhousing, and athletic proficiency. Additional factors are tendencies toward aggressiveness with peers and toward having discipline problems in school. Taken together, these various characteristics suggest that children who have repeated accidents are more likely than their classmates to expose themselves to risky situations and are less able to cope with them once they have committed themselves.

Boys who are active, extroverted, daring, and athletic likely to be accident prone

While parents and teachers may be able to prevent some accidents to children with the tendencies just summarized, they will not be able to control all of a child's behavior. Parents can forbid a boy to use savings to purchase a secondhand trail bike with a fifty-horsepower engine, for instance, but they can't stop him from a spontaneous impulse to see how far he can propel himself off a swing in a neighbor's backyard. Accordingly, some parents of accident-prone boys have made deals with their sons: if you don't have an accident that requires medical attention during the next 6 months, we will give you five dollars. Sometimes this works, sometimes it doesn't, but at least some parents have felt it was worth a try.

The fact that boys are much more likely than girls to be accident prone is just one manifestation of the increasing impact of physiological factors on behavior. Thus, it is appropriate to discuss sex-typed behavior in this chapter on physical development.

Relationships Between Puberty and Sex Typing

As noted earlier, the beginning of menstruation is bound to cause a girl to become aware of the impact of sexual maturity. She will not only begin to develop secondary sex characteristics that will cause her to appear more feminine; she may also experience a changed attitude toward boys. If Money and Ehrhardt (1972) are correct in generalizing from the results of their studies of androgenized girls (summarized in Chapter 13), changes in the production of sex hormones at puberty will cause girls to think increasingly about romantic attachments, marriage, and having children. The interest of girls in the housewife-mother role, however, is also strongly influenced by observation, imitation, and indoctrination.

Factors that begin to influence sex-typed behavior starting in the preschool years continue to shape behavior more intensely during the elementary school years. Cognitive awareness of male and female behavior, which Kohlberg (1966) suggests is established by the age of five, becomes more pervasive. The observation and imitation of male and female models, which was demonstrated by Bandura and his colleagues (1963a), also continues. Furthermore, many elementary school texts and other books depict boys and girls engaging in different activities. C. Tavris and C. Offir (1977), for example, describe the results of a survey of children's books carried out in 1972: "Boys make things. They rely on their wits to solve problems. They are curious, clever, and adventurous. They achieve; they make money. Girls and women are incompetent and fearful. They ask other people to solve their problems for them. . . . In story after story, girls are the onlookers, the cheerleaders" (p. 177).

The impact of such indoctrination was revealed in interviews carried out by W. R. Looft (1971). Looft asked first and second graders what they would like to be when they grew up. Of the thirty-three boys who responded, nine chose football player and four chose policeman. Less frequent nominations went to doctor, dentist, priest, pilot, and astronaut. Of the thirty-three girls who responded, fourteen chose nurse and eleven chose teacher. Less frequently mentioned were mother, stewardess, and salesgirl. *One* girl said she would like to be a doctor.

Starting in the early 1970s, various feminist groups encouraged school districts to select texts that did not reinforce such sex stereotypes. But children still read other books and watch television for several hours a day. (In a survey made in 1974, Sternglanz and Serbin reported that males on television programs were portrayed as aggressive, constructive, and helpful; females as deferential and passive.) Although many television series now feature women who possess traits equal to or exceeding those of the most daring, brilliant, and resourceful men (or supermen), it is possible that commercials may at least partially counteract the impact of such shows. Many of the women depicted in commercials are primarily interested in making themselves attractive to males. Even more are made to appear singlemindedly dedicated to cleaning house, washing clothes, and generally making life as comfortable as possible for husbands and children.

To determine if the women's liberation movement had overcome some of the influence of "sexist" books, television commercials, and the like on career choices, R. F. Biehler repeated the Looft survey (extending it through the sixth grade) in 1979. The career choices of children attending a middle-income elementary school in a medium-sized California city are indicated in Table 14.1. As you can see, by the end of the 1970s, girls appear to have overcome many sex-stereotyped ideas about careers for women. Only one girl specified "housekeeping" (which may or may not be the same as "homemaker") and only one mentioned being a mother, and both of these girls took pains to point out that they intended to pursue a career as well. While teacher and nurse were still popular choices for girls at the end of the 1970s, girls also expressed interest in a wide variety of other occupations, including many that were traditionally considered to be men's jobs (for example, nuclear scientist). Being a professional athlete was the most popular choice for boys, which is probably traceable to the impact of televised sports coverage.

Contemporary elementary school girls aspire to a variety of careers

Thus, some of the same general trends reported by Looft in 1971 still seemed to prevail in 1979. The interest of girls in teaching and nursing careers might be attributed as much to mature and realistic appraisals of career opportunities, though, as to the impact of sex stereotypes. In terms of actual job opportunities, particularly for females who hope to combine motherhood and a career, teaching and nursing are very sensible choices. The career choices of boys, by contrast, are much less realistic and seem to reflect a romanticized conception of the "macho"

TABLE 14.1

CAREER CHOICES OF ELEMENTARY SCHOOL CHILDREN

	Boys	Girls
1st Grade	Professional athlete (or coach) 6 Race car driver 5 Police officer 4 Truck driver 3 Construction worker 3 Mechanic, fireman, tree trimmer, welder, computer operator, diamond worker, balloon man at the zoo	Nurse 10 Teacher 7 Ballerina 2 Policewoman 2 Ice skater, person who sells cosmetics
2nd Grade	Motorcycle racer 6 Scientist 5 Professional athlete 4 Police officer 4 Truck driver 2 UPS driver 2 Artist 2 Astronaut 2 Inventor 2 Pilot, cowboy, coffee maker, store clerk, little boy	Teacher 5 Ice skater 4 Artist 3 Jockey 2 Archaeologist, nutritionist, dancer, missionary, ice cream store owner, plant nursery owner, don't know
3rd Grade	Professional athlete 2 Lawyer 2 Doctor, architect, business manager, spy, house builder, physics (fisecx) teacher, army officer, chef, fence builder	Teacher 5 Gymnast 2 Movie actress 2 Nurse 2 Veterinarian 2 Horse trainer 2 Artist, college professor, jockey, ice skater, donut maker, zoo keeper, dental assistant, housekeeper (and artist), paleontologist (and baseball player and mother)
4th Grade	Professional athlete 7 Police officer 5 Truck driver 4 Builder 2 Race car driver 2 Stuntman 2 Scientist 2 Fireman 2 Cowboy, lumberjack, sky diver, photographer, meter reader, detective, my self	Nurse 9 Teacher 6 Veterinarian 4 Stewardess 3 Secretary 2 Singer 2 Movie star 2 Gymnast 2 Dancer, jockey, dental assistant, scientist, nutritionist, plant nursery owner, president (or doctor)

TABLE 14.1
CAREER CHOICES OF ELEMENTARY SCHOOL CHILDREN *(cont.)*

	Boys	**Girls**
5th Grade	Professional athlete 4 Truck driver 2 Police officer 2 Cartoonist 2 Race car driver, motorcycle racer, driver of street sweeper, bus driver, Air Force pilot, artist, doctor, lawyer, owner of a Mercedes Benz, actor, cabinetmaker, glass blower, space scientist, I think I am too young to know	Teacher 9 Actress, model, singer 5 Veterinarian 4 Jockey 2 Psychologist 2 Lawyer, hairdresser, horse trainer, scientist, nurse, head waitress, athlete, rancher, nuclear scientist, piano teacher
6th Grade	Professional athlete 7 Police officer 3 Architect 3 Veterinarian 2 Contractor 2 Racing car driver, engineer, doctor, demolition expert, forest ranger, artist, author, astronomer, movie star, Playboy photographer	Veterinarian 4 Stewardess 4 Horse trainer 2 Artist 2 Surgeon, nurse, scientist, teacher, model, mechanic, pilot, policewoman, lawyer (and hairdresser on the side), beautician (butishion), owner of an answering service

Source: Unpublished study by R. F. Biehler. Information collected by Lotys Gibb and the teachers of Citrus Elementary School, Chico, California.

image. Only a tiny proportion of the elementary school boys who aspire to play professional football or make a living racing motorcycles, for instance, will actually pursue those careers. The hypothesis that girls are more realistic is supported by the greater tendency for them to hedge their bets. Girls in 1979 were more likely than boys (by a ratio of about five to one) to say that they wanted to be, for example, an actress *or* a beautician.

Varying Conclusions Regarding Sex-typed Behavior

Since sex-typed behavior becomes more apparent in the elementary school years than at earlier stages of development, this is an appropriate place to summarize research and conclusions relating to differences in the behavior of males and females. One of the most complete summaries of research on sex differences was carried out by Eleanor Maccoby and Carol Jacklin (1974), who examined sixteen hundred studies published between 1966 and 1973. They summarized their conclusions (pp. 349–352) under three headings:

Well-established sex differences: girls more verbal; boys better in math, more aggressive

Well-established differences: girls excel in verbal ability; boys excel in visual-spatial ability and mathematical ability, and are more aggressive.

Types of behavior where there is insufficient evidence to clearly establish sex differences: tactile sensitivity; fear, timidity, and anxiety; activity level; competitiveness; dominance; compliance; nurturance and "maternal" behavior.

Types of behavior where the evidence suggests that no sex differences exist: sociability, suggestibility, self-esteem, complex cognitive abilities, ability to analyze problems, relative impact of heredity and experiences on personality development, motivation toward achievement, and auditory or visual orientation.

Maccoby and Jacklin also concluded that there was little evidence that parents treat girls and boys in different ways (p. 338).

Jeanne H. Block (1976) analyzed many of the same studies as Maccoby and Jacklin, as well as their interpretations, and came to some different conclusions. Block felt that some of the inferences made by Maccoby and Jacklin could be questioned for the following reasons (pp. 289–298): they may have been too demanding in deciding when evidence was conclusive or indicative of tentative differences; Maccoby and Jacklin did not take into account certain significant studies that might have altered some of their conclusions; and many of the studies surveyed were done on preschool children, whose sex-typed behavior is not clearly established.

After making her own analysis, Block concluded that there is some, although not conclusive, evidence that the following sex differences exist:

Boys are better at solving insight problems.

Some evidence that boys more dominant, curious; girls more fearful, compliant

Boys are more dominant and have a stronger, more potent, self-concept.

Boys are more curious, active, and impulsive.

Girls express more fear and are more susceptible to anxiety.

Girls seek more help and reassurance.

Girls are more compliant with adults (at early ages).

Even when an element of control is established, such as in the Money and Ehrhardt investigation of androgenized girls (summarized in Chapter 13), it is not possible to determine the causes of such types of behav-

ior. Money and Ehrhardt suggest that the brain of each child is programmed to release hormones in certain ways. They believe that this
accounts for some of the differences between the behavior of males and
females. But all types of behavior are also shaped by observation of
models, experiences, reinforcement, and cultural expectations. Maccoby
and Jacklin did not find sufficient scientific evidence to support the view
that parents treat boys and girls in different ways, but other researchers
have come to different conclusions. Inge Broverman and several associates (1972), for example, summarized studies where adults were
asked to describe their perceptions of "typical" masculine and feminine
traits. Broverman and her colleagues found strong consensus from
groups of respondents who differed in sex, age, religion, marital status,
and educational level: typical masculine traits centered on competence,
rationality, and assertiveness; typical feminine traits reflected warmth
and expressiveness. Because these stereotyped conceptions were considered desirable to the majority of men and women from all types of
backgrounds, it would seem reasonable to expect that boys and girls
would be treated differently by their parents. The hypothesis that
stereotyped views of masculinity and femininity lead to differential
treatment of daughters and sons is supported, in fact, by a number of
research investigations.

In her reanalysis of the research evaluated by Maccoby and Jacklin,
Block concluded that the studies on which they based their conclusions
regarding parental socialization practices featured very young children.
Block also found that the measures used were inappropriate or too
broadly defined. Support for Block's contention is provided by Beverly I.
Fagot (1978), who observed preschoolers and their parents interacting in
their homes. She concluded that parents often responded negatively
when girls engaged in physical or athletic activities, but responded positively when girls engaged in dependent, adult-oriented behavior. She
also found that girls asked for help three times more frequently than
boys. Fagot speculates that the tendency for parents to respond positively to requests for help from girls, but not from boys, strengthens
dependent behavior in girls and weakens it in boys. Furthermore, the
parents themselves were not aware that they responded differently to
daughter and son requests for help. Nor were the parents aware that
they responded negatively when girls manipulated objects and that they
permitted boys to explore more. Fagot concluded that it is only when the
subtleties of parent-child interactions are taken into account that differences in socialization practices become clear.

In her reanalysis of studies of socialization, Block concluded that both
mothers and fathers emphasize achievement, competition, and independence in boys and stress warmth and physical closeness in dealing
with girls. In addition, parents seem to discourage rough-and-tumble

Parents may not be
aware they are
shaping sex-stereo-
typed behavior

Parents may reduce the tendency for children to accept sex-role stereotypes if they occasionally demonstrate their willingness to engage in activities traditionally associated with the opposite sex.
Mark Antman/The Image Works.

play in daughters, are reluctant to punish them, and encourage them to think more about life. These conclusions reaffirmed observations Block had made in an earlier article on sex typing. After reviewing studies of socialization practices, Block (1973) concluded that boys in our society are encouraged to achieve and be competitive, to control expression of feelings, and to conform to rules. Girls, on the other hand, are encouraged to develop close interpersonal relationships, talk about their troubles, show affection, and give comfort to others. (If you will re-examine Table 14.1 you will note that many of the occupational choices of elementary school boys center on achievement and competition and that many of the choices of girls reflect concern for others.)

In discussing the significance of the differential treatment of boys and girls in our society, Block notes that compared with adults in other technological societies, Americans put more emphasis on sex typing, with particular stress on competitive achievement in males. Americans also seem less concerned about controlling aggression in males. She points out that because of current trends in our society, it would be desirable for children to acquire a conception of sex roles that combines what are presently identified by many people as masculine *or* feminine traits. Boys would seem likely to benefit, for instance, if they became more sensitive to the needs of others. Many girls would benefit if they were encouraged to be less docile and more achievement-oriented. Block also suggests that too much stress on traditional sex-appropriate behavior inhibits introspection and self-evaluation and impedes the development of the ego and of social maturity. She concludes, however, that because of the extent to which sex stereotypes are entrenched in the minds of most Americans (as reported by Broverman and her associates), it may be difficult for children in our society, particularly girls, to develop flexible conceptions of sex-appropriate behavior. Accordingly, parents and teachers might make efforts to encourage elementary school children of both sexes to achieve a balance between self-assertiveness and concern for and relations with others. (Changes in physical development during adolescence and youth are discussed in Chapter 18, beginning on page 531.)

> Boys should be encouraged to become sensitive, girls to desire to achieve

Summary

1. Two facts stand out about human biological development. The first is that girls mature at a more rapid rate than boys. The second is that some individuals have completed their adolescent development before others have started theirs. A growth spurt that precedes puberty occurs in girls about two years earlier than in boys. The average age of puberty for American females is 12.5 years; for boys it is 14 years. Girls who mature early tend to be taller in their teens but shorter and heavier as adults.

2. During the elementary school years, children should be encouraged to engage in physical activities since there is evidence that many young children, especially girls, do not exercise sufficiently to facilitate cardiovascular health. Some children, however, tend to overindulge in physical activity in the sense that they engage in potentially dangerous forms of behavior. Boys who are active, extroverted, daring, and athletic are most likely to be accident prone.

3. The growth spurt and the fact that some elementary school girls achieve puberty increase awareness of sex differences, which, in turn, tends to make children more aware of sex-typed behavior. In terms of early career aspirations, though, there is some evidence that

contemporary American girls are eager to enter a variety of occupations not tied to traditional sex-role patterns.

4. Hundreds of studies of sex differences in various types of behavior have been published. Well-established differences are that girls are more verbal whereas boys are better in math and are more aggressive. There is also some evidence that boys are more dominant and curious, and girls are more fearful and compliant.

5. Parents and teachers often are not aware that they are shaping sex-stereotyped behavior by the way they respond to the activities of boys and girls. It would be advantageous if adults tried to guard against such tendencies and at the same time encouraged boys to become more sensitive to the needs and feelings of others and girls to become more achievement oriented.

Suggestions for Further Study

Physical Development

Perhaps the leading authority on physical development, particularly at the time of puberty, is J. M. Tanner. He describes aspects of adolescent development in "Physical Growth," Chapter 2 in *Carmichael's Manual of Child Psychology* (Volume 1, 1970, pp. 77–155), edited by Paul H. Mussen; and in "Sequence, Tempo, and Individual Variation in Growth and Development of Boys and Girls Aged Twelve to Sixteen" in *Twelve to Sixteen: Early Adolescence* (1977, pp. 1–24), edited by Jerome Kagan and Robert Coles.

Observing the Nature of Growth and Physical Development Firsthand

A simple and direct way to gain understanding of growth and physical development from six to twelve is to station yourself near the playground of an elementary school either just before school begins or at lunchtime. Observe the appearance and behavior of children who emerge from the kindergarten and first-grade rooms and those who come out of the fifth- and sixth-grade rooms. After you have noted your own impressions, carry out the following exercises. First, compare the youngest and oldest children in terms of appearance and coordination, and then begin to look for sex differences. Are boys more aggressive and active than girls, particularly at the lower grade levels? Do you notice a tendency for girls at the sixth grade level to be taller than boys? Finally, see if you can pick out some boys in the midgrade levels who might be good candidates for the accident-proneness prize in their school.

Looking for Sex-Role Stereotyping

You might find it interesting to carry out your own observations of the extent to which boys and girls in our society are subjected to sex-role indoctrination. One way to do this would be to be on the alert for differences in the ways parents treat boys and girls. You can often observe parent-child interactions in such public places as parks, shopping malls or supermarkets. In a shopping mall, go into a toy store and note the kinds of toys and games that are purchased for and by girls and boys. (A particularly enlightening way to gain insight into the way games and toys may lead girls in one direction, boys in another, is to carry out an analysis of the pages of gifts for children included in the Christmas catalogues sent out by Sears, Ward's, and similar mail-order companies. If parents and grandparents buy "typical" presents, will girls be encouraged to take care of babies and do housework? Will boys be encouraged to be adventurous and to build things?) A different way to look for sex-stereotyping would be to examine children's books in a local public library or the curriculum section of your college library. Check to see if girls are still depicted as cheerleaders for boys, who do things and achieve goals. Finally, if you have the chance to interview some elementary school children, you might ask them what kind of job they would like to have when they grow up. If girls mention a job, but not marriage, you might ask them if they have thought about whether they want to be a housewife along with having a job, or whether they would rate a career as more important than being a wife and mother.

KEY POINTS

The Nature of Concrete Operational Thought

Concrete operational thinking: decentration, classification, seriation

From Egocentric to Socialized Speech and Thought

Socialized thinking leads to awareness of feelings of others, self-consciousness

The Impact of Cognitive Style

Impulsive and reflective cognitive styles
Analytic and thematic cognitive styles
Convergent and divergent cognitive styles

The Importance of Academic Achievement

Girls may earn higher grades because of desire to please adults
Stress on grades leads to competition, anxiety, pressure

Moral Development

Moral behavior depends on circumstances
Being able to recite principles has no effect on moral behavior

Around ten: from sacred and imposed rules to mutual agreements

Morality of constraint: sacred rules; no exceptions; no allowance for intentions; consequences determine guilt

Preconventional morality: avoid punishment, receive benefits in return

Conventional morality: impress others, respect authority

Postconventional morality: mutual agreements, consistent principles

Kohlberg: stages of morality universal, sequential

No strong support for hypotheses of universal, sequential stages

Better to discuss real rather than hypothetical moral dilemmas

Many moral decisions must be made on spur of moment

A strong conscience leads to "right" moral decisions but may cause guilt feelings

Children may acquire visible moral attributes through imitation but not acquire judgment

CHAPTER

15

SIX
TO
TWELVE

COGNITIVE DEVELOPMENT

*T*he cognitive abilities of preschool children are primarily preoperational. An operation (to refresh your memory) is a mental action that can be reversed. Before they enter school, most children are unable to mentally reverse actions that they have seen performed (such as pouring water from one container to another of a different size and shape). About the time children enter the first grade, though, they do begin to mentally reverse actions, provided they are asked to deal with concrete objects and experiences that are actually present or have been experienced directly in the past. That is why Piaget refers to the stage of cognitive development that follows the preoperational period as **concrete operational.** However, if asked to apply what they have learned in a concrete (or actually experienced) situation to a hypothetical situation, most elementary school children will be unable to generalize. The ability to make such generalizations is one of the characteristics of formal thought, which typically does not begin to appear until toward the very end of the elementary school years. During most of the elementary school years, therefore, most children function as concrete operational thinkers.

The Nature of Concrete Operational Thought

Key aspects of concrete operational thought can be illustrated by the way children respond to the kinds of situations Piaget presented in his clinical interview sessions.

When six-year-olds are confronted with the problem where equal amounts of water are poured into a vase and a bowl, most are able to explain that the amount of water stays the same. If they are asked to apply the same basic principle (of conservation) to a situation where one of two equal-size pieces of clay is flattened, they may be able to supply the correct answer. But if asked to explain what will happen if heavy and light weights of equal size are placed in tubes containing equal amounts of water, they are likely to fail. Six-year-olds are able to solve problems of conservation only if they have had concrete experience with the objects involved. As they mature, they will gradually comprehend similarities and recognize relationships and be able to solve many different types of conservation problems. Until they reach the point where they can solve such problems in a fairly consistent way (around age twelve), they have not demonstrated capability of formal thought.

The same point is illustrated by the way the six- to twelve-year-old masters classification. The six-year-old who can explain when actually confronted with flowers of different types and colors that a yellow tulip is at the same time not only yellow and a tulip but also a flower may be unable to understand similar hypothetical situations. For example, if asked (just after explaining about flowers that are physically present) if a person can be a Catholic and a television star at the same time, a six-year-old may confidently state that it is *not* possible and not see any inconsistency.

Decentration—the ability to avoid centering attention on just one aspect of a situation—is a key factor in the development of concrete operational thinking. Decentration makes it possible for children to think of both the similarities and differences between objects. When children are capable of decentering their thinking, they realize that it *is* possible for a person or object to be classified in more than one category at the same time. Another important aspect of the development of concrete operational thinking is the emergence of **seriation,** the ability to order objects or events along some dimension. Seriation makes it possible for children to follow directions and understand quantitative concepts such as number and length.

Concrete operational thinking: decentration, classification, seriation

When children reach the point of being able to make some consistent generalizations, they have shown that they are beginning to develop their capacity for formal thought. But an incomplete grasp of this kind of thinking is revealed by the way they set about solving problems. If asked to explain how to predict what will happen if objects of varying sizes and weights are placed on a balance, eleven-year-olds are likely to proceed in a disorganized manner. They may make wild guesses before they begin to experiment and then proceed to engage in haphazard trial and error in searching for a solution. Not until they have gained sufficient experience with formal thought will they be able to plan mentally a systematic approach to solving the problem. Only after a considerable amount of experience will they be able to carry out a plan evolved entirely in their minds and then accurately predict the results before they actually balance objects. This kind of intellectual behavior illustrates the essence of formal thought: the ability to solve never-before-encountered problems entirely by mental manipulation of variables. (Formal thinking, which is characterized by a systematic approach to problem solving, consideration of several variables at the same time, skill in forming hypotheses, and the ability to generalize by applying principles to many different situations, will be discussed more completely in Chapter 19.)

From Egocentric to Socialized Speech and Thought

Preschoolers who are in the process of developing a repertoire of schemes tend to organize and adapt to experiences in their own way. As a consequence, their view of a particular object or situation may be quite different from the perception of others. They may also be incapable of decentration and will concentrate on only one aspect of a situation at a time. These conditions lead to egocentric speech and thought, where children tend to assume that everyone else sees things their way and understands their point of view. Conversely, they fail to comprehend that others may have different points of view.

Around the age of eight, most children have gained enough experience and interacted with enough people to grasp the idea that views of the world differ and that it is often wise to find out what others think and to pay close attention to what they say. When this occurs, Piaget says, the child has become capable of socialized speech and thought.

Socialized thinking leads to awareness of feelings of others, self-consciousness

While the ability to see things as others see them helps children interact more effectively in many school and social situations, it also tends to make children self-conscious. A first-grade boy who falls off a swing on the playground or splashes paint on his face while at the easel may continue about his business in an unconcerned way. If the same boy does something awkward when he reaches the sixth grade, he is likely to immediately check to see if others have seen him—and if they are laughing at him. One consequence of cognitive development in the elementary school years, therefore, is that children move from being more or less immune to the reactions of others to feeling as if they are "on stage" most of the time. This tendency reaches a peak in early adolescence and will be discussed more completely in Chapter 19.

The Impact of Cognitive Style

Piaget's description of cognitive development provides an outline of general trends that reflect age changes in intellectual functioning found in children in all parts of the world. It has been found, however, that while all children go through the stages of sensorimotor, preoperational, and concrete operational thought in essentially the same sequence, they may differ in cognitive style.

Impulsive and reflective cognitive styles

Jerome Kagan (1964b, 1964c) has performed a series of studies on the styles of conceptualization manifested by different children. He has concluded that some children seem to be characteristically **impulsive,** whereas others are characteristically **reflective.** He notes that impulsive children have a fast conceptual tempo; they tend to come forth with the first answer they can think of and are concerned about giving quick responses in school situations. Reflective children, on the other hand, take time before they speak; they seem to prefer to evaluate alternative answers and to give correct responses rather than quick ones. When taking tests, impulsive pupils may answer more questions but also make more errors than reflective pupils. Kagan also concluded that impulsiveness appears to be a general trait that appears early in a person's life and is consistently revealed in a variety of situations. Other types of thinking Kagan refers to as **analytic** and **thematic.** Analytic students tend to note details when exposed to a complex stimulus, whereas thematic students respond to the pattern as a whole (or in global fashion).

Analytic and thematic cognitive styles

Tamar Zelniker and Wendell Jeffrey (1976) carried out several experiments to check on Kagan's observations regarding cognitive styles. They

Jerome Kagan found that some students are impulsive thinkers who tend to react quickly when asked a question. Other pupils are reflective thinkers who prefer to mull things over before responding.
Charles Harbutt/Archive Pictures.

found that reflective children perform better on tasks requiring analysis of details, while impulsive children seem to do better on tasks requiring global interpretations. They concluded that impulsive children are not necessarily inferior to reflective children in problem-solving ability, as some earlier students of cognitive style had concluded. Impulsive thinkers may do less well on many school and test situations that require analysis of details primarily because they prefer to look at problems in a thematic, or global, way. The impulsive thinker may often be a thematic thinker as well, possessing a fast conceptual tempo combined with a tendency to look at the big picture. Reflective thinkers are more deliberate, but their tendencies toward analytic thinking cause them to concentrate on details.

Samuel Messick (1976) has summarized research on other cognitive styles. He notes that some children more than others seem to experience things vividly and also are aware of many more aspects of a situation at a given moment. Some children are more likely than others to be distracted by conflicting ideas. Other children appear to place things in broad categories, compared with age-mates who classify experiences into many separate categories. Still other children seem to have a ten-

Convergent and di-
vergent cognitive
styles

dency to "level" memories by merging similar recollections, as contrasted with peers who retain distinct recollections of separate experiences. J. P. Guilford (1967) has concluded that some individuals appear
to be **convergent** thinkers—they respond to what they read and observe
in conventional, typical ways. Others are **divergent** thinkers—they respond in unexpected or idiosyncratic ways. Some children memorize
much more easily than others; some are more capable than others of
grasping ideas and evaluating their accuracy or appropriateness in a
particular situation.

Still another type of cognitive style is referred to as **field dependence**
or **field independence.** Herman Witkin and others (1962) developed a
technique for measuring how individuals perceive situations and respond to problems. He seated subjects in a specially constructed chair in
a darkened room. An illuminated rod and frame that could be moved
independently were placed in front of the subject, who was instructed to
tell the experimenter how to move the rod so that it would appear
vertical. Sometimes the frame would be tilted; in other cases the chair
would be tilted; sometimes both would be placed at an angle. Witkin
and several associates (Witkin, Dyk, Faterson, Goodenough, and Karp,
1962) carried out a series of studies with subjects of varying ages and
found that some individuals were better able than others to perceive the
rod independent of the frame (the *field* or background). A *field-dependent*
person depends on the visual field (the frame) to make deductions about
the position of the rod. If the frame is tilted, the field-dependent person
will instruct the experimenter to align the rod so that it is parallel to the
side of the frame. The *field-independent* person, by contrast, using body
position as a guide, does not need to depend on visual cues and is better
able to disregard the position of the frame in aligning the rod. Witkin
and his colleagues found that as children mature they tend to become
more field independent. Individual differences, however, remain quite
stable. That is, some children tend to be field dependent throughout
their school years; others tend to be field independent. Witkin also
discovered that males at all age levels tend to be more field independent
than females.

In subsequent investigations, Witkin and Goodenough (1976) found
that field-independent individuals tend to be active and self-motivated;
they assume a participant role and prefer physical science subjects.
Field-dependent individuals tend to assume a spectator role; they are
more sensitive to social situations, and they prefer social science subjects. The fact that males in many cultures tend to be more field independent than females (Witkin and Berry, 1975) may be an indication that
there is a genetic factor involved. On the other hand, it is possible that
the differential treatment of boys and girls (noted in discussing parental
responses to infants and young children in earlier chapters) may favor

general independence in males and cause females to function more as spectators who also become concerned about social relationships. (Efforts to determine if specific child-rearing practices are related to field dependence or independence [for example, Witkin, 1969] have not yielded clear-cut results.)

The Importance of Academic Achievement

Sex Differences in School Achievement

Sex differences in field dependence and independence suggest that as soon as boys and girls enter the primary grades and are asked to learn basic skills and acquire information, they show different interests and abilities. Some of these center on specific subjects and skills; others involve general attitudes toward school and teachers. Helen L. Bee (1974, p. 7) analyzed sex differences in cognitive functioning and found evidence (similar to that reported by Maccoby and Jacklin [1974] and by Block [1976]) that during the elementary school years girls, on the average, are superior in verbal fluency, spelling, and reading and that they earn higher grades. Boys, on the average, are superior in mathematical reasoning and in tasks involving understanding of spatial relationships. One possible explanation for boys' superior ability in mathematical reasoning is that their greater tendency toward field independence helps them to concentrate on specific aspects of a situation without being confused by background information. Possible explanations for the verbal superiority of females include the following (some of which have already been noted): girls interact more with their mothers, they are more likely to use words than actions to express their needs, and they mature more rapidly.

Females earn higher grades in school, but males are more likely to achieve at a higher level in many activities later in life. Lois Wladis Hoffman (1972) suggests that the better school performance of girls may be due, in part at least, to their desire to please. Boys, by contrast, appear more interested in working on tasks that interest them and less concerned about earning approval. Because of these tendencies, girls may want to earn high grades in order to arouse a positive response from parents and teachers, and boys may engage in more self-motivated study. If a boy does not find a particular subject interesting, he may not make much of an effort to learn it, which will lead to poorer overall evaluations on report cards. But the tendency for a boy to study something for its own sake may be beneficial later in life, when prolonged self-directed study is called for.

Girls may earn higher grades because of desire to please adults

Researchers have reported a consistent tendency for girls to be more eager than boys to earn the approval of teachers.
© *James H. Karales/Peter Arnold, Inc.*

Hoffman speculates that girls may be motivated by a desire to please because they are not encouraged to strive for independence early in life. On the basis of research carried out by Howard Moss (1967), she suggests that mothers tend to think of male infants as sturdy and active and female infants as delicate dolls (despite the fact that female infants are more mature and better able to cope with many forms of stress than male infants). As a result, mothers overprotect female infants and treat them as dependent. This process continues throughout childhood. Hoffman also hypothesizes that a girl may find it more difficult to develop autonomy and independence because she identifies more completely with the primary caretaker (almost always the mother) and her first teachers (almost all of whom are women) and also experiences less conflict with them.

The Significance and Ramifications of Academic Achievement

America is a meritocratic society in which persons from the humblest origins can achieve success through their own efforts. In many cases, success later in life depends on doing well in school. And a child who does not get a good start during the elementary school years may have an extraordinarily difficult time overcoming this handicap later on. Upper- and middle-class parents tend to be more aware of the importance of early success in school than lower-class parents, partly because they are more likely to have benefited themselves from successful educational experiences. Early intervention, Head Start, and Follow Through programs have been established in an effort to supply children from impoverished backgrounds with the kinds of experiences and motivation that give more favored children advantages in school. A basic premise of such programs is that if disadvantaged children are helped to a good start in responding to educational experiences, they are more likely to later qualify for jobs that will permit them to improve their economic and social standing.

These comments suggest the opportunities provided by school achievement. But the fact that doing well in school is such an important prerequisite to later success causes six- to twelve-year-olds to experience pressure and anxiety. As they move through the elementary grades, children become increasingly aware that in order to succeed they must compete against others. They also learn that certain types of abilities contribute more to success than others. A child who learns to read rapidly and easily, for example, will have a substantial advantage in schoolwork over one who experiences problems acquiring that skill. Cognitive style may take on increasing significance as children are asked to deal with more complex aspects of the school curriculum. A field-independent child, for example, may enjoy advantages over a field-dependent pupil when the time comes to learn geometry or to engage in self-directed study.

Stress on grades leads to competition, anxiety, pressure

Because of individual differences in intelligence, background, motivation, specific types of abilities, cognitive style, and related characteristics, some children do better in school than others. As children become aware of differences in academic performance and of the significance of earning high grades, they are likely to experience conflicts centering on morality. Elementary school children become progressively aware of the nature and significance of moral norms, school rules, and the laws of society. One reason for this developing awareness is that they increasingly interact with others and realize that in order to get along with others certain common understandings and regulations must be established. Another reason is that the gradual transition from concrete operational to formal thinking makes it possible for them to grasp and apply general principles. But even as they become aware of the necessity for codes and rules and capable of understanding how and when to apply them, elementary school children are faced with temptations to ignore moral codes or break rules or laws that interfere with their needs and desires. A child who finds a wallet must decide whether or not to return it to the owner. A child who needs a particular score on an important test in order to earn an A may feel driven to cheat. A child who covets a toy that is as impressive as that recently given to a friend is tempted to steal it. To complicate matters further, elementary school children become increasingly aware that many adults, sometimes including highly regarded public officials or perhaps their own parents, occasionally behave in thoughtless, immoral, or illegal ways. Furthermore, only a fraction of adolescents who commit crimes are caught and punished. Accordingly, elementary school children are quite likely to observe or hear about the escapades of peers who committed an illegal act, got away with it, benefited from it, bragged about it, and were admired for it.

Moral development during the six- to twelve-year span is therefore of great significance. During this period of development children acquire the cognitive abilities to begin to comprehend the underlying reasons for honoring moral norms and obeying laws. They also become aware of conflicts between regulations and personal desires that are particularly acute in a competitive, affluent, meritocratic society. And they may also be confused and dismayed by the realization that many adults and older children set a negative example. For all these reasons, psychologists and educators have been interested in finding ways to encourage moral behavior in children. Such concern is not new, though. The topics of moral development and moral education have been studied for more than fifty years.

Moral Development

The Hartshorne and May Studies of Character

In 1922 the leaders of the Religious Education Association felt so concerned about immorality in America that they passed a resolution to attempt a scientific investigation of the question "How is religion being taught to young people, and with what effect?" They asked Hugh Hartshorne, a professor of religious education, and Mark May, a professor of psychology, to help them find answers to these questions. Hartshorne and May were provided with a substantial budget and supervised a comprehensive series of ingenious studies to discover how children reacted when placed in situations that centered on deceit, generosity, charitableness, and self-control (1929, 1930a, 1930b).

Thousands of children at different age levels were observed reacting in situations that revealed their actual moral behavior. The same children were also asked to respond to questions about hypothetical situations to reveal how much they understood about right and wrong behavior. Elementary school children, for example, were allowed to correct their own papers or record their own scores on measures of athletic skill without being aware that accurate measures were being made independently by adult observers. They were also asked what they *thought* was the right thing to do in similar situations. A comparison of the two sets of data made it possible to determine, among other things, if children practiced what they preached. Hartshorne and May wanted information about these two aspects of moral development to discover if the immoral behavior of young children was due to ignorance. They discovered, however, that many children who were able to describe right kinds of behavior in hypothetical situations indulged in wrong behavior in real-life situations.

One significant discovery of Hartshorne and May was that children behave in situations that call for moral judgment by reacting in specific rather than consistent ways. Even a child who was rated as among the most honest in a group would behave in a dishonest way under certain circumstances. A boy who was an excellent student but an indifferent athlete, for example, would not cheat when asked to correct his own paper, but he *would* inflate scores on sports skills. A girl who was an excellent athlete but a terrible speller would alter dozens of misspelled words on a paper, but be completely accurate in recording her physical performance.

Moral behavior depends on circumstances

After reviewing research carried out in the forty-five years since Hartshorne and May published their findings, Thomas Lickona reported that "A huge and ever-expanding body of research . . . has replicated Hartshorne and May's basic finding: Variations in the situation produce variations in moral behavior" (1976, p. 15). Lickona adds, though, that recent research also supports another conclusion of Hartshorne and May, that some children are more "integrated" (or consistent) than others in reacting to moral situations. It would appear to be a mistake, therefore, to assume that there is *no* consistency in moral thinking and behavior. If that hypothesis is endorsed, there would be little reason to assume that a child develops any kind of personal code of ethics or that parents and teachers should try to promote the development of a strong conscience in children.

Another factor to consider regarding consistency of moral behavior is that the various descriptions of stages in moral reasoning that will be summarized later in this chapter all stress that children exhibit character-istic types of thinking at different age levels. Some of the theories, more-over, are based on the assumption that particular children at any given stage will respond to moral situations in the same basic way. Perhaps the best way to summarize the issue of generality versus specificity in moral thinking and behavior, therefore, is to suggest that many children respond in quite consistent ways when confronted with moral deci-sions. But all children have a breaking point and may behave immorally when the personal stakes are high. This breaking point is prob-ably much higher for some children (who have a well-developed conscience) than it is for others.

Another significant, and dismaying, discovery of Hartshorne and May was that children who went to Sunday School or who belonged to such organizations as the Boy Scouts or Girl Scouts were just as dishon-est as children who were not exposed to the kind of moral instruction provided by such organizations. The members of the Religious Educa-tion Association learned, therefore, that the effect of religious education at that time seemed to be negligible. Hartshorne and May concluded that one explanation for the ineffectiveness of moral instruction in the 1920s was that too much stress was placed on having children memorize platitudes such as the Ten Commandments or the Boy Scout oath and law. They suggested that many children who could recite "Thou shalt not steal" or who could unhesitatingly reel off "Trustworthy, loyal, helpful, friendly, courteous, kind, obedient, cheerful, thrifty, brave, clean, and reverent" either did not understand what they were saying or saw no connection between such elegant words and actual deeds. Hartshorne and May suggested that a more effective way to arrange moral instruction would be to invite children to discuss real-life moral situations as they occurred. Instead of having children chant "Honesty is the best policy," for example, they urged teachers to call attention to the positive consequences of honest acts. If a pupil in a school reported that he or she had found money belonging to someone else, the teacher might praise the child and ask everyone in the class to think about how relieved the person who had lost the money would be to have it returned.

Partial explanations for the inability of children studied by Hartshorne and May to understand moral principles or to apply them in consistent ways were supplied by studies of moral judgment carried out by Jean Piaget.

Being able to recite principles has no effect on moral behavior

Piaget's Analysis of the Moral Judgment of the Child

Age Changes in Interpretation of Rules

About the time that Hartshorne and May were publishing their reports, Jean Piaget was carrying on a very different kind of investigation of

moral development. Instead of obtaining data from thousands of subjects, Piaget started out observing how a handful of Swiss children
played marbles. (He first took the trouble to learn the game himself so
that he would be able to understand the subtleties of the competition.)
Piaget discovered that interpretations of rules followed by participants
in marble games changed with age. Four- to seven-year-olds just learning the game seemed to view rules as interesting examples of the social
behavior of older children. They did not understand them but tried to go
along with them. Seven- to ten-year-olds regarded rules as sacred pronouncements handed down by older children or adults. At about the
age of eleven or twelve rules were seen as agreements reached due to
mutual consent. Piaget concluded that younger children see rules as
absolute and external.

Even though children from the age of four to about ten do not question rules, they may frequently break them because of incomplete
understanding. After the age of eleven or so, children become increasingly capable of grasping why rules are necessary. At that point, Piaget
concluded, they tend to lose interest in adult-imposed regulations and
take delight in formulating their own variations of rules to fit a particular
situation. Piaget illustrates this point by describing (1962, p. 50) how a
group of ten- and eleven-year-old boys prepared for a snowball fight.
They divided themselves into teams, elected officers, decided on rules to
govern the distances from which the snowballs could be thrown, and
agreed on a system of punishments for those who violated the rules.
Even though they wasted a substantial amount of play time engaging in
such preliminary discussions, they seemed to thoroughly enjoy their
newly discovered ability to make up rules to supplant those that had
previously been imposed on them by their elders.

Around ten: from sacred and imposed rules to mutual agreements

Reactions to Stories Involving Moral Decisions

The way children of different ages responded to rules so intrigued
Piaget that he decided to use the clinical-interview method to obtain
more systematic information about moral development. He made up
pairs of stories and asked children of different ages to discuss them.
Here is a typical pair of stories:

There was a little boy called Julian. His father had gone out and Julian thought
it would be fun to play with his father's ink-pot. First he played with the pen,
and then he made a little blot on the table cloth.

A little boy who was called Augustus once noticed that his father's ink-pot
was empty. One day that his father was away he thought of filling the ink-pot so
as to help his father, and so that he should find it full when he came home. But
while he was opening the ink-bottle he made a big blot on the table cloth. (1962,
p. 122)

After reading these stories Piaget asked "Are these children equally guilty? Which of the two is naughtiest, and why?" As was the case with interpretations of rules, Piaget found that younger children reacted to these stories differently than older children. The way six-year-olds interpreted rules and the answers they gave when confronted with the pairs of stories led Piaget to conclude that their moral reasoning is quite different from that of twelve-year-olds.

Piaget refers to the moral thinking of children up to the age of ten or so as **morality of constraint,** but he also calls it **moral realism** or **heteronomous morality.** (*Heteros* is Greek for *other; nomos* is Greek for *law.* Therefore, *heteronomous* means subject to external rules or laws.) The thinking of children of eleven or older Piaget calls the **morality of cooperation.** The terms *autonomous morality, morality of reciprocity, moral relativism,* and *moral flexibility* are sometimes also used. After analyzing the responses of elementary school children in clinical interviews, Piaget concluded that the two basic types of moral reasoning differ in several ways, which are summarized in Table 15.1. To clarify and illustrate some of the differences between the moralities of constraint and cooperation summarized in Table 15.1, here are some examples and explanations of types of thinking that characterize the thinking of moral realists (that is, those who use the morality of constraint).

The Nature of the Morality of Constraint

Morality of constraint: sacred rules; no exceptions; no allowance for intentions; consequences determine guilt

The younger child sees rules as *real*—ready made and external. Because rules are imposed by outside authority, it is assumed they should always be obeyed the same way. The letter of the law rather than the spirit of the law must be observed, and no exceptions are allowed. An illustration of these characteristics of moral realism is provided by reactions of younger and older children to a change in rules. Several children of elementary school age were playing baseball in a vacant lot bordered by weeds. One excellent hitter decided to get some additional batting practice by deliberately hitting several foul balls in a row. Each time a ball was hit foul, however, it took quite a bit of time to find it in the weeds. Accordingly, some of the older children proposed that anyone who hit two foul balls in a row was out. Most of the players agreed, but the youngest child in the group was so upset by this change in the official rules of baseball that he refused to play and went home in a huff. The moral realist, in addition, thinks literally and in terms of blind obedience—no allowance is made for motives or intentions. Furthermore, the degree of guilt is equated with the seriousness of the consequences. These characteristics of moral realism are illustrated by the responses of children to the inkblot stories. Younger children interviewed by Piaget maintained that Augustus was more guilty than Julian because he had

TABLE 15.1
DIFFERENCES BETWEEN MORALITY OF CONSTRAINT AND MORALITY
OF COOPERATION

Morality of Constraint (Typical of Six-year-olds)	Morality of Cooperation (Typical of Twelve-year-olds)
Single, absolute moral perspective (behavior is right *or* wrong)	Awareness of differing viewpoints regarding rules
Conception of rules as unchangeable	View of rules as flexible
Extent of guilt determined by amount of damage	Consideration of a wrongdoer's intentions when evaluating guilt
Definition of moral wrongness in terms of what is forbidden or punished	Definition of moral wrongness in terms of violation of spirit of cooperation

(Note that these first four differences call attention to the tendency for children below the age of ten or so to think of rules as sacred pronouncements handed down by external authority)

Punishment should stress atonement and does not need to fit the crime	Punishment should involve either restitution or suffering the same fate as a victim of someone's wrongdoing
Peer aggression should be punished by an external authority	Peer aggression should be punished by retaliatory behavior on the part of the victim[1]
Children should obey because rules are established by those in authority	Children should obey rules because of mutual concern for the rights of others

(Note how these last three differences call attention to the tendency for children above the age of ten or so to see rules as mutual agreements among equals)

---

[1]Beyond the age of twelve, adolescents increasingly affirm that reciprocal reactions, or "getting back," should occur in response only to good behavior, not to bad behavior.
Source: Freely adapted from interpretations of Piaget (1932) by Kohlberg (1969) and Lickona (1976b).

Piaget found that children up to the age of ten or so abide by a morality of constraint: they insist on obedience to fixed rules which they believe are established by external authority. Above the age of ten children become increasingly capable of adopting a morality of cooperation: they view rules as flexible and recognize that they are mutual agreements among equals.
Philip Jon Bailey; Nancy Hays/Monkmeyer.

made a bigger blot. No account was taken of the fact that Julian was misbehaving and that Augustus was trying to help his father.

Some aspects of these differences in the moral reasoning of younger and older children can be understood by taking into account Piaget's descriptions of cognitive development. The child of six who has not completely mastered decentration will tend to think of only one thing at a time and will therefore not be inclined to weigh alternatives. Before the age of seven, a child who has not made the transition from egocentric to socialized speech will find it difficult to consider different points of view. And a child who has not moved from concrete operational to formal thought will be unable to consider hypothetical situations and anticipate consequences. Because of the tendency to think of one thing at a time, the young child finds it difficult to comprehend situations where a rule might be revised to allow for special circumstances. The same tendency to focus on one thing at a time leads the younger child to reason that a big inkblot, regardless of how it is caused, is worse than a small inkblot.

The younger child concentrates on obvious physical properties and does not take into account nonobservable factors such as intentions.

Piaget's description of cognitive development also helps explain some of the conclusions of Hartshorne and May. Concrete operational thinking causes elementary grade children to think in terms of actual experiences, which may account, in part, for the tendency for children to be honest in one situation but not another. Furthermore, children who are not capable of formal thinking are unable to comprehend general principles or apply them in varied situations, which explains the ineffectiveness of moral instruction that stresses the memorization of abstract principles such as the Ten Commandments or the Boy Scout oath and law.

Thomas Lickona (1976b) reviewed research relating to differences between the moralities of constraint and cooperation and concluded that there is quite a bit of experimental evidence to support the general distinction Piaget has made between the moral thinking of younger and older elementary grade children. It appears, however, that these differences are most apparent when the thinking of six- and twelve-year-olds is compared. Children in the middle of this age range are likely to think sometimes as moral realists and function sometimes as moral relativists, depending on the situation and whether or not they have had experience with similar situations.

Kohlberg's Description of Moral Development

Kohlberg's Use of Moral Dilemmas

As a graduate student at the University of Chicago in the 1950s, Lawrence Kohlberg became fascinated by Piaget's studies of moral development. He decided to expand on Piaget's original research by making up stories involving moral dilemmas that would be more appropriate for older children. Here is the story that is most often mentioned in discussions of his work:

In Europe a woman was near death from cancer. One drug might save her, a form of radium that a druggist in the same town had recently discovered. The druggist was charging $2000, ten times what the drug cost him to make. The sick woman's husband, Heinz, went to everyone he knew to borrow the money, but he could only get together about half of what it cost. He told the druggist that his wife was dying and asked him to sell it cheaper or let him pay later, but the druggist said "No." The husband got desperate and broke into the man's store to steal the drug for his wife. Should the husband have done that? Why? (Kohlberg, 1969, p. 376)

Kohlberg's Six Stages of Moral Reasoning

After analyzing the responses of ten- to sixteen-year-olds to this and similar moral dilemmas, Kohlberg eventually (1963) developed a description of six stages of moral reasoning. Be forewarned, however, that Kohlberg has revised some of his original stage designations, and descriptions of the stages have been modified since he first proposed them. In different discussions of his stages, therefore, you may encounter varying descriptions. The outline presented in Table 15.2 is a composite summary of the sequence of moral development as it has been described by Kohlberg, but you should expect to find differences if you read other accounts of his theory.

The scoring system Kohlberg developed to evaluate a given response to a moral dilemma is extremely complex. Furthermore, the responses of subjects are lengthy and may feature arguments about a particular decision. To help you understand a bit more about each Kohlberg stage, simplified examples of responses to a dilemma such as that faced by Heinz are noted below. For maximum clarity, only brief typical responses to the question "Why shouldn't you steal from a store?" are mentioned.

Stage 1 Punishment-Obedience Orientation. "You might get caught." (The physical consequences of an action determine goodness or badness.)

Stage 2 Instrumental Relativist Orientation. "You shouldn't steal something from a store and the store owner shouldn't steal things that belong to you." (Obeying laws should involve an even exchange.)

Stage 3 Good Boy—Nice Girl Orientation. "Your parents will be proud of you if you are honest." (The right action is one that will impress others.)

Stage 4 Law and Order Orientation. "It's against the law and if we don't obey laws our whole society might fall apart." (To maintain the social order, fixed rules must be obeyed.)

Stage 5 Social Contract Orientation. "Under certain circumstances laws may have to be disregarded—if a person's life depends on breaking a law, for instance." (Rules should involve mutual agreements, the rights of the individual should be protected.)

Stage 6 Universal Ethical Principle Orientation. "You need to weigh all the factors and then try to make the most appropriate decision in a given situation. Sometimes it would be morally wrong *not* to steal." (Moral decisions should be based on consistent applications of self-chosen ethical principles.)

TABLE 15.2
KOHLBERG'S STAGES OF MORAL REASONING

Level 1   Preconventional Morality. (Typical of children up to the age of nine. Called preconventional because young children do not really understand the conventions or rules of a society.)

    Stage 1   Punishment-Obedience Orientation. The physical consequences of an action determine goodness or badness. Those in authority have superior power and should be obeyed. Punishment should be avoided by staying out of trouble.

    Stage 2   Instrumental Relativist Orientation. An action is judged to be right if it is instrumental in satisfying one's own needs or involves an even exchange. Obeying rules should bring some sort of benefit in return.

Level 2   Conventional Morality. (Typical of nine- to twenty-year-olds. Called conventional since most nine- to twenty-year-olds conform to the conventions of society because they *are* the rules of a society.)

    Stage 3   Good Boy—Nice Girl Orientation. The right action is one that would be carried out by someone whose behavior is likely to please or impress others.

    Stage 4   Law and Order Orientation. To maintain the social order, fixed rules must be established and obeyed. It is essential to respect authority.

Level 3   Postconventional Morality. (Usually reached only after the age of twenty and by only a small proportion of adults. Called postconventional because the moral principles that underlie the conventions of a society are understood.)

    Stage 5   Social Contract Orientation. Rules needed to maintain the social order should be based not on blind obedience to authority but on mutual agreement. At the same time, the rights of the individual should be protected.

    Stage 6   Universal Ethical Principle Orientation. Moral decisions should be made in terms of self-chosen ethical principles. Once principles are chosen, they should be applied in consistent ways.[1]

Preconventional morality: avoid punishment, receive benefits in return

Conventional morality: impress others, respect authority

Postconventional morality: mutual agreements, consistent principles

---

[1]In an article published several years after he originally described the six stages, Kohlberg (1978) indicated that he had concluded that the last stage is essentially a theoretical ideal and is rarely encountered in real life.
Source: Based on descriptions in Kohlberg, 1969, and Kohlberg, 1976.

Similarities and Differences Between Piaget and Kohlberg

As you examined this list of stages and the examples of responses at each type, you may have detected similarities between Piaget's and Kohlberg's descriptions of age changes in moral development. The first four of Kohlberg's stages are roughly equivalent to moral realism as described by Piaget. Kohlberg's preconventional and conventional moral thinkers and Piaget's moral realists all tend to think of rules as edicts handed down by external authority. The letter of the law is observed and not much allowance is made for intentions or circumstances. The postconventional thinker of Kohlberg shares some similarities with the older children observed by Piaget: rules are established by individuals who come to mutual agreement, each moral decision is made by taking into account special circumstances.

While there are similarities in the conclusions drawn by Piaget and Kohlberg, there are also important differences. Piaget believes that moral thinking changes as children mature. He does not believe that the changes are clearly related to age nor are they considered to be sequential. Piaget feels that the different types of moral thinking he described often overlap and that a child might sometimes function as a moral realist, sometimes as a more mature moral decision maker. Kohlberg (1969), by contrast, maintains that the order of the stages he has described is universal and fixed and that a person moves through the stages in sequence. Not everyone reaches the top stages, but all individuals begin at stage one and work their way upwards.

Kohlberg: stages of morality universal, sequential

In some respects, there are greater similarities between Piaget's description of *cognitive* development and Kohlberg's description of moral development than between the two outlines of moral development. Piaget describes preoperational, concrete operational, and formal operational stages. Kohlberg describes preconventional, conventional, and postconventional levels. Even though he does not stress an orderly sequence of *moral* development, Piaget does believe that children go through the stages of *cognitive* development in definite order. Piaget's formal operational stage and Kohlberg's postconventional level both stress understanding and application of abstract principles and taking into account unique circumstances in a given situation. A person cannot engage in postconventional moral reasoning, in fact, until after formal thinking is mastered, but only a small proportion of formal thinkers consistently apply universal ethical principles. While postconventional moral reasoning is not found in persons who are not also formal thinkers, many formal thinkers show little or no evidence of postconventional moral reasoning. This has led researchers to conclude that formal thinking is *necessary but not sufficient* for the development of postconventional moral reasoning.

Evaluations of Kohlberg's Theory

In the years since he first proposed his theory, Kohlberg has performed extensive research using the moral dilemmas he wrote and the scoring scheme he devised to evaluate levels of moral thinking. Dozens of other investigators have carried out similar studies. (For a comprehensive review, see Rest, 1983.) Some psychologists have reported evidence that substantiates Kohlberg's hypotheses that the stages he has described are fixed, sequential, and universal. Other investigators, however, have reported evidence that does not support these hypotheses and have raised questions about Kohlberg's basic approach and some of his conclusions. Some researchers believe Kohlberg's theory is culturally biased, that is, the changing value orientations described in his sequence of six stages are those subscribed to by persons in our culture, but not necessarily by persons in other cultures (Simpson, 1974). Other researchers, notably Carol Gilligan (1982), believe that Kohlberg's theory is sexually biased. They believe this bias contributes to the tendency for females to earn lower moral reasoning scores than males. Gilligan argues that the differing socialization histories of males and females cause them to develop somewhat different value orientations. Females are socialized to value interpersonal harmony and communal goals, while males are socialized to value individual goals. Gilligan points out that most of Kohlberg's dilemmas focus on males resolving male-oriented value conflicts and that all of the subjects in Kohlberg's original sample were males. She believes that Kohlberg's theory of moral development might have evolved quite differently if the original stage descriptions had been based on responses from both males and females. In support of this position, she has collected empirical data that indicate that women score higher on issues of concern to women (e.g., abortion). In his review of research on Kohlberg's theory, however, Rest reports that other investigators have *not* found evidence of sex bias. It would appear, therefore, that the issue of sex bias is yet to be resolved. Kohlberg has also been criticized for portraying more continuity in moral reasoning than actually exists. Recent research (reviewed by Rest) suggests that moral reasoning scores are influenced by a variety of factors, including the types of measure used, the particular dilemmas presented, the scoring criteria, and the instructions. Rest points out that an individual's moral reasoning scores typically fall within a somewhat restricted range or band of stage scores. Thus it is misleading to speak of persons as being "in" a given moral stage.

In a review of research on moral development, Martin L. Hoffman comments, "The research, by and large, provides little support for the main tenets of [Kohlberg's] theory" (1980, p. 299). He later adds, though, "whether the theory is confirmed or not, Kohlberg must be given credit for sensitizing researchers to the highly complex nature of moral development and the cognitive dimensions that may be necessary for a mature moral orientation" (p. 301). And he goes on to say, "Although Kohlberg's stages may not form a universal invariant sequence, as he claims, they may nevertheless provide a valid description of the changes in moral thought that occur in our society."

No strong support for hypotheses of universal, sequential stages

Educational Implications of Kohlberg's Theory

Despite serious questions about the validity of Kohlberg's theory, some individuals (including Kohlberg himself) have speculated about the possibility of using the conception of stages to foster moral development. Several psychologists have undertaken to help or teach children to proceed through the stages of moral development faster and further than they would on their own. Even though most adolescents engage in some aspects of formal operational thinking, very few adolescents or adults reach the postconventional level of moral reasoning. This is unfortunate because postconventional thinkers adapt their responses to unique situations. Elliot Turiel (1966) made the first attempt to induce changes from lower to higher stages. The subjects were twelve- and thirteen-year-old boys with equivalent IQs, drawn at random from a seventh-grade class. The boys were divided into groups and exposed to arguments for and against moral dilemmas that emphasized reasoning one stage below, one stage above, and two stages above their initial stage of moral thinking. The results indicated that arguments one level above a given stage produced more of an effect than the other arguments. The improvement in moral reasoning was quite modest, however.

In a later study, Moshe Blatt (1975) used group discussions instead of arguments to try to improve the moral reasoning of ten- to twelve-year-old boys attending a Reform Jewish Sunday School and four public school classrooms. Asking the children to carry on their own analyses (with supervision by Blatt) led to significant increases in the moral thinking of children attending the Sunday School (most of whom came from academic and professional families). The children in the public school groups registered less impressive improvement. Control group children who had not participated in discussion showed no change. A follow-up investigation (Blatt and Kohlberg, 1978) concluded that the increases were permanent (although the moral reasoning of the children when they were older might have been attributed, in part, to a greater number of intellectual and moral experiences).

Encouraging Moral Development at the Elementary School Level

Hartshorne and May found that moral instruction stressing memorization of platitudes was ineffective. Piaget found that younger children practice the morality of constraint, that ten- to twelve-year-olds enjoy making up their own rules, and that types of moral behavior can be related to cognitive development. Kohlberg believes that there is an invariant sequence of moral development and that discussion techniques help children move to more advanced stages of moral reasoning. Turiel and Blatt reported that discussions of moral dilemmas led to modest improvements in moral reasoning. These various observations point to factors that need to be considered by parents and teachers of elementary school children who would like to encourage such traits as honesty, integrity, and consideration for others. Many of the factors just noted can be put into perspective by considering Piaget's descriptions of cognitive development.

During the elementary school years, children are primarily concrete operational thinkers. They can solve problems involving factors that they have actually experienced, but they find it difficult to grasp abstractions. They cannot apply a general principle to many different situations and may be unable to deal with hypothetical situations. These characteristics of concrete operational thought help explain why Hartshorne and May found that stress on abstract principles and concepts had little impact on actual moral behavior. They also lead to doubts about the value of asking children below the age of twelve to spend a great deal of time discussing Kohlberg's moral dilemmas.

The characteristics of concrete operational thinkers suggest that discussions of moral dilemmas must be carefully arranged if they are to be successful. Richard Hersh, Diana Paolitto, and Joseph Reimer (1979) have developed techniques of moral education, based on the observations of Piaget and Kohlberg, that are more elaborate and sophisticated variations of the basic approach recommended by Hartshorne and May in the 1930s. Hartshorne and May recommended (1930, p. 413) that teachers promote discussions of actual situations in detail so that children who found themselves in similar situations would recognize commonalities and be helped to choose a desirable course of action. Hersh, Paolitto, and Reimer recommend to teachers the following procedures for implementing what they refer to as developmental moral education:

1. Recognize that younger children will respond to moral conflicts differently than older children.
2. Try to take the perspective of students and stimulate their perspective-taking abilities.
3. Develop awareness of moral issues by using a variety of real and hypothetical moral dilemmas and by using daily opportunities in the classroom to heighten moral awareness. (Moral education should be an integral part of the curriculum; it should not take place during "Moral Education Period.")
4. Create a classroom atmosphere that will enhance open discussion (for example, arrange face-to-face groupings, be an acceptant model, foster listening and communication skills, encourage student-to-student interaction).

Specific suggestions for supervising classroom discussions offered by Hersh, Paolitto, and Reimer include the following:

1. Highlight the moral issue to be discussed. (Describe a specific real or hypothetical moral dilemma.)
2. Ask "Why" questions. (After asking students what they would do if they were faced with the moral dilemma under discussion, ask them to explain *why* they would act that way.)
3. Complicate the circumstances. (After students have responded to the original dilemma, mention a factor that might complicate matters, for example, if the dilemma involved a best friend.)
4. Use personal and naturalistic examples. (Invite students to put themselves in the position of individuals who are confronted by moral dilemmas described in newspapers or depicted on television.)

Parents might use similar techniques, particularly when encouraging children to think about the consequences of real moral dilemmas. In addition, parents might take into account the points emphasized in the discussion of ways to encourage prosocial behavior in two- to five-year-olds that was presented in Chapter 13. To refresh your memory, studies of the prosocial behavior of preschoolers revealed that young children are more likely to understand the plight of others if they have had similar experiences and have thought about those experiences. The impact of models and of reinforcement of prosocial behavior has also been stressed. The guidelines for encouraging prosocial behavior in preschoolers presented in Chapter 13 can be revised as follows to apply to the fostering of moral behavior in elementary school children:

Better to discuss real rather than hypothetical moral dilemmas

1. Invite children to talk about real (not hypothetical) situations where they have had to make moral decisions (to make them aware of their feelings and to encourage them to become aware of factors that lead to dishonest behavior).
2. Express pleasure when behaving in a moral manner and encourage children to become aware of and to express the pleasure they feel when they behave in an honest or helpful way.
3. Do not berate a child for failing to apply a general moral principle in consistent ways. If a child is honest in one situation but not another, try to take into account circumstances, pressures, and feelings. If possible (and appropriate), help the child think about the factors that led him or her to commit a dishonest act. Awareness of causes of one type of immoral behavior may help the child resist temptation in a similar situation in the future.
4. Try to serve as a positive model to be imitated by exuding warmth and pleasure when acting in honest and helpful ways. Be as consis-

tent as possible in displaying moral behavior and praise children for behaving in similar ways.

A basic reason for asking children to discuss real rather than hypothetical moral dilemmas becomes apparent when the need for a conscience is examined.

The Importance of the Superego (Conscience)

One of the characteristics of many real-life moral decisions is that they often have to be made on the spur of the moment. The child wrestling with a hypothetical moral dilemma in a discussion has the opportunity to think over responses and is also likely to feel that the decision need not be final. But consider an actual moral dilemma that might be faced by an eleven-year-old boy. Assume he has had his allowance cut for failing to get sufficiently high grades. A few minutes after school has been dismissed on the fateful day, he returns to his classroom to pick up a forgotten book. He hears the school secretary call his teacher to the telephone, and as he approaches his room, he sees the teacher hurrying down the empty hall in the opposite direction. When he enters the room, he notices the week's lunch money on the teacher's desk. He is quite sure no one saw him enter the room, and he realizes the teacher will be back in a minute or two, so he must make a snap decision. Should he grab some of the money, or wait by the door until the teacher returns?

The response of a person in such a situation is almost "reflexive," since there is no time to weigh the relative merits of different courses of action. The person must act first and think later. In many cases, making an *immoral* decision may permit the person to engage in more analysis and to have more of a choice than making a moral decision. For example, if the boy decides not to take the money, he may never have another opportunity like it; but if he does take it, he can think things over and still exercise the option of returning it to his teacher. He cannot be sure how she will react, however, and since the deed is an accomplished fact, the successful culprit might be inclined to rationalize, "The teacher gave me a lousy grade and that's the reason my allowance was cut, so she really owes me the money," or "They get money for the lunch program from the government, so a couple of dollars won't make any difference."

Snap decisions and later evaluations of them that represent postconventional thinking both bring into play one's conscience (or in Freudian terminology, one's superego): the internalized values that govern much of a person's behavior. In order to make the right decision in emergency

Many moral decisions must be made on spur of moment

Many moral decisions must be made on the spur of the moment. In a situation such as this one, a child's conscience—rather than the ability to evaluate moral dilemmas at a sophisticated level of understanding—may be the key factor.
Philip Jon Bailey.

A strong conscience leads to "right" moral decisions but may cause guilt feelings

situations, a person needs a strong, clear conscience so that the "reflexive" reaction will be the correct one. But such a conscience can be a source of considerable anxiety when postmortem analyses are made. A person with a weak conscience who acts in a flagrantly dishonest way will shrug it off and suffer no pangs of guilt. The individual with a strong conscience, however, may brood for weeks about such a mild thing as an ungracious remark or gesture. This leads to questions regarding the kinds of factors and experiences that lead to the development of the conscience of a child.

Factors Leading to the Development of a Child's Conscience

Martin L. Hoffman, who specializes in the study of moral development, has summarized types of experiences that seem to favor the internalization of moral norms (which might also be referred to as the formation of a child's conscience, or superego).

The Impact of Disciplinary Techniques

He reports (1979) that moral internalization appears to be initially fostered by disciplinary techniques used by parents when a child is guilty of immoral behavior. Children are most likely to internalize moral norms when the parents point out the harmful consequences of the behavior. Such explanations are most likely to be effective, though, if the parents frequently show affection for the child outside of disciplinary encounters. These two techniques are similar to those Diana Baumrind (1967, 1971) found were used by parents who promoted general competence in children. *Authoritative* parents, to review her findings, explained restrictions and also frequently showed their children that they loved and respected them. And just as Baumrind reported that parents who were *authoritarian* seemed to coerce their children into adopting acceptable forms of behavior, Hoffman found that parents who used excessive power-assertive discipline caused children to behave morally out of fear of punishment, not because of internalized standards. It appears, though, that parents who explain rather than physically punish need to make sure that the child pays attention to the explanation. If children who have just committed a moral offense are not impressed enough by their parents' attitude and behavior, they may ignore what they are told. If they are aroused too much, on the other hand, fear or resentment may interfere with their response to the parents' explanation. Therefore, if a child has committed a moral transgression, it would seem wise for parents to treat the matter seriously and sympathetically but not casually or in an extreme or punitive way.

The Impact of Imitation

In addition to showing their children affection and explaining how immoral behavior may cause others to suffer, parents should do everything possible to set a good example. Freud was the first theorist to stress the significance of identification with parents. He proposed that children imitate their parents' moral behavior because of anxiety over either physical attack or loss of love. To reduce anxiety, Freud reasoned, the child tries to be like the parent through defensive (or "If you can't lick 'em, join 'em") identification. In his review, Hoffman notes that there is some evidence that children may acquire certain types of moral reasoning and behavior (for example, helping others) by identifying with their parents. However, identification is not likely to cause them to feel guilty after violating moral standards. One reason guilt is not likely to be learned through identification is that children up to the age of eight or so are egocentric thinkers. Another reason is that parents rarely communicate their own guilt feelings to children.

Freud's observations on identification were later interpreted by American psychologists such as Sears and Bandura in terms of social learning theory as imitation. Hoffman concludes that experiments by social learning theorists reveal that imitation may be an effective way for children to learn visible moral attributes that require little self-denial (for example, helping others). But these attributes are not likely to lead to the acquisition of moral standards children use in judging their own behavior (for example, resisting the temptation to steal something). Research by social learning theorists also discloses that if children observe a peer who behaves aggressively or yields to temptation and is *not* punished, they are likely to imitate that behavior. Even if the peer model *is* punished, however, children may not be deterred from acting the same way.

Children may acquire visible moral attributes through imitation but not acquire judgment

These findings suggest that there may not be much value in parents and teachers making an example of children who have committed moral transgressions by punishing them in front of siblings or classmates. Direct experience seems to be more effective than observation at all ages. It is probably especially important for egocentric thinkers, who are still unable to put themselves in the place of the child whose behavior they have observed. (Changes in cognitive development that occur during adolescence and youth are discussed in Chapter 19, starting on page 555.)

Summary

1. During most of the elementary school years, children function as **concrete operational** thinkers. They are able to deal with operations (by mentally reversing actions) but may be unable to generalize from one situation to another. Concrete thought develops because children become capable of thinking of more than one quality of an object or situation at a time **(decentration),** of grouping objects into categories **(classification),** and of placing objects in order **(seriation).** During the elementary school years, children also exhibit increasing tendencies to engage in **socialized,** rather than egocentric, thinking. The ability to see things the way others see them leads to greater awareness of the feelings of others, which, in turn, leads to greater self-consciousness.

2. As children grapple with the elementary school curriculum, differences in cognitive style become apparent. Some children are **impulsive** thinkers, tending to give quick answers; others are **reflective,** preferring to mull things over before responding. Some children tend to **analyze** subject matter and concentrate on details whereas others are **thematic** and look for general patterns. Some children are **convergent** thinkers, responding to instruction in conventional ways, and others are **divergent** thinkers who respond in idiosyncratic ways.

3. Quite early in their school careers, children realize that academic achievement is valued by parents, teachers, and many peers. While adult males, on the average, are more achievement oriented than females, girls typically earn higher grades in school than boys. One explanation for this tendency is that girls have a stronger desire to please adults than boys. Stress on grades leads to progressively increasing competition, anxiety, and pressure, as well as to awareness of conflicts between rules, moral codes, and desires.

4. In a classic study of morality, Hartshorne and May found that moral behavior often depends on the circumstances. They also reported that being able to recite moral principles has no observable effect on moral behavior. Piaget observed that around the age of ten children begin to switch from the **morality of constraint** to the **morality of cooperation.** Below the age of ten or so, children tend to see rules as sacred, permit no exceptions, make no allowances for intentions, and concentrate on consequences when determining guilt.

5. After asking subjects of different ages to respond to moral dilemmas, Kohlberg concluded that there are three basic stages in the development of moral reasoning: **preconventional** morality (desire to avoid punishment or to receive benefits in return), **conventional** morality (desire to impress others or respect authority), and **postconventional** morality (come to mutual agreements and apply principles). While there is some research support for the existence of these different types of moral reasoning, Kohlberg's hypotheses that the stages are universal and invariably followed in sequence have not been upheld by research.

6. Techniques of moral instruction derived from research indicate that it seems preferable to ask children to think about and discuss real, rather than hypothetical, moral dilemmas. Many moral decisions must be made on the spur of the moment. In such cases, a strong conscience may lead to a "right" moral decision, but it may also cause children to feel excessively guilty about things they should not—or should—have done. Parents should try to set a good moral example since many forms of moral behavior are acquired through imitation. Moral judgment, on the other hand, is more likely to be fostered by discussion of real moral dilemmas.

Piagetian Experiments: Concrete Operational to Formal Thought

Suggestions for Further Study

To gain greater understanding of differences between concrete operational and formal thought, you might carry out some of the experiments Piaget devised for children in the eight- to fifteen-year age range. If possible, ask a child of eight or so and one of over twelve to solve the following problems. First, ascertain the age of your subject; then follow these instructions.

Approaches to Problem Solving: Physical Science

Purpose: To discover how a child attempts to solve a problem. Children at the level of concrete operations are able to solve problems if they have had actual experience with the kinds of objects and situations involved, but they are likely to experience difficulty handling new and unique situations. In addition, they are likely to approach a problem in a haphazard, unsystematic way. The children at the level of formal operations, on the other hand, can deal with combinations of ideas in a systematic way, propose and test hypotheses, and imagine what might happen in situations never before encountered.

Equipment: A piece of string about six feet long and three fishing weights, one small, one medium, and one large. (Any objects of different weights to which a string can be attached may be substituted for the fishing weights.)

Procedure: Take three pieces of string eighteen inches long, and attach to the end of each a small, medium, and large weight. Pick up the string with the smallest weight and swing it back and forth as a pendulum; hold the string at different positions along its length and let the weight drop (when the string is held taut) from different positions on an arc; push the weight as well as simply letting it fall. Also, call attention to the fact that the strings are equal in length but the weights are different.

Then say "There are four factors involved here: the length of the string, the difference in weight at the end of the string, the height from which the weight is released, and the force with which the weight is pushed. I want you to figure out which of these factors—or what combination of them—determines how fast the weight swings. Experiment with these pieces of string any way you like, and when you think you have it figured out, tell me what your solution is. Or, if you can, give me your solution without actually handling the strings." Describe the subject's procedure and solution.

Ask the subject to prove the solution to you. If you detect an oversight, demonstrate the nature of the error and observe the subject's reaction. (Note: the *length* of the string is the major determinant of the speed of the swing.)

Approaches to Problem Solving: Behavioral Science

Purpose: The problem in the previous exercise involved principles of physical science. Some students may have had courses in science or have done considerable reading in that subject, which will have given them sufficient background to solve the problem. Accordingly, you may also wish to ask your subject to wrestle with this *behavioral* science problem.

Procedure: Ask the subject to explain how to test this hypothesis: "Because many advertisers make exaggerated claims in their television commercials, the government is beginning to ask them to provide con- clusive proof that what they say is true. Suppose a fruit company is planning to use the slogan 'An apple a day keeps the doctor away.' In anticipation of being approached by the government, they ask you to set up an experiment to either prove or disprove this statement. You have an unlimited budget and you can proceed any way you like. How would you set about getting conclusive evidence to prove or disprove the state- ment 'An apple a day keeps the doctor away'? Tell me all the ideas you get as they come into your mind." Describe the subject's proposed procedure.

Hartshorne and May's Studies of Character

The series of studies on character development carried out by Hugh Hartshorne and Mark May have never been equaled in terms of in- genuity, thoroughness, or depth. Even though they were done in the 1920s, the results of these studies are still well worth examining. The authors give detailed descriptions of how they developed and adminis- tered their various measures, as well as their results and conclusions, in a three-volume series published under the general title *Studies in the Nature of Character*. Volume I, *Studies in Deceit* (1930), gives the back- ground of the study and then provides a description of the methods and results of the studies of honesty. Volume II, *Studies in Service and Self- Control* (1929), describes methods and conclusions regarding those types of behavior. Volume III, *Studies in the Organization of Character* (1930), reports a follow-up study of interrelationships between the types of behavior reported in Volumes I and II. (The final summary begins on page 382.)

Piaget's Description of Moral Development

Piaget describes his observations on moral development in *The Moral Judgment of the Child* (1932). Thomas Lickona summarizes research inves- tigations stimulated by Piaget's conclusions in "Research on Piaget's

Theory of Moral Development'' on pages 219–240 of *Moral Development and Behavior* (1976), an excellent compilation of articles on all aspects of morality, which he edited.

Morality of Constraint

Piaget has suggested that children tend to be *moral realists* until about the end of the elementary school years, when they become capable of a morality of cooperation. For insight into this distinction, obtain permission to ask pupils at lower and upper grades in an elementary school to explain how they would react to these situations:

1. Suppose your mother had bought a new dress. She was very proud of it, but you thought it looked terrible. If she asked you what you thought about it, what would you say?
2. Suppose two boys had stolen candy bars in a supermarket. One boy had plenty of money to pay for them, and the other came from a poor family, had no money, and was very hungry. Should both boys be punished in the same way if they are caught?
3. Suppose John was playing ball on the playground and accidentally hit Mary and gave her a bloody nose. During the same recess period, David got mad at Jane and hit her. It hurt, but it wasn't nearly so bad as Mary's bloody nose. John caused greater injury to Mary than David did to Jane. Does this mean John should be punished more severely than David?

According to Piaget, younger children are more likely to apply the letter of the law (*never* tell a lie) than the spirit of the law (it is all right to tell a white lie); they are less likely to take into account circumstances (such as hunger and poverty); and they are more likely to judge a person by the practical consequences of the act committed rather than by the motivation behind the act (a child who causes a more serious injury should be more severely punished even if it was an accident). Did the responses from younger and older students fit these predictions? Summarize and comment on your results.

Kohlberg's Stages of Moral Development

If you would like to read Kohlberg's own account of the stages of moral development, examine ''Moral Stages and Moralization: The Cognitive-

Developmental Approach" in *Moral Development and Behavior* (1976), edited by Thomas Lickona. A review and critique of research on Kohlberg's stage theory is presented in "The Development of Moral Thought: Review and Evaluation of Kohlberg's Approach" by William Kurtines and Esther Blank Greif in *Psychological Bulletin*, 1974, *81*, (8). Techniques for encouraging moral development by taking account of Kohlberg's stages are described in *Promoting Moral Growth* (1979) by Richard Hersh, Joseph Reimer, and Diana Paolitto.

KEY POINTS

Relationships with Parents

Authoritarian techniques become less effective with age

Authoritative parents likely to adapt techniques to changes in child

Boys from father-absent homes may fail to acquire masculine traits, be immature

Single parent may have economic problems, be forced to play multiple roles

Working mothers may be more satisfied, serve as appropriate model

Relationships with Siblings and Peers

Firstborn children more achievement-oriented, may experience more stress

Firstborn children may benefit from acting as "teachers"

Roles established as early as first grade

Rejected children antisocial, neglected children shy and inept

Peer rejection appears to be persistent

The Development of Interpersonal Reasoning

By twelve, children understand subtleties of feelings, can take societal perspective

By twelve, children can empathize deeply, accurately

CHAPTER 16

SIX TO TWELVE

RELATIONSHIPS WITH OTHERS

*D*uring the preschool years, children typically interact with their parents much more than with peers. If a child is cared for at home by the mother and does not attend nursery school, contact with peers may be restricted to occasional interactions with playmates in a backyard. If a child is first placed in a day care arrangement and then attends nursery school, an adult other than the mother may interact with the child to a considerable extent, but the mother is still likely to remain at the top of the hierarchy of attachment figures. Even though a child has contact with peers starting as early as the age of two, most of these relationships are transitory and fairly superficial compared to interactions with parents. Thus, children feel much closer to their parents than to peers and more have intensive and intimate interactions with parents than with age-mates. Between the years of six and twelve, the nature of parent and peer relationships may pretty much reverse, at least for many children. By the time they reach the sixth grade, most children spend much more time with peers than with parents. If a sixth-grader has developed a close relationship with a particular friend, the age-mate might be on more intimate terms with the child than either parent. When faced with a decision between doing something that might displease parents but please peers (e.g., smoking cigarettes smuggled out of someone's home), the twelve-year-old may choose the peer-sanctioned activity. Thus, quite significant changes in relationships between children, their parents, and their peers take place during the elementary school years.

Relationships with Parents

Reactions to Child-rearing Styles

In Chapter 8, the beginning of the process of socialization was described. The same factors that lead the preschool child to begin to acquire culturally accepted forms of behavior continue to exert an influence throughout the elementary school years. It seems reasonable to assume, for instance, that parents who function in authoritative, authoritarian, or permissive ways when dealing with two- to five-year-olds will use essentially the same basic approach in their interactions with six- to twelve-year-olds. It is not reasonable to assume, however, that these different parenting patterns will have the same effects on older children that they had on younger ones. For example, the authoritarian parent's power-assertive methods of control (threats, physical punishment, withholding privileges) seem better adapted to preschool children, who frequently lack the linguistic and cognitive skills necessary to profit from a parent's reasoning and are generally impulsive and unable to coordinate their actions with those of others in a well-planned way (Maccoby, 1984). However, the effectiveness of authoritarian techniques probably declines rapidly during middle childhood and adolescence, as impulse control, language, and perspective-taking skills increase. Once children have developed these skills, inductive techniques of the au-

Authoritarian techniques become less effective with age

thoritative parent (explanations, calling attention to the relevant factors in the situation and to the harmful consequences of the child's actions on others) are just as likely to result in compliance and are much less likely to produce undesirable side effects. A number of investigators (Dienstbier, Hillman, Lehnhoff, Hillman, and Valkenaar, 1975; Hoffman, 1970) have suggested that when parents use power-assertive discipline, children are likely to attribute the cause of their negative emotional arousal to the parent. When parents use inductive discipline, however, children are more likely to accept personal responsibility for their transgressions, which leads to greater self-control.

While parents might be expected to continue to use the same basic approach to child rearing, there is some evidence that parenting practices exhibit both continuity and change. In a recent follow-up of a longitudinal study (Roberts, Block, and Block, 1984), mothers and fathers provided information about the child-rearing techniques they were using when their children were twelve. This information was compared with a similar set of responses provided when the children were three. The researchers found significant correlations across the nine-year period for nearly three-fourths of the mothers' responses and one-half of the fathers' responses. Where changes did occur, they tended to be on items where change would be considered developmentally appropriate (for example, a shift from physical punishment to withholding privileges). It seems, therefore, that many parents are able to adapt their parenting practices to the changing capabilities of their children. This capacity for change may be especially important in families where the parents differ in their child-rearing orientations, since Block and his colleagues also found that parental disagreement on methods of child rearing was predictive of subsequent marital disruption and was "significantly related to the quality of psychological functioning in boys and in girls over a 4-year age range, from age 3 to age 7" (Block, Block, and Morrison, 1981).

It appears that authoritarian parents are not likely to modify their parenting behavior as a function of developmental changes in their children. Authoritative parents, on the other hand, appear to be more child-centered and responsive. They are more likely to adapt their levels of intervention to the changing capabilities of their children. J. A. Armentrout and G. K. Burger (1972) asked fourth- to eighth-graders to describe the kinds of control they felt their parents used. The children reported that their parents' use of threats to withhold love decreased steadily but that establishing and enforcing rules increased from the fourth to the sixth grade and then decreased. The researchers hypothesized that as parents recognize that their children are becoming more autonomous, they make less use of techniques intended to make the child feel depen-

Authoritative parents likely to adapt techniques to changes in child

dent on them. In place of such techniques of control, they substitute rule making and limit setting. Once control has been established, however, rules are relaxed to a certain extent.

Research on parenting styles, as is true of much of the research in child development, has proceeded on the assumption that a typical family consists of a mother, a father, and children. Until recently, this assumption dominated theories about the impact of identification, imitation, and modeling on child behavior. Freud's psychosexual stages, for example, describe shifts in identification with the mother or father depending on the sex of the child and the phase of development, assuming that both parents would be available in the home for children to identify with. Social learning theorists, too, have revealed ways children learn sex-appropriate behavior by imitating models, particularly the mother *or* father, during the early years of their lives. In the 1980s, however, the traditional family pattern may not exist for almost half of all school-age children. Many American children now spend at least part of their school years living with one parent, primarily because of divorce. But even in homes where both parents are available as child rearers, the arrangement of mother as homemaker and father as sole breadwinner may no longer be typical because more and more women are becoming employed outside the home. These two deviations from the traditional family pattern will be discussed separately.

The Impact of Divorce

It is estimated that 40 to 50 percent of the children born in America in the 1980s will spend an average of six years living in a single-parent home because of marital disruption. The great majority of these children will live with the mother, but about 10 percent of school-age children will live with the father (Glick and Norton, 1978). Many of these children will eventually reenter a two-parent family involving a stepparent.

In a review of research, E. Mavis Hetherington (1979) stresses that the impact of divorce on a child depends on a number of factors including the timing of the divorce, the age of the child, the sex of the child, and the attitudes and subsequent interactions of the divorced parents toward each other. The impact of divorce is greatest, for instance, immediately after the disruption of the family occurs. After the first year most children appear to adjust quite satisfactorily to living with only one parent. Young children, though, are less capable of evaluating the impact of divorce and may harbor unrealistic hopes for reconciliation or fears of total abandonment. They may also fail to comprehend their parents' needs, emotions, and behavior.

The impact of divorce appears to be more pervasive and enduring for

A divorced mother may be forced to play multiple roles, particularly if she has a son who has little contact with his father.
© *Elizabeth Crews/Stock, Boston.*

boys than for girls, although girls from father-absent homes may experience difficulties interacting with males in adolescence (Hetherington,
1972). A basic explanation for this sex difference is that the father's
leaving home (the most common pattern) deprives the boy of a male
model. If the mother continues to be hostile and critical of the father
after they separate, boys are particularly likely to experience difficulties.
They may either fail to develop masculine traits or make exaggerated
attempts to prove their masculinity, have problems relating to peers,
and act in immature ways (Biller and Davids, 1973). When divorced
mothers have a positive attitude toward ex-husbands (and other males),
however, and encourage their sons to be independent and mature, no

Boys from father-ab-
sent homes may fail
to acquire masculine
traits, be immature

significant differences between the behavior of boys reared in father-present and father-absent homes are found (Hetherington, Cox, and Cox, 1977). This may be the case because fatherless boys may find adequate substitutes in older brothers, male teachers, youth-group leaders, and the like.

On the basis of his studies of modeling behavior, Albert Bandura concluded that "when children are exposed to multiple models they may select one or more of them as the primary source of behavior, but rarely reproduce all the elements of a single model's repertoire or confine their imitation to that model" (Bandura, Ross, and Ross, 1963, p. 534). With the hundreds of male models available in the form of characters and sports figures seen on TV, acquaintances, and neighbors, the absence of a father need not mean that a boy will fail to develop masculine traits. Even if a father is present, in fact, he may not serve as a significant model for masculine behavior.

While virtually all children appear to be upset during the first few months after a divorce takes place, they are likely to be better off in the long run if conflict between parents ceases to be an everyday occurrence. In her review, Hetherington reports that consistent evidence shows that "children in single parent families function more adequately than children in conflict-ridden nuclear families" (1979, p. 855). Even so, there are a number of problems that the single parent must cope with. In a harmonious nuclear family, mother and father can alternate in taking care of child-rearing problems, support and encourage each other, and serve as dual models for the child to imitate. Moreover, the positive traits of one parent may offset some of the negative traits of the other

Single parent may have economic problems, be forced to play multiple roles

and vice versa. A single parent, however, must try to play all of the roles that are split between mother and father in a nuclear family. Another frequent difficulty is downward economic mobility, which occurs when a divorced mother seeks employment and finds that she is able to secure only low-paying part-time jobs. These indirect consequences of divorce place additional stress on both parents and frequently lead to what Wallerstein and Kelley (1981) call "diminished parenting." The noncustodial parent often abdicates responsibility as a disciplinarian and becomes overly indulgent, perhaps as a way of compensating for having left the family.

This summary of research findings on the impact of divorce leads to the conclusion that if parents do feel obliged to separate, they can minimize the negative impact of divorce on their children by maintaining reasonably cordial (or at least neutral) rather than hostile relations with each other. As Hetherington notes, a child may be better off living in a single-parent home than in a conflict-ridden two-parent home. This may not be the case, however, if the parents are still in active conflict after they terminate their marriage.

The Impact of Maternal Employment

As noted in earlier discussions of day care, at present over half of all America's mothers who live with their husbands and have school-age children are employed. Employment rates are even higher for mothers in single-parent families. In Chapter 12, mention was made of the conclusion that the development of preschool-age children does not seem to suffer if the mother works and that there may be certain advantages to maternal employment. What applies at the preschool level continues to apply during the elementary school years.

After reviewing studies of the impact of maternal employment on child development, Lois Wladis Hoffman (1979) noted that there are a number of positive factors that may operate when a mother has a job outside the home. First of all, working mothers report that they are more satisfied with their lives, on the average, than nonworking mothers. Second, a working mother may serve as a more appropriate model for her children by exemplifying contemporary views of the feminine role and thus contradicting the traditional expectation that women should spend most of their lives as homemakers. Career homemakers may be more likely to overparent, and their indulgence may actually retard their children's development of responsibility-assumption skills. The school-age children of working mothers are more often required to assume household responsibilities. Taking such responsibilities, in turn, often means that the home runs more smoothly when either or both parents are absent and that children learn to become more independent and to develop self-esteem. Finally, it appears that daughters of working mothers admire them more than do daughters of nonworking mothers and are more likely to become higher achievers later in life.

Hoffman notes, however, that the impact of maternal employment on the behavior of boys is not as uniformly favorable as it is for girls. In some studies, boys of working mothers have been rated above average in social and personality adjustment. But boys from lower-class families may experience a strain in father-son relationships when the mother works. Apparently, the fact that she has a job implies that the father is a failure. There is also some evidence that in middle-class homes the sons of working mothers may be somewhat below average in intellectual functioning and in academic achievement. Hoffman notes that on the basis of available data it is not possible to trace the cause of this slight decrease in the cognitive behavior of sons of working mothers. Perhaps future research might indicate that while middle-class boys may not exhibit strained relationships with their fathers (as is the case with lower-class boys), they may be less likely to view the father as a highly competent person when the mother works. (This might be especially true if the mother has a "better" job than the father.) Failure to think of

Working mothers may be more satisfied, serve as appropriate model

males as competent might, in turn, cause boys to be less motivated to achieve.

Even though there are certain exceptions, then, the general conclusion regarding the impact of maternal employment on the school-age child seems to be that in most cases it is not likely to cause excessive negative behavior and that in some instances it may lead to positive forms of behavior. Group statistics can never be the sole basis for deciding whether a mother should work, however. The costs and benefits vary widely from family to family. Some mothers need to be home with their children as much as other mothers need to work outside the home. Some children thrive on the increased independence that results from their mothers' employment, while others become insecure and demand increased attention. Some fathers welcome the opportunity to share home and child care more equally with their working wives, while others tolerate the wife's working only so long as she can handle two full-time jobs. In the last analysis, a mother's decision to work outside the home must be based on a careful analysis of her own needs and the needs of her family.

Relationships with Siblings and Peers

The Impact of Birth Order and Siblings

The behavior of the child after entering school may be influenced not only by how parents establish and enforce discipline in the home, by the presence or absence of the father, and by the fact that the mother has a job, but also by relationships with siblings. Helen Koch (1956) studied nearly 400 five- and six-year-olds from two-child families and analyzed aspects of family constellations. She found that, compared to girls with older sisters, girls with older brothers were aggressive and tomboyish; compared to boys with older brothers, boys with older sisters were less aggressive and daring. These findings suggest that older siblings serve as models that influence the behavior of their younger brothers and sisters.

A substantial number of studies of the significance of birth order have been carried out. The results are often difficult to evaluate because of the number of possible combinations of siblings and also because of the difficulty of taking into account such factors as genetic differences, family size, spacing of children, socioeconomic status, and special conditions, such as preference of parents for a particular child. Even so, some trends are apparent. Firstborn children are rated as more achievement-oriented (Altus, 1966) and more cooperative, responsible, and more con-

Firstborn children more achievement-oriented, may experience more stress

forming to social pressures (Becker, Lerner, and Carroll, 1966). They are also more likely to experience guilt feelings (Cobb, 1943) and to encounter psychological problems (Garner and Wenar, 1959). It should be stressed that these are *trends;* many of the great achievers of history were later-born children, and many firstborn children do not possess any of the characteristics just noted. Furthermore, after carrying out a review of dozens of studies, C. Schooler (1972) concluded that "The general lack of consistent findings [regarding birth order effects] leaves real doubt whether the chance of positive results is worth the heavy investment needed to carry out definitive studies" (p. 174).

A number of explanations have been proposed to account for differences between first- and later-born children. One hypothesis (White, Kaban, and Attanucci, 1979) is that parents spend more time with firstborn children and also engage in more language interchanges with them than they do with later-born children. Parents may also be eager to prove to themselves and others that they are skillful and capable child rearers and may instill in the child a strong need for achievement. When a second child joins the family, the parents are likely to be more relaxed, consistent, and confident about child rearing and less likely to feel compelled to prove themselves.

Another hypothesis (Schachter, 1959) is that firstborn or only children will have greater exposure to adult models and will pattern and evaluate their behavior with reference to adult standards, which are not only more demanding but also more consistent than the behavioral standards of siblings. While this may be true during the preschool years, it would seem that as soon as children enter school they would be more likely to evaluate themselves, and be evaluated, with reference to peers. Perhaps tendencies established during the preschool years will be maintained, but a switch to peer standards may be more likely.

Still another hypothesis is that the firstborn child will feel driven to regain the parents' undivided attention enjoyed before brothers and sisters entered the family. (In her study of two-child families, Koch found that a two- to four-year difference in the ages of first- and second-born children was most threatening to the older child.)

Competition with siblings might account for some of the higher achievement of oldest children, but it does not explain the equally high achievement of only children. The higher achievement of some only children might be attributed to the fact that middle- and upper-class parents tend to have smaller families than lower-class parents. It might be hypothesized that if individuals in positions of responsibility and wealth are more intelligent and capable than those who work at less demanding and lower-paid jobs, some only children may become high achievers because of superior genetic potential and a richer and more stimulating environment. Another explanation for the higher achievement (and also guilt and adjustment problems) of firstborn children is that they may be seen as the primary perpetuators of the "family name" and that parents *expect* more of them.

A final factor that may account for some differences in the behavior of first- and later-born children centers on "tutor-pupil" relationships. R. B. Zajonc and G. B. Markus (1975) report that a study of all of the males in the Netherlands who attained nineteen years of age in the years 1963–1966 revealed that firstborn boys with slightly younger siblings earned the highest scores, on the average, on an intelligence test. A similar tendency for American firstborn children was reported by H. M. Breland (1974), who analyzed scores on Merit Scholarship examinations. Zajonc and Markus hypothesize that the superior test performance of firstborn children may be due, in part, to a tendency for them to act as "teachers" for siblings who are slightly younger. These experiences contribute to understanding of the kinds of concepts stressed on intelligence and achievement tests.

Firstborn children may benefit from acting as "teachers"

Hierarchies and Popularity

As soon as organisms interact in groups, they tend to arrange themselves in hierarchies. As chickens in a farmyard establish a pecking order, so children in the elementary grades become interested in discovering who is the best in the class with respect to different qualities. Freedman (1971) found that as early as the first grade both boys and girls showed substantial agreement about who was the "toughest" in their class. Not until later grades, however, was agreement reached regarding who was "nicest" and "smartest." (Perhaps this was the case because toughness shows up fast and needs to be recognized for reasons of survival, whereas it takes a while to find out who the nice and smart people are.)

Roles established as early as first grade

In addition to sorting themselves out with reference to specific qualities, children also develop likes and dislikes for each other. Popularity in middle childhood is associated with a number of factors, including physical attractiveness (especially for girls), high intelligence and academic achievement, and having a common rather than an unusual name. Early maturation is associated with popularity in males but not in females. Popularity is typically determined by sociometric techniques that require children to nominate their favorite and least favorite peers. The categories generated from such procedures vary somewhat from one researcher to another, but children who receive frequent positive nominations are often called **populars** or **stars.** Children who receive frequent negative nominations are called **rejects.** Children who receive neither positive nor negative nominations are designated as **neglected**

One explanation for the tendency for first-born children to score high on achievement tests and do well in school is that they act as teachers for younger siblings. These tutorial experiences may solidify their own understanding of many concepts.
Peter Vandermark/Stock, Boston.

or **isolates.** A fourth category composed of peers who receive both positive and negative nominations has been called **controversials** (Dodge, 1983). Early research on peer popularity identified a significant relationship between social interaction style and popularity, with rejected children displaying more aggressive behavior and popular children displaying more prosocial behavior. However, because these studies observed children interacting with familiar peers, it was impossible to determine whether the style of social interaction observed was the cause or the consequence of peer status.

More recent research has focused on how peer status evolves in newly formed groups, and the results strongly support the view that interaction style is a basic cause of peer status. Putallaz (1983) found that unpopular children had more difficulty gaining entry to groups. They were less likely than popular children to adapt to the ongoing frame of reference of the group's participants and they were more likely to engage in inappropriate attention-getting behavior. Dodge (1983) found that second-grade boys who were later designated as popular engaged in less socially unacceptable behavior (including aggression) and more cooperative play and social conversation. Boys who were later identified as rejected exhibited high levels of antisocial behavior, including insults, threats, and exclusion of peers. Neglected boys were as socially inept as the rejected boys, but they tended to be shy and refrained from antisocial behavior. They were also less physically attractive. Finally, boys later identified as controversials exhibited high levels of both prosocial and antisocial behaviors.

Sometimes parents and teachers attribute the social problems a child encounters to the particular social group the child is in. While this is undoubtedly the case in some situations, the danger in making such an attribution is that children with real social skill deficits will not be helped. Coie and Kupersmidt (1983) found that fourth-grade boys' status in school was highly correlated with their status in a play group of previously unacquainted peers after only three one-hour play sessions. It appears, then, that a child's social problems are likely to persist even when the child's peer group is changed. Peer rejection is a relatively persistent phenomenon; researchers have documented its stability over five-year periods starting as early as the third grade (Coie and Dodge, 1983). Given the importance of peer interaction for the development of mature interpersonal relations in adulthood and given the fact that social skill deficits are amenable to intervention (Asher and Renshaw, 1981), negative peer status in middle childhood should not be ignored.

The importance of interpersonal relationships has stimulated researchers to try to discover ways children exhibit sensitivity to the feelings of others. If favorable traits of interpersonal reasoning can be discovered, it has been hypothesized, it should be possible to help children experiencing difficulties getting along with others to acquire increased social sensitivity.

The Development of Interpersonal Reasoning

The psychologist who has been most active in the study of interpersonal reasoning is Robert L. Selman (1976a, 1976b, 1980). Selman developed **interpersonal dilemmas** similar to the moral dilemmas used by Kohlberg, which he presents in the form of sound filmstrips. Here is the description of one of the interpersonal dilemmas he uses in his research:

Eight-year-old Tom is trying to decide what to buy his friend Mike for his birthday party. By chance he meets Mike on the street and learns that Mike is extremely upset because his dog, Pepper, has been lost for two weeks. In fact, Mike is so upset that he tells Tom, "I miss Pepper so much I never want to look

Marginal notes:

Rejected children antisocial, neglected children shy and inept

Peer rejection appears to be persistent

at another dog again." Tom goes off, only to pass a store with a sale on puppies; only two are left and these will soon be gone. (Selman, 1980, p. 94)

After showing the filmstrip depicting this dilemma, Selman asked six- to twelve-year-old children to respond to a series of standard but open-ended questions designed to elicit their reasoning about interpersonal relationships. Selman concluded that children become progressively more aware of the subtleties of interpersonal relationships as they move through the elementary grades. He describes five stages of interpersonal reasoning, which are summarized in Table 16.1.

Some of these changes can be illustrated by responses of children to questions Selman asked after showing the filmstrip about Mike and Tom. When asked, "Can Mike be both happy and sad at the same time if

---

TABLE 16.1
STAGES OF INTERPERSONAL REASONING DESCRIBED BY SELMAN

Stage 0: The Egocentric Level (About ages four to six)
   Children do not recognize that other persons may interpret the same social event or course of action differently than they do. They do not reflect on the thoughts of self or others. They can label the overtly expressed feelings of others but do not comprehend cause-and-effect relations of social actions.

Stage 1: Social Information Role Taking (About ages six to eight)
   Children are able to differentiate between their own interpretations of social interactions and the interpretations of others but in limited ways. They cannot simultaneously think of their own view and the view of others.

Stage 2: Self-Reflective Role Taking (About ages eight to ten)
   Interpersonal relations are interpreted in relation to specific situations, where each person understands the expectations of the other in that particular context. Children are not yet able to view the two perspectives at once, however.

Stage 3: Multiple Role Taking (About ages ten to twelve)
   Children become capable of taking a third-person view which permits them to understand the expectations of themselves and of others in a variety of situations as if they were spectators.

Stage 4: Social and Conventional System Role Taking (About ages twelve to fifteen +)
   Each individual involved in a relationship with another understands many of the subtleties of the interactions involved. In addition, a societal perspective begins to develop. That is, actions are judged by how they might influence *all* individuals, not just those who are immediately concerned.

> By twelve, children understand subtleties of feelings, can take societal perspective

Source: Adapted from discussions in Selman 1976a and Selman 1976b.

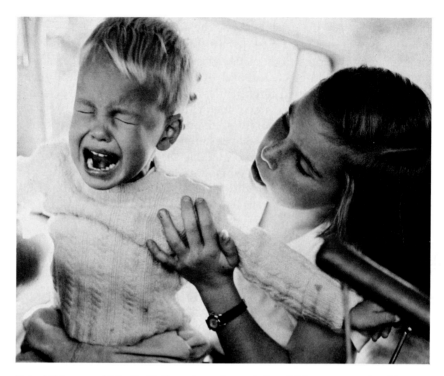

Robert Selman and Martin Hoffman have observed that children may not be able to completely understand someone else's distress, or provide appropriate sympathy or help, until after they reach the age of twelve or so.
Suzanne Szasz.

he gets a new puppy for a gift?'' six-year-olds deny that this is possible (probably because they find it difficult to decenter and therefore concentrate on only one type of feeling at a time). Children of nine years or so recognize that Mike can be sad about the lost puppy and happy about getting a new one, but they picture these feelings as more or less distinct and sequential. That is, Mike will be sad first and then happy. It is not until they approach the end of the elementary grades that children are able to grasp that Mike can feel happy and sad at the same time.

Other aspects of the development of interpersonal reasoning are brought out by the question ''Does Mike really mean it when he says he never wants to see another puppy again?'' Six-year-olds tend to take Mike's statement literally—he meant it because he said it. Twelve-year-olds begin to realize that Mike is trying to find an outlet for his grief and that he may not really feel the way he says he feels. Still another question, "What sort of boy is Mike?" reveals additional aspects of the development of interpersonal understanding. Six-year-olds tend to describe Mike's personality in terms of observable physical characteristics and actions, for example, "Mike is a boy who lost his puppy." Twelve-year-olds reveal a more comprehensive understanding of Mike. They are more likely to describe his psychological attributes; for example, Mike shows he is sensitive because he is so upset, but he also seems to want others to feel sorry for him.

These various responses reveal that during the elementary school years children gradually grasp that a person's overt actions and words do not always reflect inner feelings. They also come to comprehend that there are often multiple facets to a person's reaction to a distressing situation. Toward the end of the elementary grades and increasingly during adolescence, children become capable of taking a somewhat detached and analytic view of their own behavior as well as the behavior of others.

Not surprisingly, the interpersonal sensitivity and maturity of a child seems to have an impact on relationships with others. Comparing the responses of seven- to twelve-year-old boys who were attending schools for children with learning and interpersonal problems with the responses of a matched group of boys attending regular schools, Selman found that the special-schools boys were below average for their age in understanding the feelings of others.

Selman believes that teachers and therapists might be able to aid children who are not as advanced in role-taking skills as their age-mates by helping them become more sensitive to the feelings of others. If an eight-year-old boy is still functioning at the egocentric level, for example, he may fail to properly interpret the behavior of classmates and become a social isolate. Selman describes (1976a, p. 314) how such a boy was encouraged to think continually about the reasons behind his social actions and those of others and acquired sufficient social sensitivity to learn to get along with others.

Stages in the Development of Empathy and Sympathy

Selman's description of stages in interpersonal reasoning may be clarified by a very similar analysis Martin L. Hoffman (1976) has made of the development of empathy and sympathy. Hoffman suggests that there are three stages in the development of understanding of the feelings of others and in the reactions and motives of children who offer assistance to those in distress.

1. **Level of Person Permanence**   Children have acquired a sense of other individuals only as physical entities. They are capable of sensing another's distress, and of wanting to help, but they do not understand causes or know exactly *how* to help. Their efforts to help may be motivated primarily by a desire to end their own distress at seeing someone else suffer. (This is essentially the same as Selman's Egocentric Level.)

2. **Level of Role Playing**   Children realize that others have feelings and that these feelings may differ from their own, but their understanding is confined to a particular situation. They make an active effort to put themselves in another's place, and their efforts to help may no longer be based on a desire to relieve their own vicarious discomfort but on an altruistic wish to relieve the other person's distress. Efforts to help may proceed in trial-and-error fashion, however, and often feature frequent requests for feedback (for example, "Is there anything I can do?") (This level corresponds to Stages 1 and 2 in Selman's outline.)

By twelve, children can empathize deeply, accurately

3. **Level of Identity**   Children realize that others are continuous persons, with their own histories and identities, and they grasp distinctions between immediate and chronic distress. When children at this level respond to distress, they can take into account not only situation-specific distress but also the particular characteristics of an individual. There is increasing development of the ability to generalize from one distress experience to another and to understand the plight of an entire group of people who possess different characteristics. (This level is similar to Stage 4 in Selman's outline.)

The observations of Selman and Hoffman reveal that elementary school children not only become increasingly capable of understanding the feelings of others; they also respond sympathetically when they realize other people are in distress. But even as they become more capable of sympathizing with others, six- to twelve-year-old children also may experience such reactions as envy and spite. A child who is an excellent student or one who is elected to a class office, for example, may arouse resentment rather than empathy. When seeking to understand the behavior of elementary school children, therefore, it is not only important to consider relationships between cognitive, moral, and social development, but also to keep in mind some of the conflicts that children face when they sort out their thoughts regarding cooperation and competition, admiration and envy, sympathy and the hope that a more fortunate classmate's luck will change. (Changes in relationships with others that occur during adolescence and youth are discussed in Chapter 20, starting on page 577.)

Summary

1. Authoritarian techniques of child rearing, which tend to induce preschoolers to become hostile and insecure, seem to become even less effective as school-age children acquire abilities to understand and control their behavior. Authoritative child rearing techniques, which stress personal responsibility, are preferable. In addition, parents who choose to use authoritative techniques seem particularly likely to alter child-rearing approaches as their children mature.

2. About half of all American children spend at least a few years living in a single-parent home. The impact of divorce is typically more pervasive and enduring for boys, often because the absence of the father (the most common pattern) deprives them of a male model in the home, which may lead to immaturity and failure to acquire masculine traits. Both boys and girls may experience adjustment problems because a single parent may be forced to cope with economic difficulties and also be required to attempt to play multiple roles.

3. There may be certain advantages for a mother of elementary school-age children to be employed. Working mothers typically report that they are more satisfied with their lives than career housewives, and they serve as models for their daughters to emulate in terms of an orientation toward achievement.

4. Many studies of the impact of birth order on child behavior have been published. While there are frequent exceptions, there appears to be a tendency for firstborn children to be more achievement oriented than later-born siblings. Perhaps because of a stronger desire to achieve, firstborns are also more likely to experience stress than other children in a family. Firstborn children tend to earn slightly higher scores on intelligence tests than later-born children, perhaps because they benefit from acting as "teachers" of their younger siblings.

5. As they interact with peers during the elementary school years, children assume roles within groups. Recognition by others of certain roles (such as who is the toughest person in a class) are established as early as the first grade. When children are asked to select classmates they like and dislike, children who are rejected by peers are rated as antisocial, and those who are ignored appear to be shy and inept. The tendency for a child to be rejected by peers seems to be quite persistent and may extend over a period of years.

6. Efforts to help socially inept children to improve their abilities to get along with others have stemmed from studies of the development of interpersonal reasoning. By the age of twelve, most children are capable of understanding subtleties of feelings and can judge how what they do might influence all individuals (a societal perspective). In

addition, by the time they leave the elementary grades, children are able to empathize deeply and accurately. Children who do not seem to use their understanding of the feelings of others constructively might be shown how to increase their social sensitivity.

Suggestions for Further Study

Father Absence

For a review of studies of the impact of father absence on child behavior, examine "The Effects of Father Absence on Child Development" by E. Mavis Hetherington and J. L. Deur in *The Young Child: Review of Research* (1972, Volume 2), edited by W. W. Hartup; or "Children in Fatherless Families" by E. Herzog and C. E. Sudia in *Review of Child Development Research* (1973, Volume 3), edited by B. M. Caldwell and H. M. Ricciuti.

Divorce

For a concise review of studies of the impact of divorce on child development, see "Divorce: A Child's Perspective" by E. Mavis Hetherington in *American Psychologist*, 1979, 34 (10), 851–858. For more comprehensive analyses see *Marital Separation* (1975) by R. Weiss; or "Marital Disruption as a Stressor: A Review and Analysis" by B. L. Bloom, S. J. Asher, and S. W. White, *Psychological Bulletin*, 1978, 85, 867–894.

Maternal Employment

For a concise summary of research on the impact of maternal employment on child development, examine "Maternal Employment: 1979" by Lois Wladis Hoffman in *American Psychologist*, 1979, 34 (10), 859–865. For more comprehensive analyses, consult "Effects of Maternal Employment on the Child: A Review of Research," also by Hoffman, in *Developmental Psychology*, 1974, 10, 204–228; or "Developmental Comparisons Between 10-Year-Old Children with Employed and Non-employed Mothers" by D. Gold and D. Andres in *Child Development*, 1978, 49, 75–84.

Social-Cognitive Understanding and Empathy

Robert L. Selman describes his conclusions regarding the development of understanding of the feelings of others in "Social-Cognitive Understanding: A Guide to Educational and Clinical Practice" on pages 299–316 of *Moral Development and Behavior* (1976), edited by Thomas Lickona. Martin L. Hoffman discusses "Empathy, Role-Taking, Guilt, and the Development of Altruistic Motives" on pages 124–143 of the same volume. Carolyn U. Shantz reviews research on all aspects of the development of understanding of the thoughts and feelings of others in "The Development of Social Cognition" in *Review of Child Development Research*, 1975, 5, 257–324, edited by E. Mavis Hetherington.

KEY POINTS

The Emergence of a Concept of Self

Successfully doing things beside and with others leads to a sense of industry

Attempts to be successful *and* popular may lead to conflicts

Problems of Adjusting to Independent Existence

"Law of the jungle" atmosphere sometimes prevails during elementary school years

First real taste of independent existence during elementary school years

Extent and Nature of Behavior Disorders

Clinic referral rates highest in nine- to fifteen-year age span

Some children must cope with more risk factors than others

Views of Adjustment

Defense mechanisms protect ego

Repression as an explanation for abnormal behavior

Learning theory view of adjustment: abnormal tendencies shaped by reinforcement

Using behavior modification to control nervous habits

Child must feel comfortable, secure, and loved before experiencing urges to know and appreciate

CHAPTER 17

SIX TO TWELVE

PERSONALITY DEVELOPMENT

*S*igmund Freud and two of his students who later developed theories of their own described aspects of personality development during the elementary school years. In Freud's description of stages of psychosexual development, this is the latency period—a time when the libido is not concentrated on any particular part of the body or person, as it was during the oral, anal, and phallic stages. Some critics have interpreted "latency" in a literal way and have argued that

Freud was wrong since elementary school children continue to show an interest in sex. Peter Blos, a leading American psychoanalyst, points out, however, that such criticisms betray a lack of understanding of what Freud meant; he emphasized "the lack of a new sexual aim . . . rather than the complete lack of sexual activity" (1962, p. 5). Freud theorized that at the beginning of the elementary school years (and during the latency period), the boy admires his mother and female teachers but identifies with his father and other male adults. The girl has repressed her feelings toward her father and identifies with her mother and older females (such as teachers). If you will think back to your own feelings about your parents (and teachers) during the elementary school years and also take into account research on parent-child relationships summarized earlier, you may realize that Freud's observations are quite accurate. Even so, they do not reveal a great deal about personality development during the elementary school years. The speculations of Erikson provide deeper insights.

The Emergence of a Concept of Self

Erikson's Emphasis on Industry Versus Inferiority

In Erikson's outline of psychosocial stages of development, this is the stage of industry versus inferiority. Erikson points out that children gain their first experience with life outside the home when they enter school. In the classroom, they get their first taste of what will be a critical part of their lives: applying themselves "to given skills and tasks which go far beyond the mere playful expression of organ modes or the pleasure in the function of limbs" (1963, p. 259). That is, children learn that they need to work and "to win recognition by producing things" (p. 259). A child whose efforts in school are successful will develop a sense of industry. Erikson notes, "This is socially a most decisive stage: since industry involves doing things beside and with others, a first sense of division of labor and of differential opportunity, that is, a sense of the technological ethos of the culture develops at this time" (p. 260). The child who does not do well in school, has no confidence in being able to do things "beside and with others," and fails to achieve any status with peers will develop a sense of inadequacy and inferiority.

Successfully doing things beside and with others leads to a sense of industry

The American child with a sense of the competitive nature of our culture may recognize the opportunities available in a meritocracy but at the same time be intimidated or overwhelmed by what must be done to make the most of these opportunities. This point is emphasized by Erikson, but it was a central argument in the theory developed by another student of Freud, Karen Horney.

Horney's Emphasis on Success Versus Acceptance

Horney (pronounced "Horn-eye") was born and educated in Germany. After earning an M.D. degree, she became a member of the Berlin Psychoanalytic Institute. She soon found, however, that she was unable to accept some of Freud's teachings, particularly his belief that successful women are motivated primarily by penis envy. In time, professional relationships became uncomfortably strained. This situation, along with the realization that she and her husband had drifted apart, led Horney to decide to make a clean break with all ties in Berlin and come to the United States.

She settled in Chicago during the height of the gangster era of the 1930s, and on her first night in that city a gun duel occurred during a holdup in her hotel. That introduction to America, plus the discovery that mental illness in this country seemed to be substantially different from neurosis in Europeans, led her to have further doubts about orthodox Freudian theory.

Horney became convinced that the culture in which a person lives has a profound influence on behavior, a conclusion also reached by Erikson after he contrasted aspects of European and American culture. But while Erikson came to emphasize how the individual needs to establish a sense of identity, Horney focused on the American preoccupation with success. In her initial contacts with American patients, she was struck by the extent to which they focused on winners and losers. She became aware that this caused a basic conflict: individuals in a meritocratic society who achieve success do so at the expense of many others, who thereby become failures. As she treated American patients, she became convinced that hardly anyone seemed really to win. Some successful individuals developed insecurities because of their awareness that they were both admired and hated by their peers, while unsuccessful people were torn by envy and self-hate.

Horney therefore emphasizes many of the same ideas as Erikson. In Erikson's view, during the years six to twelve, American children must become aware that mastery of basic learning skills is essential to existence in a meritocracy. If they are successful, they will develop a sense of industry; if they do not do well, they will acquire a sense of inadequacy and inferiority. Horney emphasizes that American children experience conflicting feelings because they are told to do everything possible to be better than others but at the same time are enjoined to be popular and get along with others. Children who achieve success and feel guilty about it or those who do not and feel defeated may experience feelings of inadequacy and inferiority similar to those described by Erikson.

Attempts to be successful *and* popular may lead to conflicts

When they compare report cards, play games, compete for class offices, and the like, children during the years from six to twelve discover in no uncertain terms that some people are more successful at some things than others. As they interact in school, children acquire definite roles—class "brain," best athlete, class clown, and so forth. One of the reasons that roles become more important as children progress through the elementary grades is that they become increasingly capable of discerning the thoughts of others. Piaget has described preschoolers as egocentric to emphasize the point that young children are usually so busy sorting out their own thoughts that they find it difficult to also take into account the thoughts of others. Early in the elementary school years, however, children become capable of socialized thinking. When that occurs, they become much more aware of how their behavior affects others. By the end of the elementary school years, many children are very much concerned about what others think of them.

Erikson and Horney call attention to some of the problems faced by the elementary school child, but the list of developmental tasks for this age period provides a more complete picture.

Problems of Adjusting to Independent Existence

Review of Developmental Tasks for the Elementary School Years

The developmental tasks listed by Robert Havighurst for different stages of development were summarized in the discussion of continuity and change in personality presented in Chapter 5. The tasks children are expected to master before they leave the sixth grade include these:

1. Learning physical skills necessary for ordinary games
2. Building wholesome attitudes toward oneself as a growing organism
3. Learning to get along with age-mates
4. Learning an appropriate masculine or feminine social role
5. Developing fundamental skills in reading, writing, and calculating
6. Developing concepts necessary for everyday living
7. Developing conscience, morality, and a scale of values
8. Achieving personal independence
9. Developing attitudes toward social groups and institutions

(Havighurst, 1952, pp. 15–28)

In addition to calling attention to the many kinds of tasks the elementary grade child is expected to achieve, this list also reveals reasons why Kagan and Moss referred to the elementary school years as a "crystallization period." As noted in Chapter 5, Kagan and Moss evaluated the longitudinal data accumulated by researchers at the Fels Institute and concluded that experiences during the elementary school years "crystallize behavioral tendencies that are maintained through young adulthood" (1962, p. 272). You are also reminded that several psychologists (including Kagan, 1980) have questioned that the first years of a child's life are a critical period in development in the sense that forms of behavior that appear during the preschool years exert a permanent influence on personality. Both of these arguments can be evaluated by once again contrasting the kinds of behavior that are important at the preschool and elementary grade levels, and then comparing significant types of behavior at the elementary school and adult stages of development.

Differences Between the Preschool and Elementary School Years

Differences between kinds of behavior expected of preschool and elementary grade children were discussed in Chapter 5 after presentation of the complete list of developmental tasks. To review:

The self-concept of a preschooler is often "insulated" by support and supervision from parents as well as by egocentric thinking. The self-concept of the elementary school child is influenced by the kinds of factors noted by Erikson and Horney in the more "jungle-like" environments of the classroom, playground and neighborhood.

"Law of the jungle" atmosphere sometimes prevails during elementary school years

The preschooler is not expected to perform academically nor be evaluated publicly. The elementary school child is expected to master academic subjects, and performance is compared with standards, as well as with the achievements of others.

Preschool children almost always play under supervision and, because of egocentric thinking, are only partially aware of the reactions of others. Elementary-grade children interact with peers in unsupervised ways, assume or are assigned roles, care about how others feel about them, and are sensitive to negative reactions.

The games of preschool children (as noted in Chapter 10) are loosely organized and do not typically require a great deal of skill. The games played by elementary-grade children often are complex and competitive. Differences between the best and worst players are obvious.

Preschool children have a rudimentary understanding of moral codes, but misbehavior may often be excused because of allowance for immaturity. Elementary-grade pupils are expected to conform to several sets of rules and are much more capable of experiencing confusion or guilt about discrepancies between moral codes and behavior.

Before they enter school, children interact with others in a supervised, supportive environment. By the time they leave the elementary grades, children are expected to function as independent beings.

Children get their first taste of independent existence during the elementary school years when they interact with peers in unsupervised situations.
Mark A. Wiklund.

First real taste of in-
dependent existence
during elementary
school years

This review emphasizes the point that during the elementary school years children get their first taste of many aspects of existence in an adult world: the expectation of productive performance, public comparison and competition with others, the assumption of roles based on the unrestrained responses of others, and awareness of nuances of written and unwritten rules and codes of conduct. While some attributes lead to favorable behavior and adjustment at both the preschool and elementary school levels (e.g., sensitivity to the feelings of others), it seems clear that there are also many aspects of personality that first take on significance during the elementary school years. Many traits that are needed for a child to master the developmental tasks of the elementary school years (e.g., the ability to engage in sustained intellectual effort) are traits that are also important in adulthood. It is not surprising, therefore, that Kagan and Moss found that behavior during the years from six to twelve was a much better predictor of adult behavior than behavior observed during the preschool years. The fact that many traits and abilities become important for the first time during the elementary school years also helps account for the suggestion by Kagan and others that the first years of life may not be as crucial as they have been assumed to be. Perhaps the most direct way to summarize the overall significance of differences between preschool and elementary school behavior and expectations is to use the phrase "It's a whole new ball game." This is not to say that experiences that occur during the first five years of a child's life are of little significance. Theories and evidence presented in earlier chapters make it clear that this is not the case. The use of that phrase is simply a direct way of emphasizing that even children who get off to an excellent start the first five years of their lives have to make many adjustments when they begin school. The great majority of children *do* make the necessary adjustments, which might be considered a tribute to the resiliency and adaptability of the human organism. Some children, however, are unable to cope with the demands placed upon them and develop behavior disorders of various kinds.

Extent and Nature of Behavior Disorders

Extent of Behavior Disorders

An extensive survey (Rosen, Bahn, and Kramer, 1964) of referrals to psychiatric clinics in all parts of the country revealed that the highest referral rates occur during the nine-to-fifteen age span, with peaks at nine and ten, and fourteen and fifteen. The referral rates and peaks varied for males and females: boys were twice as likely as girls to receive psychiatric treatment; peak referral years for boys were nine and fourteen, and peak years for girls were ten and fifteen. The records of psychiatric clinics provide detailed data regarding behavior disorders, but such figures should be interpreted with caution because of the impossibility of making allowance for selective factors of various kinds (for example, characteristics of parents that cause them to seek the aid of a therapist). The data on referral peaks are supported, however, by teacher evaluations made for an extensive mental health survey of Los Angeles County (1960). Ten- and eleven-year-olds were rated as emotionally disturbed more frequently than those at other age levels.

Estimates of the prevalence of behavior disorders are difficult to make

Clinic referral rates highest in nine- to fifteen-year age span

because of the problem of determining a precise point at which a particular form of behavior becomes "abnormal" or "severe." But a number of
surveys have been made. R. Lapouse and M. Monk (1964) carried out
intensive interviews with the mothers of a large representative sample
of apparently normal six- to twelve-year-olds. They found that mothers
reported that 80 percent of the children had temper tantrums; approximately half manifested many fears and worries; about one-third had
nightmares and bit their nails; and between 10 to 20 percent sucked their
thumbs, wet their beds, or showed tics and other physical signs of
tension. The researchers concluded that their findings might be interpreted more as an indication of the pressures of meeting the demands of
a complex, modern society than as a sign of widespread psychiatric
disorders. In another study (Stennett, 1964), data accumulated on a
sample of fifteen hundred children between the ages of nine and eleven
(a peak period of clinic referrals) led to the estimate that between 5 and
10 percent had "adjustive difficulties" severe enough to warrant professional attention and that 22 percent might be classified as emotionally
handicapped.

Researchers who have studied incidence rates often conclude that
many supposedly normal children exhibit symptoms that would be
judged pathological *if* the children were referred to a clinic for observation. An extensive mental health survey carried out in England
(Shepherd, Oppenheim, and Mitchell, 1966), for example, revealed that
mothers who sought clinical help were rated as anxious, nervous, and
likely to seek consolation. The researchers concluded that many children
not referred to clinics suffered from behavior disorders as serious as
those of children who were receiving professional help.

One phase of the longitudinal research carried out at the University of
California provides evidence of adjustment problems in a typical group
of children. When the subjects of the Guidance Study were fourteen,
Jean Walker Macfarlane, Lucile Allen, and Marjorie Honzik (1954) issued a report of behavior problems shown at different age levels up to
that time. Between the years of six and twelve, the following types of
behavior were noted in one-third or more of the cases: overactivity,
oversensitiveness, fears, temper tantrums, jealousy, and excessive re-
serve. At all age levels, boys were found to be more likely than girls to
show these problems: overactivity, attention demanding, jealousy, competitiveness, lying, selfishness in sharing, temper tantrums, and steal-
ing. Girls were more likely than boys to suck their thumbs; be excessively modest and reserved; fuss about their food; be timid, shy, fearful,
oversensitive, somber; and to have mood swings. (The researchers comment that these differences were undoubtedly due to untraceable interactions between biological and cultural factors.)

Children vary in their susceptibility to behavior disorders. An "easy to care for" child with loving parents who grows up in a rich and stimulating environment has advantages over a child with opposite characteristics. At the same time, having to overcome adversity as a child may equip the adult to deal with adversity later.
© *Barbara Pfeffer/Peter Arnold, Inc.*

Susceptibility to Behavior Disorders

Even an exceptionally fortunate and well-adjusted child (or adult) is almost sure, at some time or another, to have headaches, possess little desire for food, experience a nightmare, stumble over words, engage in nervous habits, suffer pangs of jealousy, feel anxious, become preoccupied about health, or experience similar symptoms that sometimes indicate serious problems of adjustment. In many situations these responses are appropriate, and a person who did not develop such symptoms would be abnormal. A child about to undergo surgery, for example, or go to camp for the first time, or participate in a piano recital, is almost sure to experience a degree of physical and emotional upheaval. Adults usually decide for themselves whether any form of behavior has become extreme or lasting enough to require medical or psychotherapeutic attention. The decision is made *for* the child. As the researchers in the mental health survey in England discovered, some parents have a much greater tendency to seek help than others.

In making a decision about the seriousness of a behavior disorder, parents may not only weigh circumstances and be influenced by their own personalities; they are also likely to take into account their estimate of the child's ability to cope with stress. Some children seem much more capable than others of finding their own solutions to problems. E. James Anthony notes an analogy proposed by Jacques May, a disease ecologist, to account for differences in human vulnerability and resistance to disease. May observed, "It is as though I had on a table three dolls, one of glass, another of celluloid, and a third of steel, and I chose to hit the three dolls with a hammer, using equal strength. The first doll would break, the second would scar, and the third would emit a pleasant musical sound" (1970, p. 692). Anthony notes that this analogy is helpful in clarifying certain points, but that it is an oversimplification.

Anthony suggests that an evaluation of a child's adjustment should involve the appraisal of several types of risks: genetic, constitutional, environmental, and situational—which are similar to the constitutional, group membership, and situational determinants of personality described by Murray and Kluckhohn (1948). Another consideration proposed by Anthony involves critical points in development, which can be related to the critical-period concept, Freud's stages of psychosexual development, Erikson's stages of psychosocial development, and Havighurst's developmental tasks. May's analogy, Murray and Kluckhohn's set of personality determinants, and Anthony's list of risk factors serve as frames of reference for speculations about why some children are much more likely than others to develop extreme forms of behavior disorders.

Some children must cope with more risk factors than others

A "glass" child, for example, might inherit tendencies to engage in odd and difficult-to-control behavior. From the moment of birth he or she might resist cuddling and be easily irritated. The parents might have had doubts about having the child in the first place, and their attitude toward the child might be cold and resentful. These tendencies might be reinforced by the baby's strange and unresponsive behavior. And the insecurity and indecision of the parents might cause the child to develop a sense of mistrust. The parents might resort to strict toilet training and punitive discipline out of a sense of desperation, which would be likely to produce doubt and shame on the part of the child. At the preschool level the parents might be bothered by the child's tendencies to explore and ask questions. Their discouragement of such forms of behavior might produce in the child feelings of guilt and inferiority. The child might find it difficult to make friends in school, might take little interest in learning, and might mature late and be especially self-conscious at the time of puberty. Such a child might well be characterized as made of fragile crystal, likely to break if handled roughly.

A "steel" child, on the other hand, might inherit a strong physique and a well-functioning body and be exceptionally easy to care for. He or she might be responsive to others and reinforce the confidence of parents who eagerly awaited the birth of the baby and are well adjusted, warm, loving, and supportive. Such a child would begin life with a sense of trust. If the parents use techniques of child rearing such as those described by the Harvard Preschool Project researchers and Diana Baumrind, the child would be likely to develop competence as well as autonomy and initiative. If the child did well in school, industry would be established. If the child experienced few problems at puberty and made an early decision about a career, identity would become clearly established. In terms of theories of adjustment, such an individual would be much better equipped to cope with stress as an adult than the "glass" child.

As Anthony points out, however, human behavior is extremely complex. Some children who had personal histories every bit as unfortunate as those of the hypothetical "glass" child did not break under stress but responded with "highly superior modes of behavior such as creativity, productivity, and constructiveness." Several cases of this type are described by Victor and Mildred Goertzel in *Cradles of Eminence* (1962), an analysis of the biographies and autobiographies of four hundred of the most eminent people of the twentieth century. Here, for example, is a capsule description of a child who seems destined to become preoccupied with behavior problems later in life:

Boy, senior year secondary school, has obtained certificate from physician stating that nervous breakdown makes it necessary for him to leave school for six months. Boy not a good all-around student; has no friends—teachers find him a problem—spoke late—father ashamed of son's lack of athletic ability—poor adjustment to school. Boy has odd mannerisms, makes up own religion, chants hymns to himself—parents regard him as "different." (1962, p. xiii)

Instead of spending his adult life as a patient in a mental hospital, which might have been predicted from the information just provided, this child—Albert Einstein—became, in many people's consideration, the most creative, productive, and constructive thinker of the twentieth century. Insight into different ways children adapt—and why theories of adjustment do not always permit accurate predictions—is provided by an analysis of psychoanalytic, learning theory, and third-force views of adjustment.

On the basis of ratings and observations of subjects in one of the longitudinal studies at the University of California, researchers made predictions of how successful and well-adjusted each child would be as an adult. If Albert Einstein had been one of their subjects, it is quite likely that his behavior as an adolescent would have led to a prediction that he would encounter extreme problems later in life. Yet Einstein, as well as many of the ''poor risk'' subjects of the California study, turned out to be a successful and well-adjusted adult. It appears that painful early experiences sometimes have a maturing and stabilizing effect. Furthermore, certain traits that lead to adult achievement may not become apparent until an individual becomes fully mature.
United Press International.

Views of Adjustment

The Psychoanalytic View of Adjustment

Defense Mechanisms

Defense mecha-
nisms protect ego

In Freudian theory, the ego and superego are engaged in a constant struggle with the id. In some situations, the primitive impulses of the id may be so strong that the conscious and rational forces of an individual's personality cannot completely contain them. The most common result is that the individual resorts to defense mechanisms that permit partial expression of the impulses of the id but do not completely compromise the ego. Imagine that a fourth-grade boy is confronted on the same day with an important test and a class election. His id, governed by the pleasure principle, seeks the easy gratification of a high grade on the test and election to the presidency of the class. A struggle between the id

One of the defense mechanisms described by Freud is regression: the tendency to respond to stress by engaging in a form of behavior that provided comfort at an earlier stage of development.
Charles Harbutt/Magnum.

and superego may take place if the boy is tempted to cheat on the test or insert some extra slips in the ballot box. If both of these impulses are satisfactorily checked by the superego, the boy may get a low grade on the exam and receive only one vote (his own) in the election. These are both ego-shattering experiences. In efforts to patch up his self-concept, the child might resort (usually in an unconscious way) to some or all of these defense mechanisms:

He might say, "The stupid test wasn't really important, and if I'd won the stupid election, I would have had to do a lot of extra work." (Rationalization)

If the boy came very close to cheating on the test, he might say to himself, "I got a low score on the test because I didn't cheat. I saw others cheat, but I was honest and I'm going to do everything I can to be the most honest person in the class. In fact, I think I'll organize a campaign for everyone to be honest." (Reaction formation)

If the boy desperately wanted to be elected class president because he loved being the center of attention and half recognized this very strong urge, he might say to himself, "It's a good thing Mary was elected president because now maybe she won't be so wild about trying to get everybody's attention all the time." (Projection)

During recess just after the exam and election, the child might engage in some sensational and reckless stunts on the swings. (Compensation and attention getting)

After recess, the teacher might invite the child to choose a partner to work with on a project. The child might select Mary, who got an A on the test and was elected president of the class. (Identification)

On the way home from school, the double disappointment might suddenly overwhelm his thoughts, and the boy might begin to suck his thumb, a habit he had not indulged in since kindergarten days. (Regression)

A bit further along, when disappointment had turned to frustration and anger, the boy might encounter a sassy first-grader whose previous taunts had never aroused a response in him. On this occasion, the first-grader's first wisecrack is answered with a sharp cuff administered to the back of the head. (Displacement)

The Significance of Repression

As these illustrations reveal, defense mechanisms are common forms of behavior, and most of us probably resort to one or more of them every day of our lives. Only repeated and extensive use of behavior intended to protect the ego is likely to lead to unfortunate consequences. A child of demanding parents who is unable to meet their standards of school-work, for example, may be constantly torn by the urge to cheat and the fear of being caught. One solution to this conflict might be a tendency to say or think or write over and over again "Honesty is the best policy" (obsession). Another solution might be excessive concern about cleanliness (compulsion), where the "dirty" thought of cheating is symbolically purified.

Perhaps the most important contribution Freud made toward the understanding of behavior was his insight that memories repressed at the conscious level but retained in the unconscious may continue to influence thoughts and actions. A child who arouses parental fury by some flagrant act of misbehavior at an early age, for example, and is screamed at, spanked, and then locked in a dark closet as further punishment may suffer from that time on from fear of the dark and enclosed places. The pain, shame, guilt, and anxiety of the incident will be repressed, and the individual will not be able to remember what happened. The experience, however, will be retained at the unconscious level of memory and will influence behavior. If fear of the dark and of enclosed places become so extreme that they dominate the person's life, a psychotherapist's help may be called for. If the individual can be

Repression as an explanation of abnormal behavior

helped to recall the incident, talk about it, and understand why being in a dark, enclosed place was—and is—associated with pain, fear, and guilt that is no longer appropriate, the phobia may be brought under control.

The phobias just described are conditioned fears. Other phobias may be due to displaced anxiety. The child may experience a feeling of intense anxiety because of some threatening or disagreeable feature of relations with parents. If the actual cause of the anxiety is vague, incompletely understood, or threatening to the child, the anxiety may be transferred to some specific object or situation. An example of this type of reaction is **school phobia,** where the child will resist leaving home or find excuses for coming home early. The cause of school phobia may be anxiety about being separated from the mother, but fear is displaced to the school. Another common type of displaced anxiety is **death phobia,** sometimes referred to as "eight-year anxiety" because it typically occurs at that age. E. James Anthony (1967, p. 1395) has suggested that at this age the child first becomes aware of the irreversibility of death, which leads to a sense of helplessness. This vague but intense feeling of uneasiness is expressed as a fear of the child's own death or the death of parents.

School (and sometimes death) phobias may be caused by parent-child relationships that involve dependency and hostility. L. Eisenberg (1958) and S. Davidson (1961) hypothesize that while parents overtly urge a child to go to school, they may also give subtle nonverbal cues, communicating that the child should stay home. Or a child may develop a sense of hostility toward the parents (perhaps as a result of a conflict between feelings of dependency and urges to assert independence) and experience an urgent need to go home, to make sure vaguely sensed wishes for the parents' death or injury have not come true (Lassers, Nordan, and Bladholm, 1973).

Learning Theory View of Adjustment

Psychoanalysts trace behavior disorders to early experiences, particularly at critical stages of psychosexual development. Compulsive tendencies in a ten-year-old, for example, may be attributed to coercive toilet training and to the fixation of libidinal energy (that ordinarily might be available for coping with adjustment problems) at the anal stage of development. Learning theory explanations of adjustment and maladjustment also stress the impact of certain types of experiences, but emphasis is on how certain tendencies have been shaped by reinforcement rather than on fixation or the influence of unconscious memories. Compulsiveness in a ten-year-old might be explained, for instance, by

Learning theory view of adjustment: abnormal tendencies shaped by reinforcement

the hypothesis that parents frequently rewarded tendencies toward neatness early in life, particularly when the child was dependent on them and eager for their approval. An older child's excessive concern about neatness might be explained as an effort to re-experience the pleasurable sensations associated with early praise.

Learning theory explanations of certain types of behavior are usually much less intimidating than psychoanalytic explanations. As a consequence, attempts to eliminate or lessen unfortunate traits do not need to be restricted to the efforts of psychoanalysts or clinical psychologists, but can sometimes be made by parents. The psychoanalytic explanation of a phobia or of a nervous habit, for instance, may lead parents to believe that the only way they can help their child is to arrange for a specialist to uncover repressed memories. Instead of assuming that it is essential to trace causes (which is often extremely difficult to do with children because they are unable to verbalize their feelings, even when a skilled therapist endeavors to help them overcome repression), learning theorists concentrate on reinforcing positive types of behavior. Some theorists specialize in the use of **behavior therapy,** which is based on the principles of learning theory. Quite often, though, parents can use the same techniques in the home.

If a six-year-old boy has such a fear of dogs that he is afraid to go out and play, for example, parents might use the technique developed by Albert Bandura and his associates (1967) and arrange for the child to observe playmates having positive experiences with dogs. If an eight-year-old girl bites her nails almost constantly, her parents might help her use techniques recommended by Nathan Azrin and Gregory Nunn (1977). With parental encouragement and assistance, the girl might keep a record of the number of times she bites her nails each day (before she starts on her behavior modification program), list all the annoyances and inconveniences nail biting causes, list all the mannerisms that immediately precede her nail biting, describe exactly how she bites her nails, note situations and activities that seem to lead to nail biting, and identify people who seem to cause her to bite her nails. After she has used these techniques to become thoroughly aware of what was previously an "unconscious" habit, the girl should practice a competing reaction, such as clenching her hands, each time she feels the urge to bite her nails. She should mentally rehearse how she will clench her hands when she feels the impulse to bite her nails and ask her parents and friends to comment on her progress (and gently remind her when she backslides). This approach to dealing with a nervous habit such as nail biting is obviously much more simple and direct than brooding about unfortunate infantile experiences that might have fixated libidinal energy at the oral stage of psychosexual development. (A psychoanalyst

Using behavior modification to control nervous habits

might argue, however, that if the underlying causes of the nail biting are not uncovered, the girl is likely to develop some substitute form of oral activity such as thumb sucking or compulsive gum chewing. A behavior therapist might reply that those habits could also be controlled through use of behavior modification techniques.)

While the learning theory view of adjustment (and therapy) often makes it possible to replace unfortunate habits or reactions with neutral or constructive forms of behavior, it does not shed much light on more pervasive reactions such as anxiety or depression. Positive and negative personality traits that influence behavior in a variety of ways can sometimes be understood, though, by interpreting behavior in terms of a description of needs proposed by Abraham Maslow. Maslow's observations call attention to causes of positive and negative forms of behavior, but in a way that may make it possible for parents and teachers (not just psychotherapists) to become aware of inadequacies in a child's life and bring about improvements. Maslow developed his theory because he was dissatisfied with the two prevailing "forces" in psychology— psychoanalysis and learning theory. Accordingly, he referred to his interpretation of adjustment as the **third force** view.

The Third Force View of Adjustment

Maslow suggests that "We have, each one of us, an essential inner nature which is instinctoid, intrinsic, given, 'natural,' i.e., with an appreciable hereditary determinant, and which tends strongly to persist" (1968, p. 190). This inner nature is shaped by experiences and interactions with others, but it is also self-created. "Every person is, in part, 'his own project' and makes himself" (p. 199). Because individuals are unique and make themselves, Maslow reasons, they should be allowed to make many of their own choices. Parents and teachers should have faith in children and let them grow and *help* them grow, not try to *make* them grow or attempt to shape their behavior. The best way to help a child grow, Maslow suggests, is to take into account the nature of human motivation.

To explain motivation, Maslow has proposed a hierarchy of needs and a basic principle that binds them together. The principle is: "The tendency for a new and higher need to emerge as the lower need fulfills itself by being sufficiently gratified" (p. 55). At the lower level of the hierarchy are **deficiency** (or D) needs: physiological, safety, belongingness and love, and esteem. The higher level of the hierarchy is made up of **growth** or **being** (or B) needs: self-actualization, knowing and understanding, and aesthetic. (See Figure 17.1.)

FIGURE 17.1
Maslow's hierarchy
of needs

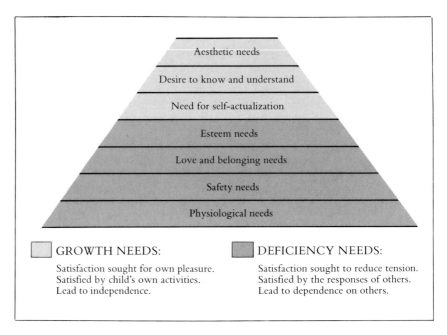

Redrawn, with permission, from Abraham H. Maslow, "A Theory of Human Motivation," *Psychological Review*, 1943, 50, 370–396. Copyright 1943 by the American Psychological Association.

There are several significant differences between deficiency and growth needs. Individuals act to get rid of deficiency needs in order to reduce disagreeable tension. Such needs can be satisfied only by other people and therefore make individuals other-directed and dependent on others when in difficulty. By contrast, people seek the pleasure of the growth needs, and their satisfaction arouses a pleasurable form of tension. Such needs can be self-satisfied, which means that individuals are self-directed and able to find their own solutions to difficulties.

Maslow's basic principle of motivation, his hierarchy of needs, and the distinctions he makes between deficiency and growth needs can be illustrated by contrasting two hypothetical third-grade boys.

One boy comes from a broken home, where he is alternately ignored and physically abused by a bitter, alcoholic mother. The mother stays up late every night, drinks, and watches television. The child gets little sleep and must get ready for school by himself each morning. He eats no breakfast and must search to find sufficient clothes to wear. He is aware that his mother despises him, and his shabby appearance and lack of confidence prevent him from making friends. Instead, he is the butt of many jokes and the chief victim of the class bully. His teacher is repelled by his appearance, bothered by his habit of falling asleep, and well aware that he is the poorest student in the class. When she plays a recording during music-appreciation period, she notes his lack of response and attributes it to low intelligence.

A second boy comes from a home where the parents provide excellent physical care and make it abundantly clear that they love and esteem him. He goes to school feeling physically fit and emotionally secure. These qualities, plus other aspects of his personality and appearance, make him attractive to classmates, and he is elected class president. He is eager to do schoolwork and takes pleasure in delving into things. When the teacher plays a record, he comments excitedly on what the music might mean.

Maslow would explain the behavior of the first boy by pointing out that none of his deficiency needs are being satisfied. He is hungry, tired, afraid of being physically abused, has rarely experienced love or a sense of belonging, and is constantly made to feel inferior. Since a higher need emerges only when lower needs are sufficiently gratified, such an unfortunate child could not desire to learn or develop an appreciation for music. The second boy, by contrast, is in the enviable position of having all the deficiency needs well satisfied. He is therefore primed to devote himself wholeheartedly to learning and to enjoying aesthetic and other self-fulfilling experiences.

Child must feel comfortable, secure, and loved before experiencing urges to know and appreciate

If the first boy is not helped to satisfy his deficiency needs, he is almost sure to become what Maslow refers to as a **bad chooser.** If left entirely to his own devices, he will very likely develop one or more types of problem behavior. Only if some sympathetic and understanding adult helps him to satisfy his deficiency needs is he ever likely to become a good chooser, capable of making his own growth decisions. This is a significant aspect of Maslow's theory that is sometimes overlooked. He recommends freedom of choice only for children who have had deficiency needs well satisfied. This is what he means when he urges parents and teachers to *help* children grow. (Changes in personality development during adolescence and youth are discussed in Chapter 21, starting on page 597.)

Summary

1. Erikson stressed that during the elementary school years it is important for children to develop a sense of industry by successfully doing things by and with others. Children who fail to do reasonably well in school and/or who are not accepted by others are likely to experience

a sense of inferiority. Karen Horney, who followed a career pattern quite similar to that of Erikson, pointed out that attempts to be successful and popular may lead to conflicts because American children are told that they should strive to do better than others, and, at the same time, to get along favorably with others. Few children satisfy both demands with complete success.

2. Between the ages of six and twelve, children in our society are expected to achieve a formidable set of developmental tasks. Many of these tasks must be achieved in a comparatively unprotected and unsupervised "jungle-like" atmosphere. Thus it is during the elementary school years that children become initiated into a life of independent existence.

3. Because they are expected to try to achieve independently many demanding tasks, some children inevitably experience adjustment problems, and the rate of clinic referrals is highest in the nine- to fifteen-year span. Understanding of why some children encounter problems while others do not can be increased by taking into account the fact that some children must cope with more demands (or **risk factors**) than others.

4. Various views of the adjustment process have been proposed. Freud called attention to ways **defense mechanisms** are resorted to in order to protect the ego and also pointed out that allowing for the possibility of **repressed memories** may explain certain types of abnormal behavior. Learning theorists view abnormal tendencies as forms of behavior that have been shaped because they provided satisfaction and recommend use of behavior modification techniques to weaken undesirable types of behavior and strengthen preferred forms of reacting. Abraham Maslow developed a hierarchy of needs to explain positive and negative forms of behavior. He suggested that before children experience urges to learn, appreciate, and make the most of themselves, they must feel comfortable, secure, and loved. The lower-level needs can be satisfied only by others, which means that the positive influence of parents and teachers is essential.

Suggestions for Further Study

Horney's View of Behavior

If Karen Horney's observations on the conflict between success and acceptance of self arouse your interest, you may wish to read a section of one of her books. These not only provide many insights into behavior; they are also a pleasure to read because Horney has a clear, direct style. Her best-known work is *The Neurotic Personality of Our Time* (1937). For a sample of the points made in this book, you might read pages 35–40 for a concise description of a neurotic personality; pages 75–78 for an analy-sis of how Horney's view of anxiety differs from Freud's (a complete description of which is presented in Horney's book *New Ways in Psychoanalysis* [1939]); and pages 80–90 for a description of environmen-tal characteristics leading to neurosis. Neurotic competitiveness is dis-cussed in Chapter 11; "Recoiling from Competition" in Chapter 12; "Culture and Neurosis" in Chapter 15. Other books by Horney are *Our Inner Conflicts* (1945) and *Neurosis and Human Growth* (1950).

Types of Maladjustment

For more complete information about causes and symptoms of behavior problems, neuroses, and psychoses, refer to *Child Psychiatry* (4th ed., 1972) by Leo Kanner. The first edition of this classic text was published in 1935, and Kanner might be thought of as the dean of American psy-chiatrists. He outlines the history of child psychiatry (Part 1), discusses how physical, environmental, and interpersonal factors influence be-havior (Part 2), describes clinical methods (Part 3), and provides detailed descriptions of personality problems arising from physical illness, psychosomatic disorders, and disorders of behavior (Part 4). Essentially the same topics are covered in *Behavior Disorders in Children* (4th ed., 1972) by Harry and Ruth Morris Bakwin. Another excellent reference is *Manual of Child Psychopathology* (1972), edited by Benjamin B. Wolman. A comprehensive but quite technical discussion of developmental psychopathology is provided by Michael Rutter and Norman Garmezy in *Socialization, Personality, and Social Development*, edited by E. Mavis Hetherington, Volume IV of the *Handbook of Child Psychology* (4th ed., 1983), edited by Paul H. Mussen.

Psychotherapy with Children

If you would like information about techniques of psychotherapy used with children, a general review of methods is presented in the Kanner and Wolman books mentioned above. For detailed information about specific techniques, consult the following:

The *Psychoanalytic Treatment of Children* (1946) by Anna Freud and *The Psychoanalysis of Children* (1937) by Melanie Klein describe the psychoanalytic approach. Carl Rogers describes his nondirective or client-centered approach in *Client-Centered Therapy* (1951) and *On Becom-ing a Person: A Therapist's View of Psychotherapy* (1970). Two case histories in which nondirective techniques are used with children are *One Little Boy* (1952) by Dorothy W. Baruch; and *Dibs: In Search of Self* (1964) by

Virginia Axline. Behavior therapy is discussed in the *Handbook of Psychotherapy and Behavior Change* (2nd ed., 1978), edited by S. L. Garfield and A. E. Bergin. Group therapy is discussed in *The Theory and Practice of Group Psychotherapy* (1970) by I. D. Yalom. Family therapy is described in *Progress in Group and Family Therapy* (1972), edited by C. J. Sager and H. S. Kaplan. Milieu therapy is described in *The Empty Fortress* (1966) and *A Home for the Heart* (1974) by Bruno Bettelheim. A fictional account of the reactions of a sixteen-year-old girl to institutionalization and psychotherapy is offered in *I Never Promised You a Rose Garden* (1964) by Hannah Green (a pseudonym used by Joanne Greenberg).

Encouraging Parent-Child Understanding

Carl Rogers (1951) developed techniques of nondirective therapy because he wanted to help his patients learn to cope with their own problems. In his sessions with clients, Rogers accepts, reflects, and clarifies the feelings expressed so that people gain insights into their own behavior. A number of psychologists who used nondirective techniques in therapeutic sessions concluded that it might be beneficial to help parents use variations of the basic method in interacting with their children. One of the first therapists to do this was Haim Ginott, author of *Between Parent and Child* (1965), *Between Parent and Teenager* (1969), and *Teacher and Child* (1971). In all these books, Ginott urges those who deal with children to accept, reflect, and clarify feelings expressed by children.

Thomas Gordon has expanded the basic technique outlined by Ginott into a more complete program described in *P.E.T.: Parent Effectiveness Training* (1970). He calls his approach the "No-Lose" method because it involves having parent and child discuss problems and come up with compromise solutions. If a girl refuses to wear a raincoat to school, for example, the parent may force her to wear it (the parent wins) or give in and permit the child to go out in the rain without a coat (the child wins). A no-lose solution involves having the parent and child discuss the problem (the girl doesn't want to wear her raincoat because it is plaid and no one else at school wears a plaid coat) and find a mutually satisfying solution (the girl is allowed to wear her mother's white coat).

If you would like to find out more about how parents and teachers might use techniques derived from nondirective therapy, examine one of the books by Ginott or Gordon's description of P.E.T. (Gordon trains and "licenses" individuals to conduct P.E.T. workshops. You might wish to examine his book for a preview of what would be covered in the eight-week program, so that if a course is offered in your area, you would know whether you would like to take it.) For critical evaluations of the Ginott and Gordon books, examine "Popular Primers for Parents" by K. Alison Clarke-Stewart in *American Psychologist* (1978, *33*, 359–369) and "The Validity of Popular Primers for Parents" by Robert J. Griffore in *American Psychologist* (1979, *34*, 182–183).

Maslow's View of Motivation

If the account of Abraham H. Maslow's views of motivation in this chapter aroused your interest more than earlier descriptions of his work, you might wish to read sections of *Toward a Psychology of Being* (2nd ed., 1968) or *Motivation and Personality* (2nd ed., 1970).

PART
6

ADOLESCENCE AND YOUTH

KEY POINTS

The Nature and Impact of Puberty

Girls achieve puberty 1.5 years earlier than boys, on the average

Appearance becomes extremely important after puberty is achieved

Popularity due to appearance only for most attractive

Bulimia: insatiable appetite during eating binges

Anorexia nervosa: abnormal preoccupation with not eating

Anorexia may be due to a desire to resist growing up

The Impact of Early and Late Maturation

Early-maturing boys self-confident; late-maturing boys seek attention

Early-maturing girls out of step in high school; self-possessed as adults

The Impact of Sexual Maturity

Contemporary adolescents expected to be interested in sex

Aspects of sexuality imbued with vague but powerful moral tones

Substantial increase in premarital intercourse by females

Double standard has diminished but has not disappeared

Less than one-third of teen-agers who engage in premarital sex use contraceptives

Failure to use contraceptives due to ignorance, unpredictability, desire for spontaneity

To be effective, sex education courses for females should be given in junior high

Illegitimacy rate has declined but public concern has increased

Early childbearing often leads to physical, psychological, and economic problems

Early pregnancy and/or early marriage reduce(s) chances for stable marital relationship

CHAPTER
18

ADOLESCENCE AND YOUTH

PHYSICAL DEVELOPMENT

*T*hese four chapters are devoted to descriptions of development during adolescence *and* youth for reasons spelled out succinctly by Kenneth Keniston. In the opening paragraphs of *Youth and Dissent* (1971), Keniston observes, "Millions of young people today are neither psychological adolescents nor sociological adults; they fall into a psychological no man's land, a stage of life that lacks any clear definition" (p. 3). He goes on to argue that "the unprecedented prolongation of education has opened up opportunities for an extension of psychological development, which in turn is creating a 'new' stage of life." Keniston suggests that the word *youth* is preferable to terms such as *protracted adolescence* as a designation for this new stage of development. He notes (p. 5) that in 1900 only 6.4 percent of young Americans completed high school and that there were only 238,000 college students. Today, almost 80 percent of American youth complete high school and approximately 10 million—about half of all Americans in their late teens and early twenties—attend college. Largely because so many young Americans continue their education beyond high school, Keniston feels that discussions of development should not stop at adolescence (typically defined as the years between twelve and eighteen) but should continue through the midtwenties. Because Keniston's point seems accurate, these chapters summarize information and speculations about development through the midtwenties.

Some psychologists agree with Keniston that *youth* should refer to a transitional stage, but they use the term to describe all individuals between the ages of fourteen and twenty-four. This alternative definition is used by the authors of *Youth: Transition to Adulthood* (1974), a report by the Panel on Youth of the President's Science Advisory Committee. The

Kenneth Keniston suggests that youth has become a new stage of life in our society because about half of all young Americans prolong their education beyond high school. Many college students, Keniston notes, are "neither physiological adults nor sociological adults . . . they fall into a psychological no-man's land."
Paul Conklin/Monkmeyer.

writers of this report also suggest that whereas young people in simple agricultural societies appear to be eager to *hurry* through childhood in order to begin to function as adults, young people in technological societies may be *reluctant* to leave the youth subculture. Many American youth may feel obliged to attend college in order to prepare for an occupation. But as college students they are segregated in many ways from adult society. Because of this segregation, they may prefer to remain in the youthful subculture as long as possible.

In these chapters, references to youth will be based more or less on Keniston's interpretation of the term. That is to say, the word **youth** will refer primarily to college students who are in a transitional stage between adolescence and adulthood. The term **adolescent** will be used to refer to high school students between the ages of twelve and eighteen.

The Nature and Impact of Puberty

A brief analysis of puberty and the impact it has on behavior was presented in Chapter 14 in the discussion of physical development during the six- to twelve-year span. A more complete analysis follows. The earlier brief comments were appropriate since many girls reach puberty before they leave the sixth grade. The more complete discussion of puberty in this chapter reflects the fact that the overwhelming majority of males and females reach sexual maturity some time during the junior and senior high school years.

Physiological Changes That Occur at Puberty

As noted in Chapter 14, most girls experience the growth spurt that precedes puberty at eleven or twelve. Boys are likely to have their most rapid period of growth between thirteen and fourteen (Tanner, 1970). The spurt and changes that accompany it are caused by increased output of the growth hormone and gonadotropic hormones controlled by the pituitary gland. The gonadotropic hormones stimulate the sex glands (gonads) so that they not only increase in size but also produce increased amounts of sex hormones: androgens in males and estrogens in females. These in turn act on the pituitary to lead first to an increase and then to a gradual diminution of output of the growth hormone. Thus, there is a reciprocal interaction between the pituitary and the sex hormones, an interaction that produces an increase in overall size and several other physical changes as well. The proportions of the body change, and it assumes close to adult form. The shape of the face alters and comes closer to adult appearance. Internally, the heart and lungs in-

534

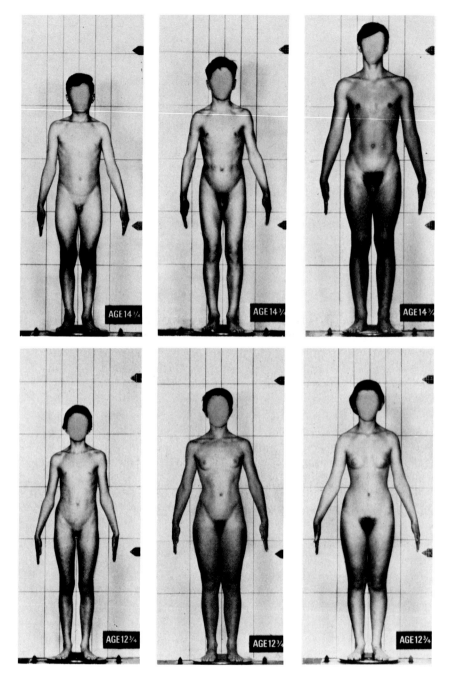

Differing degrees of pubertal development at the same chronological age. The three boys in the upper row are 14.75 years of age. In the lower row, the three girls are 12.75 years of age.
From J. M. Tanner, "Growth and Endocrinology in the Adolescent," in L. I. Gardner, ed., Endocrine and Genetic Diseases of Childhood *(W. B. Saunders Company, 1969).*

crease in size, and the digestive system assumes almost its final size and shape. The sex organs mature rapidly and secondary sex characteristics appear. To review the description presented in Chapter 14, secondary sex characteristics include breast development, rounded hips, and the appearance of a waistline in girls; broadening of shoulders and replacement of fat with muscle tissue in boys. Pubic, axillary, facial, and body hair appear. The texture of the skin changes (often with temporary malfunctioning of the oil-producing glands, which leads to acne). The voice deepens, a change that is much more apparent in males, since the larynx enlarges and the vocal cords lengthen to such an extent that the voice drops an octave in pitch.

Strictly speaking, the term **puberty** refers to the time when a person becomes physiologically capable of reproduction. It might be assumed that in females this occurs at the time menstruation begins. There is evidence (Tanner, 1972), however, that a period of sterility occurs just after menstruation begins and that conception is not likely to take place until at least ten months after that time. There is, therefore, some vagueness about the age of puberty in females, but there is even more confusion about when boys become sexually mature. As a result, a commonly used index of masculine puberty is the emergence of pigmented pubic hair, although some authorities suggest that capability of ejaculation is a more useful indicator. Thus, the figures given earlier about average ages for puberty are approximate. With that reservation in mind, note again that the average age at which American girls reach menarche is between twelve and thirteen, with a range from nine to sixteen years. For boys the average age of puberty is fourteen years, with a range from eleven to eighteen years.

Girls achieve puberty 1.5 years earlier than boys, on the average

Concern About Appearance

The timing of puberty and the development of characteristics signaling sexual maturation are extremely important to both boys and girls for many reasons, but an especially compelling one is concern about appearance, particularly attractiveness to members of the opposite sex. During the elementary school years, children tend to prefer the company of peers of the same sex. If boys and girls do engage in similar activities such as neighborhood games, they are more likely to judge each other on the basis of skill than any other quality. But growth spurt, sexual maturity, and the discovery that particular members of the opposite sex arouse feelings never before experienced lead many recently pubescent boys and girls to think seriously for the first time about male-female relationships. A boy who delighted in provoking the girls in his sixth-grade class by a well-phrased gibe may strive to win their approval

Concern about appearance reaches a peak during the junior high school years, just after most adolescents achieve puberty.
Richard Kalvar/Magnum Photos.

Appearance becomes extremely important after puberty is achieved

by what he says and does in high school. A girl who treated boys with ill-concealed contempt in the fifth grade may take great pains to make herself appear attractive to them in junior high school. Suddenly, physical appearance becomes extremely important. When Aaron Hass (1979) asked fifteen- to eighteen-year-old males, "What are the most important qualities that a girl must have for you to want to go out with her?" the five most frequently mentioned qualities were: good looks and a good body, friendly, intelligent, sense of humor, and honest ("not into game playing"). When females were asked what they looked for in a boy, the five qualities they mentioned most frequently were: intelligent, good looks and good body, good conversationalist, sincere ("not just out for sex"), and confident but not conceited.

Other evidence indicating that appearance is of great concern just after puberty is supplied by studies in which adolescents are asked what they like and dislike about themselves (for example, Lerner and Karabenick, 1974). Physical characteristics are mentioned more frequently than either intellectual or social ones. But the proportion of disliked appearance characteristics decreases as students move from junior high into senior high school. Such studies also reveal that girls tend to be more concerned about their appearance than boys.

The standards against which teen-agers measure their relative appeal to members of the opposite sex both reflect and enhance their increasing concern about appearance. For girls, the qualities displayed by models in magazine advertisements and TV commercials, contestants in beauty pageants, and stars of films and television series present a clear standard of the qualities of face and figure considered desirable. For boys, signs of early maturity (for example, face and body hair) and strength may be more of an asset than facial features.

Ellen Berscheid and Elaine Walster (1972) studied reactions to appearance and concluded that for both sexes physical attractiveness exerts a positive impact on many aspects of a child's life and that it may be the single most important factor in determining popularity among college students. Furthermore, they discovered that attractiveness was associated with many positive traits (such as adaptability and academic ability) and unattractiveness with some negative traits. Teachers, for example, were more likely to give attractive children higher ratings and higher grades.

In a review of studies of friendship, however, John C. Coleman (1980) reports that there is evidence that appearance influences popularity (or lack of it) only for adolescents and youth who are the most and least attractive members of a group. He concludes that appearance has little effect on the popularity of most young people who are between the extremes. He also concludes that attractiveness alone is neither a necessary nor a sufficient cause for popularity.

Popularity due to appearance only for most attractive

Problems with Weight Control

Weight is an aspect of appearance that may be particularly likely to become a source of concern during the adolescent years. Before children enter junior high school, being overweight may not cause too much anguish, partly because younger children do not treat appearance as an especially important characteristic and partly because of egocentric thinking. During the secondary school years, however, appearance *does* become important and adolescents become very much concerned about what others think of them. Weight control is much more of a problem for females than males. Girls are more likely than boys to be placid and inactive early in life (due to genetic as well as environmental causes). As a consequence, female infants are more likely to be fat, and (as noted earlier) early tendencies toward fatness are likely to be perpetuated. During the preschool and elementary school years, the typical girl is more likely than the typical boy to engage in sedentary as opposed to athletic activities. Thus, a habit of overeating coupled with lack of exercise is likely to cause girls to become overweight, but the condition might not be reacted to as a problem until after puberty. Once fatness *is* perceived as a problem, the adolescent girl may feel that she has less control over the condition than boys the same age. An overweight high school boy, for example, can take the initiative (because of social traditions) to ask a girl for a date. By contrast, an overweight adolescent girl who is unattractive to males because she is fat, may feel that she can do nothing about the situation. Consequently, she may develop feelings of resignation, fatalism, and self-pity. Such a reaction may lead to the establishment of a vicious circle. An overweight adolescent girl who is rejected by males (and perhaps females as well) may feel humiliated and isolated to the point that she suffers severe adjustment problems. Her own "solution" to these problems may be to turn to eating as "therapy," which perpetuates, or even intensifies, the condition.

The number of books and articles in magazines and newspapers about diets and dieting, together with the number of advertisements for diet centers and plans, attests to the fact that many overweight females are concerned about their condition and want to do something about it. If a series of "miracle" diets all turn out to be ineffective or if a diet program seems to be too difficult to maintain, the overweight girl may develop conditions that are harmful physically as well as psychologically.

Bulimia

Bulimia: insatiable appetite during eating binges

One reaction to concern about fatness is called **bulimia.** This condition is characterized by eating binges that may become so extreme that the young woman feels she cannot stop. The binge may come to an end when the voracious eater experiences abdominal pain, which she may attempt to relieve by self-induced vomiting. The woman with bulimia may eat normally for a few days or weeks, only to succumb to the urge to embark on another eating binge. In quite a few cases, the female who has developed bulimia may become so uncomfortable after an eating orgy that she makes a resolution to go to the opposite extreme. This sometimes leads to a situation where the cure is worse than the disease.

Anorexia Nervosa

Some young women who conclude that they are overweight, either because of bulimia or for a variety of other reasons, make a firm resolution to go on a diet. Once they begin to restrict their intake of food, however, they seem unable to stop. If the dieting becomes so extreme

Females who suffer from anorexia nervosa perceive themselves as fat even though they appear abnormally underweight to others.
© *Susan Rosenberg/Photo Researchers.*

Anorexia nervosa:
abnormal preoccupation with not eating

that the young woman becomes abnormally thin, she may be said to be suffering from **anorexia nervosa.** (*An* is the Greek word for without, *orexis* means longing, so *anorexia* indicates that someone is without a longing for food.) Some anorexics become so preoccupied with not eating that they die, but most maintain their weight at far below average levels. An interesting aspect of anorexia is that even though others see the underweight young woman as unattractively emaciated in appearance, she perceives herself as either just the right weight or perhaps a bit on the fat side. Another common trait of anorexics is that they become preoccupied with food preparation. They collect recipes, avidly read cookbooks, and prepare gourmet meals—for others to eat.

A number of explanations have been proposed to account for anorexia. One hypothesis is that growing up seems so threatening to some high school age females that they try to make themselves appear like little girls by, in effect, "shrinking" themselves (Bruch, 1973). Girls who fear growing up are often dependent and compliant and they may fear that their parents will withdraw support if it becomes obvious that they are mature. In an effort to "resist" the physiological changes that occur at the time of puberty, the girl may reduce food intake so that maturation will not seem so apparent (Levenkron, 1978). (If a post-pubertal girl reduces food intake beyond a certain point, menstruation ceases.) If the parents of an anorexic female express concern about her condition, they may unwittingly reinforce feelings of dependency, as well as the girl's conviction that not eating is a desirable form of behavior.

Anorexia may be due to a desire to resist growing up

Because relationships with parents are often a key factor in the treatment of anorexic high school girls, therapy appears to be most effective when the entire family is involved (Minuchin et al., 1978). In extreme cases, high school girls, as well as older females who no longer have contact with their parents, may need to be hospitalized for physical, as well as psychotherapeutic care.

The Impact of Early and Late Maturation

Over a period of years, a number of investigators at the University of California examined longitudinal data to determine the impact of early and later maturation on adolescents. Then, when the subjects were in their thirties, their adult behavior and adjustment were compared to the ratings made when they were in high school. These various investigations are summarized in Table 18.1.

The characteristics noted in Table 18.1 cannot be interpreted too literally for several reasons. First of all, different groups of subjects were studied, and the types of behavior various investigators found typical of

TABLE 18.1
THE IMPACT OF EARLY AND LATE MATURATION

	Characteristics as Adolescents	Characteristics as Adults
Early-maturing Boys	Self-confident, high in self-esteem, likely to be chosen leaders. (But leadership tendencies more likely in lower-class than middle-class boys.)	Self-confident, responsible, cooperative, sociable. But also rigid, moralistic, humorless, conforming
Late-maturing Boys	Energetic, bouncy, given to attention-getting behavior, not popular	Impulsive and assertive. But also insightful, perceptive, creatively playful, able to cope with new situations
Early-maturing Girls	Not popular or likely to be leaders, indifferent in social situations, lacking in poise. (But middle-class girls more confident than those from lower class.)	Self-possessed, self-directed, able to cope, likely to score high in ratings of overall psychological health
Late-maturing Girls	Confident, outgoing, assured, popular, likely to be chosen leaders	Likely to experience difficulty adapting to stress, likely to score low in ratings of overall psychological health

Sources: H. E. Jones, 1946; M. C. Jones, 1957, 1965; P. H. Mussen and M. C. Jones, 1957; Peskin, 1967, 1973; Clausen, 1975; Livson and Peskin, 1980; Petersen and Taylor, 1980.

early and later maturers were not always consistent. Second, as indicated by the parenthetical notes regarding leadership in early-maturing adolescent males and confidence in later-maturing adolescent girls, the impact of the timing of puberty sometimes varied depending on social class. Third, comparatively small groups of subjects were studied. And thus factors such as attractiveness may have had an influence on some of the characteristics (for example, popularity) studied. Finally, the subjects of these studies attended high school in the 1930s and 1940s. Changes in conceptions of sex roles and sexual behavior in the last few years may have altered the significance of early and later maturation in the 1980s.

It does seem safe to conclude, however, that the behavior and development of individuals who mature substantially earlier or later than most of their peers may be influenced in significant and permanent ways. The exact nature of this influence may be difficult to predict, though, for reasons that become clear in interpretations of the data in Table 18.1. After reviewing research on early and later maturation, Norman Livson and Harvey Peskin (1980) speculate that the early-maturing male is likely to draw favorable responses from adults (because of his adult appearance), which promotes confidence and poise (contributing to leadership and popularity with peers). The late-maturing boy, by contrast, may feel inferior and attempt to compensate for his physical and social frustration by engaging in bossy and attention-getting behavior. The very success of the early-maturing boy in high school, however, may cause him to develop an inflexible conception of himself, leading to problems when he must deal with new or negative situations later in life. The need for the early-maturing boy to cope with difficult adjustment situations in high school, on the other hand, may equip him with the ability to adapt to adversity and change later in life.

Livson and Peskin observe that the late-maturing boy is psychologically and socially out of step with peers, and the same applies to the *early*-maturing girl. The *late*-maturing girl, whose growth is less abrupt and whose size and appearance are likely to reflect the petiteness that is a feature of stereotyped views of femininity, shares many of the characteristics (poise, popularity, leadership tendencies) of the early-maturing boy. The advantages enjoyed by the late-maturing girl are not permanent, however. Livson and Peskin report that "The stress-ridden early-maturing girl in adulthood has become clearly a more coping, self-possessed, and self-directed person than the late-maturing female in the cognitive and social as well as emotional sectors. . . . It is the late-maturing female, carefree and unchallenged in adolescence, who faces adversity maladroitly in adulthood" (1980, p. 72).

This discussion of the significance of the timing of puberty leads to the broader questions of the impact of sexual maturation on behavior.

The Impact of Sexual Maturity

Conflicting Feelings About Sexuality

In a discussion of the development of sexuality in adolescence, Patricia Y. Miller and William Simon (1980) point out that puberty, a biological event, causes adolescents to function as "self-motivated sexual actors," which is a social event. They go on to comment that in technological societies "young people are defined as sexually mature while simultaneously being defined as socially and psychologically immature" (1980, p. 383). The confusion resulting from conflicts between sexual, social, and psychological conceptions of maturity is intensified by contemporary attitudes toward sex. Miller and Simon observe that, compared to previous cohorts, "contemporary adolescents are expected to be more interested in sex, to become experienced earlier, and once experienced, to approach regular sociosexual activity with greater competence" (p. 390). They go on to observe that "the contemporary adolescent must

*The psychoanalyst Peter Blos suggests that much adolescent behavior can be under-
stood by thinking of it as a "struggle to regain or retain a psychic equilibrium which
has been jolted by the crisis of puberty."*
*The Norwegian painter, Edvard Munch, offered his interpretation of a girl's discovery of her
sexual maturity in* Puberty. *Nasjonalgalleriet, Oslo.*

fashion an interpersonal sexual script from materials provided by a society that is nearly obsessed with the sexual possibilities of adolescence."
They add that because of the high rate of divorce and the large number
of adults on the "sexual marketplace," the adolescent in contemporary
America "increasingly sees the surrounding adult social world as itself
more sexually active and sexually interested than it used to be" (p. 390).

  In addition to difficulties caused by such factors, the young person
may be further confused because "the sex education of the adolescent is

emphatically attached to moral education" (p. 392). Miller and Simon believe this is the case because gender-role expectations establish attitudes toward sexual morality. (The traditional view of the "good girl," for example, is that she does not engage in premarital sex.) They note, "Many of the specific images that form the core of the individual's earliest sense of the sexual are thoroughly imbued with vague but powerful moral tones" (p. 392). Evidence to support the point that sex and morality are intertwined was supplied by R. C. Sorensen (1973), who found that 76 percent of the thirteen- to fifteen-year-old girls he interviewed and 43 percent of the sixteen- to nineteen-year-olds reported sometimes or often feeling guilty about masturbation. The corresponding figures for males were 43 percent at thirteen to fifteen, 47 percent at sixteen to nineteen. Sorensen also asked his subjects to express their psychological reactions to their first sexual experience. Thirty-six percent of the girls reported that they had felt guilty (compared to 3 percent of the boys); 31 percent of the girls said they felt embarrassed (compared to 7 percent of the boys).

Aspects of sexuality imbued with vague but powerful moral tones

It appears, then, that quite a few adolescents and youth feel guilty about sexual activities. Even though they may endorse the traditional view that premarital sex is wrong, however, adolescents and youth are motivated to engage in such relationships. As Miller and Simon observe, contemporary adolescents or youth may feel that they are *expected* to have early sexual experience and to develop a high level of competence. In addition to sexual attraction, engaging in sexual relations may be reinforcing for reasons that have been outlined by S. Jessor and R. Jessor (1975). These researchers point out that adolescents and youth may be motivated to have sexual relations as early as possible because of one or more of these reasons: to prove to themselves and others that they have achieved a mature status, to establish a sense of independence, to affirm sexual identity, to gain support for the belief that they are attractive to others, to reject social conventions or behave in a socially unacceptable manner, and to gain respect from peers.

These factors explain why premarital sex may seem appealing to adolescents and youth, even when they at least partially endorse the view that such activity is morally wrong. Jessor and Jessor found, for example, that while 60 percent of their female respondents mentioned fear of pregnancy as a reason for not engaging in premarital sex, 60 percent also mentioned fear of parental disapproval and 55 percent mentioned fear of damaging their reputation.

Premarital Intercourse and Birth Control

Melvin Zelnik has collaborated with several colleagues in accumulating information about teen-age sexual behavior. Three extensive surveys were carried out under his direction in 1971 (Zelnik and Kantner, 1972), 1976 (Zelnik and Kantner, 1977), and 1979 (Zelnik, Kantner, and Ford, 1981; Zelnik and Shah, 1983; Zelnik, Koenig, and Kim, 1984). Zelnik and his associates found that the percentage of young women fifteen to nineteen years of age who reported having had premarital sex increased from 30 to 50 percent between 1971 and 1979. When Albert Kinsey and his colleagues (1953) interviewed females in the 1940s, only 20 percent reported having had premarital sex before the age of nineteen. While percentages for males increased somewhat between 1940 and 1980, percentages for females, it is clear, increased substantially.

Substantial increase in premarital intercourse by females

When asked about their attitudes regarding premarital sex, 28 percent of the white females surveyed in the late 1970s expressed the opinion that sex was "always all right"; 40 percent said it was "all right if planning to marry"; and 32 percent said it was "never all right." Six in ten females had intercourse for the first time—at an average age of just over sixteen—with a male they were "committed to" (engaged or going steady). Zelnik observes that while the double standard condoning premarital sex for males but not for females has diminished, it has not disappeared. His findings reveal that contemporary teen-age males follow a pattern similar to previous generations of young men—they are likely to have premarital sex for the first time with a "casual" acquaintance. The proportion of teen-age females who are sexually active has increased, but they are still much more likely than males to restrict premarital sexual relations to partners they are seriously considering as husbands.

Double standard has diminished but has not disappeared

Zelnik and his colleagues found that females from upper economic and higher educational level homes, where the natural mother and father were both present for at least the first fifteen years of the respondent's life, were much more conservative than the hypothetical "average" females depicted by the statistics just cited. Other factors contributing to more traditional views regarding premarital sex were having a religious orientation (not necessarily involving church attendance), having close friends with similar conservative views, and having high educational and career aspirations. Conversely, females most likely to approve of and/or engage in premarital sex exhibited one or more of these characteristics: single-parent or second-marriage home, indifferent attitude toward religion, close friends with similar backgrounds and/or views on premarital sex, and low educational and career aspirations. There were a number of variations on these general trends. Black females, for example, were found to engage in premarital sex at earlier ages and in greater numbers than white females, and white females from unstable families had premarital sex more frequently and with more partners than average.

Perhaps the most perplexing aspect of the increased premarital sexual activity of American youth centers on birth control. Zelnik and his as-

Less than one-
third of teen-agers
who engage in pre-
marital sex use
contraceptives

sociates provide evidence that reinforces findings of earlier studies that less than one-third of all contemporary teen-agers who engage in pre-marital sex make use of contraceptives. (At the same time, Zelnik estimates that approximately 700,000 teen-age pregnancies a year are now prevented by the use of contraceptives.) Although the proportion who reported using contraceptives increased between 1971 and 1977, in the 1980s two out of five births to women under twenty have been illegitimate. This figure would be even higher if it were not for 375,000 legal abortions to women under twenty (one-third of the total), and the fact that many teen-age marriages occur because of pregnancy. In an analysis of teen-age sexuality and childbearing, Frank F. Furstenberg, Jr., Richard Lincoln, and Jane Menken (1981) observe, "While most teen-agers who have babies are married when the birth occurs, if present trends continue it will not be long before most adolescent births occur outside of marriage" (p. 2).

Two aspects of this situation merit consideration: reasons that teen-agers fail to use contraceptives and the consequences of teen-age birth and marriage.

Reasons for Not Using Contraceptives

To try to determine why so few teen-agers make use of contraceptives, Donn Byrne (1977) asked eighteen- and nineteen-year-old girls attending a Midwestern university to fill out an anonymous questionnaire. Information about birth control methods was provided via films and lectures at the university, and various contraceptives could be obtained at the student health service. Despite the fact that students were knowledgeable about methods of birth control and aware of the availability of contraceptives, only a third of those who were sexually active made systematic efforts to prevent pregnancy. Byrne hypothesizes (on the basis of related research on sexual behavior) that many adolescents and youth may be reluctant to use contraceptives because they feel anxious or negative about sex. He suggests that they avoid planning ahead and obtaining contraceptives because such thoughts and actions lead to guilt. In order to reduce the number of unwanted pregnancies in teen-age girls, Byrne recommends (p. 68) that adolescents be exposed to the view that contraception is a significant and legitimate part of sexuality.

While Byrne's recommendation might lead to somewhat fewer illegitimate births, the results of a survey and analysis by C. Lindemann (1974) leads to the conclusion that not all adolescent and youthful females would accept the view that contraception should be a part of sexuality. Lindemann interviewed and counseled more than twenty-five hundred young women in public health clinics, high schools, and colleges. When he asked those who failed to use contraceptives why they followed such

There is quite consistent evidence that early pregnancy and/or marriage reduces chances for a stable marital relationship.
Polly Brown/The Picture Cube.

a policy, he found that some young women stressed unpredictability, uncertainty, and spontaneity; others seemed to be ignorant of the need for birth control. Some of his respondents pointed out, for example, that having sexual relations is often unpredictable and cannot always be anticipated. Others agreed with a young woman who said, "Sex is better if it is natural. I didn't like the idea of birth control because sex should be spontaneous" (1974, p. 15). Still others endorsed the view of a high school girl who pointed out that she had been having sexual relations for two years without getting pregnant and therefore saw no reason to bother with contraceptives.

Teen-age girls who favor these points of view might not be interested in information about birth control or take advantage of opportunities to obtain contraceptives. Lindemann found, however, that many girls and young women he interviewed were simply ignorant of the need for birth control. Such females would probably be more likely to welcome information about contraception and come to think of it as a part of sexuality.

Additional factors that may determine if an adolescent or youthful female will use birth-control techniques were reported by I. L. Reiss, A. Banwart, and H. Foreman (1975). These investigators found that the lifestyle of a young woman most likely to use contraceptives included

Failure to use contraceptives due to ignorance, unpredictability, desire for spontaneity

these elements: a high degree of commitment to a particular heterosex-
ual relationship, a view of sexuality stressing the right of a woman to
make decisions about her own sex life, self-assurance concerning her
body image, and a history of early acquisition of sex information inside
and outside her family. In regard to the last point, H. D. Thornburg
(1970) asked female college students how they had acquired information
about sex. Female acquaintances seemed to be the primary source, with
articles in magazines and books and school sex education programs next
in line, and parents at the bottom of the list. Unfortunately, peers were
often poorly informed about many aspects of sex, and Lindemann found
in his survey that many girls hesitated to ask their mothers for information because they assumed that their parents were opposed to premarital sex. He also discovered, though, that contrary to the expectation
of adolescent girls, quite a few parents had permissive attitudes about
premarital sex. These permissive parents hesitated to offer information
to girls about birth control, however, for fear that this would be interpreted as a sign that they were encouraging unrestrained sexual activity.
Those who oppose sex education programs in the schools by arguing
that adolescents should learn about sex from their parents are usually
not aware of the kinds of factors noted by Thornburg and Lindemann.

   In their interpretation of survey responses regarding use of contraceptives, Zelnik and his colleagues note many of the points just mentioned.
They emphasize that perhaps the most basic problem is that premarital
sex is typically irregular and often unplanned. (In the 1979 survey, only
17 percent of the females and 25 percent of the males reported that they
had planned their first act of intercourse.) They note, "The effective
methods [of birth control] provide continuous protection, but are most
appropriate when sex is regular and contraception routinized. The
young sexually active woman therefore faces a dilemma: She is interested in reliable protection against pregnancy, yet the most effective
methods are poorly adapted to her sex life; the methods that are adapted
to her sex life do not provide the same degree of protection" (Zelnik,
Kantner, and Ford, 1981, p. 180).

   Zelnik suggests that improved sex education courses and more information and greater availability of medical methods of contraception (the
pill, the diaphragm) might reduce dependency on less reliable methods
(rhythm, withdrawal, or douche). He notes, however, that even though
significantly more females reported using contraceptives in 1976 and
1979 than 1971, the number of teen-age pregnancies out of wedlock
remained essentially constant during those years. The best explanation
to account for this paradox seems to be that the age at which the first
intercourse takes place has become lower, and younger girls are less
knowledgeable about birth control than older ones. Furthermore, half of
all teen-age pregnancies occur during the first six months of sexual
activity. It would appear, therefore, that sex education courses for fe-

males should be given in the junior high school years if they are to be effective. This policy is advocated by Furstenberg, Lincoln, and Menken in summing up research on teen-age pregnancy (1981, p. 304). These researchers counter the argument that such courses would *encourage* early sexual promiscuity by suggesting that because of factors such as those mentioned by Simon and Miller at the beginning of this section on sexuality, many young Americans are going to engage in sex before marriage regardless of courses about sex *or* admonitions by various individuals and groups that it is immoral. They mention the results of a Gallup poll of the late 1970s, which indicated that only 43 percent of the teen-agers surveyed reported having had a course in sex education. But even those who had such courses frequently were not given any explicit information about contraception. Freya L. Sonenstein and Karen J. Pittman (1984) found that only 14 percent of the sex education courses in large school districts included in-depth discussions of ways to prevent pregnancy. Less than 20 percent mentioned sources of contraceptives at the high school level, and only 7 percent at the junior high school level. (It appears that information about sexually transmitted diseases also is either ignored entirely or presented ineffectively in sex education courses. A bulletin of the U.S. Department of Health and Human services entitled *Sexually Transmitted Diseases: 1980 Status Report* notes that "gonorrhea has become epidemic." Furthermore, it is estimated that 10 million Americans suffer from genital herpes, and many more suffer from labial herpes. In the *Status Report for 1980,* King K. Holmes, M.D., characterizes the American approach to sexually transmitted diseases in three words: ignorance, apathy, and neglect.) Furstenberg, Lincoln, and Menken note, "It is difficult to avoid the conclusion that when it comes to birth control, most teenagers are functional illiterates"; (p. 302). They suggest that the key to the problem of inadequate sex instruction in the schools "is the reluctance on the part of society at large to acknowledge that teenagers are going to have sexual relations" (p. 302). Even so, they comment that liberalization, during the last twenty years, of laws and practices restricting teen-agers from obtaining information, contraceptives, or abortions without parental or other control amounts to a "revolution."

To be effective, sex education courses for females should be given in junior high

Problems Associated with Teen-age Pregnancy and Marriage

According to the National Center for Health Statistics figures, teen-age childbearing in the United States has been on the decline during the last ten years. As noted earlier, Zelnik and his associates found that, due to greater use of medical methods of contraception, the illegitimacy *rate* for teen-agers also declined during the 1970s. Because the number of teen-

Illegitimacy rate has declined but public concern has increased

age females who were sexually active increased, however, the number of illegitimate births has not decreased to any appreciable extent. Estimates of illegitimacy that do not take into account the increased number of sexually active females often give the erroneous impression, therefore, that America is in the throes of an epidemic of out-of-wedlock births. As a consequence, many individuals and groups have only recently expressed great concern about a situation that has remained more or less constant for many years. Furstenberg, Lincoln, and Menken speculate (1981, p. 6) that current concern about teen-age pregnancy might be traced in large part to the controversy over abortion. As noted earlier, one-third of all legal abortions are obtained by teen-age females, a fact that has drawn attention only recently to an aspect of adolescent sexuality (conception out of wedlock) that has always existed. While many American adults express concern about teen-age pregnancy for moral reasons, researchers have found that there are also physical, psychological, and economic problems associated with early childbearing, particularly when the mother remains unmarried.

Early childbearing often leads to physical, psychological, and economic problems

As noted in the discussion of prenatal development and birth in Chapter 4, mothers younger than twenty have a greater than average chance of experiencing problems during pregnancy and birth. Maternal and infant mortality rates are higher for young mothers, and infants born to teen-age mothers are more likely to have birth defects. Premature birth is more common, and the problems typical of low-birth-weight infants, summarized in Chapter 4, are likely to occur. (There is some evidence, reported by the Institute of Medicine of the National Academy of Science, that legalized abortion has led to an improvement in the overall health of infants born to teen-age mothers because of a decrease in the number of low-birth-weight infants delivered.)

Even if a teen-age mother is married, experiences no problems during pregnancy, and delivers a healthy, full-term baby, she is likely to encounter difficulties in child rearing and in the control of her personal destiny. If she elects not to marry, the difficulties are magnified. (Zelnik and his associates [1984] estimate that the proportion of teen-age girls who elect not to marry after a child is conceived out of wedlock has increased to over 40 percent.)

Between one-half and two-thirds of all female high school dropouts cite pregnancy and/or marriage as the principal reason they left school. Many females who drop out of school because of pregnancy later return and graduate (Furstenberg, 1976), but because women who have their first child early tend to have additional children soon after, education beyond high school is often the exception rather than the rule. Equipped only with a high school diploma, the young mother is likely to encounter problems finding employment—provided she is not tied down by child-care responsibilities. Furstenberg and Albert C. Crawford (1981) found, however, that when the unmarried teen-age mother is given support by her family, she can often overcome problems associated with limited education. Interestingly, teen-age females who marry are likely to drop out of school even if they do not become pregnant before or shortly after marriage. Furstenberg (1976) speculates that this may be the case because high school girls who have little interest in pursuing careers may conclude that marriage will make it unnecessary for them to seek work. Unfortunately, girls who reason this way fail to take into account that many teen-age marriages end in divorce.

Both early pregnancy and/or early marriage reduce(s) the chances for a stable marital relationship. The marriage least likely to succeed is one that occurs after a child has been conceived. (It has been estimated [O'Connell and Moore, 1981], that 60 percent of firstborns of white teenagers and 90 percent of firstborns of black teen-agers are premaritally conceived.) Such marriages often may involve couples who were initially drawn together primarily by sexual attraction. But even marriages between high school couples who have had time to become acquainted, who share similar interests, and who have not begun a pregnancy before the ceremony, often are fraught with difficulties. These include psychological immaturity and lack of preparation for roles of husband and wife. The most potent problem faced by young married couples, however, is typically economic, particularly if one or more children are born before the parents reach their twenties. The need for earning a livelihood is likely to force one or both parents to drop out of school and enter the labor market prematurely. As a consequence, family income is likely to be limited, leading to difficulties in maintaining a household and causing friction between husband and wife.

> Early pregnancy and/or early marriage reduce(s) chances for stable marital relationship

The impact of sexual maturity has been treated at length in this chapter because, as figures cited on the preceding pages reveal, it has become a particularly significant aspect of adolescent development in contemporary American society.

Summary

1. One important point about physical development during adolescence is that girls achieve puberty a year and one-half earlier, on the average, than boys. Another is that awareness of the importance of social and sexual attractiveness causes most postpubescent adolescents to become extremely concerned about their appearance. It seems, though, that appearance influences popularity only for those who are the most and least attractive members of a group.

2. A number of adolescents, particularly females, become excessively preoccupied with weight control. Some young women, for instance, develop **bulimia,** a condition characterized by the development of an insatiable appetite during eating binges. Others suffer from **anorexia**

nervosa, an abnormal preoccupation with not eating that may become so extreme that malnutrition or even death may result. One explanation for anorexia is that it represents an attempt on the part of a young woman to resist growing up.

3. Some adolescents mature at a faster or slower rate than the average. Early-maturing boys are often self-confident, perhaps because they draw favorable responses as a result of their adult appearance. Late-maturing boys, by contrast, may try to compensate for their immaturity by seeking attention. Early-maturing girls may experience problems in high school because they are out of step with peers, but as adults they are often more confident and better adjusted than girls who were late maturers.

4. As a result of recent social trends in our society, contemporary adolescents may feel that they are *expected* to be interested in sex. At the same time, many aspects of sexuality are still imbued with vague but powerful moral overtones. During the last thirty years, there has been a substantial increase in premarital intercourse by females. The double standard, which stipulated that premarital sex was acceptable for males but not for females, has diminished but has not completely disappeared.

5. One of the most apparent manifestations of the greater sexual activity of females is a substantial number of births to unwed mothers, due in large part to the fact that less than one-third of all teen-agers who engage in premarital sex use contraceptives. Failure to use contraceptives may be due to ignorance, the unpredictable nature of sexual relations, a desire for spontaneity (or a desire to have a child even if not married).

6. Because American adolescents begin to engage in sexual relationships at early ages, sex education courses for females, to be effective, should be given during the junior high school years. Improved sex education courses are desirable but controversial because even though the illegitimacy rate has declined, public concern about out-of-wedlock births has increased. More effective sex education programs might make young women more aware that early childbearing often leads to physical, psychological, and economic problems and that early pregnancy or marriage or both reduce chances for a stable marital relationship.

Suggestions for Further Study

Impact of the Growth Spurt and Puberty

To appreciate the nature and magnitude of changes that take place at the time of puberty, arrange to visit a seventh-grade and a ninth-grade classroom. Observe the students not only in class, but also in the halls and after school. Describe differences in physical appearance and in behavior between the seventh- and ninth-graders, paying particular attention to differences between boys and girls. You might also try to pick out the most and least mature students in a group and concentrate on their behavior in and out of the classroom. If you make an observation of this type, note your reactions and comment on the implications of the differences you detect.

Biological and Physiological Aspects of Adolescence

For more complete information about biological changes at adolescence, consult *Growth at Adolescence* (2nd ed., 1962) by J. M. Tanner, whose condensed versions of the material in this book can be found in Chapter 3 of *Carmichael's Manual of Child Psychology* (3rd ed., 1970), edited by Paul H. Mussen; and in Chapter 1 of *Twelve to Sixteen: Early Adolescence* (1972), edited by Jerome Kagan and Robert Coles. Another source you might consult is "The Biological Approach to Adolescence: Biological Change and Psychological Adaptation" by Anne C. Petersen and Brandon Taylor in the *Handbook of Adolescent Psychology* (1980, pp. 117–155), edited by Joseph Adelson.

Adolescent Sexuality

The impact of sexual maturity is briefly explained in "The Development of Sexuality in Adolescence" by Patricia Y. Miller and William Simon in the *Handbook of Adolescent Psychology* (1980, pp. 383–407), edited by Joseph Adelson. More extensive analyses are presented in *Sexuality in Contemporary America* (1973) by R. C. Sorensen; *Sexual Behavior in the 1970s* (1973) by Morton Hunt; and *The Sexual Experience* (1976), edited by B. J. Saddock, H. I. Kaplan, and A. M. Freedman.

Unwanted Pregnancy

Perhaps the major change in the sexual habits of Americans that has taken place in the last twenty years is the increase in the number of women who engage in premarital intercourse. Despite the availability of birth-control devices, many women, married as well as unmarried, become pregnant by mistake. Katrina Maxtone-Graham interviewed several women who found themselves in this predicament and recorded their reactions in *Pregnant by Mistake: The Stories of Seventeen Women* (1973). In their accounts, the women interviewed express their thoughts and feelings about such options as abortion, adoption, and single parenthood.

KEY POINTS

The Nature and Impact of Formal Thinking

Formal thought: possibilities, hypotheses, future, thoughts, speculations

Unrestrained theorizing when formal thought achieved

Adolescent egocentrism: extreme concern about reactions of others

Transition to formal thinking not abrupt, influenced by schooling and background

The Development of Political Thinking

Political thinking of older adolescents more abstract, less authoritarian

Influence of parents on political thinking likely to be indirect

Moral and Interpersonal Development

Morality of cooperation: mutual agreements, allowance for intentions

Understanding of interpersonal subtleties, societal perspective in adolescence

Kohlberg: regressions in moral thinking due to awareness of inconsistencies

Turiel: inconsistencies in moral thinking due to differences in values

The Nature and Significance of Values

Values: beliefs that guide and determine attitudes and actions

Values of adolescents and youth likely to be similar even though tastes differ

Parents influence plans; peers influence immediate status

Conservative youth stay that way even if exposed to liberal views in college

CHAPTER

19

ADOLESCENCE AND YOUTH

COGNITIVE DEVELOPMENT

*A*lmost all discussions of cognitive development during adolescence are based on, derived from, or related to Piaget's description of formal thought. As noted in the discussion of cognitive development during the elementary school years (Chapter 7), the transition from concrete operational thinking to formal thought typically begins before children leave elementary school. During the high school years, this transition is completed (for many adolescents) and represents a basic reorganization of cognitive abilities.

The Nature and Impact of Formal Thinking

Characteristics of Formal Thought

Daniel P. Keating (1980, pp. 212–215) summarizes the characteristics of formal thinking by noting that it is based on these abilities:

Formal thought:
possibilities, hypotheses, future, thoughts, speculations

Thinking about possibilities

Thinking about hypotheses

Thinking ahead

Thinking about thoughts

Thinking beyond limits

Piaget (and his chief collaborator, Barbel Inhelder) place particular stress on the ability to **think about possibilities.** They state, "There is no doubt that the most distinctive feature of formal thought stems from the role played by statements about possibility relative to statements about empirical reality" (Inhelder and Piaget, 1958, p. 245). The concrete operational thinker concentrates on what can be or has been observed. The formal thinker is able to manipulate abstract ideas and imagine all kinds of possible situations, including those that have never been encountered. These cognitive skills not only influence an adolescent's ability to solve problems and consider contrary-to-fact propositions; they may also influence the process of identity formation. When older adolescents can anticipate the results of a decision to prepare for a particular job and what it might be like to be employed, they may feel so threatened and confused that they postpone the final choice. Or young people who try to weigh all the possibilities available may find it difficult to choose among them. For youth who attend college, the preoccupation with such possibilities may be extended for four or more years.

Thinking about hypotheses is illustrated most clearly by experiments in which subjects are asked to solve problems such as figuring out relationships between weights and pendulums. As noted in the discussion of the thinking of elementary school children, concrete operational thinkers typically try to solve problems by trial and error and without following any discernible plan. Adolescents who have mastered formal thought, by contrast, are likely first to plot a course of action and then test hypotheses in a systematic manner by observing and perhaps recording the results of different actions. (Because of the abilities to think about possibilities and think ahead, they may also be able to solve the problem in their heads.)

Thinking about thought and **thinking beyond limits** are illustrated by a fascination with abstractions that often characterizes adolescent thinking. Two leading interpreters of Piagetian theory describe this preoccupation with the abstract in the following way:

> In the intellectual sphere, the adolescent has a tendency to become involved in abstract and theoretical matters, constructing elaborate political theories or inventing complex philosophical doctrines. The adolescent may develop plans for the complete reorganization of society or indulge in metaphysical speculation. Having just discovered capabilities for abstract thought, he then proceeds to exercise them without restraint. Indeed, in the process of exploring these new abilities the adolescent sometimes loses touch with reality, and feels that he can accomplish everything by thought alone. In the emotional sphere the adolescent now becomes capable of directing his emotions at abstract ideals and not just toward people. Whereas earlier he could love his mother or hate a peer, now he can love freedom or hate exploitation. The adolescent has developed a new mode of life: the possible and the ideal captivate both mind and feeling. (Ginsburg and Opper, 1979, p. 201)

Unrestrained theorizing when formal thought achieved

Adolescent Egocentrism

David Elkind suggests that unrestrained theorizing about ideals without complete understanding of realities tends to make the young adolescent a militant rebel having little patience with parents or other adults who fail to find quick solutions to personal, social, and other problems. Only when the older adolescent begins to grasp the complexities of interpersonal relationships and of economic and social problems will more tempered understanding appear. Elkind also suggests that the egocentrism of early childhood that gave way to socialized speech and thought at the end of the elementary grade years reappears in a different form as **adolescent egocentrism.** This occurs when high school students turn their new powers of thought upon themselves and become introspective. The strong tendency to analyze the self is projected upon others, which helps explain why adolescents are so self-conscious—they assume their thoughts and actions are as interesting to others as to themselves. The major difference between the egocentrism of childhood and of adolescence is summed up in Elkind's observation: "The child is egocentric in the sense that he is unable to take another person's point of view. The adolescent, on the other hand, takes the other person's point of view to an extreme degree" (1968, p. 153).

Adolescent egocentrism: extreme concern about reactions of others

Elkind believes that adolescent egocentrism also explains why the peer group becomes such a potent force in high school. He observes:

> Adolescent egocentrism . . . accounts, in part, for the power of the peer group during this period. The adolescent is so concerned with the reactions of others toward him, particularly his peers, that he is willing to do many things which

G. V. Brittain proposes that while parents influence the long-range plans of the adolescent sons and daughters, peers have a greater impact on immediate status and identity needs.
© *George Gardner*

are opposed to all of his previous training and to his own best interests. At the same time, this egocentric impression that he is always on stage may help to account for the many and varied adolescent attention-getting maneuvers. . . .

Toward the end of adolescence, this form of exploitative egocentrism gradually declines. The young person comes to realize that other people are much more concerned with themselves and their problems than they are with him and his problems. (1968, p. 154)

Evaluations of Piaget's Description of Formal Thought

Researchers (for example, Neimark, 1975) who have reviewed investigations of Piaget's hypotheses on the basic characteristics of formal thought have found support for many of his speculations. But there are certain aspects of Piaget's theory that have been questioned. Criticisms have centered on whether there is a qualitative change in thinking at adolescence, whether this change is gradual or abrupt, and whether the change is universal. In his analysis of Piaget's theory, Keating (1980) concludes that each of these assumptions can be questioned. He interprets the available evidence as indicating that there are *not* distinct stages that distinguish the thinking of older elementary school children from the thinking of adolescents. He also argues that the change is gradual rather than abrupt and that cognitive development is not universal because it is influenced by such factors as schooling and cultural background. It should be noted, however, that Neimark reports greater support for Piaget's hypothesis regarding stages than does Keating.

Even if strong and consistent support for certain aspects of Piaget's description of formal thinking is lacking, his basic description of cognitive development during preadolescence and adolescence can be used to clarify certain types of behavior. Parents and teachers, for instance, might sympathize with, rather than criticize, the disorganized efforts of embryonic formal thinkers to solve problems. And they also might try to be more understanding and tolerant of the tendency for adolescents who have just "discovered" formal thinking to engage in unrestrained theorizing. Still another way to benefit from Piaget's observations is to use them to comprehend certain forms of political and moral thinking that become apparent during adolescence.

Transition to formal thinking not abrupt, influenced by schooling and background

The Development of Political Thinking

Adelson's Study of Political Thinking

Joseph Adelson (1971) used the interview approach to obtain information about the development of political thought during the adolescent years. With the assistance of several colleagues and graduate students, he conducted interviews with 450 eleven- to eighteen-year-olds from all social and intellectual levels in the United States, Great Britain, and West Germany. Fifty members of this original sample were chosen for more intensive, longitudinal analyses. At the start of the interviews, the subjects were requested to imagine that a thousand people ventured to an island in the Pacific for the purpose of establishing a new society. The respondents were then asked to explain how these people might establish a political order, devise a legal system, and deal with other problems of public policy.

The analysis of the interview responses showed no significant sex differences in understanding political concepts and no significant differences attributable to intelligence and social class, although brighter students were better able to deal with abstract ideas and upper-class students were less likely to be authoritarian. The most striking and consistent finding was the degree to which the political thinking of the adolescent changes in the years between twelve and sixteen. Adelson concluded that the most significant changes were (1) an increase in the

Political thinking of older adolescents more abstract, less authoritarian

ability to deal with abstractions; (2) a decline in authoritarian views; and (3) an increase in political knowledge.

The increase in the ability to deal with abstractions is a function of the shift from concrete to formal operational thought. When thirteen-year-olds were asked "What is the purpose of laws?" a typical answer was "So people don't steal or kill" (1972, p. 108). A fifteen- to sixteen-year-old, by contrast, was more likely to say "To ensure safety and enforce the government" (p. 108). The young adolescent who thinks in concrete terms concentrates on individuals and finds it difficult to take into account society as a whole. When asked about the purpose of laws to require vaccination of children, for example, the twelve-year-old is likely to say that it is to prevent sickness in the child who receives the treatment. The fifteen-year-old, who has mastered formal thought, is likely to consider how it will protect the community at large.

Thinking in concrete terms also causes the twelve-year-old to concentrate on the immediate present because of the inability to analyze the significance of past events or to project ideas into the future. And as Piaget noted in his analysis of moral development, the younger child (who is a moral realist) is not likely to take motives into account. When asked to explain why many prisoners are repeat offenders, for example, only older adolescents would mention such motives as having a grudge against society. Adelson and his colleagues found that when twelve-year-olds were asked how prisoners should be treated, many of them recommended that they be punished and taught a stern lesson. Adelson speculates that the tendency for younger adolescents to be punitive and authoritarian might be attributed to several factors: preoccupation with wickedness, the inability of the young adolescent to grasp the concept of rights, and the conviction that laws are immutable. By fourteen or fifteen, the adolescents interviewed by Adelson were more likely to weigh circumstances and the rights of the individual and to recommend rehabilitation rather than punishment.

While Adelson's findings were consistent with Piaget's observations on shifts from morality of constraint to morality of cooperation, Adelson questioned Ginsburg and Opper's conclusion that the young person who has just "discovered" formal thought has a tendency to engage in uncontrolled theorizing. Adelson was led to question this hypothesis by the discovery that respondents rarely discussed utopian schemes. Instead, they demonstrated their grasp of political knowledge. The structured nature of the interviews might have influenced these results and Adelson's conclusions, since a high school student might feel threatened when questioned by a formidably intelligent adult from a prestigious university. Instead of expressing utopian political theories and risking the possibility of appearing naive, the student might simply recite facts.

If Adelson had been able to tape-record spontaneous political discussions between fifteen- and sixteen-year-olds (which would have been closer to Piaget's approach), perhaps he would have found greater support for the hypothesis that adolescents who have just become capable of formal thought have a tendency toward unrestricted theorizing. (Even mature and confident adults who have devoted years of thought to developing utopian schemes hesitate to publish them for fear of being ridiculed by critics. Exchanging ideas in an informal bull session is an entirely different matter.)

Even though they did not discuss utopian schemes in the interviews, older adolescents revealed that they felt a keen sense of involvement in political matters. Subjects who were especially intense about politics were found to come, not surprisingly, from homes where parents were politically active. Other evidence of the influence of parental (and cultural) factors on political thinking was revealed by nationality differences. Adelson concluded that German adolescents disliked confusion and admired a strong leader; British subjects stressed the right of the individual citizen and the need to equalize wealth; American respondents were concerned about finding ways to balance individual rights and community needs.

The Adelson study has been described in some detail because it focuses on the development of political thinking in ways that can be related to Piaget's description of formal thought. Hundreds of other studies of the political thinking of adolescents and youth have been published. A few brief comments on some of the conclusions of these studies will be noted.

Conclusions of Other Studies of Political Thinking

Although it sometimes has been found that many adolescents may not know basic political facts of life, such as whether Republicans are more conservative than Democrats, after analyzing many studies, Judith Gallatin (1980) concluded that most eighteen-year-olds are quite capable of functioning as well-informed voters.

There is evidence (Gallatin, 1980) that parents often have a significant influence on the political thinking of their sons and daughters. R. W. Connell (1972) speculates that parents do not directly mold the political views of their children but that they place them in a sociopolitical context that leads them to acquire attitudes in subtle and indirect ways. The influence of the parents is most likely to be felt, according to Gallatin, when both parents agree on basic political issues and when there are opportunities for free communication and discussion in the home. Adolescents from such homes tend to earn above-average scores on tests of

Influence of parents on political thinking likely to be indirect

political knowledge, and they are more inclined to assume civic responsibilities than are adolescents from permissive or authoritarian homes (to use the terms favored by Baumrind in her studies of child-rearing practices).

There is little evidence that high school teachers have much of an impact on the political views of adolescents (Beck, 1977), but it appears that the mass media do have significant effect. During the elementary school years, television appears to be the most influential medium of communication. Newspapers tend to become a more important source of information about political developments during the high school years (Chaffee et al., 1977).

Moral and Interpersonal Development

Piaget's View of Moral Development: A Review

In Chapter 15, some of Piaget's observations on moral development were noted. After observing how children devised rules to govern play and listening to them respond to stories involving moral dilemmas, Piaget concluded that younger children are governed by a morality of constraint. At around the age of ten or so, however, when some children begin to function as formal thinkers, a shift to the morality of cooperation begins to occur. Starting around the fifth or sixth grade, children enjoy making up their own rules to supplant those that were formerly imposed on them by adults or older playmates. They think of rules as mutual agreements established to protect the rights of all participants. Children of that age also may evaluate moral situations by taking into account circumstances and intentions. A well-meaning child who makes a big blot of ink on a tablecloth will be considered less guilty than a misbehaving child who makes a small blot.

Morality of cooperation: mutual agreements, allowance for intentions

All these changes in moral reasoning can be explained by taking into account features of formal thought. The older child is no longer egocentric and can consider another person's point of view, which makes it possible to come to mutual agreement about rules. The older child can think of more than one thing at a time (for example, the physical results of an action and the motives behind that action) and take into account extenuating circumstances.

In an analysis of the transition from the morality of constraint to the morality of cooperation, Martin L. Hoffman (1980, p. 296) observes that "Moral growth requires that the child give up egocentrism and realism and develop a concept of self as distinct from others who have their own independent perspectives about events" (1980, p. 296). He suggests that

When adolescents become capable of the morality of cooperation, they often seek to participate in making group decisions.
Michael Heron/Woodfin Camp.

this shift occurs because of two basic developments in cognitive ability and in social interactions that begin in late childhood and continue through adolescence. First, as adolescents mature, they realize that they are gradually attaining equality with adults. As a consequence, they are less inclined to think of regulations as sacred pronouncements handed down by infallible grown-ups and more inclined to feel that they are just as qualified as anyone else to make up or change rules. A second factor that contributes to the emergence of the morality of cooperation is that interactions with peers make it necessary to assume alternate and reciprocal roles. Assuming a variety of roles in different situations and with different acquaintances leads to the realization that while one person often reacts to situations as others do, sometimes individuals react differently. Awareness of this fact leads the adolescent to become increasingly aware of the inner states that underlie the behavior of others.

Interactions with peers also cause adolescents to think a great deal about relationships with others, particularly when the behavior of friends contradicts expectations. If a friend does not respond in the expected manner, a high school student may brood about it for days.

Changes in Interpersonal Reasoning at Adolescence

Hoffman's observation on the tendency for adolescents to become concerned about the thoughts and feelings of others are similar to Robert Selman's description of the final stages of interpersonal reasoning. To review points noted in Chapter 16, Selman (1976a,b) suggests that ten- to twelve-year-olds are at the **multiple role-taking stage.** They become capable of taking a **third person** view in that they are able to evaluate their own behavior and that of others as if they were spectators. From the age of twelve to fifteen and beyond, adolescents move into the stage of **social and conventional system role taking.** They increasingly come to understand subtleties of interpersonal relationships and toward the end of the high school years they may begin to take a **societal perspective.** They realize that their actions might influence *all* individuals, not just those who are immediately concerned or affected.

Understanding of interpersonal subtleties, **societal perspective** in adolescence

Some of the most interesting examples of this societal perspective take the form of what Hoffman (1980, p. 314) refers to as **existential guilt.** Such guilt occurs when a person who has done nothing wrong still feels culpable because of circumstances that cannot be controlled. Kenneth Keniston (1968) reported that some upper-class activists of the 1960s, for example, occasionally explained that they participated in demonstrations favoring programs for the oppressed or disadvantaged because they felt guilty about their favored backgrounds. In other cases, Hoffman suggests, the existential guilt of 1960s-vintage youth from affluent homes may have caused them to renounce material possessions and join the hippie movement.

In making some final comments on existential guilt, Hoffman speculates that it may be less common in the 1980s than it was in the 1960s. On the basis of informal interviews with upper- and middle-class contemporary youth, he concluded that they place a high value on success, and even though they may come from affluent backgrounds, they do not feel they are in a privileged position as they strive to become successful. Two reasons were frequently mentioned by the youth Hoffman interviewed to support their conviction that they are not favored individuals: (1) they expect to have to work hard to find a decent job; and (2) because of equal opportunity regulations and affirmative action programs, they feel that many "disadvantaged" individuals now enjoy a privileged position in the job market.

Information that might be used to evaluate Hoffman's speculations has been provided by J. G. Bachman and L. D. Johnston (1979). They asked seventeen thousand students who entered college in 1979 to describe "important things in my life." Here are some of the results of the survey, expressed in terms of the percentage of respondents who rated each of the following goals as important:

Strong friendships	69
Finding purpose and meaning in my life	66
Finding steady work	65
Being successful in my work	63
Making a contribution to society	23

The results of this survey seem to support Hoffman's impression that many contemporary youth are more interested in finding a good job and a satisfying life for themselves than in "contributing to society."

Piaget's description of the transition from the morality of constraint to the morality of cooperation has stimulated much research and many speculations about adolescent morality and interpersonal relationships. The theory proposed by Lawrence Kohlberg has been even more provocative.

Kohlberg's Theory of Moral Development

A Brief Review of Kohlberg's Theory

On the basis of responses of ten- to sixteen-year-olds to moral dilemmas such as the story of Heinz (Chapter 15), Kohlberg proposed six stages of moral development:

Stage 1 Punishment-Obedience Orientation. The physical consequences of an action determine goodness or badness.

Stage 2 Instrumental Relativist Orientation. Obeying laws should bring some sort of benefit in return.

Stage 3 Good Boy–Nice Girl Orientation. The right action is the one likely to impress others.

Stage 4 Law and Order Orientation. To maintain the social order, fixed rules must be established and obeyed.

Stage 5 Social Contract Orientation. Rules should be based on mutual agreement, but the rights of the individual must be taken into account.

Stage 6 Universal Ethical Principle Orientation. Moral decisions should be based on consistently applied self-chosen principles. (As noted in Chapter 15, Kohlberg has come to view the last stage as a theoretical concept that is rarely encountered in real life.)

Kohlberg believes these stages are universal, fixed, and sequential; that individuals move through the stages in order. He also believes that moral development can be enhanced by exposing children and adolescents to arguments and discussions of moral concepts that are one stage above their present level.

Speculations About "Regression" in Moral Development

An example of how Kohlberg's theory gives insight into both the nature and the complexity of moral development is provided by research and interpretations of "regressions" in moral thinking. The subjects of Kohlberg's original research, who supplied the answers to moral dilemmas that were used in establishing the stages, were retested at four-year intervals. Kohlberg and Kramer (1969) reported that most of the respondents followed the predicted pattern and moved through the stages in sequence. About 20 percent of them who had obtained Stage 4 scores at sixteen, however, dropped to Stage 2 at twenty. Most of those subjects moved to higher-than-original levels of Stage 4 by twenty-four, though, and some advanced to Stage 5.

Kohlberg and Kramer concluded that the drop from Stage 4 to Stage 2 reflected a consistent regression in moral thinking. They hypothesized that it was attributable to the impact of the liberal arts curriculum in the colleges the subjects had attended. The youth who slipped from Stage 4 to Stage 2 typically came from middle-class homes. During their college years they came to question and examine their beliefs. Kohlberg and Kramer theorize that the college students who regressed were faced with two developmental challenges. First, they learned that the conception of morality they had accepted and formulated as adolescents was

Kohlberg: regressions in moral thinking due to awareness of inconsistencies

just one of many possible conceptions. Second, they discovered that there are frequent inconsistencies between moral expectations and the actual behavior of adults. The difficulty of coping with these two challenges caused the young men to regress to a simpler level of moral reasoning. By the time they had completed college, though, they had resolved these conflicts to their satisfaction and emerged with more sophisticated conceptions of morality than they had begun with.

Elliot Turiel (1974) offers a different explanation for apparent regressions in moral thinking. He acknowledges that adolescents and youth may sometimes give answers to moral dilemmas that are below their typical stage of development, but he is not convinced that this means they have moved back to a lower stage. Instead, he suggests, they may simply be rejecting certain types of moral thinking as they become aware of contradictions and of differences between types of moral decisions.

Turiel argues that adolescents may develop two distinct value systems. One encompasses principles that are universal and that can be objectively validated (for example, honesty). The other is made up of values (for example, sexual mores) that need to be formulated (up to a point) by each individual living in a particular cultural environment at a particular time. Some of the "regressions" reported by Kohlberg and Kramer, therefore, might not have indicated a consistent shift to simpler moral thinking but merely a tendency for the young men attending college to be in the process of distinguishing between universal-objective and personal-subjective values.

Turiel: inconsistencies in moral thinking due to differences in values

After analyzing data supplied by Turiel, Hoffman concluded (1980, p. 303) that there appears to be more evidence to support the universal-personal conflict hypothesis of Turiel than the regression hypothesis of Kohlberg and Kramer.

Turiel's distinction between two types of values calls attention to the nature of values and how they influence behavior.

The Nature and Significance of Values

The Nature of Values

One of the most widely respected definitions of values has been proposed by M. Rokeach.

To say that a person has a value is to say that he has an enduring prescriptive or proscriptive belief that a specific mode of behavior or end-state of existence is preferred to an opposite mode of behavior and end-state. This belief transcends attitudes toward objects and toward situations; it is a standard that guides and determines action, attitudes toward objects and situations, ideology, presentation of self to others, evaluations, judgments, justifications, comparisons of self with others, and attempts to influence others. Values serve adjustive, ego-defensive, knowledge, and self-actualizing functions. Instrumental and terminal values are related yet are separately organized into relatively enduring hierarchical organizations along a continuum of importance. (1973, p. 25)

Values: beliefs that guide and determine attitudes and actions

In his definition, Rokeach mentions instrumental and terminal values, and he has developed a survey device to obtain information about them. Respondents are asked to rank the two types of values presented in Table 19.1 in order from the most important to least important. To gain a bit of insight into your own values, take a sheet of paper and list the numbers 1,2,3,4 and 15,16,17,18. Then select and record the four top and four bottom values from the two columns in Table 19.1. As you will realize when you peruse the lists, terminal values describe general con-

TABLE 19.1
VALUES INCLUDED IN THE ROKEACH VALUE SURVEY

Terminal Values	Instrumental Values
A comfortable life (a prosperous life)	Ambitious (hard working, aspiring)
An exciting life (a stimulating, active life)	Broad-minded (open-minded)
A sense of accomplishment (lasting contribution)	Capable (competent, effective)
A world at peace (free of war and conflict)	Cheerful (lighthearted, joyful)
A world of beauty (beauty of nature and the arts)	Clean (neat, tidy)
Equality (brotherhood, equal opportunity for all)	Courageous (standing up for your beliefs)
Family security (taking care of loved ones)	Forgiving (willing to pardon others)
Freedom (independence, free choice)	Helpful (working for the welfare of others)
Happiness (contentedness)	Honest (sincere, truthful)
Inner harmony (freedom from inner conflict)	Imaginative (daring, creative)
Mature love (sexual and spiritual intimacy)	Independent (self-reliant, self-sufficient)
National security (protection from attack)	Intellectual (intelligent, reflective)
Pleasure (an enjoyable, leisurely life)	Logical (consistent, rational)
Salvation (saved, eternal life)	Loving (affectionate, tender)
Self-respect (self-esteem)	Obedient (dutiful, respectful)
Social recognition (respect, admiration)	Polite (courteous, well mannered)
True friendship (close companionship)	Responsible (dependable, reliable)
Wisdom (a mature understanding of life)	Self-controlled (restrained, self-disciplined)

Source: M. Rokeach, *The Nature of Human Values* (New York: Free Press, 1973), pp. 358–361. Reproduced with permission of Halgren Tests, 873 Persimmon Ave., Sunnyvale, CA 94087.

ditions—ultimate goals of life; instrumental values refer to personality traits that might be instrumental in achieving goals.

Values and the Cohort Effect

In the discussion of continuity and change in development in Chapter 5, some of the problems of interpreting longitudinal research findings were noted. Among the problems mentioned was the **cohort effect,** the influence of rapidly changing political, cultural, and social trends on children and adolescents just a few years apart. The cohort effect usually has a much greater impact on the behavior of adolescents and youth than on younger children. The dress, games, hobbies, and favorite books of succeeding generations of preschool and elementary school children, for instance, stay essentially the same despite cultural upheavals. There are some changes, of course, but basic interests remain quite constant. As these words are being written, for instance, mothers are making pilgrimages to department and toy stores or putting their names on waiting lists to acquire Cabbage Patch dolls for their preschool age

In contrast to youth of the 1960s, who often engaged in campus protests and were contemptuous of those who studied diligently, youth of the 1980s tend to recognize that it is important to take full advantage of educational opportunities.
© *Jerry Berndt/Stock, Boston;* © *Alex Webb/Magnum Photo.*

children. By the time you read these words, a different type of doll may be the rage, but it will still be a doll. The dress, favorite musical groups and songs, dance steps, and free-time pursuits of adolescents, on the other hand, are extremely susceptible to change. If, as a college senior, you were to return to the high school from which you graduated, you might be dismayed about how out of touch you had become in just four years. At the same time, you would probably conclude that older high school students had values very similar to yours, even though some of those values differed from the ones you honored in your high school days. To put it a different way, values change in response to current events but high school and college students are likely to endorse many of the same values at any given time.

> Values of adolescents and youth likely to be similar even though tastes differ

Each generation of high school students may favor different styles of dress, music, and dance to prove to themselves and others that they are on their own, not just docile imitators of older siblings and peers. But because older high school and college students are both capable of formal thought and are being influenced by the same cultural and political trends, they are likely to think the same way, depending on their personality traits and home environments. The interactions of these various

TABLE 19.2
POLITICAL EVENTS AND YOUTH MOVEMENTS: 1950–1979

Period of Time	Decisive Political Events	Youth Movements
1950–1959	The Cold War—Eisenhower years Growth of "military-industrial complex" Dulles foreign policy Recession McCarthyism 1954 Supreme Court desegregation decision House Un-American Activities Committee	"The silent generation"
1960–1968	Kennedy-Johnson years "New Frontier" Civil rights demonstrations Peace Corps, poverty programs Vietnam escalation Assassinations of Kennedy brothers and Martin Luther King "Great Society" programs Ghetto riots and campus disruption	New Left New Right Civil rights and Black Power Protest demonstrations, strikes, violence
1969–1976	Nixon-Ford years Emphasis on "law and order" Voting Rights Act Vietnam War ends Kissinger foreign policy Inflation, job squeeze Growth of multinational corporations Watergate OPEC and Middle East oil embargo	Women's rights Ecology movement Charismatic religious movements Quiet seventies
1977–1979	Early Carter administration Conciliatory, practical, informal mood in White House Emphasis on government reorganization National energy crisis Inflation, job squeeze continues	"No-Nuke" movement Gay liberation

Source: Richard G. Braungart, "Youth Movements," in J. Adelson (ed.), *Handbook of Adolescent Psychology* (New York: Wiley, 1980), p. 565.

factors can be illustrated by noting some of the political and cultural changes that have produced various youth movements in recent years. In Table 19.2, you will find lists of political events and youth movements for the decades from 1950 to 1980. Youth movements reveal ways sets of values coalesce, so they call attention to general tendencies. To complete the table, you might note your own interpretation of major concerns of youth during the second Reagan administration. What do you think are the basic concerns of adolescents and youth during the mid-1980s?

Factors That Influence the Development of Values

Factors That Influence Value Development in Adolescence

A number of attempts have been made to compare the beliefs, attitudes, and values of parents and their children, and also compare the extent to which parent-peer and peer-peer opinions agree and conflict. Studies of values (reviewed by Feather, 1980), of political thinking (reviewed by Gallatin, 1980), of moral development (reviewed by Hoffman, 1980), and of occupational choice (reviewed by Rogers, 1972) lead to the conclusion that high school students are probably influenced in these areas of their lives more by parents than by peers. A visit to any high school, on the other hand, will reveal that in terms of dress, hair styles, interests, social relationships, and the like, the influence of peers is also extremely potent. The hypothesis that parents and peers influence different aspects of adolescent behavior has been developed by G. V. Brittain (1968), who suggests that parents have a greater impact on decisions that have implications for the future (choice of a career) while peers influence decisions that involve current status and identity needs (choice of friends). L. E. Larsen (1972) evaluated Brittain's hypothesis and concluded that the influence of parents was greatest when there was mutual affection and respect. It might be concluded, then, that values, moral and political beliefs, and the long-range plans of high school students are likely to be influenced by their parents. When they seek to establish an immediate sense of identity or status, however, adolescents are more likely to be influenced by peers.

Parents influence plans; peers influence immediate status

This distinction might be clarified by considering principles of social learning theory that center on observation, imitation, and reinforcement. Sears and other social learning theorists emphasize the importance of the peer group during adolescence because of the extent to which the behavior of high school students is shaped by the behavior and reactions of classmates. Adolescents may adopt styles of dress or mannerisms of speech and behavior they observe in age-mates they admire. If they receive a positive response from peers when they dress or act in similar ways, such behavior will be strengthened. Only rarely, however, can values or attitudes be acquired by imitating the overt behavior of others. Such beliefs are more likely to be acquired through long-term contact with particular individuals who have expressed opinions or displayed characteristics over a period of time. Most often this description fits the parents more than other adults, although certain high school teachers may have a lasting impact on their students.

Factors That Influence Value Development in Youth

The relative influence of parents and peers on the attitudes and behavior of youth is more difficult to assess than adolescent-parent similarities. But it seems reasonable to expect that many college students will be more inclined than they were in high school to form their own set of values. As they formulate a philosophy of life, they may select beliefs that have been encouraged by parents. They will also be likely to take into account attitudes and values favored by peers and by adults other than their parents.

There are a number of reasons for expecting youth to be more self-selective than adolescents in formulating a personal code for making decisions. First, and most obvious, youth are more socially, cognitively, and politically sophisticated than adolescents. They have also become legally and perhaps economically responsible for their own behavior, and may no longer feel a strong sense of allegiance to their parents. Furthermore, if they conclude that they are members of a subculture that is between adolescence and adulthood, they may feel an obligation to rethink earlier convictions about values. Finally, to a much greater extent than in high school, college students are likely to be exposed to teachers who espouse values that differ from those of most parents. Some of the courses that college students take (either as requirements or electives), in fact, may force assessment and questioning of traditional beliefs. For all these reasons, it seems logical to expect that parent-youth values will be more divergent than parent-adolescent values. At the same time, it seems reasonable to assume that even older youth will continue to be influenced by the extended contacts they have had with their parents.

Norman T. Feather (1980) supplies evidence in support of these two expectations in a review of research on values. He reports that researchers have found that as college students move from the freshman to the senior class they become increasingly open to new experiences and display greater tolerance. There is also a tendency for them to become more liberal, *provided* they were either a liberal or a moderate to begin with. Students who were conservative when they entered college, though, tend to become more conservative by the time they graduate, even though they have been exposed to liberal ideas. These findings reveal that the extent to which youth will or will not continue to share the

Conservative youth stay that way even if exposed to liberal views in college

Researchers who have asked students to record their values during their college careers have discovered that liberal and moderate youth become more liberal but that conservative youth become more conservative—even though they have been exposed to liberal ideas.
J. P. Laffont/Sygma.

values of their parents will depend on a complex group of interacting variables. It may be difficult to predict what will happen in the development of any particular individual because of the interaction of many factors: sex, social class, marital compatibility of the parents, type of discipline used by the parents, geographic area, political background of the home and the home town, the influence of particular peers or teachers, and dozens of other factors.

The nature of some of the push-pull forces that act on youth as they engage in the process of forming their own set of values is illustrated by this statement by a young college woman:

Up to a certain age, I believed everything my parents said. Then, in college, I saw all these new ideas and I said, "Okay, I'm not going to believe all that stuff you told me," and I rejected everything and said to myself, "Okay, now I'm going to make a new Debbie which has nothing to do with my mother and father. I'm going to start with a clean slate" and what I started to put on it were all new ideas. These ideas were opposite to what my parents believed. But slowly, what's happened is that I'm adding on a lot of the things which they've told me and I'm taking them as my own and I'm coming more together with them. (Josselson, 1973, p. 37)

Summary

1. During the high school years, most adolescents become at least partially capable of formal thought, which is characterized by thinking about possibilities, hypotheses, the future, thoughts, and speculations. An aspect of formal thinking that may cause problems in high school classes featuring discussion is a tendency toward **unrestrained theorizing.** Another aspect of formal thinking that may cause difficulties is **adolescent egocentrism,** or extreme concern about the reactions of others. Criticisms of Piaget's description of formal thinking include doubts that there is an abrupt switch to such thinking and evidence that cognitive development is influenced by schooling and cultural factors to a greater extent than he acknowledged.

2. As they approach voting age, adolescents are more inclined to engage in political thinking. The political thinking of older adolescents is more abstract and less authoritarian than that of younger adolescents. The influence of parents on political thinking appears to be indirect rather than due to "indoctrination."

3. Starting in early adolescence, the **morality of cooperation** is practiced, with stress on coming to mutual agreements and making allowance for intentions. Parallel changes in interpersonal reasoning occur as adolescents become increasingly capable of understanding subtleties of relationships and also take into account how their actions might influence *all* individuals.

4. When adolescents and youth are asked to respond to moral dilemmas over a period of time, regressions in moral reasoning sometimes occur. Kohlberg hypothesizes that such regressions are due to awareness of inconsistencies between expectations and actual behavior. Other theorists suggest that regressions in moral reasoning are due to changes in values as a result of experiences.

5. Values are beliefs that guide and determine attitudes and actions. When asked to respond to survey questions, adolescents and youth are likely to reveal that they endorse similar values even though their tastes for such things as popular music are different. Parents are more likely than peers to influence the values of their adolescent offspring, but peers are more likely to influence factors that involve immediate status (such as friendships). An interesting aspect of value development is that youth who enter college as political conservatives tend to stay that way even though they are exposed to liberal views in classes and in campus discussions.

The Nature of Formal Thought

Analyses of formal thinking are presented in *Piaget's Theory of Intellectual Development: An Introduction* (2nd ed., 1979) by Herbert Ginsburg and Sylvia Opper; and in "Thinking Processes in Adolescence" by Daniel Keating in the *Handbook of Adolescent Psychology* (1980, pp. 211–246), edited by Joseph Adelson. A review of research on formal thinking is provided by E. D. Neimark in "Intellectual Development During Adolescence," in *Review of Child Development Research*, 1975, 4, edited by F. D. Horowitz.

Political Thinking

"Political Thinking in Adolescence" is discussed by Judith Gallatin in Chapter 10 (pp. 344–382) of the *Handbook of Adolescent Psychology* (1980), edited by Joseph Adelson. A collection of articles on various aspects of political thinking is provided in the *Handbook of Political Socialization: Theory and Practice* (1977), edited by S. A. Renshon.

Moral Development

Perhaps the best brief discussion of moral development during adolescence is provided by Martin L. Hoffman in Chapter 9 (pp. 295–343) of the *Handbook of Adolescent Psychology* (1980), edited by Joseph Adelson. A collection of articles on moral development is presented in *Moral Development and Behavior: Theory, Research, and Social Issues* (1976), edited by Thomas Lickona.

Values

For information about values, peruse "Values in Adolescence" by Norman T. Feather, and "Youth Movements" by Richard G. Braungart, Chapters 8 and 18 of the *Handbook of Adolescent Psychology* (1980), edited by Joseph Adelson.

KEY POINTS

Relationships with Parents

Parents must allow adolescent to abandon them without feeling abandoned

Generation gap appears to be exception rather than rule

Autonomy favored by moderate but sincere interest, participation in decisions

Democratic approach to encouraging autonomy appears to be most effective

Relationships with Peers

Middle adolescence time of greatest insecurity about friendships

Girls develop closer relationships, more likely to experience anxiety

Dating sequence: looks and popularity, personality, dependability and sensitivity

Intimate behavior strengthened by reinforcements beyond those previously received

Desire to maintain equity when establishing an intimate relationship

Factors That Complicate Male-Female Relationships

Achievement motivation influenced by past experiences with success and failure

Fear-of-success stories influenced by variety of factors

Capable women may experience conflicts between success and acceptance by males

Both males and females benefit from psychological androgyny

CHAPTER
20

ADOLESCENCE AND YOUTH

RELATIONSHIPS WITH OTHERS

*H*uman beings have a longer period of dependence on parents than any other species. This leads to special difficulties when the time comes for the young person to be independent, partly because the long period of interaction has led to strong emotional ties and partly because the adolescent is mature and sensitive enough to comprehend the magnitude and significance of what is happening. In our society, these already substantial problems are magnified by a lack of any clear set of guidelines indicating when a young person has achieved maturity. In many simpler societies, initiation rituals have been established, and once a boy or girl successfully masters or experiences the prescribed forms of behavior, adulthood is proclaimed by dress or ornament or some other tangible sign. But in America, there is considerable confusion about the rights and privileges of adulthood. The most obvious example, up until 1972, was that an eighteen-year-old male was considered to be man enough to engage in warfare but not man enough to vote. At present, many legislative bodies are debating the age at which liquor can be legally purchased or consumed. This varies from state to state, as do the ages at which a marriage license or a driver's license can be obtained, property owned, or even cigarettes purchased.

Relationships with Parents

These inconsistencies in society at large make the task facing parents and their close-to-adult children even more difficult than it is to begin with. Douvan and Adelson provide an eloquent description of the nature of the problem.

The family must take on tasks of socialization more subtle than they have met before; at the same time it must know how to yield gracefully to such competing socializers as the peer group. It must accommodate itself to the implications and dangers of the child's sexual maturity; it must adjust to his extraordinary, nerve-wracking ambivalence; it must face and respond to his clamor for autonomy, distinguishing those demands which are real and must be granted from those which are token and are used to test the parents or to bargain with them. Above all, the family must allow the child to abandon it without allowing him to feel that he is himself abandoned or an abandoner. (1966, p. 119)

Parents must allow adolescent to abandon them without feeling abandoned

Because ours is a melting-pot society, there is no single, well-established code of behavior, such as that found in homogeneous and self-contained cultures. Because ours is a technological society, culture change is extremely rapid. Because ours is a meritocratic society, parents are eager to insure that their children will be prepared to compete effectively with others. For all these reasons, the peer group may exert a degree of influence on parental decisions about adolescent behavior. In the absence of a single set of guidelines, parents who must make decisions about what their teen-age sons and daughters can and cannot do may fall back on their own adolescent experiences. But rapid cultural change has made some of the parents' experiences obsolete or irrelevant. In addition, they may feel apprehensive that too many restrictions—or old-fashioned ones—may handicap their children when the time comes for career and marriage competition with the children of neighbors. Recognizing the parents' uncertainty, the adolescent may try to gain as much freedom and autonomy as possible by describing what peers with the fewest restrictions are allowed to do. Parents, for the most part, will want to continue to exert a degree of control and may disbelieve or discount descriptions of what other families are doing.

Evaluations of the "Generation Gap" Hypothesis

The term **generation gap** is frequently used to explain that the factors just noted may lead to substantial differences between the views of parents and of their adolescent offspring. While such a gap probably exists in some families, it is not inevitable and may be the exception rather than the rule. Daniel Offer (1969) discovered this when he made his comprehensive study of seventy-three normal adolescent boys and their families. Offer felt that too many conclusions about adolescence were based on extreme cases, and he deliberately chose subjects who were *not* identified as maladjusted. He and his associates conducted 6 forty-five-minute interviews with each subject over a period of three years, administered projective and other tests, and also interviewed parents.

Generation gap appears to be exception rather than rule

They found that disagreements with parents reached a peak in the seventh and eighth grades, but even at that time these were not severe. Eighty-eight percent of the boys felt home discipline was fair, and there were few strong complaints about parents (inconsistent discipline was one of the most common factors mentioned). Most parents were pleased with the behavior of their sons, particularly because they felt that pressure on adolescents had increased since their youth. While the boys were most rebellious at twelve and thirteen, argued with their parents about hair and clothes at thirteen and fourteen, and about the car at sixteen, Offer found that by and large they endorsed the same middle-class values as their parents. He concluded that there was little evidence of parent-child conflict or a generation gap. Apparently, parents recognized cultural changes influencing the behavior of their teen-age sons and adjusted their attitudes accordingly.

Although Offer's results and conclusions may have been significantly influenced by his deliberate choice of "normal" subjects (who might have emphasized their normality because of their awareness that he was a psychiatrist), it does seem reasonable to say that conflict between parents and teen-agers is far from inevitable. The conclusions reached by Offer in 1969 regarding lack of evidence of a generation gap have been reaffirmed more recently by A. Tolor (1976), Joseph Adelson (1979), R. Josselson (1980), and J. Gallatin (1980).

Daniel Offer concluded that a "generation gap" between parents and their adolescent children may be the exception rather than the rule.
Cary Wolinski/Stock, Boston.

Parent-Child Relationships That Favor Autonomy

On the basis of the finding of their comprehensive study of adolescence, Douvan and Adelson (1966) concluded that four aspects of parent-adolescent relationships were involved in the development of autonomy: parental interest and involvement, the emotional intensity of family interaction, the degree and nature of family conduct, and the nature of parental authority. They note that an adolescent is more likely to achieve a satisfactory sense of at least some aspects of autonomy under these conditions: parents manifest a moderate degree of sincere interest; relationships are neither cold nor intense; parents allow a certain amount of conflict (by listening to children explain *their* point of view); and adolescents participate in making decisions. They also discovered

Autonomy favored by moderate but sincere interest, participation in decisions that girls seemed to progress steadily toward independence but that boys were likely to experience a certain amount of strain. Boys were also more likely to assume an objective-critical view of their parents. In summarizing their analysis, Douvan and Adelson note, "the autonomous have the opportunity for individualism [while the nonautonomous do not]" (p. 173).

G. H. Elder, Jr. (1962) investigated parent-adolescent relationships and autonomy by a method similar in many respects to the Douvan and Adelson investigations. He asked over seven thousand adolescents to rate their parents' behavior. He found that when asked about *fairness,* the most positive ratings were given to parents characterized as **democratic** (the adolescent was invited to participate in discussions, but final decisions were made by the parents) or **equalitarian** (parents and adolescents had equal say). The lowest rating was given to parents who were **autocratic** (the adolescent was not consulted at all). The democratic approach also seemed to foster confidence and independence. Thus, the results of the Elder study are consistent with the findings of Douvan and Adelson—and with the results of Baumrind's research (1971) on authoritative, authoritarian, and permissive styles of child rearing. Parents who use a democratic approach give their children a chance to gain some experience in making decisions. At the same time they supply a degree of guidance and control. The final move toward autonomy appears to be less threatening under such a regime.

> Democratic approach to encouraging autonomy appears to be most effective

In using a democratic approach with adolescents, however, it appears to be desirable for parents not to exhibit affection too strongly. Douvan and Adelson concluded that sincere (but not smothering) interest and relationships that were neither cold nor intense seemed most likely to promote healthy independence. These conclusions are in harmony with the opinion expressed by Peter Blos that adolescents who come from very close and affectionate homes may be "burdened by family ties" (1962, p. 19) when the time comes to move from dependence to independence.

Differences in the Influence of Peers and Parents

It seems clear that parents may influence their teen-age sons and daughters in a variety of ways. But the peer group also has a significant impact, particularly on some types of behavior. Peers may influence adolescent behavior because most teen-agers spend much more time in the company of peers than with their parents. In addition, many types of social behavior can be learned only by interacting with others of the same age. Furthermore, the very fact that peers are experiencing similar physical and psychological changes tends to bring them together because they can identify with each other's problems and concerns. (As noted earlier, adolescents report that they are much more likely to learn about sex from peers than from parents.) Because adolescence is a period of rapid change in physical, cognitive, and social development, teen-agers must engage in a considerable amount of trial and error in order to adapt to alterations in their physiological and psychological functioning. Such experimentation takes place largely in the peer group.

Relationships with Peers

Relationships with age-mates during adolescence differ in a number of ways from earlier friendships. The achievement of puberty triggers hormonal changes that arouse feelings of sexual attraction, causing both males and females to see each other in a new light. Increasing awareness of eventual marriage stimulates dating and courtship interactions with members of the opposite sex. Self-consciousness due to formal thinking and adolescent egocentrism causes teen-agers to be more deeply concerned about the reactions of others than they were during the elementary school years. Growing independence often leads teen-agers to discuss personal problems and concerns more with age-mates than with parents. For all these reasons, the nature of friendships change during the high school years.

Changes in Adolescent Same-Sex Friendships

The most complete analysis of same-sex friendships during adolescence was included in the comprehensive study of Douvan and Adelson (1966). Even though they obtained information primarily from girls and even though several cohorts of adolescence have come and gone since their study was done, the results are still worth examining. Subsequent, less comprehensive, studies (reviewed by Coleman, 1980) have not produced any contradictory findings, and many of the trends described seem unlikely to be drastically influenced by cultural and political events. Douvan and Adelson found that in the early phase of adolescence (ages eleven, twelve, and thirteen), friendships seemed to center more on mutual activities than on social interactions. Friends were chosen not so much because of their personality characteristics, but because they participated in similar activities. In the middle adolescent years (ages fourteen, fifteen, and sixteen), friendships seemed to be based primarily on feelings of security. The ninth- and tenth-grader seems to want someone who can be confided in and trusted. One explanation for stress on loyalty at this stage is that it reflects a need for more than superficial reactions from others at a time when a sense of personal identity is being formed. Another explanation is that severance of ties with parents is becoming more complete. Yet another explanation is that this is a time when a girl is likely to first begin to date, and she wants a close friend as a confidant and source of support and guidance. Because loyalty is so important at this age, and because personal thoughts and feelings are likely to be shared more intimately than ever before, the middle adolescent period is the time of greatest insecurity and fear of rejection. In late adolescence (age seventeen and older) friendships become more relaxed and, as in the early stage, are likely to be based primarily on mutual interests.

Middle adolescence time of greatest insecurity about friendships

Differences in the Friendships of Males and Females

While Douvan and Adelson found that this basic sequence was similar in males and females, they also discovered differences. Girls were much more concerned about having a sensitive, sympathetic female friend to talk to; boys were more interested in a buddy who would enjoy similar activities and provide help when needed. In a different study of adolescent friendships, John C. Coleman (1974) found support for the conclusions of Douvan and Adelson. He reported that tensions, jealousies, and conflicts were much more apparent when girls were asked to describe friendships and that anxiety about friendships reached a peak around the age of fifteen. Coleman agreed with Douvan and Adelson that a logical explanation for greater anxiety about friendships on the part of girls can be traced to socialization influences. Girls in our society are encouraged to be sensitive to the feelings of others and to develop close interpersonal relationships. Boys are encouraged to be independent and self-sufficient. Thus, boys may resist developing too strong a relationship with other males during the high school years because they want to prove that they do not need to depend on others. Boys may also be less likely to form intimate same-sex friendships because of concern about homosexuality. A male with homosexual tendencies may eventually feel uninhibited about forming a relationship with another male, but during the high school years this tendency may be suppressed because social interactions are so public and likely to attract attention and arouse comment. If two girls in a high school corridor are observed engaging in an earnest conversation, it will be reacted to by classmates as normal behavior. Two boys observed in a similar situation may be teased or ridiculed.

Girls develop closer relationships, more likely to experience anxiety

Adolescent females are more likely than males to develop close same-sex friendships. They also are more likely to experience anxiety if such relationships appear to deteriorate.
Owen Franken/Stock, Boston.

Aspects and Ramifications of Dating

While friendships with members of the same sex are a significant part of adolescent social behavior, male-female relationships become increasingly important as teen-agers move through the grades. Some adolescents begin to date early and make a career out of it; others leave school without having had a single date. Douvan and Adelson point out that "the dating mechanism serves in defining and testing of identity; it is a laboratory for training in the social graces; it provides occasion for sexual experimentation and discovery; it is used to chart popularity and success" (p. 203). They suggest that dating is a better mechanism for the purposes just noted than for encouraging social maturity or preparing for marriage.

Douvan and Adelson conclude that one reason dating may interfere with, rather than encourage, social development is that it often begins too early. Under ideal circumstances, dating behavior takes place over a period of time and provides a gradual introduction to male-female relationships. If dating starts early, adolescents may be prevented from developing more mature relations with peers of the same sex. And if a couple starts to go steady too early, they may develop only a superficial relationship with each other.

Studies of dating behavior by Douvan and Adelson and others (e.g., Hansen, 1977) have revealed that there are often three stages that can be discerned. At first, the primary goal of dating seems to be a desire for social prestige. During this initial phase, both males and females indicate that good looks and popularity are the most important attributes of a dating partner. In the second stage, physical appearance is considered to be less important than personality traits and social sophistication. In the final stage, dating partners are selected for deeper qualities such as reliability, dependability, and being considerate. J. Roy Hopkins (1983) points out that these three stages are very neatly summarized by a passage from *Loose Change: Three Women in the Sixties* by Sara Davidson:

Dating sequence: looks and popularity, personality, dependability, and sensitivity

Looking back, I can see that at sixteen I had a willowy, beautifully proportioned body but at the time I was only aware of what I considered its unnatural elongation. When . . . I grew to be 5′10″, I calculated that 90 percent of the men in the world were inaccessible to me because they were shorter. I day dreamed of going to Sweden to have an operation on my legs that would diminish me by three inches. When friends offered to fix me up, my first question was always "Is he tall?" followed by "Is he cute?" (Later I would ask, "Is he bright?" and still later, "Is he sensitive?") (1977, pp. 24–25)

Aspects of Youthful Intimacy

Many of the trends in relationships with peers that characterize older high school students continue for youth who go on to college. As Keniston has observed, however, young people who attend college are not just experiencing protracted adolescence; they are engaged in a separate stage of life. One of the most important aspects of this new phase of life for many youth involves establishing an intimate relationship with an age-mate of the opposite (or same) sex. Before so many high school graduates went on to college (and before sexual freedom became widely accepted), opportunities for developing a close premarital relationship were restricted. Today many young Americans feel that they have at least two to four years after graduation from high school to explore the ramifications of a close relationship with another person. Because of cultural trends, such a relationship no longer needs to involve formal marriage vows, nor does it always involve male-female pairs.

As an outgrowth of social learning theory, a number of psychologists have developed what is referred to as **social exchange** theory to explain intimate relationships. T. L. Huston and R. L. Burgess (1979), for instance, suggest that people become intimate when the outcome of a relationship exceeds the outcome they are accustomed to receiving. If two individuals get more reinforcement from each other than they have previously received when interacting with age-mates, intimate behavior will be strengthened. Using that basic premise as a guide, Burgess and Huston suggest that the following tendencies are likely to characterize intimate relationships. (To test the validity of these observations, first think of the most intimate relationship you have with another person, then evaluate that relationship in terms of the following points.)

Intimate behavior strengthened by reinforcements beyond those previously received

1. Intimate relationships involve frequent interaction over a long period of time in a wide variety of settings.
2. Intimates are eager to regain proximity to each other when they are separated and feel comforted when proximity is regained.
3. Intimates engage in extended self-disclosure, including physical intimacies.
4. Communication—both positive and negative—between intimates is comparatively uninhibited.
5. Intimates tend to develop their own systems of communication.
6. Partners in an intimate relationship show increased abilities to predict each other's point of view.
7. Intimates tend to synchronize goals and to develop stable patterns of reaction.
8. As they interact, intimates tend to increase their investment in the relationship.
9. Intimates tend to see the relationship between them as more nearly irreplaceable than relationships between those who are not close to each other.
10. Others tend to relate to intimates as a couple more than as individuals.

Huston and Burgess believe that in seeking someone to develop intimacy with, individuals look for others who are attractive to them, but who, they also feel, will reciprocate positive feelings. Before individuals are willing to fall in love, in other words, they would like to feel that they are going to get something back.

A variation of social exchange theory is called **equity theory.** Those

According to equity theory, both partners in a male-female relationship should feel that characteristics such as attractiveness, poise, popularity, and potential should be about equal in each member of the pair.
Eli Heller/Stock, Boston.

Desire to maintain equity when establishing an intimate relationship

who favor this view reason that in addition to wanting to get reinforcement out of an intimate relationship, individuals want to maintain equity. A college male who is considered to be handsome, intelligent, and talented, for example, will strive to become intimate with a female who possesses an assortment of traits of equivalent value. They do not need to be the same traits, but the partner's attributes should add up to the same number of "points." If there is a marked discrepancy between the "desirability quotient" of members of an intimate pair, equity theorists predict it will not last. Thus, if the campus idol quixotically chooses to live intimately with a rather plain, shy, and diffident (but adoring) coed, he is likely to feel cheated after a while, and she will feel guilty because she is getting more than her share. While equity theory often can be used to explain the success or failure of short-term relationships, it may not be as applicable to long-term commitments. And even though it is interesting to try to analyze love in terms of the principles of social learning theory, there are many exceptions to the sort of relationship predicted. Even so, equity theory does call attention to a significant factor in contemporary marriage relationships: the achievement levels of husbands and wives. In order to understand why achievement may be such an important factor in male-female relationships, a bit of background about the concept of achievement motivation is called for.

Factors That Complicate Male-Female Relationships

Speculations About Achievement Motivation

J. W. Atkinson (1964) has developed a view of occupational aspirations that is derived from the conception of **achievement motivation** proposed by David McClelland (1961). McClelland believes that in the course of development people acquire a **need for achievement,** and he has conducted research to demonstrate the degree to which the need varies among individuals. His basic research technique is to show subjects pictures of individuals in different situations (a boy sitting at a desk with a book in front of him, for example) and ask them to write stories about what is happening. Individuals with a high need for achievement tend to write stories emphasizing work, getting things done, and success; those with a low need for achievement do not mention such types of behavior. Atkinson proposes that differences in the strength of the need for achievement can be explained by postulating a contrasting need to avoid failure. Atkinson believes that the tendency to achieve success is influenced by the probability of success and the attractiveness of achieving it. A strong need to avoid failure is likely to develop when

Achievement motivation influenced by past experiences with success and failure

people experience repeated failure and set goals beyond what they think they can accomplish.

Research on Fear of Success

Some Females May Perceive Achievement as Inappropriate

As she read reports of research inspired by the work of McClelland and Atkinson, Matina S. Horner became intrigued by the finding that the need for achievement in males seemed to be more fully developed than in females. She decided to make this the subject of her Ph.D. dissertation (1968) and, using a technique derived from studies by Atkinson, asked 178 university students to write a four-minute story from this cue: "At the end of first-term finals Anne finds herself at the top of her medical school class." When she analyzed the stories, Horner found three recurrent themes: (1) fear that Anne would lose friends; (2) guilt about success; (3) unwillingness to come to grips with the question of Anne's success (in some stories, the cue was more or less ignored). She concluded that all three of these themes reflected a general *fear of success* and discovered that 65.5 percent of the stories written by women could be classified under this heading, contrasted with only 9 percent of those written by men.

As a second part of her study, she placed men and women in competitive and noncompetitive situations. She found that women who wrote fear-of-success stories performed much better when working alone than when competing against others. She reasoned that fear of success motivates many women to avoid achievement, particularly in competitive situations.

Reports of Horner's study (1970) attracted attention, and a number of articles in newspapers and magazines led readers to believe that there is a well-established tendency for almost all women to fear success. Because of the publicity and the topicality of the concept, over sixty studies derived from or similar to Horner's original research were carried out in the next three years. David Tresemer (1974, 1977) reviewed these and also analyzed the techniques used by Horner. He concluded that fear-of-success stories may be influenced by a variety of factors, including the type of cues supplied. For example, when a woman in a story is described as the best *psychology* student rather than as the best medical student, Tresemer reports, males write more fear-of-success stories than females.

Fear-of-success stories influenced by variety of factors

Females May Try to Protect the Male Ego

In *The Adolescent Society* (1961), James S. Coleman reported that bright high school girls did not try to qualify for the honor roll because they were afraid it might make them unpopular, particularly with boys. While it appears that more young women of the 1980s have a greater desire to achieve success in school and in a career than their predecessors, there are still many adolescent (and adult) females whose primary goal is marriage and a family. For thousands of years bright and capable women have accepted that marriage may be possible only when a male is attracted to but not threatened by a woman. Recognizing that many males are sensitive about their "masculinity," generations of practical women have avoided display of their abilities and resorted to subtle and indirect ways of achieving success in marriage and life. Awareness of this aspect of male-female relationships may account for at least some of the fear-of-success stories written by females in studies such as Horner's. Perhaps some stories stressing Anne's discomfort about "finding" (a word which leads the reader to believe that Anne is bothered) herself at the top of her class could be attributed to recognition of the need to protect the male ego. (Philip H. Dreyer reports [1975, p. 214], though, that the percentage of women who admit that they pretend to be dumb on dates has dropped considerably in the last thirty years.)

Conflicts Between a Career and Marriage

Additional insight into career problems encountered by females is provided by the observations of Karen Horney. It seems significant that a woman was the first psychoanalyst to reveal the conflict between a desire to achieve success and the desire to be accepted by others. (Maslow's hierarchy of needs calls attention to the fact that the needs for love and belonging usually must be satisfied before the need for esteem emerges.) Perhaps the disintegration of her own marriage led Horney to

Capable women may experience conflicts between success and acceptance by males

emphasize the significance of such conflicts. As a young woman she was attracted to her husband and desired to maintain a loving relationship with him, but she also felt impelled to use her exceptional intelligence and abilities. After she had achieved notable success in her career, her relationship with her husband became less meaningful and they separated, a predicament that may confront many successful women in the 1980s. Today, more than at any time in history, choices concerning career and marriage for both males and females may be inextricably intertwined.

In *The Adolescent Experience* (1966), Douvan and Adelson emphasized the extent to which the future of a high school girl of the mid-1950s would depend on the man she married. In the 1980s this is still true of many adolescent females. A significant number of high school and college females, however, are determined to try to alter this pattern by establishing themselves in careers. A young woman's decision to prepare for a career will influence other decisions, particularly those regarding marriage and having children. If she hopes to combine a career and a

Douvan and Adelson found that in the 1950s most high school girls had a "diffuse and misty" identity because they assumed that what they would become would depend on the man they would eventually marry.
Burt Glinn/Magnum Photo.

family, she must decide whether to devote full time to rearing children before or after pursuing a career, whether to interrupt a career only long enough to give birth and then place the child in the care of baby sitters or a day care center, or whether to ask her husband to share or take over the responsibility for child rearing. This last option, in particular, emphasizes how decisions about a career will have a profound influence on the choice of a husband. A woman who wants to combine a full-time career with marriage will need to try to choose a husband who is willing and able to adapt to deviations from the traditional pattern. While a contemporary young man might profess to be above male chauvinism and be confident in his ability to adjust to marriage with a career-oriented woman, both he and his prospective spouse might not consider some of the practical difficulties that could arise in such a relationship. They may discover that traditional role assignments of female as homemaker and child rearer and male as provider are not easy to disregard.

The Advantages of Psychological Androgyny

Broverman and her colleagues (1972) reveal the extent to which traditional conceptions of sex roles are ingrained in the minds of many Americans. Sandra Bem's research (1975, 1976) supports those findings. In discussing early child-parent relationships in Chapter 8, Bem's studies were cited as indicating that adults vary in the extent to which they can be classified as **sex-typed** or as high in **psychological androgyny.** Sex-typed females (who endorse stereotyped conceptions of femininity) may refuse to nail two boards together, for instance, because they feel it is a "masculine" rather than a "feminine" form of behavior. Sex-typed males may refuse to handle a baby or do household chores presumably because engaging in such behavior will make them appear effeminate or at least unmasculine. Only adults rated high in psychological androgyny appear able to move between masculine and feminine roles without difficulty or self-consciousness.

On the basis of available evidence, it is not possible to trace or precisely evaluate all the factors that lead to sex-typed behavior or to psychological androgyny. The report of Money and Ehrhardt (1972) comparing androgenized and normal girls leads to the assumption that at least some forms of sex-typed behavior (for example, the tendencies for adolescent girls to be interested in marriage and motherhood) may be due to hormonal balances established at the time of conception. The study by Fagot and the analysis of research by Block, on the other hand, call attention to the extent to which sex-typed behavior is shaped by the responses of parents and teachers. Furthermore, the various studies carried out by social learning theorists such as Sears and Bandura suggest that observation of models will have a significant impact on sex-typed behavior. A boy who watches his father unselfconsciously care for an infant or wash the dishes would seem more likely to acquire a flexible view of sex roles than a boy whose father is a sex-typed male. And a girl who observes her mother go off to work should be less inclined to picture women solely as mothers and homemakers.

Thus, even if a girl has tendencies toward sex-typed feminine behavior due to hormonal balances that were programmed at the time of conception, it would seem likely that she could be encouraged to develop psychological androgyny. Parents and teachers might try to favor the development of flexible conceptions of sex roles by following suggestions offered by Block. Girls might be urged to be more competitive and achievement oriented; boys might be encouraged to be more sensitive to the feelings of others and to engage in other than traditional masculine activities without self-consciousness. Without such encouragement, a sex-typed male might experience many problems if he later marries a career-oriented woman or is ever asked to share in childrearing and housekeeping responsibilities.

Both males and females benefit from **psychological androgyny**

Summary

1. Human beings have a longer period of dependence on parents than any other species. As a consequence, difficulties may be experienced when the time comes for a young person to function independently. It has been suggested that the parents must allow an adolescent daughter or son to abandon them without feeling abandoned. Contrary to a popular opinion that is sometimes expressed, a generation gap between parents and their teen-age sons and daughters appears to be the exception rather than the rule. The achievement of autonomy seems to be favored by parents who take moderate but sincere interest in the activities of their offspring and who use a democratic approach, permitting their children to participate in making decisions.

2. Many adolescents confide more in close friends than in parents. Middle adolescence (ages fourteen, fifteen, and sixteen) appears to be the time of greatest insecurity about friendships because this is a period when the trust of a close friend is particularly important. Adolescent females typically develop closer relationships with same-sex friends than males. Because girl-girl relationships are more intense, females are more likely than males to experience anxiety when friction between friends develops.

3. When adolescents first begin to date, looks and popularity are the most important attributes sought in the partner. A bit later, personality traits and social sophistication are the most desired characteristics. Eventually, qualities such as dependability and sensitivity are considered to be most important.

4. The development of intimate relationships between young adults has been explained by social exchange theorists in terms of the following hypothesis: two individuals become intimate when the outcome of their relationship exceeds the outcome they have been accustomed to receiving from relationships with others. Other theorists suggest that those who establish intimate relationships are guided by a desire to

maintain **equity,** each member of the pair possessing traits of equal desirability.

5. Male-female relationships in contemporary America may be influenced by aspects of achievement motivation—the desire to achieve, which has been influenced by past experiences with success and failure. Because of sex-role stereotypes, some young adults (particularly females) perceive achievement as an inappropriate form of behavior for women in our society. When asked to respond to stories where females exhibit a high level of achievement in traditionally male fields of endeavor, women may express a **fear of success.** Capable women, in particular, may experience conflicts between achieving success and being accepted by males. Potential conflicts that might be caused by the vocational success of a wife compared with a husband seem to be least harmful when both rate high in psychological androgyny.

Suggestions for Further Study

The Influence of Parents and Peers on Adolescents

Ways parents and peers influence adolescents are examined in several chapters of the *Handbook of Adolescent Psychology* (1980), edited by Joseph Adelson. Peruse Chapter 8 ("Values"), Chapter 9 ("Moral Development"), Chapter 10 ("Political Thinking"), and Chapter 12 ("Friendships and the Peer Group").

Feelings and Attitudes of Adolescents

In *The Adolescent Experience* (1966), Elizabeth Douvan and Joseph Adelson report on surveys they conducted for the Boy and Girl Scouts of America. They devised extensive questionnaires and used them in interviewing approximately 1,000 fourteen- to sixteen-year-old boys and 2,000 sixth- to twelfth-grade girls. Their results and interpretations reveal many interesting aspects of adolescent development. Almost any chapter of *The Adolescent Experience* makes interesting reading, particularly since the authors write exceptionally well.

Interviewing Adolescents

If you are interested in the revealing insights that the interview technique often yields, you may wish to try this method of obtaining information from adolescents. Douvan and Adelson carried out their interviews in 1955 and 1956. If you would like to use some of their questions to interview adolescents of the 1980s, examine pages 429–449 of *The Adolescent Experience* and pick out provocative questions. Then ask some high school students to respond to them (you can compare the responses of your subjects with those of adolescents of the 1950s). (If you are unable to find the Douvan and Adelson book, examine the Interview Schedule in the Suggestions for Further Study in Chapter 1 of this book [page 44] for a sample of questions you might ask.) You may prefer, however, to make up your own questions. In any case, if you carry out some interviews, you might describe how you proceeded, record the responses, summarize trends that emerge, and comment on the implications.

KEY POINTS

Erikson: The Stage of Identity Versus Role Confusion

Identity: acceptance of body, goals, recognition from those who count

Identifications at adolescence involve sense of urgency

Sex-role confusion may complicate formation of identity

Choice of career has significant impact on identity

Psychosocial moratorium: delay of commitment

Negative identity: adopting forms of behavior considered undesirable by family and society

The Nature and Significance of Identity Statuses

Identity-status criteria: extent of crisis, degree of commitment

Identity-diffusion types avoid thinking about goals, roles, and values

Moratorium types suffering identity crises of various kinds

Foreclosure types unquestioningly endorse goals and values of parents

Identity-achievement types have made self-chosen commitments

Adjustment Problems

Identity problems, hostility and rivalry factors may lead to academic underachievement

Delinquency may be caused by poverty, unemployment, hostile parent-child relationships

Drug use may be due to parental factors, low self-esteem, problem proneness, imitation

Preschizophrenic boys negativistic, aggressive; girls shy, inhibited

Depression may be caused by negative set, learned helplessness, sense of loss

Suicide triggered by inability to solve problems, deterioration of relationships

The Adaptive Capacity of the Human Organism

Many mature and competent adults were troubled and confused as adolescents

Stages in Occupational Choice

Search for satisfying career may extend to thirties

CHAPTER 21

ADOLESCENCE AND YOUTH

PERSONALITY DEVELOPMENT

*I*nterpretations of personality development during adolescence and youth vary considerably. Starting with G. Stanley Hall, who wrote a pioneering two-volume text on adolescence in 1904, some theorists have stressed that adolescence is a period of turmoil. Sigmund Freud emphasized adolescent "storm and stress" twenty years after the publication of Hall's text, and his daughter, Anna, agreed with her father, observing, "the upholding of a steady equilibrium during the ado-

lescent process is in itself abnormal" (1958, p. 275). Among contemporary American psychologists, Peter Blos, who studied with Freud and
then came to this country to specialize in psychoanalyzing adolescents,
observed, "Late adolescence is a decisive turning point and consequently a time of crisis" (1962, p. 130). Erik Erikson, who studied with
Freud at the same time as Blos and who also settled in America, has
attracted considerable attention with his suggestion that adolescents
experience an identity crisis (1968). (These views were noted in Chapter
5, in the evaluation of the hypothesis that infancy is more important
than any other stage of development.)

Other psychologists who have studied adolescents, however, have
questioned whether turmoil is inevitable during the teen years. Daniel
Offer, for instance, carried out a study of normal high school boys in the
early 1960s (mentioned in Chapter 20) and subsequently developed and
used the Offer Self-Image Questionnaire with thousands of adolescents.
He found little evidence in either his original study (Offer, 1969) or in
follow-up investigations using the questionnaire (Offer, Ostrov, and
Howard, 1981) that most adolescents experience a "crisis."

In a more comprehensive study of normal teen-agers in Great Britain,
however, the researchers concluded that nearly half of the subjects reported "some appreciable misery or depression" and that "there can be
no doubt from these findings that many 14–15 year olds experience
quite marked feelings of affective disturbance which could well be described as 'inner turmoil'" (Rutter, Tizard, and Whitmore, 1981, p. 42).
Ozzie Siegel (1981) observed that Offer's conclusions, which have frequently been cited as "proof" that adolescent turmoil is a myth, are
somewhat misleading because the boys studied were screened for indications of behavioral problems. Siegel summed up a review of research
on the question of adolescent crisis by noting, "while maintaining and
underscoring the importance of distinguishing between adolescent turmoil on the one hand and psychopathology on the other, it seems a
reasonable conclusion that the adolescent process is an interruption of
peaceful growth and is normatively attended by anxiety, worry, and
concerns regarding self-esteem, physical appearance, and body image"
(1982, p. 542).

Thus, the apparent contradictions between psychoanalytic interpretations and Offer's conclusions are not as extreme as they have sometimes
been made to appear. Sigmund and Anna Freud and Peter Blos and Erik
Erikson spent all or part of their professional lives treating disturbed
individuals. Those who study abnormal behavior often reason that
traits and tendencies found in extreme form in individuals needing
psychotherapy probably exist in less extreme form in "normal" individuals. Thus, when Blos and Erikson suggest that all adolescents experience a "crisis," they do not necessarily mean that every teen-ager expe-

riences wrenching personal turmoil. As used by Blos and Erikson, in fact, the word *crisis* refers to a struggle to achieve a more mature and committed conception of self, not to the equivalent of a nervous break-down. In addition, theorists are influenced by personal experiences and recollections of their own adolescence. Some contemporary adolescents will have experiences and perceptions similar to those of a given theorist and will "fit" that theory; others will not. Simply because a theory does not accurately describe *all* adolescents is no reason to reject it entirely. Erikson, for example, spent several years wandering rather aimlessly around Europe in his early twenties before he became acquainted with Freud, was accepted as a student, and decided on a career. It is not surprising, then, that he emphasizes that occupational choice plays a significant role in identity formation. Research to be reported later in this chapter indicates that contemporary adolescents and youth who experience considerable difficulty establishing occupational goals for themselves are likely to experience an identity crisis as defined by Erik-son. Adolescents who make firm career choices early in high school, however, do not experience any difficulty with that aspect of identity formation.

Therefore, instead of attempting to judge whether some of the theoretical interrelations of adolescence and youth to be discussed in the first part of this chapter are "right" and others "wrong," it will be more constructive to focus on the insights each supplies on particular aspects of this stage of development.

Erikson: The Stage of Identity Versus Role Confusion

Because earlier stages serve as the framework for later ones, a brief review of Erikson's concept of development will clarify the description of adolescence that follows.

Review of Erikson's Theory of Development

Erikson based his view of development on the epigenetic principle illus-trated by the biological maturation of the embryo and fetus. He hy-pothesized that there is a ground plan for personality development and that out of this parts arise, "each part having its time of special ascen-dancy, until all parts have arisen to form a functioning whole" (1968, p. 92). He described the "parts" as stages where "ego qualities which emerge from critical periods of development . . . integrate the time table of that organism within the structure of social institutions" (1963, p. 246). The first four of these stages were described in preceding chapters. Infants must develop a sense of trust based on recognition of consistency and continuity in their own behavior and in interactions with their parents. When two- to three-year-olds become capable of mastering their muscles and nerves so that locomotion and toilet control are achieved, they need to experience a sense of autonomy or independence and to avoid feeling shame or doubt about their abilities. At the preschool level, when children energetically engage in many activities, they need to develop a sense of initiative, without feeling guilty about trying new things on their own. During the elementary school years, a sense of industry must emerge as children learn to do things with others and to engage in sustained activities involving specific goals. If children are not accepted by peers or feel that they have failed in efforts to meet standards, they will develop a sense of inferiority.

The Significance of Identity

A child who has had favorable experiences during these four stages will develop a stable and positive self-concept. But this is no guarantee that the individual will successfully cope with the problems of the next stage. As noted in earlier discussions of Erikson's theory, he stressed that the adolescent must "refight many of the battles of earlier years" (1963, p. 261).

In all the preceding stages, Erikson stressed the importance of "continuity and sameness." These qualities take on special significance when the child moves toward adulthood because the integration of the ego is perceived to take on aspects of finality, just as physical appearance does. Consequently, the key characteristic of this stage is a search for **identity,** and the primary danger is **role confusion.**

The terms *identity* and *identity crisis* have become so popularized that it is important to review Erikson's original meanings. Here is how Erikson described the basic concept of identity: "An optimal sense of identity . . . is experienced merely as a sense of psychosocial well-being. Its most obvious concomitants are a feeling of being at home in one's body, a sense of 'knowing where one is going,' and an inner assuredness of anticipated recognition from those who count" (1968, p. 165). Erikson suggested that adolescence is a critical period in development for the following reasons:

Identity: acceptance of body, goals, recognition from those who count

Adolescence is the last stage of childhood. The adolescent process, however, is conclusively complete only when the individual has subordinated his childhood identifications to a new kind of identification, achieved in absorbing sociability and in competitive apprenticeship with and among his age mates. These new identifications are no longer characterized by the playfulness of childhood and the experimental zest of youth: with dire urgency they force the young individ-

Identifications at adolescence involve sense of urgency

ual into choices and decisions which will, with increasing immediacy, lead to commitments "for life." (P. 155)

In Erikson's view, two aspects of behavior are of special significance to the young person on the verge of adulthood: sex roles and occupational choice. Sex roles are particularly important because they establish a pattern for many types of behavior. Until recently, there was little confusion about appropriate characteristics and activities for males and females in our society. While such certainty provided a clear code of behavior for those who possessed or were eager to develop these characteristics, it created problems for those who did not. Sex stereotypes also led to the kinds of abuses and forms of discrimination objected to by feminists. With recognition of these abuses has come a blurring of sex roles and a trend toward unisex views. This trend may remove pressure from those who reject or are unable to develop "traditional" male and female traits, but it may create problems for the adolescent trying to develop a clear sense of identity.

> *Sex-role confusion may complicate formation of identity*

While sex-role confusion causes problems for many adolescents, occupational choice may be of greater concern and significance. The occupation we choose influences other aspects of our lives perhaps more than any other single factor. Our job determines how we will spend a sizable proportion of our time; and that, in turn, determines where and how we live. These last two factors determine, to a considerable extent, with whom we interact socially. All of these factors influence the reactions of others, and these reactions lead us to develop perceptions of ourselves. Erikson notes that occupational choice is particularly difficult in America because of our technological orientation, which features the assembly line and corporate organization, both of which limit individuality. Other complicating factors are the amount of training needed for many jobs in a technological society and the rapidly changing job market.

> *Choice of career has significant impact on identity*

When confronted with the realization that the time has come to make some sort of career choice, that many careers pose a threat to personal identity, and that the job market fluctuates rapidly, the young person seeking to avoid role confusion by making a firm vocational choice is faced with many unsettling complications. Because of this, Erikson suggests that for many young people a **psychosocial moratorium** may be desirable.

The Concepts of Psychosocial Moratorium and Negative Identity

A psychosocial moratorium is a period marked by a delay of commitment, which is illustrated very clearly by Erikson's own youthful experiences. Under ideal circumstances, such a psychosocial moratorium

> **Psychosocial moratorium:** delay of commitment

The tendency for mothers and fathers to sometimes reverse traditional roles helps prevent the development of sex-role stereotypes in young children but may lead to sex-role confusion during adolescence.
© *Erika Stone/Peter Arnold, Inc.*

should be a period of adventure and exploration with a positive (or at least neutral) impact on the individual and society. A young person who is unable to overcome role confusion—or unable to postpone choices leading to identity formation by engaging in a positive psychosocial moratorium—may attempt to resolve inner conflict by choosing what Erikson refers to as a **negative identity.**

The loss of a sense of identity is often expressed in a scornful and snobbish hostility toward the roles offered as proper and desirable in one's family or immediate community. Any aspect of the required role, or all of it—be it masculinity or femininity, nationality or class membership—can become the main focus of the young person's acid disdain (1968, pp. 172–173).

An adolescent boy whose parents have constantly stressed how important it is to do well in school so that he will be admitted to a prestige college, for example, may deliberately act in an unscholarly way or quit school entirely and join a commune. Erikson explains such choices by suggesting that the young person finds it easier to "derive a sense of identity out of total identification with that which he is least supposed to be than to struggle for a feeling of reality in acceptable roles which are unattainable with his inner means" (p. 176). If the young person who chooses a negative identity plays the role only long enough to gain greater self-insight, it may be a positive experience. But in some cases, the negative identity may be "confirmed" by the way the adolescent is treated by those in authority. If forms of behavior adopted to express a negative identity bring the teen-ager into contact with excessively punitive parents, teachers, or law enforcement agencies, for example, the "young person may well put his energy into becoming exactly what the careless and fearful community expects him to be—and make a total job of it" (p. 196). Erikson's concept of identity, with its stress on sex roles and occupational choice, has inspired substantial discussion and research. Some of the most intriguing studies involve evaluating the **identity status** of individual adolescents and youths.

Negative identity: adopting forms of behavior considered undesirable by family and society

The Nature and Significance of Identity Statuses

The Nature of Identity Statuses

James E. Marcia (1966, 1980) has proposed *identity statuses* that "were developed as a device by means of which Erikson's theoretical notions about identity might be subjected to empirical study. . . . The identity statuses are four modes of dealing with the identity issue characteristic of late adolescents" (1980, p. 161). (Marcia's use of the term *late adoles-*

cents is essentially the same as Keniston's use of the word *youth,* and most research on identity statuses has been carried out with college students.)

Marcia established the four identity statuses after he had conducted semistructured interviews with a selected sample of male youth. All of the interviewees were asked their thoughts about a career, their personal value system, sexual attitudes, and religious beliefs. Marcia proposes that the criteria for the attainment of a mature identity are based on two variables: crisis and commitment. "Crisis refers to times during adolescence when the individual seems to be actively involved in choosing among alternative occupations and beliefs. Commitment refers to the degree of personal investment the individual expresses in an occupation or belief" (1967, p. 119). After analyzing interview records with these two criteria in mind, Marcia established four identity statuses:

Identity-status criteria: extent of crisis, degree of commitment

Identity Diffusion: No apparent commitment to an occupation or to a particular set of values.

Moratorium: Currently struggling with occupational or ideological issues.

Foreclosure: Committed to occupational or ideological positions chosen by or similar to those of parents.

Identity Achievement: Committed to occupational and ideological positions that are self-chosen.

Factors to Consider in Evaluating Identity Status Descriptions

There are a number of factors that ought to be considered when evaluating rapidly accumulating research on identity statuses. Some of these interpretive limitations are unique to the identity-status concept; some are due to limitations of any system of classification.

One of the most vexing problems of classification schemes is that *pure* types are rare or even nonexistent. The psychologist who establishes a typology may tend to smooth out the differences of various types and become convinced that most individuals will fit neatly into one category or another. When classifications are made of large numbers of subjects, though, this pigeonholing effect may not be taken into account.

Marcia based his original description of identity statuses on semistructured interviews with a small number of male subjects. While this technique makes it possible for an interviewer to probe for subtleties of attitudes, it also increases the possibility that subjective interpretations will be introduced as the interview proceeds. As was the case with Kohlberg's original stage descriptions of moral reasoning (which were also based on interviews with a small number of male subjects), the tentative classification Marcia made of identity statuses was prematurely treated as if it were a well-established typology because it served as a convenient frame of reference for researchers. As data have accumulated, it has become clear that not very many youth can be placed into only one category. The mixed-type problem seems particularly acute with the identity-status approach since identity (as defined by Erikson and Marcia) consists of a combination of somewhat unrelated traits: acceptance of one's appearance, occupational choice, attitudes toward sex roles, feelings of acceptance by others, moral religious values. A young person may experience commitment in one or more of these facets of identity but not in others. Consider just a few examples of possible combinations:

A young man who has made a firm occupational choice feels insecure about his social acceptance because the woman he loves has rejected his proposal of marriage.

An attractive young woman who is very satisfied with her appearance is confused about how she feels about her boyfriend's suggestion that she leave the Catholic church.

A young woman who plans to earn a Ph.D. is elected to Phi Beta Kappa. She is very attracted to a male admirer but gradually becomes aware that he is extremely competitive and that he becomes visibly upset whenever she does anything better than he does.

Each of these individuals is "committed" in one area of identity but "in crisis" in another. Accordingly, they could not be classified in only one of the four identity statuses described by Marcia.

Still another difficulty with the identity-status scheme is that it does not apply nearly as well to females as to males. Marcia has acknowledged this point (1980, p. 179), noting that females are often more concerned about interpersonal relationships than about occupational choice. He also explains that because of marriage-career complications, identity formation typically takes much longer for females than for males. (Elizabeth Douvan has observed that "the thirty-five-year-old woman who returns to school or work when her last child goes to school undergoes an identity process in many ways comparable to the selection and adaptation process experienced by males in adolescence and early adulthood" [1975, p. 207].)

Despite all the cautions and limitations just noted, though, identity-status descriptions *do* make it possible to interpret and understand the behavior of different types of college students.

Elizabeth Douvan has observed, "The thirty-five-year-old woman who returns to school or work when her child goes to school undergoes an identity process in many ways comparable to the selection and adaptation process experienced by males in adolescence and early adulthood."
Frank Siteman/The Picture Cube.

Using Identity Status Descriptions to Understand Youthful Behavior

Identity-diffusion types avoid thinking about goals, roles, and values

Identity-diffusion types have yet to experience a crisis because they have not given much serious thought to an occupation, sex roles, or values. They give the impression that they may be trying to distract themselves from confronting such issues. They have little self-direction, are disorganized and impulsive, and tend to avoid getting involved in either schoolwork or interpersonal relationships. If these characteristics are displayed only briefly by young people who have just entered college, they might be attributed to immaturity and the initial impact of embarking on an entirely new kind of existence free of parental control. If older students continue to exhibit these forms of behavior, though, they are likely to experience adjustment problems of varying degrees of severity. (Some of these problems will be discussed later.)

Moratorium types suffering identity crises of various kinds

Moratorium types *have* given a certain amount of thought to identity questions, but they have not come up with any satisfactory answers. They are *aware* that they are "in crisis." They are dissatisfied with college, change majors often, daydream a great deal, and engage in intense but short-lived relationships with others. They may also temporarily reject parental values. After a period of experimentation and restless searching, most moratorium types are likely to come to grips with themselves and achieve a satisfactory sense of identity.

Foreclosure types are not experiencing a crisis and may never suffer any doubts about key aspects of their identity (particularly occupational choice, sex roles, and values). They are satisfied with the goals they have chosen, have good relationships with their parents, and seem able to take stress in stride. In a sense, they might be said to possess an **ultrapositive** identity because they endorse and want to acquire traits favored by their parents, which is the opposite of youth who defy their parents by fashioning a negative identity. Some research findings on foreclosure types suggest, however, that they may tend to be rigid and dependent.

Foreclosure types unquestioningly endorse goals and values of parents

Identity-achievement types have made self-chosen commitments in at least some aspects of their identity. But because of the variety of factors that make up identity, it is not likely that too many individuals experience a triumphant sense of having "put it all together." As the examples provided earlier illustrate, it may be more likely that commitments will have been made in some but not all facets of identity. Furthermore, identity achievement is not a once-and-for-all accomplishment. If an ego-shattering event (loss of a job, being divorced) occurs, identity-achievement types may be propelled back into a crisis and be faced with the task of rebuilding self-esteem. Because they have already accomplished it once, however, they might be expected to achieve a satisfactory identity again.

Identity-achievement types have made self-chosen commitments

In a review of research on identity statuses, Richard M. Lerner and Judy A. Shea (1982) conclude that some studies support Marcia's hypothesis that there are recognizable differences between the four identity-status types; other studies do not. Not surprisingly, foreclosure and identity-achievement types are more easily categorized than identity-diffusion and moratorium types. Lerner and Shea sum up their conclusions by noting that "most people move adaptively toward identity achievement, and hence crisis resolution, by virtue of occupational and ideological role commitment. However, it is clear that there is variability in this pattern. Not all people go through this sequence" (1982, p. 511). Lerner and Shea also mention research findings that support the observations just made about variability in any particular individual's identity status. That is, a young person may be classified as an identity-achievement type in some, but not all, aspects of personal development. Even though the identity-status concept is not always applicable to all youth and even though inconsistencies are common, it does help explain various adjustment problems experienced by adolescents and youth.

Adjustment Problems

Problems Relating to Failure to Achieve Identity

Some of the identity status descriptions just summarized point to types of problems adolescents and youth may encounter if they have not achieved a sense of identity. Identity-diffusion and moratorium types have no clear academic or vocational goals; they may be confused about sex roles and unsure of how they feel about values. Because of uncertainties about such factors, they may feel estranged from at least one of their parents, fail to do well in school, and have problems engaging in satisfying relationships with others. (Moratorium types engage in deeper relationships than identity-diffusion types, but those classified in the moratorium category may seek intensive relationships primarily to satisfy their own needs without giving much in return.) If adolescents or youth do not feel they are working toward a meaningful academic or vocational goal and/or if they have not established mutually rewarding relationships with others, they may experience a variety of problems traceable at least in part to failure to achieve a satisfying sense of identity. Reactions of this type may include academic underachievement, delinquency, and use of drugs.

Academic Underachievement

Between one-third and one-half of young people seen in psychological clinics are referred primarily because of learning problems (Schechter, 1974). Among youth, concern about college grades accounts for over half of all requests for counseling (Blaine and McArthur, 1971). Many academic problems are due to poor study habits and could be alleviated if more students would ask for instruction on ways to become more efficient information processors. Some academic difficulties, though, are traceable to learning disabilities of various kinds (perceptual disorders, difficulties in forming concepts, hyperactivity, distractibility), but others appear to be caused by identity or adjustment problems. For instance, both moratorium and identity-diffusion types who have made no clear choice of an academic or occupational goal find it difficult to settle down in college. Lack of a clear academic goal undoubtedly is an important cause of poor schoolwork in high school as well, but other factors may contribute to underachievement at both levels. Irving B. Weiner (1980) comments on two causes (other than failure to achieve identity) of poor schoolwork: hostility toward parents and concerns about rivalry.

Weiner reports that many adolescents and youth who seek counseling because of academic performance problems express resentment about parental demands they cannot or prefer not to try to meet. If the resent-

Identity problems, hostility and rivalry factors may lead to academic under-achievement

*A common problem during adolescence and youth is academic underachievement.
School problems may be due to identity confusion, hostility toward parents, concerns
about rivalry, or poor study habits.*
Ann Chwatsky/Art Resource.

ment is strong enough, the young person may retaliate by making little
effort to earn high grades (perhaps as a means for establishing a negative identity). Such attitudes are revealed by characteristics of identity
diffusion and moratorium types. The most unfortunate aspect of such
retaliation is that even if moratorium and identity diffusion types eventually *do* focus on self-chosen academic or occupational goals, they may
not be able to overcome the low grade point average they became
saddled with during the pre-identity phase of their college careers.

Delinquency

One general explanation for delinquency is supplied by Erikson's concept of negative identity. Other explanations to account for criminal acts
of adolescents include overpopulation, increased mobility leading to the

disruption of family and neighborhood ties, frequent separations and divorce making it necessary for the parent with custody of children to hold down a job (and have less time for child care), increasing callousness and indifference to human and property rights, and the general "immoral" tone of our society exemplified by highly publicized acts of dishonesty on the part of public officials and business executives.

Explanations for delinquency also vary depending on the background of particular adolescents. A major cause of delinquent acts by lower-class youth, particularly in inner cities, is unemployment, which may be as high as 70 percent. (Bachman, O'Malley, and Johnston [1978] found that unemployment had a crippling impact on self-esteem.) Other causes of lower-class delinquency center on the conditions of slum living—poverty, rapid population turnover, broken homes, general disorganization. James Coleman (1966) and Michael Harrington (1965) have called attention to the pessimism and despair of inner-city adolescents who feel that they have no control over their future lives and are doomed to remain where they are. Finally, it appears that indulging in delinquent acts is an approved tradition in many inner-city neighborhoods (G. F. Jensen, 1973).

Delinquency may be caused by poverty, unemployment, hostile parent-child relationships

A major cause of delinquent acts by middle-class urban youth may be parent-child conflicts, a point emphasized by a distinction that has been made between **sociologic** delinquency, which is molded by environmental conditions (as in the case of slum youth) and **individual** delinquency caused primarily by parent-child relationships (A. Johnson, 1959).

W. M. Ahlstrom and R. J. Havighurst (1971) found that adolescents who engage in delinquent acts are likely to have been subjected to erratic and overly strict discipline with physical punishment used instead of reasoning. Furthermore, relationships between delinquent adolescents and their parents are frequently characterized by mutual hostility. The parents of delinquents are more likely to ignore or reject their children, to have personal problems of their own, and to have police records. A final point noted by Ahlstrom and Havighurst is that adolescents from nonbroken homes characterized by hostility or apathy are more likely to commit delinquent acts than adolescents from broken homes where the remaining parent shows affection and provides support.

Drug Use

Several theorists have offered explanations why some adolescents and youth are more inclined than others to use drugs. Erikson's concept of negative identity has already been mentioned. An adolescent or youth who is experiencing problems establishing a satisfying sense of identity may turn to drugs because parents and school authorities stress that such behavior is undesirable. Howard B. Kaplan (1980) has proposed an explanation for drug use (and other deviant behavior) that also centers on the self-concept. He suggests that forms of deviant behavior can often be understood as attempts to restore a sense of self-esteem previously damaged by self-devaluing experiences in established groups. Deviant behavior may foster self-esteem if it facilitates avoidance of self-devaluing experiences, attacks the group or institutional structures that were the source of the self-rejection, and offers substitute sources of self-enhancement. An adolescent who suffers humiliation in the classroom because of an uninterrupted series of low grades, for example, may drop out of school, join other dropouts in ridiculing teachers and students who earn high grades, and begin to use drugs to win prestige from out-of-school peers.

Richard Jessor and Shirley L. Jessor (1977) propose that drug use can be understood by evaluating **problem-behavior proneness.** Adolescents and youth who possess several of the personality, familial, and demographic characteristics noted above are likely to be predisposed to use drugs. An unemployed high school dropout in an inner-city area, who comes from a broken home where the mother provides little support and who spends his time with peers who all use drugs (to note just a few factors) will be much more prone to use drugs than a male with essentially opposite characteristics.

Drug use may be due to parental factors, low self-esteem, problem proneness, imitation

R. L. Akers (1977) has proposed a social learning theory view of drug use that stresses imitation and reinforcement. An adolescent who observes friends use drugs and who finds that drugs supply satisfaction and prestige will "learn" to use them.

Denise B. Kandel (1978) also emphasizes imitation and reinforcement, as well as the interaction between individual characteristics and competing influences of parents and peers. She suggests that there are often three stages in the emergence of drug use:

1. Use of hard liquor, typically in the home, involving imitation of and approval by parents.
2. Use of marijuana, typically away from home, involving imitation of and approval by peers.
3. Use of drugs other than liquor and marijuana. This stage is most likely to follow the first two if there are conflicts with parents about discipline.

Kandel points out that parents and peers influence drug use directly, as models and reinforcers, and indirectly by the kinds of attitudes and values they exhibit and communicate. Factors such as those listed in describing characteristics of adolescents and youth most likely to use drugs contribute to susceptibility. Finally, opportunities to use drugs will vary depending on circumstances such as availability and proportion of peers who serve as models and who supply reinforcement.

The types of behavior just discussed can often be classified, at least in part, as problems due to failure of adolescents and youth to achieve a positive sense of identity. Other, more serious, problems take the form of behavior disorders. Severe disorders that occur during the adolescent years include schizophrenia, depression, and suicidal behavior.

Behavior Disorders in Adolescence and Youth

Schizophrenia

Irving B. Weiner describes schizophrenia, the most common single type of severe psychological disturbance, as "perhaps the major mental health problem in the United States" (1980, p. 450). Schizophrenia (along with autism) was briefly discussed in Chapter 9 in the analysis of interactions between inherited and environmental influences on personality development. Characteristics of schizophrenia noted by Weiner include impaired capacity to think coherently, distorted perceptions of reality, difficulty in establishing and maintaining satisfactory relationships with others, and weakened control over impulses. These characteristics are found in both adolescent and adult schizophrenics, but they may be less clearly defined in younger individuals, which means that the onset of abnormal behavior is more difficult to detect in teenagers.

Types of behavior that may indicate the likelihood that an adolescent of either sex will later exhibit schizophrenic patterns of abnormality center on withdrawal and lack of interest in social relations. Adolescent boys who later become schizophrenic have been characterized by irritability, aggressiveness, negativism, and defiance of authority. Preschizophrenic adolescent girls tend to be emotionally immature, shy, and inhibited. If an adolescent displays such characteristics in high school and is later diagnosed as a schizophrenic, the prognosis for recovery is less favorable than if abnormal symptoms appear later in life. Weiner notes that follow-up studies reveal that 23 percent of adolescents hospitalized for schizophrenia recover, 25 percent improve but suffer lingering symptoms or occasional relapses, and the remaining 53 percent make little or no progress and remain hospitalized indefinitely. (A fictionalized account of a young woman's experiences with schizophrenia and hospitalization is presented in *I Never Promised You a Rose Garden* [1964] by Hannah Green, a pseudonym for Joan Greenberg. Mark Vonnegut provides an autobiographical account of similar experiences in *The Eden Express* [1975].)

Preschizophrenic boys negativistic, aggressive; girls shy, inhibited

Feelings of depression during adolescence and youth may be due to a negative set, learned helplessness, or a sense of loss.
Melissa Shook/The Picture Cube.

Depression

About 2 percent of the population may be diagnosed as schizophrenics at some time in their lives but about 10 percent of all high school students seen in psychiatric clinics suffer from depression. Common symptoms of depression include self-deprecation, crying spells, and suicidal thoughts and attempts (Masterson, 1967). Additional symptoms of depression found in adolescents below the age of seventeen involve fatigue, hypochondriasis, and concentration difficulty (Weiner, 1980, p. 455). High school students who experience such symptoms typically try to ward off their depression by restless activity or flight to or from others. They may also engage in problem behavior or delinquent acts carried out in ways that make it clear they are appealing for help. (A depressed fifteen-year-old boy may carry out an act of vandalism, for instance, at a time when a school authority or police officer is sure to observe the incident.) Adolescents over the age of seventeen who suffer from depression are likely to show little self-confidence and feel worthless and discouraged. To combat such feelings, they may join antiestablishment groups, manifest a "what's the use of it all?" attitude, or turn to sex and drugs.

A. T. Beck (1970) suggests that depression consists of a **cognitive set** made up of negative views toward oneself, the world, and the future. Martin Seligman (1975) has proposed that depression is caused by **learned helplessness** due to feelings of having no control over one's life. Irving Weiner (1975) emphasizes that depression typically involves a **sense of loss,** sometimes caused by the abrupt end of a personal relationship through death, separation, or broken friendship. Or an individual may undergo a sharp drop in self-esteem due to failure or guilt. Or the person may experience a loss of bodily integrity following illness, incapacitation, or disfigurement.

Depression may be caused by negative set, learned helplessness, sense of loss

Any or all of these factors that lead to depression may eventually lead to thoughts about suicide.

Suicide

Between 1961 and 1975 the suicide rate among fifteen- to twenty-four-year-olds increased 131 percent. Since that time the rate has more or less stabilized. Explanations for the increase in suicide by adolescents and youth include overcrowding caused by the postwar baby boom, increase in a sense of social isolation, earlier age of puberty, and an upsurge in self-centered tendencies in parents. Michael Peck (1982) suggests that those who contemplate and/or commit suicide can be classified into six categories: the very young, the loner, the depressed, psychotics, those who experience crisis, and those who choose it as a form of communication.

It appears that there is a quite typical sequence of experiences that culminates in the attempt of an adolescent to commit suicide (Jacobs, 1971, p. 64):

1. The individual is likely to have experienced adjustment problems starting in childhood and continuing through adolescence. Many of these problems may have been caused by marital discord between parents, harsh and erratic discipline, and similar negative and ineffective forms of parent-child relationships.

Suicide triggered by inability to solve problems, deterioration of relationships

2. A few weeks or days prior to the suicide attempt, problems are perceived to increase.

3. Attempts to deal with the problems are unsuccessful, leading the young person to conclude that he or she has no control over them.

4. Meaningful relationships with others, particularly parents, seem to deteriorate completely. The depressed and desperate adolescent is likely to feel that parents (and others) do not understand his or her problems or that they are unwilling to provide support.

The Adaptive Capacity of the Human Organism

This discussion of behavior disorders is more than a bit misleading since it tends to imply that a great many adolescents and youth succumb to the pressures of moving toward independence. Such is obviously not the case. Even though Rutter and his colleagues concluded (as noted at the beginning of this chapter) that nearly half of the adolescents they studied reported "some appreciable misery or depression" by the time they left school, most young Americans have found their own successful ways to adapt to the demands made on them. The ability of human beings to overcome "misery and depression" during the adolescent years was discovered by the researchers at Berkeley who made predictions (on the basis of observations made of their subjects up to the time of adolescence) about how successful and well adjusted they would be as adults. As noted in Chapter 5, the researchers were surprised to discover that 50 percent of the subjects in the sample who were later studied as adults became more stable and effective individuals than predicted. Jean Walker Macfarlane spoke for her colleagues when she observed, "Many of our most mature and competent adults had severely troubled and confusing childhoods and adolescences" (1964, p. 125). She also noted, "We had not appreciated the maturing utility of many painful, strain-producing, and confusing experiences which in time, if lived through, brought sharpened awareness, more complex integration, better skills in problem solving, clarified goals, and increasing stability" (p. 124).

Many mature and competent adults were troubled and confused as adolescents

It appears that the impact of physiological changes at the time of puberty, as well as the complexity of the developmental tasks of adolescence, cause the teen years to be a period of struggle, experimentation, adjustment, and consolidation. Calling adolescence a period of "storm and stress" may be a bit extreme, but it certainly appears to be a period of unsettled behavior. Norman Livson and Harvey Peskin (1980) provide support for this view in an analysis of data from the longitudinal studies at Berkeley. In a preliminary comparison of records of behavior over the years, Livson and Peskin thought that they had discovered that behavior during the elementary school years is a better predictor of adult behavior than behavior during adolescence. After re-evaluating the data, however, Livson and Peskin concluded that when characteristics at eleven and thirteen were *combined* with characteristics at fourteen to sixteen, predictions became even more precise. Girls most likely to display psychological health as adults, for example, were characterized by independence, self-confidence, and controlled temper, and were disinclined to whine about disappointments as ten- to twelve-year-olds. *But,* at the ages of fourteen to sixteen, they were characterized as dependent, low in self-confidence, possessed of explosive tempers, and given to frequent whining. Putting the two sets of characteristics together improved predictions of adult adjustment. Boys who were stolid and had hearty appetites between ten and twelve *and* who were irritable and had poor appetites between fourteen and sixteen often turned out to have excellent psychological health as adults. While such *stage reversals* quite frequently turned out to improve prediction in girls, this was not as true for boys. The best predictions of psychological health in males occurred when they were rated high in expressiveness, social comfort, and cheerfulness at *both* the ten-to-twelve- and fourteen-to-sixteen-year age spans.

The conclusions of Livson and Peskin, as well as the findings of the impact of early and late maturation summarized in Chapter 18, point to some of the difficulties of predicting precisely what sort of adult a child or adolescent will become. One explanation for lack of stability or predictability centers on differences between the developmental tasks that must be mastered at different age levels. Different kinds of traits and skills are needed to handle the tasks of adolescence than were appropriate for mastering the tasks of childhood. Another possible explanation is based on a point noted in discussing the goodness-of-fit concept in Chapter 5: a mother or father may possess an ideal set of characteristics for engaging in meaningful play with a baby but not be able to handle heart-to-heart talks with an adolescent.

Still another explanation is offered by Mary Cover Jones (1965), one of the leading researchers at Berkeley. After repeated analyses of the longitudinal data that had been accumulated at the University of California, she became impressed by the extent to which adolescents became *constructive actors* in creating new situations to explore their own capacities to survive and develop. It seems reasonable to expect that this tendency to control one's own destiny becomes even more significant during youth and in adulthood.

Moving Through the No-Person's Land of Youth

Even though more and more individuals in the 1980s take college courses in midadulthood, chances are you entered college shortly or immediately after you graduated from high school. If so, you may feel a bit in limbo as you finish these chapters on adolescence and youth and anticipate the next chapter about adulthood. As noted at the beginning of Chapter 18, these four chapters have been devoted to a discussion of development during adolescence and youth for reasons stressed by Kenneth Keniston. Youth, as defined by Keniston, is a psychological no-person's land for millions of young people who are "neither psychological adolescents nor sociological adults." Because youth has not been recognized as a separate stage of life until recently (and because not all psychologists who study development agree about definitions of youth), there is much more scientific information about adolescence than about development during the college years. The distribution of pages devoted to adolescence and youth in these chapters pretty much reflects the degree of research emphasis on the two stages. Consequently, you may have felt a bit slighted. You might have found yourself thinking, "I've been through puberty, gone through all of Piaget's stages, and become pretty much independent of my parents. This material on adolescence is all past history." In an effort to redress this imbalance of material on adolescence, the remaining pages of this chapter are devoted to comments on aspects of development that are particularly significant for those in the stage of youth.

In terms of physical and cognitive development, you are presently at the apogee of your efficiency (Troll, 1975; Horn, 1976). Physical strength reaches a peak in the twenties. Growth has been completed and the physiological functioning of a person's body is as efficient as it will ever be (assuming habits of diet and exercise remain about the same). As information processors, individuals in their twenties are also as efficient as they will ever be, although for cognitive activities that depend on knowledge and experience, the peak years of intellectual achievement lie ahead (Horn and Donaldson, 1980). Most students of college age are in the process of becoming emotionally, as well as financially, independent of parents or have achieved such independence. The peer group still exerts an influence on social behavior but with less urgency than in the high school years. Friendships are typically less intense and relationships with others more mature. The aspect of development during youth that is typically of greatest concern centers on the formation of identity. In terms of physical, cognitive, and social development, you are in peak form and ready to go. The problem with many college students is that they aren't sure which *way* to go.

As you read the identity-status descriptions a bit earlier in this chapter, you may have tried classifying yourself. Perhaps you decided that you are either a foreclosure type or an identity-achievement type, with a clear idea of what you are going to do after graduation. In that case, you are not bothered about future plans regarding a job. If you concluded that you are either a moratorium or an identity-diffusion type, on the other hand, you may still be undecided about a career (or even a college major). At this stage of your life, you may feel that you have established quite clear personal conceptions of sex roles. You may not, however, have made a decisive occupational choice. For many youthful Americans, therefore, the aspect of identity that is probably of greatest concern is occupational choice. Accordingly, the remainder of this chapter is devoted to a description of the nature of career selection.

Stages in Occupational Choice

Super's Description of Vocational Developmental Tasks

Donald Super (1957, 1963) has offered a description of vocational choice that is similar in many respects to Erikson's emphasis on the significance of the selection of an occupation on the formation of identity. Super proposes that patterns of behavior emerge during the school years and are expressed in academic performance, peer-group activities, athletics, and part-time work. (In the elementary school years, Erikson would refer to this as the development of a sense of industry or inferiority.) Success and failure in these various activities lead eventually to a concept of self that is publicly proclaimed when the person seeks a more or less permanent occupation.

Evidence to support Super's hypothesis regarding interrelationships among self-concept, success in school, and later occupational attainment is provided in a summary of the results of a longitudinal study of two thousand boys who entered high school in 1966 (Bachman, O'Malley, and Johnston, 1978). Starting in the tenth grade, the boys were studied intensively and their careers were followed for several years after they graduated. Boys rated high in self-esteem in the tenth grade did well academically, and the high grades they earned served to reinforce their confidence in themselves. If they succeeded in finding a satisfying job as soon as they entered the labor market, their self-esteem remained high. But if they remained unemployed for any length of time, their self-concept suffered.

Super proposes that there are vocational developmental tasks similar to the more general developmental tasks described by Havighurst. These tasks are listed and described in Table 21.1. Super's outline of vocational developmental tasks suggests that Erikson's statement about the choice of occupation being "commitment for life" should not be interpreted too literally, particularly in the volatile occupational world of the 1980s. Super's view of an extended period of searching for the "right" job, a search that may often extend into one's thirties, appears to be an accurate reflection of the present occupational situation in America. Because of rapid advances in technology and abrupt reversals in the economic situation in this country and the world, many adults may change careers several times either out of choice or out of necessity.

Search for satisfying career may extend to thirties

TABLE 21.1
VOCATIONAL DEVELOPMENTAL TASKS DESCRIBED BY SUPER

Age	Designation of Task	Description of Task
14–18	Crystallization of a vocational preference	Evaluation of self-concept and formulation of initial ideas about work
18–21	Specification of a vocational program	Choice of a college curriculum that leads toward a particular career
21–24	Implementing the vocational preference	Acceptance of an initial job
24–35	Stabilization	Narrowing an area of specialization and searching for personal satisfaction in a career
35–	Consolidation	Developing expertise, strengthening job skills, and acquiring status

Source: D. E. Super, "Vocational Development in Adolescence and Early Childhood: Tasks and Behaviors." Reprinted with permission from *Career Development: A Self-Concept Theory,* copyright © 1963 by the College Entrance Examination Board, New York.

Summary

1. Identity, as defined by Erikson, is experienced as a sense of psychosocial well-being due to feeling at home in one's body, having a sense of knowing where one is going, and expecting recognition from those who count. Concern about identity is particularly strong at adolescence because of a sense of urgency about important decisions. Failure to develop a satisfactory personal conception of sex roles and/or to make a firm occupational choice is likely to lead to **role confusion.** If problems in establishing identity are experienced, the young person may engage in a **psychosocial moratorium** by delaying commitment or assume a **negative identity** by adopting forms of behavior considered undesirable by family and society.

2. A person's **identity status** is evaluated by taking into account the degree of commitment to decisions centering on sex roles, occupational choice, and values. **Identity-diffusion** types avoid thinking about roles, goals, and values. **Moratorium** types postpone making decisions and experience identity confusion. **Foreclosure** types endorse the goals and values of their parents without question and have

few doubts about identity formation. **Identity-achievement** types have made satisfying self-chosen commitments.

3. Some of the adjustment problems of adolescents and youth can be traced to failure to achieve identity. Academic underachievement, for example, may be due to indecision about a college major or career but may also be a result of hostility toward parents or to indecision stemming from rivalry with others. Conflicts with parents may lead to drug use, although low self-esteem, problem-proneness, and imitation of peers are also typical of those who habitually use drugs.

4. Adolescent males who later develop schizophrenic symptoms are often negativistic; preschizophrenic females are often shy and inhibited. Depression is a common form of behavior disorder in adolescence and may be caused by a negative set, learned helplessness, or a sense of loss. Young people who become so depressed that they contemplate suicide are likely to have experienced the feeling that they are unable to solve problems and/or to have suffered recent deterioration in important relationships.

5. Many individuals experience emotional upheaval and adjustment problems to a greater or lesser degree during adolescence, but the adaptive capacity of the human organism is impressive. Longitudinal researchers at Berkeley found that many of their subjects who had been troubled and confused as adolescents turned out to be mature and competent adults.

6. Although Erikson stressed that occupational choice was a significant factor contributing to adolescent identity, studies of career patterns lead to the conclusion that the search for a satisfying career may extend into the thirties or beyond.

Suggestions for Further Study

Erikson on Adolescence

The special significance of the stage of identity versus role confusion in Erikson's scheme is explained in *Identity: Youth and Crisis* (1968). In the preface, Erikson notes that identity is so unfathomable and all-pervasive that "I will not offer a definitive explanation of it in this book" (p. 9). (The explanation he offers on page 165 may not be definitive, but it is quite clear.) In Chapter 1, he describes how he first came to use the phrase *identity crisis* and gives a general description of what he means by it. In Chapter 2 he explains how his anthropological studies and treatment of war veterans led him to reinterpret Freud's original explanations of development. Chapter 3 is an overview of all his stages of psychosocial development and emphasizes how they lead up to the stage of identity versus role confusion. Chapter 4 presents brief descriptions of identity crises experienced by George Bernard Shaw, William James, and Freud, and the meaning of *psychosocial moratorium* is explained (pages 156–158). *Negative identity* is described on pages 173–176.

Identity Statuses

James Marcia reviews research on identity statuses in Chapter 5 (pp. 159–187) of the *Handbook of Adolescent Psychology* (1980), edited by Joseph Adelson. Related research on ego development is summarized by Ruthellen Josselson in Chapter 6 (pp. 188–210) of the same volume.

Behavior Disorders

A brief description of "Psychopathology of Adolescence" is provided by Irving Weiner in Chapter 14 (pp. 447–471) of the *Handbook of Adolescent Psychology* (1980), edited by Joseph Adelson. More comprehensive analyses of severe behavior disorders during adolescence are supplied in *Psychiatric Disorders in Adolescents* (1974) by R. W. Hudgens; and *Current Issues in Adolescent Psychiatry* (1973), edited by J. C. Schooler.

Various interpretations of depression are offered in *Depression: Causes and Treatment* (1970) by A. T. Beck; *Helplessness: On Depression, Development, and Death* (1975) by Martin E. Seligman; and *The Nature and Treatment of Depression* (1975), edited by F. F. Flach and S. C. Draghi.

Suicide is analyzed in *The Gamble with Death* (1971) by Gene Lester and David Lester; *Adolescent Suicide* (1971) by J. Jacobs; and *Suicide* (1972) by Jacques Choron.

PART 7

ADULTHOOD AND AGING: AN OVERVIEW

KEY POINTS

Stages and Tasks of Adulthood

Levinson's "seasons" provocative and widely discussed but not universal

Physical Development

At fifty, 90 percent of strength at twenty (with regular exercise)

Eyes first sense organs to be affected by aging

Older adults rate health as most important life satisfaction factor

Aerobic exercise reduces chances of cardiovascular problems, may improve cognitive functioning

Cognitive Development

Cross-sectional studies indicating decline in intelligence often involve contaminating factors

Longitudinal studies may be difficult to interpret but IQ decline appears to be slight

Crystallized intelligence: store of knowledge that does not necessarily diminish

Fluid intelligence: efficient problem-solving abilities that decline with age

Creativity and productivity peak in thirties but decline only gradually thereafter

Relationships with Others

Erikson: true intimacy depends on fusing of identities

To avoid stagnation, adults need to guide, help, or be creative

Females more cautious about falling in love than males

Marital satisfaction tends to decline after birth of a child

Impact of divorce more severe for parents, older adults, males

Most divorced individuals remarry, those without children most likely to be happy

Personality Development

Personality more influenced by experiences than physical appearance and functioning

Social readjustment depends on number and timing of stressful situations

Ego-resilient types better able to handle stress than ego-brittle types

CHAPTER
22

ADULTHOOD

*I*n Chapter 5, various opinions about continuity and change in development were summarized. As noted in that discussion, until recently there was considerable unanimity of opinion that early experiences exerted a profound and lasting impact on personality. The implication emerged from such stress on early experiences that while a certain amount of change took place during the adolescent years, once a person became an adult, little additional development would take place. The stage theories of Freud and Piaget, for example, both terminate with descriptions of adolescent development. Starting with Erikson, however, more and more psychologists have come to endorse the view that development continues throughout the life span. This point of view is reflected by a trend in texts in developmental psychology, such as the book you are now reading. Up until quite recently most texts used in courses in development discussed changes in behavior through adolescence and abruptly stopped there. Today, many texts on human development, including this one, continue with chapters on adulthood and later maturity.

Erik Erikson was one of the first psychologists to acknowledge that important stages in development occur beyond adolescence, and his stage descriptions serve as an organizational frame of reference for this and the next chapter. Because Havighurst's developmental tasks emerged as an outgrowth of Erikson's theory, they also provide a basic outline of important developments during stages of life beyond adolescence.

Stages and Tasks of Adulthood

Psychosocial Stages Described by Erikson

The psychosocial stage Erikson described for young adulthood is intimacy versus isolation. He suggests that if twenty- to forty-year-olds develop an intimate relationship with another person they will experience a sense of fulfillment. Isolation may be experienced not only because of lack of shared intimacy but also because of competitive interactions (as in occupational situations) with others. Erikson proposes that during middle age the stage of generativity versus stagnation occurs. Establishing and guiding the next generation through child rearing and civic responsibilities gives satisfaction; concern primarily with oneself leads to a sense of arrested development.

"Seasons of Man" Proposed by Levinson

Erikson proposed his stages of psychosocial development over thirty years ago, paving the way for many similar descriptions of stages by others. Daniel J. Levinson (1978), for instance, has offered a different outline of stages of adulthood. After carrying out extensive interviews with forty middle-aged men (ten executives, ten biologists, ten factory workers, and ten novelists), Levinson concluded that he had found evidence for a series of stages (outlined in Figure 22.1) characterized by

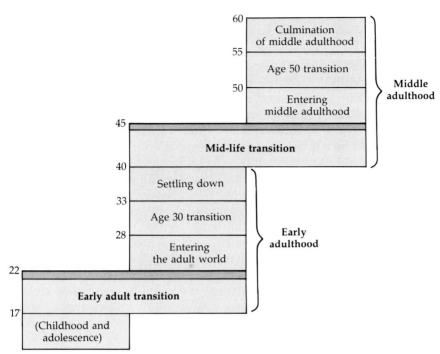

FIGURE 22.1
Stages of adulthood proposed by Levinson

Source: From *The Seasons of a Man's Life* by Daniel J. Levinson et al. Copyright © 1978 by Daniel J. Levinson. Reprinted by permission of Alfred A. Knopf, Inc.

alternating periods of stability and change. Early adulthood begins with the **early adult transition,** marked by separation from parents, career choice, and marriage (for many). This period of significant choices typically occurs between the age of seventeen and twenty-two, according to Levinson, although for individuals included under the category of youth as defined in Chapter 18 it would occur a few years later. That phase is followed by a stable period called **entering the adult world** (twenty-two to twenty-eight years) during which men strive to fulfill commitments made to careers and marriage partners. Next comes the **age thirty transition** (twenty-eight to thirty-three years). For some men only moderate changes may occur during this span. For many others, however, this is a time of crisis, when the individual's life structure (to use Levinson's term) is reworked. A man who had dreamed of becoming highly successful, for instance, may have to accept the fact that he has not achieved goals set earlier. The **settling down** period (ages thirty-three to forty) is typically a stable time, only to be followed by the **midlife transition** (forty to forty-five years), which is again a time of crisis. At this point in their development many men evaluate what they have done with their lives and may sometimes desperately seek to express talents and desires that have not been fulfilled. The **entering middle adulthood** period (ages forty-five to fifty) often involves commitment to new tasks, but the **age fifty transition** (fifty to fifty-five years) once again may be a time of crisis, particularly for men who did not experience upheaval during the midlife transition period. The **culmination of middle adulthood** period (fifty-five to sixty years) is often a period of stability, when decisions made during earlier periods are fulfilled.

Levinson's description of stages is intriguing, provocative, and frequently referred to in books and articles on adulthood, but it should be remembered that it is based on interviews with a small number of males, who expressed and recollected their feelings about experiences during a particular period of American history. Females, and men who were and are influenced by different cohort effects, may depart from the pattern described by Levinson. Furthermore, while the neat arrangement of periods of stability and change depicted in Figure 22.1 serves as a convenient way to summarize conclusions, it should not be accepted too literally. It is doubtful that all, or even most, adults actually go through such predictable periods exactly "on schedule." Many adults, in fact, do not seem to experience *any* upheavals severe enough to merit being called "crises" (Brim, 1976). Perhaps the safest conclusion to draw from Levinson's analysis is that many individuals go through periods of stability and sometimes rather extreme change between the years of twenty and sixty but that the nature, severity, and timing of such changes as do occur will depend on a combination of idiosyncratic personal, economic, political, and social factors. You should not feel, therefore, that having a "midlife" crisis is obligatory or "normal," as intimated by books (e.g., Sheehy, 1976) and magazine articles derived from Levinson's publications. While Levinson's description of stages has aroused considerable interest, Havighurst's developmental tasks provide a more complete outline of significant types of behavior during early adulthood and middle age.

Levinson's "seasons" provocative and widely discussed but not universal

Developmental Tasks Described by Havighurst

The developmental tasks Havighurst listed for early adulthood are

1. selecting a mate.
2. learning to live with a marriage partner.
3. starting a family.
4. rearing children.
5. managing a home.
6. getting started in an occupation.
7. taking civic responsibility.
8. finding a congenial social group.

Several of the most significant developmental tasks for early adulthood center on starting a family, rearing children, and managing a home.
Karen Rosenthal/Stock, Boston.

The tasks for middle age are

1. achieving adult civic and social responsibility.
2. establishing and maintaining an economic standard of living.
3. assisting teen-age children to become responsible and happy adults.
4. developing adult leisure-time activities.
5. relating oneself to one's spouse as a person.
6. accepting and adjusting to physiological changes of middle age.
7. adjusting to aging parents.

The descriptions of stages and tasks by Erikson, Levinson, and Havighurst provide a general picture of development during adulthood, and they will frequently be referred to in the following discussion. The organization of this chapter, though, follows the sequence of sets of chapters covering the preceding stages from infancy through adolescence and youth. That is, physical, cognitive, social, and personality factors will be described. In selecting topics to be discussed under each heading, age trends, as well as aspects of life likely to be of concern to most adults, have been selected for emphasis.

Physical Development

Physical Functioning Declines Gradually

Through adolescence, discussions of physical development center on changes that occur as the body matures. By the time we reach our twenties, though, most of us have pretty much completed our physical growth. Perhaps the main question that comes to a person's mind starting in the twenties is "How soon am I going to slow down and begin to deteriorate?" The answer seems to be "Not for awhile." Physical strength and endurance reach their peak in the twenties, as do most bodily functions, but the decline of both strength and general functioning is gradual up to the age of fifty. If you exercise regularly, for example, at the age of fifty you should have 90 percent of the strength you had at twenty (Hodgson and Buskirk, 1981). If you will think of the activities engaged in by spry and healthy older men and women of your acquaintance, you will realize that you should be capable of functioning physically at an acceptable level until at least your seventies.

At fifty, 90 percent of strength at twenty (with regular exercise)

While physical functioning may decline gradually, physical appearance may deteriorate too rapidly for comfort since signs of age may tend to make us feel older, particularly when advertisers do their best to convince us that we must try to appear eternally youthful rather than mature. Wrinkles and gray hair often appear as early as the twenties. The frequency of magazine ads and television commercials touting products that will give skin and hair a youthful appearance persuade us that we should resist looking as old as we are.

Eyes first sense organs to be affected by aging

The eyes are usually the first sense organs to be affected by the aging process. Both visual acuity and the capacity of the eyes to adjust from near to far vision usually change around forty, prompting many adults to wear glasses for the first time or switch to bifocal lenses. (Perhaps you recall seeing advertisements announcing the availability of bifocal glasses that did not have the telltale separation halfway down the lenses. The biggest selling point when these glasses were introduced was that others would not realize that you had reached the point in life where you needed bifocals—until you tilted your head back to read print.) Peripheral vision decreases with age, too, and it also takes longer for eyes to adjust to the dark. In addition, the lights may have to be turned up for older persons because their corneas and the fluid in their eyes become less transparent and let in less light. The other senses do not age quite as rapidly, but hearing, in particular, may be affected by environmental experiences. Listening to rock music or the equivalent at high decibel levels, for instance, or frequently operating noisy equipment without hearing protectors may lead to premature and permanent hearing decrements. For the most part, though, gradual loss of sensitivity of the senses can be compensated for through use of readily available corrective devices (e.g., glasses and hearing aids).

The Effects of Hormonal Changes

Perhaps the most obvious physical changes that occur at middle age are produced by decreased production of the sex hormones. Such changes usually occur earlier and more rapidly in women than in men. The achievement of puberty is more apparent to an adolescent girl than to an adolescent boy because of the beginning of menstruation. Changes in the sex hormones at midlife are more apparent to women than to men because of the cessation of menstruation, or **menopause.** Changes in the menstrual cycle typically begin between the ages of forty and fifty-five, with the average being approximately forty-eight (Timiras, 1972). Menstruation usually stops completely within two to three years after that time. During the period when menstruation tapers off, many women experience irregular expansion and constriction of blood vessels that maintain body temperature, which leads to tingling sensations ("hot flashes") or blushing and sweating ("flushes"). Other symptoms include breast tenderness, nervousness, mood changes, and depression. It appears, however, that if depression does occur, it is more likely to be due to psychological than to physiological factors (Notman, 1980).

During the 1970s many physicians routinely prescribed **estrogen replacement therapy** (ERT): the use of synthetic estrogen to offset the loss of the female sex hormone caused by changes in the glandular system at the time of menopause. ERT alleviated many of the symptoms of menopause and was believed to preserve attractiveness (e.g., fullness of breasts) and also to reduce the impact of hormonal changes leading to brittle bones and hardening of the arteries. In 1979, however, the National Institute of Health announced that use of synthetic estrogen increased the risk of uterine cancer. Accordingly, in the 1980s, ERT is often restricted to temporary use by women who experience rather severe problems with the symptoms of menopause.

The reactions of women to menopause vary considerably. Many accept it as a natural phase of the life cycle. Others have severe problems coping with the physical symptoms associated with the change of life, with their inability to bear children, and with other psychological symptoms that may be related to menopause (e.g., the fear that they will no longer be sexually attractive to their husbands).

The effects of hormonal changes in men are less abrupt. Despite reduced levels of testosterone, sperm production continues at fairly high levels in middle age, and many men have fathered children at seventy, eighty, or even ninety. Decreases in testosterone levels may reduce the sex drive, however, and with advancing age many men experience decreases in the frequency, strength, and duration of erections. Males, like females, may also experience a variety of physical and psychological symptoms as they approach old age. These include headaches, weight gain, mood swings, and memory lapses (Mourad, 1980). As is the case with women, responses to these symptoms vary considerably.

Health, Diet, and Physical Fitness

Older adults rate health as most important life satisfaction factor

In a longitudinal study of five hundred adults ranging in age from forty-five to sixty-nine (Palmore and Luikart, 1974), the participants were asked to rate eighteen variables contributing to life satisfaction. The factor that was rated far above all the rest was health, with involvement in social organizations a distant second. There is evidence, however, that adults aged forty to fifty-nine are three times as likely as adults aged twenty-five to thirty-nine to indicate that they have recently attempted to improve their health habits (Tough, 1982). Thus, it appears that health becomes more precious to us as we grow older, but that we may take it for granted when we are younger. A potential unfortunate consequence of that attitude is that we may make life difficult for ourselves later if we don't take good care of ourselves earlier. Habits (such as smoking) established early in life may be extraordinarily difficult to change later. Furthermore, attention to diet and exercise can substantially reduce the risk of being early victims of the most common causes of death: cardiovascular problems and cancer. An analysis of causes of death and factors that contribute to longevity will be presented in the next chapter. At this point, brief mention will be made of the values of eating prudently and exercising regularly during the adult years.

Diet

Adults who are overweight increase the likelihood that they will develop cardiovascular problems, diabetes, and arthritis. *What* you eat may be even more important than *how much* you eat, however, because of the negative impact of excessive amounts of fats, sugar, and salt on various organs of the body and on blood cholesterol levels. Because what you eat is so important, it would be wise to learn more about the role nutrition plays in contributing to health and longevity. Pamphlets about proper diet can be obtained at county and state health agencies. Here are some general guidelines offered by the National Institute of Health (1985):

Choose more vegetables, fruits, cereal grains, and starches.

Choose fish, poultry, and lean cuts of meat, and serve moderate portions.

Trim fat from meats and skin from chicken before cooking.

Eat less or avoid organ meats such as liver, brain, and kidney.

Eat less commercial baked goods made with lard, coconut oil, palm oil, or shortening.

Eat less sausage, bacon, and processed luncheon meats.

Use skim or low fat milk.

Choose low fat cheeses.

Eat less cream, ice cream, and butter.

Use low fat yogurt.

Eat less food fried in animal fats or shortening.

Eat fewer eggs or eat fewer egg yolks.

Exercise

The number of exercise machines advertised in magazines and newspapers and the number of joggers encountered on American roads and paths suggests that many adults engage in exercise. In order for exercise to be truly effective, however, it should be *regular*. Regular exercise often adds years to a person's life (Physical Fitness Research Digest, 1977) for a variety of reasons: reduction of feelings of stress due to various kinds of pressure, increase in heart and lung capacity, reduction of ratio of body fat to body weight, and development of a sense of well-being. As is often the case, though, it is difficult to separate cause and effect. Do people who exercise experience a sense of well-being because they exercise, or do they exercise because they already possess a sense of well-being? There is virtual unanimity of opinion in the medical profession, though, that exercise has extremely beneficial effects. To gain such benefits, you should indulge at least three times a week in some form of exercise during which your maximum attainable heart rate reaches 70 to 85 percent of its potential for fifteen to thirty minutes. Pushing the heart and lungs close to capacity is called **aerobic** exercise and is strongly recommended by most physicians. The maximum attainable heart rate varies from over 200 heartbeats per minute at the age of twenty-five to around 150 at the age of sixty-five, so the proper pulse rate will vary

Regular aerobic exercise, which involves pushing the heart and lungs close to capacity for 15 to 30 minutes every other day, has been found to contribute to health and longevity.
© *John Maher/EKM–Nepenthe.*

Aerobic exercise reduces chances of cardiovascular problems, may improve cognitive functioning

with age. For that reason (and to determine if you have any physical idiosyncrasies that would make strenuous exercise potentially harmful), it is usually wise to obtain some expert advice before embarking on an aerobic exercise program. If you do exercise regularly, though, you will increase the amount of high-density lipoprotein (HDL) in your blood (Williams et al., 1980). HDL picks up excess fat and cholesterol from the blood vessels and carries them to the liver where they are excreted. Lower amounts of fat and cholesterol in the blood reduce the possibility of cardiovascular problems. There is also some evidence (Elsayed et al.,

1980) that increased amounts of HDL in the blood circulating in the brain may improve cognitive functioning, particularly in middle-aged and older adults.

Cognitive Development

From the 1920s to the 1960s there was general agreement among psychologists that intelligence reached a peak between the ages of eighteen and twenty-one and then declined. For a time in the 1950s there was also substantial support for the hypothesis that creative productivity reached a peak in the twenties and thirties and then declined. During the last few years both of these conclusions have been questioned and a number of investigators have provided evidence to support the view that intelligence, productivity, and creativity do not necessarily decline until toward the very end of a person's life. Various opinions and interpretations of research on intelligence and creativity during the adult years will be examined separately.

Research and Opinions About Declines in Intelligence

The conclusion that intelligence reached a peak in early adulthood and then declined was based largely on the results of comprehensive testing programs during both World Wars and by patterns of intelligence test scores revealed by cross-sectional studies in which samples of individuals of different ages were tested at the same time. Eventually, however, psychologists realized that a number of contaminating factors were introduced when the cross-sectional approach was used. The typical forty-year-old draftee during World Wars I and II, for instance, had fewer years of schooling than the typical twenty-year-old draftee. Thus, it was suggested that a basic reason older individuals scored lower than younger ones was that they were less well educated. Other explanations for the poorer performance of older individuals centered on their approach to taking tests. If twenty-year-olds and sixty-year-olds were asked to take a group intelligence test in the same room on the same day, the younger subjects would benefit from recent experience in taking tests. Because they would be used to taking tests, they would be familiar with how to record answers on answer sheets and likely to be familiar with the values of working rapidly and using a guess-when-in-doubt approach. Older individuals, by contrast, often experience quite a bit of anxiety when taking tests (Whitbourne, 1976), to the point that they may have difficulty concentrating. In addition, older individuals are more deliberate and cautious in their approach to almost all tasks

Cross-sectional studies indicating decline in intelligence often involve contaminating factors

Cross-sectional studies purporting to show a decline in intellectual performance with age have been criticized for failure to take into account that older persons often experience anxiety when taking tests. Such anxiety, together with a tendency to be cautious, may lead to lower scores.
Michael Weisbrot and Family.

(Birren et al., 1980). Both of those tendencies might limit the number of questions examined and answers recorded, thus lowering the test score.

Because of the potential influence of such factors on cross-sectional research, the results of longitudinal studies were examined. Some studies in which the same individuals were repeatedly tested at intervals (reviewed by Botwinick, 1977), provided evidence of only slight declines with age. These results were criticized, however, partly because of a possible practice effect and partly because of the attrition of subjects. It was suggested that when the same test was given repeatedly, the subjects might remember at least some questions (and answers). More importantly, critics pointed out that fewer subjects were included in each test cycle because some individuals died and some others could not be found after an interval of a few years. It was argued that only the healthiest and most reliable subjects were tested over a long period of time, which may have contributed to the stability of their scores.

Because of the kinds of factors just noted, strong differences of opinion were expressed regarding the question of stability of intelligence.

Longitudinal studies may be difficult to interpret but IQ decline appears to be slight

Some theorists (e.g., Baltes and Schaie, 1974), who devised techniques for correcting for weaknesses of longitudinal studies, noted little or no decline with age. Others (e.g., Horn and Donaldson, 1976) maintained just as emphatically that decline *did* occur. Eventually, the conflicts became resolved to a certain extent when account was taken of the complex nature of intelligence.

Differences Between Crystallized and Fluid Intelligence

Some of the conflicts between findings and conclusions regarding what happens to intellectual abilities as we grow older are a function of how intelligence is defined and measured. One common definition of intelligence is that it is what is measured by an intelligence test. This definition may seem merely evasive at first glance, but it does emphasize the point that different tests measure different aspects of intellectual abilities. J. P. Guilford (1967), for instance, has proposed that there are over fifty different mental abilities, and any test will measure only a few of these. John L. Horn and Raymond B. Cattell (1967) offered a description of two basic types of intelligence that is far easier to grasp than multifactorial conceptions such as that of Guilford. Horn and Cattell make a distinction between **crystallized** and **fluid** intelligence.

Crystallized intelligence, as the term implies, refers to intellectual abilities that have accumulated (or crystallized) into a store of knowledge based on formal and informal educational experiences. Fluid intelligence refers to the capacity to devise solutions when confronted with never-before encountered problems. Crystallized intelligence depends to a considerable extent on experiences in and out of school. Fluid intelligence, by contrast, is assumed to be based on such constitutional factors as memory, creativity, and cognitive style. We may continually augment crystallized intelligence as we grow older and become more experienced and wiser. Aspects of our fluid intellectual capacity that are dependent on neurological efficiency, though, reach a peak in the twenties and decline thereafter. Problem-solving abilities that depend on experience, on the other hand, may increase.

Thus, if individuals of different ages were asked to take an intelligence test that featured many tricky problems that had to be solved as rapidly as possible, twenty-year-olds would almost certainly earn higher scores than fifty-year-olds. If the same subjects took an intelligence test made up of just a few complex problems that were to be evaluated in depth over an extended period of time, older individuals might do as well as or better than younger ones. If the same subjects took an intelligence test that measured understanding of general information, there might not be any significant differences between the scores of twenty- and fifty-year-olds.

Crystallized intelligence: store of knowledge that does not necessarily diminish

Fluid intelligence: efficient problem-solving abilities that decline with age

The questions of whether and how intellectual functioning changes with age, then, are complex and not easy to answer in simple terms. As far as intellectual efficiency goes, the evidence is quite consistent that we reach a peak in our twenties and then decline (Horn and Donaldson, 1980). Fluid intelligence, or problem-solving ability, also seems to decline with age when cognitive speed and agility are called for. But crystallized intelligence, or a person's accumulation of general knowledge, does not necessarily decline with age, and practical knowledge and experience often permit older individuals to solve many types of problems that are important in their lives. Thus, you may not be as quick at solving certain types of problems twenty or more years from now as you are today, but you should be able to compensate for losses in intellectual efficiency because of wider experience.

Research and Opinions About Decline in Creativity

In 1953 H. C. Lehman wrote *Age and Achievement*, in which he presented evidence that the peak period of creative achievement in most fields occurs early in life and declines markedly thereafter. He reported, for example, that forty-year-old chemists produced only half as many significant contributions per person as chemists in their thirties. By the age of sixty, Lehman maintained, chemists produced only one-fifth as many reports as they had in their thirties. Similar results were reported for virtually all other areas of endeavor. Lehman's conclusions were uncritically accepted when his book first appeared, particularly by journalists and authors of magazine articles.

Quite soon, however, behavioral scientists who carefully examined *Age and Achievement* began to question a number of the procedures Lehman had followed in compiling his results. He determined output, for example, by noting when a creative person's works were cited in texts or histories. While this strategy is simple and seems logical at first glance, it does not take into account the possibility that a younger person's first works are more likely to attract attention than later contributions. Furthermore, because the number of producers in any field increases every year, the number of individuals competing for recognition increases. A chemist who was twenty-five in 1940, for instance, might have been mentioned frequently by other writers because he was one of a half-dozen specialists in a new field. At the age of sixty-five, he might produce work that is even better than his early discoveries but might not receive a great deal of recognition because several hundred other chemists now specialize in studying the same problem. A final criticism of Lehman's approach was that he failed to take into account longevity in compiling his figures. Many of the individuals he studied died in their forties and fifties. They failed to produce impressive work beyond middle age not because of a decline in abilities, but because they were denied the opportunity to continue working.

When researchers have allowed for the kinds of contaminating factors just described, it has been found (Dennis, 1966; Simonton, 1975) that while creativity and productivity typically peak in the thirties, many individuals continue to do impressive work until the seventies or beyond. The decline in both quantity and quality of work is gradual, rather than precipitous, as Lehman had reported. You should not assume, therefore, that you will be a spent force as a creative and productive person after you have celebrated your thirty-fifth birthday.

Creativity and productivity peak in thirties but decline only gradually thereafter

Relationships with Others

The Need to Revise Stages and Tasks

The discussion of stages and tasks of adulthood presented at the beginning of this chapter called attention to the significance of relationships with others between the years of twenty and sixty. Erikson emphasizes that during that span of years it is important for an adult to first experience intimacy rather than isolation, then generativity rather than stagnation. Developmental tasks listed by Havighurst include selecting a mate, learning to live with a marriage partner, starting a family, rearing children, and finding a congenial social group. Both Erikson and Havighurst developed their descriptions in the 1950s, when the "traditional" family was the typical social arrangement in which relationships with others occurred. Furthermore, during that period of American history, there was still quite a bit of emphasis on interaction between generations of families. Thus, generativity for fifty-year-olds was often achieved through frequent interactions with grandchildren. In the last thirty years so many alterations of that pattern have occurred that it may be necessary to partially revise interpretations of the stages and tasks described by Erikson and Havighurst.

U. S. Census data for 1980 reveal that only 31 percent of all households in America now comprise a traditional family arrangement (husband, wife, children of those parents). The number of single parent homes doubled between 1965 and 1980 largely due to the fact that approximately half of all marriages contracted now end in divorce (Huyck, 1982). (Perhaps we have reached the point where "Adjusting to divorce" should be added as a developmental task for adulthood.) Since most divorced individuals remarry, many households now are made up of sometimes bewildering combinations of children of present and previous spouses. Lack of clear relationships between particular grandchildren and grandparents, together with the high degree of mobility in our culture, probably has reduced the tendency for grandparents to have frequent, close contact with their children and grandchildren. The number of adults sharing a household with a member of the opposite sex to whom they were not married doubled between 1965 and 1980. The number of young adults who live on intimate terms with a member of the same sex cannot be specified with any degree of accuracy, but it seems safe to say that it has increased since the 1950s.

Taken together, these various developments lead to the conclusion that instead of establishing a single long-term intimate relationship with an individual of the opposite sex (which was the typical pattern when Erikson and Havighurst devised their outlines of development), adults of the 1980s may engage in a series of less intimate and less lasting relationships with others. Even so, the latest census data indicate that young adults of this period of American history are more likely to marry and have children than those of previous cohorts, but they are likely to marry at a later age. However, if the trend toward divorce stays the same, only half of the marriages (and families) currently established will remain intact.

The outline of trends just presented serves as background for more complete analyses of Erikson's stages and Havighurst's tasks.

The Advantages of Intimacy and Generativity

Erikson: true intimacy depends on fusing of identities

Erikson stresses that intimacy, as he defines it, involves "fusing of identities." Therefore, before a person can achieve true intimacy with another, it is presumably necessary for him or her to first develop a satisfactory sense of personal identity to fuse with the identity of another. Erikson notes, "The youth who is not sure of his identity shies away from interpersonal intimacy or throws himself into acts which are 'promiscuous' without true fusion or real self-abandon" (1968, p. 135). Because such a person fails to develop a sense of true intimacy with another, he or she experiences a sense of isolation. Erikson also suggests that for many couples, sexual relations are either self-serving or a form of "genital combat" because the participants are unwilling to share true intimacy for fear of "taking chances" with their own identity. The unwillingness of many young adults to take chances with their own identity might explain, in part at least, why so many marriages fail.

As for generativity, Erikson notes that dependency and maturity are reciprocal in nature since mature individuals need to be needed and experience a desire to guide those who require care and instruction. He points out that the mere act of having children does not automatically lead to a sense of generativity and that those who do not have any contact with younger individuals may experience generativity through altruistic acts or creativity. Failure to either guide others or to be productive may cause adults to pamper themselves as if they were their own infant or pet. Such preoccupation with self leads to personal impoverishment and stagnation, amounting in some cases to what might be called a form of self-pollution.

To avoid stagnation, adults need to guide, help, or be creative

Developmental tasks involving relationships with others during adulthood include mate selection, marriage, and child rearing (with divorce and remarriage added as tasks for about half of all adults).

Selecting a Mate

Stages of Mate Selection

In discussing dating behavior during adolescence in Chapter 20, this pattern was described: initial interest in good looks and prestige, followed by interest in personal traits and social sophistication, followed by interest in deeper qualities such as being reliable and considerate. In an analysis of a number of descriptions of the way mate selection occurs, Bernard Murstein (1976) suggests that quite similar stages often occur. First, each member of the pair notices the other, with physical attractiveness being a major attention getter. If initial interactions are positive and reinforcing, the couple then begin to indirectly and directly compare sexual, social, cultural, and perhaps political values. If such comparisons do not reveal obvious incompatibilities, the couple may then explore how they perceive the roles of husband and wife: how they feel about having children, jobs for both, division of labor in home and family, and the like. (Sometimes, of course, people just fall in love and get married.)

In the discussion of adolescent relationships with others in Chapter 20, the observations of Douvan and Adelson (1966) on sex differences in destiny control were noted. They pointed out that during the 1950s the youthful male typically felt that his destiny was in his own hands. He was free to select both a job and a wife. Females of the 1950s, on the other hand, tended to feel that what they would become as adults would depend to a significant extent on what their husbands would do for a living. While this pattern has become less common during the last thirty years, it still applies to many couples of the 1980s. Contemporary females, for instance, tend to take into account many more characteristics of a potential marriage partner than males, and they are more cautious about falling in love (Hill et al., 1974). A young man may fall in love with a girl almost entirely because of her attractiveness, for example, but the girl may not reciprocate until after she has evaluated not only attrac-

Females more cautious about falling in love than males

It has been found that when couples date each other as a possible prelude to marriage, females tend to be more cautious about falling in love than males.
© *Chip Henderson/Woodfin Camp.*

tiveness but also the kind of job the young man has (or is working toward), as well as such traits as thoughtfulness and consideration for the feelings of others. It seems fair to say, therefore, that even today, the female may feel that her future will depend to an important extent on what her husband does and how he behaves.

Some of the differences between the ways males and females select a spouse might also be explained by social exchange theory and equity theory (which were mentioned in Chapter 20). Before they fall in love and seriously contemplate marriage, both males and females (according to social exchange theorists) would like to make sure that they are going to get something back. They also want marriageability strengths to be equal. Thus, an attractive, successful female may feel that she should consider as husband candidates only men who have proved that they can earn a high income and a high-salaried male executive may feel that he should marry an extremely attractive woman.

If either member of a pair contemplating marriage is cautious about falling in love, the couple may interact over an extended period of time to discover if there are incompatibilities or conflicts before they commit themselves to marriage.

Cohabitation

Finding out in advance about potential incompatibilities is the major argument in favor of trial marriage, or **cohabitation,** which is practiced by many contemporary couples. Perhaps the major disadvantage of cohabitation is that one member of the pair (most likely the female, according to Simenauer and Carroll, 1982) may feel that the unwilling-ness of the other person to make a commitment before marriage will prevent what Erikson might call true intimacy. Even if the couple even-tually marry, there always may be a feeling of regret on the part of one or both partners that they did not feel confident enough about their relationship to publicly formalize it before living together.

There may be a few rare perfect marriages involving couples who, through luck, divine intervention, or accurate computer data, hardly ever experience dissatisfaction with the behavior of a spouse. Most mar-riages, however, are less than perfect, and conflicts are inevitable. Ac-cordingly, in most marriage relationships, each member of the pair will need to make allowances and adjustments. Often this involves simul-taneous attempts on the part of one partner to try to control or change certain aspects of behavior and attempts on the part of the other partner to accept or learn to live with certain annoyances. It seems possible that a couple who pledged marriage vows before living together might be expected to be more willing to make a concerted effort to reconcile differences than a couple who did not feel completely committed to each other.

Marriage and Child Rearing

The first few years following marriage that was not preceded by cohabi-tation typically involve the task that Havighurst describes as "learning to live with a marriage partner." It is during this stage that premarital estimates of compatibility are thoroughly tested. Analyses of family life cycles (e.g., Duvall, 1977) suggest that if the couple are compatible, this is often the happiest period of a marriage, as well as the period of greatest sexual activity. However, because the first years of a marriage feature sexual activity, if conflicts between husband and wife develop, this may also be the period when extramarital affairs are most likely to occur, particularly for males (Athanasiou et al., 1970).

If the marriage survives the initial testing period, a second phase begins when the first child is born. Census data indicate that while the percentage of couples who do not have children has increased during the last twenty years, only 7 percent of married adults in 1980 were childless. The birth of a first child is least likely to lead to feelings of dissatisfaction if the parents have thought realistically about the responsibilities of child care and if they have planned to have the child. Even

Marital satisfaction tends to decline after birth of a child

under ideal circumstances, however, marital satisfaction often declines after children enter the family partly because of the demands of child care and partly because of loss of opportunities for sexual and social intimacy (Leifer, 1980). If the baby was unplanned, if the parents have not given much thought to child care, and/or if the baby is of the type that Thomas and his associates would have classified as difficult, the initial period of child care is likely to be stressful. If the parents have not thought about how they intend to share responsibilities for child care or if conflicts arise about such matters, the marriage relationship may suffer. On the other hand, the fascination and sense of fulfillment achieved by observing the evolution of a unique human being may be sufficient to counteract any negative impact of child rearing on marriage (LeMasters, 1977).

When the first child reaches the age of two or so, conflicts may develop over choice of a permissive, authoritative, or authoritarian style of child rearing or because of inconsistencies caused by the use of one approach by one parent and of a different approach by the other. Marriage roles that worked out well during the prechild period of the marriage may need to be revised, particularly if the mother assumes primary responsibility for day-to-day care (Galinsky, 1981). A wife who deferred to her husband's ideas about buying a home or car, for instance, may feel that she has the right to assert herself more aggressively after she has assumed primary responsibility for child rearing.

After all the children in a family have entered school, some of the pressure of child rearing on a marriage may diminish, although new problems may emerge when offspring reach high school. Reactions to the departure of an adolescent from the home may vary from a sense of loss or depletion to feelings of satisfaction and/or relief. Kiyo Morimoto, for example, has expressed the view that "Parenthood is the experience of inevitable defeat" (quoted in Kegan, 1982, p. 217), calling attention to the sense of loss parents may feel when children go off on their own. On the other hand, many parents have indicated that they experience considerable stress when youthful or even adult children do *not* leave home (Datan, 1980). Instead of feeling defeated, therefore, many parents may feel relieved when child-rearing responsibilities are completed. Rearing children and watching them develop can provide a special sense of fulfillment, but marital satisfaction is often reported to be highest by newlyweds, couples without children, and older couples (Huyck, 1982). Marital satisfaction often is lowest among parents who have teen-agers still living at home.

Marriage After the Children Leave Home

The years after the last child leaves home may be the most satisfying period of a couple's life, although both husband and wife may experience some sort of midlife crisis. For males, the time when adolescents leave home for college or a job coincides with the midlife transition (forty to forty-five years), which Levinson found to be a time of crisis for many of his subjects. Perhaps the fact that their children were beginning to function as independent beings caused some of the men interviewed by Levinson to examine their own careers and seek ways to express unfulfilled talents and desires. For the wife, the reaction to the end of active motherhood may depend on whether she engaged in some form of work while the children were in school. A woman who started or resumed a career as soon as infant-care responsibilities were completed may find that no adjustment is necessary at midlife and may even feel relieved that she can concentrate on her job. A woman who had functioned as a full-time mother and homemaker, on the other hand, may experience a crisis much more severe than that of a man, who merely evaluates his career in his early forties. It has been found (Newberry et al., 1979) that mothers who work tend to express greater satisfaction with their lives than full-time mothers. Even when they are employed at rather tedious jobs, working mothers receive tangible proof that they are accomplishing something and earning money. The housewife's work is never done, on the other hand, and a woman who functions only as a homemaker may resent feeling financially dependent on her husband. When the job of rearing children and maintaining a home for them is completed, moreover, the forty-five-year-old woman may find it difficult to find a job or start a career. Accordingly, the "retired" mother may try to immerse herself in such activities as sports, bridge, politics, or community activities.

Divorce and Remarriage

As noted earlier, at present approximately half of all marriages end in divorce, but most divorced adults remarry. Most divorces occur during the first seven years of marriage; most remarriages occur within three years after a divorce. The current rate of divorce is about two and one-half times as high as it was just twenty years ago (according to U.S. Census figures). One explanation for this sharp increase is that state laws now make it much easier for couples to obtain divorces that do not entail penalties for either spouse, so-called no-fault divorces. It is often difficult to trace cause and effect relationships, so it is impossible to determine to what extent liberalized divorce laws led to more liberal views about marriage dissolution and remarriages and to what extent changes in divorce laws were a manifestation of the emergence of more liberal views about sex and relationships between adults.

Thirty years ago, when divorce laws were much stricter than they are today, many couples who experienced marital difficulties would try to reconcile their differences or just live with them. Today couples may not feel that the effort is worth the trouble because it is so easy to get a divorce. On the other hand, thirty years ago couples who were so ill-matched that they made each other (and their children) miserable often felt compelled to stay together and thus prolonged and intensified their misery. Today such couples are much more likely to call off the marriage and try to start again with someone else.

In addition, thirty years ago there were comparatively few unattached adults in the thirty- to fifty-year-age range. Today there are substantial numbers of potential second husbands or wives (or cohabitation partners) of the same age to choose from, and abundant opportunities to meet them. Furthermore, unattached adults are motivated to meet other unattached adults because of the extent and nature of the "sexual marketplace," to use the term of Miller and Simon (1980) noted in discussing sexuality during adolescence. Teen-agers are motivated to be sexually active, according to Miller and Simon, because they perceive that adults are more sexually active than they used to be. Adults perceive the same thing and react the same way, and the category "adults" includes husbands and wives, as well as unattached singles. Thus, contemporary husbands and wives may be tempted to engage in potentially marriage-destroying affairs to a greater extent than their parents. They may also be less hesitant about considering divorce because they are aware that there are lots of other potential partners available in the "sexual marketplace."

Because attempting to fuse one's identity with that of another is complex and demanding, there are many reasons why one or both marriage partners may seek a divorce. Among the most common reasons given by contemporary couples who file for divorce is lack of communication and understanding (Kitson and Sussman, 1982). In one recent interview study of divorced and married males at midlife (Davis, 1985), an analysis of the subjects' level of interpersonal understanding was carried out. The majority of married males were able to integrate their own needs and feelings with those of their wives and work collaboratively with their wives to resolve conflicts and problems. Divorced males, on the other hand, resorted to less effective strategies for conflict resolution. Because of their lower level of intra- and interpersonal awareness, they tended either to deny problems existed or to find unilateral solutions, sometimes giving in to their wives and sometimes imposing their own wishes. These results corroborate the findings of other studies of marital adjustment: mutual satisfaction in marriage often depends heavily on the husband's level of psychosocial maturity (Newman and Newman, 1984).

The impact of divorce is rarely mild and often may be quite severe, particularly for couples with children, for older adults, and for males (Kitson, 1982). The presence of children calls attention to the fact that a *family*, as well as a marriage, is being dissolved. Furthermore, the ties between husband and wife cannot be severed completely because arrangements for child custody and care must be maintained. Older adults may react to divorce as more of a crisis than younger ones because they have lived on intimate terms for a longer period of time and because they may feel it will be too late to start over. Males may be more upset by a divorce than females because their lives are more likely to be disrupted (in the sense that they move out of the home and away from the children). The husband may also be more likely than the wife to experience feelings of rejection and a bruised ego. In most cases, the male proposes marriage and "wins" his bride. If he "loses" his wife, therefore, he may think of it as a reflection on his masculinity, sex appeal, and overall performance as a husband. By contrast, the wife, who may have assumed (as noted by Douvan and Adelson) that what she would become as an adult would depend on her husband, may have fewer misgivings about divorce because she may reason that the husband failed to meet her expectations. On the other hand, a wife's feelings of dependency on her husband—even in the case of a wife who is physically abused by her spouse—may prevent her from seeking a divorce. An unhappy and/or abused wife in her midthirties or beyond may feel that she has no choice but to stay with her husband because she lacks confidence in her ability to support herself or find a second marriage partner.

> Impact of divorce more severe for parents, older adults, males

While the initial shock of divorce is often severe, most divorced individuals recover within a few years, and as noted, most remarry. There is some evidence (Glenn and Weaver, 1977) that many adults, particularly women, find greater happiness in a second marriage than in a first failed marriage. A number of possible explanations can be noted: greater wisdom about picking a partner with the "right" characteristics, experience with day-to-day details of marriage, awareness of the need to make adjustments and compromises, and a strong desire to make the second marriage work. Not all second marriages turn out well, of course, partic-

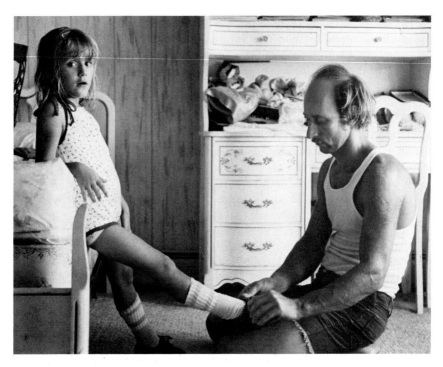

Males may be more upset by divorce than females because their lives are more likely to be disrupted. The male typically moves out of the home, for instance, and has only occasional (and perhaps somewhat strained) interactions with his children.
© *Deborah Kahn/Stock, Boston.*

Most divorced individuals remarry, those without children most likely to be happy

ularly when one or both members of a couple marry on the rebound. The divorce rate for second marriages, in fact, is slightly higher than for first marriages. Couples with children are most likely to have problems with second marriages; young adults without children are most likely to enjoy success.

Personality Development

Continuity and Change in Adult Personality

At the very beginning of this chapter, you were reminded that until recently there was virtual unanimity of opinion that there would be few major changes in personality after the first few years of life. Within the last few years, however, several psychologists have argued that personality traits *do* change throughout the life span and that the impact of early experiences on personality may be counteracted by later experiences. Levinson's conclusion that many of his subjects experienced a midlife crisis in their forties and fifties is one example of this trend. Even though a man or woman experiences a midlife crisis that has a profound influence on behavior, however, does not necessarily mean that his or her personality has undergone substantial change. Recall that psychologists such as Jack Block, who have analyzed exceptionally detailed longitudinal data with painstaking thoroughness, are convinced that "the unity or consistency of personality is compellingly apparent" (1971, p. 268).

Several researchers (e.g., Labouvie-Vief, 1982; Vygotsky, 1978) have suggested that discontinuities in personality functioning can often be understood by taking into account fundamental differences between biological and psychological development. When our physical growth is completed in the late teens or early twenties, we remain in a quite stable physical condition for many years, except for periods of change due to illness, substantial alteration in eating habits, and the like. There is often a tendency to equate personality functioning with physical functioning and to assume that since the physical body stays essentially the same during adulthood, personality also will remain essentially unchanged. This line of reasoning fails to take into account the fact that our physical appearance and functioning are determined to a significant extent by inherited factors. We can alter our appearance, of course, and either care for or abuse our bodies, but many physical and physiological characteristics emerge according to a genetic timetable programmed at conception and tend to remain more or less stable after we reach maturity. Constitutional determinants, however, are only one set of factors that influence personality. Our behavior is also influenced by group membership, role, and situational determinants. Thus, personality is much more likely to be influenced by experiences and relationships with others than is our physical appearance and functioning.

Personality more influenced by experiences than physical appearance and functioning

As noted in Chapter 2, B. F. Skinner has maintained that psychologists should concentrate on studying environmental experiences because they can be altered and arranged, while inherited predispositions are usually beyond control. As noted in Chapter 3 in the discussion of behavioral genetics, it is not always possible to identify the extent to which many behavioral traits are determined by heredity or environment. Longitudinal studies of personality summarized in Chapter 5 indicate that certain traits (such as activity level and passivity) seem to be traceable to genetic factors and remain stable throughout the life span. Other traits (such as achievement motivation) may be stable partly because of inherited predispositions and partly because they are types of behavior reinforced by social interactions and expectations throughout the life span. Still other traits (such as attitudes) may be highly susceptible to change because they are influenced by cultural factors and cohort effects. Thus, it might be expected that manifestations of certain person-

ality traits will stay quite consistent throughout the life span while manifestations of other traits will very likely change.

The Unpredictable Impact of Experiences on Personality

As noted in earlier chapters, several researchers who have analyzed the
data of longitudinal studies have discovered that it is often difficult to
predict how a person will behave later in life on the basis of behavior
during childhood or adolescence. The researchers at Berkeley, for instance, found that predictions of adult behavior made when their subjects were teen-agers often turned out to be inaccurate. An explanation
for such unpredictability emphasized in Chapter 5 was based on a comparison of developmental tasks for different age levels. A comparison of
the behavior of preschool and elementary school children revealed that
achievement of early tasks does not necessarily equip a child to master
later tasks. A similar point can be made in comparing the tasks for
adolescence and adulthood. There are certain continuities between the
two sets of tasks, but even quite similar tasks at the two levels may
require different traits and abilities. High school students who "prepare
for marriage and family life" by dating, for instance, do not necessarily
gain experience in many of the types of behavior that will be of benefit
when they "learn to live with a marriage partner." Many of the qualities
that lead to social popularity and success in high school do not really
prepare a person for the kinds of hour-by-hour and day-to-day interactions that play a significant role in the success of a marriage. The ability
of a person to handle some of the tasks of marriage, therefore, cannot be
predicted on the basis of previous experience because the adjustments
required in marriage are somewhat unique.

Furthermore, successful achievement of developmental tasks early in
adulthood does not mean that those tasks have been permanently mastered. A marriage may suddenly disintegrate, or an abrupt change in
economic conditions may cause a man or woman to lose a high-paying
and prestigious job. While all individuals experience certain stresses and
crises during their adult years, some experience much more upheaval
than others. Aspects of life that require readjustment also change with
age. Moreover, some individuals are better able than others to handle
stress.

Differences in Social Readjustment

A number of researchers have investigated the extent and nature of
stressful situations during different periods of development. M. F. Low-

Everyone must make certain social readjustments during their lives. Some individuals, however, such as a woman with a family who is widowed early in life, are faced with more severe adjustments to stress than others.
Jim Whitmer/Nawrocki Stock Photo.

enthal, M. Thurnher, and D. Chiriboga (1975), for instance, interviewed high school seniors, newlyweds, middle-aged adults, and preretirement adults and asked them to note the most significant events of their lives. Not surprisingly, high school seniors most frequently mentioned educational factors (e.g., changing schools). Newlyweds mentioned changing their living location. Consistent with Levinson's findings, middle-aged men mentioned work-related factors (e.g., getting fired, changing jobs). Middle-aged women, by contrast, mentioned health (not necessarily their own), despite the fact that many of them were employed and might have been expected to be as concerned about job factors as males.

In an effort to make the study of stressful situations more systematic, T. H. Holmes and R. H. Rahe (1967) developed the Social Readjustment Rating Scale, summarized in Table 22.1. The mean value opposite each "life event" in that table represents an estimate of the degree of stress that might be experienced when such an event occurred. The values assigned to each life event are obviously average estimates and will vary depending on each individual's life situation and style, as well as cohort

TABLE 22.1
ITEMS FROM THE SOCIAL READJUSTMENT SCALE

Death of a spouse 100	Sex difficulties 39
Divorce 73	Business readjustment 39
Marital separation 65	Change in financial state 38
Jail term 63	Death of a close friend 37
Death of a close family member 63	Change to a different line of work 36
Personal injury or illness 63	Foreclosure of mortgage or loan 30
Marriage 50	Change in responsibilities at work 29
Fired at work 47	Son or daughter leaving home 29
Marital reconciliation 45	Begin or end of school 26
Retirement 45	Change in living conditions 25
Change in health of family member 44	Trouble with boss 23
Pregnancy 40	Change in residence 20

Source: T. H. Holmes and R. H. Rahe, "The Social Readjustment Rating Scale," *Journal of Psychosomatic Research,* 1967, *11*, 213–218. Reprinted by permission of Pergamon Press, Ltd.

effects and timing. Divorce may not be as much of a crisis in the lives of contemporary adults, for example, as it was in the 1960s when the scale was devised. Divorce that occurs after thirty years of marriage and several children will be a more significant upheaval than divorce that occurs after six months of marriage. Even so, the scale calls attention to several interesting points. If you will examine Table 22.1, you will realize that while certain of the life events listed are inevitable, some individuals—because of the nature of their lives and the intervention of "fate"—are bound to encounter a larger number of stressful situations than others.

Social readjustment depends on number and timing of stressful situations

In addition, stressful situations may be spaced out or bunched together in a person's life. An individual might be able to handle a divorce, loss of a job, and a foreclosed mortgage with a certain degree of equanimity if these events occur at five-year intervals. If all three happen at once, the problems of readjustment may seem overwhelming.

Individual Differences in Reactions to Stress and Crises

While certain individuals are bound to encounter more stressful situations than others in the course of their adult lives, there is evidence that because of basic personality traits some adults are likely to be better able than others to cope with crises. In discussing personality development during the school years in Chapter 13, the glass, celluloid, and steel doll analogy of Jacques May was mentioned. Because of inherited predispositions, treatment by parents, favorable or unfavorable sequences of experiences, and the presence or absence of a tempering process of dealing with problems, some adults are likely to resemble the glass, celluloid, and steel dolls described by May. If exposed to the same basic crisis in their lives, each type would respond with varying degrees of control. The May analogy is hypothetical, but there is evidence to support it.

Jack and Jeanne H. Block (1979) analyzed data on subjects of the Berkeley longitudinal studies and concluded that a distinction could be made between individuals classified as **ego-brittle** or **ego-resilient.** Ego-brittle types exhibit the following characteristics: fixed in patterns of adaptation, stereotyped in responding to new situations, rigid under stress, anxious when confronted by competing demands, slow to recover from stress, disquieted by changes in life. Ego-resilient types, by contrast, exhibit these characteristics: resourceful, able to improvise when confronted by new situations, maintain integrated performance under stress, able to handle conflicting demands, quick to recover after stress, take changes of life in stride. These descriptions refer to "pure" types, and most individuals fall somewhere between these two extremes. Even so, it seems reasonable to assume that the reactions to a change in life structure of a person with ego-brittle characteristics would be quite different from those of an ego-resilient type. One would experience a crisis; the other might take care of the problem without giving it a great deal of thought.

> **Ego-resilient** types better able to handle stress than **ego-brittle** types

Levinson reported that about 80 percent of his subjects told him they had experienced "tumultuous struggle" (1978, p. 199) during their forties or fifties. Differences between his conclusion that a midlife crisis is almost inevitable and the conclusion of others (e.g., Neugarten and Datan, 1974) that middle age is a time of stability and satisfaction might be attributed to a number of factors: more upsetting life events (as listed on the Social Readjustment Rating Scale), different definitions of "crisis," a cohort effect due to unstable economic conditions, and the presence of an atypical proportion of ego-brittle types in Levinson's sample. The safest conclusion to draw from conflicting research reports on crises during middle adulthood is probably that some people are going to experience more upheaval than others and that some are going to be able to handle crises better than others.

Summary

1. Daniel Levinson's description of "seasons of a man's life," which features a midlife crisis, has attracted considerable attention and has been widely popularized. While some individuals seem to go through the stages approximately as described, many do not.
2. For individuals who are active and healthy, physical functioning typi-

cally declines gradually during adulthood. If you exercise regularly, for instance, at the age of fifty you should still have 90 percent of the strength you had at twenty. The eyes are usually the first sense organs to be affected by aging, but both sight and hearing losses can often be easily corrected. Older adults rate health as the single most important life satisfaction factor. One way to promote good health throughout adulthood is to engage in aerobic exercise, which reduces the risk of cardiovascular problems and may improve cognitive functioning.

3. The question of whether intellectual functioning declines with age has been studied and debated intensively. Cross-sectional studies, in which individuals of different ages are tested at the same time, introduce contaminating factors such as age differences in education and test-taking skills and attitudes. The results of longitudinal studies are sometimes difficult to interpret, but there is fairly general agreement that any decline in intelligence that takes place as we grow older is slight. Some of the conflicts between conclusions of studies of changes in cognitive functioning can be resolved by noting differences between two types of intelligence. **Crystallized intelligence,** or a person's store of knowledge, does not necessarily diminish with age and may increase. **Fluid intelligence,** or problem-solving abilities that stress quickness and efficiency, *do* seem to decline with age. Creativity and productivity, which do not depend on quick solutions, peak when individuals are in their thirties but decline only gradually thereafter.

4. Erikson proposed that for satisfactory adjustment during adulthood an individual should first develop a sense of **intimacy** by fusing her or his identity with another person and then experience a sense of **generativity** by guiding the next generation, helping others, or engaging in creative activities. For most people, a sense of intimacy occurs after falling in love. It appears that females are more cautious about falling in love than males, perhaps because females consider more characteristics of a potential marriage partner than males.

5. For many couples the first few months or years after marriage are satisfying. Marital satisfaction tends to decline, however, after the birth of a child. Many couples report that satisfaction in marriage is greatest after children have left home.

6. Approximately half of all contemporary marriages end in divorce. The impact of divorce is most severe for those who have children, males, and older adults. Most divorced individuals remarry. Those without children are most likely to have a successful second marriage.

7. The question of how consistent personality remains throughout the adult years is difficult to answer with any degree of certainty, but it

seems logical to expect that personality, which is influenced by a variety of determinants, may be altered by experiences. All individuals must adjust to stressful situations at different times in their lives. The number and timing of such traumatic incidents influence the frequency and degree of readjustments that are made. Some individuals seem to have greater **ego resiliency** than others, though, regardless of the number of stressful experiences they must deal with.

Varying Views About the Midlife Crisis

Suggestions for Further Study

Perhaps the most controversial aspect of contemporary life during adulthood centers on just how common a midlife crisis is. If you are curious about this question, you might sample one or more of these books:

The Seasons of a Man's Life (1978) by Daniel J. Levinson, the book that is probably referred to most often when the midlife crisis topic is debated; *Adaptation to Life* (1977) by George E. Vaillant, a book very similar to Levinson's based on an analysis of the careers of a group of Harvard graduates; *Passages* (1977) and *Pathfinders* (1982) by Gail Sheehy and *Turning Points* (1979) by Ellen Goodman, variations on the basic theme suggested by Levinson written in journalistic style, with interview data used as the basis for generalizations; *The 40-to-50-Year Old Male* (1980) by Michael McGill, who concludes that most men probably do *not* experience a midlife crisis; *Women of A Certain Age: The Midlife Search for Self* (1979) by Lillian Rubin, an analysis of midlife crises experienced by women.

Asking Fifty-Year-Old Adults to Assess Their Lives

A more direct way to find out about how common midlife crises are would be to ask a number of adults in their fifties or so to talk about how they feel about the present state of their lives. Without mentioning the term midlife crisis, ask your interviewees if there were any particular periods during the years between thirty and fifty when life seemed to change.

KEY POINTS

The Stage and Tasks of Later Maturity

Integrity: satisfied acceptance of one's life as own responsibility

Decreasing Physical Health and Strength

Increase in life expectancy has led to distinction between young-old and old-old

Type A behavior: constant drive, competitiveness, hostility, tension

Most memory problems of elderly involve long-term memory

Behavioral slowing most significant general change as we grow older

Slower behavior due to physiological decline, desire to avoid mistakes, cautiousness

Each individual genetically programmed to reach a point of deterioration

Longevity increased by exercise, diet, useful work

Alterations of DNA due to aging lead to error catastrophe

Loss of efficiency of glandular system reduces immunities, leads to physical decline

Retirement

Retirement least satisfactory for those who are disappointed with lives, bitter

Females more likely than males to change life style in later years

Adjusting to the Death of a Loved One

Ageism: prejudice against older people

Dementia: intellectual deterioration due to organic brain causes

Alzheimer's disease: destruction of brain tissue because of abnormal cellular formations

Awareness of impending death often involves denial, anger, bargaining, depression, acceptance

Bereavement: grief, guilt, preoccupation with deceased, anger against others

Grief work: advantages of expressing grief freely and openly

Many widows take pride in being independent

CHAPTER
23

LATER
MATURITY

You may have responded with interest to the discussion of adulthood in the preceding chapter because you are either in that stage of development or about to enter it. Later maturity, the final stage of development, and the topic of this chapter, may seem (at first glance) to be too remote from your present existence to have similar personal interest. A moment's reflection, however, should convince you that it is worth reading about old age. You will inevitably have contact with individuals older than yourself. You are quite likely to have contact with your parents as they grow older, for instance. In addition, the number of Americans over sixty-five has increased to 25 million, representing about 11 percent of the total population. Projections based on numbers of children born after World War II (as well as vital statistics and medical data) suggest that there will be more than 40 million Americans over the age of sixty-five by the end of the century. Accordingly, there will be an ever-increasing number of older people you are likely to have contact with in your daily activities. Finally, even though you are probably at least several decades away from your sixty-fifth birthday, you may find it not only intriguing but valuable to learn about the process and impact of aging. There are several things you can do—starting now—to increase your chances of living a long life and enjoying your retirement.

As with earlier stages of development, the speculations of Erik Erikson and Robert Havighurst will be summarized to serve as an introduction to the discussion that follows.

The Stage and Tasks of Later Maturity

Erikson's Stage of Integrity versus Despair

The final psychosocial stage of development described by Erikson is integrity versus despair. In a recent re-evaluation of his theory, Erikson notes that when he first described psychosocial stages in the 1950s, it was still possible to think of *elders:* "the few wise men and women who quietly lived up to their stage-appropriate assignment and knew how to die with some dignity in cultures where a long survival appeared to be a divine gift to and a special obligation of a few" (1982, p. 62). He then suggests that the elders of just a few years ago have been replaced by a "quite numerous, fast-increasing and reasonably well-preserved group of mere 'elderlies.'" He then suggests that this switch from elders to elderlies calls for a modification of his original description of the stage of integrity versus despair to include a continuation of generativity. He observes, "old people can and need to maintain a grand-generative function" (p. 63).

Integrity: satisfied acceptance of one's life as own responsibility

In his earlier description of integrity versus despair (1968, p. 139), Erikson emphasized that **integrity** involves a feeling of emotional integration and satisfaction with one's life experiences, as well as acceptance of responsibility for those experiences. Those who take stock of their lives in their sixties and beyond and find themselves dissatisfied are likely to experience a sense of despair. The sense of despair may increase when the person realizes that it is too late to make a new start, and contempt for oneself may be converted into expressions of contempt for others. Older persons who fail to experience integrity also might be expected to blame others for many things that went wrong with their lives.

Developmental Tasks for Later Maturity

Havighurst listed these developmental tasks for later maturity:

1. Adjusting to decreasing physical strength and health
2. Adjusting to retirement and reduced income
3. Adjusting to death of spouse
4. Establishing an explicit affiliation with one's age group
5. Meeting social and civic obligations

   Because the first three of these tasks call attention to basic concerns of older Americans, they will be used as the organizational frame of reference for this chapter (instead of the previously used scheme of discussing physical, cognitive, social, and personal behavior).

Decreasing Physical Health and Strength

There has been a tendency for researchers in the fields of medicine, psychology, and sociology to study older people, who are easily accessible as subjects (Butler and Lewis, 1982). The easiest way to accumulate a large amount of data on older people in a short period of time is to go to places where they congregate in groups made up of more or less captive subjects. Hospitals and institutions are such places and until recently the results of many studies of the effects of aging were based on an atypical sample and often led to erroneous conclusions that Americans over the age of sixty-five were a lot worse off physically and mentally than they really are. In a poll conducted by the National Council on Aging in 1975, for instance, respondents of all ages estimated that one out of every three Americans over the age of sixty-five is cared for in a hospital or nursing home. The actual figure is one out of every twenty.
   Today greater efforts are made to study older individuals in a variety of settings and the results of such research have led to the suggestion that there may be an advantage to distinguishing between the **young-old** and the **old-old** (Neugarten, 1975). Many Americans between the age of sixty-five and seventy-five are healthy and active. It is only after the age of seventy-five that the process of aging becomes apparent in many individuals. Differences between the young-old and the old-old

An older person who looks back over his or her life with satisfaction is likely to experience a sense of integrity.
© *Jean-Claude Lejeune.*

are based not just on chronological age, however; they also depend on attitudes, interests, health, and activities. Some sixty-five-year-olds, as you can probably attest from personal experience, look and act much older than some eighty-five-year-olds.

Life Expectancy

Increase in life expectancy has led to distinction between **young-old** and **old-old**

Making a distinction between the young-old and the old-old is in large part a consequence of the longer life-span of contemporary Americans (which led Erikson to distinguish between elders and elderlies). The life expectancy of the average American in 1900 was forty-seven years; today it is about seventy-four years. These figures (which are based on Census data for whites) are approximate because the average person born in

1970 will live longer than the average person born in 1920, the average woman lives about seven years longer than the average man, the average white lives longer than the average black, and the average upper- and middle-income person lives longer than the average lower-income person. Even so, they are accurate enough to reveal that more old-old Americans are alive today than at any other time in our history. And because they *are* alive, they make individuals who previously were old-old look and act like young-old senior citizens.

Mention of life expectancy may have caused you to speculate a bit about how long you (and those you know well) will live. Diana Woodruff (1977) has compiled data that make it possible to estimate the extent to which various factors and conditions are likely to extend or shorten a person's life. Selected figures that she supplies are summarized below.

Family Factors

Grandparents lived to 80—add 1 year for each

Mother lived to 80—add 4 years

Father lived to 80—add 2 years

Grandparent, parent, or sibling died of cardiovascular disease before age of 50—subtract 4 years for each incidence; before age of 60—subtract 2 years

Grandparent, parent, or sibling died of diabetes or peptic ulcers before age of 60—subtract 3 years for each incidence; if died of stomach cancer—subtract 2 years

Mother under 18 or over 35 when born—subtract 1 year

Personal Factors

Work as a professional—add 1.5 years; as a manager, administrator, or agricultural worker—add 1 year

Active job—add 2 years

Live most of life in urban area—subtract 1 year

Live most of life in rural area—add 1 year

Married and living with spouse—add 1 year

Male separated or divorced and living alone—subtract 9 years

Male separated or divorced not living alone—subtract 4 years

Male who never marries—subtract 2 years for every 10 years beyond the age of 25

Female separated or divorced and living alone—subtract 4 years

Female separated or divorced not living alone—subtract 2 years

Female who never marries—subtract 1 year for every 10 years beyond the age of 25

Aggressive personality—subtract up to 5 years

Health Factors

More than 30 percent overweight—subtract 5 years

More than 10 to 30 percent overweight—subtract 2 to 4 years

Eat plenty of vegetables and fruits, stop eating before full—add 1 year

Smoke two or more packages of cigarettes a day—subtract 12 years

Smoke between one and two packs of cigarettes a day—subtract 7 years

Smoke less than a pack of cigarettes a day—subtract 2 years

Heavy drinker—subtract 8 years

Moderate or light consumption of alcohol—add 2 years

Exercise regularly at least 3 times a week—add 3 years

Regular physical check-ups—add 2 years

The year values just given are based on census figures and other actuarial data, which make it possible to make group, but not individual, predictions. Insurance companies make predictions about the likelihood that individuals with certain characteristics will experience certain events (e.g., accidents, death) at a particular rate during a particular period of time, but they cannot specify *which* individuals will be affected. The same holds true for the figures you just examined. Even though you cannot make a precise estimate of how long you (or anyone else) will live, you might note how some of the figures illustrate points discussed in earlier chapters. You might also note factors that could lead to an extension of your life span.

The entries under "family factors" call attention to points mentioned in the discussion of behavioral genetics in Chapter 3. Because you received your unique combination of genes from your grandparents and parents, you share some, and perhaps many, of their characteristics. At least some of those characteristics will directly or indirectly affect your health and longevity. That is why a doctor who gives you a thorough physical checkup will probably ask you questions about the health of your parents and grandparents, as well as the cause of their deaths.

Entries under "personal factors" might be related to aspects of Erikson's psychosocial stages for adulthood and old age. Individuals who stay married presumably have established a reasonably satisfying intimate relationship with another person. Individuals who are divorced (or who never marry) and live alone may suffer first from feelings of isolation, then experience a sense of stagnation to the point that lack of fulfillment leads to physical and psychological stress. If they live beyond their sixties, they may brood about what might have been, blame others for their failures, and become weighted down by despair.

Aggressive individuals, including those who manifest what has been dubbed **Type A behavior** (Friedman and Rosenman, 1974), may shorten their lives because their behavior increases the possibility of a heart attack. Those who exhibit Type A behavior give the impression that they are always trying to do more in less time and react to situations and interactions with other people in hostile and competitive ways. Because they find it difficult to relax, and are often in a state of constant tension, they put stress on the cardiovascular system.

Type A behavior: constant drive, competitiveness, hostility, tension

The list of points under "health factors" may have been of greatest interest to you because such factors are under your control. The values of holding weight down and being careful about what you eat were outlined in the preceding chapter. A series of reports from the Surgeon General has conclusively established that smoking leads to lung, mouth, bladder, kidney, and stomach cancer, as well as to emphysema and strokes. The major potentially lethal condition associated with heavy drinking is cirrhosis of the liver, but the heart, stomach, and even the brain may be affected. If you wondered whether the suggestion that you *add* two years to your projected life span if you are a moderate drinker was a misprint, it is not. There is evidence (St. Leger et al., 1979) that adults who drink moderate amounts of wine are somewhat less likely to suffer heart attacks than teetotalers and significantly less likely to suffer such attacks than heavy drinkers. One explanation for this finding is that moderate amounts of alcohol increase the amount of high density lipoprotein (HDL) in the blood, and, as noted in the preceding chapter, HDL prevents clogged arteries. Another explanation is that moderate amounts of alcohol lead to relaxation of tension and induce sleep. Thus, an abstainer with tendencies toward Type A behavior may never be able to relax. A Type A person who has a glass of wine in the evening, on the other hand, may at least partially ease tension and perhaps sleep more restfully. Alcohol tends to increase appetite, though, so the wine drinker may need to resist the temptation to have a second helping in order to avoid putting on weight and increasing the likelihood of health problems due to obesity.

Exercise may add years to a person's life for the variety of reasons noted in the preceding chapter: reduction of stress, increase in heart and lung capacity, reduction of ratio of body fat to body weight, development of a sense of well-being.

Decline in Physiological Functioning

Even if you do your best to slow down the process of aging by watching your diet and exercising regularly, you will not be able to avoid certain changes.

Loss of Sensory Acuity

The process of slow decline in acuity of the sense organs that begins in the twenties accelerates with age. At forty a person may need to start to

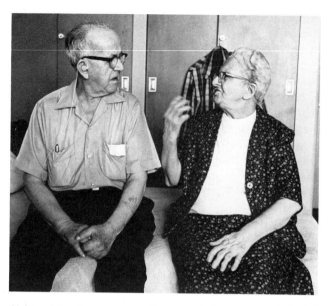

Sight and hearing are among the more obvious aspects of physiological functioning that decline as we grow older. In many cases, however, the decline can be offset by corrective devices.
© *Sepp Seitz/Woodfin Camp.*

wear bifocals, in the seventies the lens of one or both eyes may cloud over, forming a cataract. Just as corrective glasses can counteract the earlier problem, surgery, together with corrective lenses inserted in the eye or worn as contact lenses of regular glasses, can often restore vision.

Hearing losses increase quite sharply after the age of sixty, particularly for high frequency sounds. About 19 percent of adults in the forty-five to fifty-five age group experience some hearing loss. About 75 percent of those in the seventy-five to eighty range experience hearing difficulties (Corso, 1977), but hearing aids often bring about improvement.

Sensitivities to taste and smell decrease gradually, with the ability to sense sweet and salty flavors declining before awareness of sour and bitter flavors.

Memory Problems

While loss of sensory acuity can be a bothersome byproduct of aging, problems with memory often are more irritating and sometimes potentially harmful. If you have had any contact with older individuals, you know that many of them experience memory lapses of various kinds. They may be unable to remember names of people or objects. They may tell an anecdote at the beginning of a meal and then repeat it verbatim when dessert is served. All of us have such memory lapses occasionally (a psychoanalyst might offer to explain some of them on the basis of repression), but as we grow older, such lapses become more frequent. If memory problems become so severe that they limit the older person's ability to function satisfactorily in everyday situations, they may be signs of dementia (which will be discussed a bit later).

In an effort to determine precisely how much memory declines in old age, many psychologists have carried out experiments of various kinds. Unfortunately, the same kinds of problems (described in the preceding chapter) faced by those who attempt to study the "decline" of intelligence with age confront memory researchers. Cross-sectional studies, for example, may yield untrustworthy data because younger Americans are better educated than older ones. Younger subjects also are used to taking exams and often have had previous experience as subjects in psychological experiments. Older subjects may be unfamiliar with test situations and either anxious or unmotivated when asked to perform under experimental conditions. As a consequence of the many methodological complications inherent in memory research, there is little unanimity of opinion about conclusions. Even so, a few trends are worth noting.

There is fairly wide agreement that most older people show little deficit in the first two stages of the information processing system described in Chapter 2. They do quite well in processing sensory impressions and in handling short-term memory (Craik, 1977). Most memory problems that are experienced by older people seem to involve long-term memory, but researchers are not yet sure about the extent to which such problems are due to faulty encoding, storage, or retrieval. It is often difficult or impossible to make a distinction between these processes, and the results of different studies are sometimes contradictory (Poon et al., 1980). Perhaps the simplest way to summarize findings on memory research with older subjects is to say that they need ample time to learn new material and that they may also benefit from instruction on how to use memory aids. In the course of your education, for example, you have probably been introduced to (or "picked up") various **mnemonic devices** (memory aids). You may be aware of the values of **chunking,** for instance, which involves grouping unrelated bits of information. When you look up a telephone number, for instance, you may reduce the four numbers after the prefix to a single number by converting 1–9–4–2 into the date nineteen-forty-two. Older people are less likely to know about these techniques, but they are able to improve their memories when they are told about them.

Most memory problems of elderly involve long-term memory

Intellectual Functioning

The question of how much intelligence declines with age was discussed at some length in the preceding chapter. As noted in that discussion, there has been quite a bit of controversy about methods and the meaning of results, but the general conclusion seems to be that the decline of intelligence is slight and gradual. Evidence that intelligence does not necessarily or inevitably deteriorate is provided by the accomplishments of famous men and women of past and present who produced outstanding works of literature, music, art, and architecture in their eighties and nineties. For example, Goethe completed *Faust* when he was eighty-two, Richard Strauss composed his hauntingly beautiful "Four Last Songs" a few months before his death at eighty-five, Michelangelo supervised the construction of St. Peter's when he was in his nineties, and Grandma Moses was still painting at a hundred. While some older individuals are capable of functioning at an incredibly high intellectual level in old age, even they tend to work at a slower pace. The slow pace of all activities, including intellectual activities, has been proposed as perhaps the most distinctive characteristic of old age.

Behavioral Slowing with Age

Psychologists who have specialized in the study of aging (e.g., Birren and Schaie, 1977) have decried the lack of a theoretical perspective. The only developmental theory discussed in Chapter 2 that includes any mention of behavior beyond young adulthood is Erikson's outline of psychosocial stages. While Erikson's stage of integrity versus despair is insightful, it is also very limited. **General behavioral slowing with age** has been suggested by James Birren, Anita Woods, and M. V. Williams (1980) as a basic frame of reference of wider utility. Birren and his associates note:

Behavioral slowing: most significant general change as we grow older

Perhaps the most ubiquitous and significant change observed in the older organism is slowness of behavior. Slowness is not limited to motor responses or to peripheral sensory phenomena . . . it appears to be even more evident the more complex the behavior observed and the higher the mediating neural structures in the nervous system. (1980, p. 293)

The most obvious manifestations of slowness of behavior with age are physical signs such as speed of walking and speech. A less apparent but potentially more harmful aspect of physical slowing down involves **reaction time.** An older driver, for example, is likely to move his or her foot from the accelerator to the brake at a slower rate than a younger driver when confronted by an unexpected obstacle. The same slower rate of response is also found in verbal processes, which in turn are mediated by cognitive functioning. Older individuals tend to move through the various "boxes" of the information processing model depicted in Chapter 2 at a slower rate than younger ones. The decline in perceptual sensitivity reduces the effectiveness of processing stimuli in the sensory register. While the capacity of short-term memory may not decline with age (Craik, 1977), the speed at which information held in short-term memory can be processed (or scanned) does slow with age. In addition, both storage and retrieval processes for long-term memory appear to be influenced by behavioral speed (Birren et al., 1980).

General behavioral slowing with age is significantly influenced by changes in the central nervous system but may also be affected by certain diseases, behavior disorders, and environmental factors. Individuals with cardiovascular disorders, for example, often react at a slower rate than others of the same age, as do individuals suffering from schizophrenia and depression. Older individuals who exercise regularly, on the other hand, have faster reaction times than those who do not (Botwinick, 1978), and often have superior cognitive functioning. Exercise increases the amount of oxygen in the blood, the amount of blood flow to the brain, and may even have an impact on neural tissue.

Implications of Slowing with Age

A number of hypotheses have been offered to account for slowing with age (Birren et al., 1980). One explanation is physiological—the nerves and muscles of the body function less effectively as a person grows older. Another hypothesis is that older people are wiser and therefore more cautious. Instead of acting impulsively in trial and error fashion, as younger people are inclined to do, they prefer to reason out actions ahead of time. Having made so many mistakes earlier in their lives, they may be eager to avoid making more mistakes. A related explanation is that cautiousness about reacting impulsively in situations where there is a risk of error generalizes into a habit centering on cautiousness. Thus, an older person in a supermarket may block the aisle and infuriate younger shoppers while deliberating about which brand of salad dressing to put in the basket.

Speculating about causes of slowing with age leads to consideration of more general theories of aging.

Slower behavior due to physiological decline, desire to avoid mistakes, cautiousness

Theories of Aging

Scientists seek causes, and several psychologists have speculated about factors that lead to the process of aging.

Hypotheses Based on Genetic Factors

One hypothesis about aging is that we are genetically programmed at the time of conception to reach a point of deterioration at a certain age. The cells of the body have been found to be capable of reproducing themselves just so many times (Hayflick, 1979), and when cells that

Some theorists suggest that slowing of behavior is the most ubiquitous and significant general change as we grow older. One explanation for this change is a tendency for older people to be cautious—even about such everyday decisions as which brand to buy in the supermarket.
© *Gabor Demjen/Stock, Boston.*

Each individual genetically programmed to reach a point of deterioration

control bodily functions reach the point of nonreproduction due to faulty biochemical processes, death will occur. Some lucky individuals will receive a more favorable set of cells and genetic instructions that lead to a longer period of cell reproduction than others. That is one reason why the estimate of personal longevity you were asked to make earlier may not be accurate. You cannot know for sure whether you have been ''programmed'' to live to be seventy or one hundred. The concept that cells have a limited reproduction cycle helps explain a point emphasized by Hayflick (1979), who notes that the life span of humans, which is somewhere between ninety-five and one hundred ten years, has remained unchanged over the last 100,000 years, while life expectancy has increased substantially. Hayflick estimates that two thousand years ago life expectancy was about twenty-two years. In the late 1600s, it was about thirty-three years. As noted earlier, the life expectancy of the

Death is the end result of the causes just listed, but before death occurs, certain conditions—particularly **dementia**—are likely to develop.

The Nature and Impact of Dementia

Dementia is defined by the American Psychiatric Association (1980) as intellectual deterioration of sufficient severity to interfere with social or occupational functioning due to organic brain causes. It is estimated (Butler and Lewis, 1982) that one person in ten over sixty suffers from dementia, which typically progresses through three phases. The first sign of dementia is forgetfulness. Older persons may begin to experience difficulty remembering recent events or actions such as having gone shopping or putting a cake in the oven. In the second phase, the forgetfulness becomes worse and abstract reasoning may also deteriorate. When faced with a decision that must be made by weighing options, such people may find the task impossible. Furthermore, problems in communication may develop because of inability to consider the other person's point of view. The final phase involves almost total disorientation. Those who reach this stage may be unable to tell who or where they are or even supply their own name. Many individuals who reach the final phase may need nursing care, and it has been estimated (Blazer, 1980) that 70 percent of patients in long-term care facilities suffer from dementia. In most cases (as indicated by the definition just noted) dementia is attributed to organic brain changes. Indications (other than forgetfulness and disorientation) that organic brain changes have occurred include dizziness, headaches, decreased physical and mental vigor, and a variety of physical complaints (Butler and Lewis, 1982). Types of dementia are determined by causes, some of which can be determined only by examination of the brain during autopsy.

Dementia: intellectual deterioration due to organic brain causes

Alzheimer's Disease

A specific form of dementia that has attracted a great deal of attention during the last few years is Alzheimer's disease. It is estimated that as many as 1.2 million Americans suffer from this condition, and that many more experience the disease before death (Katzman, 1976). It is a leading cause of death due to disease, but, until recently, was not reported as such on death certificates (Katzman and Karasu, 1975). The symptoms of Alzheimer's disease are similar to those just described but the onset of the condition has been traced to destruction of brain tissue because of abnormal cellular formations called *plaques* and *tangles* that interfere with normal functioning of the brain. Hypotheses about the cause of Alz-

Alzheimer's disease: destruction of brain tissue because of abnormal cellular formations

heimer's disease include the following: genetic predisposition, errors in DNA duplication, a virus contracted early in life that has remained dormant, exposure to toxic agents (particularly aluminum), insufficient amounts of certain enzymes, a combination of some or all of these. Whatever the cause, more women than men suffer from Alzheimer's disease.

The condition has become so common that **Alzheimer's Disease Support Groups** have been formed in many communities: individuals whose relatives suffer from the condition meet to share techniques of care and provide psychological support for each other. There is optimism that the disease may be alleviated by drugs that influence *neurotransmitters*—substances that are important in the formation of synapses between brain cells that lead to learning and memory. An enzyme called *choline acetyltransferase* (C.A.T.) may be in short supply or lacking in individuals who suffer from Alzheimer's disease. Administration of drugs that favor the formation of neurotransmitters has provided at least temporary improvement (Davis and Mohs, 1982), and may be effective on a long-term basis.

Multi-infarct Dementia

A condition related to (and sometimes associated with) Alzheimer's disease is **multi-infarct dementia** (MID), so-called because an *infarct* (obstruction) of blood vessels leads to destruction of brain tissue. Persons with Alzheimer's disease tend to move through the stages of dementia in progessive steps. The pattern in MID is uneven. A person with MID may display sudden forgetfulness and disorientation when an infarct leads to destruction of brain tissue in one part of the brain. Quite often, though, other parts of the brain take over the function of the destroyed area, and the victim will appear to bounce back, only to suffer another decline when another infarct occurs. Eventually, after multiple blockages have occurred, the brain can no longer compensate. Older people who have cardiovascular problems and diabetes are prone to MID. The likelihood that brain damage will occur can be reduced by exercise and control of hypertension and diabetes by drugs.

Reactions to Awareness of Impending Death

Because of ageism and gerontophobia, there has been considerable resistance to study or speculations about death. The work of Elisabeth Kubler-Ross (1969) has led to greater awareness of the attitudes and experiences of individuals who are in the process of dying. On the basis of interviews with hospital patients who were close to death, Kubler-

Elisabeth Kubler-Ross interviewed elderly patients in hospitals and found that awareness of impending death often followed a pattern that involved these stages: denial, anger, depression, acceptance.
© *Martine Franck/Magnum Photos.*

Ross concluded that many individuals go through five emotional stages when they become aware of impending death:

Denial: The diagnosis of a doctor may be dismissed as inaccurate, a symptom may be perceived as lessening in intensity, or miracle cures may be desperately sought.

Anger: Impending death may be accepted as a fact but reacted to with anger, sometimes directed against "fate," sometimes directed against relatives or medical personnel.

Bargaining: The person may try to bargain with God or fate, expressing a desire for death to be postponed.

Depression: Fatalistic resignation is experienced, accompanied by feelings of sadness, self-pity, and depression.

Acceptance: Death is understood as the culminating stage of life and accepted in an essentially emotionless way.

Awareness of impending death often involves denial, anger, bargaining, depression, acceptance

Publication of the original conclusions of Kubler-Ross led other investigators (e.g., Schulz and Alderman, 1974) to conduct similar studies, and their reports, together with follow-up reports by Kubler-Ross her-self (1975), have led to revisions of the original description of stages. It now seems clear that not all dying patients go through all the stages in the order originally described. Depression is the most common reaction, bargaining the least common. Furthermore, some patients seem to ex-hibit aspects of two or three stages at a time.

The pioneering research of Kubler-Ross has led to the establishment of seminars for doctors and hospital personnel, as well as death-education programs for students and adults of all age levels. One reason for seminars for hospital personnel is that Kubler-Ross found that many doctors were at a loss as to the most effective ways to tell their terminally ill patients about their condition or to interact with them in satisfying ways as death became imminent.

A significant part of the physician-patient relationship as death nears centers on the patient's **right to know.** A related problem that has emerged as life support systems have become standard equipment in most hospitals centers on a patient's **right to die.** There have been a number of well-publicized cases where parents or spouses have felt compelled to go to court in efforts to obtain permission to have a life support system removed from a patient with no hope of recovery. In order to give individuals an opportunity to perhaps have some control over their own death, an organization called Concern for Dying has developed a *Living Will* (Figure 23.1). As you can see, it makes it possible for individuals to make decisions while they are healthy that they might not be in a condition to make when they are close to death.

Bereavement

The statistics on life expectancy given earlier reveal that whereas most of us will be alive when our parents die, wives will outlive their husbands by an average of about seven years (assuming they stay married and are the same age). Death of one's spouse is at the top of the Social Readjust-ment Scale, indicating the magnitude of the adjustment required. Just as Elisabeth Kubler-Ross paved the way for sympathetic study of the feel-ings of dying individuals, E. Lindemann (1944) carried out a pioneering investigation of the bereavement of individuals who were forced to ad-just to the death of someone they loved. Lindemann, a psychiatrist, was curious about whether there was a normal pattern of mourning. He felt that discovering what was normal was a necessary first step to being able to determine when bereavement became abnormal. Accordingly, he observed and interviewed a large number of recent widows. (Al-though Lindemann's conclusions, and most of the other conclusions to be summarized in this section, are based on interviews with widows,

To My Family, My Physician, My Lawyer and All Others Whom It May Concern

Death is as much a reality as birth, growth, maturity and old age—it is the one certainty of life. If the time comes when I can no longer take part in decisions for my own future, let this statement stand as an expression of my wishes and directions, while I am still of sound mind.

If at such a time the situation should arise in which there is no reasonable expectation of my recovery from extreme physical or mental disability, I direct that I be allowed to die and not be kept alive by medications, artificial means or "heroic measures". I do, however, ask that medication be mercifully administered to me to alleviate suffering even though this may shorten my remaining life.

This statement is made after careful consideration and is in accordance with my strong convictions and beliefs. I want the wishes and directions here expressed carried out to the extent permitted by law. Insofar as they are not legally enforceable, I hope that those to whom this Will is addressed will regard themselves as morally bound by these provisions.

Signed_____

Date _____

Witness_____

Witness_____

Copies of this request have been given to _____

_____

_____

_____

By permission of Concern for Dying.

FIGURE 23.1
A living will

679

they also apply to husbands, children, and others who must adjust to the death of someone they knew intimately.) He discovered that common indications of grief—such as crying, disturbed sleep, and loss of appetite—were often accompanied by some unexpected psychological reactions. Many of his subjects felt guilty that they had not done enough for their husbands, for instance, and sometimes became so preoccupied with the image of the deceased person that they almost experienced hallucinations that he was present. In addition, there was a tendency to feel distant from or angered by others, including close friends and relatives.

Bereavement: grief, guilt, preoccupation with deceased, anger against others

Later observations by other researchers (e.g., Parkes, 1972) corroborated Lindemann's conclusions and also revealed that another common aspect of bereavement was preoccupation with the events surrounding the death of the husband. Furthermore, in many cases the following bereavement sequence was typical:

An initial phase of numbness, shock, and emptiness lasting for a few weeks.

An intermediate phase consisting of periods of intense yearning alternating with periods of depression, lasting for about a year after death occurred. It is during this phase that the tendency for the widow to search for or hallucinate about her husband is most likely to occur.

A recovery phase, beginning around the second year, when periods of grief are most likely to be triggered by reminders of the husband.

The nature, duration, and intensity of each of these phases depends on factors such as personality traits and the circumstances surrounding the husband's death. Some women (whom Block might classify as ego-brittle) have an extraordinarily difficult time adjusting to the loss of the husband. In addition, the shock and magnitude of adjustment appear to be greatest when death occurs unexpectedly at an early age.

Grief work: advantages of expressing grief freely and openly

It appears that there are advantages to expressing initial grief freely and openly. (Lindemann called such behavior **grief work**.) Widows who made an effort to control or repress their grief seemed to show emotional disturbance for a longer time after the death of their husbands than those who expressed their grief more openly (Parkes, 1972).

Many texts on development through the life span end with discussions of death and bereavement. It seems more logical, however, to continue with consideration of the behavior of those who survive the deceased. Because the wife is much more likely to survive than the husband, the following discussion once again focuses on widowhood.

Adjusting to Widowhood

The last three developmental tasks for later maturity are establishing an affiliation with one's age group, meeting social and civic responsibilities, and establishing satisfactory living arrangements. The last of these is the most essential from a practical point of view, but it often turns out that widows also do an effective job of achieving tasks involving affiliation and social obligations.

Independent Living

According to the latest U. S. Census figures, 52.8 percent of all females over the age of sixty-five live alone (compared to 21.8 of males over sixty-five). Most older women seem to prefer it that way since widows interviewed in two comprehensive studies (Lopata, 1973, 1979) indicated that they took pride in being independent. Many widows reported that they did not wish to live with children for fear it would cause friction. Most of them stated that they did not wish to remarry for a variety of reasons: age, a desire to avoid repeating experiences associated with illness and death of a husband, the conviction that they would not be able to find another man as good as their first husband. (The researchers who conducted the interviews concluded that there was often a tendency for widows to romanticize their lives with their husbands and to concentrate on positive qualities while overlooking negative ones.)

Many widows take pride in being independent

The desire to be independent was often so strong that relationships with children and siblings were limited and sometimes impersonal. The pattern of friendships established by widows was often a function of education and social class. Many recently widowed women found that friendships involving couples were difficult to maintain, at least in the same ways as when the husband was alive. Shortly after the death of their husbands, for instance, many women tend to be invited to socialize with friends who had been in the habit of engaging in activities as couples. Quite often, such interactions may be dismaying or unsatisfying because the widow is reminded of the absence of her husband, partly because an odd number added to a couple may be awkward. Accordingly, many widows prefer to form new friendships.

Better-educated women seem to have greater success revising old friendships and forming new ones. Poorly educated, lower-income widows are most likely to feel socially isolated and dissatisfied with their lives. It has been hypothesized (Lopata, 1979) that such women were the victims of socializing influences that stressed dependence on the husband and conformity to the traditional feminine role of housewife and

After adjusting to the loss of their husbands, many widows take pride in demonstrating their independence by engaging in venturesome activities.
© *Sybil Shelton/Peter Arnold, Inc.*

mother. When their children left home and their husbands died, such women felt poorly equipped to make adjustments.

Even well-educated widows who make an excellent adjustment after the death of their husbands seem to lead lonely lives, however. Four out of ten reported that they never entertained and that they always ate lunch alone. Half said they never went to public places such as restaurants. Community programs specifically planned for widows seem to be scarce, but a trend toward adult education may provide opportunities for widows and other older Americans to make new friends as well as develop new interests. According to the latest U. S. Census figures, one out of every twenty adults over sixty-five is enrolled in a class of some kind.

Social and Civic Obligations

Many widows (and older couples) engage in a variety of social service activities. Lists of organizations and meetings in newspapers reveal the nature and extent of such activities: church groups and events, interest groups of various kinds, senior citizen organizations. In addition, there is an increasing tendency for older Americans to be active politically, particularly when reports from Washington indicate that changes in the Social Security system are being considered. At the age of sixty-seven, Maggie Kuhn founded a group imaginatively dubbed the *Gray Panthers* that has generated a considerable amount of political clout.

The fact that so many widows and other older Americans manifest a desire to be independent calls attention to an interesting parallel with the behavior of two-year-olds. As soon as they learn to walk and talk and become capable of doing things on their own, young children strive to assert their independence. The very same tendency seems to be reasserted at the other end of the span of life, which is a quite reassuring point to think about at the end of a book on human development.

Summary

1. The final psychosocial stage described by Erikson stresses **integrity:** satisfied acceptance of one's life as one's own responsibility. Older individuals who look back on their lives with disappointment experience a sense of despair.
2. Because of an increase in life expectancy due to improved nutrition and medical care, a distinction is sometimes made between the **young-old** and the **old-old.** While some aspects of life expectancy are due to genetic factors, there are many things a person can do to prevent premature death. Some individuals, for instance, exhibit **Type A** behavior, which is characterized by constant drive, competitiveness, hostility, and tension. Such individuals may reduce the possibility of having a stroke shorten their lives by seeking ways to reduce stress.
3. Physiological and cognitive processes gradually decline in efficiency as we age. Older individuals, for example, may experience losses in long-term memory. Perhaps the most distinctive change with age, though, is general behavioral slowness. Slower behavior may be due to physiological decline, to a desire to avoid mistakes, and to cautiousness.
4. Each individual appears to be genetically programmed to reach a point of deterioration. Studies of individuals who have much longer than average life spans reveal that they exercise regularly, have low-calorie diets, and keep constructively busy. One explanation for obvious signs of aging that precede death attributes them to alterations in DNA that lead to **error catastrophe** in cells. Another explanation

emphasizes loss of efficiency of the glandular system, which reduces immunities.

5. Reactions to retirement vary considerably and often reflect how a person has responded to previous life events. Retirement appears to be least satisfactory for those who are disappointed with their lives and are bitter about lost opportunities. While most men seem to follow retirement patterns that reflect earlier behavior, women may adopt dramatically different life styles in later years.

6. **Ageism,** or prejudice against older people, may be due in large part to reluctance to think about death. Such prejudice is likely to be strengthened by observation of conditions such as **dementia:** intellectual deterioration due to organic brain causes. A form of dementia that has come to public attention in recent years is **Alzheimer's disease,** a condition caused by deterioration of brain tissue because of abnormal cellular formations. Regardless of the cause, as death approaches, many individuals go through a series of emotional stages in this sequence: denial, anger, depression, and acceptance.

7. After the loss of a loved one, bereavement typically begins with intense grief, which may be followed by feelings of guilt about not having done enough, preoccupation with thoughts of the deceased person, and anger directed against others. There is evidence that **grief work,** or the expression of grief freely and openly, is advantageous. After an initial period of bereavement, many widows take great pride in functioning as independent individuals.

Suggestions for Further Study

General Books on Later Maturity

The following books discuss aspects of growing old in a manner appropriate for a general audience: *Why Survive?: Growing Old in America* (1975) by Robert Butler, *A Good Age* (1978) by Alex Comfort, and *Prime of Your Life: A Practical Guide to Your Mature Years* (1983) by Joseph Michaels.

Scholarly Books on Later Maturity

The following books summarize research on aging: *Handbook of the Psychology of Aging* (1977) edited by J. E. Birren and W. K. Schaie, *The Psychology of Aging* (1984) by Janet Belsky, and *Aging and Behavior* (3rd ed., 1984) by Jack Botwinick.

Death and Bereavement

The following books discuss aspects of death and bereavement: *On Death and Dying* (1969) by Elisabeth Kubler-Ross; *Death and the Family: The Importance of Mourning* (1976) by Lily Pincus; *Women as Widows: Support Systems* (1979) by Helen Lopata; and *Widow* (1975) by Lynn Caine.

Obtaining an Oral History from an Older Person

If you have the opportunity to talk with one or more older persons, you might ask them to provide an oral history of aspects of their lives that they want to describe. Using a tape recorder, ask them to describe how they felt about their first job and subsequent jobs, their marriage, having children, and retirement, how they feel at the present time, and any other topics you or they select to reminisce about.

GLOSSARY

Accommodation Piaget's term for the modification of existing concepts or ways of thinking in order to encompass new information.

Adaptation Piaget's term for the innate tendency of human beings to adjust to the environment by enlarging or modifying existing concepts or ways of thinking. The other innate tendency is *organization*.

Adaptation level As a result of repeated social interaction, persons develop mutual expectations for one another's behavior. Behaviors that fall within this predicted range are less likely to be attended to than behaviors that fall outside this range or adaptation level.

Adolescent egocentrism Heightened self-consciousness that results from the tendency of adolescents to turn their new powers of formal thought inward and become preoccupied with how they appear to others.

Aerobic exercise Exercises designed to improve health by pushing the cardiovascular system to near peak levels of performance.

Ageism Prejudice against the elderly.

Allele Information found at a particular location of a hereditary unit in a chromosome.

Alzheimer's Disease A cognitive disorder, affecting primarily the elderly, that results from the destruction of brain tissue due to abnormal cellular formation.

Amniocentesis A medical procedure for extracting and analyzing amniotic fluid to detect possible abnormalities in the unborn child.

Amnion A fluid-filled sac that serves to protect and cushion the developing organism throughout the prenatal period.

Anaclitic identification Freud's term for the tendency of children up to the age of three or four to attach libidinal energy to the primary caretaker (usually the mother) and to pattern their behavior after that person.

Anal stage   Freud's second stage of psychosexual development, occurring typically between two and four years. During this period the child focuses on gaining control of bodily functions, as in toilet training.

Androgyny   A sex-role orientation in which a person feels comfortable engaging in both sex-typed masculine and sex-typed feminine behaviors and is, therefore, able to adapt his or her behavior to the particular demands of the situation.

Anorexia nervosa   An eating disorder in which the person, most often an adolescent female, severely restricts caloric intake, sometimes to the point of starvation.

Anoxia   A shortage of oxygen in the fetus that can occur during the final stage of labor and may result in brain damage and some form of cerebral palsy.

Anticipatory control   The ability to control one's own behavior by imagining what might happen under given circumstances and then choosing between different situations and experiences.

Apgar score   An overall measure of a neonate's physical functioning. A newborn baby's appearance, pulse, grimace, activity, and respiration are individually rated on a scale from 0 to 2, and the ratings are combined to form the *Apgar score*.

Assimilation   Piaget's term for the process of incorporating new information to fit existing categories or ways of thinking.

Associative play   An unorganized form of social play in which children interact with each other but have no mutual goals or designated roles.

Attachment   The emotional bond that develops between an infant and caretaker. When caregiving is sensitive and consistent, this bond enables the infant to use the caregiver as a secure base from which to explore the world.

Authoritarian parenting   A style of parenting in which parents set absolute standards that are enforced with punitive techniques. Such parents often lack warmth and are unresponsive, seldom taking their children's wishes into account.

Authoritative parenting   A style of parenting in which parents establish firm control but give reasons for restrictions. These parents are willing to listen to their children's points of view and to make compromises.

Autism   A form of childhood psychosis whose chief symptom is a lack of social responsiveness.

Autonomy vs. doubt   Erikson's second stage of psychosocial development, occurring at around two to three years of age. The goal during this period is to develop a sense of competence in manipulating the environment. Too much protection or too little support may lead to a sense of doubt.

Baby biography   A detailed record of a single infant's behavior and development, such as the one Charles Darwin wrote to chart the development of his firstborn son.

Base-line experiment   A strategy for assessing change due to experimental treatment that involves comparing subjects' behavior before and after exposure to the experimental treatment.

Behaviorism   A school of psychology advocating that the study of human behavior and development should focus on observable behaviors as opposed to conscious or unconscious processes.

Behavior modification   The systematic application of behavioral principles, such as contingent reinforcement, for the purpose of increasing or decreasing the frequency of specific behaviors.

Bereavement The period of mourning following the death of a loved one. It is characterized by indications of grief such as disturbed sleep, loss of appetite, depression, anger, guilt, and a preoccupation with the deceased.

Brazelton Neonatal Behavioral Assessment Scale A technique for evaluating infants on factors such as neurological intactness, interactive capacities, social attractiveness, and need for stimulation.

Bulimia An eating disorder characterized by eating binges followed by self-induced vomiting. It occurs most frequently in females.

Centration In Piaget's theory, the tendency of a young child to focus perceptual attention on one aspect of an object or situation at a time.

Cephalocaudal growth A developmental pattern characterized by the acquisition of physical and motor control beginning first with the head region and progressing gradually toward the lower extremities of the body.

Chromosomes Threadlike particles that are contained in the cell nucleus and each contains up to twenty thousand genes.

Chunking A strategy for enlarging memory capacity that involves encoding isolated bits of information in larger units. For example, a nine-digit Social Security number typically is stored as three consecutive units of three, two, and four digits.

Classical conditioning A form of learning in which a neutral stimulus acquires the capacity to evoke a response after having been paired repeatedly with another stimulus that already evokes the response (also called *Pavlovian conditioning*).

Classification In Piaget's theory, the concrete operational ability to group objects into distinct categories on the basis of shared characteristics. For example, shirts, pants, and dresses are all articles of clothing.

Clinical interview Technique developed by Piaget in which questions may vary from one subject to another because each subject's initial responses determine later questions. This method is more flexible than the questionnaire or standardized interview, but it is also more subjective.

Coefficient of correlation A numerical index ranging from $+1$ to -1 that measures the strength and direction of the relationship between two variables. The relationship is positive if both variables increase or decrease simultaneously; it is negative if one variable increases as the other decreases.

Cognitive map A mental representation that influences behavior. An example is the cognitive map of sex roles that typically develops in the three- to four-year-old child and facilitates the rapid acquisition of sex-typed behavior.

Cohort A group of persons who, by virtue of having been born at approximately the same time, have been influenced by a set of cultural, social, economic, and political factors that may be quite different from those factors influencing persons born somewhat earlier or later.

Collective monologue Piaget's term for the discourse that occurs between two or more young children who, although appearing to have a conversation, are not actually responding to the content of each other's speech.

Concrete operations   In Piaget's theory, the stage of cognitive development that begins between the ages of five and seven and is characterized by a logical, organized pattern of cognitive skills that can be used to solve problems involving concrete objects and experiences. These skills include classification, seriation, decentration, and reversibility of thought.

Conscious level   In Freud's theory, the level of consciousness that consists of all mental processes that a person is aware of at a given moment.

Conservation   In Piaget's theory, the recognition that certain properties of objects (such as their number, weight, or volume) remain unchanged despite transformations in the objects' superficial appearance.

Conventional morality   The second of Kohlberg's levels of moral reasoning; a moral orientation in which decisions about right and wrong are based primarily on the standards of others, either on the standards of those persons with whom one has close interpersonal relations or on societal standards that are typically embodied in a system of laws.

Cooperative play   An organized form of social play in which children share a common goal and assume separate but complementary roles.

Coordinated scheme   In Piaget's theory, the deliberate combining of separate skills learned in interacting with the environment for the purpose of achieving a specific goal.

Critical period   A short period of time, early in development, during which certain traits or tendencies are thought to be influenced by experiences (such as imprinting in goslings).

Cross-sectional approach   A research method in which the same behaviors are studied in children of different ages at one point in time.

Crystallized intelligence   Knowledge gained largely from social experience, especially in school. Examples include vocabulary and reading comprehension.

Death phobia   A preoccupation with death that typically occurs at around eight years of age, when children first understand the irreversibility of death and fear their own death or the death of their parents.

Decentration   In Piaget's theory, the concrete operational ability to focus simultaneously on more than one aspect of a stimulus event (for example, the height and width of two beakers containing water).

Defense mechanisms   In Freud's theory, unconscious mechanisms used by the ego to screen, block, or deflect impulses from the id that the ego deems inappropriate. Examples of such mechanisms include repression, projection, displacement, and regression.

Defensive identification   In Freud's theory, the tendency for children of approximately four years to recognize sex differences and begin to identify with the parent of the same sex.

Dementia   Intellectual deterioration that results from organic causes.

Deoxyribonucleic acid (DNA)   Complex chemical molecules that make up the genes; their structure is in the form of a double helix.

Developmental task   Culturally defined tasks that are expected to be accomplished by all persons at a particular age level. Examples include toilet training, talking, and reading.

Discrimination   In learning theory, the ability to distinguish and respond differently to two or more stimuli that are similar but distinct.

Displacement   In Freud's theory, a defense mechanism used by the ego to divert hostility from its source onto others. For example, a boy who is angry at an older and more powerful neighbor boy may take out this anger on his own younger sister.

Divergent thinker   Guilford's term for a person who tends to think by connecting different ideas and often finds novel and unexpected solutions to problems.

Dizygotic (DZ)   Fraternal twins who originate from separate eggs fertilized by separate sperm. Such twins are no more similar than two siblings born at different times.

Dominant gene   A gene that expresses its trait in the phenotype regardless of whether it is paired with like or unlike genes.

Down's syndrome   A common form of mental retardation caused by chromosomal abnormalities.

Ego   In Freud's theory, the largely conscious part of the mind that mediates between the superego and the largely unconscious impulses emanating from the id. The ego is governed by the reality principle, which involves a rational analysis and coordination of internal and external forces.

Egocentrism   In Piaget's theory, a lack of differentiation between some aspect of self-other relations. During the preoperational stage, egocentrism is exemplified by the young child's inability to understand the points of view of others or to coordinate their views with his or her own.

Embryo   The name given to the prenatal organism during the period from two to eight weeks after conception, when the major organ systems and structures of the body are being formed.

Emotional desensitization   A decrease in behavioral and physiological responsiveness resulting from repeated exposure to an affect-laden stimulus such as aggression.

Epigenetic model   A model of development that follows the principle that anything that grows has a ground plan causing the various parts to arise at different stages of development and eventually form a functioning whole.

Epistemology   A branch of philosophy concerned with the study of knowledge and how it is acquired. Piaget's lifelong study of cognitive development reflects his basic interest in genetic epistemology.

Equilibration   In Piaget's theory, a form of self-regulation that occurs through the complementary processes of assimilation and accommodation. It is used to restore balance and stability to conflicting perceptions and experiences and is the underlying mechanism responsible for cognitive development.

Equity theory   A variation on social exchange theory that suggests that from an intimate relationship a person wants not only reinforcement but also a partner who possesses an assortment of traits equivalent in value to one's own.

Error catastrophe   Alterations in DNA due to the aging process which lead to garbled instructions and accumulated imperfections in reproduced cells.

Existential guilt   Feelings of guilt that occur when persons who have done nothing wrong still feel culpable because of circumstances beyond their control. Such guilt is believed to prompt many children from wealthy families to join the Peace Corps or to engage in altruistic activities.

Extinction   In theories of learning, the gradual elimination of a conditioned response as a result of withdrawal of reinforcement.

Fear of success   An emotional conflict felt by persons who perceive that their success puts them in a position to lose something of value. For example, a woman may believe that her occupational success will damage her relationship with her spouse by engendering feelings of jealousy and competition.

Fetus   The name given to the prenatal organism from about eight weeks after conception until birth.

Field dependence   A cognitive style in which the person interprets situations in terms of the immediate environment and finds it difficult to ignore misleading perceptual cues.

Field independence   A cognitive style in which the person interprets situations by maintaining an accurate spatial orientation and is able to ignore misleading perceptual cues.

Fluid intelligence   Cognitive abilities that make learning rapid and efficient and contribute to skill in solving unique problems.

Formal operational thought   Piaget's fourth and final stage of cognitive development. Characterized by abstract and hypothetical thought, for some persons this stage may begin in early adolescence but for many persons it may never be reached at all.

Free association   A therapeutic technique developed by Freud that involves encouraging clients to talk about whatever thoughts pop into their heads, thereby reducing the chances that thoughts that are unpleasant or undesirable, but important, could be screened out by the ego's defenses.

Functional assimilation   In Piaget's theory, the inherited tendency for persons to use and repeat activities they have become capable of performing.

Functional lateralization   The localization of different functions in the two hemispheres of the cerebral cortex. It is believed, for example, that for most persons language abilities are localized in the left hemisphere, whereas spatial abilities are localized in the right hemisphere.

Gene   The hereditary unit that is a segment of a chromosome; also, the information contained in one particular copy of that unit.

Generation gap   A gap in understanding between generations that is thought to occur because of different life experiences and life tasks.

Generativity vs. stagnation   The seventh of Erikson's psychosocial stages. Generativity results when a person, by functioning as a mentor or raising a family, is able to guide the next generation through creative activity. Failure to achieve this developmental task leads to a sense of stagnation.

Genetic counseling   Advice given to couples contemplating parenthood that is based on estimates of the likelihood that persons with their particular genetic make-ups will produce offspring with genetic defects.

Genital stage   The last of Freud's stages of psychosexual development. Libidinal satisfaction centers on the genital organs, and pleasure is derived from intimate sexual relations with another person. This stage begins with puberty and continues throughout adulthood.

Genotype The genetic make-up of an individual. It is not always expressed in observable traits (phenotypic expression), because many genes are recessive.

Gerontophobia A fear of growing old.

Goodness of fit The degree of similarity between the temperamental traits exhibited by young children and the characteristics and attitudes valued by the children's caregivers. Harmonious relations are most likely when the parents value the traits expressed by their children, such as a hard-driving father taking pride in his son's high activity level and assertiveness.

Grief work The free and open expression of grief that is believed to shorten the duration of emotional disturbance after the death of a loved one.

Growth spurt The rapid increase in a person's rate of growth that occurs at puberty.

Habituation The tendency for persons to lose interest in a stimulus that has been presented repeatedly over an extended period.

Hemophilia A blood disease that occurs in males and is caused by a sex-linked recessive gene. Clotting is retarded, with the result that relatively minor injuries may cause uncontrollable hemorrhaging and even death.

Holophrastic speech One-word utterances that are intended to convey complex meanings. They are used by children who are beginning to learn language and are not yet capable of more complex patterned speech. For example, a one-year-old child may say, "Ball!" and mean, "Throw me the ball."

Hostile aggression Aggression directed at persons with an intent to injure. Such aggression is often provoked when a person perceives the behavior of others as intentional or threatening to his or her self-esteem.

Id In Freud's theory, the unconscious part of the personality that is the source of libidinal energy. The *id* is governed by the pleasure principle and seeks immediate gratification of impulses.

Identity Erickson's term for a person's sense of psychosocial well-being produced by acceptance of one's appearance, clear goals, recognition by others.

Identity achievement According to Marcia, the identity status in which a young person has become committed to occupational and ideological positions that are self-chosen.

Identity crisis In Erikson's theory, the basic conflict of adolescence that occurs when the young person fails to achieve identity because of uncertainty about sex roles and occupational choice.

Identity diffusion According to Marcia, the identity status in which there is no apparent commitment to either an occupation or a particular set of values and no apparent effort to seek such a commitment.

Identity foreclosure According to Marcia, the identity status in which young persons commit themselves to occupational or ideological positions that are identical or similar to those chosen by others, typically their parents.

Imprinting A tendency for specific types of behavior to develop quickly and become firmly established during a particular brief (critical) period in development.

Inborn (innate) Any predisposition toward activity or growth that reflects an inherent plan.

Industry vs. inferiority Erikson's fourth stage of psychosocial development, which spans the years from six to eleven. A sense of industry results when children do and make things and are praised for their accomplishments. Limitations on activities and frequent criticism of performance may lead to feelings of inferiority.

Information processing An approach to the study of thinking that focuses on how humans perceive things, store their perceptions, process them, and retrieve them to solve problems.

Initiative vs. guilt Erikson's third stage of psychosocial development, occurring around four to five years of age. Initiative results when children are given freedom to engage in activities and express new understandings through language. Restrictions on activities or parental unresponsiveness may lead to feelings of guilt.

Instrumental aggression Aggression aimed at attaining or retrieving an object or privilege. Such aggression is usually provoked when a goal-directed activity is blocked.

Integrity vs. despair The eighth and final stage of Erikson's psychosocial therapy. Integrity results when persons can accept and be satisfied with their lives. Failure to do so results in a sense of despair.

Intelligence quotient (IQ) A measure of intelligence calculated by statistically establishing the relationship between mental age and chronological age.

Interpersonal dilemmas A method developed by Selman to study interpersonal reasoning in children and adolescents.

The structure is similar to that used in moral reasoning research, in that stories and open-ended questions are used to elicit awareness of the subtleties of interpersonal relationships.

Intimacy vs. isolation The sixth stage of Erikson's psychosocial theory. Interpersonal sharing during this period leads to mutuality and a shared identity with a partner. Failure to develop such relationships results in a sense of isolation.

Klinefelter's syndrome A genetic abnormality occurring in males with an extra X chromosome (XXY) that results in undeveloped secondary sex characteristics and is, in some cases, accompanied by mental retardation.

Language acquisition device (LAD) According to Chomsky, the innate capacity of humans to acquire language. It includes both the ability to derive the grammatical rules governing the relations among words and the ability to produce meaningful speech.

Latency Freud's fourth stage of psychosexual development, lasting from about six to twelve years, during which the libidinal energy is not focused on a particular part of the body.

Learned helplessness According to Seligman, a belief that one is unable to control events or persons in one's life. This conviction is often found in persons raised in punitive or unresponsive environments.

Libido In Freud's theory, the basic instinctual energy, which is present at birth, that drives human behavior.

Living will A will written by healthy persons in which they advocate their right to die and request that they not be kept alive by artificial means or ''heroic measures'' if they should become terminally ill.

Longitudinal approach A research method in which the same children are studied over a period of time in order to reveal both continuities and discontinuities in behavior.

Long-term memory Storehouse of permanently recorded information in one's memory.

Marasmus A disorder displayed by infants that is characterized by listlessness, apathy, and unresponsiveness.

Matched-group experiment A type of experiment in which similar groups (matched by age, sex, skills, or other common characteristics) are exposed to different conditions, and the effects of these conditions on behavior are observed.

Meiosis A special kind of cell division in which the number of chromosomes is reduced so that one-half of the original forty-six chromosomes are retained in each new germ cell.

Mental age A measure of intelligence based on how a person's score on a particular test compares with the scores of other persons of the same and different ages.

Metamemory Knowledge about one's own memory processes; the ability to understand and use techniques that aid in storing information.

Midlife transition The period between forty and forty-five years when persons are moving from early to middle adulthood. Emotional distress frequently accompanies this transition, as persons reevaluate various aspects of the life course they have chosen for themselves and either reaffirm or redirect these aspects.

Minimum sufficiency principle According to Lepper, the strategy that parents apply no more external pressure than is necessary to ensure compliance from their children.

Mnemonic devices Strategies, such as rhymes and codes, for improving memory.

Monozygotic (MZ) Identical twins who originate from the same fertilized egg and have the same genotype.

Morphemes The smallest units of meaning in a language, including entire words (*milk*) or parts of words (*-ing*).

Motherese A form of speech used by mothers when talking to their infants and young children. When contrasted to the speech used with older children and adults, the sentences are shorter and are spoken more slowly and in a higher-pitched voice (also called *baby talk*).

Multifactorial inheritance Refers to traits whose expression in the phenotype depends on a complex combination of genes rather than on a single gene (also called *polygenic traits*).

Mutual imitation In Piaget's theory, the ability of a child to imitate sounds made by someone else, provided the child has just made the sounds himself or herself.

Myelination The process of coating nerve fibers with a fatty substance (*myelin*) that functions to insulate nerve impulses and speed up neural transmission.

Natural childbirth Any approach to childbirth that stresses the preparation of the mother and father for childbirth and their participation in the process. The term *prepared birth* has been suggested as an alternative.

Negative identity In Erikson's theory, an

adolescent's adoption of roles and behaviors that are opposite to those preferred by parents and, more generally, by society.

Neonate An infant, from birth to the age of one month.

Neurotransmitters Chemical substances that affect learning and memory because of their role in the formation of synapses between brain cells.

Object permanence In Piaget's theory, the understanding, developed gradually by the child between six and eighteen months of age, that objects continue to exist even when they are not physically present (also called *object concept*).

Oedipus complex In Freud's theory, the love that young boys in the phallic stage feel for their mothers and the accompanying feelings of rivalry and fear that these feelings will be discovered and punished by their fathers. The comparable conflict in girls is called the *Electra complex*.

Onlooker behavior A form of social interaction in which children watch others play but do not join in themselves.

Operant conditioning A form of learning, first elucidated by B. F. Skinner, in which the frequency of voluntary behavior is increased or decreased gradually through the systematic use of rewards and punishments.

Operation In Piaget's theory, a mental action that can be reversed.

Oral stage Freud's first stage of psychosexual development, which encompasses the period from birth to two years of age. In this period infants concentrate their attention on feeding and use their mouths to explore the world.

Organization In Piaget's theory, the human organism's innate tendency to systematize and combine processes into coherent systems.

Overextension The tendency for children to generalize their use of new words to refer to similar but distinct objects and events. For example, having learned the word *bird*, a child may apply it to all flying objects.

Paradigm A model that serves as a frame of reference in inquiry on human behavior and scientific theory building.

Parallel play A form of play in which children play beside but not with other children. They often use identical toys in close proximity to others, but in an independent way.

Permissive parenting A style of parenting in which parents are nonpunitive, accepting, and make few attempts to influence the behavior of their children.

Personality The unique combination of physical and psychological characteristics that determine an individual's behavior.

Phallic stage Freud's third stage of psychosexual development, encompassing the ages from four to six years. In this period children learn about anatomical differences between the sexes and about the origin of babies, and they may begin manipulating their genital organs for pleasure.

Phenotype The observable characteristics that result from a person's genotype.

Phenylketonuria (PKU) A metabolic disorder caused by a recessive gene. Following delivery, newborn infants are routinely tested for PKU, since the mental retardation that may result from the disorder can, if diagnosed early, be prevented or minimized through dietary control.

Phoneme The smallest unit of sound in a particular language.

Pleasure principle According to Freud, the id's primitive and illogical guiding principle, the prime directive of which is to seek pleasure and avoid pain.

Postconventional morality In Kohlberg's theory, the most advanced form of moral reasoning based on mutual agreements and consistent application of principles.

Practice play In Piaget's theory, a form of play in which satisfying bodily activities are repeated. It is typical of infants during the first part of the sensorimotor period.

Preconscious In Freud's theory, the level of consciousness that consists of stored memories that can be readily recalled.

Preconventional morality In Kohlberg's theory, the lowest level of moral reasoning based on a desire to avoid punishment or to receive some sort of reward in return for proper behavior.

Prehension The ability to use the thumb and forefinger in opposition to pick up small objects.

Preoperational stage Piaget's second stage of cognitive development, which usually spans the ages from two to seven years. During this period, children become capable of representational thought, which is exemplified in their ability to use language and engage in symbolic play.

Preterm birth Births that occur before full term (approximately 260 days after the beginning of the mother's last menstrual period). The terms *low birth weight infant* and *short gestation period infant* are frequently substituted for *preterm infant*.

Primary circular reactions In Piaget's theory, a substage of the sensorimotor period during which infants derive considerable pleasure from repeating a variety of actions that are focused on parts of their own bodies (kicking their legs, sucking, opening and closing their hands).

Projection In Freud's theory, a defense mechanism used by the ego whereby negative behaviors or feelings about oneself are attributed to others.

Projective techniques Methods of assessing personality functioning that involve asking subjects to respond to ambiguous stimuli. Examples include inkblots and pictures that might be interpreted in a variety of ways.

Prosocial behavior Behaviors such as helping, cooperation, and sharing that lead to positive relationships between individuals.

Proximodistal growth A developmental pattern characterized by the gradual acquisition of physical and motor control, beginning first with the interior of the body and moving outward to the exterior.

Psychoanalysis A form of therapy developed by Freud that combines free association, dream interpretation, and analysis of resistance. The term also is used to refer to Freud's theory of behavior and development.

Psychosocial moratorium In Erikson's theory, a period during adolescence or youth in which young persons explore occupational alternatives without the pressure of making a final commitment.

Puberty The onset of sexual maturity, which occurs at about 12.5 years for girls and 14 years for boys. It is marked by changes in the sex organs (primary sex characteristics) and by the appearance of secondary sex characteristics such as breast development in girls and facial hair in boys.

Questionnaire   A form of data collection in which subjects reveal their knowledge or opinions by responding to a standardized set of written questions.

Rating scale   A form of data collection in which behavior is observed and rated on scales representing gradations between opposite types of behavior, such as passive-aggressive or dependent-independent.

Rationalization   In Freud's theory, a defense mechanism used by the ego to reframe and justify one's unacceptable behaviors in terms of "good" causes.

Reaction formation   In Freud's theory, a defense mechanism that an individual uses to resist succumbing to strong desires by behaving in ways that are opposite to those desires.

Reaction range   According to Gottesman, the amount of variability that can be expected in a person's phenotype as a result of environmental factors that exert an influence on the genotype.

Readiness   A preparedness to learn that is based on factors such as physical and neurological development and experience.

Reality principle   In Freudian theory, the tendency for the ego to control the expression of libidinal energy in terms of rational analysis of situations.

Recessive gene   A gene that expresses its trait in the phenotype only when paired with another recessive gene.

Reflex   An unlearned, involuntary response to an external stimulus that infants are capable of making at birth. Examples include the grasp and Moro reflexes.

Regression   In Freud's theory, a defense mechanism used by the ego whereby individuals resort to forms of behavior that have provided satisfaction at earlier stages of psychosexual development.

Reinforcement   In Skinner's theory of operant conditioning, an object or event that, when presented immediately after a voluntary behavior has been performed, functions to increase the frequency of that behavior in the future.

Repression   In Freud's theory, a defense mechanism that involves the tendency to be unable to recall painful memories.

Reversibility   In Piaget's theory, the ability to mentally reverse an action. For example, a child who observes a row of poker chips being spread out on a table can imagine the chips being moved back together again, without having to move them physically.

Rh disease   The destruction of red blood cells in a fetus, which occurs when the blood of a Rh-negative mother mixes with the Rh-positive blood of her unborn child. Afflicted infants are typically given a new supply of blood by transfusion. Mothers can be treated medically to prevent the build-up of harmful antibodies, thereby decreasing the risk of disease during subsequent pregnancies.

Role confusion   In Erikson's theory, a distressing uncertainty as to appropriate and preferred roles, including sexual, social, and vocational roles. This confusion is typical among adolescents (also called *identity confusion*).

Scaffolding   The support provided to a child learning a complex behavior by a more knowledgeable adult or peer, who assists the child in mastering the various components of the task.

Scheme In Piaget's theory, an organized pattern of action or thought that structures how one thinks about and interacts with the environment.

Schizophrenia The most common single type of severe psychological disorder. Characteristics include impaired capacity to think coherently, distorted perceptions of reality, and weakened control of impulses.

School phobia A reluctance or refusal to go to school because of extreme anxiety experienced in relation to the school setting or in separating from the caretaker.

Secondary circular reactions In Piaget's theory, a substage of the sensorimotor period, occurring between four and eight months of age, during which infants derive considerable pleasure from endlessly repeating a variety of actions focused on objects in their environment.

Secondary sex characteristics Physical signs of masculinity or femininity that develop during puberty but are not directly involved in reproduction. Examples include facial and pubic hair, breast development in girls, and voice changes in boys.

Sensorimotor stage The first of Piaget's stages of cognitive development, which extends typically from birth to two years of age. During this period infants understand the world through their senses and the motor actions they are capable of performing on objects in their environment. The period ends when infants become capable of symbolic or representational thought.

Sensory register Memory structure that holds sense impressions temporarily for possible further processing.

Separation anxiety The signs of emotional distress exhibited by infants when their caretakers leave. Such responses begin to be exhibited during the second half of the first year.

Seriation In Piaget's theory, the concrete operational ability to order objects or events in a logical sequence. For example, events may be placed in chronological order, and a group of objects may be placed in a sequence from smallest to largest.

Sex cleavage The tendency for children to prefer interacting with same-sex peers. This preference is often evident by three years of age and persists throughout middle childhood and into adolescence.

Sex-typed A tendency in both males and females to engage in behaviors that are more common in members of their own sex.

Short-term memory Memory structure that functions as one's working memory, where information is temporarily stored.

Sickle cell anemia A blood disease common in black persons that has been traced to a recessive gene. Its symptoms include swollen joints, fatigue, and chest pain.

Social cognition Knowledge about the social world; it includes the ability to infer another's perspective and coordinate it with one's own, as well as an understanding of social norms and rules that govern social interaction.

Social learning theory A behavioral theory that focuses on the acquisition of new behaviors through the processes of identification with and imitation of other persons.

Socialization The process by which children acquire the attitudes, values, abilities, and behaviors that are considered desirable or appropriate by their family and their culture.

Socialized speech In Piaget's theory, speech in which the responses of each partner follow logically from the comments of the other. Socialized speech is clearly established in most children by seven years of age, replacing egocentric speech which is typical up to that time.

Sociometric techniques Measures of popularity derived by asking members of a group to indicate which peers they like best and least.

Solitary play A form of play in which children play alone with toys not shared with other children.

Standardized interviews A research method in which all subjects are asked to respond to the same series of questions.

Stimulus generalization A situation in which a response is elicited by stimuli similar to the stimulus that originally provoked the response. The most famous example involved Watson's experiment with an infant whose conditioned fear of a white rat was generalized to all white, furry objects.

Stranger anxiety Signs of emotional distress in infants when in the presence of unfamiliar persons. This response is first observed around six months of age.

Subcortical reflexes Reflexes, such as the grasp reflex, that are controlled by the lower brain. These reflexes disappear gradually as the cerebral cortex develops.

Sublimation In Freud's theory, a defense mechanism used by the ego to divert libidinal energy away from socially unacceptable behaviors into creative or constructive activities.

Sudden infant death syndrome (SIDS) The sudden, unexplained death of an otherwise healthy infant. SIDS most frequently occurs between the second and fourth month after birth; its immediate cause is the cessation of breathing, usually during sound sleep.

Superego In Freud's theory of personality, the equivalent of one's conscience.

Symbolic play In Piaget's theory, a common form of play among preoperational children in which one object is used to stand for something else (as when a broom is used as a horse).

Synapse The relay point between adjacent neurons. The *synapse* is responsible for the transmission of nerve impulses from one neuron to another.

Target-seeking tendency The tendency for children whose growth has been interrupted by illness or malnutrition to "catch up" to their initial growth curve.

Telegraphic speech The two-word utterances used by young language learners, so named because they resemble telegrams in which nonessential words have been left out.

Teratogens Harmful agents such as drugs and X rays that may cause abnormalities to the prenatal organism, especially during the embryonic period.

Tertiary circular reactions In Piaget's theory, the substage of the sensorimotor period occurring between twelve and eighteen months. The infant in this period is characterized by active experimentation. Although the infant still enjoys repeated actions, these actions are now varied slightly to observe what will happen.

Theory of development A systematic framework of principles that is based on organized observations of changes in behavior over time. Such theories help to explain and predict behavior as well as guide research.

Third-force psychology A general term used to refer to humanistic theories such as Maslow's conception of growth, which emphasizes the self-actualizing needs of human beings.

Time sampling A procedure for collecting data in which subjects are observed at specified intervals, and their behavior at that time is recorded.

Trust vs. mistrust Erikson's first stage of psychosocial development. From birth to one year of age, infants who experience consistency and continuity of care develop trust. Inconsistent or unresponsive care may lead to mistrust.

Turner's syndrome A genetic abnormality resulting in incomplete sexual maturation. It occurs in females who have one rather than two X chromosomes.

Type A personality Behavioral disposition characterized by constant drive, competitiveness, hostility, and tension.

Unconscious In Freud's theory, the level of consciousness that consists of memories that may influence thinking and behavior but cannot be recalled (except through special circumstances such as dreams or free association).

Unoccupied behavior A category of social participation, described by Parten, in which children stand around, glance at each other, or engage in aimless activities without ever interacting.

Values Beliefs that guide and determine attitudes and actions.

Vocal contagion In Piaget's theory, the tendency for children to be stimulated to vocalize in response to sounds made by another person.

Wear-and-tear theory An explanation for aging based on an analogy between the body and a machine. Just as the parts of a machine wear out through constant use, the parts of the body are also thought to gradually become nonfunctional.

XYY syndrome A genetic abnormality in which males have an extra Y chromosome. Its victims are often unusually tall, impulsive, and antisocial.

BIBLIOGRAPHY

Abramson, E. E. (Ed.). (1977). *Behavioral approaches to weight control.* New York: Springer.

Adelson, J. (1970, January 18). What generation gap? *New York Times Magazine,* pp. 101–108.

Adelson, J. (1971). The political imagination of the young adolescent. In J. Kagan & R. Coles (Eds.), *Twelve to sixteen: Early adolescence.* New York: Norton.

Adelson, J. (Ed.). (1980). *Handbook of adolescent psychology.* New York: Wiley.

Adelson, J., & Dochrman, M. J. (1980). The psychodynamic approach to adolescence. In J. Adelson (Ed.), *Handbook of adolescent psychology.* New York: Wiley.

Ahlstrom, W. M., & Havighurst, R. G. (1971). *Four hundred losers.* San Francisco: Jossey-Bass.

Ainsworth, M. D. S. (1962). The effects of maternal deprivation: A review of findings and controversy in the context of research strategy. In *Public Health Papers, 14.* Geneva: World Health Organization.

Ainsworth, M. D. S. (1967). *Infancy in Uganda: Infant care and the growth of attachment.* Baltimore: Johns Hopkins University Press.

Ainsworth, M. D. S. (1972). Attachment and dependency: A comparison. In J. L. Gewirtz (Ed.), *Attachment and dependency.* Washington, D.C.: Winston.

Ainsworth, M. D. S. (1974). The development of infant-mother attachment. In B. M. Caldwell & H. N. Ricciuti (Eds.), *Review of child development research* (Vol. 3). Chicago: University of Chicago Press.

Ainsworth, M. D. S. (1979a). Attachment as related to mother-infant interaction. In J. S. Rosenblatt, R. A. Hinde, C. Beer, & M. C. Busnel (Eds.), *Advances in the study of behavior* (Vol. 9). New York: Academic Press.

Ainsworth, M. D. S. (1979b, March). Attachment: Retrospect and prospect. Presidential address to the biennial meeting of the Society for Research in Child Development, San Francisco.

Ainsworth, M. D. S., Blehar, M. C., Waters, E., & Wall, S. (1978). *Patterns of attachment: A psychological study of the strange situation.* Hillsdale, NJ: Erlbaum.

Ainsworth, M. D. S., & Wittig, B. A. (1972). Attachment and exploratory behavior of one-year-olds in a strange situation. In B. M.

Foss (Ed.), *Determinants of infant behavior* (Vol. 4). New York: Wiley.

Akers, R. L. (1977). *Deviant behavior: Social learning approach.* Belmont, CA: Wadsworth.

Aldrich, C. A., Norval, M. A., Knop, C., & Venegas, F. (1946). The crying of newly born babies. IV. A follow-up study after additional nursing care had been provided. *Journal of Pediatrics, 27,* 89–96.

Aldrich, C. A., Sung, C., & Knop, C. (1945). The crying of newly born babies. II. The individual phase. *Journal of Pediatrics, 26.*

Aldrich, C. A, Sung, C., Knop, C., Stevens, G., & Burchell, M. (1945). The crying of newly born babies. I. The community phase. *Journal of Pediatrics, 26,* 313–326.

Allport, G. W. (1937). *Personality: A psychosocial interpretation.* New York: Holt.

Altus, W. D. (1966). Birth order and its sequelae. *Science, 151,* 44–49.

Anderson, C. M. (1974). *Classroom activities for modifying misbehavior in children.* Nyack, NY: Center for Applied Research in Education.

Anderson, J. E. (1948). Personality organization in children. *American Psychologist, 3,* 409–416.

Annis, L. F. (1978). *The child before birth.* NY: Cornell University Press.

Anthony, E. J. (1957). An experimental approach to the psychopathology of childhood: Encopresis. *British Journal of Medical Psychology, 30*(3), 146–175.

Anthony, E. J. (1967). Psychoneurotic disorders. In A. M. Freedman & H. I. Kaplan (Eds.), *Comprehensive textbook of psychiatry.* Baltimore: Williams & Wilkins.

Anthony, E. J. (1970). Behavior disorders. In P. H. Mussen (Ed.), *Carmichael's manual of child psychology* (3rd ed., Vol. 2). New York: Wiley.

Apgar, V., & Beck, J. (1972). *Is my baby all right?* New York: Trident Press.

Apgar, V., Holoday, D. A., James, L. S., Weisbrot, I. M., & Berrien, C. (1958). Evaluation of the newborn infant: Second report. *Journal of the American Medical Association, 168,* 1985–1988.

Armentrout, J. A., & Burger, G. K. (1972). Children's reports of parental child-rearing behavior at five grade levels. *Developmental Psychology, 7,* 44–48.

Aronfreed, J. (1968). *Conduct and conscience: The socialization of internalized control over behavior.* New York: Academic Press.

Asher, S. R., & Renshaw, P. (1981). Children without friends: Social knowledge and social skill training. In S. R. Asher & J. M. Gottman (Eds.), *The development of children's friendships.* New York: Cambridge University Press.

Asimov, I. (1962). *The genetic code.* New York: Signet.

Aslin, R. N., Pisoni, D. B., & Jusczyk, P. W. (1983). Auditory development and speech perception in infancy. In M. M. Haith & J. J. Campos (Eds.), *Infancy and developmental psychology.* Vol. 2 of P. H. Mussen (Ed.), *Handbook of child psychology* (4th ed.). New York: Wiley.

Athanasiou, R., Shaver, P., & Tavris, C. (1970). *Psychology Today* reports back to readers on what they told when they filled out the sex questionnaire. *Psychology Today, 4*(2), 39–52.

Atkinson, J. W. (1964). *An introduction to motivation.* Princeton, NJ: Van Nostrand.

Atkinson, R. C., & Shiffrin, R. M. (1968). Human memory: A proposed system and its control processes. In K. W. Spence & J. T. Spence (Eds.), *Advances in the psychology of learning and motivation research and theory* (Vol. 2). New York: Academic Press.

Axline, V. (1964). *Dibs: In search of self.* New York: Ballantine Books.

Azrin, N. H., & Foxx, R. (1976). *Toilet training in less than a day.* New York: Pocket Books.

Azrin, N. H., & Nunn, R. G. (1977). *Habit control in a day.* New York: Simon & Schuster.

Bachman, J. G., & Johnston, L. D. (1979). The freshmen, 1979. *Psychology Today, 13*(4), 78–87.

Bachman, J. G., O'Malley, P. M., & Johnston, J. (1978). *Youth in transition: Vol. 6. Adolescence to adulthood: Change and stability in the lives of young men.* Ann Arbor: Institute for Social Research.

Baldwin, A. L. (1980). *Theories of child development* (2nd ed.). New York: Wiley.

Baldwin, W., & Cain, V. S. (1981). The children of teenage parents. In F. F. Furstenberg, Jr., R. Lincoln, & J. Menken (Eds.), *Teenage sexuality, pregnancy, and childbearing*. Philadelphia: University of Pennsylvania Press.

Baltes, P. B., & Schaie, K. W. (1984, March). The myth of the twilight years. *Psychology Today*, 35–40.

Bandura, A. (1973). *Aggression: A social learning analysis*. Englewood Cliffs, NJ: Prentice-Hall.

Bandura, A. (1974). Behavior theory and the models of man. *American Psychologist, 29*, 859–869.

Bandura, A. (1977). *Social learning theory*. Englewood Cliffs, NJ: Prentice-Hall.

Bandura, A., Grusec, J. E., & Menlove, F. L. (1967). Vicarious extinction and avoidance behavior. *Journal of Personality and Social Psychology, 5*, 16–23.

Bandura, A., & Menlove, F. L. (1968). Factors determining vicarious extinction of avoidance behavior through symbolic modeling. *Journal of Personality and Social Psychology, 8*, 99–108.

Bandura, A., Ross, D., & Ross, S. A. (1963a). A comparative test of the status envy, social power, and secondary reinforcement theories of identificatory learning. *Journal of Abnormal & Social Psychology, 67*, 527–534.

Bandura, A., Ross, D., & Ross, S. A. (1963b). Imitation of film mediated aggressive models. *Journal of Abnormal & Social Psychology, 66*, 3–11.

Bandura, A., Ross, D., & Ross, S. A. (1963c). Vicarious reinforcement and imitative learning. *Journal of Abnormal & Social Psychology, 67*, 601–607.

Bandura, A., & Walters, R. H. (1963). *Social learning and personality development*. New York: Holt, Rinehart & Winston.

Banks, M. S., & Salapatek, P. (1983). Infant visual perception. In M. M. Haith & J. J. Campos (Eds.), *Infancy and developmental psychobiology*, Vol. 2 of P. H. Mussen (Ed.), *Handbook of child psychology* (4th ed.). New York: Wiley.

Barnes, K. E. (1971). Preschool play norms: A replication. *Developmental Psychology, 5*, 99–103.

Barrett, D. E. (1979). A naturalistic study of sex differences in children's aggression. *Merrill-Palmer Quarterly, 25*, 193–203.

Baruch, D. W. (1952). *One little boy*. New York: Dell.

Baumrind, D. (1967). Child care practices anteceding three patterns of preschool behavior. *Genetic Psychology Monographs, 75*, 43–88.

Baumrind, D. (1971). Current patterns of parental authority. *Developmental Psychology Monographs, 1*, 1–103.

Baumrind, D. (1973). The development of instrumental competence through socialization. In A. Pick (Ed.), *Minnesota symposia on child psychology* (Vol. 7). Minneapolis: University of Minnesota Press.

Bayley, N. (1965). Comparisons of mental and motor test scores for ages 1–15 months by sex, birth order, race, geographical location, and education of parents. *Child Development, 36*, 379–411.

Bayley, N. (1969). *Bayley scales of infant development*. New York: Psychological Corporation.

Bean, C. A. (1983). *Methods of childbirth*. Garden City, NY: Doubleday.

Beck, A. T. (1970). *Depression: Causes and treatment*. Philadelphia: University of Pennsylvania Press.

Beck, P. A. (1977). The role of agents in political socialization. In S. A. Renshon (Ed.), *Handbook of political socialization: Theory and research*. New York: Free Press.

Becker, S. W., Lerner, M. J., & Carroll, J. (1966). Conformity as a function of birth order and type of group pressure: A verification. *Journal of Personality and Social Psychology, 3*, 242–244.

Becker, W. C. (1964). Consequences of different kinds of parental discipline. In M. L. Hoffman & L. W. Hoffman (Eds.), *Review of child development research* (Vol. 1). New York: Russell Sage Foundation.

Bee, H. (Ed.). (1977). Social issues in developmental psychology (2nd ed.). New York: Harper & Row.

Bell, R. Q., & Harper, L. V. (Eds.). (1977). *Child effects on adults.* Hillsdale, NJ: Erlbaum.

Bell, R. Q., Weller, G. M., & Waldrop, M. F. (1971). Newborn and preschooler: Organization of behavior and relations between periods. *Monographs of the Society for Research in Child Development, 36*(1–2, Serial No. 142).

Beller, E. K. (1979). Early intervention programs. In J. D. Osofsky (Ed.), *Handbook of infant development.* New York: Wiley.

Belsky, J. K. (1984). *The psychology of aging: Theory, research, and practice.* Monterey, CA: Brooks/Cole.

Bem, S. L. (1975). Sex-role adaptability: One consequence of psychological androgyny. *Journal of Personality and Social Psychology, 31,* 634–643.

Bem, S. L. (1976). Sex-typing and androgyny: Further explorations of the expressive domain. *Journal of Personality and Social Psychology, 34*(5), 1016–1023.

Bem, S. L. (1981). Gender schema theory: A cognitive account of sex-typing. *Psychological Review, 88,* 354–364.

Bergner, S., & Susser, M. W. (1970). Low birthweight and parental nutrition: An interpretive review. *Pediatrics, 46,* 946–966.

Berko, J. (1958). The child's learning of English morphology. *Word, 14,* 150–177.

Berscheid, E., & Walster, E. (1972). Beauty and the best. *Psychology Today, 5*(10), 42–74.

Bettelheim, B. (1967). *The empty fortress.* New York: The Free Press.

Bettelheim, B. (1974). *A home for the heart.* New York: Knopf.

Biehler, R. F. (1979). Unpublished study. California State University, Chico.

Biller, H. B., & Davids, A. (1973). Parent-child relations, personality development, and psychopathology. In A. Davids (Ed.), *Abnormal child psychology.* Belmont, CA: Brooks/Cole.

Binet, A., & Simon, T. (1905). Méthodes nouvelles pour le diagnostic du niveau intellectuel des anormaux. *Année Psychologie, 11,* 191–244.

Bing, E. (1967). *Six practical lessons for an easier childbirth.* New York: Grossett & Dunlap.

Birnbaum, J. A. (1971). *Life patterns, personality style, and self-esteem in gifted family-oriented and career-committed women.* Unpublished doctoral dissertation. Ann Arbor, MI: University of Michigan.

Birns, B. (1965). Individual differences in human neonates' responses to stimulation. *Child Development, 36,* 249–256.

Birns, B., Blank, M., & Bridger, W. H. (1966). The effectiveness of various soothing techniques on human neonates. *Psychosomatic Medicine, 28,* 316–322.

Birren, J. E., & Schaie, K. W. (Eds.) (1977). *Handbook of the psychology of aging.* New York: Van Nostrand Reinhold.

Birren, J. E., Woods, A. M., & Williams, M. V. (1980). Behavioral slowing with age: Causes, organization, and consequences. In L. W. Poon (Ed.), *Aging in the 1980s.* Washington, DC: American Psychological Association.

Blatt, M. (1975). Studies on the effects of classroom discussion upon children's moral development. *Journal of Moral Education, 42,* 129–161.

Blatt, M., & Kohlberg, L. (1978). The effects of classroom moral discussion upon children's level of moral judgment. In L. Kohlberg & E. Turiel (Eds.), *Recent research in moral development.* New York: Holt, Rinehart & Winston.

Blazer, D. (1980). The epidemiology of mental illness in later life. In E. W. Busse & D. Blazer (Eds.), *Handbook of geriatric psychiatry.* New York: Van Nostrand Reinhold.

Blehar, M. C. (1974). Anxious attachment and defensive reactions associated with day care. *Child Development, 45,* 683–692.

Block, J. (1971). *Lives through time.* Berkeley, CA: Bancroft Books.

Block, J. H. (1973). Conceptions of sex role: Some cross-cultural and longitudinal perspectives. *American Psychologist, 28,* 512–529.

Block, J. H. (1976). Issues, problems and pitfalls in assessing sex differences. *Merrill-Palmer Quarterly, 22,* 283–308.

Block, J. H., & Block, J. (1979). The role of ego control and ego resiliency in the organization of behavior. In W. A. Collins (Ed.),

Minnesota Symposia on Child Psychology (Vol. 11). Hillsdale, NJ: Erlbaum.

Block, J. H., Block, J., & Morrison, A. (1981). Parental agreement-disagreement on child rearing orientations and gender-related personality correlates in children. *Child Development, 52,* 965–974.

Bloom, B. L., Asher, S. J., & White, S. W. (1978). Marital disruption as a stressor: A review and analysis. *Psychological Bulletin, 85,* 867–894.

Bloom, B. S. (1964). *Stability and change in human characteristics.* New York: Wiley.

Bloom, L. (1975). Language development review. In F. D. Horowitz (Ed.), *Review of child development research* (Vol. 4). Chicago: University of Chicago Press.

Bloom, L. (Ed.). (1978). *Readings in language development.* New York: Wiley.

Blos, P. (1962). *On adolescence.* New York: Free Press.

Blos, P. (1979). *The adolescent passage.* New York: International Universities Press.

Boccia, M., & Campos, J. (1983, April). *Maternal emotional signalling: Its effect on infants' reaction to strangers.* Paper presented at the meeting of the Society for Research in Child Development, Detroit.

Botwinick, J. (1984). *Aging and behavior* (3rd ed.). New York: Springer.

Bower, T. G. R. (1977a). *The perceptual world of the child.* Cambridge, MA: Harvard University Press.

Bower, T. G. R. (1977b). *A primer of infant development.* San Francisco: Freeman.

Bower, T. G. R., Broughton, J. M., & Moore, M. K. (1970). Infants' responses to approaching objects: An indicator of response to distal variables. *Perception and Psychophysics, 9,* 193–196.

Bowerman, M. F. (1976). Semantic factors in the acquisition of rules for word use and sentence construction. In D. M. Morehead & A. E. Morehead (Eds.), *Normal and deficient language.* Baltimore: University Park Press.

Bowes, W. A., Jr., Brackbill, Y., Conway, E., & Steinschneider, A. (1970). The effects of obstetrical medication on fetus and infant.

Monographs of the Society for Research in Child Development, 35(4), 1–38.

Bowlby, J. (1952). *Maternal care and mental health* (Monograph No. 2). Geneva: World Health Organization.

Bowlby, J. (1969). *Attachment and loss: Vol. 1. Attachment.* New York: Basic Books.

Bowlby, J. (1973). *Attachment and loss: Vol. 2. Separation: Anxiety and anger.* New York: Basic Books.

Brackbill, Y. (1979). Obstetrical medication and infant behavior. In Joy D. Osofsky (Ed.), *Handbook of infant development.* New York: Wiley.

Braine, M. D. S. (1963). The ontogeny of English phrase structure: The first phase. *Language, 39,* 1–13.

Braine, M. D. S. (1976). Children's first word combinations. *Monographs of the Society for Research in Child Development, 41* (1, Serial No. 164).

Brainerd, C. J. (1978). *Piaget's theory of intelligence.* Englewood Cliffs, NJ: Prentice-Hall.

Braungart, R. G. (1980). Youth movements. In J. Adelson (Ed.), *Handbook of adolescent psychology.* New York: Wiley.

Brazelton, T. B. (1970). Effect of prenatal drugs on the behavior of the neonate. *American Journal of Psychiatry, 126,* 1261–1266.

Brazelton, T. B. (1973). *Neonatal behavioral assessment scale.* (Clinics in Developmental Medicine, No. 50.) London: Heinemann Medical Publications.

Brecher, E. M., & the editors of *Consumer Reports.* (1973). *Licit and illicit drugs.* Boston: Little, Brown.

Breland, H. M. (1974). Birth order, family size, and intelligence. *Science, 184,* 114.

Bridges, K. M. (1932). Emotional development in early infancy. *Child Development, 3,* 324–341.

Brill, A. A. (Ed. and Trans.). (1938). *The basic writings of Sigmund Freud.* New York: Random House.

Brim, O. G. (1976). Life-span development of the theory of oneself: Implications for child development. *Advances in Child Development and Behavior, 11,* 241–251.

Brim, O. G., Jr., & Kagan, J. (Eds.). (1980). *Con-*

stancy and change in human development. Cambridge, MA: Harvard University Press.

Brittain, C. V. (1968). An exploration of the bases of peer-compliance and parent-compliance in adolescence. *Adolescence, 2,* 445–458.

Brody, S. (1959). *Bio-energetics and growth.* New York: Reinhold.

Broman, S. H. (1984). The collaborative perinatal project: An overview. In S. A. Mednick, M. Harway, & K. M. Finello (Eds.), *Handbook of longitudinal research: Vol. 1. Birth and childhood cohorts.* New York: Praeger.

Broverman, I. K., Vogel, S. R., Broverman, D. M., Clarkson, F. E., & Rosenkrantz, P. S. (1972). Sex-role stereotypes: A current appraisal. *Journal of Social Issues, 28*(2), 58–78.

Brown, R. (1973). *A first language: The early stages.* Cambridge, MA: Harvard University Press.

Brown, R., & Bellugi, U. (1964). Three processes in the child's acquisition of syntax. *Harvard Educational Review, 34,* 133–151.

Bruch, H. (1973). *Eating disorders: Obesity, anorexia nervosa, and the person within.* New York: Basic Books.

Bruner, J. S. (1973). *Beyond the information given* (J. M. Anglin, Ed.). New York: Norton.

Bruner, J. S., Jolly, A., & Sylva, K. (Eds.). (1976). *Play: Its role in development and evolution.* New York: Basic Books.

Brush, S. G. (1974). Should the history of science be rated X? *Science, 183,* 1164–1172.

Bryan, J. H. (1975). Children's cooperation and helping behaviors. In E. M. Hetherington (Ed.), *Review of child development research* (Vol. 5). Chicago: University of Chicago Press.

Bryant, R. D., & Danforth, D. N. (1978). The conduct of normal labor. The first and second stages. In D. N. Danforth (Ed.), *Textbook of obstetrics and gynecology* (6th ed.). New York: Hoeber.

Burks, B. S. (1928). The relative influence of nature and nurture upon mental development: A comparative study of foster parent–foster child resemblance and true parent–true child resemblance. *Yearbook of the National Society for the Study of Education, 27*(II), 248–353.

Butler, R. N., & Lewis, M. I. (1982). *Aging and mental health* (3rd ed.). St. Louis: Mosby.

Butler, R. N. (1975). *Why survive? Growing old in America.* New York: Harper & Row.

Byrne, D. (1977). A pregnant pause in the sexual revolution. *Psychology Today, 11*(2), 67–68.

Caine, L. (1975). *Widow.* New York: Bantam Books.

Cairns, R. (1983). The emergence of developmental psychology. In W. Kessen (Ed.), *History, theory, and methods.* Vol. 1 of P. H. Mussen (Ed.), *Handbook of child psychology* (4th ed.). New York: Wiley.

Campos, J. J., Barrett, K. C., Lamb, M. E., Goldsmith, H. H., & Stenberg, C. (1983). Socioemotional development. In M. M. Haith & J. J. Campos (Eds.), *Infancy and developmental psychobiology.* Vol. 2 of P. H. Mussen (Ed.), *Handbook of child psychology* (4th ed.). New York: Wiley.

Campos, J. J., Haitt, S., Ramsay, D., Henderson, D., & Svejda, M. (1978). The emergence of fear on the visual cliff. In M. Lewis & L. A. Rosenblum (Eds.), *The development of affect.* New York: Plenum.

Cancro, R. (Ed.) (1971). *Intelligence: Genetic and environmental influences.* New York: Grune & Stratton.

Carew, J. B., Chan, I., & Halfer, C. (1976). *Observing intelligence in young children.* Englewood Cliffs, NJ: Prentice-Hall.

Carey, S. (1977). The child as word learner. In M. Halle, J. Bresnan, & G. A. Miller (Eds.), *Linguistic theory and psychological reality.* Cambridge, MA: MIT Press.

Carpenter, F. (1974). *The Skinner primer.* New York: Free Press.

Cazden, C. (1968). The acquisition of noun and verb inflections. *Child Development, 39,* 433–438.

Chabon, I. (1966). *Awake and aware: Participating in childbirth through prophylaxis.* New York: Delacorte.

Chaffee, S. H., Jackson-Beeck, M., Durall, J., & Wilson, D. (1977). Mass communication in political socialization. In S. A. Renshon

(Ed.), *Handbook of political socialization: Theory and research.* New York: Free Press.

Chomsky, N. (1965). *Aspects of the theory of syntax.* Cambridge, MA: MIT Press.

Chomsky, N. (1968). *Language and the mind.* New York: Harcourt, Brace, Jovanovich.

Choron, J. (1972). *Suicide.* New York: Scribner's.

Christensen, A., Phillips, S., Glasgow, R. E., & Johnson, S. M. (1983). Parental characteristics and interactional dysfunction in families with child behavior problems: A preliminary investigation. *Journal of Abnormal Child Psychology, 11,* 153–166.

Clarizio, H. F., & McCoy, G. F. (1983). *Behavior disorders in children* (3rd ed.). New York: Harper & Row.

Clark, E. V. (1973). What's in a word? On the child's acquisition of semantics in his first language. In T. E. Moore (Ed.), *Cognitive development and the acquisition of language.* New York: Academic Press.

Clark, H. H., & Clark, E. V. (1977). *Psychology and language.* New York: Harcourt, Brace, Jovanovich.

Clarke, A. M., & Clarke, A. D. B. (Eds.). (1976). *Early experience: Myth and evidence.* London: Open Books.

Clarke-Stewart, A. (1982). *Daycare.* Cambridge, MA: Harvard University Press.

Clarke-Stewart, A., & Fein, G. G. (1983). Early childhood programs. In M. M. Haith & J. J. Campos (Eds.), *Infancy and developmental psychobiology.* Vol. 2 of P. H. Mussen (Ed.), *Handbook of child psychology* (4th ed.). New York: Wiley.

Clarke-Stewart, K. A. (1978). Popular primers for parents. *American Psychologist, 33*(4), 359–369.

Clausen, J. (1975). The social meaning of differential physical and sexual maturation. In S. Dragastin & G. H. Elder, Jr. (Eds.), *Adolescence in the life cycle.* New York: Wiley.

Cobb, E. A. (1943). Family press variables. *Monographs of the Society for Research in Child Development, 8,* 327–361.

Cohen, J. H., & Filipczak, J. (1971). *A new learning environment.* New York: Jossey-Bass.

Coie, J. D., & Dodge, K. A. (1983). Continuities and changes in children's social staus: A five-year longitudinal study. *Merrill-Palmer Quarterly, 29*(3), 261–282.

Coie, J. D., & Kupersmidt, J. B. (1983). A behavior analysis of emerging social status in boys' groups. *Child Development, 54,* 1400–1416.

Coleman, J. C. (1980). Friendship and the peer group in adolescence. In J. Adelson (Ed.), *Handbook of adolescent psychology.* New York: Wiley.

Coleman, J. S. (1961). *The adolescent society.* New York: Free Press.

Coleman, J. S. (1966). *Equality of educational opportunity.* Washington, DC: U.S. Department of Health, Education, and Welfare, Office of Education.

Coles, R. (1970). *Erik H. Erikson: The growth of his work.* Boston: Little, Brown.

Comfort, A. (1976). *A good age.* New York: Crown.

Committee on Maternal Nutrition, National Research Council. *Maternal nutrition and the course of pregnancy.* (1970). Washington, DC: National Academy of Sciences.

Connell, R. W. (1972, fall). Political socialization in the American family: The evidence reexamined. *Public Opinion Quarterly, 36,* 323–333.

Corso, J. (1977). Auditory perception and communication. In J. E. Birren & K. W. Schaie (Eds.), *Handbook of the psychology of aging.* New York: Van Nostrand Reinhold.

Craik, F. I. M. (1977). Age differences in human memory. In J. E. Birren & K. W. Schaie (Eds.), *Handbook of the psychology of aging.* New York: Von Nostrand Reinhold.

Crandall, V. J., Orleans, S., Preston, A., & Rabson, A. (1958). The development of social compliance in young children. *Child Development, 29,* 429–443.

Cravioto, J., DeLicardie, E. R., & Birch, H. G. (1966). Nutrition, growth, and neurointegrative development: An experimental and ecologic study. *Pediatrics, 38* (1, Pt. 2, Supplement), 319–372.

Cromer, R. F. (1974). The development of language and cognition. In B. M. Foss (Ed.),

New perspectives in child development. Baltimore: Penguin.

Cross, T. G. (1978). Mother's speech and its association with rate of linguistic development in young children. In N. Waterson & C. E. Snow (Eds.), *The development of communication*. New York: Wiley.

Crowell, D. H. (1967). Infant motor development. In Y. Brackbill (Ed.), *Infancy and early childhood*. New York: Free Press.

Crystal, S. (1982). *America's old age crisis: Public policy and the two worlds of aging*. New York: Basic Books.

Danforth, D. N. (Ed.). (1982). *Textbook of obstetrics and gynecology* (4th ed.). New York: Hoeber.

Danforth, D. N., and Hughey, M. J. (1983). *The complete guide to pregnancy*. New York: Hoeber.

Darwin, C. (1859). *The origin of species*. London: Murray.

Darwin, C. (1872). *The expression of emotions in man and animals*. London: Murray.

Darwin, C. (1877). A biographical sketch of an infant. *Mind, 2*, 285–294.

Datan, N. (1980). Midas and other midlife crises. In W. H. Norman & T. J. Scaramella (Eds.), *Midlife: Developmental and clinical issues*. New York: Brunner/Mazel.

Davidson, S. (1961). School phobia as a manifestation of family disturbance: Its structure and treatment. *Journal of Child Psychology and Psychiatry, 1*, 270–287.

Davidson, S. (1977). *Loose change: Three women of the sixties*. Garden City, NJ: Doubleday.

Davis, K. L., & Mohs, R. C. (1982). Enhancement of memory processes in Alzheimer's disease with multiple-dose intravenous physostigmine. *American Journal of Psychiatry, 139*, 1421–1423.

Davis, K. L. (1985). *Intra- and inter-personal awareness of married and divorced males in midlife: A structural analysis*. Unpublished master's thesis, University of Toledo, Toledo, OH.

De Casper, A. J., & Fifer, W. P. (1980). Of human bonding: Newborns prefer their mothers' voices. *Science, 208*, 1174–1176.

Dennis, W. (1940). Historical beginnings of child psychology. *Psychological Bulletin, 46*, 224–235.

Dennis, W. (Ed.). (1951). *Readings in child psychology*. New York: Prentice-Hall.

Dennis, W. (1966). Creative productivity between the ages of 20 and 80 years. *Journal of Gerontology, 21*, 1–8.

Dennis, W. (Ed.). (1972). *Historical readings in developmental psychology*. New York: Appleton-Century-Crofts.

de Nouy, P. (1937). *Biological time*. New York: Macmillan.

Deutsch, M. (1964). Facilitating development in the pre-school child: Social and psychological perspectives. *Merrill-Palmer Quarterly of Behavior and Development, 10*, 277–296.

de Villiers, P., & de Villiers, J. (1979). *Early language*. Cambridge, MA: Harvard University Press.

Diament, L. (1970). Premarital sexual behavior, attitudes, and emotional adjustment. *Journal of Social Psychology, 82*, 75–80.

Dick-Read, G. (1959). *Childbirth without fear: The principles and practice of natural childbirth* (rev. ed.). New York: Harper.

Dienstbier, R. A., Hillman, D., Lehnhoff, J., Hillman, J., & Valkenaar, M. C. (1975). An emotion-attribution approach to moral behavior: Interfacing cognitive and avoidance theories of moral development. *Psychological Review, 82*, 299–315.

Dodge, K. A. (1983). Behavioral antecedents of peer social status. *Child Development*, 1386–1399.

Dollard, J., Doob, L. W., Miller, N. E., Mowrer, O. H., & Sears, R. R. (1939). *Frustration and aggression*. New Haven, CT: Yale University Press.

Doman, G. (1964). *How to teach your baby to read*. New York: Random House.

Donaldson, M. (1979). *Children's minds*. New York: Norton.

Donaldson, M., and Wales, R. (1970). On the acquisition of some relational terms. In J. R.

Hayes (Ed.), *Cognition and the development of language.* New York: Wiley.

Douvan, E. (1975). Sex differences in the opportunities, demands, and development of youth. In R. J. Havighurst & P. H. Dreyer (Eds.), *Youth* (74th Yearbook of the National Society for the Study of Education). Chicago: University of Chicago Press.

Douvan, E., & Adelson, J. (1966). *The adolescent experience.* New York: Wiley.

Dreyer, P. H. (1975). Sex, sex roles, and marriage among youth in the 1970s. In R. J. Havighurst & P. H. Dreyer (Eds.), *Youth* (74th Yearbook of the National Society for the Study of Education). Chicago: University of Chicago Press.

Dubnoff, S. J., Yeroff, J., & Kulka, R. A. (1978, August). *Adjustment to work.* Paper presented at the meeting of the American Psychological Association, Toronto.

Duvall, E. M. (1971). *Family development.* Philadelphia: Lippincott.

Ebbs, J. H., Brown, A., Tisdale, F. F., Moyle, W. J., & Bell, M. (1942). The influence of improved prenatal nutrition upon the infant. *Canadian Medical Association Journal, 126,* 6–8.

Eimas, P. D., Siqueland, E. R., Jusczyk, P., & Vigorito, J. (1971). Speech perception in infants. *Science, 171,* 305–306.

Eisenberg, L. (1958). School phobia: A study in the communication of anxiety. *American Journal of Psychiatry, 114,* 712–718.

Ekman, P., and Friesen, W. (1978). *Facial action coding system.* Palo Alto, CA: Consulting Psychologists Press.

Elder, G. H., Jr. (1962). Structural variations in the child rearing relationship. *Sociometry, 25,* 241–262.

Elder, G. H., Jr. (1980). Adolescence in historical perspective. In J. Adelson (Ed.), *Handbook of adolescent psychology.* New York: Wiley.

Elkind, D. (1968). Cognitive development in adolescence. In J. F. Adams (Ed.), *Understanding adolescence.* Boston: Allyn & Bacon.

Elkind, D. (1974). *Children and adolescents: In-*

terpretive essays on Jean Piaget (2nd ed.). New York: Oxford University Press.

Elkind, D. (1970, April 5). Erik Erikson's eight ages of man. *New York Times Magazine,* pp. 25–76.

Elkind, D. (1968, May 26). Giant in the nursery—Jean Piaget. *New York Times Magazine,* pp. 25–80. [Reprinted in D. Elkind, 1974, *Children and adolescents: Interpretive essays on Jean Piaget* (2nd ed.). New York: Oxford University Press.]

Elsayed, M. I., Ismail, A. H., & Young, R. J. (1980). Intellectual differences of adult men related to age and physical fitness before and after an exercise program. *Journal of Gerontology, 35,* 383–387.

Endler, H. S., Rushton, J. P., & Roediger, H. L. III. (1978). Productivity and scholarly impact (citations) of British, Canadian, and U.S. departments of psychology (1975). *American Psychologist, 33,* 1064–1082.

Engelmann, S. (1969). *Preventing failure in the elementary grades.* Chicago: Science Research Associates.

Engelmann, S., & Engelmann, T. (1968). *Give your child a superior mind.* New York: Simon & Schuster.

Epstein, H. T. (1974). Correlated brain and intelligence development in humans. In M. E. Hahn, C. Jensen, & B. C. Dudek (Eds.), *Development and evolution of brain size: Behavioral implications.* New York: Academic Press.

Erikson, E. H. (1951). Sex differences in the play configurations of preadolescents. *American Journal of Orthopsychiatry, 21,* 667–692.

Erikson, E.H. (1963). *Childhood and society* (2nd ed.). New York: Norton.

Erikson, E. H. (1968). *Identity: Youth and crisis.* New York: Norton.

Erikson, E. H. (1982). *The life cycle completed.* New York: Norton.

Etaugh, C. (1980). Effects of nonmaternal care on children: Research evidence and popular views. *American Psychologist, 35*(4), 309–319.

Etzel, B. C., & Gewirtz, J. L. (1967). Experimental modification of caretaker-maintained high rate operant crying in 6- and 20-week old infants. Extinction of crying with reinforcement of eye contact and smiling. *Journal of Experimental Child Psychology, 5,* 303–317.

Evans, R. I. (1967). *Dialogue with Erik Erikson.* New York: Harper & Row.

Fagan, J. F. (1982). Infant memory. In T. M. Field, A. Huston, H. C. Quay, L. Troll, & G. E. Finley (Eds.), *Review of human development.* New York: Wiley.

Fagot, B. I. (1978). The influence of sex of child on parental reactions to toddler children. *Child Development, 49,* 459–465.

Falkner, F., Pernot-Roy, M. P., Habich, H., Sénécal, J., & Massé, G. (1958). Some international comparisons of physical growth in the first two years of life. *Courier, 8,* 1–11.

Fantz, R. L. (1958). Pattern vision in young infants. *The Psychological Record, 8,* 43–47.

Fantz, R. L. (1961). The origin of form perception. *Scientific American, 204*(5), 66–72.

Fantz, R. L. (1963). Pattern vision in newborn infants. *Science, 140,* 296–297.

Fantz, R. L., Fagan, J. F., & Miranda, S. B. (1975). Early visual selectivity as a function of pattern variables, previous exposure, age from birth and conception, and expected cognitive deficit. In L. B. Cohen & P. Salapatek (Eds.), *Infant perception: From sensation to cognition: Vol. 1. Basic visual processes.* New York: Academic Press.

Feather, N. T. (1980). Values in adolescence. In J. Adelson (Ed.), *Handbook of adolescent psychology.* New York: Wiley.

Feshbach, S. (1970). Aggression. In P. H. Mussen (Ed.), *Carmichael's manual of child psychology* (3rd ed., Vol. 2). New York: Wiley.

Fetters, W. B. (1976). *National longitudinal study of the high school class of 1972.* Washington, DC: National Center for Health Statistics, Department of Health, Education, and Welfare, Bulletin Numbers 197, 208.

Fitzgerald, H. E., & Brackbill, Y. (1976). Classical conditioning in infancy: Development and constraints. *Psychological Bulletin, 83*(3), 353–376.

Flach, F. F., & Draghi, S. C. (Eds.). (1975). *The nature and treatment of depression.* New York: Wiley.

Flavell, J. H. (1963). *The developmental psychology of Jean Piaget.* Princeton: Van Nostrand.

Flavell, J. H. (1977). *Cognitive development.* Englewood Cliffs, NJ: Prentice-Hall.

Flavell, J. H. (1982). On cognitive development. *Child Development, 53,* 1–10.

Ford, M. E. (1979). The construct validity of egocentrism. *Psychological Bulletin, 86,* 1169–1188.

Fraiberg, S. (1959). *The magic years.* New York: Scribner's.

Freedman, D. C. (1971, June 28–July 3). *The development of social hierarchies.* Paper presented at meeting of World Health Organization, Stockholm.

Freud, A. (1946). *The psychoanalytic treatment of children.* New York: International Universities Press.

Freud, A. (1965). *Normality and pathology in children: The writings of Anna Freud.* New York: International Universities Press.

Freud, A. (1968). Adolescence. In A. E. Winder & D. L. Angus (Eds.), *Adolescence: Contemporary studies.* New York: Modern Library.

Freud, S. (1935). *An autobiographical study.* New York: Norton.

Freud, S. (1936). *The problem of anxiety.* New York: Norton.

Freud, S. (1949). *An outline of psycho-analysis.* New York: Norton.

Friedman, M., and Rosenman, R. H. (1974). *Type A behavior and your heart.* New York: Knopf.

Furstenberg, F. F., Jr. (1976). *Unplanned parenthood: The social consequences of teenage childbearing.* New York: Free Press.

Furstenberg, F. F., Jr., & Crawford, A. G. (1981). Family support: Helping teenage mothers to cope. In F. F. Furstenberg, Jr., R. Lincoln, & J. Menken (Eds.), *Teenage sexuality, pregnancy, and childbearing.* Philadelphia: University of Pennsylvania Press.

Furstenberg, F. F., Jr., Lincoln, R., & Menken, J. (Eds.). (1981). *Teenage sexuality, pregnancy and childbearing.* Philadelphia: University of Pennsylvania Press.

Furth, H. (1970). *Piaget for teachers.* Englewood Cliffs, NJ: Prentice-Hall.

Galinsky, E. (1981). *Between generations: The six stages of parenthood.* New York: Berkley.

Gallatin, J. (1980). Political thinking in adolescence. In J. Adelson (Ed.), *Handbook of adolescent psychology.* New York: Wiley.

Galton, F. (1890). Statement made in footnote to an article by J. M. Cattell, Mental tests and measurements. *Mind, 15,* 373.

Garai, J. E., & Scheinfeld, A. (1968). Sex differences in mental and behavioral traits. *Genetic Psychology Monographs, 77,* 169–299.

Garfield, S. L., & Bergin, A. E. (Eds.). (1978). *Handbook of psychotherapy and behavior change* (2nd ed.). New York: Wiley.

Garn, S. M. (1980). Continuities and change in maturational timing. In O. Brim & J. Kagan (Eds.), *Constancy and change in human development.* Cambridge, MA: Harvard University Press.

Garner, A. M., & Wenar, C. (1959). *The mother-child interaction in psychosomatic disorders.* Urbana, IL: University of Illinois Press.

Garnica, O. K. (1977). Some prosodic and paralinguistic features of speech to young children. In C. Snow & C. Ferguson (Eds.), *Talking to children: Language input and acquisition.* Cambridge: Cambridge University Press.

Garvey, C., & Hogan, R. (1973). Social speech and social interaction: Egocentrism revisited. *Child Development, 44,* 562–568.

Geber, M., & Dean, R. F. A. (1957). The state of development of newborn African children. *Lancet, 272,* 1216–1219.

Geis, G., & Monahan, J. (1975). The social ecology of violence. In T. Lickona (Ed.), *Man and morality.* New York: Holt, Rinehart & Winston.

Gelfand, D. E., & Olson, J. K. (1979). *The aging network: Programs and services.* New York: Springer.

Gelles, R. J. (1973). Child abuse as psychopathology: A sociological critique and reformula-
tion. *American Journal of Orthopsychiatry, 43,* 611–621.

Gelman, R. (1969). Conservation acquisition: A problem of learning to attend to relevant attributes. *Journal of Experimental Child Psychology, 7,* 167–187.

Gelman, R. (1979). Preschool thought. *American Psychologist, 34*(10), 900–905.

Gelman, R., & Baillargeon, E. E. (1983). A review of some Piagetian concepts. In J. H. Flavell & E. M. Markman (Eds.), *Cognitive development.* Vol. 3 of P. H. Mussen (Ed.), *Handbook of child development* (4th ed.). New York: Wiley.

Gesell, A. L. (1928). *Infancy and human growth.* New York: Macmillan.

Gesell, A. L. (1954). The ontogenesis of infant behavior. In L. Carmichael (Ed.), *Manual of child psychology* (2nd ed.). New York: Wiley.

Gesell, A. L., & Thompson, H. (1929). Learning and growth in identical infant twins: An experimental study by the method of co-twin control. *Genetic Psychology Monographs, 6,* 1–124.

Gibson, E. J., & Walk, R. R. (1961). The "visual cliff." *Scientific American, 202,* 2–9.

Gibson, J. J. (1979). *The ecological approach to visual perception.* Boston: Houghton Mifflin.

Gilliam, T. B., Freedson, P. S., Geenen, D. L., & Shahraray, B. (1981). Physical activity patterns determined by heart-rate monitoring in 6–7 year-old children. *Medicine and Science in Sports and Exercise, 13*(1), 65–67.

Gilligan, C. (1982). *In a different voice: Psychological theory and women's development.* Cambridge, MA: Harvard University Press.

Ginott, H. (1965). *Between parent and child.* New York: Macmillan.

Ginott, H. (1969). *Between parent and teenager.* New York: Macmillan.

Ginott, H. (1971). *Teacher and child.* New York: Macmillan.

Ginsburg, H., & Opper, S. (1979). *Piaget's theory of intellectual development* (2nd ed.). Englewood Cliffs, NJ: Prentice-Hall.

Glass, R. H., & Kase, N. G. (1970). *Woman's*

choice: A guide to contraception, fertility, abortion, and menopause. New York: Basic Books.

Glenn, N. D., & Weaver, C. N. (1977). The marital happiness of remarried divorced persons. *Journal of Marriage and the Family, 39,* 331–337.

Glick, P. G., & Norton, A. J. (1978). Marrying, divorcing, and living together in the U.S. today. *Population Bulletin, 32,* 3–38.

Glynn, T. J. (1981). From family to peer: A review of transitions of influence among drug-using youth. *Journal of Youth and Adolescence, 10*(5), 363–383.

Goertzel, V., & Goertzel, M. (1962). *Cradles of eminence.* Boston: Little, Brown.

Gold, D., & Andres, D. (1978). Developmental comparisons between 10-year-old children with employed and non-employed mothers. *Child Development, 49,* 75–84.

Gold, M. (1970). *Delinquent behavior in an American city.* Monterey, CA: Brooks/Cole.

Gold, M., & Petronio, R. J. (1980). Delinquent behavior in adolescence. In J. Adelson (Ed.), *Handbook of adolescent psychology.* New York: Wiley.

Goldfarb, W. (1970). Childhood psychosis. In P. H. Mussen (Ed.), *Carmichael's manual of child psychology* (3rd ed., Vol. 2). New York: Wiley.

Goldsmith, H. H. (1983). Genetic influence on personality from infancy to adulthood. *Child Development, 54,* 331–355.

Golub, M. S., & Golub, A. M. (1981). Behavioral teratogenesis. In A. Milunsky, E. A. Friedman, & L. Gluck (Eds.), *Advances in perinatal medicine* (Vol. 1). New York: Plenum.

Goodman, E. (1979). *Turning points.* New York: Fawcett Crest.

Goodrich, F. W., Jr. (1969). *Preparing for childbirth: A manual for expectant parents.* Englewood Cliffs, NJ: Prentice-Hall.

Gordon, I. J. (1969). *Early childhood stimulation through parent education* (Final report to the Children's Bureau, Social and Rehabilitation Service, Department of Health, Education, and Welfare). Gainsville, FL, University of Florida, Institute for Development of Human Resources.

Gordon, I. J., & Guinagh, B. J. (1974). *A home learning center approach to early stimulation* (Final report to the National Institute of Mental Health). Gainesville, FL: Institute for Development of Human Resources, University of Florida.

Gordon, T. (1970). *P.E.T.: Parent effectiveness training.* New York: Wyden.

Gottesman, I. I. (1963). Heritability of personality: A demonstration. *Psychology Monographs, 77* (No. 572).

Gray, S. W., & Klaus, R. E. (1970). The early training project: A seven year report. *Child Development, 41,* 909–924.

Graziano, A. M., De Giovanni, I. S., & Garcia, K. A. (1979). Behavioral treatment of children's fears: A review, *Psychological Bulletin, 86,* 804–830.

Green, H. [Joanne Greenberg]. (1964). *I never promised you a rose garden.* New York: Holt, Rinehart & Winston.

Greenfield, P. M., & Smith, J. (1976). *The structure of communication in early language.* New York: Academic Press.

Griffore, R. J. (1979). The validity of popular primers for parents. *American Psychologist, 34*(2), 182–183.

Groos, K. (1898). *The play of animals.* New York: Appleton.

Groos, K. (1901). *The play of men.* New York: Appleton.

Grossman, K., Thane, K., & Grossman, K. E. (1981). Maternal tactual contact of the newborn after various postpartum conditions of mother-infant contact. *Developmental Psychology, 17,* 159–169.

Gruber, H. E., & Vonèche, J. J. (Eds.). (1977). *The essential Piaget: An interpretive reference and guide.* New York: Basic Books.

Guilford, J. P. (1967). *The nature of human intelligence.* New York: McGraw-Hill.

Guttmacher, A. F. (1969). *Birth control and love.* New York: Macmillan.

Guttmacher, A. F. (1973). *Pregnancy, birth, and family planning: A guide for expectant parents in the 1970s.* New York: Viking Press.

Hafez, E. S. E., & Evans, T. N. (Eds.). (1973). *Human reproduction: Conception and contraception.* New York: Harper & Row.

Haith, M. M. (1980). *Rules that babies look by. The organization of newborn visual acuity.* Hillsdale, NJ: Erlbaum.

Haith, M. M., & Campos, J. J. (Eds.). (1983). *Infancy and developmental psychobiology.* Vol. 2 of P. H. Mussen (Ed.), *Handbook of child psychology* (4th ed.). New York: Wiley.

Hall, C. S. (1979). *A primer of Freudian psychology.* New York: New American Library.

Hall, G. S. (1891). The contents of children's minds. *Pedagogical Seminary, 1,* 139–173.

Hall, G. S. (1904). *Adolescence: Its psychology and its relations to physiology, anthropology, sociology, sex, crime, religion, and education* (2 vols.). New York: Appleton.

Hall, M. C. et al. (1977). *Responsive parent program.* Lawrence, KS: H & H Enterprises.

Hall, R. V. (1974). *Managing behavior: Applications in home and school.* Lawrence, KS: H & H Enterprises.

Halliday, M. A. K. (1975). *Learning how to mean: Explorations in the development of language.* London: Arnold.

Halverson, H. M. (1931). An experimental study of prehension in infants by means of systematic cinema records. *Genetic Psychology Monographs, 10.*

Hansen, S. L. (1977, April). Dating choices of high school students. *The Family Coordinator,* 133–138.

Hanson, J. W. (1977). Unpublished manuscript.

Hanson, J. W., Jones, K. L., & Smith, D. W. (1976). Fetal alcohol syndrome: Experience with 41 patients. *Journal of the American Medical Association, 235,* 1458–1460.

Harbison, R. D. (Ed.). (1975). *Perinatal addiction.* New York: Halsted Press.

Hardin, G. J. (1970). *Birth control.* New York: Pegasus.

Harlap, S., & Shlono, P. H. (1980). Alcohol, smoking, and incidence of spontaneous abortion in the first and second trimester. *Lancet, 2,* 173–176.

Harrington, M. (1965). *The other America.* Baltimore: Penguin.

Harris, P. L. (1983). Infant cognition. In M. M. Haith & J. J. Campos (Eds.), *Infancy and developmental psychobiology.* Vol. 2 of P. H. Mussen (Ed.), *Handbook of child psychology* (4th ed.). New York: Wiley.

Hartshorne, H., & May, M. A. (1929). *Studies in service and self-control.* New York: Macmillan.

Hartshorne, H., & May, M. A. (1930a). *Studies in deceit.* New York: Macmillan.

Hartshorne, H., & May, M. A. (1930b). *Studies in the organization of character.* New York: Macmillan.

Hartup, W. W. (1974). Aggression in childhood: Developmental perspectives. *American Psychologist, 29,* 336–341.

Hartup, W. W. (1983). Peer relations. In E. M. Hetherington (Ed.), *Socialization, personality, and social development.* Vol. 4, of P. H. Mussen (Ed.), *Handbook of child psychology* (4th ed.). New York: Wiley.

Hartup, W. W., & Coates, B. (1967). Imitation of a peer as a function of reinforcement from the peer group and rewardingness of the model. *Child Development, 38,* 1003–1016.

Hass, A. (1979). *Teenage sexuality: A survey of teenage sexual behavior.* New York: Macmillan.

Hausknecht, R., & Heilman, J. R. (1978). *Having a caesarean baby.* New York: Dutton.

Havighurst, R. (1952). *Developmental tasks and education.* New York: Longmans, Green.

Hayflick, L. (1979). Cell aging. In A. Cherkin (Ed.), *Physiology and cell biology of aging.* New York: Raven Press.

Heinonen, O. P., Slone, D., & Shapiro, S. (1976). *Birth defects and drugs in pregnancy.* Littleton, MA: Publishing Sciences Group.

Herron, R. E., & Sutton-Smith, B. (1971). *Child's play.* New York: Wiley.

Hersh, R. H., Paolitto, D. P., & Reimer, J. (1979). *Promoting moral growth: From Piaget to Kohlberg.* New York: Longman.

Herzog, E., & Sudia, C. E. (1973). Children in fatherless families. In B. M. Caldwell & H. M. Ricciuti (Eds.), *Review of child development research* (Vol. 3). Chicago: University of Chicago Press.

Hess, R. D., & Shipman, V. (1965). Early experience and the socialization of cognitive modes in children. *Child Development, 36,* 869–886.

Hetherington, E. M. (1972). Effects of father absence on personality development in adolescent daughters. *Developmental Psychology, 7,* 327–336.

Hetherington, E. M. (1979). Divorce: A child's perspective. *American Psychologist, 34*(10), 851–858.

Hetherington, E. M., Cox, M., & Cox, R. (1977, June). *The development of children in mother headed families.* Paper presented at the Families in Contemporary America Conference, George Washington University, Washington, DC.

Hilgard, J. R. (1932). Learning and maturation in school children. *Journal of Genetic Psychology, 41,* 40–53.

Hill, R. M. (1973). Drugs ingested by pregnant women. *Clinical Pharmacology Therapeutics, 14,* 654–659.

Hill, R. M., & Stern, L. (1979). Drugs in pregnancy: Effects on the fetus and newborn. *Drugs, 17,* 182–197.

Hill, T., Rubin, Z., & Peplau, L. A. (1974). Breakups before marriage. The end of 103 affairs. In G. Levinger & O. C. Moles (Eds.), *Divorce and separation.* New York: Basic Books.

Hinde, R. (1963). The nature of imprinting. In B. M. Foss (Ed.), *Determinants of infant behavior* (Vol. 2). London: Methuen.

Hinde, R. (1983). Ethology and child development. In M. Haith & J. Campos (Eds.), *Infancy and developmental psychobiology.* Vol. 2 of P. H. Mussen (Ed.), *Handbook of child psychology* (4th ed.). New York: Wiley.

Hindley, C. B., Filliozat, A. M., Klackenberg, G., Nicolet-Meister, P., & Sand, E. A. (1966). Differences in age of walking in five European longitudinal samples. *Human Biology, 38,* 364–379.

Hirsch, J. (1975). Cell number and size as a determinant of subsequent obesity. In M. Winick (Ed.), *Childhood obesity.* New York: Wiley.

Hodapp, R. M., Goldfield, E. C., & Boyatzis, C. J. (1984). The use and effectiveness of

maternal scaffolding in mother-infant games. *Child Development, 55,* 772–781.

Hodgson, J. L., & Buskirk, E. R. (1981). The role of exercises in aging. In P. Danon, N. W. Schoek, and M. Marois (Eds.), *Aging: A challenge to science and to society.* Vol. I. London: Oxford University Press.

Hoffman, L. W. (1972). Early childhood experiences and women's achievement motives. *Journal of Social Issues, 28*(2), 129–156.

Hoffman, L. W. (1974a). Effects of maternal employment on the child: A review of the research. *Developmental Psychology, 10,* 204–228.

Hoffman, L. W. (1974b). Fear of success in males and females: 1965 and 1971. *Journal of Consulting and Clinical Psychology, 42,* 353–358.

Hoffman, L. W. (1979). Maternal employment: 1979. *American Psychologist, 34*(10), 859–865.

Hoffman, M. L. (1975). Developmental synthesis of affect and cognitions and its implications for altruistic motivation. *Developmental Psychology, 11,* 607–622.

Hoffman, M. L. (1976). Empathy, role-taking, guilt, and development of altruistic motives. In T. Lickona (Ed.), *Moral development and behavior.* New York: Holt, Rinehart & Winston.

Hoffman, M. L. (1978). Toward a theory of empathic arousal and development. In M. Lewis & L. A. Rosenblum (Eds.), *The development of affect.* New York: Plenum.

Hoffman, M. L. (1979). Development of moral thought, feeling, and behavior. *American Psychologist, 34*(10), 958–966.

Hoffman, M. L. (1980). Moral development in adolescence. In J. Adelson (Ed.), *Handbook of adolescent psychology.* New York: Wiley.

Hogan, R. (1974). The terror of solitude. *Merrill-Palmer Quarterly, 21,* 67–74.

Holden, C. (1980). Identical twins reared apart. *Science, 21,* 1323–1327.

Holinger, P. C. (1980). Violet deaths as a leading cause of mortality: An epidemiological study of suicide, homicide, and accidents. *American Journal of Psychiatry, 137,* 472–476.

Hollender, J. W. (1967). Development of a realistic vocational choice. *Journal of Counseling Psychology, 14,* 314–318.

Holmes, T. H., & Rahe, R. H. (1967). The social

readjustment rating scale. *Journal of Psychosomatic Research, 11,* 212–218.

Honzik, M. P. (1954). *A developmental study of persistence, change, and recurrences of behaviors over certain age periods.* Paper presented at the Western Psychological Association, Long Beach, CA.

Hopkins, J. R. (1983). *Adolescence: The transitional years.* New York: Academic Press.

Horn, J. L. (1976). Human abilities: A review of research and theory in the early 1970s. *Annual Review of Psychology, 27,* 437–485.

Horn, J. L. (1978). Human ability systems. In P. B. Baltes (Ed.), *Life-span development and behavior.* New York: Academic Press.

Horn, J. L., & Cattell, R. B. (1967). Age differences in fluid and crystallized intelligence. *Acta Psychologica, 26,* 107–129.

Horn, J. L., & Donaldson, G. (1976). On the myth of intellectual decline in adulthood. *American Psychologist, 31,* 701–719.

Horn, J. L., & Donaldson, G. (1980). Cognitive development in adulthood. In O. G. Brim & J. Kagan (Eds.), *Constancy and change in human development.* Cambridge, MA: Harvard University Press.

Horn, J. M. (1983). The Texas adoption project: Adopted children and their intellectual resemblance to biological and adoptive parents. *Child Development, 54,* 268–275.

Horner, M. S. (1968). *Sex differences in achievement motivation and performance in competitive and noncompetitive situations.* Unpublished doctoral dissertation. Ann Arbor: University of Michigan.

Horner, M. S. (1970). Femininity and successful achievement: A basic inconsistency. In J. M. Bardwick, E. Douvan, M. S. Horner, & D. Guttman (Eds.), *Feminine personality and conflict.* Belmont, CA: Brooks/Cole.

Horney, K. (1937). *The neurotic personality of our time.* New York: Norton.

Horney, K. (1939). *New ways in psychoanalysis.* New York: Norton.

Horney, K. (1945). *Our inner conflicts.* New York: Norton.

Horney, K. (1950). *Neurosis and human growth.* New York: Norton.

Hotchner, T. (1979). *Pregnancy and childbirth.* New York: Avon.

Hunt, M. (1970, July). Special sex education survey. *Seventeen,* p. 94.

Huntington, D. S. (1979). Supportive programs for infants and parents. In J. D. Osofsky (Ed.), *Handbook of infant development.* New York: Wiley.

Huston, A. C. (1983). Sex-typing. In E. M. Hetherington (Ed.), *Socialization, personality, and social development.* Vol. 4 of P. H. Mussen (Ed.), *Handbook of child psychology* (4th ed.). New York: Wiley.

Huston, T. L., & Burgess, R. L. (1979). Social exchange in developing relationships: An overview. In T. L. Huston & R. L. Burgess (Eds.), *Social exchange in developing relationships.* New York: Academic Press.

Huyck, M. H. (1982). From gregariousness to intimacy: Marriage and friendship over the adult years. In T. M. Field, A. Huston, H. C. Quay, L. Troll, & G. E. Finley (Eds.), *Review of human development.* New York: Wiley.

Ilg, F. L., & Ames, L. (1955). *Child behavior.* New York: Dell.

Inhelder, B., & Piaget, J. (1958). *The growth of logical thinking from childhood to adolescence.* New York: Basic Books.

Izard, C. E. (1977). *Human emotions.* New York: Plenum.

Izard, C. E., Kagan, J., & Zajonc, R. B. (Eds.). (1984). *Emotions, cognition, and behavior.* Cambridge: Cambridge University Press.

Jacklin, C.N., & Maccoby, E. E. (1978). Social behavior at thirty-three months in same-sex and mixed-sex dyads. *Child Development, 49,* 557–569.

Jackson, D. D. (1980). Reunion of identical twins, raised apart, reveals some astonishing similarities. Smithsonian, *11*(7), 48–56.

Jacobs, J. (1971). *Adolescent suicide.* New York: Wiley.

Janeway, E. (1971). *Man's world, woman's place.* New York: Morrow.

Jelliffe, D., & Jelliffe, E. (Eds.) (1971). Symposium: The uniqueness of human milk. *American Journal of Clinical Nutrition, 24,* 968–1024.

Jensen, G. F. (1973). Parents, peers, and delinquent action: A test of the differential association perspective. *American Journal of Sociology, 78,* 562–575.

Jersild, A. T. (1954). Emotional development. In L. Carmichael (Ed.), *Manual of child psychology* (2nd ed.). New York: Wiley.

Jersild, A. T. (1968). *Child psychology* (6th ed.). Englewood Cliffs, NJ: Prentice-Hall.

Jersild, A. T., & Holmes, F. B. (1935a). Children's fears. *Child Development Monographs,* No. 20. New York: Teachers College, Columbia University.

Jersild, A. T., & Holmes, F. B. (1935b). Methods of overcoming children's fears. *Journal of Psychology, 1,* 75–104.

Jessor, R., and Jessor, S. (1977). *Problem behavior and psychosocial development: A longitudinal study of youth.* New York: Academic Press.

Jessor, S., & Jessor, R. (1975). Transition from virginity to nonvirginity among youth: A social-psychological study over time. *Developmental Psychology, 11,* 473–484.

Jones, E. (1953). *The life and work of Sigmund Freud: Vol. 1. The formative years and the great discoveries.* New York: Basic Books.

Jones, E. (1961). *The life and work of Sigmund Freud* (Abridged version edited by L. Trilling & S. Marcus). New York: Basic Books.

Jones, H. E. (1939). The adolescent growth study. I. Principles and methods. II. Procedures. *Journal of Consulting Psychology, 3,* 157–159, 177–180.

Jones, H. E. (1946). Physical ability as a factor in social adjustment in adolescence. *Journal of Educational Research, 39,* 287–301.

Jones, K. L., Smith, D. W., Ulland, C. N., & Streissguth, A. P. (1973). Pattern of malformation in offspring of chronic alcoholic mothers. *Lancet, 1* (7815), 1267–1271.

Jones, M. C. (1924). A laboratory study of fear: The case of Peter. *Pedagogical Seminary and Journal of Genetic Psychology, 31,* 308–315.

Jones, M. C. (1957). The later career of boys who were early or late maturing. *Child Development, 28,* 113–128.

Jones, M. C. (1965). Psychological correlates of somatic development. *Child Development, 36,* 899–911.

Jones, M. C., Bayley, N., Macfarlane, J. W., & Honzik, M. P. (Eds.). (1971). *The course of human development.* Waltham, MA: Xerox.

Jones, M. C., & Mussen, P. H. (1958). Self conceptions, motivations and interpersonal attitudes of early and late maturing girls. *Child Development, 29,* 491–501.

Josselson, R. (1973). Psychodynamic aspects of identity formation in college women. *Journal of Youth and Adolescence, 2,* 3–52.

Josselson, R. (1980). Ego development in adolescence. In J. Adelson (Ed.), *Handbook of adolescent psychology.* New York: Wiley.

Kagan, J. (1964a). *Developmental studies of reflection and analysis.* Cambridge, MA: Harvard University Press.

Kagan, J. (1964b). Impulsive and reflective children. In J. D. Krumbolz (Ed.), *Learning and the educational process.* Chicago: Rand McNally.

Kagan, J. (1971). *Change and continuity in infancy.* New York: Wiley.

Kagan, J. (1979). Structure and process in the human infant. The ontogeny of mental representation. In M. H. Bornstein & W. Kessen (Eds.), *Psychological development from infancy: Image to intention.* Hillsdale, NJ: Lawrence Erlbaum.

Kagan, J. (1980). Perspectives on continuity. In O. G. Brim & J. Kagan (Eds.), *Constancy and change in human development.* Cambridge, MA: Harvard University Press.

Kagan, J., Kearsley, R. B., & Zelazo, P. R. (with the assistance of C. Minton). (1978). *Infancy: Its place in human development.* Cambridge, MA: Harvard University Press.

Kagan, J., & Moss, H. A. (1962). *Birth to maturity: A study in psychological development.* New York: Wiley.

Kamii, C., & Dermon, L. (1972). The Engelmann

approach to teaching logical thinking: Findings from the administration of some Piagetian tasks. In D. R. Green, M. P. Ford, & G. Flamer (Eds.), *Piaget and measurement*. New York: McGraw-Hill.

Kandel, D. B. (1978). *Final report: Family processes in adolescent drug use*. Rockville, MD: National Institute on Drug Abuse, Division of Research.

Kandel, D. B. (1978). Similarity in real-life adolescent friendship pairs. *Journal of Personality and Social Psychology, 36,* 306–312.

Kandel, D. B. (1980). Drug and drinking behavior among youth. In A. Inkeles, J. Coleman, & R. H. Turner (Eds.), *Annual Review of Sociology* (Vol. 6). Palo Alto, CA: Annual Review Press.

Kanner, L. (1941). *In defense of mothers*. Springfield, IL: Thomas.

Kanner, L. (1943). Autistic disturbances of affective content. *Nervous Child, 2,* 217–250.

Kanner, L. (1972). *Child psychiatry* (4th ed.). Springfield, IL: Thomas.

Kaplan, H. B. (1980). *Deviant behavior in defense of self*. New York: Academic Press.

Karmel, M. (1959). *Thank you, Dr. Lamaze: A mother's experience in painless childbirth*. Philadelphia: Lippincott.

Karmiloff-Smith, A. (1979). A functional approach to child language: A study of determiners and reference. *Cambridge Studies in Linguistics*, No. 24. Cambridge, MA: Cambridge University Press.

Karoly, P., & Kanfer, F. (Eds.). (1978). *The psychology of self-management: From theory to practice*. Elmsford, NY: Pergamon Press.

Katzman, R. (1976). The prevalence and malignancy of Alzheimer's disease. *Archives of Neurology, 33,* 217–218.

Katzman, R., & Karasu, T. B. (1975). Differential diagnosis in dementia. In W. Fields (Ed.), *Neurological and sensory disorders in the elderly*. New York: Stratton.

Keating, D. P. (1980). Thinking processes in adolescence. In J. Adelson (Ed.), *Handbook of adolescent psychology*. New York: Wiley.

Kegan, R. (1982). *The evolving self: Problem and process in human development*. Cambridge, MA: Harvard University Press.

Kelly, E. L. (1955). Consistency of adult personality. *American Psychologist, 10,* 659–681.

Kempe, R. W., & Kempe, C. H. (1978). *Child abuse*. Cambridge, MA: Harvard University Press.

Keniston, K. (1968). *Young radicals*. New York: Harcourt, Brace, & World.

Keniston, K. (1971). *Youth and dissent: The rise of the new opposition*. New York: Harcourt, Brace, Jovanovich.

Kennell, J. H., & Klaus, M. H. See Klaus and Kennell (1976).

Kennell, J. H., Voos, D. K., & Klaus, M. H. (1979). Parent-infant bonding. In J. D. Osofsky (Ed.), *Handbook of infant behavior*. New York: Wiley.

Kessen, W. (1965). *The child*. New York: Wiley.

Kessler, S. (1980). The genetics of schizophrenia: A review. *Schizophrenia Bulletin, 6,* 404–416.

Keys, A. J., Brozek, J., Henschel, A., Mickelsen, O., & Taylor, H. L. (1950). Growth and development. In *The biology of human starvation* (Vol. 2). Minneapolis: University of Minnesota Press.

Kinkade, K. (1973). *A Walden Two experiment: The first five years of Twin Oaks community*. New York: Morrow.

Kinsbourne, M., & Hiscock, M. (1983). The normal and deviant development of functional lateralization of the brain. In M. M. Haith & J. J. Campos (Eds.), *Infancy and developmental psychobiology*. Vol. 2 of P. H. Mussen (Ed.), *Handbook of child psychology*. New York: Wiley.

Kinsey, A. C., Pomeroy, W. B., & Martin, C. E. (1948). *Sexual behavior in the human male*. Philadelphia: Saunders.

Kinsey, A. C., Pomeroy, W. B., Martin, C. E., & Gebhard, P. H. (1953). *Sexual behavior in the human female*. Philadelphia: Saunders.

Kitson, G. C. (1982). Attachment to the spouse in divorce: A scale and its application. *Journal of Marriage and Family, 44,* 379–393.

Kitson, G. C., & Sussman, M. B. (1982). Marital complaints, demographic characteristics and symptoms of mental distress in divorce. *Journal of Marriage and the Family, 44,* 87–101.

Klaus, M. H., & Kennell, J. H. (1976). *Maternal-infant bonding.* St. Louis: Mosby.

Klausner, S. Z. (1968, October). *Two centuries of child rearing manuals* (Technical report submitted to the Joint Commission of Mental Health of Children, Inc.). University Park, PA: University of Pennsylvania, Project "Hydra."

Klein, M. (1937). *The psychoanalysis of children.* London: Hogarth.

Klinnert, M., Emde, R. N., Butterfield, P., & Campos, J. J. (1983, April). Emotional communication from familiarized adults influences infants' behavior. Paper presented at the meeting of the Society for Research in Child Development, Detroit.

Koch, H. L. (1956). Some emotional attitudes of the young child in relation to characteristics of his siblings. *Child Development, 27,* 393–426.

Kohlberg, L. (1958). *The development of modes of moral thinking and choice in the years ten to sixteen.* Unpublished doctoral dissertation, University of Chicago.

Kohlberg, L. (1963). The development of children's orientations toward a moral order. I. Sequence in the development of moral thought. *Vita Humana, 6,* 11–33.

Kohlberg, L. (1966). A cognitive-developmental analysis of children's sex-role concepts and attitudes. In E. E. Maccoby (Ed.), *The development of sex differences.* Stanford, CA: Stanford University Press.

Kohlberg, L. (1969). Stage and sequence: The cognitive-developmental approach to socialization. In D. A. Goslin (Ed.), *Handbook of socialization theory and research.* Chicago: Rand McNally.

Kohlberg, L. (1976). Moral stages and moralization: The cognitive-developmental approach. In T. Lickona (Ed.), *Moral development and behavior: Theory, research, and social issues.* New York: Holt, Rinehart, & Winston.

Kohlberg, L. (1978). Revisions in the theory and practice of moral development. In W. Damon (Ed.), *Moral development: New directions for child development* (No. 2). San Francisco: Jossey-Bass.

Kohlberg, L., & Kramer, R. (1969). Continuities and discontinuities in childhood and adult moral development. *Human Development, 12,* 93–120.

Kohlberg, L., & Turiel, E. (Eds.). (1972). *Recent research in moral development.* New York: Holt, Rinehart & Winston.

Kohn, R. R. (1979). Biomedical aspects of aging. In D. D. Van Tassel (Ed.), *Aging, death, and the completion of being.* Philadelphia: University of Pennsylvania Press.

Kopp, C. B., & Parmelee, A. H. (1979). Prenatal and perinatal influences on infant behavior. In J. D. Osofsky (Ed.), *Handbook of infant development.* New York: Wiley.

Korner, A. F., & Thoman, E. B. (1970). Visual alertness in neonates as evoked by maternal care. *Journal of Experimental Child Psychology, 10,* 67–78.

Kraus, P. (1984). A longitudinal study of children into the adult years. In S. A. Mednick, M. Narway, & K. M. Finello (Eds.), *Handbook of longitudinal research: Vol. 1. Birth and childhood cohorts.* New York: Praeger.

Kron, R. E. (1966). Instrumental conditioning of nutritive sucking behavior in the newborn. *Recent Advances in Biological Psychiatry, 9,* 295–300.

Krumboltz, J. D., & Thoreson, C. E. (1972). *Changing children's behavior.* Englewood Cliffs, NJ: Prentice-Hall.

Kubler-Ross, E. (1969). *On death and dying.* New York: Macmillan.

Kubler-Ross, E. (1975). *Death: The final stage of growth.* Englewood Cliffs, NJ: Prentice-Hall.

Kuhn, T. S. (1962). *The structure of scientfic revolutions.* Chicago: University of Chicago Press.

Kurtines, W., & Greif, E. B. (1974). The development of moral thought: Review and evaluation of Kohlberg's approach. *Psychological Bulletin, 81*(8), 453–470.

Labouvie-Vief, G. (1980). Beyond formal operations: Uses and limits of pure logic in life-span development. *Human Development, 23*(3), 141–161.

Lakin, M. (1957). Personality factors in mothers of excessively crying (colicky) infants. *Monographs of the Society for Research in Child Development, 22* (64).

Lamaze, F. (1958). *Painless childbirth: Psychoprophylactic method.* London: Burke.

Lamb, M. E. (Ed.). (1976). *The role of the father in child development.* New York: Wiley.

Lamb, M. E. (1979). Paternal influences and the father's role. *American Psychologist, 34*(10), 938–943.

Lamb, M. E., Thompson, R. A., Gardner, W. P., Charnov, E., & Estes, D. (1983). *Patterns of attachment reassessed.* Hillsdale, NJ: Erlbaum.

Langer, J. (1975). Interactional aspects of cognitive organization. *Cognition, 3,* 9–28.

Lapouse, R., & Monk, M. (1964). Behavior deviations in a representative sample of children: Variation by sex, age, race, social class and family size. *American Journal of Orthopsychiatry, 34,* 436–446.

Larsen, L. F. (1972). The influence of parents and peers during adolescence: The situation hypothesis revisited. *Journal of Marriage and the Family, 34,* 67–74.

Lassers, E., Nordan, R., & Bladholm S. (1973). Steps in the return to school of children with school phobia. *American Journal of Psychiatry, 130*(3), 265–268.

Leahy, A. M. (1935). Nature-nurture and intelligence. *Genetic Psychology Monographs, 17,* 236–308.

Leboyer, F. (1975). *Birth without violence.* New York: Knopf.

Lehman, H. C. (1953). *Age and achievement.* Philadelphia: American Philosophical Society.

Leiderman, H., & Leiderman, G. (1974). Affective and cognitive consequences of polymatric infant care in the East African highlands. In A. Pick (Ed.), *Minnesota symposium on child development* (Vol. 8). Minneapolis: University of Minnesota Press.

Leiderman, P. H. (1978). The critical period hypothesis revisited. Mother to infant social bonding in the neonatal period. In F. D. Horowitz (Ed.), *Early development hazards: Predictors and precautions.* Washington, DC:

American Association for the Advancement of Science.

Leifer, A., Leiderman, P., Barnett, C., & Williams, J. (1972). Effects of mother-infant separation on maternal attachment behavior. *Child Development, 43,* 1203–1218.

Leifer, M. (1980). *Psychological effects of motherhood: A study of first pregnancy.* New York: Praeger.

LeMasters, E. E. (1977). *Parents in modern America* (3rd ed.). Homewood, IL: Dorsey.

Lepper, M. R. (1982). Social control processes, attributions of motivation, and the internalization of social values. In E. T. Higgins, D. N. Ruble, & W. W. Hartup (Eds.), *Social cognition and social behavior: Developmental perspectives.* Cambridge: Cambridge University Press.

Lerner, R. M., & Karabenick, S. A. (1974). Physical attractiveness, body attitudes, and self-concept in late adolescents. *Journal of Youth and Adolescence, 3,* 307–316.

Lerner, R. M., & Shea, J. A. (1982). Social behavior in adolescence. In B. B. Wolman (Ed.), *Handbook of developmental psychology.* Englewood Cliffs, NJ: Prentice-Hall.

Lester, G., & Lester, D. (1971). *Suicide: The gamble with death.* Englewood Cliffs, NJ: Prentice-Hall.

Levenkron, S. (1978). *The best little girl in the world.* Chicago: Contemporary Books.

Levinson, D. J. (1978). *The seasons of a man's life.* New York: Knopf.

Lewis, M. (1967). The meaning of a response or why researchers in infant behavior should be Oriental metaphysicians. *Merrill-Palmer Quarterly, 13,* 7–18.

Lewis, M. (1972). Culture and gender roles: There's no unisex in the nursery. *Psychology Today, 5*(12), 54–57.

Lewis, M., & Brooks, J. (1975). Infants' reactions to people. In M. Lewis & L. A. Rosenblum (Eds.), *The origins of fear,* New York: Wiley.

Lewis, M., & Brooks, J. (1978). Self-knowledge and emotional development. In M. Lewis & L. A. Rosenblum (Eds.), *The development of affect.* New York: Plenum.

Lewis, M., & Rosenblum, L. A. (Eds.). (1974).

The effect of the infant on its caregiver. New York: Wiley.

Lewis, M., & Rosenblum, L. A. (Eds.). (1978). *The development of affect.* New York: Plenum.

Lewis, M., & Starr, M. D. (1979). Developmental continuity. In J. D. Osofsky (Ed.), *Handbook of infant development.* New York: Wiley.

Lickona, T. (1976a). Research on Piaget's theory of moral development. In T. Lickona (Ed.), *Moral development: Current theory and research.* New York: Holt, Rinehart & Winston.

Lickona, T. (Ed.). (1976b). *Moral development and behavior: Theory, research, and social issues.* New York: Holt, Rinehart & Winston.

Liebert, R. M., & Neale, J. M. (1972). TV violence and child aggression: Snow on the screen. *Psychology Today, 5*(11), 38–40.

Liebert, R. M., Neale, J. M., & Davidson, E. S. (1973). *The early window: Effects of television on children and youth.* New York: Pergamon.

Lindemann, C. (1974). *Birth control and unmarried women.* New York: Springer.

Lindemann, E. (1944). Symptomatology and management of acute grief. *American Journal of Psychiatry, 101*, 141–148.

Lipsitt, L. P. (1979). Critical conditions in infancy: A psychological perspective. *American Psychologist, 34*(10), 973–980.

Livson, N., & Peskin, H. (1980). Perspectives on adolescence from longitudinal research. In J. Adelson (Ed.), *Handbook of adolescent psychology.* New York: Wiley.

Loehlin, J. C., Horn, J. M., & Willerman, L. (1981). Personality resemblance in adoptive families. *Behavior Genetics, 3*, 309–330.

Looft, W. R. (1971). Sex differences in the expression of vocational aspirations by elementary school children. *Developmental Psychology, 5*, 366.

Lopata, H. Z. (1973). *Widowhood in an American city.* Cambridge, MA: Schenkman.

Lopata, H. Z. (1979). *Women as widows: Support systems.* New York: Elsevier/North Holland.

Lorenz, K. (1937). Über die Bildung des Instinkbegriffes. *Naturwissenschaften, 25*, 289–300, 307–318, 324–331.

Lorenz, K. (1943). Die angeborenen formen mö-

glicher Erfahrung. *Zeitschrift für Tierpsychologie, 5*, 235–409.

Lorenz, K. (1952). *King Solomon's ring.* New York: Crowell.

Lorenz, K. (1966). *On aggression.* New York: Harcourt, Brace & World.

Lorenz, K. (1970, 1971). Studies in animal and human behavior (2 vols.). Cambridge, MA: Harvard University Press.

Lovaas, O. I. (1974). Interview with Paul Chance. *Psychology Today, 7*, 76–84.

Lowenthal, M. F., Thurnher, M., & Chiriboya, D. (1975). *Four stages of life.* San Francisco: Jossey-Bass.

Lynn, D. B. (1974). *The father: His role in child development.* Belmont, CA: Brooks/Cole.

Lytton, H. (1979). Disciplinary encounters between young boys and their mothers: Is there a contingency system? *Developmental Psychology, 15*, 256–268.

Maas, H. S., & Kuypers, J. A. (1975). *From thirty to seventy: A forty-year study of adult life styles and personality.* San Francisco: Jossey-Bass.

McCall, R. B. (1981). Nature-nurture and the two values of development. A proposed integration with respect to mental development. *Child Development, 52*, 1–12.

McClelland, D. C. (1961). *The achieving society.* Princeton, NJ: Van Nostrand.

Maccoby, E. E. (1980). *Social development. Psychological growth and the parent-child relationship.* New York: Harcourt, Brace, Jovanovich.

Maccoby, E. E. (1984). Socialization and developmental change. *Child Development, 55*, 317–328.

Maccoby, E. E., & Jacklin, C. N. (1974). *Psychology of sex differences.* Stanford, CA: Stanford University Press.

Maccoby, E. E., and Martin, J. A. (1983). Socialization in the context of the family: Parent-child interaction. In E. M. Hetherington (Ed.), *Socialization, personality, and social development.* Vol. 2 of P. H. Mussen (Ed.), *Handbook of child psychology* (4th ed.). New York: Wiley.

McDonald, R. C. (1968). The role of emotional factors in obstetric complications: A review. *Psychosomatic Medicine, 30*, 222–237.

Macfarlane, J. W. (1964). Perspectives on personality consistency and change from the Guidance Study. *Vita Humana, 7,* 115–126.

Macfarlane, J. W., Allen, L., & Honzik, M. P. (1954). *A developmental study of the behavior problems of normal children between twenty-one months and fourteen years.* Berkeley: University of California Press.

McGill, M. E. (1980). *The 40 to 50 year old male.* New York: Simon and Schuster

McGlothlin, W. H., Sparkes, R. S., & Arnold, D. O. (1970). Effect of LSD on human pregnancy. *Journal of the American Medical Association, 212,* 1483–1487.

McGraw, M. (1935). *Growth: A study of Johnny and Jimmy.* New York: Appleton-Century-Crofts.

McGraw, M. (1939). Later development of children specially trained during infancy. *Child Development, 10,* 1–19.

McGraw, M. (1943). *The neuromuscular development of the human infant.* New York: Columbia University Press.

McGurk, H. (Ed.). (1978). *Issues in childhood social development.* London: Methuen.

McIntire, R. W. (1970). *For love of children.* Del Mar, CA: CRM.

Magnusson, D., Duner, A., & Zetterblom, G. (1975). *Adjustment.* New York: Wiley.

Malina, R. M. (1979). Secular changes in size and maturity: Causes and effects. In A. F. Roche (Ed.), Secular trends in human growth, maturation, and development. *Monographs of the Society for Research in Child Development, 44* (3–4, Serial No. 179).

Manheimer, D., & Mellinger, G. (1967). Personality characteristics of the child accident repeater. *Child Development, 38,* 491–513.

Marcia, J. E. (1966). Development and validation of ego identity status. *Journal of Personality and Social Psychology, 3*(5), 551–558.

Marcia, J. E. (1967). Ego identity status: Relationship to change in self-esteem, "general adjustment," and authoritarianism. *Journal of Personality, 35*(1), 119–133.

Marcia, J. E. (1980). Identity in adolescence. In J. Adelson (Ed.), *Handbook of adolescent psychology.* New York: Wiley.

Maslow, A. H. (1943). A theory of human motivation. *Psychological Review, 50,* 370–396.

Maslow, A. H. (1968). *Toward a psychology of being* (2nd ed.). Princeton, NJ: Van Nostrand.

Maslow, A. H. (1970). *Motivation and personality* (2nd ed.). New York: Harper & Row.

Maslow, A. H. (1972). *The farther reaches of human nature.* New York: Viking.

Masterson, J. F. (1967). *The psychiatric dilemma of adolescence.* Boston: Little, Brown.

Maternity Center Association. (1964). *A baby is born.* New York: Author.

Maternity Center Association. (1969). *Guide for expectant parents.* New York: Grosset & Dunlap.

Maxtone-Graham, K. (1973). *Pregnant by mistake: The stories of seventeen women.* New York: Liveright.

Medvedev, Z. (1974). Caucasus and Atlay longevity: A biological or social problem? *The Gerontologist, 14,* 381–387.

Menyuk, P. (1977). *Language and maturation.* Cambridge, MA: MIT Press.

Merminod, A. (Ed.). (1962). *The growth of the normal child during the first three years of life.* Basel: Karger.

Messick, S., & associates. (1976). *Individuality in learning.* San Francisco: Jossey-Bass.

Michaels, J. (1983). *Prime of your life: A practical guide to your mature years.* Boston: Little, Brown.

Miller, N. E., & Dollard, J. (1941). *Social learning and imitation.* New Haven, CT: Yale University Press.

Miller, P. H. (1983). *Theories of developmental psychology.* San Francisco: Freeman.

Miller, P. Y., & Simon, W. (1980). The development of sexuality in adolescence. In J. Adelson (Ed.), *Handbook of adolescent psychology.* New York: Wiley.

Miller, S. W. (1973). Ends, means, and galumphing: Some leitmotivs of play. *American Anthropologist, 75,* 87–98.

Milstein, R. M. (1978). *Visual and taste responsiveness in obese-tending infants.* Unpublished manuscript, Yale University, Department of Psychology, New Haven, CT.

Minuchin, S., Rosman, B. L., & Baker, L. (1978). *Psychosomatic families: Anorexia nervosa in context*. Cambridge, MA: Harvard University Press.

Mischel, W. (1968). *Personality and assessment*. New York: Wiley.

Mischel, W. (1970). Sex-typing and socialization. In P. H. Mussen (Ed.), *Carmichael's manual of child psychology* (3rd ed., Vol. 2). New York: Wiley.

Mitchell, J. E. (Ed.). (1984). *Anorexia nervosa and bulimia: Diagnosis and treatment*. Minneapolis: University of Minnesota Press.

Moerk, E. L. (1975). Piaget's research as applied to the explanation of language development. *Merrill-Palmer Quarterly, 21,* 151–169.

Moerk, E. L. (1976). Processes of language teaching and training in the interaction of mother-child dyads. *Child Development, 47,* 1064–1078.

Money, J., & Ehrhardt, A. A. (1972). *Man and woman, boy and girl*. Baltimore: Johns Hopkins University Press.

Moore, K. L. (1982). *The developing human: Clinically oriented embryology* (3rd ed.). Philadelphia: Saunders.

Moore, T. W. (1975). Exclusive early mothering and its alternatives. *Scandinavian Journal of Psychology, 16,* 256–272.

Moreno, J. L. (1934). *Who shall survive?* Washington, DC: Nervous and Mental Disease Publishing Co.

Moss, H. A. (1967). Sex, age, and state as determinants of mother-infant interaction. *Merrill-Palmer Quarterly, 13,* 19–36.

Moss, H. A. & Susman, E. J. (1980). Longitudinal study of personality development. In O. H. Brim & J. Kagan (Eds.), *Constancy and change in human development*. Cambridge, MA: Harvard University Press.

Mourad, L. A. (1980). Biophysical development during middlesence. In C. S. Schuster & S. S. Ashburn (Eds.), *The process of human development*. Boston: Little, Brown.

Murphy, L. B. (1937). *Social behavior and child personality*. New York: Columbia University Press.

Murray, H. A. (1943). *Thematic apperception test: Manual*. Cambridge, MA: Harvard University Press.

Murray, H. A., & Kluckhohn, C. (1948). *Personality in nature, society and culture*. New York: Knopf.

Murray, H. W., Royce, J. M., Lazar, I., & Darlington, R. B. (1984). The consortium for longitudinal studies: A follow-up of participants in early childhood programs. In S. A. Mednick, M. Harway, & K. M. Finello (Eds.), *Handbook of longitudinal research: Vol. 1. Birth and childhood cohorts*. New York: Praeger.

Murstein, B. (1973). Self-ideal, self-discrepancy, and choice of marital partner. In M. E. Lasswell & T. E. Lasswell (Eds.), *Love, marriage and family: A developmental approach*. Glenview, IL: Scott, Foresman.

Mussen, P. H. (Ed.). (1960). *Handbook of research methods in child development*. New York: Wiley.

Mussen, P. H. (Ed.). (1970). *Carmichael's manual of child psychology* (3rd ed.). New York: Wiley.

Mussen, P. H. (Ed.). (1983). *Manual of child psychology* (4th ed.). New York: Wiley.

Mussen, P. H., & Jones, M. C. (1957). Self-conceptions, motivations, and interpersonal attitudes of late and early maturing boys. *Child Development, 28,* 245–256.

Myers, C. R. (1970). Journal citations and scientific eminence in contemporary psychology. *American Psychologist, 25,* 1041–1048.

Naeye, R., Messmer, J., III, Specht, T., & Merritt, F. (1976). Sudden infant death syndrome temperament before death. *Journal of Pediatrics, 88,* 511–515.

National Institute of Health. (1985). Facts about blood cholesterol levels. Washington, DC: Public Health Service.

Neimark, E. D. (1975). Intellectual development during adolescence. In F. D. Horowitz (Ed.), *Review of child developmental research* (Vol. 4). Chicago: University of Chicago Press.

Neisser, U. (1967). *Cognitive psychology*. New York: Appleton-Century-Crofts.

Nelson, K. (1973). Structure and strategy in

learning to talk. *Monographs of the Society for Research in Child Development, 38,* (No. 149).

Nelson, K. (1981). Individual differences in language development: Implications for development and language. *Developmental Psychology, 17,* 170–187.

Nesselroade, J. R., & Baltes, P. B. Adolescent personality development and historical change: 1970–1972. *Monographs of the Society for Research in Child Development, 39* (1, Serial No. 154).

Neugarten, B. L. (1975). The future and the young-old. *Gerontologist, 15,* 4–9.

Neugarten, B. L., & Datan, N. (1973). Sociological perspectives on the life cycle. In P. B. Baltes & K. W. Schaie (Eds.), *Lifespan developmental psychology: Personality and socialization.* New York: Academic Press.

Newberry, P., Weissman, M., & Myers, J. K. (1979). Working wives and housewives: Do they differ in mental status and social adjustment? *American Journal of Orthopsychiatry, 49,* 282–291.

Newman, B. M., & Newman, P. R. (1984). *Development through life: A psychosocial approach.* Homewood, IL: Dorsey Press.

Newman, H. H., Freeman, F. N., & Holzinger, K. J. (1937). *Twins: A study of heredity and environment.* Chicago: University of Chicago Press.

Nichols, R. C. (1978). Heredity and environment: Major findings from twin studies of ability, personality, and interests. *Homo, 29,* 158–173.

Nilsson, L., Ingelman-Sundberg, A., & Wirsén, C. (1966). *A child is born.* New York: Delacorte.

Nisbet, R. (1969). *Social change and history.* New York: Oxford University Press.

Notman, M. T. (1980). Changing roles at midlife. In W. H. Norman & T. J. Scaramella (Eds.), *Midlife: Developmental and clinical issues.* New York: Runner/Mazel.

Novak, M. A., & Harlow, H. F. (1975). Social recovery of monkeys isolated for the first year of life. I. Rehabilitation and therapy. *Developmental Psychology, 11,* 453–465.

Null, G., & the staff of the Nutrition Institute of America. (1977). *Successful pregnancy.* New York: Pyramid Publications.

O'Connell, M., & Moore, M. J. (1981). The legitimacy status of first births to U.S. women aged 15–24, 1939–1978. In F. F. Furstenberg, Jr., R. Lincoln, & J. Menken (Eds.), *Teenage sexuality, pregnancy, and childbearing.* Philadelphia: University of Pennsylvania Press.

Offer, D. (1969). *The psychological world of the teenager: A study of normal adolescent boys.* New York: Basic Books.

Offer, D., Ostrov, E., & Howard, K. I. (1981). *The adolescent: A psychological self-portrait.* New York: Basic Books.

Oliver, C. M., & Oliver, G. M. (1978). Gentle birth: Its safety and its effect on neonatal behavior. *Journal of Obstetrical, Gynecological, and Neonatal Nursing.*

Olson, G. M., & Sherman, T. (1983). Attention, learning, and memory in infants. In M. M. Haith & J. J. Campos (Eds.), *Infancy and developmental psychobiology.* Vol. 2 of P. H. Mussen (Ed.), *Handbook of child psychology* (4th ed.). New York: Wiley.

Ostrea, E. M., & Chavez, C. J. (1979). Perinatal problems (excluding neonatal withdrawal) in maternal drug addiction. A study of 830 cases. *The Journal of Pediatrics, 94,* 292–295.

Palmore, E., & Luikart, C. (1974). Health and social factors related to life satisfaction. In E. Palmore (Ed.), *Normal aging.* Durham, NC: Duke University Press.

Papoušek, H. (1961). Conditioned head rotation reflexes in infants in the first months of life. *Acta Pediatrika, 50,* 565–576.

Parke, R. D. (1977). Punishment in children: Effects, side effects and alternative strategies. In H. Hom & P. Robinson (Eds.), *Psychological processes in early education.* New York: Academic Press.

Parke, R. D. (1979). Perspectives on father-infant interaction. In J. D. Osofksy (Ed.), *Handbook of infant development.* New York: Wiley.

Parke, R. D., & Collmer, C. W. (1975). Child abuse: An interdisciplinary analysis. In

E. M. Hetherington (Ed.), *Review of child development research* (Vol. 5). Chicago: University of Chicago Press.

Parke, R. D., & Slaby, R. G. (1983). The development of aggression. In E. M. Hetherington (Ed.), *Socialization, personality, and social development.* Vol. 4 of P. H. Mussen (Ed.), *Handbook of child psychology* (4th ed.). New York: Wiley.

Parkes, C. M. (1972). *Bereavement: Studies of grief in adult life.* New York: International Universities Press.

Parmalee, A. H., Jr., & Sigman, M. D. (1983). Perinatal brain development and behavior. In M. M. Haith & J. J. Campos (Eds.), *Infancy and developmental psychobiology.* Vol. 2 of P. H. Mussen (Ed.), *Handbook of child psychology* (4th ed.). New York: Wiley.

Parten, M. B. (1932). Social participation among preschool children. *Journal of Abnormal and Social Psychology, 27,* 243–269.

Patterson, G. R. (1976). *Living with children: New methods for parents and teachers.* New York: Research Press.

Patterson, G. R. (1982). *Coercive family process.* Eugene, OR: Castalia Press.

Patterson, G. R., Littman, R. A., & Bricker, W. (1967). Assertive behavior in children: A step toward a theory of aggression. *Monographs of the Society for Research in Child Development, 32*(5, Serial No. 113).

Pavlov, I. P. (1927). *Conditioned reflexes.* New York: Oxford University Press.

Peck, M. (1982). Youth suicide. *Death Education, 6,* 29–47.

Peskin, H. (1967). Pubertal onset and ego functioning: A psychoanalytic approach. *Journal of Abnormal Psychology, 72,* 1–15.

Peskin, H. (1973). Influence of the developmental schedule of puberty on learning and ego functioning. *Journal of Youth and Adolescence, 2,* 273–290.

Petersen, A. C., & Taylor, B. (1980). The biological approach to adolescence. In J. Adelson (Ed.), *Handbook of adolescent psychology.* New York: Wiley.

Physical fitness research digest. (1977). Washington, DC: President's Council on Physical Fitness.

Piaget, J. (1932). *The moral judgment of the child.* New York: Harcourt, Brace. (Collier Books edition, 1962).

Piaget, J. (1952a). *The language and thought of the child.* London: Routledge & Kegan Paul.

Piaget, J. (1952b). *The origins of intelligence in children.* New York: International Universities Press.

Piaget, J. (1967). *Biologie et connaissance.* Paris: Gallimard.

Piaget, J. (1970). *Science of education and the psychology of the child.* New York: Grossman.

Piaget, J., & Inhelder, B. (1956). *The child's conception of space.* London: Routledge & Kegan Paul.

Piaget, J., & Inhelder, B. (1969). *The psychology of the child.* New York: Basic Books.

Piaget, J., & Inhelder, B. (1973). *Memory and intelligence.* London: Routledge & Kegan Paul.

Pincus, L. (1974). *Death and the family: The importance of mourning.* New York: Vintage.

Plomin, R. (1983). Developmental behavioral genetics. *Child Development, 54,* 253–259.

Plomin, R., DeFries, J. C., & Loehlin, J. C. (1977). Genotype-environment interaction and correlation in the analysis of human behavior. *Psychological Bulletin, 84,* 309–322.

Plomin, R., & Rowe, D. (1977). A twin study of temperament in young children. *Journal of Psychology, 97,* 107–113.

Poon, L. W., Fozard, J. L., Cermak, L. S., Arenberg, D., & Thompson, L. W. (Eds.). (1980). *New directions in memory and aging.* Hillsdale, NJ: Erlbaum.

Pratt, K. C. (1954). The neonate. In L. Carmichael (Ed.), *Manual of child psychology* (2nd ed.). New York: Wiley.

Presidential Science Advisory Commission, Panel on Youth. (1974). *Youth: Transition to adulthood.* Washington, DC: U.S. Government Printing Office.

Pulaski, M. A. (1971). *Understanding Piaget: An introduction to children's cognitive development.* New York: Harper & Row.

Purtillo, D. F., & Sullivan, J. L. (1979). Immunological basis for superior survival of females. *American Journal of Diseases of Children, 133,* 1251–1253.

Putallez, M. (1983). Predicting children's sociometric status from their behavior. *Child Development, 54,* 1417–1426.

Radke-Yarrow, M., Campbell, J. D., & Burton, R. V. (1968). *Child rearing.* San Francisco: Jossey-Bass.

Radke-Yarrow, M., Zahn-Waxler, C., & Chapman, M. (1983). Children's prosocial dispositions and behavior. In E. M. Hetherington (Ed.), *Socialization, personality, and social development.* Vol. 4 of P. H. Mussen (Ed.), *Handbook of child psychology* (4th ed.). New York: Wiley.

Reed, E. W. (1975). Genetic anomalies in development. In F. D. Horowitz (Ed.), *Review of child development research* (Vol. 4). Chicago: University of Chicago Press.

Reichard, S., Livson, F., & Peterson, P. G. (1968). Adjustment to retirement. In B. Neugarten (Ed.), *Middle age and aging: A reader in social gerontology.* Chicago: University of Chicago Press.

Reiss, I. L., Banwart, A., & Foreman, H. (1975). Premarital contraceptive usage: A study and some theoretical explorations. *Journal of Marriage and the Family, 37,* 619–630.

Rest, J. (1983). Morality. In J. H. Flavell & E. M. Markman (Eds.), *Cognitive development.* Vol. 3 of P. H. Mussen (Ed.), *Handbook of child psychology* (4th ed.). New York: Wiley.

Reynolds, S. R. M., & Danforth, D. N. (1966). The physiology and course of labor. In D. N. Danforth (Ed.), *Textbook of obstetrics and gynecology.* New York: Hoeber.

Rhead, W. J. (1977). Smoking and SIDS. *Pediatrics, 59,* 791–792.

Rheingold, H. L. (1973). Independent behavior of the human infant. In A. D. Pick (Ed.), *Minnesota symposia on child psychology* (Vol. 7). Minneapolis: University of Minnesota Press.

Rheingold, H. L., & Cook, K. V. (1975). The contents of boys' and girls' rooms as index of parents' behavior. *Child Development, 46,* 459–463.

Rheingold, H. L., & Eckerman, C. U. (1973). Fear of the stranger: A critical examination. In H. W. Reese (Ed.), *Advances in child development and behavior* (Vol. 8). New York: Academic Press.

Ribble, M. (1943). *The rights of infants.* New York: Columbia University Press.

Riessman, F. (1962). *The culturally deprived child.* New York: Harper & Row.

Ringler, N. (1978). A longitudinal study of mothers' language. In N. Waterson & C. E. Snow (Eds.), *The development of communication.* New York: Wiley.

Roberts, G. C., Block, J. H., & Block, J. (1984). Continuity and change in parents' child-rearing practices. *Child Development, 55,* 586–597.

Robinson, A., Lubs, H. A., Nielsen, J., & Sorensen, K. (1979). Summary of clinical findings: Profiles of children with 47, XXY, 47, XYY karyotypes. *Birth Defects, 15,* 261–266.

Roche, A. (Ed.). (1979). Secular trends in human growth, maturation, and development. *Monographs of the Society for Research in Child Development, 44*(3–4, Serial No. 179).

Roche, A. (1981). The adipocyte-number hypothesis. *Child Development, 52,* 31–43.

Rogers, C. R. (1951). *Client-centered therapy.* Boston: Houghton Mifflin.

Rogers, C. R. (1963). Learning to be free. In S. Farber & R. H. L. Wilson (Eds.), *Conflict and creativity: Control of the mind.* New York: McGraw-Hill.

Rogers, C. R. (1970). *On becoming a person: A therapist's view of psychotherapy.* Boston: Houghton Mifflin.

Rogers, C. R., & Skinner, B. F. (1956). Some issues concerning the control of human behavior. *Science, 124,* 1057–1066.

Rogers, D. (1972). *The psychology of adolescence* (2nd ed.). New York: Appleton-Century-Crofts.

Rokeach, M. (1973). *The name of human values.* New York: Free Press.

Rosen, B. M., Bahn, O. K., & Kramer, M. (1964). Demographic and diagnostic characteristics of psychiatric clinic outpatients in the U.S.A., 1961. *American Journal of Orthopsychiatry, 24,* 455–467.

Rosett, H. L., & Sander, L. W. (1979). Effects of

maternal drinking on neonatal morphology and state regulation. In J. D. Osofsky (Ed.), *Handbook of infant development.* New York: Wiley.

Rowe, D. C., & Plomin, R. (1978). The Burt controversy: A comparison of Burt's data on IQ with data from other studies. *Behavior Genetics, 8,* 81–84.

Rowe, D. C., & Plomin, R. (1981). The importance of nonshared (E.) environmental influences in behavioral development. *Developmental Psychology, 17,* 517–531.

Rubin, K. H. (1977). The play behaviors of young children. *Young Children, 32,* 16–24.

Rubin, K. H. (Ed.). (1980). *Children's play.* San Francisco: Jossey-Bass.

Rubin, K. H., Fein, G. G., & Vandenberg, B. (1983). Play. In E. M. Hetherington (Ed.), *Socialization, personality, and social development.* Vol. 4 of P. H. Mussen (Ed.), *Handbook of child psychology* (4th ed.). New York: Wiley.

Rubin, L. B. (1979). *Women of a certain age: The midlife search for self.* New York: Harper & Row.

Rutter, M. (1972). *Maternal deprivation reassessed.* Hammondsworth, England: Penguin.

Rutter, M. (1979). Maternal deprivation, 1972–1978: New findings, new concepts, new approaches. *Child Development, 50,* 283–318.

Rutter, M., & Garmezy, N. (1983). Developmental psychopathology. In E. M. Hetherington (Ed.), *Socialization, personality, and social development.* Vol. 4 of P. H. Mussen (Ed.), *Handbook of child psychology* (4th ed.). New York: Wiley.

Rutter, M., Tizard, J., & Whitmore, K. (Eds.). (1981). *Education, health, and behavior.* Huntington, NY: Krieger. (Originally published 1970.)

Saddock, B. J., Kaplan, H. I., & Freedman, A. M. (Eds.). (1976). *The sexual experience.* Baltimore: Williams & Wilkins.

Sager, C. J., & Kaplan, H. S. (Eds.), (1972). *Progress in group and family therapy.* New York: Brunner/Mazel.

Salapatek, P. (1975). Pattern perception in early infancy. In L. B. Cohen & P. Salapatek (Eds.), *Infant perception: From sensation to cognition: Vol. 1. Basic visual processes.* New York: Academic Press.

Sameroff, A. J. (1974). Early influences on development: Fact or fancy? *Merrill-Palmer Quarterly, 21*(4), 267–294.

Sameroff, A. J. (1983). Developmental systems: contexts and evolution. In W. Kessen (Ed.), *History, theory, and methods.* Vol. 1 of P. H. Mussen (Ed.), *Handbook of child psychology.* New York: Wiley.

Sameroff, A. J., & Cavanagh, P. J. (1979). Learning in infancy: A developmental perspective. In J. D. Osofsky (Ed.), *Handbook of infant development.* New York: Wiley.

Sameroff, A. J., & Chandler, M. J. (1975). Reproductive risk and the continuum of caretaking causality. In F. D. Horowitz (Ed.), *Review of child development research* (Vol. 4). Chicago: University of Chicago Press.

Scanlan, J. V. (1975). *Self-reported health behavior and attitudes of youths 12–17 years.* U. S. Department of Public Health Service. Health, Education, and Welfare, Series II, Number 147, Publication No. (HRA) 75–1629.

Scarr, S., & Kidd, K. K. (1983). Development behavior genetics. In M. M. Haith & J. J. Campos (Eds.), *Infancy and developmental psychobiology.* Vol. 2 of P. H. Mussen (Ed.), *Handbook of child psychology.* New York: Wiley.

Scarr, S., & McCartney, K. (1983). How people make their own environments: A theory of genotype environment effects. *Child Development, 54,* 424–435.

Scarr, S., and Weinberg, R. A. (1980). Calling all camps! The war is over. *American Sociological Review, 45,* 859–865.

Scarr, S., and Weinberg, R. A. (1983). The Minnesota adoption studies: Genetic differences and malleability. *Child Development, 54,* 260–267.

Schachter, S. (1959). *The psychology of affiliation.* Stanford, CA: Stanford University Press.

Schaefer, S. (1959). A circumplex model for maternal behavior. *Journal of Abnormal and Social Psychology, 59,* 226–235.

Schaffer, H. R. (1977a). *Mothering.* Cambridge, MA: Harvard University Press.

Schaffer, H. R. (1977b). (Ed.). *Studies in mother-infant interaction.* New York: Academic Press.

Schaffer, H. R., & Emerson, P. E. (1964). The development of social attachments in infancy. *Monographs of the Society for Research in Child Development, 29*(3).

Schaie, K. W. (1977–1978). Toward a stage theory of adult cognitive development. *International Journal of Aging and Human Development, 8,* 129–138.

Schechter, M. D. (1974). Psychiatric aspects of learning disabilities. *Child Psychiatry and Human Development, 5,* 67–77.

Scheinfeld, A. (1958). The mortality of men and women. *Scientific American, 1981*(2), 22–27.

Scheinfeld, A. (1965). *Your heredity and environment.* Philadelphia: Lippincott.

Scheinfeld, A. (1972). *Heredity in humans.* Philadelphia: Lippincott.

Schooler, C. (1972). Birth order effects: Not here, not now! *Psychological Bulletin, 78,* 161–175.

Schooler, J. C. (ed.). (1973). *Current issues in adolescent psychiatry.* New York: Brunner/Mazel.

Schramm, D. G. J. (1935). Direction of movements of children in emotional responses. *Child Development, 6,* 26–51.

Schulz, R., & Alderman, D. (1978–1979). Physicians' death anxiety and patient outcomes. *Omega, 9,* 327–332.

Schuster, C. S. (1980). Biophysical development of the school-age child. In C. S. Schuster & S. S. Ashburn (Eds.), *The process of human development.* Boston: Little, Brown.

Schwartz, R. H., & Yaffe (Eds.). (1980). *Drugs and chemical risks to the fetus and newborn.* New York: Alan R. Liss.

Sears, R. R. (1975). Your ancients revisited: A history of child development. In E. M. Hetherington (Ed.), *Review of child development research* (Vol. 5). Chicago: University of Chicago Press.

Sears, R. R., Maccoby, E. E., & Levin, H. (1957). *Patterns of child rearing.* Evanston, IL: Row, Peterson.

Sears, R. R., Rau, L., & Alpert, R. (1965). *Identification and child rearing.* Stanford, CA: Stanford University Press.

Seligman, M. E. P. (1975). *Helplessness: On depression, development, and death.* San Francisco: Freeman.

Selman, R. L. (1976a). Social-cognitive understanding: A guide to educational and clinical practice. In T. Lickona (Ed.), *Moral development and behavior: Theory, research, and social issues.* New York: Holt, Rinehart & Winston.

Selman, R. L. (1976b). Toward a structural analysis of developing interpersonal relations concepts. In A. Pick (Ed.), *Minnesota symposia on child psychology* (Vol. 10). Minneapolis: University of Minnesota Press.

Selman, R. L. (1980). *The growth of interpersonal understanding.* New York: Academic Press.

Senn, M. J. E. (1975). Insights on the child development movement in the United States. *Monographs of the Society for Research in Child Development, 40*(3–4, Serial No. 161).

Sever, L. E. (1981). Reproductive hazards of the workplace. *Journal of Occupational Medicine, 23,* 685–691.

Shantz, C. U. (1975). The development of social cognition. In E. M. Hetherington (Ed.), *Review of child development research* (Vol. 5). Chicago: University of Chicago Press.

Sheehy, G. (1976). *Passages.* New York: Dutton.

Sheehy, G. (1982). *Pathfinders.* New York: Bantam.

Shepherd, M., Oppenheim, A. N., & Mitchell, S. (1966). Childhood behavior disorders and the child guidance clinic: An epidemiological study. *Journal of Psychology and Psychiatry, 7,* 39–52.

Sherman, J. A., & Bushell, D., Jr. (1975). Behavior modification as an educational technique. In F. D. Horowitz (Ed.), *Review of child development research* (Vol. 4). Chicago: University of Chicago Press.

Shirley, M. M. (1931). The first two years: A study of twenty-five babies: Vol. I. Posture and locomotor development. *Institute of Child Welfare Monograph Series,* No. 6. Minneapolis: University of Minnesota Press.

Shirley, M. M. (1933a). The first two years: A study of twenty-five babies: Vol. II. Intellectual development. *Institute of Child Welfare Monograph Series*, No. 7. Minneapolis: University of Minnesota Press.

Shirley, M. M. (1933b). The first two years: A study of twenty-five babies: Vol. III. Personality manifestations. *Institute of Child Welfare Monograph Series*, No. 8. Minneapolis: University of Minnesota Press.

Shirley, M. M. (1938). Development of immature babies during the first two years. *Child Development, 9,* 347–360.

Shirley, M. M. (1939). A behavior syndrome characterizing prematurely born children. *Child Development, 10,* 115–128.

Shock, N. W. (1977). Biological theories of aging. In J. E. Birren & K. W. Schaie (Eds.), *Handbook of the psychology of aging.* New York: Van Nostrand Reinhold.

Siegel, O. (1982). Personality development in adolescence. In B. B. Wolman (Ed.), *Handbook of developmental psychology.* Englewood Cliffs, NJ: Prentice-Hall.

Siegler, R. S. (1983). Information processing approaches to development. In W. Kessen (Ed.), *History, theory, and methods.* Vol. 1 of P. H. Mussen (Ed.), *Handbook of child psychology* (4th ed.). New York: Wiley.

Simenauer, J., & Carroll, D. (1982). *Singles: The new Americans.* New York: Simon & Schuster.

Simonton, D. K. (1975). Age and literary creativity: A cross-cultural and transhistorical survey. *Journal of Cross-Cultural Psychology, 6,* 259–277.

Simpson, E. L. (1974). Moral development research: A case of scientific cultural bias. *Human Development, 17,* 81–106.

Siqueland, E. R., & DeLucia, C. A. (1969). Visual reinforcement of nonnutritive sucking in human infants. *Science, 165,* 1144–1146.

Skinner, B. F. (1948). *Walden Two,* New York: Macmillan.

Skinner, B. F. (1953). *Science and human behavior.* New York: Macmillan.

Skinner, B. F. (1957). *Verbal behavior.* New York: Appleton-Century-Crofts.

Skinner, B. F. (1971). *Beyond freedom and dignity.* New York: Knopf.

Skinner, B. F. (1974). *About behaviorism.* New York: Knopf.

Skinner, B. F. (1976). *Particulars of my life.* New York: Knopf.

Skinner, B. F. (1979). *The shaping of a behavorist.* New York: Knopf.

Skodak, M. (1939). Children in foster homes: A study of mental development. *University of Iowa Studies of Child Welfare, 16*(1).

Skodak, M., & Skeels, H. M. (1945). A follow-up study of children in adoptive homes. *Journal of Genetic Psychology, 66,* 21–58.

Skodak, M., & Skeels, H. M. (1949). A final follow-up of one hundred adopted children. *Journal of Genetic Psychology, 75,* 85–125.

Smilansky, S. (1968). *The effects of sociodramatic play on disadvantaged preschool children.* New York: Wiley.

Smith, P. K. (1978). A longitudinal study of social participation in preschool children: solitary and parallel play reexamined. *Developmental Psychology, 14,* 517–523.

Smoking and Health: A Report of the Surgeon-General. (1979). Washington, DC: U.S. Department of Health, Education, & Welfare.

Sonenstein, F. L., & Pittman, K. J. (1984). The availability of sex education in large school districts. *Family Planning Perspectives, 16,* 19–25.

Sontag, L. W. (1941). The significance of fetal environmental differences. *American Journal of Obstetrics and Gynecology, 42,* 996–1003.

Sontag, L. W. (1971). The history of longitudinal research: Implications for the future. *Child Development, 42,* 987–1002.

Sorensen, R. C. (1973). *Adolescent sexuality in contemporary America: Personal values and sexual behavior.* New York: World.

Sorrells-Jones, J., 1982. Cited in A. Clarke-Stewart and J. B. Koch, *Children: Development through adolescence.* New York: Wiley, 1983.

Speert, H. (1966). Historical highlights. In D. N. Danforth (Ed.), *Textbook of obstetrics and gynecology.* New York: Hoeber.

Spence, M. J., & De Casper, A. J., (1982, March). Human fetuses perceive maternal speech. Paper presented at the meeting of the International Conference on Infant Studies. Austin, TX.

Spinetta, J. J., & Rigler, D. (1972). The child-abusing parents: A psychological review. *Psychological Bulletin, 77,* 296–304.

Spitz, R. A. (1945). Hospitalism: An inquiry into the genesis of psychiatric conditions in early childhood. In A. Freud (Ed.), *The psychoanalytic study of the child* (Vol. 1). New York: International Universities Press.

Spitz, R. A. (1965). *The first year of life.* New York: International Universities Press.

Sroufe, L. A. (1977). Wariness of strangers and the study of infant development. *Child Development, 48,* 731–746.

Sroufe, L. A. (1979). Socioemotional development. In J. D. Osofsky (Ed.), *Handbook of infant development.* New York: Wiley.

Starfield, B., & Pless, I. B. (1980). Physical health. In O. G. Brim & J. Kagan (Eds.), *Constancy and change in human development.* Cambridge, MA: Harvard University Press.

Stark, R., & McEvoy, J. (1970). Middle class violence. *Psychology Today, 4,* 52–65.

Starr, R. H., Jr. (1979). Child abuse. *American Psychologist, 34*(10), 872–878.

Stein, A. H., & Friedrich, L. K. (1975). Impact of television on children and youth. In E. M. Hetherington (Ed.), *Review of child development research* (Vol. 5). Chicago: University of Chicago Press.

Steinmetz, S. K. (1977). *The cycle of violence: Assertive, aggressive, and abusive family interaction.* New York: Praeger.

Steinschneider, A. (1975). Implications of the sudden infant death syndrome for the study of sleep in infancy. In A. D. Pick (Ed.), *Minnesota Symposia on Child Psychology* (Vol. 9). Minneapolis: University of Minnesota Press.

Stendler, C. B. (1950). Sixty years of child-training practices. *Journal of Pediatrics, 36,* 122–134.

Stern, D. (1977). *The first relationship: Mother and infant.* Cambridge, MA: Harvard University Press.

Sternglanz, S. H., & Serbin, L. A. (1974). Sex-role stereotypes in children's television programs. *Developmental Psychology, 10,* 710–715.

Stewart, A. H., Weiland, I. H., Leider, A. R., Mangham, C. A., Holmes, T. H., & Ripley, H. S. (1954). Excessive infant crying (colic) in relation to parent behavior. *American Journal of Psychiatry, 110,* 687–699.

St. Leger, A. S., Cochrane, A. L., & Moore, F. (1979). Factors associated with cardiac mortality in developed countries with particular reference to the consumption of wine. *Lancet, 1*(8124), 1017–1020.

Stone, L. J., Smith, H. T., & Murphy, L. B. (Eds.). (1973). *The competent infant.* New York: Basic Books.

Stoneman, Z., Brody, G. H., & MacKinnon, C. (1984). Naturalistic observations of children's activities and roles while playing with their siblings and friends. *Child Development, 55,* 617–627.

Stott, D. H. (1971). The child's hazards in utero. In J. G. Howells (Ed.), *Modern perspectives in international child psychiatry.* New York: Brunner/Mazel.

Strean, L. P., & Peer, A. (1956). Stress as an etiologic factor in the development of cleft palate. *Plastic and Reconstructive Surgery, 18,* 1–8.

Streib, G., & Schneider, C. J. (1971). *Retirement in American society: Impact and process.* Ithaca, NY: Cornell University Press.

Streissguth, A. P., Landesman-Dwyer, S., Martin, J. C., & Smith, D. W. (1980). Teratogenic effects of alcohol in humans and laboratory animals. *Science, 209,* 353–361.

Sulzer-Azaroff, B., & Mayer, G. R. (1977). *Applying behavior analysis procedures with children.* New York: Holt, Rinehart & Winston.

Super, D. E. (1957). *The psychology of careers.* New York: Harper & Row.

Super, D. E. (1963). Vocational development in adolescence and early childhood: Tasks and behaviors. In D. E. Super, R. E. Starishevsky, N. Matlin, & J. P. Jordan (Eds.), *Career development: A self-concept theory.* New York: College Entrance Examination Board.

Super, D. E., & Hall, D. T. (1978). Career development: Exploration and planning. *Annual Review of Psychology, 29,* 333–372.

Swift, J. W. (1964). Effects of early group experience: The nursery school and day nursery. In M. L. Hoffman & L. W. Hoffman (Eds.), *Review of child development research* (Vol. 1). New York: Russell Sage Foundation.

Tanner, J. M. (1962). *Growth at adolescence* (2nd ed.). Philadelphia: Davis.

Tanner, J. M. (1970). Physical growth. In P. H. Mussen (Ed.), *Carmichael's manual of child psychology* (3rd ed., Vol. 1). New York: Wiley.

Tanner, J. M. (1972). Sequence, tempo, and individual variation in growth and development of boys and girls aged twelve to sixteen. In J. Kagan & R. Coles (Eds.), *Twelve to sixteen: Early adolescence.* New York: Norton.

Tanner, J. M., Taylor, G. R., & the Editors of Time-Life Books. (1969). *Growth* (rev. ed.). New York: Time-Life Books.

Tanzer, D., & Block, J. L. (1972). *Why natural childbirth?* Garden City, NY: Doubleday.

Tavris, C., & Offir, C. (1977). *The longest war: Sex differences in perspective.* New York: Harcourt, Brace, Jovanovich.

Television and growing up: The impact of televised violence. (1972). Washington, DC: U.S. Government Printing Office.

Television and social behavior. (1972). Washington, DC: U.S. Government Printing Office.

Terman, L. M., et al. (1925). *Genetic studies of genius: Vol. 1. Mental and physical traits of a thousand gifted children.* Stanford, CA: Stanford University Press.

Terman, L. M., & Oden, M. (1954). *Genetic studies of genius: The gifted group at mid-life. Thirty-five years' follow-up of the superior child.* Stanford, CA: Stanford University Press.

Teuber, H. L., & Rudel, R. G. (1962). Behavior after cerebral lesions in children and adults. *Developmental Medicine and Child Neurology, 4,* 3–20.

Thomas, A., & Chess, S. (1977). *Temperament and development.* New York: Brunner/Mazel.

Thomas, A., Chess, S., & Birch, H. G. (1970). The origin of personality. *Scientific American, 223*(2), 102.

Thomas, A., Chess, S., Birch, H. G., Hertzig, M. E., & Korn, S. (1963). *Behavioral*

individuality in early childhood. New York: New York University Press.

Thomas, R. M. (1979). *Comparing theories of child development.* Belmont, CA: Wadsworth.

Thompson, R. A., & Lamb, M. E. (1983). Security of attachment and stranger sociability in infancy. *Developmental Psychology, 19,* 184–191.

Thompson, W. R., & Grusec, J. (1970). Studies of early experience. In P. H. Mussen (Ed.), *Carmichael's manual of child psychology* (3rd ed., Vol. 1). New York: Wiley.

Thornburg, H. D. (1970). Age and first sources of sex information as reported by 88 college women. *Journal of School Health, 40,* 156–158.

Timaras, P. S. (1972). *Developmental physiology and aging.* New York: Macmillan.

Tinbergen, N. (1974). Interview with Elizabeth Hall. *Psychology Today, 7*(10), 65–80.

Tinklenberg, J. R. (Ed.). (1975). *Marijuana and health hazards: Methodological issues in current research.* New York: Academic Press.

Tolor, A. (1976). The generation gap: Fact or fiction? *Genetic Psychology Monographs, 94,* 35–130.

Tough, A. (1982). *Intentional changes: A fresh approach to helping people change.* Chicago: Follet.

Tresemer, D. (1974). Fear of success: Popular but unproven. *Psychology Today, 7*(10), 82–85.

Tresemer, D. (1977). *Fear of success.* New York: Plenum Press.

Troll, L. E. (1975). *Early and middle adulthood.* Monterey, CA: Brooks/Cole.

Tronick, E. Z., Als, H., Adamson, L., Wise, S., & Brazelton, T. B. (1978). The infant's response to entrapment between contradictory messages in face-to-face interaction. *Journal of the American Academy of Child Psychiatry, 17,* 1–13.

Truhon, S. A., McKinney, J. P., & Hotch, D. F. (1980). The structure of values among college students: An examination of sex differences. *Journal of Youth and Adolescence, 9,* 189–297.

Turiel, E. (1966). An experimental test of the sequentiality of developmental stages in the child's moral judgments. *Journal of Personality and Social Psychology, 3,* 611–618.

Turiel, E. (1974). Conflict and transition in adolescent moral development. *Child Development, 45,* 14–79.

U. S. Department of Health and Human Services. (1980). *Sexually transmitted diseases: 1980 status report.* Washington, DC.

Vaillant, G. E. (1977). *Adaptation to life.* Boston: Little, Brown.

Vincent, C. E. (1951). Trends in infant care ideas. *Child Development, 22,* 199–209.

Vonnegut, M. (1975). *The Eden express.* New York: Praeger.

Vygotsky, L. (1962). *Thought and language.* Cambridge, MA: MIT Press.

Vygotsky, L. (1978). *Mind in society: The development of higher psychological processes.* Cambridge, MA: Harvard University Press.

Wachs, T. D. (1983). The use and abuse of environment in behavior-genetic research. *Child Development, 54,* 396–407.

Waddington, C. H. (1962). *New patterns in genetics and development.* New York: Columbia University Press.

Waddington, C. H. (1966). *Principles of development and differentiation.* New York: Macmillan.

Wadsworth, B. J. (1979). *Piaget for the classroom teacher* (2nd ed.). New York: Longman.

Walker, C. E., & Roberts, M. C. (Eds.). *Handbook of clinical child psychology.* New York: Wiley.

Wallerstein, J. S., & Kelley, J. B. (1980). *Surviving the breakup: How children and parents cope with divorce.* New York: Basic Books.

Wanderer, Z., & Cabot, T. (1978). *Letting go: A twelve week personal action program to overcome a broken heart.* New York: Putnam.

Warner, D. A. (1978). Personal communication.

Waters, E., Vaughn, B., & Egeland, B. (1980). Individual differences in infant-mother attachment relationships at age one: Antecedents in neonatal behavior in an urban, economically disadvantaged sample. *Child Development, 51,* 208–216.

Watson, J. B. (1903). *Animal education: The psychical development of the white rat.* Unpublished doctoral dissertation, University of Chicago.

Watson, J. B. (1913). Psychology as the behaviorist views it. *Psychological Review, 20,* 158–177.

Watson, J. B. (1919). *Psychology from the standpoint of a behaviorist.* Philadelphia: Lippincott.

Watson, J. B. (1928a). *Psychological care of infant and child.* New York: Norton.

Watson, J. B. (1928b). *The ways of behaviorism.* New York: Harper.

Watson, J. B. (1930). *Behaviorism* (rev. ed.). Chicago: University of Chicago Press. (Originally published 1925).

Watson, J. B. (1936). Autobiographical sketch. In C. Murchison (Ed.), *A history of psychology in autobiography* (Vol. 3). Worcester, MA: Clark University Press.

Watson, J. B., & Morgan, J. J. B. (1917). Emotional reactions and psychological experimentation. *American Journal of Psychology, 28,* 163–174.

Watson, J. B., & Rayner, R. (1920). Conditioned emotional reactions. *Journal of Experimental Psychology, 3,* 1–14.

Watson, J. D. (1968). *The double helix: Being a personal account of the discovery of the structure of DNA.* New York: Atheneum.

Webster, R. L. (1967). Postnatal weight and behavior changes as a function of components of prenatal material injection procedures. *Science, 7,* 191–192.

Weikart, D. P., & Schweinhart, L. J. (1984). Two decades of research: The high-scope longitudinal preschool evaluations. In S. A. Mednick, M. Harway, & K. M. Finello (Eds.), *Handbook of longitudinal research: Vol. 1. Birth and childhood cohorts.* New York: Praeger.

Weiner, I. B. (1975). Depression in adolescence. In F. F. Flach & S. C. Draghi (Eds.), *The nature and treatment of depression.* New York: Wiley.

Weiner, I. B. (1980). Psychopathology in adolescence. In J. Adelson (Ed.), *Handbook of adolescent psychology.* New York: Wiley.

Werner, E. E., Bierman, J. M., & French, F. E. (1971). *The children of Kauai: A longitudinal study from the prenatal period to age ten.* Honolulu: University of Hawaii Press.

Wessel, H. (1963). *Natural childbirth and the Christian family.* New York: Harper & Row.

Whitbourne, S. K. (1976). Test anxiety in elderly and young adults. *International Journal of Aging and Human Development, 7,* 201–220.

White, B. L. (1967). An experimental approach to the effects of experience on early human behavior. In J. P. Hill (Ed.), *Minnesota symposia on child psychology* (Vol. 1). Minneapolis: University of Minnesota Press.

White, B. L. (1975). *The first three years of life.* Englewood Cliffs, NJ: Prentice-Hall.

White, B. L., & Castle, P. W. (1964). Visual exploratory behavior following postnatal handling of human infants. *Perceptual and Motor Skills, 18,* 497–502.

White, B. L., & Held, R. (1966). Plasticity of sensori-motor development in the human infant. In J. F. Rosenblith & W. Allinsmith (Eds.), *The causes of behavior* (2nd ed.). Boston: Allyn & Bacon.

White, B. L., Kaban, B. T., & Attanucci, J. S. (1979). *The origins of human competence. The final report of the Harvard Preschool Project.* Lexington, MA: Lexington Books.

White, B. L., Watts, J. C., et al. (1973). *Experience and environment: Major influences on the development of the young child.* Englewood Cliffs, NJ: Prentice-Hall.

White, R. W. (1959). Motivation reconsidered: The concept of competence. *Psychological Review, 66,* 297.

Whiting, J. W., & Whiting, B. B. (1975). *Children of six cultures: A psycho-cultural analysis.* Cambridge, MA: Harvard University Press.

Williams, R. S., Logue, E. E., Lewis, J. L., Stead, N. W., Wallace, A. G., & Pizzo, S. V. (1980). Physical conditioning augments the fibrinolytic response to venous occlusion in healthy adults. *New England Journal of Medicine, 302,* 987–991.

Wilson, J. G. (1977). Current status of teratology. In J. G. Wilson & F. C. Fraser (Eds.), *Handbook of teratology.* New York: Plenum.

Wilson, J. G., & Fraser, F. C. (Eds.). (1977).

Handbook of teratology: Vol. 1. General principles and etiology. New York: Plenum.

Wilson, R. S. (1983). The Louisville twin study: Developmental synchronies in behavior. *Child Development, 54,* 298–316.

Winick, M. (1976). *Malnutrition and brain development.* New York: Oxford University Press.

Winnicott, D. W. (1965). *The maturational process and the facilitating environment.* New York: International Universities Press.

Witkin, H. A. (1969). Social influences in the development of cognitive style. In D. A. Goslin (Ed.), *Handbook of socialization theories and research.* Chicago: Rand McNally.

Witkin, H. A., & Berry, J. W. (1975). Psychological differentiation in cross-cultural perspective. *Journal of Cross-Cultural Psychology, 6,* 84–87.

Witkin, H. A., Dyk, R. B., Faterson, H. F., Goodenough, D. R., & Karp, S. A. (1962). *Psychological differentiation.* New York: Wiley.

Witkin, H. A., & Goodenough, D. R. (1976). *Field dependence revisited* (Research Bulletin 76–39). Princeton, NJ: Educational Testing Service.

Wolfenstein, M. (1953). Trends in infant care. *American Journal of Orthopsychiatry, 33,* 120–130.

Wolman, B. B. (Ed.). (1972). *Manual of child psychopathology.* New York: McGraw-Hill.

Woodruff, D. (1977). *Can you live to be 100?* New York: Chatham Square Press.

Wright, H. F. (1960). Observational child study. In P. H. Mussen (Ed.), *Handbook of research methods in child development.* New York: Wiley.

Yalom, I. D. (1970). *The theory and practice of group psychotherapy.* New York: Basic Books.

Zajonc, R. B., & Markus, G. B. (1975). Birth order and intellectual development. *Psychological Review, 82*(1), 74–88.

Zelnik, M., & Kantner, J. F. (1972). The probability of premarital intercourse. *Social Science Research, 1,* 335–341.

Zelnik, M., & Kantner, J. F. (1977). Sexual and contraceptive experience of young unmarried women in the United States, 1976 and 1971. *Family Planning Perspectives, 9*, 55–71.

Zelnik, M., Kantner, J., & Ford, K. (1981). *Sex and pregnancy in adolescence.* Beverly Hills: Sage Publications.

Zelnik, M., Koenig, M. A., & Kim, Y. J. (1984). Sources of prescription contraceptives and subsequent pregnancy among young women. *Family Planning Perspectives, 16,* 6–13.

Zelnik, M., & Shah, F. K. (1983). First intercourse among young Americans. *Family Planning Perspectives, 15,* 64–70.

Zelniker, T., & Jeffrey, W. E. (1976). Reflective and impulsive children: Strategies of information processing underlying differences in problem solving. *Monographs of the Society for Research in Child Development, 41*(5, Serial No. 168).

Zigler, E. (1975, January 18). Letter to the editor. *New York Times Magazine.*

Zuckerman, M. (1979). *Sensation seeking: Beyond the optimal level of arousal.* Hillsdale, NJ: Erlbaum.

INDEX

WHAT DO YOU THINK OF THIS BOOK?

We would like to know what you think of this edition of *Developmental Psychology: An Introduction*. Your comments will help us not only in improving the next edition of this book but also in developing other texts. We would appreciate it very much if you would take a few minutes to respond to the following questions. When you have finished responding, please return the form to: College Marketing, Houghton Mifflin Company, One Beacon Street, Boston, MA 02108.

On a ten-point scale, with 10 as the highest rating and 1 as the lowest, how do you rate the following features of *Developmental Psychology: An Introduction*?

Overall rating compared to all other texts you have read. _____

Interest level compared to all other texts you have read. _____

Readability compared to other texts. _____

Clarity of presentation of concepts and information. _____

Value of the *Key Points* as a study and learning aid. _____

Helpfulness of summary *tables* and *diagrams*. _____

Interest level and pedagogical effectiveness of the *illustrations*. _____

Usefulness of the *Suggestions for Further Study*. _____

Do you intend to sell this book _____ or keep it for future reference _____? (Please insert an X in the appropriate space.)

Do you expect to have contact with children or adolescents in any of these capacities during the next ten years? (Check more than one, if appropriate.) Parent _____ Teacher _____ Nurse _____ Social worker _____ Recreational leader _____ Other (Please specify) _____

Please turn to the table of contents and list here the number of all chapters that were assigned by your instructor. _____

If not all chapters were assigned, did you read any others on your own? Please indicate chapter numbers you read on your own. _____

Please indicate the numbers of chapters you found most interesting. _____

Allowing for the fact that some topics are more intrinsically interesting than others, did you find any chapters particularly "deadly" and in need of more effective presentation? Please specify chapter numbers. _____

Were there any topics that were not covered that you thought should have been covered? _____

Please indicate the number of each of the following types of exams that your instructor asked you to take: multiple choice _____ short answer _____ essay _____ oral _____ other (please specify) _____

Did your instructor give you the opportunity to compare your test answers to the answers provided by the person who wrote the questions? Yes _____ No _____

Were you required to write a term paper _____ or complete some sort of term project? (Please specify nature of term project) _____

Did you use the Study Guide? Yes _____ No _____. On a ten-point scale, how do you rate the usefulness of the Study Guide _____? Did your instructor ask you to use the Study Guide _____ or did you obtain it on your own _____?

Are you attending a 2-year college _____, 4-year college _____, university _____?

Is your college or university on the quarter system _____ or the semester system _____?

If you had the chance to talk to the authors of this book just before they started to prepare the next edition, what suggestions would you give them for improving *Developmental Psychology: An Introduction?*